form•Z 4

3D Modeling, Rendering, and Animation

form•Z 4

3D Modeling, Rendering, and Animation

Lachmi Khemlani, Ph.D.

Foreword by **Dr. Mark D. Gross**

McGraw-Hill

New York Chicago San Francisco Lisbon London Madrid
Mexico City Milan New Delhi San Juan Seoul
Singapore Sydney Toronto

Cataloging-in-Publication Data is on file with the Library of Congress

1 2 3 4 5 6 7 8 9 0 DOC/DOC 0 9 8 7 6 5 4 3

P/N 142517-9
PART OF
ISBN 0-07-142516-0

The sponsoring editor for this book was Cary Sullivan, the editing supervisor was Stephen M. Smith, and the production supervisor was Sherri Souffrance. The art director for the cover was Anthony Landi.

Printed and bound by RR Donnelley.

This book is printed on recycled, acid-free paper containing a minimum of 50% recycled de-inked fiber.

To Pran, Sarisha, and Sahil

Contents

Foreword

With this new book on form•Z, Lachmi Khemlani updates her excellent guide on computer graphics model-making to cover the latest enhancements in one of the best CAD modeling programs on the market today.

From its innovative experimental start in a research lab at The Ohio State University's School of Architecture, form•Z has steadily evolved into a sophisticated tool for representing design ideas in three dimensions. form•Z was originally designed to serve the special requirements of architectural modeling, in which understanding the spaces in a design is as important as understanding its material shape and assembly of components. Over the years, the software has grown to serve the diverse needs of all kinds of designers, from product and industrial design to mechanical engineers to scene and game design, as well as architectural and urban design. Today form•Z is a powerful professional tool for geometric modeling, rendering, and animation.

Anyone who has learned to draw with pencil and paper, or to construct models with basswood, chipboard, or clay, knows that skill comes with experience. There are tricks and techniques, and through practice one learns when and how to use them. Gradually one gets good. So it is with form•Z. Getting started is easy; but true mastery of any complex software application requires time and effort. Here is where this book will help: by guiding you through the program's diverse capabilities, from basic modeling functions to subtle variations of the software's more esoteric operations. To become an effective model-maker with form•Z (or any CAD application), you must learn to approach any modeling problem strategically: What is the simplest sequence of modeling operations that will best yield the desired result? Based on a thorough understanding of how the software is designed to work most effectively, *form•Z 4: 3D Modeling, Rendering, and Animation* will save you time and frustration by teaching you to think strategically about CAD.

Whether you are a practicing professional using form•Z for work or a student learning the software for school, you will find this book an easy yet comprehensive introduction to this powerful software package. The Workshops approach that Lachmi Khemlani has adopted to organize the material offers a natural learning sequence. The many examples and illustrations make it easy to follow along as you try things out on the screen. And long after you've worked your way through the lessons presented here, you'll keep the book ready at hand. You will no doubt find that *form•Z 4: 3D Modeling, Rendering, and Animation* will serve you as a desktop reference for the application as well.

Like exercising any creative skill, once you get good at it, making computer graphics models is fun. Certainly, it is work to master the mechanics of the software, but after you get into the swing of it, you will find yourself enjoying the challenges of making sophisticated and elegant models. And, as you can see from some of the models in the later chapters of this book, you can make some quite amazing models with form•Z. Enjoy!

Mark D. Gross, Ph.D.

Professor of Architecture
University of Washington, Seattle

Preface

Welcome to the world of 3D modeling, rendering, and animation! Imagine yourself as a sculptor, a carpenter, an architect, an interior designer, a product designer, or any kind of form-giver. You have visions of forms that you want to create and you'd like to visualize them accurately in all their three-dimensional reality. You could build small-scale physical models for each of them, but you find that to be not only a cumbersome and time-consuming process, but limiting in several ways. Different shapes need vastly different materials to be modeled, and not all forms can be created with wood and paper. Also, you are frustrated by the lack of malleability of a physical model, which makes the model so difficult to change as your design ideas develop; you find yourself having to start from scratch every time. You'd like a tool that enables you to create three-dimensional forms just as easily as your pencil moves across a piece of paper sketching them, and that can make changes and revisions to these forms as quickly as your mind goes through them. Welcome to form•Z!

form•Z is one of the most popular programs for 3D design available today, widely used both in schools and in the professional world. Its sophistication and versatility coupled with ease of use has attracted over 100,000 users. No longer are designers content to use the computer to merely draft out their designs while doing their conceptualizing solely on paper; they're taking advantage of the tremendous potential offered by 3D modeling software to enhance their designing capabilities. They're discovering that being able to actually visualize their creations interactively in 3D while designing them becomes an incentive to explore so many more alternative solutions than is possible using the traditional paper-and-pencil and physical model-building methods.

3D modeling motivates you to begin conceptualizing your design along the same lines as you'd build it in real life, complete in all dimensions, rather than with projections like plans, elevations, and sections. If you want a sphere, you create a sphere. If you want a cylindrical hole punched into the sphere, that's exactly what you do. You do not try to imagine how it would look like from a particular direction and orientation. You simply build it as it would be, and apply appropriate textures and simulate the desired lighting conditions,; then you have the choice to look at it from any angle, any perspective that you want. Therein lies the real power of 3D modeling. It's the closest that you can get to visualizing your design short of actually going out and creating it in real life, without having to resort to the unwieldy and inflexible process of physical model-building. What's more, form•Z provides all these powerful capabilities while still being a lot of fun to work with—as most designers comment when they are introduced to the program.

This book aims to give you a comprehensive understanding of how to use form•Z for 3D modeling, rendering, and animation. It comes directly from my several years of experience as an instructor in the Architecture department at University of California, Berkeley, teaching courses in which students learned how to use form•Z to explore diverse shapes and forms for their studio design projects.

The Approach

The content of this book is primarily organized into seven chapters—I refer to these as *workshops*. They're structured according to the way I taught the program to students at UC Berkeley, in a seven-week module. Each workshop follows a similar format—it contains a series of exercises, designed and grouped together according to the "theme" of that workshop, as reflected in its title. Each exercise consists of a sequence of steps that are described in detail. Performing these exercises as illustrated will enable you to learn about each and every one of the tools in the program and the operations that you can perform with it. Every workshop concludes with a suggested assignment, incorporating the tools learned in that session. Along with this, a demonstration of a sample design problem, based on the suggested assignment, is also provided—the main steps in the modeling process to achieve the desired form are described in detail.

This strategy has been devised to help you learn the different ways in which a design can be modeled, involving a certain sequence of operations. In the course of my teaching, I have found that many students, even after learning the use of the various tools, find the most difficult aspect of 3D modeling to be this: What approach should they take to arrive at a particular form? In form•Z, there is invariably more than one way to model something. One approach may be slow, arduous, and involved. Another may be faster, more logical, and more accurate. How can you identify which is the better way to model something? Undoubtedly, this is something that comes with practice. But for now, I anticipate that by observing the sequence of operations *I* choose to arrive at a particular form (which comes from many teaching sessions and solving the umpteen modeling problems students come up with!), you can begin to identify for yourself the easier, faster, and more efficient way to model various kinds of objects. I often have had students come to me with an overall form and ask, "Where do I start for something like this?" Some of the examples I present here come straight from such modeling problems I was asked to help with.

The content of each workshop has evolved considerably from the time I first taught the course, based on my assessment of the manner in which students responded to it, and their direct feedback and evaluation of the course after each session. In fact, I consider the sequence in which the material is presented and the manner in which the exercises are designed as two of the main strengths of this book. Without this carefully thought-out and organized sequence, one might just as well go through the manuals of the program and try to learn how to use form•Z from them.

It's important to understand the difference between a book and a manual. A manual is indispensable as a source of reference for a program. However, by virtue of its very nature, it's not the best way to learn to *use* a program. A manual has to describe everything, all the features that exist in a program, equally well in full detail—even those features that you might rarely or never ever have to use. A manual does not discriminate between important and unimportant features—it must tell you everything. Moreover, a manual describes all the tools and their operations in the sequence in which they appear in the program, rather than in the manner in which the tools are most likely to be used and need to be learned by the user.

The intent of this book is not to replace the use of the manuals altogether, for those of you who have access to them. You might need to consult them occasionally for more detailed information about certain tools and operations. What this book will do is guide you in learning to use the program easily. You'll start with the more elementary tools and create simple forms and compositions, build up your understanding of the program gradually, and learn to create more complex shapes and carry out more complicated operations as the workshops progress. By the end of the book, you will have worked with all the tools and should be well on your way towards using form•Z comfortably, confidently, with a clear understanding of what tool to use to create, render, and animate the forms you envision.

This book doesn't require you to have had prior experience with either 3D modeling or 2D drafting programs. However, basic familiarity with your operating system is assumed. This includes opening, closing, and saving files; working with windows; using the shortcut keys that appear on the pulldown menus; performing basic operations such as cut, copy, and paste that are found in almost any application; doing a page setup before printing; and so on. Refer to the manuals that came with your operating system if you need help with any of these tasks.

Overview of the Book

form•Z gives you the option of working in two different environments—*modeling* and *drafting*—each of which has its own set of tools and its own windows. The modeling environment is for working in 3D, while drafting is exclusively 2D. Although they're not synchronized, i.e., the drafting module does not automatically generate plans and sections of modeling objects, communicating between the two environments is fairly straightforward. Since the objective of this book is 3D design, we'll concentrate primarily on the modeling environment in all the workshops. An Appendix at the end of the book gives an overview of the drafting module, which provides you with tools and capabilities similar to what you can find in other conventional drafting programs.

The book starts with an introductory chapter that'll give you a basic understanding of the different types of objects you can create in form•Z. You'll also get acquainted with different aspects of the form•Z interface, from launching the program to learning how to create your own shortcuts keys for frequently used tools and commands. Then come the actual workshops, a brief overview of which is given in the following paragraphs.

Workshop 1 will introduce you to the basic modeling operations of form•Z. You'll learn how to create simple 2D and 3D objects, and perform some elementary transformations and boolean operations. You'll also learn how to interact with the program through the various palettes and dialogs associated with different tools.

In Workshop 2, you'll learn how to create models that are to scale. This includes setting up the units of measurement, using the coordinate displays effectively, and specifying values using the mouse as well as the keyboard. You'll also see how to restrain the cursor movement in various ways, create new objects with reference to existing ones, work at multiple levels ranging from points to groups, apply transformations and make copies of objects in different ways, edit parametric objects and lines, and finally, work with the insertion tools that can be used to perform some boolean operations more simply and elegantly.

Workshop 3 will teach you how to customize your working environment. You'll learn to modify the default colors used by the system, create new colors or surface styles, change the way the various display options work, use multiple layers, and create and save your own reference planes and views of the modeling world. Finally, you'll learn how to save the modified settings as preference files and template files, which you can then recall for use in other projects when needed.

In Workshop 4, you'll be introduced to several new modeling tools for creating more complex forms. You'll see how to revolve simple 2D shapes about an axis or sweep, skin, and loft them along various paths, derive new objects from existing ones in various ways, work with powerful sectioning tools, model undulating landforms and terrains, round object edges and corners, transform objects using draft angles, and create blends and fillets. You'll also learn how to build up sophisticated configurations by attaching objects to each other in various ways, align and distribute objects, extend and trim them with respect to other objects, and position them along a path to generate interesting forms.

Workshop 5 is devoted to imaging, lights, and textures. You'll study the extensive set of options available to you for rendering your models photorealistically, use the Sketch Rendering plugin to generate sketch-like renderings, and work with the Imager Set that enables you to render a set of images efficiently in a batch mode. You'll learn how to light up your objects in various ways using multiple light types, and explore the radiosity-based rendering feature which enhances lighting effects considerably. You'll also see how to map textures to objects more precisely, apply multiple textures to the same surface using decals, and look at some other object attributes that can be manipulated to achieve interesting rendering effects.

Workshop 6 covers the entire repertoire of tools available in form•Z for organic modeling, i.e., modeling of non-rectilinear forms. This includes creating meshes on the surfaces of objects in various ways, and applying movements, disturbances, various kinds of deformations, and image-based displacements to meshed objects, all of which can be used to mold objects as desired. You'll learn to create and modify smooth curves, controlled curves and meshes, nurbz (NURBS-based) surfaces, and patches, and carry out boolean operations on these kinds of objects. You'll also venture further into the realm of organic modeling using the sophisticated capabilities of metaformz, which are objects that have the ability to blend seamlessly with each other when they overlap.

In Workshop 7, you'll be introduced to the amazing realm of 3D text with which you can populate your models, and learn to create and use symbols or object libraries. You'll see how to generate and play QuickTime VR movies as well as animation sequences of your modeling world. Last but not least, you'll study some of the common options associated with importing and exporting files of different formats, and how to customize your use of form•Z with plugins and scripts.

The book concludes with an Appendix that provides you with a brief overview of the drafting module of form•Z.

About form•Z

form•Z is available as three separate programs: form•Z, form•Z RenderZone, and form•Z RadioZity. The first includes just the modeling functions; the second includes lighting, texture mapping, and rendering capabilities; and the third adds radiosity-based rendering, which simulates the lighting conditions in a scene more accurately and realistically. This book covers the features available in all three programs.

form•Z comes on both the Macintosh and Windows platforms, and using popular terminology, I will refer to these as *Mac* and *PC* respectively. The window snapshots and dialog boxes that are illustrated in this book come the PC platform on which I work. As far as usage is concerned, there are only minor differences between the two platforms, which I will mention as and when they appear. The reader of this book is by no means limited to either platform—it can be used by both the Mac and PC users of form•Z.

The recommended system requirements for running form•Z on all platforms are 256 MB memory and 200 MB hard disk space. The minimums are 64 MB and 50 MB respectively. The OS requirements for different platforms are as follows: Mac OS X—version 10.2.x recommended, 10.1 minimum; Mac OS—version 9.2 recommended, 8.6 minimum; Windows Consumer—Windows 98, Windows ME or Windows XP home edition; Windows Professional—Windows NT 4.0, Windows 2000, or Windows XP.

About Version 4

This book incorporates the latest release of form•Z, version 4, which represents a major release of the program. Long-time users will recall that the last major release, version 3, incorporated a significant overhaul of the interface. Version 4 incorporates even more dramatic changes, but many of these lie under the surface and won't be immediately apparent. The program has been completely redesigned internally to have a modular and open architecture, which can support plugins and scripts developed by both auto•des•sys and third-party vendors. Organic modeling has been vastly improved with several new tools for creating, reconstructing, and editing NURBS surfaces in various ways; a whole new toolset for also creating, reconstructing, and editing different kinds of smooth curves; and the introduction of the Loft, Blend, and Fillet tools. Other significant enhancements include the ability to include lights and lights groups in symbols for creating and reusing real world lighting fixtures, network rendering that allows a single image or animation to be rendered faster on multiple machines simultaneously, a new design for the tool icons in full color, better organized and more consistent-looking dialogs, clearer distinction between native and non-native file formats, and a new image export option to the HPGL (Hewlett Packard Graphics Language) file format for pen plotting.

Version 4's new open and modular architecture, with its plugins and scripts, will take some time to become noticeable, but it definitely represents a new beginning for form•Z and will drastically affect its future evolution.

About the Accompanying CD-ROM

An installer for the demo copy of form•Z 4 is provided in the accompanying CD-ROM in the folder called `formZ demo`. A demo copy of the latest release can also be easily downloaded from the form•Z website at *http://www.formz.com*. You can use the demo to try out all the features of the program if it's not available to you, including working with the assignment files. All that the demo does not allow you to do is print and save. Keep in mind that the minimum system requirements mentioned in an earlier section for the regular version of form•Z apply to the demo version as well.

The `formZ demo` folder also contains installation instructions for the demo in a PDF file, and several sample files, symbol libraries, and texture images supplied by auto•des•sys, Inc.

All the files related to the content of this book are organized in two folders on the CD-ROM. The `Assignments` folder contains, for the seven workshops, a separate form•Z file for every step of the assignment that appears at the end of each workshop, along with a rendered color image of the completed assignment in TIFF format. Providing a separate file for each step enables you to compare what you have to what you *should* have, as you work through an assignment. You can also simply use any of the files as a starting point and proceed on your own from there, if the preliminary steps of an assignment seem easy to you.

The other reference folder for the book on the CD-ROM is called `Workshop5 Images`. It contains color versions of all the rendered images that appear in the workshop, "Illuminating, Texturing, and Rendering Your World." These are again in TIFF format and can be opened by any program reading this format.

A Note on Notations

In this book, all menu items, tool names, dialog items, and so on are differentiated from the rest of the text by `this difference in font`.

There are three levels of hierarchy in the organization of the content: *workshop*, *exercise*, and *section*. A workshop contains a number of exercises; an exercise comprises several sections. To make cross-referencing easier, a section number is preceded by the exercise number. Thus, Section 2.4 refers to Section 4 of

Exercise 2 in the same workshop. A section from another workshop is referenced by the section number followed by the workshop number, for example, Section 2.4 from Workshop 3.

The bulleted paragraphs in the exercises indicate actual steps that you should perform, while unbulleted paragraphs provide explanations wherever necessary.

form•Z is primarily an icon-based program, where operations are carried out by selecting tool icons from various palettes. Along with a notation for locating a tool that is described in the Introduction, a tool icon is displayed to the right of the text whenever the tool is encountered in the workshops for the first time. This will enable you to easily identify the tools as you go along.

To make the book easier to read, I have avoided putting eye-catching information under multiple categories such as Tip, Hint, Note, Warning, and so on, as so many other books do. All such important information is given in a single category, Note, identified by an icon that was created in—what else but form•Z!

Contact Information

For more information about the form•Z program, including purchase and pricing, you can visit *http://www.formz.com.*

For matters related to the content of this book, including write-ups on new features that will be added in future updates of the program, visit my website at *http://www.arcwiz.com/formZbook2/formZbook.htm.* You can also contact me via e-mail at *lachmi@arcwiz.com* with any questions, comments, and feedback related to this book.

The customer service support numbers for McGraw-Hill are 1-800-217-0059 in the United States and 1-914-747-2787 outside the United States.

Trademark Information

Acknowledgments

I owe my book-writing ventures to my husband, Pran Kurup. It was he who set me on the path to becoming an author with firsthand advice coming from his own book-writing experiences, and has continued to provide tremendous support and motivation throughout this endeavor.

Long-term credit for my books goes all the way back to my parents, Rita and Shyam Khemlani, who have always encouraged my intellectual pursuits.

I am especially grateful to Cary Sullivan, Senior Editor for Architecture and Design at McGraw-Hill, who responded to my book proposal with great enthusiasm and set the stage for its publication.

Special thanks to Chris Yessios and David Kropp of auto•des•sys, Inc. for heading the development of a splendid program like form•Z, and for their support of this book and their prompt responses to my requests for clarifications and information.

I would like to thank Mark Gross, who shares my enthusiasm for form•Z and kindly agreed to write the Foreword for this book.

I could not have written this book if I had not been given the continued opportunity to teach form•Z at the University of California at Berkeley by Yehuda Kalay, Professor of Architecture.

I am grateful to all the students at UC Berkeley who have, over the years, enrolled in my form•Z workshops. Their endless barrage of questions taught me more than I could have ever hoped to learn on my own.

I greatly appreciate the efforts of all the people at McGraw-Hill who were involved in this project: Stephen M. Smith, Editing Manager; Anthony Landi, Art Director; Sherri Souffrance, Senior Production Supervisor; and Joshua Goldstein, Systems Administrator.

Above all, I'd like to acknowledge my children, Sarisha and Sahil, for their cheerful acceptance of the long hours I spent working on this book and the stress relief they provide on a daily basis.

form•Z 4

3D Modeling, Rendering, and Animation

Getting Acquainted

This introductory chapter starts with an overview of the different kinds of objects and the basic model types that can be created in form•Z, giving you a snapshot of the entire program and its repertoire. Keep this broad picture in mind when you proceed to the workshops and start exploring the individual tools. You'll find yourself working with greater clarity and a lot less confusion than you would if you just plunged into the details right away.

After the overview, the Introduction focuses on some of the key features of the form•Z interface, which you should be comfortable with before proceeding to the workshops. You'll start by launching the program, then move on to look at the different component windows which make up the interface. You'll learn how to work with the various tool palettes, get online help when you need it, and enhance your speed and efficiency with the program by creating your own shortcut keys for various tools and operations.

1. Overview of form•Z Objects and Model Types

form•Z is both a solid and surface modeler. Unlike some other modeling programs which simulate the modeling of solids by actually manipulating only surfaces, form•Z is a "true" solid modeler that lets you model even complex solids in relatively simple ways. It has the full complement of tools for modeling rectilinear forms as well as organic, free-form surfaces and forms with NURBS, Bezier/ Coon patches, and metaballs.

Figure I.1 shows a simplified chart illustrating the various types of objects you will find in form•Z. There are dedicated modeling tools for each of these objects. In addition, there are several other tools that can manipulate these objects in various ways; for instance, there's a Sweep tool that can convert a 2D surface into a 3D solid object by simply "sweeping" it along a 2D path. You'll learn more about this tool in Workshop 4 (Enhancing Your Modeling Capabilities).

As shown in Figure I.1, there are four basic categories of objects: points, wires, surfaces, and solids. Each of these object categories, as you can see, comprises several different kinds of objects. Within this broad categorization, further subtypes also exist. Thus, a wire object is *open* if its endpoints do not meet, and is *closed* if they do. A point object can be a single entity, or part of a group of points referred to as a *point cloud*. A surface can be *one-sided*, if it is a single surface that has an area; or *two-sided*, if it is actually a solid with two equal, coincident, and opposite surfaces, but no thickness. A two-sided surface is also referred to as a *surface solid*. It looks identical to a surface, but there are some operational differences between the two kinds of objects that you'll learn about subsequently in the workshops.

Notice also the objects referred to as *enclosures*, both in 2D as well as in 3D. Mathematically, these are no different from the regular objects in their respective categories. The distinction is made because form•Z has dedicated tools for creating both 2D and 3D enclosures, which is of great convenience, especially in architectural modeling.

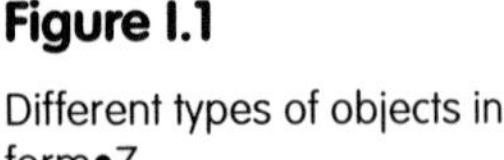

Figure I.1

Different types of objects in form•Z.

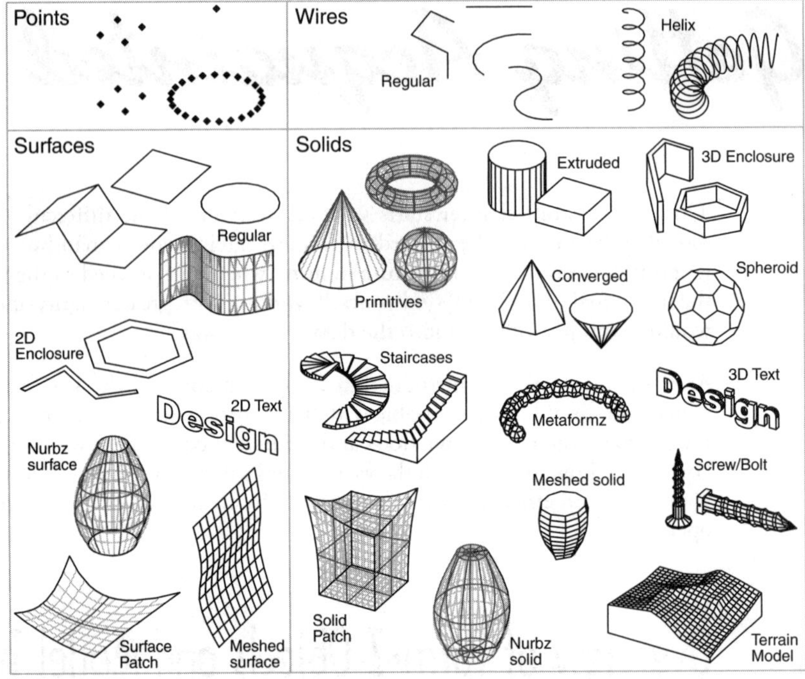

By far the largest variety of objects is in the solids category, reinforcing the emphasis of form•Z on simplifying the complicated process of solid modeling as much as possible. Some of these objects are shown in Figure I.1; a complete listing would take up too much space. All the objects shown are mathematically true solids with a definite volume, but it helps a great deal to have separate tools devoted exclusively towards creating basic primitives, simple extrusions, converged solids, spheroids, NURBS-based objects, patches, terrain models, staircases, and so on.

Most of the objects that you create in form•Z are *parametric*, that is, they're stored with their creation parameters, allowing you to edit and modify them through a preview dialog or by using a tool. Those that are not parametric are referred to as *plain* objects. Another dedicated tool exists for converting parametric objects to plain objects, which is sometimes needed to allow operations that cannot be performed on parametric objects. You'll encounter the parametric/plain distinction frequently as you work with the various modeling tools.

A parametric object is also known as a controlled *object, as it is stored with the control parameters that can be accessed and modified to reshape the object.*

Another important distinction that you need to keep in mind as you work in form•Z is the *model type* of an object, which can be *facetted* or *smooth*. The main difference between the two is in how the faces making up the object are defined. In a facetted object, the surface is made up of a series of planar faces, whereas in a smooth object, the individual faces comprising it can be curved. This impacts how the object is rendered. When a curved object of the facetted model type is rendered, the individual facets will be seen unless the resolution is very high; the same object of the smooth model type will be rendered perfectly smoothly, irrespective of the resolution. The contrast is remarkable, as you can see in Figure I.2. Earlier versions of form•Z had only facetted objects, which frequently caused rendering heartache to users. The introduction and pervasiveness of the smooth model type, starting from version 3.8, is certainly a welcome development. Moreover, the ability to combine facetted and smooth objects means that you can literally model any conceivable form in form•Z.

Now that we have a basic understanding of the different kinds of objects and model types that can be created in form•Z, let's get acquainted with the form•Z interface.

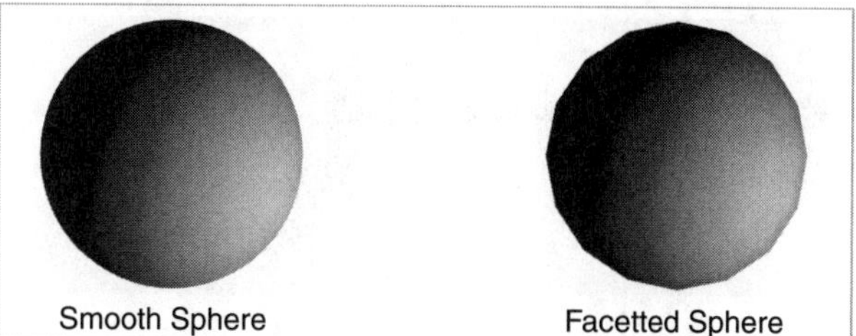

Figure I.2

The contrast in smoothness between the rendering of two spheres of the same size but of different model types: smooth and facetted.

2. Launching form•Z

After installing the application, navigate to the form•Z program folder on your desktop. It should look like the one shown in Figure I.3 if you're using a PC. The Mac icons are similar. Go ahead and launch form•Z by double-clicking on the main application icon, which is circled in the illustration. It takes a few moments for the program to go through the initialization routines, after which you'll be asked to click or press the return (Mac) or Enter (PC) key to continue. Do so. In future, you can start form•Z using any one of the usual application launching methods available on your system.

Much of the form•Z interface is visible as soon as you start the application—the main graphics window, several floating palettes, and rows and columns of various tools for different functions. At first sight, it might seem overwhelming, making you wonder how you're ever going to be able to find your way around the program without getting confused or lost. The rest of this chapter is aimed at alleviating precisely this fear—it'll help you navigate through the program easily and understand how to work with the various components that make up the form•Z program. You should come away from it with an appreciation of what is, in fact, a very lucid, easy-to-use, and elegant user interface.

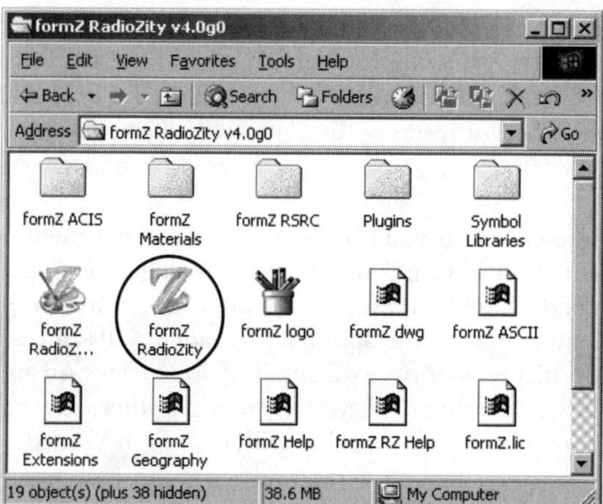

Figure I.3

The form•Z folder with its various icons. The main application icon is circled.

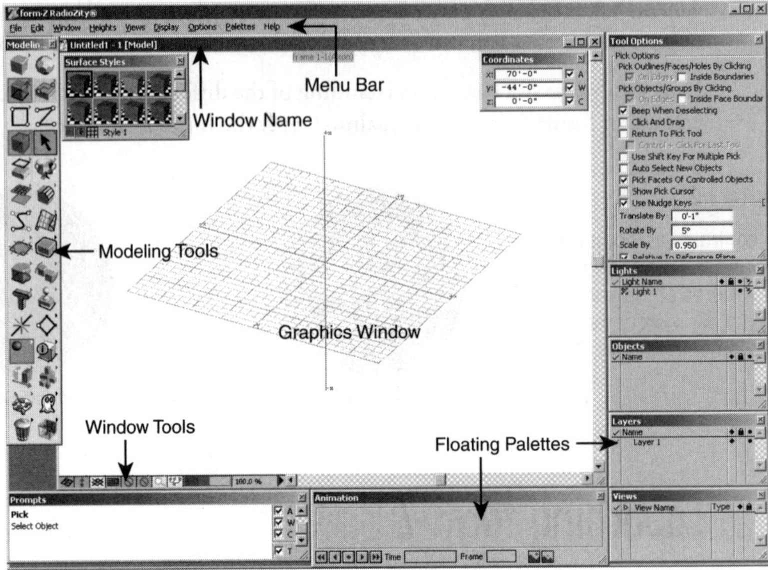

Figure I.4

The default screen layout, showing the different components making up the form•Z interface.

3. Exploring the Basic Interface

As soon as you launch the form•Z application, you'll see the default screen layout shown in Figure I.4. The basic interface is made up of several different items; these are annotated in the illustration and briefly described below. Some of the items are referred to by an abbreviation that's given in parentheses beside the name. Keep a careful note of this—the same abbreviation will be used in referring to these items throughout the book.

Menu Bar

This is the standard menu bar located at the top of the screen. In form•Z, it consists of nine pulldown menus for different functions, including Help. (On the Mac, the form•Z Help menu is incorporated into the standard Mac OS Help menu.) In this book, menu items will be referenced in the format, *main menu > submenu*. So, for instance, Display > Wire Frame refers to the Wire Frame item under the Display menu.

Glance through the menus and you'll find that some of the menu items have an asterisk (*) sign associated with them. This indicates that there's a dialogue box (called *dialog* for short) associated with the operation performed by that item, containing various options. This dialog can be accessed by selecting that menu item with the option key (Mac) or Ctrl+Shift keys (PC) pressed. On the other hand, the menu items that only bring up dialogs and do not perform any other operation are designated by three dots, for instance Options > Layers...; selecting these items brings up the associated dialog right away. You'll learn more about working with dialogs in Workshop 1 (Letting Yourself Go).

Window Name

form•Z is organized in projects. A *project* essentially corresponds to a file. By default, form•Z presents you with a new Untitled1 project when it is launched. The word Model in square brackets in the window title bar indicates that you're in the modeling environment. Of course, you also know this from the fact that all the three coordinate axes—X, Y, and Z—are visible in the window. In the drafting environment, the word [Model] in the window title would be replaced by [Draft], and you would see only the X and Y axes. This makes it possible to easily distinguish between the two window types. For most of this book, we'll be dealing with the modeling environment, and consequently, with modeling windows.

One project can have many windows associated with it, hence the window is named Untitled1-1, indicating that it's the first window of the Untitled1 project. Even though multiple windows can be opened for a particular project, only one can be *active* at any given time. Essentially, this means that you can work in only one window at a time. A window is made active by clicking on it. When a project is saved, all the windows *associated* with that project are saved. Further discussion on associated windows will appear in Workshop 3 (Personalizing Your Environment).

Graphics Window

The graphics window is where all the modeling and visualization activities take place. Initially, this is blank except for the default display of the XY reference plane grid colored in teal (a bluish-green color), and the three coordinate axes—X, Y, and Z—colored in red.

The graphics window can be divided into a number of frames, each of which can be set to a different view of the modeling world. It's possible to continue drawing from one frame to another, which provides additional flexibility and convenience in modeling. By default, the graphics window consists of a single frame, as you can see. It's indicated by the name, frame 1-1(Axon), appearing at the top of the window, just below the window title bar. The two numbers stand for the window number and frame number respectively, while the word Axon in parentheses is the name of the view to which the frame is set. We'll learn more about frames and how to work with them in Workshop 3 (Personalizing Your Environment).

Modeling Tools (M-Tool)

form•Z has a contemporary user interface where you don't have to type in commands—you just click on the tool icon of the operation you wish to perform. All the tools in form•Z are divided into two categories: those that deal with the creation and editing of entities, grouped under the *modeling tool palette*; and those that deal with manipulating some aspect of the window display, grouped under the *window tool palette*. The modeling tool palette is the vertical palette positioned by default on the left side of the graphics window. It consists of 15 rows of tools, arranged in two columns, used to carry out the various modeling operations. Each row in turn has many tool icons. The complete modeling tool palette is shown in Figure I.5, in a different icon style from the default style shown in Figure I.4. Tools aren't repeated needlessly as menu commands, which keeps the menu concise.

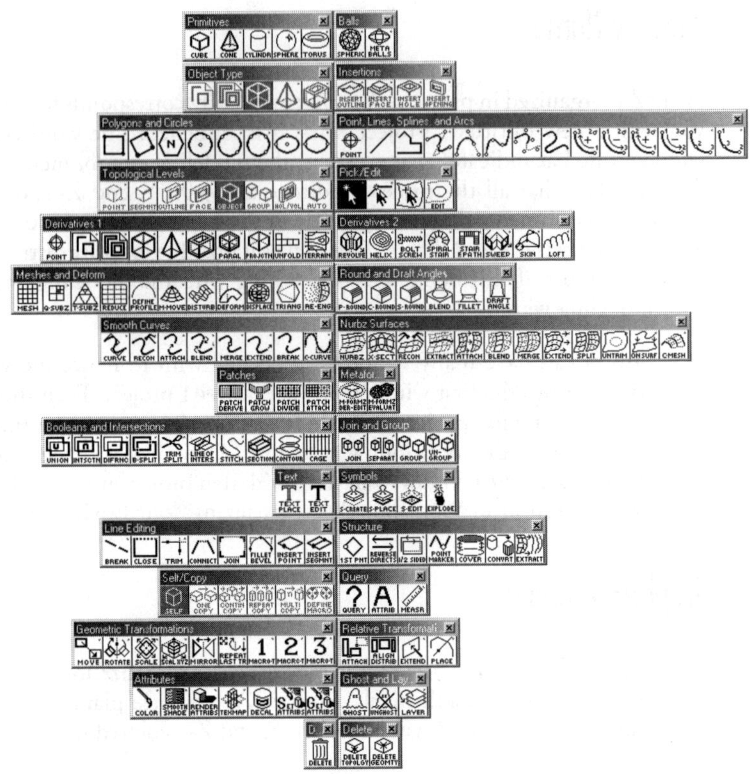

Figure I.5

All the tools in the modeling tool palette, in a different icon style from the default setting.

In this book, any tool from the modeling palette will be referred to by its row number, accompanied by an "a" or a "b" to indicate whether it's in the left column or the right column respectively, then followed by its order in that row. Thus, for example, M-Tool:5b,1 refers to the first tool, Revolve, located in the right column of the fifth row. Check it out and verify that this is indeed the case. A more comprehensive discussion on the use of the tool palettes appears a little later in Section 4.

Window Tools (W-Tool)

The window tool palette is the horizontal palette positioned in the lower left margin of the graphics window. It consists of eight vertically arranged columns of tools. As mentioned earlier, the tools here control the graphic environment of the window, so every window of the project will have its own set of window tools located at its base. The complete window tool palette is shown in Figure I.10. As with the modeling tools, the window tools will be referred to by their position in the columns. So, for instance, W-Tool:6,4 refers to the fourth tool from the bottom, Midpoint Snap, in the sixth column. Again, check it out.

If you find it inconvenient to access each one of the window tool palettes individually when you're working with multiple windows, the same set of tools is also available as a *floating palette* (described next) from the Palettes main menu. You can open this and position it anywhere on the screen for easy access. The tools activated in this floating palette will change depending upon which window is activated, keeping in sync with that window's own tool palette.

Floating Palettes

These are small floating windows that can be positioned anywhere on the screen. There are nineteen in all, arranged in two groups. The first group is comprised of the standard palettes, including the modeling and window tool palettes, while the second group is comprised of palettes that also exist as dialogs. Of these, ten are opened by default when you open a new project, and positioned as shown in Figure I.4. Any palette can be closed, if not required, by clicking on the close button in the upper left corner, and can be reopened, when required, by going to the Palettes menu and selecting the required palette.

4. Working with the Tool Palettes

We've seen that there are two kinds of tool palettes—modeling and window. Each one of these is comprised of many tools grouped together in related rows (as in the case of modeling tools) or in related columns (as in the case of window tools). Both these palettes work on similar principles, which are briefly discussed below.

All the tools in a row (or column) are not immediately visible. To see the entire set, you need to click on the first tool in that row, keeping the mouse down. This brings up the complete set of tools from which the desired one can be selected by moving to it (see Figure I.6). The selected tool will now be positioned in the beginning of the row, and it will remain there until another tool from that set is selected. This avoids the tedium of having to go over the same process again when working with one tool repeatedly. The selected tool will be highlighted to indicate that it's the currently active tool. Only one such tool can be active at any given time.

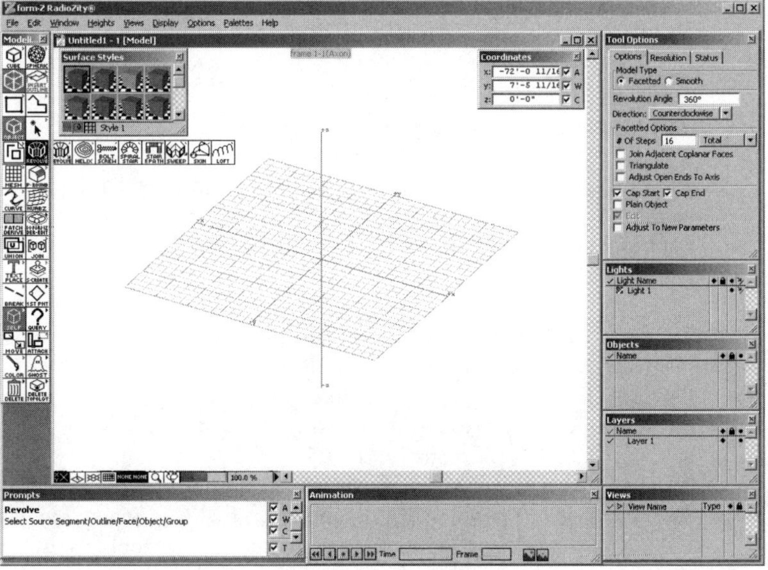

Figure I.6

Taking a look at all the tools belonging to one row of the modeling tool palette.

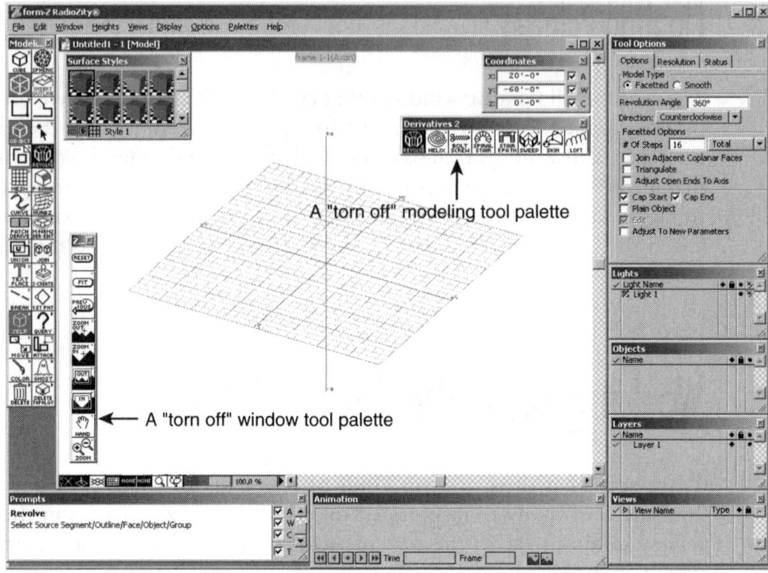

Figure I.7

Two tool palettes "torn off" and repositioned on the screen.

While most of the tools in both the modeling and window tool palettes are colored in black, you can see that some tools in three particular rows—2, 4, and 12—of the modeling palette are colored in teal or magenta. These tools function differently from the other tools—they *set a mode* for the black-colored tools to operate in, rather than *perform an operation*. You will learn more about each of these tools as the workshops progress.

Any particular row or column of tools from either palette can be "torn off" by selecting and dragging it to position it anywhere on the screen (see Figure I.7) Subsequently, all the regular window operations—moving, closing, and so on—can be applied to it. This is particularly useful when you work with a certain set of tools very frequently and require them to be constantly visible to you.

Once you've gained expertise with the program and use it extensively, you might also like to customize the tool palettes, based on your style of working and the project at hand. Customization involves reorganizing the tools in the palettes, deleting some of them if necessary. To undertake this process, select the last command from the Palettes menu, Customize Tools. This invokes the dialog shown in Figure I.8. The Category popup menu at the top of the dialog lets you select which tool palette you want to customize: drafting, modeling, or window. The default, as you can see, is the modeling tool palette.

The Icons Customization dialog contains three separate windows showing the icons of the tool palette that's selected for customization. All three windows have different functions. The Tool Bar window shows the first icon of each set of tools (row or column) in the palette, as it appears in the toolbar on the screen. An icon is selected by clicking on it; this actually selects the entire set of tools represented by that icon. Multiple icons can be selected using the Shift key. Once an icon is selected, it can be deleted by clicking on the accompanying Remove button, or it can be dragged to another location in the toolbar. If you double-click on an icon, a dialog is invoked in which you can change the default name assigned to that tool set. You can also create new tool sets using the accompanying New button; these are placed by default at the bottom of the toolbar. Thus, in the Tool Bar window, you're essentially working with *entire tool sets*.

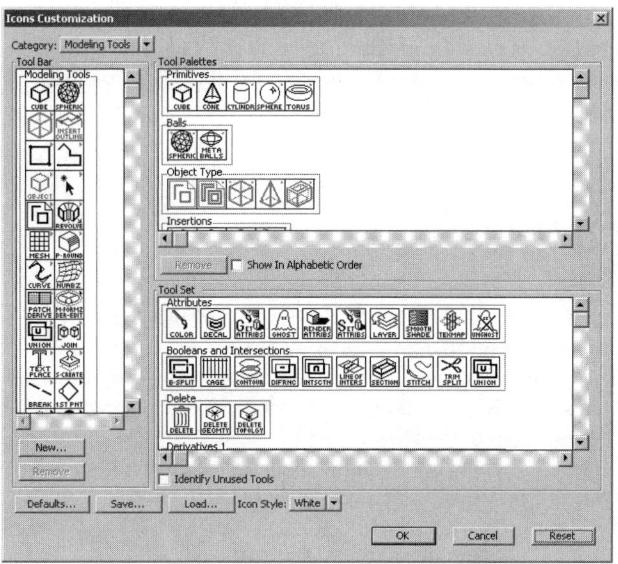

Figure I.8

The dialog invoked by the Customize Tools command.

To "fill" new tool sets that you've created with tools, use the second window in the Icons Customization dialog, Tool Palettes. This window shows the individual tools in each tool set whose first icon is depicted in the Tool Bar window. Here again, icons can be selected for repositioning or deletion by clicking on them. You can move an icon to a different location in the same palette, or move it to a different palette. Once selected, an icon can be deleted using the accompanying Remove button. Thus, you're actually working with *individual tools* here rather than with entire tool sets.

There's a third window in the dialog called Tool Set, which also displays the individual tool icons of the palette selected for customization. Unlike the Tool Palettes window, which gets updated to show the customized toolbar of that palette, the contents of the Tool Set window do not change. It retains all the available tools in their default positions in the palette; the tools cannot be deleted or repositioned. However, they *can* be copied across to the tool sets in the Tool Palettes window above by selecting and dragging. Thus, if you delete some tools in the Tool Palettes window and find out at a later stage that you need to include them again, you can always copy them across from the "permanent" collection in the Tool Set window.

The few remaining options located at the base of the Icons Customization dialog serve various functions. The Defaults button is used to reset the selected palette to the default form•Z layout. Reset, on the other hand, performs the standard task of resetting the layout to what it was when the dialog was invoked, eliminating all the subsequent changes. You can save your customized layout to a menu file, automatically given the ".mnu" extension, using the Save command. Many such menu files can be created. Any menu file can be loaded for use in subsequent sessions of form•Z using Load. The Icon Style pulldown menu lets you choose between three different types of looks for the various icons. The default of Color was shown in Figure I.4. In all the other illustrations in this book, the White option has been used for clarity.

Throughout this book, the tool icons will mostly be shown in the White icon style, as it is clearer in print.

Since there are so many tools in both the modeling and window tool palettes, remembering what each tool is used for can be a daunting task for a beginner. Although by the end of this book you'll have learned about each tool in depth, you can get a sneak preview right away by using the Help option, which is discussed in detail next.

5. Getting Help

form•Z has a comprehensive, well-organized, and user-friendly help system built into its interface. Instead of the conventional Help menus found in other applications in which you have to traverse a series of hyperlinks to ultimately get to the information you want, form•Z tells you directly what any tool or menu item is used for. Say, for instance, you want more information about the Mesh tool, which is the first tool in the left column of the sixth row of the modeling palette. Simply select it and then go to Help > General. A dialog is invoked that provides a brief synopsis about the selected tool (Figure I.9).

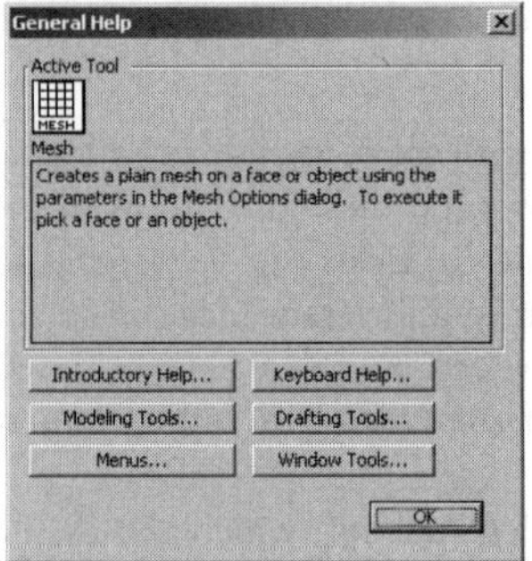

Figure I.9

The Help dialog for the Mesh tool.

You can see that this General Help dialog also gives you the option to branch off to additional information about each one of the tools and menus that make up the form•Z environment. If you click on the Window Tools button, for instance, a dialog displaying all the window tools is invoked (see Figure I.10). Information about any tool can now be obtained by simply highlighting it with the cursor. You don't need to click on a tool; merely move the mouse over it. Similarly, information about all the modeling tools can be obtained in an identical fashion by invoking the Modeling Tools option from the General Help dialog. All the options in this dialog are also directly accessible from the Help menu. So, for instance, you can access the Window Tools dialog shown in Figure I.10 directly by going to Help > Window Tools.

Spend some time at this stage browsing through the descriptions of the tools in both the modeling and window tool palettes. It will give you a feel for what the different kinds of tools are and how they are organized. Check out also the Introduction, Keyboard, and Menus options in the Help menu; you'll find them very useful. The Drafting Tools option can be explored when you go through the brief overview of the drafting module in the Appendix. The Error Messages option lets you view a log of the errors you ran into during your work, while the Project Info dialog provides you with useful information about the objects in the project.

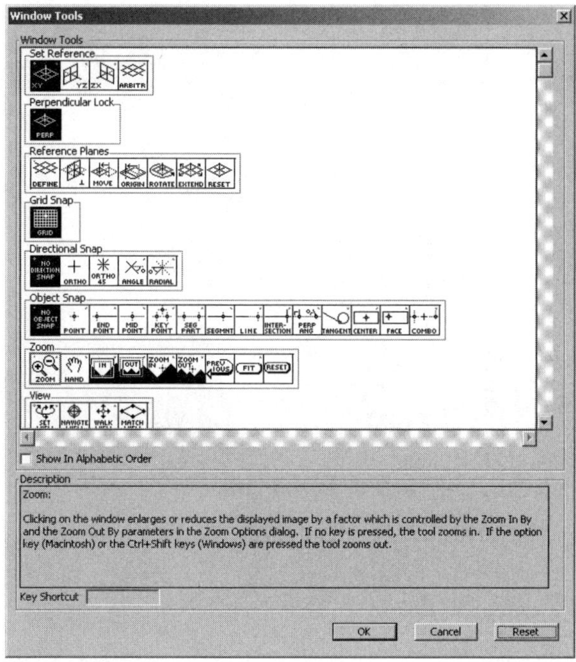

Figure I.10

The Help dialog for the window tool palette. Information is being displayed about W-Tool:7,1.

6. Creating Your Own Shortcut Keys

Many of the commands that appear in the form•Z pulldown menus have associated shortcut keys, which appear beside the name of the command, just like in any other program. Thus, the default shortcut key for File > Save, as you would expect, is command+S on the Mac and Ctrl+S on the PC. However, as you'll see from browsing through the various menus, not all commands have shortcut keys. When you start working with the tool palettes, you'll find that the various tools they contain also do not have shortcut keys associated with them by default.

form•Z, however, does provide you with a utility to create and store your own shortcut keys. With this feature, you can assign your own key combinations to the tools and commands that you use frequently, bringing them literally to your fingertips. If a shortcut key already exists for a particular command, you can also choose to overwrite it with your own combination. Users can create their own sets of shortcut keys and save them in files, which they can readily access even when they move to a different computer. The convenience of this utility can greatly enhance your speed and efficiency with the program, taking it to an altogether new level of user-friendliness.

The process of creating shortcut keys is carried out in the Key Shortcuts Manager dialog (Figure I.11-a), which you can access by going to Edit > Key Shortcuts. The window on the left lists all the menu items and tools, grouped by category. Any category can be opened or closed by clicking on the arrows (Mac) or the plus/minus signs (PC) beside its name. Figure I.11-a shows the Primitives toolset of the Modeling Tools palette expanded in this fashion. Any item from the expanded list can be selected by clicking on it. If a shortcut key is already associated with that item, it will appear in the Shortcuts window on the right side of the dialog.

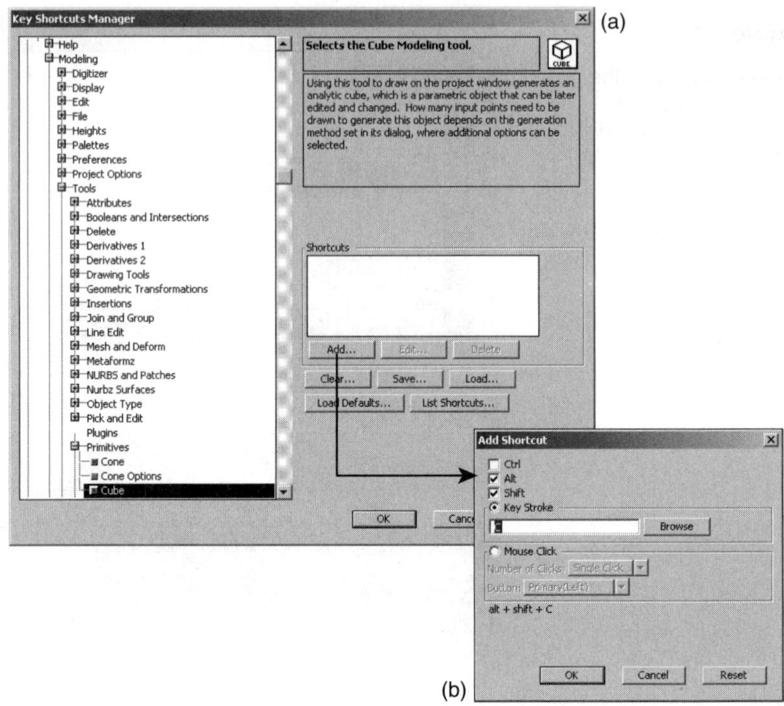

Figure I.11

The Key Shortcuts Manager dialog, showing the expanded list of tools in the Primitives toolset, and the Add Shortcut dialog, showing the shortcut created for the selected tool.

As you can see, there's no shortcut key associated with the Cube tool that's selected in Figure I.11-a. To create your own shortcut key for this tool, simply click on the Add button. This will open up the Add Shortcut dialog (Figure I.11-b), the contents of which will differ slightly depending upon which platform you're using. The idea, however, is the same: you can make up a combination of *keys* (such as Control, Option, and so on), and *key strokes* (such as A, B, 1, 2, etc.) or *mouse clicks* (single, double, etc.) that will function as the shortcut key for the selected item. Note that you can use either a key stroke or a mouse click in a shortcut, but not both.

Figure I.11-b shows how the combination of Alt+Shift+C on the PC has been assigned as the shortcut for the Cube tool. To see if it actually works, exit both dialogs by clicking on their OK buttons and test this key combination; you should find that it activates the Cube tool on the Modeling Tools palette without requiring you to select it with the mouse. Convenient, isn't it?

The Key Shortcuts Manager dialog has some additional options for managing shortcuts. You can Edit or Delete a particular shortcut, or Clear all of them. You can Save your set of created shortcuts to a file, which is automatically given the ".sct" extension. You can use the Load button to load this shortcut file in future working sessions of form•Z. The Load Defaults button will load all the default shortcuts, while the List Shortcuts button will list the current set of shortcuts in an organized fashion. It also gives you the option to print the list for easy reference.

While you may not need to create your own shortcuts while you're learning the program, you'll find this a very convenient utility once you become proficient with form•Z and start using it extensively. Be aware, therefore, that such a utility exists, so that you know how to use it once the time comes.

With this brief introduction to the form•Z interface, we are now ready to take our first plunge into the world of 3D modeling, rendering, and animation, starting with Workshop 1 (Letting Yourself Go).

WORKSHOP 1

Letting Yourself Go

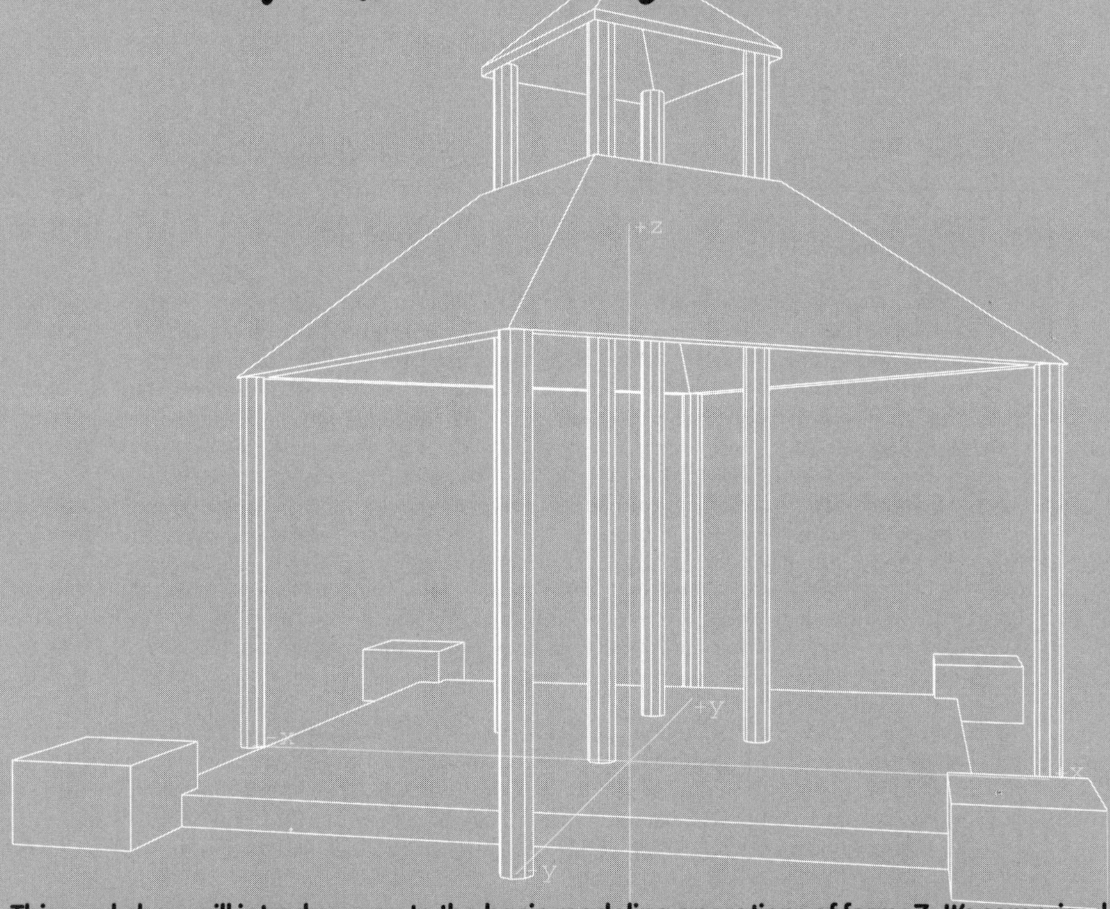

This workshop will introduce you to the basic modeling operations of form•Z. It's comprised of four exercises, covering a wide range of both modeling and window tools. You'll learn how to create simple 2D and 3D objects, along with some elementary transformations and boolean operations. You'll also learn how to interact with the program through the various palettes and dialogs associated with different tools. In this workshop, the concern will not be with aspects such as working units, drawing scale, creating objects of specific dimensions, and so on. The idea, instead, is to simply let yourself loose and create any forms you want, of any size and scale you want.

EXERCISE 1

Beginning with 2D: A Complete Session

In this exercise, we'll run through an entire session of form•Z, starting with launching the program, creating simple 2D elements, performing basic operations such as moving and deleting objects, changing viewpoints as well as the display mode, deriving 3D objects from 2D elements, and finally, printing what we have. This exercise is slightly atypical, since it deals with such a broad range of tools and functions. Most of the other exercises, particularly in later workshops, will focus on a single tool or a group of related tools. It's important, however, to start with as large a picture as possible.

1.1 Setting the Stage: Starting form•Z

- Launch form•Z. A default modeling window will appear on the screen, as you saw in Figure I.4 in the Introduction. Save it as a new project using File > Save As and specify a suitable file name. The file is saved by default in the form•Z format and an extension of ".fmz" is automatically given to the file name.

Once you start working on actual projects, make it a habit to keep saving at regular intervals so that you don't lose your work in the event of a computer crash. form•Z does have an "automatic save" option like many other programs, and we'll look at this feature in Workshop 3 (Personalizing Your Environment). However, it may not always be advisable to use such an option, for reasons we shall soon see. At any point, you can choose to go back to the last saved version of the project using File > Revert to Saved.

- The default view is axonometric. Change it to a plan view by selecting Views > Top. The graphics window will now resemble a graph sheet.

- Turn off the palettes for Coordinates, Tool Options, Lights, Objects, Layers, Views, and Animation by clicking on their close buttons. You will not be using these in most of the exercises in this workshop. Make sure that the Prompts palette is open—this is where you will interface with the program, give your input, and receive messages from the system.

- Leave the Surface Styles palette (or the Colors palette in the basic version of form•Z) open, so that you can create objects with different colors. The color that's highlighted in this palette is the *active* color; all objects are created using the active color. To designate another color from the palette as the active color, simply click on it and it will be highlighted. Change the active color frequently in this manner as you work on the rest of the exercise—having a large variety of colors on your screen will make it a lot more fun.

1.2 Single-Line 2D Mode

- Select M-Tool:2a,1. Recall from the Introduction that this notation refers to the first tool in the left column of the second row of the modeling tool palette. Make sure you've selected the icon shown on the right.

The entire second left row consists of the *object generation modes*—the mode that's selected from here will determine what kinds of objects the tools in the third row will create: 2D single or double lines, or 3D extruded, converged, or enclosed solids. The first tool on this row, which you've just selected, sets the object generation mode to 2D Surface.

1.3 Creating Closed Shapes

- Select the Rectangle tool, the first of the drawing tools in the left column of the third row. Use it to draw a rectangle anywhere on the screen. The first click of the mouse picks one end, the second click completes the figure. Don't worry about the dimensions of the shape at this stage.

Notice that you don't have to keep the mouse down and drag to draw the rectangle, as in many other drawing programs—form•Z considers the multiple-click method more user-friendly than the click-and-drag method. The same concept applies to all the other drawing operators as well.

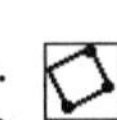

- Now select M-Tool:3a,2—the 3 Point Rectangle tool—and draw another rectangle on the screen. Notice the difference in method. Three clicks are required here, and the rectangle doesn't have to be aligned parallel to the X and Y axes, as with M-Tool:3a,1 (see Figure 1.1 to clarify the difference). The first two mouse clicks determine the alignment of the rectangle; the third determines its dimensions. Remember that your mode is still set to 2D Surface, so that's exactly the kind of object you're creating.

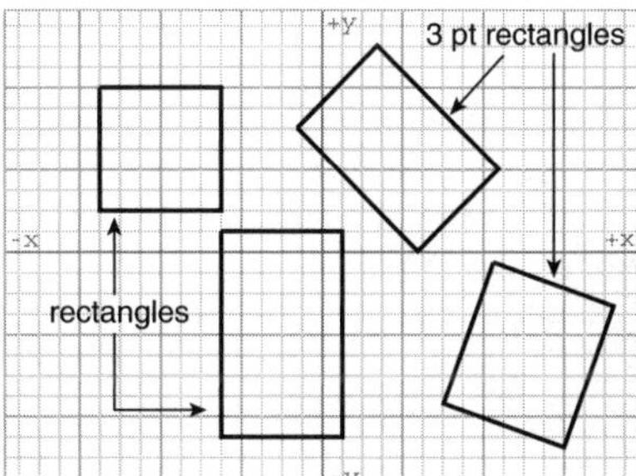

Figure 1.1

2D single-line shapes created using the first two tools in the left column of the third row.

- Continue to use all the other tools in the third left row to create different shapes: polygons, circles, and ellipses. You'll notice that there are multiple tools for drawing circles as well as ellipses, depending upon how you want the operation to be executed. Explore all of them and see how they differ. The icons of these tools do a good job of indicating how they operate, so use them as your guide.

All the objects you're creating now are one-sided surfaces, not two-sided surface solids.

- Remember to work with different colors by frequently changing the active color in the Surface Styles palette. Avoid choosing red for now as it's the color used by the program for highlighting selected objects, so it can be confusing to have objects colored in red as well. For those of you who love red—don't despair! You'll learn to change the system default colors in Workshop 3 (Personalizing Your Environment) and then be able to use all the red you want.

1.4 Working with Dialogs and the Tool Options Palette

You'll have noticed that the Polygon operator (M-Tool:3a,3) creates only six-sided shapes. Obviously, you might need to change that specification at times to be able to create polygons of other shapes. This can be done very easily:

- Double-click on the Polygon tool icon. Alternately, click on it while holding down the option key (Mac) or Ctrl+Shift keys (PC). On the PC, you can also simply click on the icon with the right mouse button. N

- In response to one of these techniques, the dialog shown in Figure 1.2-a pops up. Under the Edges tab, you can specify the number of sides you want your polygon to have. Alternately, you can select the By Size Of Segments option, which allows you to create the polygon by specifying a fixed length for its side. Following the conventional software interface, radio buttons in the dialog denote exclusive either/or choices, whereas checkboxes are for additional non-exclusive options.

Figure 1.2

Exploring polygon-creation options. (a) The dialog of the Polygon tool showing the Pattern tab. (b) A patterned polygon, created with the specifications shown in the dialog.

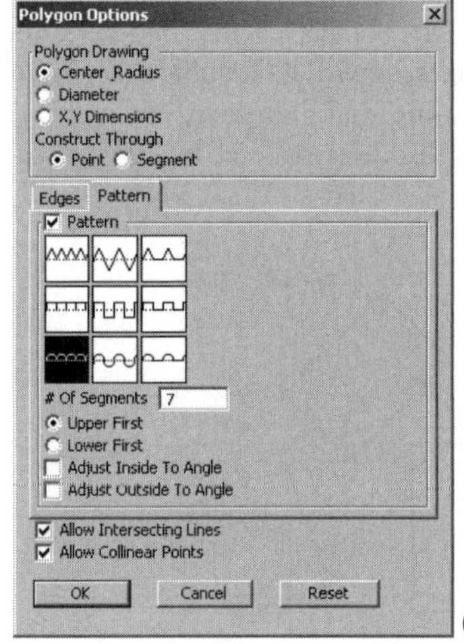

(a)

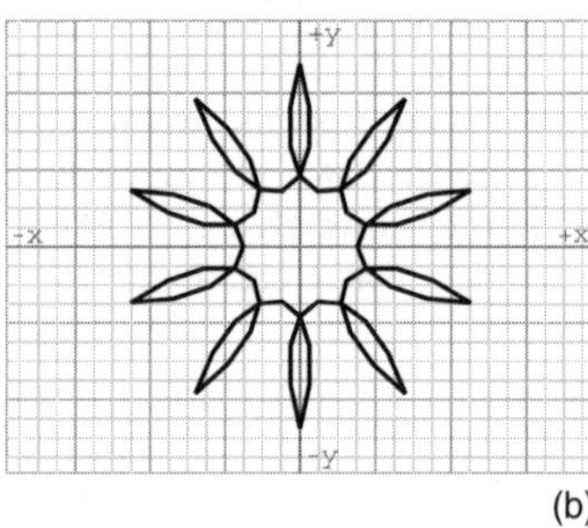

(b)

Keep in mind that a polygon is created as a plain object, so once it's created, you cannot go back and change its number of sides or segment length to some other value using the Polygon Options dialog. This is a very common misconception in the early learning process. It's important to realize that all the drawing tools you're working with now are for *creating* new objects rather than *editing* existing ones. In the same sense, most of the tool dialogs are meant to be used *before* rather than *after* the event. This also applies to objects such as circles, ellipses, etc., which are created as parametric objects. (You'll recall the difference between plain and parametric objects from Section 1 of the Introduction.) There are various means to edit existing objects, both plain and parametric, which we'll explore in detail in Exercise 5 of Workshop 2 (Bringing a Sense of Scale).

- The Polygon Options dialog has a number of additional options that you should explore. Start by experimenting with the different Polygon Drawing techniques that are listed, and find one that's best suited to your modeling needs and style.

- You can also choose to create patterned polygons by going to the Pattern tab, checking the Pattern option, and selecting one of the nine choices it contains. Figure 1.2-b shows the 10-sided polygon created by the pattern selected in Figure 1.2-a. You'll find that when you create patterned polygons, additional mouse clicks are required to define the pattern in addition to the polygon. There are some other options associated with patterned polygons available in the dialog, which will lead to additional variations of each of the nine main patterns. You can explore these in detail at leisure.

- The last two options appearing at the base of the Polygon Options dialog, Allow Intersecting Lines and Allow Colinear Points, are self-explanatory. You can let them remain selected, unless you have specific reasons for disallowing intersecting lines or coincident points in the polygons you create.
- Move on to any one of the Circle tools. Draw a circle with a large diameter and you'll find that it's displayed as a sequence of segments, almost like a many-sided polygon. Draw a large ellipse, and you'll find that it's displayed in the same manner. The number of segments in the display is referred to as the *resolution* of the curve. Smoother curves need a higher resolution, the specification of which requires accessing the tool dialog.
- Double-click on any one of the Circle or Ellipse tools to open its dialog (Figure 1.3-a). The first tab lets you specify the Model Type of the object: Smooth or Facetted. Again, refer to Section 1 of the Introduction to recall the difference between smooth and facetted objects. The default selection is Smooth, and you would usually keep it that way for smoother renderings.
- The second tab lets you specify the Display Resolution. You can choose between the Simple and the Detailed options, as shown in Figure 1.3-a. The first lets you set the resolution using a simple slider, with the lowest value corresponding with a very low resolution. By default, it is set to a middle value, which accounts for the segmented effect you saw. The Detailed option lets you specify the resolution more precisely in terms of number of segments, maximum normal deviation, or maximum edge length. Experiment with all these options and see how they affect the resolution of the circles and ellipses that you create.

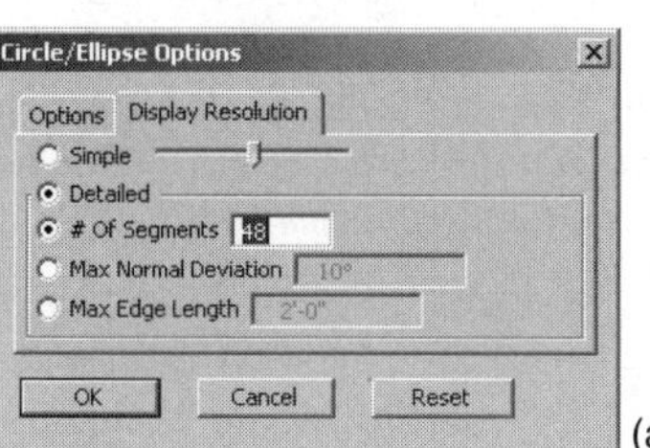

(a)

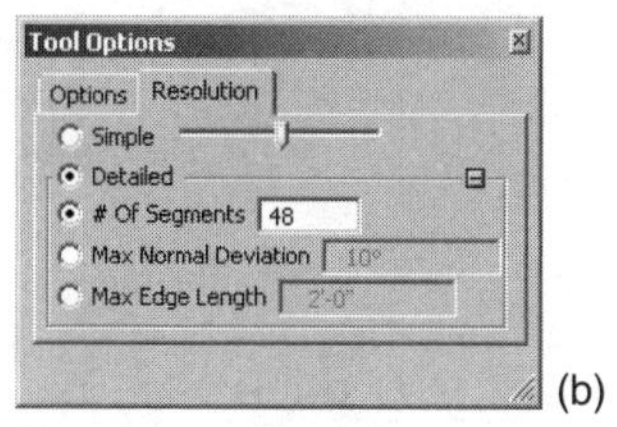

(b)

Figure 1.3

Specifying the resolution of arcs, circles, and ellipses. (a) In the tool dialog. (b) In the Tool Options palette.

The settings you make in the dialog shown in Figure 1.3-a will be applied to *all* the tools that create arcs, circles, and ellipses. Thus, if you change the model type or display resolution for one type of curve, you don't have to repeat the process for the other types of curves, unless you want to specify a different resolution.

Keep in mind also that the display resolution specification won't have any effect on the rendering of a curved object whose Model Type is Smooth, as that will be rendered perfectly smooth. The resolution settings will only influence the non-rendered display modes such as the one currently active in your graphics window. For facetted objects, however, the display resolution settings will affect the rendered image as well, so they need to be higher for smoother renderings. Be careful, however, not to increase the resolution too much, as it will make all future operations involving that object much more complex and memory intensive.

- The options contained in the dialog of a tool are also available continuously in the floating palette called Tool Options, which you had closed in the beginning of this exercise. Go ahead and reopen this palette from the Palettes menu. Then select any one of the Circle or Ellipse tools from the third left row. You'll find that the resolution options you accessed earlier by invoking the dialog of the tool (Figure 1.3-a) are now also visible in the Tool Options palette (Figure 1.3-b), and can be modified in the same fashion.

- Select the Polygon tool once again, and turn your attention to the Tool Options palette. The number of options is now considerably larger compared to the options shown in Figure 1.3-b, with the result that they do not "fit" within the palette. If you still want to use the Tool Options palette, you have to either resize it so that all the options are visible, or else navigate through it by placing the cursor within the palette and clicking and dragging in the vertical direction. This will scroll the contents of the palette upwards or downwards, letting you access all its content.

The Tool Options palette thus provides you with an alternative to accessing the dialog of a tool by the double-click or another method. It's convenient as it can always remain open. However, I recommend that while using each tool in form•Z for the first time, you invoke its dialog rather than rely on the palette. This is because the dialog shows you all the options associated with the operation of that tool without needing to scroll, so they're easier to study. Also, keep in mind that the options for the window tools, as well as for the teal- and magenta-colored modeling tools, do not appear in the Tool Options palette, so you always have to invoke their dialogs to access their options.

To conclude this section, here is some additional information on dialogs. In general, the dialog for any tool contains various options that determine how that tool will function. If a dialog *is* associated with a tool, it's indicated by a tiny red mark on the top right corner of that tool's icon. As you'll see by browsing through the tools in both the modeling as well as the window tool palettes, most of the tools do have dialogs associated with them.

While this book discusses the dialog options for most of the tools, it doesn't cover every single dialog and every single option contained in it. Such an undertaking is beyond the scope of a single book. Therefore, you should do a certain amount of exploration and discovery on your own, and determine how the dialog options that are not covered here affect the behavior of their respective tools.

1.5 Creating Open Shapes

We'll now proceed to work with the tools in the right column of the third row of the modeling tool palette. From their icons, it will be obvious that these are tools which let you draw *open* shapes, in contrast to the tools in the left column which let you create *closed* shapes only. Remember that your object generation mode is still set to 2D Surface, so you'll be continuing to create single-line 2D objects.

- Use the first and second tools in the row to create points and segments respectively. The Point tool requires the selection of a single point in the graphics window, while the Segment tool requires the selection of two points. Keep in mind that a single point object is not a "true" object; however, it can be useful as a reference for creating other kinds of objects by means of snapping, which we'll look at in Workshop 2 (Bringing a Sense of Scale).

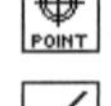

- Next, draw a sequence of lines, referred to as a *polyline*, using M-Tool:3b,3—the Vector Line tool. To end the polyline, double-click at the last point. To close the shape instead of simply ending it, use a triple-click. The last one is a little tricky; you'll learn an easier way to close shapes in Workshop 2.

Figure 1.4

Various shapes created individually with some of the tools in the right column of the third row.

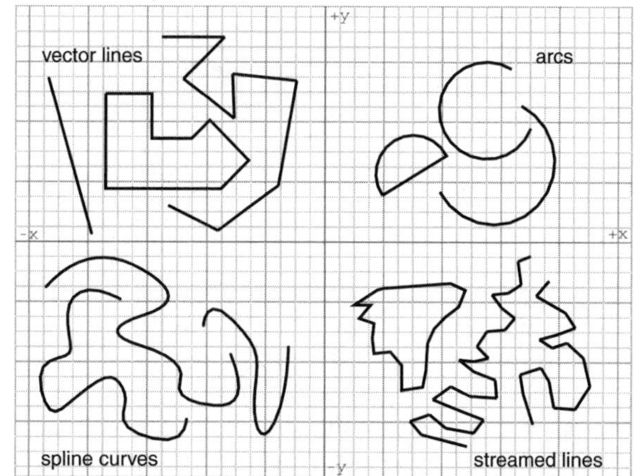

- If you disabled the Allow Intersecting Lines and Allow Colinear Points options in the Polygon Options dialog you worked with earlier, you'll find that the Vector Line tool also doesn't let you create intersecting lines or have colinear points. This shows how the dialogs of all the tools are interrelated, ensuring that the different tools behave consistently, according to the same specifications. You can access the dialog of the Vector Line tool in the usual manner to enable or disable these two options.

- Continue working with the remaining tools in the third right row to create various elements. The four tools located immediately after the Vector Line tool let you draw various kinds of spline curves in different ways. Try them all out. Just like ellipses and circles, these curves are created as smooth by default, and are affected by the Display Resolution settings in their dialogs.

- The following tool, Stream Lines, works a little differently—you hold the mouse down and use it like a pencil to do a freehand sketch in the window. The smoothness of the sketch is governed by a value called the Stream Distance that you can change in the dialog of this tool. Its value is defaulted to 2'-0", which is why the sketching might not feel very smooth at first.

- The third right row ends with six different Arc tools that enable you to create arcs in various ways. Experiment with each one of them. Here again, the icons do a good job of explaining how the tools work. So, for instance, M-Tool:3b,9 is the clockwise Arc tool for which you first select a point on the arc, then the center of the arc, and finally the endpoint of the arc. You'll find yourself relying on different arc tools for modeling different objects, depending upon what the configuration of the object is.

Figure 1.4 gives you a sampling of shapes that can be created using some of the tools in the third right row individually. These tools can also be used in *combination* with one another to create a single shape of the type shown in Figure 1.5. The process is described next.

- Select any one of the tools in the third right row and create a shape. Then, instead of double-clicking to end the shape, simply choose another tool from that row—the last point of the previous shape will act as the first point for the operation of the new tool you just selected. This process can be repeated for as long as necessary. When you're finally ready to end the process, double-click at the last point or triple-click to close. Try this out a few times, creating various shapes. It's important to learn how to do this, as you'll find yourself using it frequently.

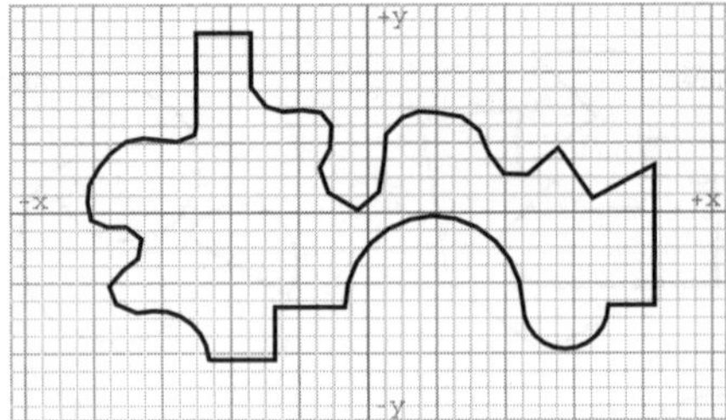

Figure 1.5

A single element created by combining the use of many tools in the right column of Row 3. A triple-click was used at the end to close the figure.

Of the 2D shapes that can be created with the tools in the third right row, spline curves, arcs, and any shape that includes them are created as parametric objects, while segments, vector lines, and stream lines are created as plain objects.

1.6 Double-Line 2D Mode

In this section, you'll be dealing with double-line rather than with single-line 2D shapes.

- Go back to the second left row of the modeling tool palette and select the second tool in this row (M-Tool:2a,2) instead of the first which you were using so far. This sets the object generation mode to 2D Enclosure. Recall from Section 1 of the Introduction that 2D enclosures are double-line 2D elements.
- Now repeat the entire sequence of steps (Section 1.3 to Section 1.5) that you've done so far, and observe the differences in the 2D elements that are created. Note that you'll still be using the drawing tools located on Row 3 to actually create the objects—the only difference is the change of mode.
- If you need to change the width of the enclosure from its default value, access the dialog for M-Tool:2a,2—a procedure you should be familiar with by now. You can change the Wall Width here to any specified value. You can also change the Justification option, which determines where the double-line will be drawn with respect to the points you select. The default selection of Center, which distributes the width of the enclosure equally on both sides of the selection point, might not be the best option in all cases.

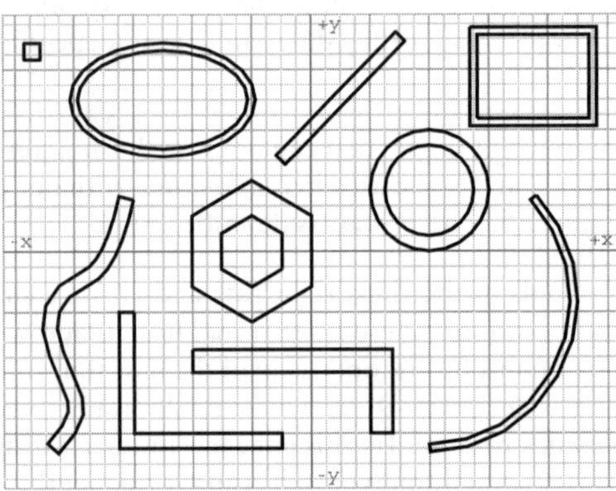

Figure 1.6

Various kinds of 2D enclosures.

Figure 1.6 shows some 2D enclosures with varied widths and justification options, created using various drawing tools from Row 3. By this time, you should be well on your way towards mastering these tools, since you'll have gone over each one of them twice so far.

1.7 Cleaning Up: Moving and Deleting

Very soon, you'll use the 2D shapes that you've created as base shapes for the generation of 3D objects. Before moving on to that, you might want to rearrange your objects in a more pleasing composition by moving them around on the gridded reference plane in the graphics window. If you have too much clutter, you may want to delete some objects. Let's see how to perform these operations.

- Turn your attention to the left column of Row 12 of the modeling tool palette. This special teal-colored row determines the *self-copy mode* and is set to Self by default. If it isn't, do so by clicking on M-Tool:12a,1, the Self tool, now. This ensures that any subsequent transformations—move, rotate, mirror, scale, etc.—that you perform are applied *to* the object selected, rather than in making a copy of it.

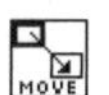

- Select Move (M-Tool:13a,1) and click on any object. You'll now be able to move the selected object around the screen—it will be rubber-banded as you move the mouse. (Note, again, that you do *not* have to keep the mouse down and *drag* the element.) When you've found an appropriate position, click a second time to establish the move. Continue using the Move tool in this manner to reorganize your collection of objects as desired.

- To delete objects, simply select the Delete tool—the only tool located in the left column of the last row. Any object that you click on will be deleted. Continue to apply the tool in this manner to all the objects you want to delete.

The Move and Delete operators can also be applied to many objects at a time rather than to each object individually as we've done. We'll see how to do this in Section 3.4. For now, let's concentrate on completing our full session of form•Z.

1.8 Changing Views

So far, we've been working in the Top view which lets us see the X and Y dimensions only. This was fine as long as we were working with 2D objects alone. But to prepare for the creation of 3D objects, let's switch to a view in which all three dimensions are visible. Such a view is referred to as a *non-planar* view, as opposed to a *planar* view, which lets you see two dimensions only. A planar view is also technically referred to as a *projection* view.

- Open up the Views menu. You'll find a √ mark against Top as well as Axonometric, indicating that the current view is looking straight down on the XY plane. There are a total of seven groups of options under the View menu; concentrate only on the first three of these for now. The first group consists of five predefined non-planar views, along with a Custom View Angles option that lets you define your own viewing angles. The second group includes the six planar views possible with respect to the coordinate system you see in the window; Top is the first of these. The third group gives you an additional five options that determine how the chosen view appears.

- We'll look at all these options in detail in Workshop 3 (Personalizing Your Environment). For now, settle for any of the non-planar Axonometric views so that you can see all three coordinate axes, X, Y, and Z. The first two, [z=30° x=60°] and [z=45° x=45°], are very common and are used for most of the illustrations in this book.

1.9 Specifying Heights

Let's move to a different dimension. After all, it *is* the 3D aspect that we're most interested in, right? What you'll do next is convert the 2D shapes you've created into various kinds of 3D objects. Before doing this, however, you need to specify the heights of these objects.

- Go to the Heights pulldown menu. By default, the height is set to a preset value—usually 10'-0" in the English measurement system—indicated by a √ mark against it in the Heights menu. You can preselect another height from among the values listed here, or go to the Custom option to define your own values. This selected value—whether preset or customized—will set the heights of objects for all subsequent 3D modeling.

- If heights need to be constantly varied and you'd like to indicate them graphically as you go along, the first option from the Heights menu, Graphic/Keyed, needs to be activated. Select this option for now, as shown in Figure 1.7. This lets you specify the height of a 3D object interactively, either with a mouse click or by typing the required value in the Prompts palette using the keyboard. In this workshop, we'll deal with the first method only, leaving numeric input through the keyboard for Workshop 2 (Bringing a Sense of Scale).

Figure 1.7

The Heights menu, with the option set to Graphic/ Keyed.

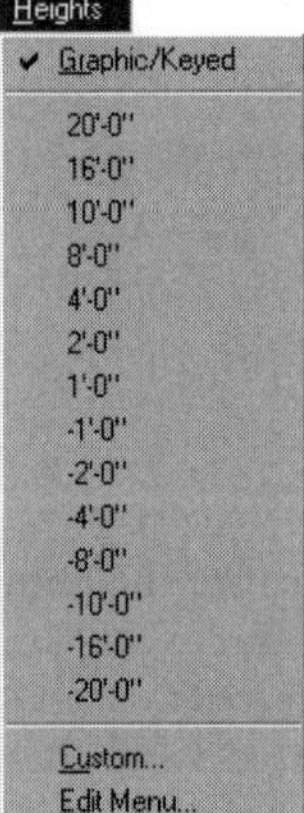

1.10 Deriving 3D Objects from 2D Shapes

Now that the heights aspect has also been settled, we're finally ready to move into the third dimension. To derive 3D objects from 2D elements, look at the left column of the fifth row of the modeling tool palette. It contains all the *derivative object* tools, used to derive new objects from existing ones in various ways. We'll work with only three of these tools for now.

Figure 1.8

Extruded, converged, and enclosed 3D objects derived from existing 2D shapes, using the 3D derivative tools in the left column of Row 5.

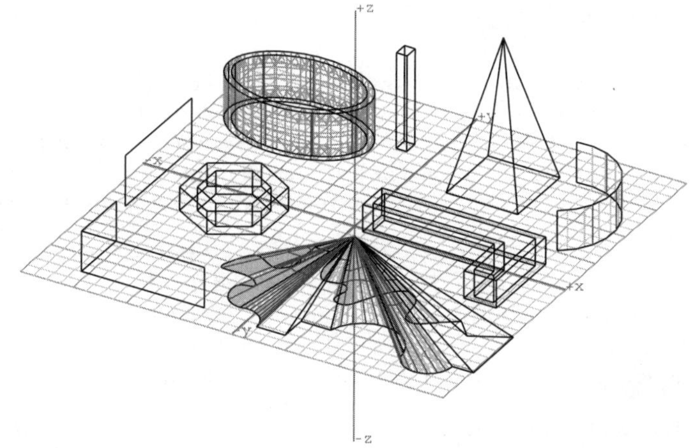

- Select M-Tool:5a,4. This is the 3D Extrusion tool, used to derive simple extruded objects from 2D shapes. Click on any element and watch the extrusion being rubber-banded as you drag the mouse in the Z direction to indicate the height of the object. Click when you get to the height you want, and your 3D object is complete. You can also go in for *negative* heights by moving in the –Z direction. Repeat this process with some more of the 2D elements that you have; however, leave some for deriving other kinds of objects as well. Keep an eye on the instructions that appear in the Prompts palette and follow them. In general, you'll find this a useful habit to cultivate.

- Repeat the same procedure using the 3D Convergence tool (M-Tool:5a,5) as well as the 3D Enclosure tool (M-Tool:5a,6), and observe the differences in the forms that are generated (see Figure 1.8). 3D Convergence creates conical or pyramidal objects, while 3D Enclosure creates the 3D equivalent of a 2D enclosure from any kind of 2D shape. Notice that if the base shape is a 2D enclosure, there's no difference between the kind of object derived by the 3D Extrusion tool or the 3D Enclosure tool.

The 3D derivation of a 2D shape will be facetted or smooth depending upon whether the original shape is facetted or smooth respectively.

- Invoke the dialogs of these three tools in turn to explore the options they contain. The 3D Extrusion and 3D Convergence tool dialogs are identical. Look at the Extrusion/Convergence Options tab. By default, the extrusion or convergence happens in a direction perpendicular to the reference plane. Thus in Figure 1.8 where XY is the reference plane, the heights are defined in the Z direction. You can also choose to extrude or converge in a direction perpendicular to the *surface* of the object, an option that is relevant only when the base 2D object is inclined with respect to the reference plane. We have no such objects yet but will be creating them soon in the next workshop (see Figure 2.11), so keep this option in mind for later use. Don't worry about the options in the Status Of Objects tab for now; we'll explore these later in Section 3.7.

- The dialog of the 3D Enclosure tool is a little different. It contains a number of options related to the justification, thickness, and configuration of the enclosure, which we'll study while working with the 3D Enclosure mode (M-Tool:2a,5) in Section 2.2. The remaining options are identical to those in the 3D Extrusion and 3D Convergence tool dialogs we just discussed. Notice that the 3D Enclosure operation can never produce a surface object since it converts an open shape to an enclosed shape before extrusion.

1.11 Changing the Display

Let's move on to briefly discuss how the objects in the graphics window are shown to us. The kind of display that you see in Figure 1.8 is called a *wireframe* display. In this mode, all the lines of the object are shown, even those that wouldn't be visible to your eye from the position in which you're viewing it. This kind of display can get a little confusing to visualize, as you can see. Also, it may not be the most attractive mode of presentation. You therefore may want to exercise the option to switch to a different display.

- Go to the Display menu. The second, third, and fourth group of items in this menu comprise the various kinds of displays available in form•Z. Switch to each one of them in turn and observe the differences. Compare what you see to Figure 1.9, which shows a relative comparison of six different display modes for the same configuration of objects.

Displays can be broadly divided into two categories: *line* and *paint*. Wire Frame is one example of a line display; Hidden Line is the other. A Wire Frame display is the only mode that displays open surfaces by default, as you can see in Figure 1.9. Thus, if your window appears blank even though you're confident you had drawn *something* (open shapes) on it, you can be sure you're no longer in the Wire Frame mode. A Hidden Line mode is similar to Wire Frame except that it hides lines that wouldn't be visible to you from your current viewpoint, and is therefore more realistic.

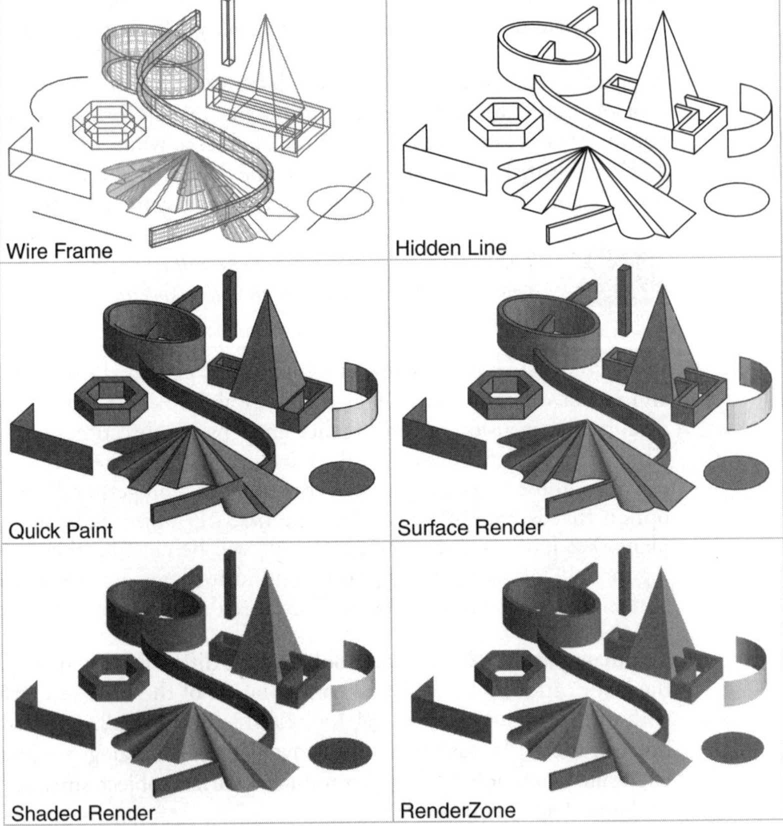

Figure 1.9

Various display modes for the same set of objects. The display of the grid and axes has been turned off in these illustrations.

All the other display modes are paint displays. Quick Paint is the fastest of these but is also the least accurate, especially for complex shapes and configurations, so don't rely on it too often. You can see the inaccuracy right away in Figure 1.9. Surface Render, Shaded Render, and RenderZone are progressively more sophisticated and accurate displays that take a long time to execute, particularly for complex models. RenderZone, especially, is best left for final presentations.

Recent versions of form•Z have an additional display mode called Interactive Shaded grouped along with Wire Frame in the Display menu. This mode enables you to carry out interactive modeling of objects using shaded surfaces rather than lines. To get a feel for this, create some objects, first using the Surface Render display mode and then the Interactive Shaded mode. The difference should be obvious at once. This display mode works faster when the window size is smaller, so keep this in mind if you use it frequently. Also, this mode is meant for interactive modeling only and cannot be used for printing, which is why it isn't shown in Figure 1.9 with the other displays.

Each one of the display modes in form•Z comes with its own options, which we'll explore in detail in subsequent workshops.

1.12 Ending the Show: Printing and Closing

We're approaching the end of our first complete form•Z session. Save the project, if you like, using File > Save. Let's see how to go about printing what we have.

- First, make sure that your display is set to a suitable mode, depending upon the desired quality of the output. A Hidden Line or Surface Render display prints well and takes less time than the higher-quality modes, so you can settle for either of these. Also, the current view is what gets printed, so make sure you switch to an appropriate view before printing.
- Go to File > Page Setup to set the paper size and orientation. This is the standard Page Setup dialog found in most programs, and its options will depend upon the printer you've selected.
- Next, go to Plot/Print Setup in the same menu. This is the key dialog for determining what will print and how, so let's look at it in some detail. It's shown in Figure 1.10. To begin with, you can specify the Plot Scale in which the file is to be printed. But since we haven't been modeling using proper dimensions yet, a plotting scale is of little consequence and will be rather arbitrary. Therefore, check the Scale to Fit Media option for now. This will fit all the objects within the specified paper size (Figure 1.11-a). Use the Page Preview command to contrast the results, before and after selecting this option.

Figure 1.10

The Plot/Print Setup dialog.

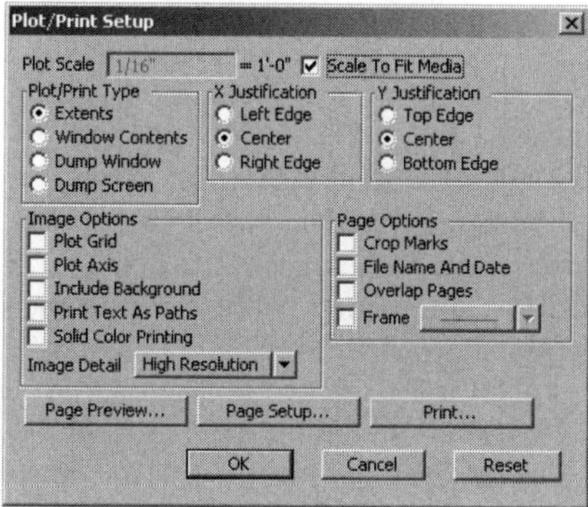

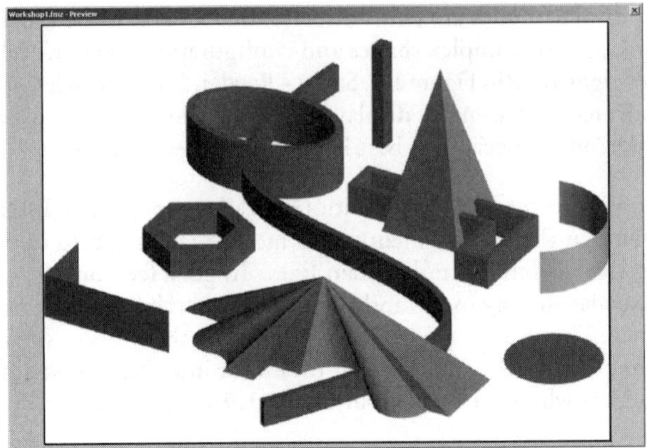
(a)

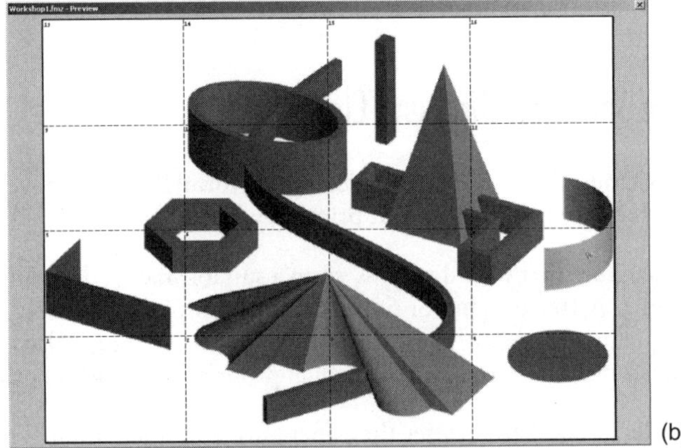
(b)

Figure 1.11

Different plot scales for printing. (a) Choosing the Scale To Fit Media option fits the plot within the specified paper size. (b) Not selecting this option uses the Plot Scale value to determine the size of the plot. A large value (1/2"=1'-0") was specified to generate this illustration, leading to a plot extending over several pages, as indicated by the dashed lines.

- Turn your attention to the other options in the Plot/Print Setup dialog. By default, the Plot/Print Type is set to Extents, which means that all the objects you created will be printed. However, you could also print out only a part of the project by first zooming in to that section of the window, then selecting Window Contents as the Plot/Print Type. (You'll learn how to use the Zoom tools a little later in Section 3.8.) The remaining two Plot/Print Type options simply create screen dumps of the window and the screen respectively, at a low resolution but faster than the first two options, and should be used for rough drafts only.

- The X and Y Justification options are used to determine the alignment of the plot with respect to the page. The most commonly used Center options are selected by default.

- Once you begin modeling to scale and specify a value for Plot Scale rather than use Scale To Fit Media, the plotting may take place on several sheets of paper (as shown in Figure 1.11-b) if it cannot fit on a single sheet in the specified scale. In this case, you'll find it useful to check both the Overlap Pages and Crop Marks options. The first will provide some overlap between neighboring pages, while the second will mark the corners of the plots on each page. This will enable you to easily collate the individual sheets into the full plot.

- The remaining options in the Plot/Print Setup dialog are fairly self-explanatory, and you can explore them on your own. For instance, you can check the Frame option and choose the frame thickness that will be used to border your plot. Activate the Solid Color Printing option to see if it yields better results, but most often it will not, in which case it's better to keep it turned off. Don't worry about the Print Text As Paths option for now—we'll come back to it when working with text objects in Workshop 7.

- A note of caution: you should *always* do a Page Preview of your plot before you issue the Print command to check if the plot is satisfactory. By a simple oversight, you might forget to select the Scale To Fit Media option, making the plot extend over several sheets of paper in the default scale. And before you realize it, the printer will be spurting out loads of paper with not more than a few lines on each! Therefore, use the environmentally friendly Page Preview option generously.
- This marks the end of Exercise 1. You can close the current project using File > Close and exit form•Z using File > Quit/Exit. However, if you'd like to continue working, don't quit now. Just move on to Exercise 2.

Exercise 2

Direct 3D

So far, we've been working with 2D shapes and creating 3D objects by applying certain operations to them. This is rather a roundabout way, though, to go about 3D modeling, isn't it? Therefore, without any further delay, let's proceed to generating 3D objects directly. We'll first look at the traditional form•Z method that involves the use of the third, fourth, and fifth object generation modes located in the left column of Row 2 of the modeling tool palette. Just like the first two modes you worked with in the last exercise, these are used in conjunction with the drawings tools on Row 3. We'll also look at the other method of directly generating 3D objects, which involves the use of five kinds of Primitive tools. Additionally, we'll learn to model various kinds of spherical objects using the dedicated tool, and use different reference planes for the creation of objects. Let's start by looking at how to use the Clear command, which we might need at this point.

2.1 Clearing the Project of All Objects

If you didn't quit form•Z at the end of the last exercise but moved on directly to this exercise, do the following:

- If you saved Exercise 1 and closed that file, open a new modeling project by going to File > New[Model].
- If you didn't close the Exercise 1 file and don't wish to save it, start with a clean slate by going to Edit > Clear, located in the third group of the menu. This will clear all the visible objects in your graphics window.
- If you went through Section 1.10 on deriving 3D objects in the last exercise, you'll find all the original 2D shapes from which 3D objects were derived still remaining in the window, even after executing Clear. These objects are colored in gray and cannot be moved or deleted. In fact, they cannot even be selected with the Pick tool (M-Tool:4b,1). Try it. Such objects are called *ghosted*

objects. How and why were these objects created? You shall have the answer to that question later in Section 3.7. For now, simply clear these objects by going to Edit > Clear All Ghosted, located just below Clear.

2.2 3D Object Generation Modes

- Select M-Tool:2a,3. This sets the object generation mode to 3D Extrusion. You can now create a 3D extrusion directly by drawing a base shape with any of the tools on Row 3 and specifying the height with an additional mouse click. If you started a new session of form•Z for this exercise, don't forget to set the Heights menu to Graphic/Keyed so that you can specify the extrusion height interactively with the mouse, rather than letting it acquire a default preset value.

- Use all the tools on Row 3 to create different kinds of solids and surfaces directly in 3D. A *solid* will be created when the base shape is closed, as with the tools in the left column of Row 3; a *surface* will be created when the base shape is open, as with the tools in the right column. The dialog of the 3D Extrusion mode has the same Extrusion/Convergence options that we studied in Section 1.10 for the 3D derivative tools.

A surface object can be converted to a surface solid and vice versa by using the Make One/Two Sided tool (M-Tool:11b,3). The conversion choice is made in the dialog of the tool.

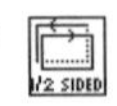

- Experiment with different colors and shapes. You can change the display mode to Interactive Shaded to visualize the objects better as you're creating them.

- Repeat the previous steps with the object generation mode set to 3D Converged (M-Tool:2a,4), and finally with it set to 3D Enclosure (M-Tool:2a,5). You'll find that you're generating the same kinds of solids that you created in Exercise 1, but now directly instead of operating on 2D shapes.

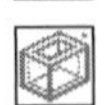

- For 3D enclosures, you can change the enclosure thickness by accessing the dialog of the 3D Enclosure mode (shown in Figure 1.12-a). You'll find the same Justification options in this dialog that you encountered for the 2D Enclosure tool in Section 1.6. For 3D enclosures, whether generated directly (by setting the mode to M-Tool:2a,5) or from 2D shapes (using M-Tool:5a,6), there are additional options in the tool dialog that control the resultant object. You can choose to have enclosures with either the top, or the bottom, or both enclosed, and specify the corresponding thicknesses. In effect, you can create a hollow volume, bounded on all sides by slabs, directly in one step by selecting the appropriate options. Such volumes are illustrated in Figure 1.12-b.

- While one of these 3D object generation modes is active, access the dialog of any of the Circle, Arc, or other curve tools to see its options. You'll see two tabs like those you saw in Section 1.4, the first for specifying the Model Type and Extrusion/Convergence Options, and the second for specifying the Display Resolution of the object. The Display Resolution again gives you the choice between a Simple and a Detailed display; however, there are a lot more options now under the Detailed display since this is a 3D rather than 2D object. The philosophy remains the same, however: the values here will not have any effect on the rendering of a curved object whose Model Type is Smooth, as that will be rendered perfectly smooth. The resolution settings will only influence the non-rendered display modes such as the Wire Frame one currently active in your graphics window. For facetted objects, however, the display resolution settings will affect the rendered image as well, so they need to be higher for smoother renderings. Experiment with the different detailed resolution settings and see how they affect the 3D curved objects you create.

Figure 1.12

The dialog for the 3D Enclosure tool, and the enclosed objects created with the set of options specified in it.

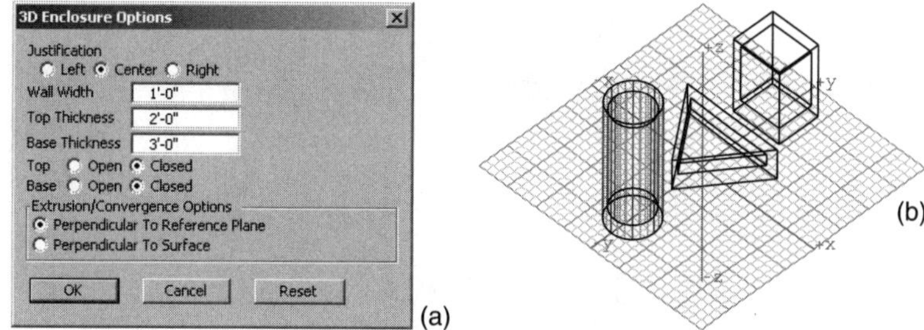

2.3 Modeling Primitive 3D Objects

form•Z gives you the ability to directly create five different types of primitive 3D objects: cube, cone, cylinder, sphere, and torus. The tools for generating these primitives are grouped together in the left column of the first row of the modeling tool palette. All the primitives, except the cube, are created as smooth objects.

- Select the first tool in the row, Cube, and invoke its dialog. You'll find three different options for creating a cube: Preset, Diagonal, and Axial. Try them all out. The Preset option lets you specify the Width, Depth, and Height of the cube in the accompanying fields. A single click of the mouse in the graphics window is then used to place the cube of the specified dimensions in the desired location. In contrast, for the Diagonal and Axial options, all three dimensions of the cube are specified graphically using the mouse. The Diagonal option, like the Rectangle tool (M-Tool:3a,1) you encountered in Section 1.3, lets you only model a cube that's aligned parallel to the coordinate axes. With the Axial option there's no such limitation, and an additional mouse click is needed to determine the alignment of the cube, as with the 3 Point Rectangle tool (M-Tool:3a,2).

CUBE

The primitive tools are not affected by the settings in the Heights menu. They always require the object height to be specified interactively, or with the Preset option.

- Move on to the next tool in the left column of the first row, Cone, and explore all its options (see Figure 1.13). Switch to the Surface Render mode to see the results better. There are five basic means to model a cone: the Preset option is similar to that for the Cube tool you just explored, while the other four options simply give you different ways of modeling the base of the cone. If you activate the Truncated Cone option, the graphical modeling process gets slightly modified to enable you to specify how the truncation happens. The Partial option, when checked, lets you create partial cones with the specified Start and End angles for the circumference of the base.

- The Cone tool also has three different types of Closure options that determine whether the resulting cone becomes a solid or surface object. The default option of Plane, as you can see, creates a solid object for both complete and partial cones by closing both the base and side surfaces. The None option does not close any surfaces, so the cone remains a surface object. The final option, Center, generates a solid cone like the Plane option, but in a slightly different fashion for partial cones. Rather than using a single face to close the side of the cone, two faces are used that extend to the axis of the cone. The difference is illustrated in Figure 1.13.

The Cone Options dialog additionally contains the same Display Resolution tab you saw in the previous section. You'll find this tab in the dialogs of the remaining primitives as well.

Figure 1.13

The Cone Options dialog, and the different types of conical objects that can be created using the various options.

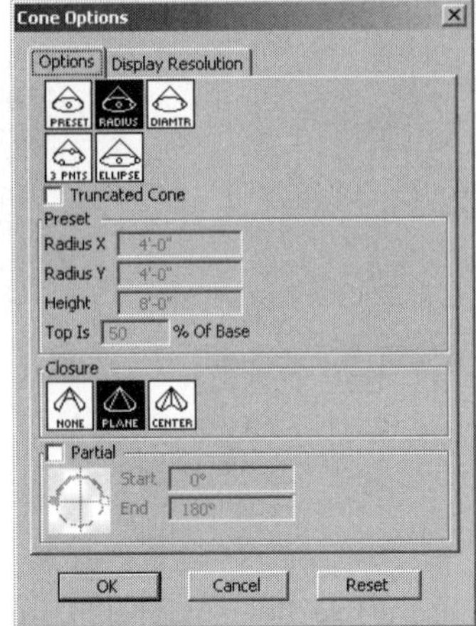

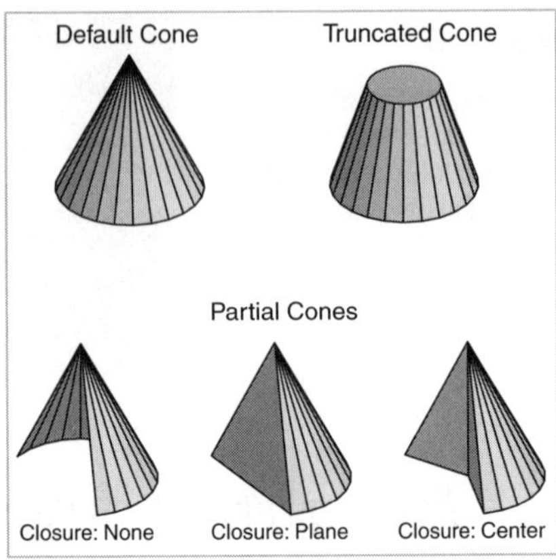

▣ Proceed to work with the remaining three primitive tools in a manner similar to the first two tools. The options for the Cylinder tool are identical to those for the Cone tool, except that there's no truncation option. The Sphere tool, again, has the same Closure and Partial options, with the latter ability being provided for both the horizontal and the vertical directions. The last primitive tool, Torus, lets you model a ring or donut-like shape. It has options similar to those of the other primitives, so exploring them should be easy. Just note the meaning of the three parametric terms, Major Radius, Minor Radius X, and Minor Radius Z, all of which are illustrated in Figure 1.14.

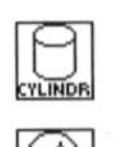

Figure 1.14

The meaning of the three parametric terms used to define a torus object.

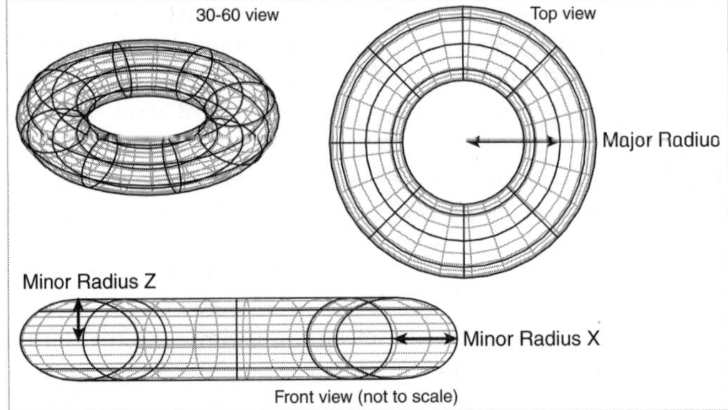

2.4 Creating Spherical Objects

In addition to the Sphere tool you just saw which lets you create primitive spheres, form•Z has a second tool for modeling various kinds of spherical objects. They are, however, created as facetted objects, unlike the smooth ones created by the Sphere tool.

▣ Select the Spherical Object tool from the right column of the first row, and invoke its dialog. It's somewhat similar to the dialogs of the primitive tools, in that it has a Preset option along with a number of other methods for modeling the spherical object (Figure 1.15-a). Try them all out. The icons do a good job of explaining how each method works.

Figure 1.15

The eight different types of spherical objects that can be created with the Spherical Object tool, shown along with the tool dialog.

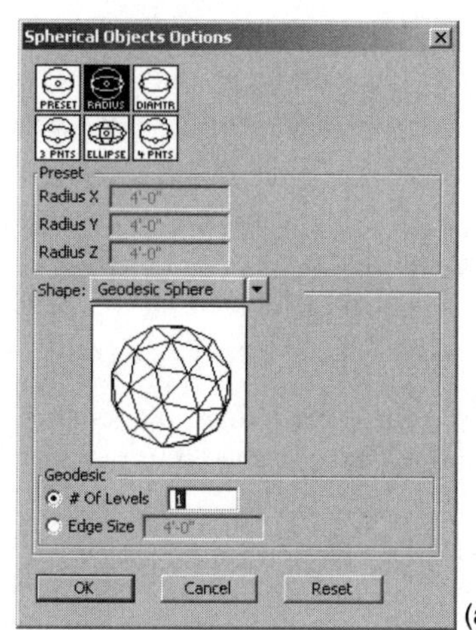

(a)

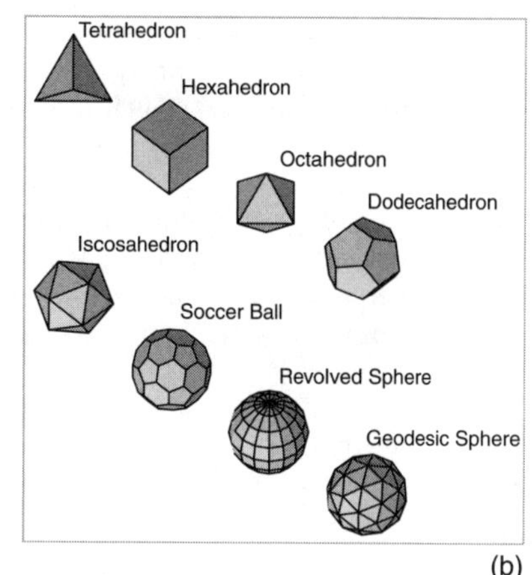

(b)

- Turn your attention to the Shape popup list in the Spherical Object Options dialog. The default selection is Geodesic Sphere, the spherical object type you just created. There are seven other types. Activate each of them in turn and create the corresponding objects. Compare your results with those illustrated in Figure 1.15-b.

- Explore also the sub-options for Revolved Sphere and Geodesic Sphere, experimenting with different values that determine the resolution, and consequently, the smoothness of the solid. Geodesic spheres can be created at four levels of resolution, indicated by the # Of Levels value. Alternately, you can specify an Edge Size, just as you did for 2D curves. Again, settle for the smallest resolution (lower levels or larger edge sizes) that you can get away with, so that subsequent operations are faster and less memory-intensive. In general, you'll find that geodesic spheres give you the smoothest rendering of all the spherical objects.

2.5 Using Predefined Reference Planes

All modeling activity takes place with reference to a plane. So far, you've been working entirely on the predefined XY plane, indicated by the teal-colored reference grid. All 2D drawing activity took place on this plane. All extrusions (i.e., defining the heights of objects) took place in the direction perpendicular to this plane, along the Z axis.

It is, of course, conceivable that using the XY plane alone may be sufficient for all your modeling activity. However, at times, it might be faster and more convenient to use some other reference plane for modeling certain objects. In addition to the XY plane, form•Z has two other predefined planes—the YZ and the ZX planes—that are defined by the three red-colored coordinate axes and are orthogonal (i.e., perpendicular) to the XY plane. We'll work with these two planes right now.

form•Z also lets you create your own customized reference planes, which can be non-orthogonal, passing through any set of lines in 3D space. We'll work with such planes in Workshop 3 (Personalizing Your Environment).

- Turn your attention to the first column of window tools at the base of the graphics window. If you like, you can "pull it out" and position it as a floating palette on the screen (Figure 1.16-a). This palette is where the selection of the active reference plane is made, and it contains four options: XY,

YZ, ZX, and ARBITR (which stands for Arbitrary). XY is active by default, which is why you've been using it all this time. Let's see what it's like working with the other two planes. Ignore the Arbitrary option for now—you'll use it when you create customized reference planes in Workshop 3.

- Select the YZ option by clicking on it. The grid will change from spanning the X and Y axes to spanning the Y and Z axes. Proceed to create any 3D object. You'll see that the base shape is now created on the active YZ plane, while the height of the object is given in the direction of the perpendicular X axis. Continue to create more objects on this plane. You should have something similar to what's shown in Figure 1.16-b.

- Finally, switch to ZX, the last of the three predefined planes, and create some 3D objects. The heights will now be defined along the Y axis, as shown in Figure 1.16-c.

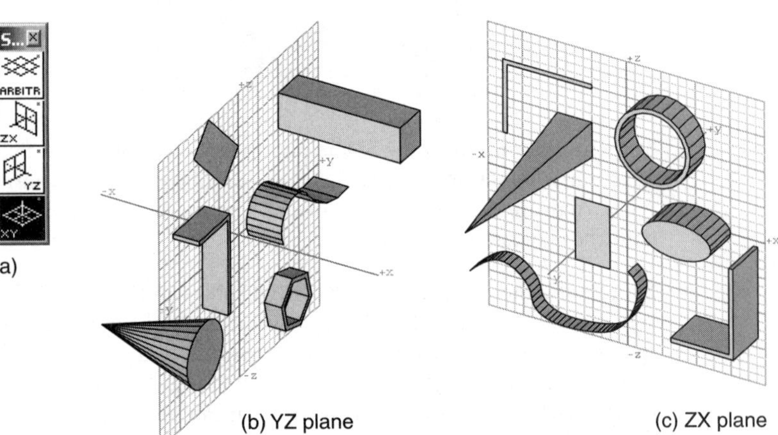

Figure 1.16

Working with predefined reference planes. (a) The window tool palette of the reference planes. XY is highlighted, indicating that it is the active plane. (b) Modeling using the YZ plane. (c) Modeling using the ZX plane.

You can see right away the flexibility and convenience afforded by being able to use additional planes for modeling. Of course, you can create simple compositions such as those shown in Figure 1.16 by using only the XY plane, and then moving or rotating the objects to the desired position. (You'll learn to use the Rotate tool in the next workshop.) However, it's faster, and more intuitive and elegant, to use the other two planes for modeling objects that relate to them better than to the XY plane. For more complex objects and configurations that you'll model later, you'll find the use of multiple reference planes absolutely indispensable.

EXERCISE 3

Some Basic Functions

Now that we've learned to create various kinds of 2D and 3D objects, it's time to look at some frequently used functions, without which we wouldn't be able to proceed very far with our modeling. These functions include changing the color of objects after they've been created, moving objects perpendicular to the reference plane, undoing and redoing operations, making multiple selections using the Pick tool, selecting and deselecting objects, ghosting and unghosting objects, and finally, zooming and scrolling through the graphics window. Let's start with the aspect of color.

3.1 Changing Colors

You already know from Section 1.1 how to create an object in a desired color. What if you want to change the color of an object *after* it's been created? Here's how you can do that.

- Select the Color tool from the modeling palette—the first icon in the left column of the fourteenth row. Then highlight the required color in the Surface Styles palette and simply "apply" it to the object whose color you wish to change. The selected object gets colored in the new color.

- You can repeat the same color for many objects or choose different colors. The Color command remains active until you select some other tool.

3.2 Using the Perpendicular Lock

So far, you've been executing only planar moves with the Move tool—moving objects horizontally on a plane. You'll often need to execute moves *perpendicular* to the active plane. Let's see how to do this.

- Make sure you're in a non-planar view, seeing all three axes, X, Y, and Z. Select the Move tool (M-Tool:13a,1) and apply it to an object. Try moving the object in a direction vertical to the currently active plane. You may think you've succeeded in doing so, but if you check the exact position of the object by switching to some of the planar views—Top, Right, Front, etc.—from the Views menu, you'll find that you've only moved the object *along* the plane rather than perpendicular to it. If your display mode is set to Interactive Shaded, you should be able to spot the error at once. Try it.

- Now click on the single tool located in the second column of the window tool palette. This is called the Perpendicular Lock. When selected, it gets highlighted in black, indicating that it's active. Use the Move tool again. You'll find that now you can move objects only in a direction perpendicular to the plane.

- When you don't want to restrict movement to the vertical direction only, deselect the Perpendicular Lock tool by clicking on it again. It will no longer be highlighted, indicating that it is not active. (Such a tool is referred to as a *toggle switch*.) Don't forget to turn it off in this manner when not needed, otherwise your regular planar moves will not be performed correctly, leaving you wondering what's going wrong!

The Perpendicular Lock is relevant only to non-planar views. When you see your project in a planar view, you'll be able to move objects along that plane only. In such views, the Perpendicular Lock automatically switches itself off.

3.3 Undoing and Redoing

form•Z has more than the two standard Undo and Redo commands that you find in most programs. It has six commands related to undoing and redoing, located in the first group of the Edit menu. Let's see how they work.

- Keep selecting the first command, Undo, to keep undoing in reverse order the operations you've just performed. You may find it more convenient to use the shortcut key for Undo, listed beside the command name in the menu.

Notice that Undo applies *only* to operations that cause *changes to the objects* (such as object creation, move, color, etc.), but not to operations that make changes to the graphic environment (such as switching reference planes) or modify options in the various dialogs (such as changing the number of sides of a polygon). Such changes cannot be reversed using the Undo command. Keep this in mind, as it often tends to be a source of some confusion.

- You can also conveniently undo multiple operations in one step. Notice the * sign next to the Undo command in the Edit menu—this indicates that a dialog containing options is associated with that command. To access this dialog, select Undo while holding down the option key (Mac) or Ctrl+Shift keys (PC). This brings up an Undo List from which you can select multiple consecutive operations to be undone, starting with the most recent operation (see Figure 1.17-a). By default, only the last 10 operations are listed. To undo more operations, open up the Undo List again after undoing the last set.

Don't expect to be able to undo only specific operations from the Undo List, for instance, only the third and sixth operations. That's an impossible demand!

- The second command in the Edit menu, Redo, simply redoes the last operation that was undone. It can be executed repeatedly to redo a sequence of undo operations, but it works only if selected immediately after an Undo command. If you did a multiple series of Undo commands, you can use the third command, Redo All, to reverse all of them in one step and restore the project to what it was before the Undo commands were performed.

- The Undo and Redo commands also work while you're in the middle of an operation. Use the Vector Line tool (M-Tool:3b,3) to draw a continuous sequence of lines, but don't double-click or triple-click to end. Select Undo instead, and you'll find that the last point you selected gets deselected, without affecting any of the points selected before it. Any number of points can be repeatedly deselected in this manner by continuing to use Undo; thereafter, selection of new points can be resumed. After the command has been executed fully (i.e., you've double-clicked or triple-clicked) and you select Undo, the complete object will be undone rather than just a single segment.

- Proceed to select the fifth command from the Edit menu, Reset Undo/Redo. Now try and Undo the last operation you performed and you'll find that you can no longer do so. The Reset Undo/Redo option sets a new starting point beyond which an Undo cannot be executed. It does this by erasing all the earlier records of the model at its various stages.

With the help of all these Undo and Redo commands, you can experiment with various modeling alternatives without the fear of making an unredeemable error. It will always be possible to go back and undo operations that weren't done correctly. The Reset Undo/Redo command can be used to mark the end of an experimentation phase—in fact, you should make it a point to do so, whenever you feel confident that you no longer need to return to any earlier stage of your modeling. This will help to free up valuable disk space, particularly for large projects

- Carry out a few more modeling operations and then select Replay, the fourth command in the Edit menu. This clears the window and plays back in sequence all the operations you performed since the Reset Undo/Redo option was selected. You can pause the playback at any time for visual inspection by holding the mouse down, and release it for resuming the replay. It's a nifty little feature that can be useful.

Figure 1.17

Using Undo. (a) The Undo List, showing multiple operations selected for undoing. (b) The Undo Options dialog.

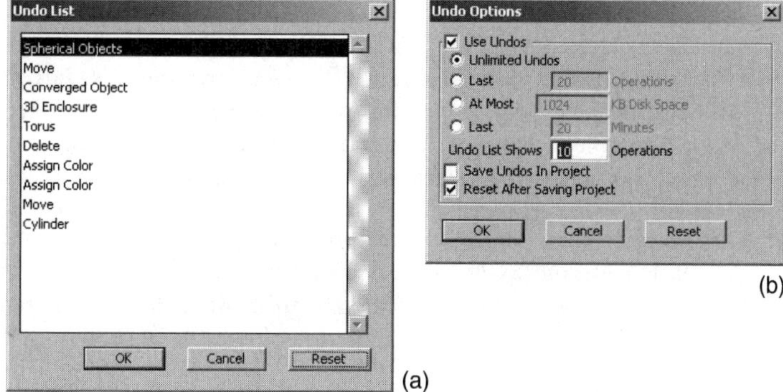

- The last item in the Undo/Redo group under the Edit menu is Undo Options. Select this command, and it will open up a dialog in which you can make various changes to how the Undo operation will work (Figure 1.17-b).

- As you can see, it's possible to completely turn off the Undo feature if disk space happens to be at a premium. Fortunately, a less drastic option is also available—you can simply choose to limit, in three different ways, the number of Undo records that will be stored, rather than have an unlimited number. You can also change the number of Undo operations that are displayed in the Undo List from the default value of 10.

- Selecting the Save Undos In Project option will save all the undo records along with a project file. This means that when you open the file again, you can also Undo operations executed in previous sessions of working on that project. However, be careful with this option as it could increase your file size substantially.

- The last option in the Undo Options dialog, Reset After Saving Project, erases the undo records every time a project is saved. It's checked by default, in which case you should be careful not to use the auto-save option (which you'll study in Workshop 3, Personalizing Your Environment)—this might save your file at some arbitrary point in time while you're still in the process of experimentation, and prevent you from using Undo to reverse something you didn't do right. If you must use the auto-save feature, remember to deselect this option and you should be fine.

3.4 Prepicking and Postpicking

All this time, we've been moving, coloring, or deleting objects by selecting them *after* choosing the Move, Color, or Delete tools respectively. This is referred to as *postpicking*, and here, the operation is executed only on one object at a time. If, however, you want to move, color, delete, or carry out any other operation on many objects at the same time, it's more convenient to use what's known as the *prepicking* method.

- Go to the Pick tool (M-Tool:4b,1) and keep selecting all the objects on which a certain operation is to be performed. The selected objects get highlighted in red. 

- Once all the desired objects have been selected, go to the tool you wish to use: Move, Color, Delete, etc. Execution of the operation will now make the required change in *all* the objects selected—they'll be moved together, or colored in the selected color, or deleted—in one single step.

- Using the Delete tool in the prepicking mode can be a little confusing at first. After you finish making the selection of objects and activate the Delete tool, the Prompts palette will instruct you to "Click to Delete Picked Objects." You *must* execute this click for the deletion to happen. You can click *anywhere* in the graphics window, even on blank space; you don't necessarily have to click on an object. Alternately, you can use the Delete key (Mac) or Backspace key (PC) on your keyboard instead of the Delete tool to carry out the deletion operation after prepicking.

- Keep in mind that you can use the prepicking method in this manner for many other operations as well. For instance, you can select a number of 2D shapes with the Pick tool, and then derive extruded 3D objects of the same height from all of them at the same time with the 3D Extrusion tool (M-Tool:5a,4). Make sure that a preset height is selected in the Heights menu and then try it.

3.5 Area Picking

Prepicking objects individually, as you did in the last section, can get quite tedious if you have many objects to select. If the targeted objects lie close together, it might be more convenient to select them by enclosing them in a boundary that's demarcated with the mouse. This is known as *area picking*.

- Make sure you have a number of objects in the graphics window; if required, create some more. Select the Pick tool. You'll now use it to draw a rectangular boundary that encloses all the objects you need to select. Click on one corner of this boundary, keep the mouse down, drag it until you define the opposite corner, and then release the mouse. All the objects that lie *completely within* this boundary will get selected. Unlike some other CAD programs, the direction of dragging—left to right, or vice versa—doesn't matter. But keep in mind that the first click should always be on blank space rather than on an object, otherwise only that object will get selected.

The rectangular boundary you just defined is referred to as a *frame*. You can also use a different kind of bounding area for selecting objects, known as a *lasso*, by choosing this option in the Pick tool dialog.

- Double-click on the Pick tool to open its dialog. It contains a large number of options that we'll explore in depth in Workshop 2 (Bringing a Sense of Scale). For now, simply look at the three Area Pick options located at the base of the dialog. Frame is selected by default. Change the selection to Lasso and exit the dialog.

- Back in the graphics window, first deselect any objects that are selected by clicking on blank space. Now click and drag to select objects using area picking as you did earlier. Notice that you're no longer restricted to defining a rectangle as the bounding area—you can draw out any freehand enclosure with the mouse, as if you were sketching. Once you release the mouse button, all the objects lying within this freehand enclosure get selected.

- Get back to the Pick Options dialog and activate the remaining Pick Crossing option in the Area Pick section. If you now use area picking, you'll find that objects crossing the bounding frame or lasso also get selected, in addition to the objects lying completely inside it.

- When area picking is used, notice that any previously selected entities get deselected automatically, since you have to start by clicking on a blank area of the window. To select additional entities while still maintaining the current selection, press the Shift key on your keyboard while area picking.

- Area picking is only available when using the Pick tool for prepicking—it cannot be used for postpicking. Thus, for instance, if you've already selected the Move tool, you cannot use area picking to select the objects you want to move. Instead, you first need to activate the Pick tool, draw a bounding area to enclose the objects you wish to select, and *after* the objects have been selected, use the Move tool to carry out the desired transformation.

3.6 Other Methods of Selection...and Deselection

In addition to the Pick tool, there are a few other commands that can be employed for making selections. These are located in the third group of the Edit menu. Let's try them all out.

- Start with Select Previous. This repicks the last round of selected entities and is useful when a number of selections are accidentally deselected. Very often while making multiple selections, it happens that you don't click close enough to an object to select it, resulting in the deselection of objects you've already selected. It can be quite tedious to make the selection all over again, so Select Previous comes in really handy in such a situation.
- Select All Unghosted will select all the visible elements in your project, as opposed to Select All Ghosted, which will select the ghosted elements only. The concept of ghosting, and the difference between visible and ghosted objects, is explained in detail in the next section.
- Next, go to the Select By command. This opens up a dialog in which you can select objects by various properties such as Object Type, Surface Style, Layer, and so on, grouped under two separate categories: Geometry and Attributes. In subsequent workshops, you'll learn more about many of the object properties that appear in this dialog, which will be unfamiliar to you right now. Figure 1.18 shows the Select By dialog in which all objects colored in two different surface styles have been targeted for selection. You can also have multiple selection criteria by activating more than one property. This kind of selection ability can be extremely convenient. It also motivates you to draw your entities systematically, differentiating them by layers, colors, and so on, to make full use of this option.

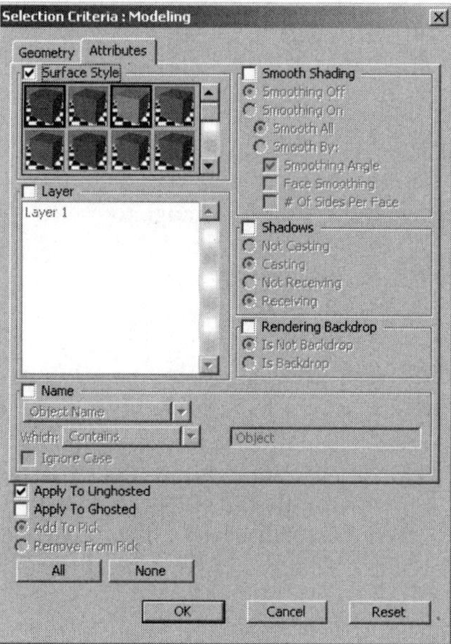

Figure 1.18

Using the Select By command to select objects that are colored in the two highlighted surface styles.

- Let's move on to deselection, the inverse process of selection. The Deselect option, located immediately after the Select By option, lets you deselect all the objects that are currently selected. You've already seen how you can achieve the same result by simply clicking on a blank area of the window, away from any object.

- To deselect only one object from a number of selected objects, click on that object itself rather than on a blank portion of the window.

3.7 Ghosting and Unghosting Objects, and the Status of Objects Options

Ghosting is an alternative attribute to visibility that objects in form•Z can have. Visible objects are those that you see in your window in the color which was assigned to them. These can be selected and operated upon in the usual manner. Another name for visible objects is *unghosted* objects. Ghosted objects, in contrast, have the default color of gray; also, they're inactive and cannot be selected for the execution of any operation. Unghosted objects can be ghosted by the Ghost tool (M-Tool:14b,1), and ghosted objects can be unghosted by the Unghost tool (M-Tool:14b,2). Unghosting is, thus, the inverse process of ghosting.

But how are ghosted objects created in the first place and what are they used for? You've already worked with three of the derivative object tools in the left column of Row 5, which derived 3D objects from 2D shapes. What happened to the original 2D elements? They were ghosted by default, and therefore retained in the project, making it possible to retrieve them at a later stage, if needed. Let's see how this can be done.

- Select any of the three derivative tools you worked with in Section 1.10, say 3D Extrusion (M-Tool:5a,4), and invoke its dialog. Click on the Status Of Objects tab to see its options. It gives you three choices of what to do with the original objects from which new objects will be derived. This Operand Status is set to Ghost by default (Figure 1.19-a), which is why ghosted objects were created when you used this tool earlier. You can choose to retain (Keep) or throw away (Delete) the original objects, but stick with Ghost for now. The New Object Status options are more relevant to the boolean operations which will be covered in Exercise 4, so ignore them at present. 

- Notice the checkbox called Global at the top of the dialog, which is selected by default. This means that the current settings of the dialog will be applied to all the tools to which the Status Of Objects option is relevant. To make the change in settings only for the tool you're invoking this dialog from, click on the checkbox and it will change to reflect the current tool.

The Status Of Objects options are also available in a separate palette accessible from the second group of the Palettes menu.

- Now go ahead and apply the 3D Extrusion tool to some 2D objects (Figure 1.19-b). Then delete the 3D objects you just derived or move them aside. If you aren't in the Wire Frame display mode, switch to it. You'll see your original 2D objects in ghosted form (Figure 1.19-c).

Suppose that you've performed a large number of subsequent operations, and you suddenly realize you want to retrieve one or more of these 2D objects. You cannot go back all the way using Undo without losing what you've subsequently done, and you would rather not have to recreate the objects. This is what you can do:

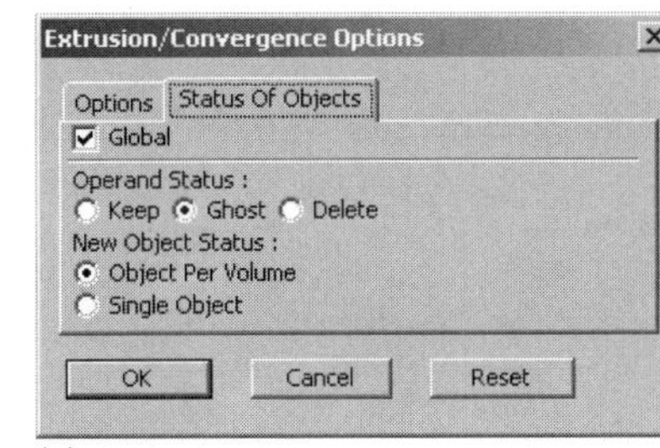

(a)

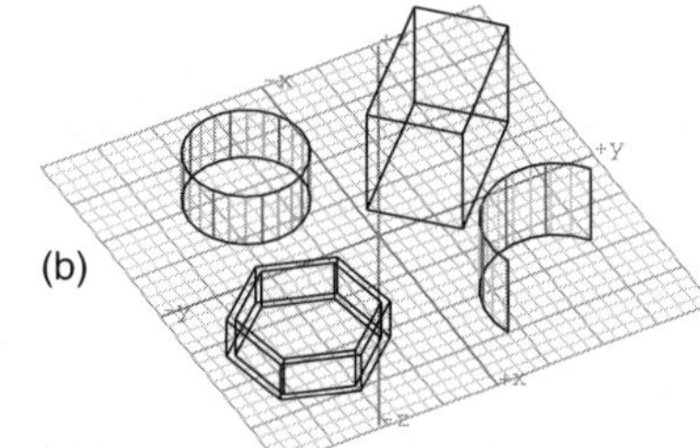

(b)

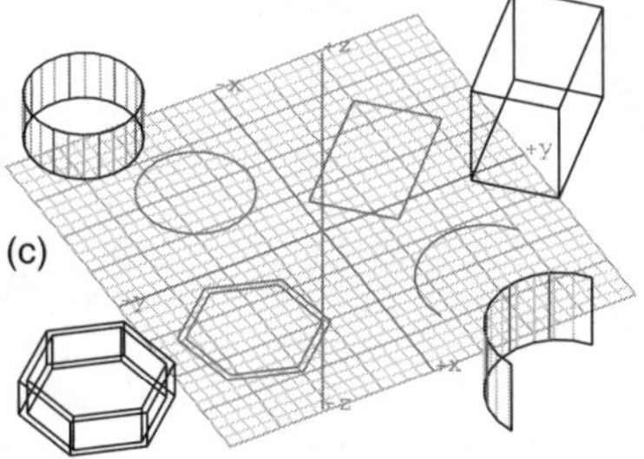

(c)

Figure 1.19

Creating ghosted objects. (a) The Status Of Objects dialog, showing the status set to Ghost. (b) Generating 3D objects with the 3D Extrusion operation. (c) Moving the objects aside to reveal the original 2D objects in ghosted mode.

- To retrieve only one or a few ghosted objects, apply the Unghost tool (M-Tool:14b,2) to them directly. They'll come back as regular objects, with their original colors, and you can now operate on them just like any other visible objects.

- When a large number of ghosted objects needs to be unghosted, it would be tedious to apply the Unghost tool to each one of them individually. It's better to apply the prepicking method. However, you cannot select them in the normal fashion by using the Pick tool. Instead, go to Edit > Select All Ghosted. All the ghosted objects get highlighted in red, indicating that they're selected. Then select the Unghost tool and click in the graphics window to unghost all the selected objects. You can reghost the ones you did not wish to retrieve by using the Ghost tool (M-Tool:14b,1).

- As emphasized, ghosted objects can only be seen in the Wire Frame display mode. If you tend to use this mode of display very often and don't want these objects cluttering up your screen, but also do not want to get rid of them irrevocably, you can choose to hide them. Select the Wire Frame display from the Display menu while holding down the option key (Mac) or Ctrl+Shift keys (PC). This will invoke the Wire Frame Options dialog. Activate the Hide Ghosted option with the default Objects sub-option, then close the dialog. (We'll explore all its other options in Workshop 3, Personalizing Your Environment.) The ghosted objects will no longer be visible in the graphics window.

- If, on the other hand, you're confident that you'll never need them again, you can delete all ghosted objects by going to Edit > Clear All Ghosted. They will now be permanently erased from the database of your project, reducing the size of the project file. Periodically clearing ghosted objects is a good practice, particularly if the file is getting too large.

3.8 Zooming and Scrolling

In all this time that you've been working, you may have, on occasion, inadvertently moved some objects out of view in the graphics window. It's time to learn how to use the zoom and scroll commands so that you can bring them back.

- Go to the seventh column of the window tool palette at the base of the graphics window. This is the Zoom & Pan palette. Drag it out and position it on one side of the graphics window as shown in Figure 1.20, and explore each one of the tools in turn.

- The first tool, Zoom, is the familiar "magnifying glass" that you find in most programs. It lets you zoom in or out of a specified area of the window by clicking in the center of that area. By default it zooms in, indicated by the + sign. Use it with the option key (Mac) or Ctrl+Shift keys (PC) to zoom out. The extent of the zooming in or zooming out is determined by percentage factors that you can modify in the dialog of this tool. This dialog actually contains options for all the zoom tools and can be accessed by going to any one of them.

- The second tool, Hand, is again the familiar tool used for scrolling through a window. Click and drag to move the displayed image in any desired direction.

- The next two tools, Zoom In By Frame and Zoom Out By Frame, allow you to zoom in and out of any part of the window by drawing a rectangular frame. By default, zoom frames are drawn from the center out. If you prefer to draw frames by demarcating their corners, select that option in the Zoom Options dialog. Keep in mind that you have to *click and drag* to indicate a frame. If you simply click, the command will not be executed.

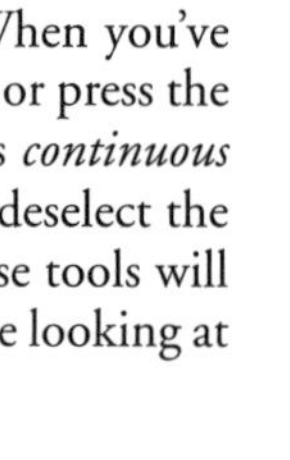

- With all these four tools, you'll notice that once selected, each remains active even after it's been applied, enabling it to be repeatedly applied any number of times. Thus, you can keep zooming in and out or scrolling without having to reselect the tool each time—you only need to do it once. During this process, all other tools become deactivated, as shown in Figure 1.20. When you've finished using the tool, simply click on it or on any one of the other grayed out tools, or press the Esc key, and the tool palette display will be restored to normal. This is referred to as *continuous window tool control.* If you want to disable this feature, go to Edit > Preferences and deselect the checkbox for this option located under the Project > General section. Thereafter, these tools will function in the regular fashion—getting deactivated after being applied once. (We'll be looking at the Preferences dialog in detail in Workshop 3, Personalizing Your Environment.)

- The next two tools, Zoom In Incrementally and Zoom Out Incrementally, do so by the same preset percentage factors specified in the Zoom Options dialog that you saw for the first Zoom tool. The difference is that these tools always zoom in or out from the center of the window. Thus, you don't need to click in the window at all for these tools to work.

- The Previous tool takes you one step back to the previous zoom/scroll view, if any.

- The Fit tool automatically adjusts the zoom level so that all the objects in the project fit within the graphics window. It's a frequently used tool. It has a few associated options in the Zoom Options dialog, which you should explore. You can choose to fit selected entities only within the window rather than all the objects in the project, as well as change the default border size between the "fitted" objects and the edge of the window. The options related to lights and camera views will be clear once you study these topics in Workshop 3 (Personalizing Your Environment).

- The last tool, Reset, takes you to the default viewing size of the reference plane and coordinate axes, the one you see when you first open a new project. You can change this default viewing size, if necessary, by going to the Display menu and choosing a different display scale from the first group of menu items. A Custom Display Scale can also be specified. This display scale is the viewing size you will return to whenever you select the Reset tool.

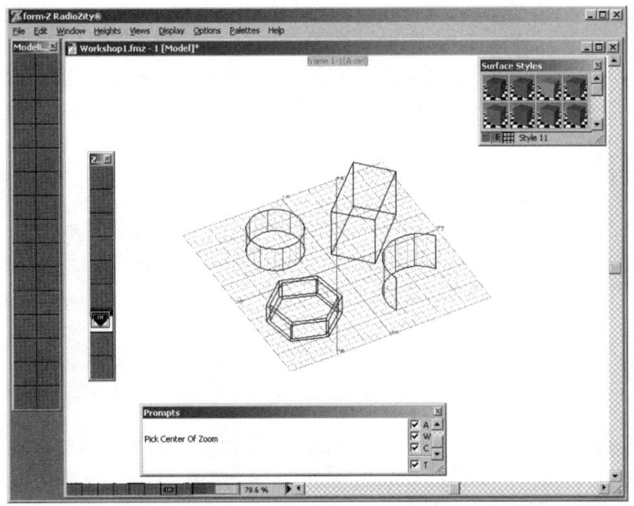

Figure 1.20

All other tools are deactivated when the Zoom In By Frame tool is selected.

Changing the display scale is an alternate way of zooming in or out, but unlike the regular Zoom tools, it also has the effect of resetting the display. Therefore, use it for the latter purpose only, and rely on the Zoom tools in the window tool palette for the regular zooming in and out operations.

- Finally, turn your attention to the percentage value displayed in the box at the right end of the window tool palette. This shows the current zoom level of the graphics window relative to the active display scale. If you click on this box, the Zoom Percentage popup menu is invoked, from which a different zoom percentage can be selected to zoom in or zoom out. It's a convenient alternative to the other Zoom tools—try it.

This marks the end of Exercise 3. You should now feel much better equipped to move on to some more complex operations, such as the booleans.

EXERCISE 4

Combining Objects in Various Ways: The Booleans

Very often, the objects that you'll need to model will be quite complex, impossible to generate directly from the various 2D and 3D modeling tools that you've learned so far. You might need to create several objects and then combine them in various ways to finally achieve the configuration you're looking for. If you're familiar with set theory, you know that there are three basic operations that can be performed on two sets: addition, subtraction, and intersection. Such operations are referred to as *boolean operations*. Objects that have an area (such as closed surfaces) or a volume (such as solids) can also be thought of as sets, and the same boolean operations can be applied to them to generate interesting and infinitely varying forms.

form•Z not only has the three basic boolean operators corresponding to addition, subtraction, and intersection—in the form of the Union, Difference, and Intersection tools respectively—but has two additional operators that are a convenient variation on the booleans—the B-Split and Trim & Stitch tools. All these tools are located in the left column of the ninth row of the modeling tool palette. In this concluding exercise for Workshop 1, we'll look at the first four of the boolean tools, along with the related Join and Separate tools which are located in the right column of the same row. The Trim & Stitch tool is a little more involved, targeted primarily towards meshed objects, so we'll leave it for Workshop 6 (Going Organic), which deals with such objects.

If a boolean operation is applied to a parametric object, it gets converted to a plain object. If it's applied to a combination of smooth and facetted objects, the result will be a smooth object.

As a rule, the boolean tools should only be applied to two or more objects that intersect each other in some manner. Let's do some preparation before we start working with them.

- Rearrange the objects in your window with the Move tool to get some intersecting groups. To position objects more accurately along the horizontal plane, change to Plan view. Then go to the Back/Front or Right/Left views to do the same in the vertical direction. Also, bring together objects of various colors within a group—this will yield very interesting and colorful results. It will also serve to demonstrate a key concept in coloring that we'll look at later on in this exercise.
- After you've finished collecting all the objects in intersecting groups, switch back to a non-planar view. This will afford a better view of the boolean operations.

4.1 Union

Activate the Union tool (M-Tool:9a,1) and follow the instructions that appear in the Prompts palette. You'll be asked to select two objects for a union. If you now select any two objects that intersect or at least touch each other (see Figure 1.21-a), the boolean operation of addition is performed and they're united into one object. Any further transformation such as moving, changing colors, and so on, will now be performed on the unioned entity rather than the individual objects.

Union is the only boolean tool that works even if the objects only touch each other. All the others require them to actually intersect.

- In a Wire Frame mode, you'll still be able to see the two original objects in ghosted mode (see Figure 1.21-b). The booleans are another instance of tools that operate on existing objects to create new ones, so the Status Of Objects options we discussed earlier are applicable to them as well. These options appear in the Tool Options palette when the Union tool is activated. You can set the Operand Status to Keep or Delete instead of Ghosted, if required. Alternately, you can hide the display of ghosted objects, as discussed in Section 3.7. You also know how to retrieve the original objects using the Unghost tool (M-Tool:14b,2), should you need to do so later.
- If you want to unite more than two objects at a time, use the prepicking method: select all the objects you wish to unite using the Pick tool first, then apply the Union tool. Keep in mind that the operation is actually executed on two consecutively selected objects at a time—in other words, you must ensure that the objects selected first and second actually intersect or touch, the object selected third intersects or touches the union of the first two, the object selected fourth intersects or touches the union of the first three, and so on.

Figure 1.21

The Union, Intersection, and Difference tools applied to a pair of facetted objects. The original objects are shown, along with the Wire Frame and Surface Render displays of the resultant objects.

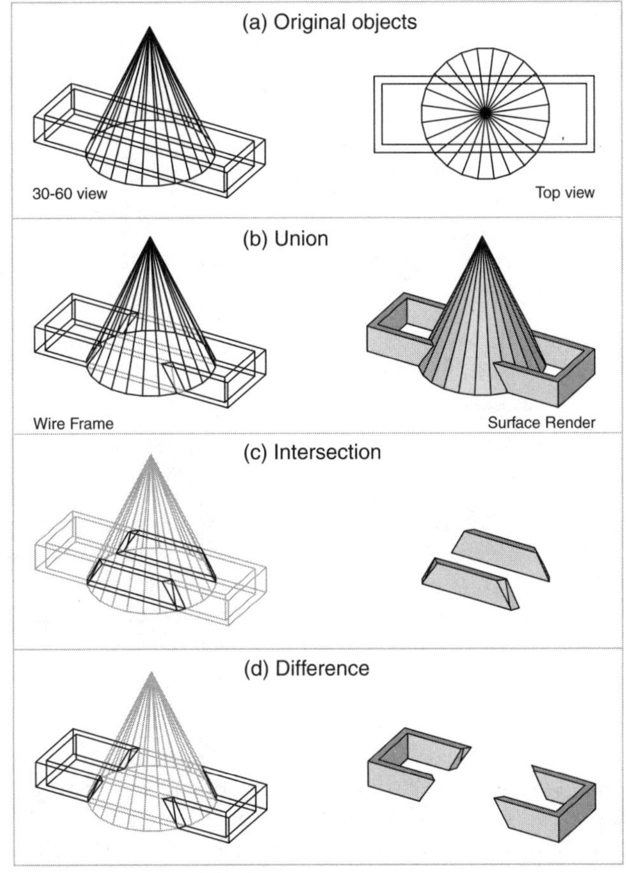

- The Union tool, along with the other booleans, also works on 2D closed surfaces with the same results and under the same conditions. Try it out. Don't expect, however, to be able to unite a surface and a solid—that's mathematically impossible and will not work.

4.2 Intersection

- Repeat the same sequence of operations you just performed, now with the Intersection tool and using the postpicking method. Intersection will create an object that's common to both the objects involved in the operation. Using the prepicking method will be quite tricky since each object needs to have some common area or volume with the intersection of the previously selected objects, otherwise the result of the operation will be a null object. It's always safer to use postpicking for this tool.

- An Intersection operation is illustrated in Figure 1.21-c. Notice that two separate volumes are created as a result of the operation, since a solid cylinder is being intersected with a 3D enclosure. Should these separate volumes be one object, or should each volume be a separate object? This is where the New Object Status item under Status Of Objects becomes relevant. It has two options, one for each of these two cases. Select the one that's appropriate to the situation. Even if you select the Single Object option for now, you can later separate the volumes, if required, by using the Separate tool (M-Tool:9b,2) which you'll soon learn about.

4.3 Difference

- Move on to explore the Difference tool in the same manner. It works just like subtraction—it returns the first object minus the second object. Thus the sequence of selection is important here, even when the postpicking method is used. If you use the prepicking method, each subsequent volume starting with the second object will be subtracted from the first object, so make the selection carefully.

- A useful "architectural" implementation of the Difference tool is to create different kinds of openings in enclosures. Try it.

- In the Difference operation illustrated in Figure 1.21-d, notice again that two separate volumes result from the operation. You already know how to deal with such a situation.

4.4 Split

- The final boolean operator is the B-Split tool, used for splitting objects against one another. Apply it to two intersecting objects. You'll find that the second object disappears, but not before it has split up the first object along their mutual lines of intersection. Figure 1.22-a shows the result of a Split operation by moving away some of the newly created objects to reveal the original ones in ghosted mode. You can see that this operation is actually equivalent to the combination of both Difference and Intersection applied to the same set of objects—you get the first object minus the second, as well as their intersection.

- What you just performed was a One Way Split operation. There is a second kind of Split operation called Two Way Split. Open the dialog of the B-Split tool and set the option to Two Way. Apply it to a pair of intersecting objects, and you'll find that it gives you *both* the objects trimmed against each other, rather than just the first object trimmed against the second. It's illustrated in Figure 1.22-b, again by moving away the newly created objects from the originals.

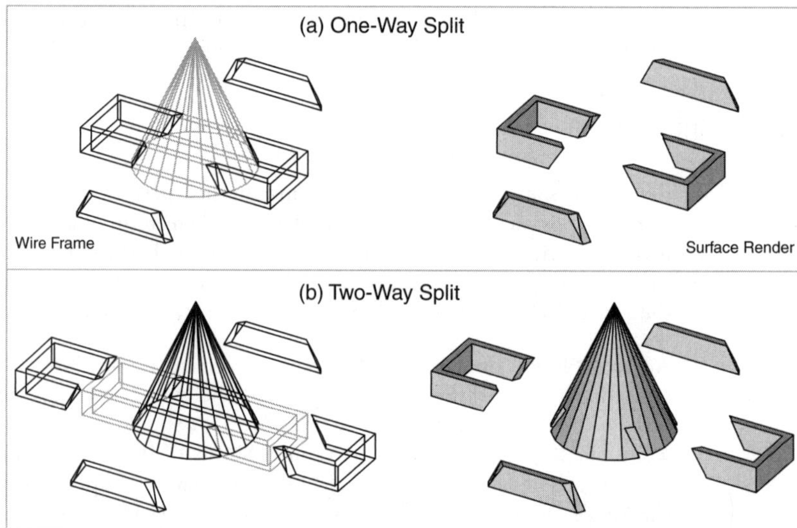

Figure 1.22

One Way and Two Way Split operations, applied to the same set of objects shown in Figure 1.21-a. The split pieces have been moved aside to reveal the original objects in ghosted mode.

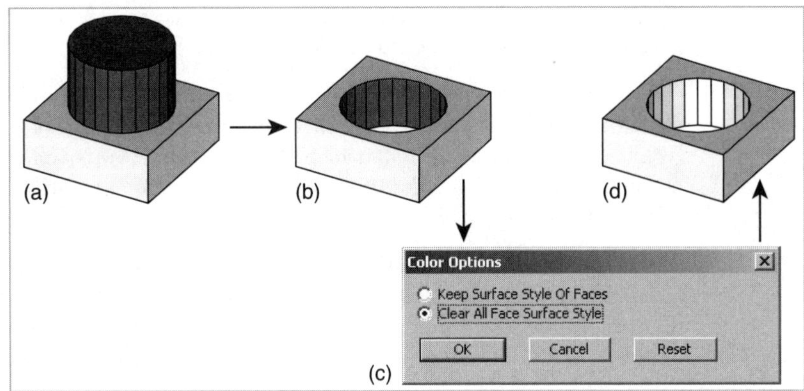

Figure 1.23

Working with multiple object colors. (a) Two intersecting facetted objects in different colors. (b) Applying the Difference tool to create an object with faces of different colors. (c) Setting the Color tool option to Clear All Face Surface Styles. (d) Applying the Color tool to the object to color all its faces in the same surface style.

4.5 The Color Tool Revisited

Now that you've worked with the boolean tools, let's look at an important concept related to object colors that comes into play when working with booleaned objects.

- Perform any of the boolean operations on two facetted objects with different colors (Figure 1.23-a). Look at the result in the Wire Frame display mode. You'll find that the new object appears fully colored in the color of the first operand object (i.e., the object which was selected first while executing the boolean operation). Now switch to the Surface Render display, and you'll find that some faces of the new object, those that were derived from the second operand object, have the color of that object (see Figure 1.23-b).
- Select a new color from the Surface Styles palette, different from those already visible in the object, and use the Color tool (M-Tool:14a,1) to change the color of the object to the selected color. You'll find that the new color gets applied to only those faces derived from the first operand object. The faces derived from the second operand object continue to have the color of that object.

What has happened here is that the faces of the object derived from the second operand have acquired a color different from the overall object color. Fortunately, there's a simple fix to this problem.

- Invoke the dialog of the Color tool and choose the second option, Clear All Face Surface Styles (Figure 1.23-c), instead of the first option that's selected by default. Now reapply the Color tool to the object that has multiple surface colors. You'll find all faces of the object seamlessly taking on the color that's currently active in the Surface Styles palette (Figure 1.23-d).

4.6 Joining and Separating Volumes

You've seen that when you apply the Union tool to objects that intersect or touch each other, their individual volumes are combined into a single volume that makes the resultant object. The Union tool cannot be applied to non-intersecting objects, since their volumes cannot be combined. form•Z, however, provides you with another tool that enables you to treat several non-intersecting objects as a single object, on which desired modeling operations can then be performed. This is the Join tool, and it's accompanied by a related but opposite tool, Separate.

- Select two or more non-intersecting objects with the Pick tool. Then apply the Join tool (M-Tool:9b,1) to them. Select one of them again with the Pick tool—you'll find that all the objects you had applied the Join tool to get highlighted. What you've effectively done is joined them into a single object. Just like the Union operation, the Join operation changes parametric objects to plain objects, and you'll get a warning message to this effect before you proceed with it.
- Next, apply the Join tool in the same fashion to two or more intersecting objects. You'll find that unlike the Union operation, the individual volumes of the objects are *retained* rather than combined. Essentially, the Join tool operates in the same way, irrespective of whether the selected objects intersect or not.

- One advantage of the Join tool over the Union tool is that the joined objects can be separated at any time using the Separate tool (M-Tool:9b,2). Apply Separate to the joined objects you just created and you'll find that you've retrieved the original objects, as they were before the Join operation was applied to them. There is one difference, however; they remain plain objects, even if they had been parametric before.
- You've already seen how the Separate tool can be applied to separate noncontiguous volumes of the same object, created by boolean tools such as Intersection and Difference. Thus, the scope of the Separate tool is not restricted to objects joined with the Join tool. Moreover, the Separate tool can also be used to separate objects along selected segments or faces. The choice of operation is made in the tool dialog. You'll be able to apply it in these other modes once you learn to work with the Segment and Face topological levels in Section 3.1 of Workshop 2 (Bringing a Sense of Scale).

With the Join tool, any number of objects, located anywhere with respect to each other, can be temporarily or permanently joined. Any modeling operation will then be performed on all of them collectively. Figure 1.24 shows a situation where the use of the Join tool is indispensable. An elliptical extrusion needs to be subtracted from a series of non-intersecting slabs. Rather than performing the Difference operation individually for each slab and unghosting the extrusion each time for use with the next slab—an incredibly tedious process!—we can simply join all the slabs with the Join tool and subtract the elliptical extrusion from the collective volume.

This concludes the exercises for Workshop 1. You've covered a lot of ground and learned enough to be able to create fairly complex configurations. You'll be guided through one such project in the suggested assignment for this workshop. Attempt at least one such modeling exercise yourself before moving on to the next workshop.

Figure 1.24

The use of the Join tool. (a) Initial configuration of objects. (b) Desired configuration, achieved by using the Join tool and then the Difference tool.

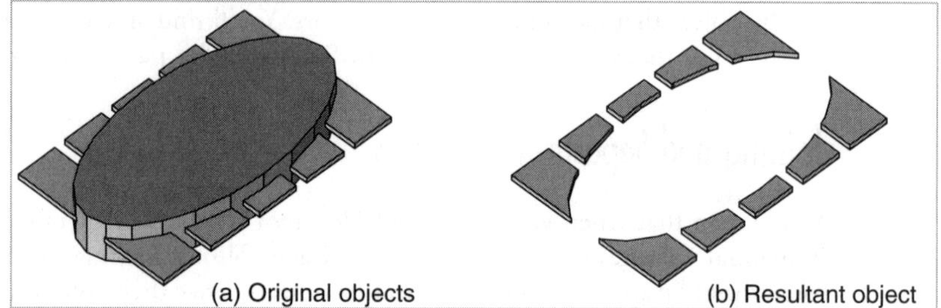

Assignment 1

A Simple Pavilion

Create a simple pavilion using all the tools you've learned so far. Don't worry about scale, dimensions, or accuracy for now. You needn't necessarily have a concept in mind before you start this exercise. You can use the medium itself to generate ideas for you as you are modeling.

The actual exercise of modeling the pavilion shown here will now be demonstrated step by step. How your graphics window should look at the end of each step is illustrated alongside, along with the modeling tools that need to be used. The CD-ROM accompanying this book has a separate form•Z file for each step of this exercise in the Assignments > Workshop1 folder, and you can always use them for reference if you get stuck. A color rendering of the completed project is in the Assignment1.tif file in the same folder.

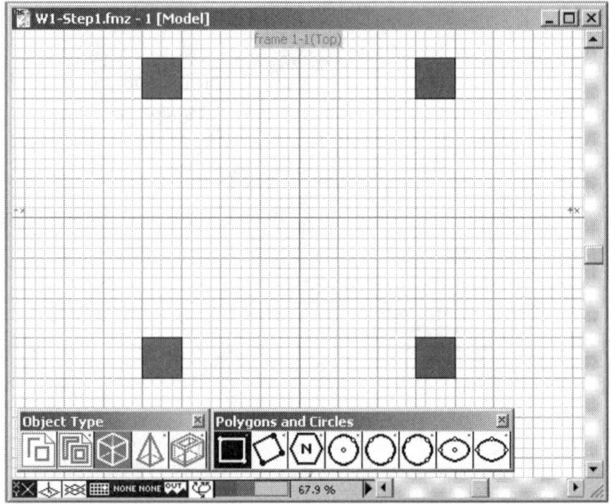

Step 1

Open a new form•Z project. Change to the Top view by going to View > Top. Set the Heights menu to Custom and specify the height as 5'-0". Set the object generation mode in the left column of the second row to 3D Extrusion.

Use Rectangle (M-Tool:3a,1) to draw four squares as shown. Use the grid lines for reference, but don't worry about perfect accuracy for now.

Step 2

Set Heights to 2'-0". While still in the Top view and 3D Extrusion mode, draw another square that intersects all of the first four blocks at their corners.

Switch to a non-planar view and Union each of the four smaller blocks with the larger slab. This becomes the base of the pavilion. (You can add the steps to climb to the base later. Let's complete the basic structure for now.)

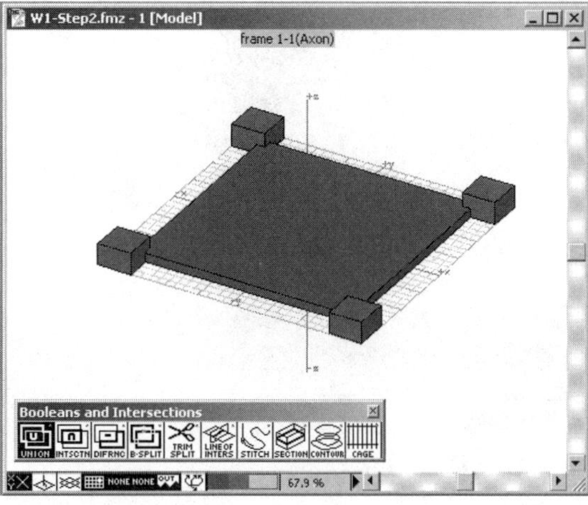

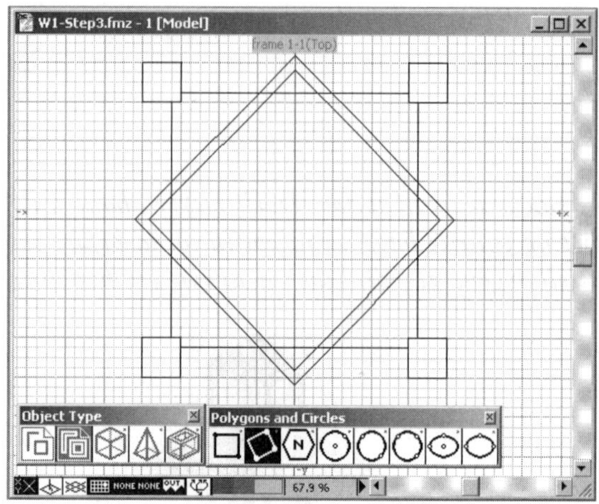

Step 3

Switch back to the Top view. Set the object generation mode to 2D Enclosure by selecting M-Tool:2a,2. Change the width of the enclosure to 2'-0" by accessing the tool dialog.

Select M-Tool:3a,2 and draw a square inclined at an angle of 45° as shown.

Step 4

Switch to a non-planar view, and set Heights to Graphic/ Keyed. Select the 3D Convergence tool (M-Tool:5a,5) and generate a 3D pyramid from the 2D enclosure, specifying an appropriate height interactively with the mouse. This object will be the roof of the pavilion.

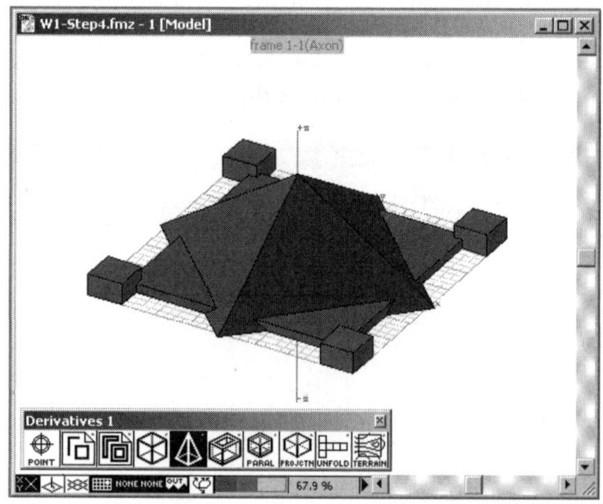

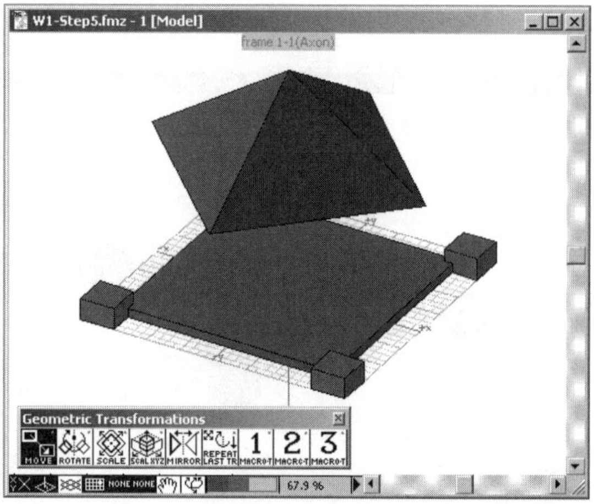

Step 5

Highlight the Perpendicular Lock tool (W-Tool:2,1) to activate it. Then use the Move tool to displace the pyramid vertically upwards by an appropriate distance.

Step 6

Switch back to the Top view and set the object generation mode to 2D Surface. Use any one of the Circle tools to draw four small circles at the four corners of the pyramid.

Change to a non-planar view and extrude each circle by the same height, up to the base of the pyramidal roof. These circular extrusions will serve as the supports for the roof.

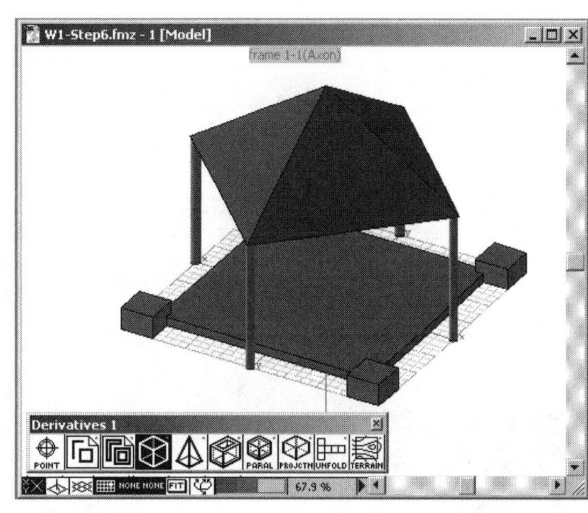

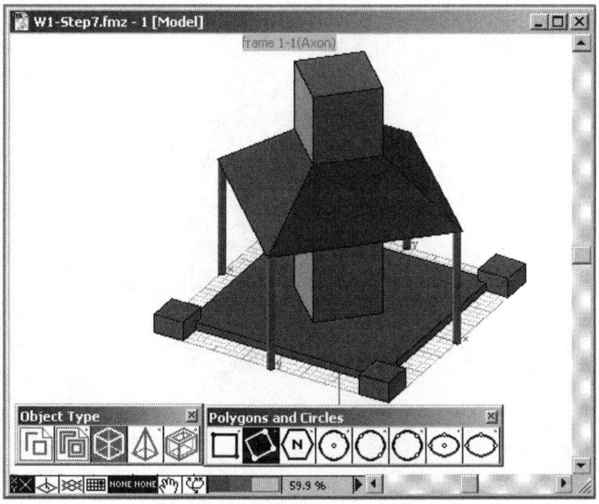

Step 7

Create an extruded solid, aligned diagonally like the pyramid and passing through its center. By now, it should be easy for you to figure out how to do this.

Step 8

Use the central solid to carry out a One Way Split of the pyramidal roof. Remember—the roof should be selected first!

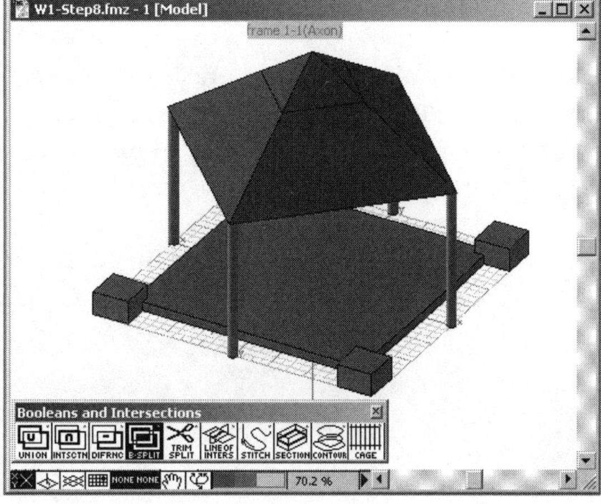

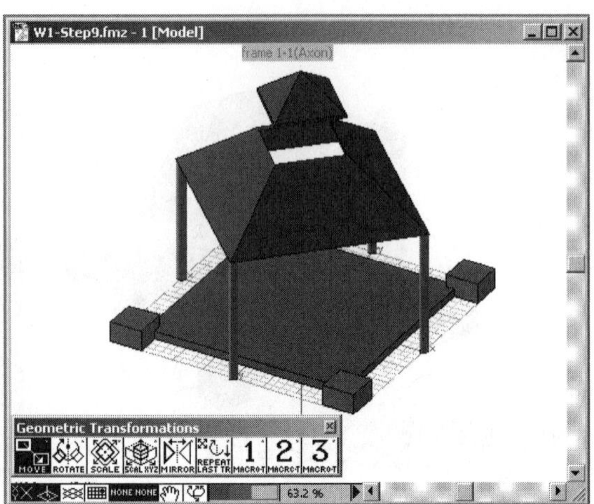

Step 9

Now use the Move tool, with the Perpendicular Lock activated, to displace the split top portion of the roof vertically upwards by a small distance.

Step 10

Finally, add circular supports for this displaced portion of the roof as well. When you're done, you should have a simple, structurally stable pavilion as shown.

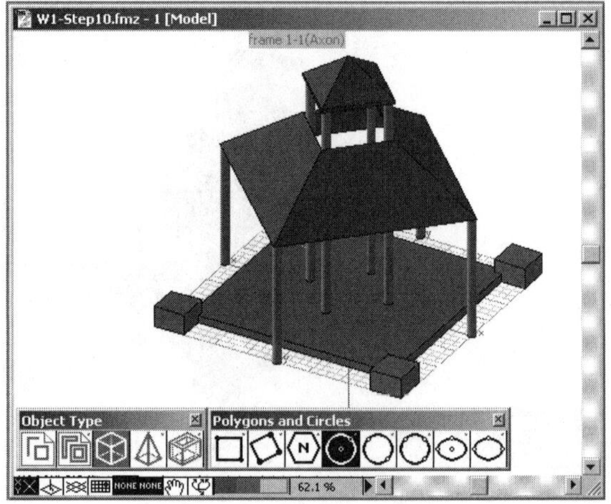

You now have the basic structure of a pavilion that you can build upon and embellish, according to your creative visions. As you can see, you were able to create a 3D model of some complexity in a relatively short sequence of steps. The process was simple and quite intuitive, and will become more so as you continue to work with the program.

Creating objects of specific dimensions, undoubtedly a more complicated task than what we've been doing so far, will be our next challenge, and we'll take it up in Workshop 2.

Workshop 2

Bringing a Sense of Scale

In this workshop, you'll learn how to create models that are of specific dimensions. The process involves setting up the units of measurement, using the coordinate displays effectively, and specifying values using the mouse as well as the keyboard. All these aspects will be covered in Exercise 1. Exercises 2 and 3 will show you how to restrain the cursor movement in your window in various ways, create new objects with reference to existing ones, and work at multiple levels ranging from points to groups.

Some additional key functions in modeling will be covered in Exercises 4 and 5. You'll learn how to apply transformations and make copies of objects in different ways, as well as edit parametric objects and lines. Finally in Exercise 6, you'll work with the Insertion tools which can be used to perform, more simply and elegantly, some of the boolean operations you mastered in Workshop 1 (Letting Yourself Go). In the concluding assignment for this workshop, you'll apply all that you've learned in creating the block model (i.e., the massing model) of a building.

EXERCISE 1

Sizing Up Your World

Throughout the last workshop, you worked without worrying about dimensions, scale, units, and so on. This may be fine in the early stages of a design when you're exploring various shapes and forms, but sooner or later, you'll have to bring scale into your modeling world. Exercise 1 will guide you through this process. You'll start by learning how to specify the measurement unit according to the requirements of the project, which may be different from the default unit settings. Then, you'll see how to track the cursor coordinates in the graphics window, using both the Coordinates and the Prompts palettes. Finally, you'll master a crucial aspect of accurate modeling—using the keyboard to specify object positions and dimensions, both in relative as well as absolute terms.

- Launch form•Z and save the default modeling window that appears as a new project. Close all palettes except Prompts, Coordinates, and Surface Styles. As usual, also set the Heights menu to Graphic/Keyed so that you can specify object heights interactively.

1.1 Specifying the Working Units

- Go to Options > Working Units. A dialog is invoked containing various options for selecting the type of measurement unit and its accuracy (Figure 2.1). Select the Data Scale appropriate to the scale of your project. There are four options, ranging from the smallest (Watch) to the largest (City). The default option is Medium (Building). Then, select the unit type—English or Metric—you want to work with, and the base unit for that type. (Throughout this book, the English system has been used, with the base unit set to Feet. If you're using the Metric system, simply substitute the appropriate metric values for feet and inches.)

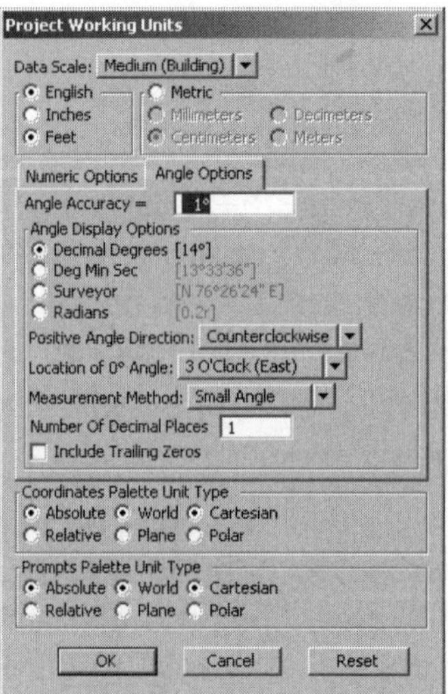

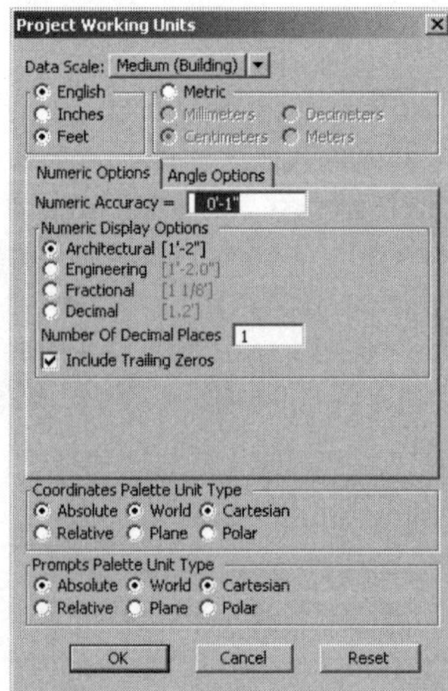

Figure 2.1

The dialog for setting the working units of the project, showing both the Numeric Options and the Angle Options tabs.

- Notice how changing the Data Scale automatically sets appropriate values for the options in the Numeric Options and Angle Options tabs. You can also change the Numeric Accuracy and Angle

Accuracy values to better suit the specific project requirements. In general, you should try and set these to *not less than the minimum levels of accuracy* you need in a project. Thus, if you're modeling small objects like furniture, a numeric accuracy of 1/8" and an angle accuracy of 0.1° might be sufficient. On the other hand, if you're modeling large projects such as a city block, you can probably get away with a numeric accuracy of 6" and an angle accuracy of 1°.

- Check out also the Numeric Display Options and Angle Display Options and set them as required. As shown in Figure 2.1, Numeric Display Options lets you select one of four different formats to see the coordinate display in, along with some decimal formatting options. Angle Display Options similarly lets you specify the format of the angle display, along with the direction of the 0° angle and the measurement method. You can stick with the defaults for now, and see how they work.
- Don't worry about the Coordinates Palette Unit Type and the Prompts Palette Unit Type in the Project Working Units dialog for now. These options can be set directly from the Coordinates and Prompts palettes respectively, and we shall see in due course what they're used for. For now, close the Project Working Units dialog.

1.2 Tracking Coordinates

- Let's assume you've set the unit type to English, the base unit to Feet, the Numeric Accuracy to 0'-1", and the Numeric Display Options to Architectural. Notice that as you now move the cursor in the graphics window, the coordinates of the current position are interactively displayed in the Coordinates palette in this format you specified (Figure 2.2-a). Carry out any modeling operation, and you'll find that the same format is also followed for the coordinate display in the Prompts palette (Figure 2.2-b).

You'll be closely following the coordinate displays in both these palettes when you create models that are to scale. It's important to remember that in a CAD system like form•Z, *all modeling is done to true scale*, i.e., in the actual size of the object. So, for example, if a box is 20' long, 15' wide, and 10' high, you're going to create it in these very dimensions: 20' by 15' by 10'. It's only when you want to *print* your project that you need to specify a scale. Thus, confusion about the best or the most appropriate scale for creating a particular drawing, usually encountered when doing drawings manually, is completely done away with in form•Z.

Moving on to the actual modeling process, suppose that we really want to create the box specified above. Let's see if we can accomplish this task by tracking coordinates alone.

- Choose the appropriate combination of tools from the toolbox—the Rectangle tool (M-Tool:3a,1) in 3D Extrusion mode (M-Tool:2a,3), or the Cube tool (M-Tool:1a,1). Let's assume you've selected the first combination. Click on a point anywhere in the window to get the first point of the box, and keep a mental note of its coordinates by reading them off the Coordinates palette.

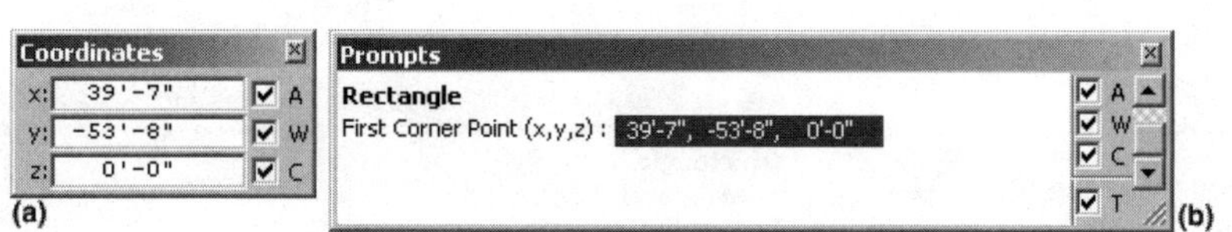

Figure 2.2

The settings for Numeric Display Options, shown in Figure 2.1, are reflected in both the Coordinates and Prompts palettes.

- Then, move the cursor to a point which is approximately 20' away on the X axis and 15' away on the Y axis, again by keeping track of the coordinate display and doing a quick calculation. This will be the diagonal point of the base of our box. Click to record it as such.
- Finally (since you haven't preset a height in the Heights menu), drag the cursor to specify the height of the box following the same procedure. This time it's easier as the z coordinate was initially 0.

Incredibly tedious, wasn't it? And this was for just a single entity. How much more tedious it would be if you had to model many more such entities, all related to one another dimensionally, you can well imagine! Obviously, this isn't the right way to go about creating scaled models.

Let's do it the proper way then, making a more intelligent use of the coordinate displays.

1.3 Direct Numeric Input

- Delete the box you just created; you'll create another, more accurate one. Make sure the same tool or tool combination is selected as before.
- Let's start from the point [0,0,0], which is generally a good starting point and can be conveniently used to locate the *origin* of the model. Try moving the cursor exactly to this position with the help of the coordinate display in the Coordinates palette. Though not impossible, this can be difficult, particularly if your Numeric Accuracy is set to a very low value (which is why you were cautioned against making it needlessly small). It would be easier to just type the coordinates in. This is referred to as *direct numeric input.*
- Turn your attention from the Coordinates to the Prompts palette. You'll find it prompting you for the *first corner point* of the extruded rectangle. Instead of clicking on a point in the window, type in the coordinate value 0',0',0' in the palette at the prompt line (see Figure 2.3) and press the return (Mac) or Enter (PC) key. The point [0,0,0] will be selected as the first point of the box. Make sure you don't move the mouse while inputting data numerically, as the new cursor position then overrides what has been typed in.
- Having specified the first point, the Prompts palette will prompt you for the *second corner point* of the extruded rectangle. This is the diagonal point of the base of the box, and it should be [20,15,0] to create a box with a base of 20' by 15'. Type in this value and hit return or Enter as before.
- Finally, you'll be prompted for the height of the box. Key this in as 10'. Your box will be complete, created according to the required dimensions.

This is how direct numeric input can be used to create precise models with accurate measurements. Practice this technique some more with other kinds of objects until you're comfortable with it, as it's a vital component of any serious modeling activity.

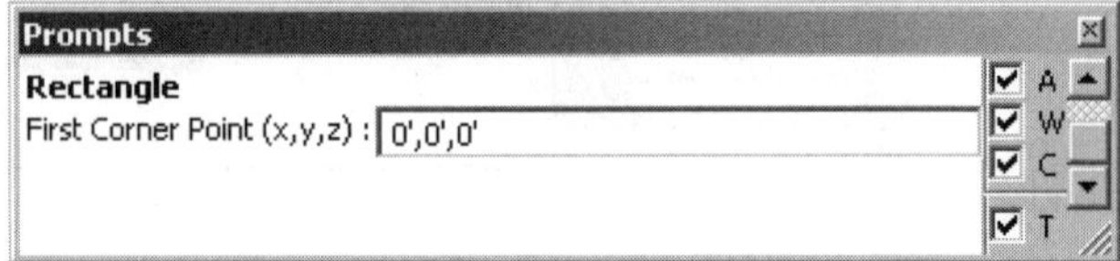

Figure 2.3

Specifying the point [0,0,0] as the first corner point of an extruded rectangle in the Prompts palette.

Something to note about direct numeric input: if the base unit's set to Feet and your coordinate input for a particular operation doesn't use inches, you can do away altogether with the quotes that you'd normally use to indicate units in feet. Also, if the z coordinate is 0, it's enough to just input the x and y coordinates. So, for instance, the point [2'-0",10'-0",0'-0"] *can be input simply as* [2,10], *the point* [2'-6",5'-0",0'-0"] *as* [2'-6",5], *and so on.*

1.4 Absolute and Relative Coordinates

In the last section, it was easy to specify the second point of the box, since we made sure that the first point coincided with [0,0,0]. However, this won't always be the case. Let's see how to deal with the situation where the first point isn't [0,0,0].

- Start the procedure for creating a new box. Type in the values 18,15 for the first point in the Prompts palette.

To specify the second corner point of a 20' by 15' by 10' box starting at [18,15,0], we need to calculate its x and y coordinates by adding the distances of 20 and 15 to the first point coordinates of 18 and 15 respectively. Such coordinates are known as *absolute coordinates*, since they're specified with respect to the origin [0,0,0] of the coordinate system. As you can see, it can get very tedious specifying absolute coordinates in this manner, because most objects in our modeling world won't conveniently start at the origin. There should be a better way.

There is! We can avoid the whole "absolute coordinate" rigmarole by using *relative coordinates*. These are essentially coordinates relative to the point last selected, which is useful because once the first point for an object has been specified, subsequent points can be measured from the previous point only. You no longer have to bother with calculating distances from the origin. Let's see how this works.

- By default, the entries you make in the Prompts palette are treated as absolute coordinates. You need to change this so that it works in relative mode. You can make this change even while you're in the *middle* of an operation, like you are now. Click on the checkbox labeled A (which stands for "absolute") that's located on the right side of the Prompts palette. The box will be unchecked, indicating that all the entries will now be treated as relative coordinates (Figure 2.4).
- Notice that for the second point of the box, you're now asked to input [Δx, Δy, Δz] (Mac) or [dx, dy, dz] (PC), instead of [x, y, z]. These new inputs represent the distance of the desired point from the *point entered previously*. Simply input 20,15 as shown in Figure 2.4, and the relative point [20,15,0] will be selected as the diagonal point of the base of the box.
- Complete the object by keying in the height of the box as 10.

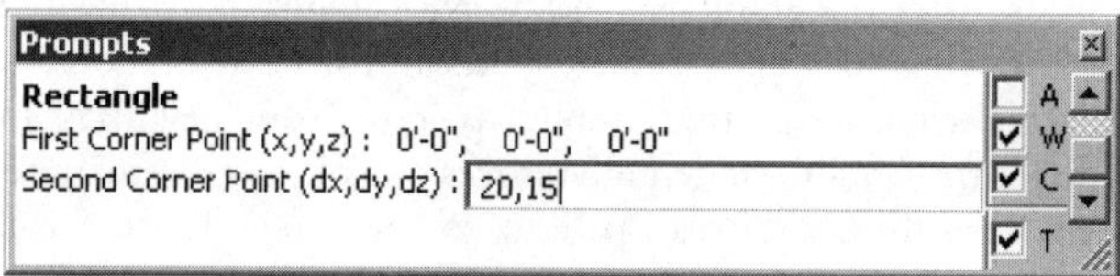

Figure 2.4

Using relative rather than absolute coordinates to specify the second corner point of the base of the box.

- In the same manner, use the other drawing tools on Row 3 as well as the primitives to create various kinds of scaled objects, using direct numeric input and relative coordinates. You might want to use absolute coordinates for specifying the first point of an object, in which case you need to click on the A box as you did earlier. It will get checked, setting the Prompts palette mode back to the default of absolute.

When you input values through the keyboard for the drawing tools in the right column of Row 3 (which create open shapes), type the character "e" in the Prompts palette to "end" the command. It thus equates a double-click of the mouse, as you learned in Section 1.5 of Workshop 1 (Letting Yourself Go). Similarly, the character "c" can be typed to "close" the figure and is thus the keyboard equivalent of a triple-click.

1.5 Switching Between the Prompts and Coordinates Palettes

You've seen that while using direct numeric input, you often have to keep switching between the absolute and relative modes while you model. The first point of a new object is usually specified using absolute coordinates (since this determines the location of the object in the coordinate space), while subsequent points are easier to specify using relative coordinates (since they determine the dimensions of the object). Rather than being forced to select and deselect the A box in the Prompts palette repeatedly as you did in the preceding section, you can follow the more convenient process described here.

- Set the Prompts palette to relative mode, but let the Coordinates palette, which has the same A checkbox, remain in absolute mode. Go through the process of creating a box again. Move the cursor to the x field in the Coordinates palette and enter the absolute x coordinate of the first point of the box. Press the Tab key (very important!) to move to the y field, and specify the absolute y coordinate. Do the same for the z field; then press return or Enter. You'll find that this point specified in absolute coordinates has indeed been selected in the graphics window as the first corner point of the box. Thus, you used the Coordinates palette rather than the Prompts palette for numeric input this time, and absolute coordinates to position your box correctly.

- For the second point which you want to specify in relative coordinates, return to the Prompts palette by clicking on it. Delete the values for this point that appear here automatically (based on the cursor movement), and enter the values you want.

- Finally, specify the height in the Prompts palette itself, in relative mode. Your box will be created accurately with the specified dimensions.

- You may occasionally find that in the process of switching back and forth between the two palettes, the values you entered in the Prompts palette are lost if the cursor is accidentally moved out of the palette. This happens because *tracking* the cursor position is on by default; therefore, whenever the cursor is inside the graphics window, the Prompts palette will display its coordinate position. If this is annoying and inconvenient, you can turn tracking off by deselecting the T checkbox in the lower right corner of the Prompts palette. Your keyboard input values will no longer be overridden if the cursor accidentally moves out of the palette on to the window. Tracking cannot be turned off in the Coordinates palette, so you can still read the current cursor position off it.

1.6 Cartesian and Polar Coordinates

In addition to absolute and relative coordinates, you can also choose between cartesian and polar coordinates. You've been using cartesian coordinates so far, which consist of three coordinate values: x, y, and z. In contrast, polar coordinates are made up of three different values: the *distance* of the new point from the origin point in absolute mode or the previous point in relative mode, the *angle* made by the line connecting these two points with the horizontal axis in the positive direction, and the *coordinate value* of the point in a direction perpendicular to the currently active plane.

- Deselect the box labeled C (standing for "cartesian") in the Prompts palette. This will set the coordinate mode to polar instead of the default of cartesian. The Coordinates palette can be set to polar mode in the same fashion; however, leave it as cartesian, so that you can easily switch between the two modes using both palettes.
- Switch to the Top view and select the Vector Line tool (M-Tool:3b,3) in 2D Surface mode (M-Tool:2a,1). You'll use polar coordinates to create an isosceles triangle with a base angle of 75° as shown in Figure 2.5, an operation that would be impossible to execute with precision using cartesian coordinates alone. (Try it if you're not convinced!)

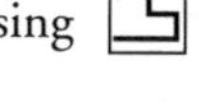

- Click anywhere to select the first point of the triangle, or locate the origin using absolute cartesian coordinates in the Coordinates palette.
- Deselect the A box in the Prompts palette so that you can use *relative* polar coordinates. For Point #2 of the triangle, you'll be prompted for [dist, ang, z]—standing for distance, angle with the +X axis, and the z coordinate (since you're using the XY plane). Delete the values that automatically appear in the Prompts palette (if tracking is on) and enter a value of say 40 for the distance, 75 for the angle, and 0 for the z coordinate.
- For Point #3, specify the same values, except that the angle value should be negative, i.e., -75. This gives us the two equal and opposite sides of our isosceles triangle, as shown in Figure 2.5.

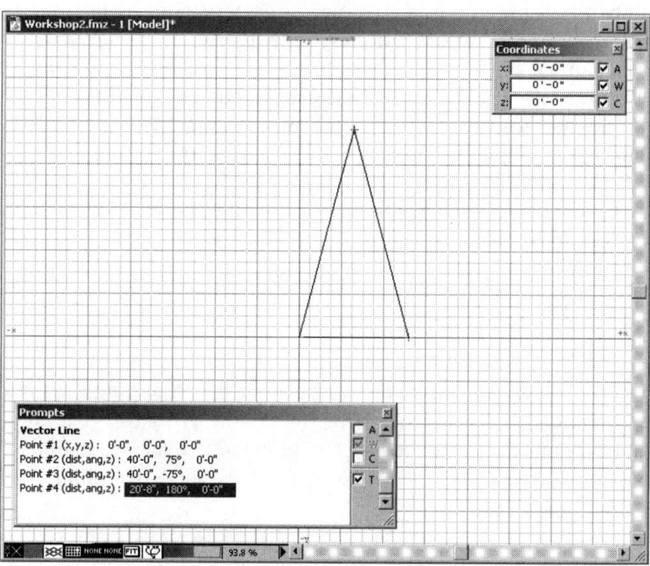

Figure 2.5

Using relative polar coordinates in the Prompts palette to accurately create an isosceles triangle of specific dimensions.

- At the prompt for Point #4, enter c or triple-click to close the figure. The base of the triangle will be added, completing the shape.

1.7 Scaled Moves

Now that you know how to model properly dimensioned shapes and objects, it's also essential to be able to perform transformations like Move accurately. Let's see how this can be done.

- Suppose the triangle you just created needs to be moved from its current position to a point 10' away along both the X and Y axes. To carry out this operation, first select the C box in the Prompts palette to change the mode back from polar to cartesian. Ensure, however, that the A box is still deselected.
- Now highlight the Move tool (M-Tool:13a,1), select the triangle, and key in 10,10,0 (or simply 10,10) as the *relative coordinates* of the move. The triangle will be moved to the desired new location.

Now that we know how to use direct numeric input to create objects that are accurately dimensioned and positioned, let's move on to look at another set of utilities that will further assist us in this process.

EXERCISE 2

Restraining the Cursor

If you're the kind of person who hates using the keyboard, direct numeric input would be something you'd like to avoid as much as possible. You *can* rely on the mouse for much of your input; however, you should then learn to do it more efficiently by restraining the mouse so that it moves only in a specified manner and not anywhere in the graphics window. This is referred to as *snapping*, and it enables you to easily and accurately select the points that are needed for carrying out any operation. form•Z provides you with three kinds of snapping: *grid* snapping, *direction* snapping, and *object* snapping. Exercise 2 is devoted to exploring these three snapping methods.

Let's first see how to change the settings of the graphics window, since some of the snap options directly depend upon it.

2.1 Setting Up the Graphics Window

The graphics window setup involves aspects such as changing the size of the reference plane grid with respect to which objects are being created, turning off the grid and axes displays when they're not needed, changing the cursor display to an extended cursor, displaying a ruler along the edge of the window, and auto scrolling. All these options are available under the Window pulldown menu. We'll explore each one of them in turn.

Figure 2.6

The Window Setup dialog with different settings from the defaults, and the resultant grid. The display of axis marks has been turned on.

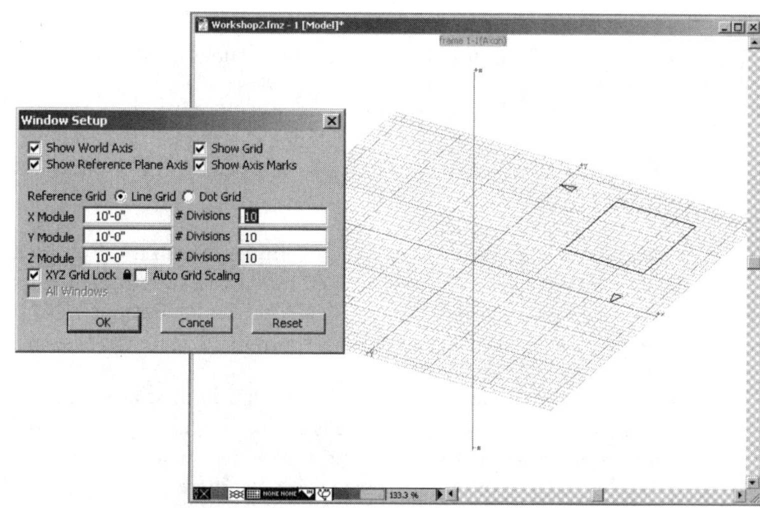

- Select the `Window Setup` command, located in the fifth group of the `Window` menu. A dialog will be invoked in which you can make various changes to the settings of the graphics window (Figure 2.6). Experiment with all the options, exiting the dialog to see the modified grid and axes displays each time. You can turn off the grid and axes displays, turn on the display of axis marks that indicate the position of the cursor with respect to the axis, and opt for a dot grid instead of the default line grid. Ignore the `Show Reference Plane Axis` option for now—it will be clear once you start dealing with arbitrary reference planes in Workshop 3 (Personalizing Your Environment).

- The most important feature in the `Window Setup` dialog is the option to change the default size of the reference grid to values more suited to a particular project. There are two aspects to this grid: a module along all three directions, X, Y, and Z; and the number of subdivisions for each module. You can see that the grid in the graphics window resembles a graph sheet, with the main modules in bold and the smaller subdivisions in fainter lines. To specify different grid settings, simply enter the new values in place of the defaults. Figure 2.6 shows the `Window Setup` dialog with grid settings of 10' modules and 10 subdivisions along all three directions. The resultant grid is also shown.

Keep in mind that the grid extends infinitely beyond what is actually displayed in the graphics window. You'll learn to modify the default extent of the grid display in Workshop 3.

- Notice that when you change the grid settings for one module, the other two modules get conveniently updated to have the same values automatically. If you need to have different module and subdivision settings along the X, Y, and Z directions, simply deselect the `XYZ Grid Lock` option and you'll be able to do so.

- The `Auto Grid Scaling` option, when selected, automatically adjusts the grid settings when you make a change to the display scale under the `Display` menu (as you learned in Section 3.8 of Workshop 1, Letting Yourself Go). The adjustment is made in such a way that the density of the grid in the window remains constant. Choosing a smaller display scale, for instance, increases the size of the main modules and vice versa. Try it.

- When you open up multiple associated windows for the same project (as you'll do in Workshop 3, Personalizing Your Environment), the `All Windows` option in the `Window Setup` dialog will be activated, allowing you to apply the modified settings simultaneously to all open windows. You'll encounter this option frequently in other dialogs as well, so keep this explanation in mind.

- Exit the Window Setup dialog after you've explored all the options. Notice that the options to turn the grid and axes displays on and off are also directly available in the fifth group of the Window menu. This saves you from the hassle of opening the Window Setup dialog repeatedly to make these changes.

- Proceed to select the Extended Cursor command from the Window menu. It gets activated, and the regular cursor switches to an extended mode that you might find more convenient to use at times (see Figure 2.7). Explore also the Extended Cursor Options item in the same menu. To turn the Extended Cursor off, simply select the command again, and it will switch back to regular mode.

- Similarly, explore the Show Rulers command, located in the sixth group of the Window menu, as well as the subsequent Ruler Options dialog. Here, you can make various changes to the default ruler display, such as the sides of the window on which it appears, the coordinate mode that's used, the text and markings on the ruler, the increments, origin, and so on. In particular, setting the Coordinate Mode to Relative is extremely useful, as it automatically repositions the origin at every currently selected point instead of leaving it fixed at [0,0,0]. This is illustrated in Figure 2.7, which also shows how the Show Ruler and Extended Cursor options work well together in planar views. Needless to say, having a ruler display around the edge of the window is most useful when you're working in a planar view rather than in a 3D view.

- Finally, let's look at auto scrolling. This is the ability of the graphics window to scroll automatically when the cursor is moved beyond its edges in the middle of an operation. Turn this feature on by selecting Window > Auto Scroll, and test it out by using any of the modeling tools you've learned so far. Select a first point in the window, then move the cursor beyond one of its edges. It will scroll automatically, allowing you to select subsequent points in areas that were previously not visible to you. It thus saves you from the bother of using the Zoom or Hand tools in the middle of an operation and can be convenient once you get used to it.

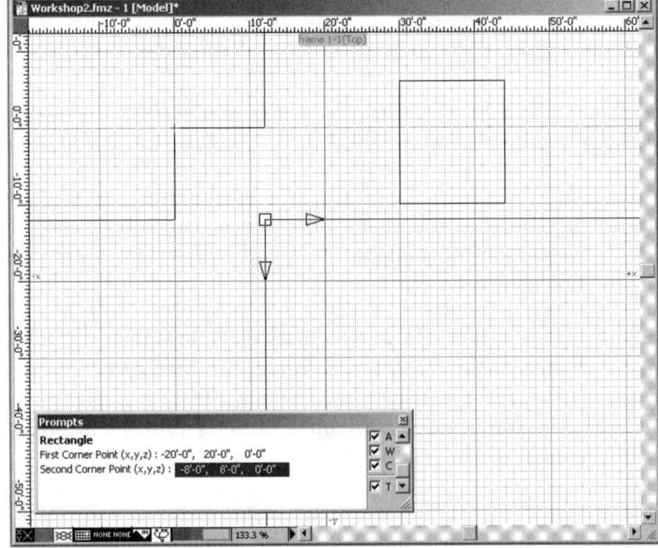

Figure 2.7

The Extended Cursor and Show Ruler options make an effective combination in a planar view. The ruler coordinate mode is set to Relative. The window settings are the same as those shown in Figure 2.6.

Having finished the task of setting up the graphics window according to our desired specifications, let's move on to look at the various snapping options, starting with Grid Snap.

2.2 Grid Snapping

Grid snapping restricts the movement of the cursor in the window to the points of an invisible rectangular grid, based on the active reference plane. It won't move to points outside this grid. This kind of snapping is particularly useful for those projects in which some underlying grid is used as the basis for modeling.

- Click on the fourth window tool located at the base of the graphics window. This is the Grid Snap tool, and just like the Perpendicular Lock (W-Tool:2,1), it works like a toggle switch. On clicking, it gets highlighted, indicating that it's active. Now move the mouse around in the window, keeping an eye on the coordinate display in the Coordinates palette. You'll find that the cursor movement isn't very smooth and that you cannot move to points below a certain increment value. GRID
- Deactivate the Grid Snap switch by clicking on it again, and notice that the cursor movement is much smoother. In the Coordinates palette, you'll now see that the cursor moves to point increments equal to the Numeric Accuracy value specified in the Project Working Units dialog in Section 1.1.
- Double-click on the Grid Snap tool to open its dialog (Figure 2.8). Here, you can change the default X, Y, and Z snap values to suit the requirements of your project. Set these now to values much higher than the defaults. The XYZ Snap Lock option in the dialog is checked by default, constraining the three directions to the same snapping value, so it's enough to change it along one of the axes only. The remaining option, Match Grid Module, can be checked if you want the snapping modules to automatically match the grid divisions specified in the Window Setup dialog. Leave this option deselected for now, but keep it in mind for later use.

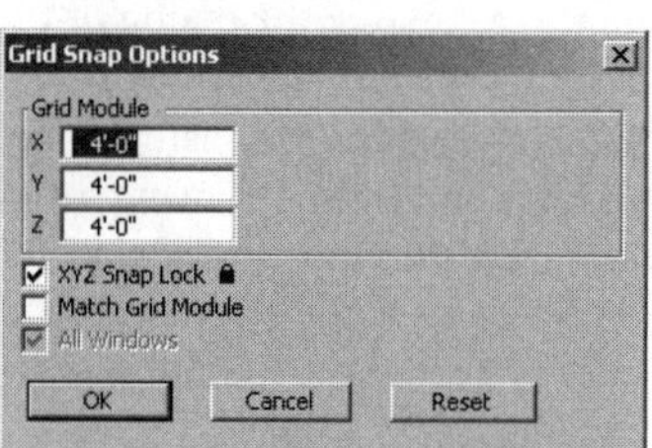

Figure 2.8

The Grid Snap Options dialog, with different settings from the defaults.

- Exit the dialog and perform any modeling operation. You'll find that you can no longer graphically select points in the window which are located at intervals less than the new grid snap values along the three axes.

Although you cannot rely on Grid Snap completely for complex modeling operations and will have to fall back on direct numeric input occasionally, it's definitely better than letting your cursor move anywhere in the graphics window, even at those fractional points you'll never want or need to select!

2.3 Direction Snapping

Direction Snap is the fifth set of window tools, located immediately after Grid Snap. Its task is to constrain the *directional position* of each input point, relative to its previous point. There are five different Direction Snap tools, of which only one can be active at any given time. We'll activate each option in turn and see how it affects the movement of the cursor during a modeling operation.

- Select the Vector Line tool—a good tool with which to explore direction snapping, as demonstrated in Figure 2.9. Turn the Grid Snap off, if it's active, so that it doesn't interfere with your understanding of the Direction Snap options.

- The default option for direction snapping is No Direction Snap (indicated by the icon displaying None in the fifth window tool position), which means that the cursor movement is free and not constrained in any particular direction. You're therefore free to draw lines in any direction, as you can test.

- Select the next option, Ortho. This restricts the cursor movement to the horizontal and vertical directions only, relative to the active reference plane. Thus, if you're working on the XY plane, you can only draw lines that are parallel to the X axis or to the Y axis.

- Switch to Ortho 45. This sets the directional snapping to the vertical, horizontal, *and* diagonal directions, relative to the active reference plane. Thus, you can draw lines parallel to the axes or diagonal to them.

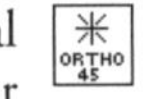

- The Angle option is next. This sets the directional snapping to a user-defined angle, set by default to 45°. Invoke the dialog of the Angle tool and change the Angle value to, say, 30°. Alternately, you can specify the angle in terms of a Slope value. Exit the dialog. You'll find that you can now move only at an angle of 30° with respect to any of the axes, as illustrated in Figure 2.9. This option is very useful when you're working on a part of the model that's tilted at a fixed angle with respect to the axes.

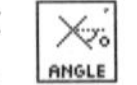

- Switch to the last option, Radial. The movement of the cursor will now be restricted to angular increments *centered* about the previous point. After the first point is selected, you can only move radially about that point at a certain angle. Invoke the dialog of the tool and change the By Angle Of value to 60° (which corresponds to 360 ÷ 30 = 12 Radial Divisions, if you prefer to do it that way). Activate also the Distance Snap option and set its value to say, 5'. Exit the dialog to get back to the graphics window. You'll find that the cursor movement is now restricted to only those points which are located at 5' intervals, radiating out at an angle of 60° from the point last selected. Obviously, this a useful option in modeling certain objects, such as the example shown in Figure 2.9.

- Finally, try combining the use of all five Direction Snap options to create a single object. You can keep alternating between these different snaps, even in the middle of an operation. In general, this applies to most of the tools in form•Z.

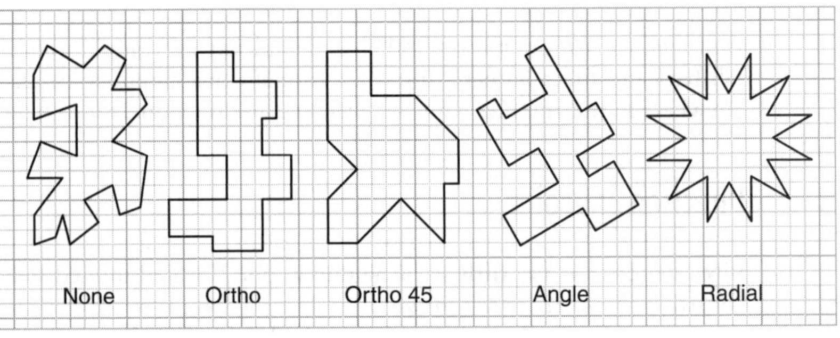

Figure 2.9

Different shapes created using each of the five Direction Snap options.

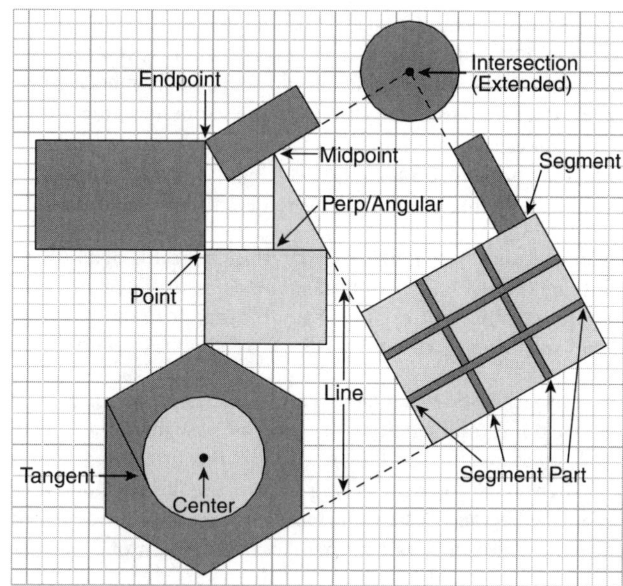

Figure 2.10

The use of the various Object Snap options.

2.4 Object Snapping

The third and final snapping mode—Object Snap—is used for selecting points *in relation to existing objects*. It's thus a crucial snapping mode, since new objects that you need to create will almost always be related in some manner to objects that you've already modeled. There are a large number of Object Snap options, located in the sixth set of window tools immediately after Direction Snap. The use of most of these options is illustrated in Figure 2.10. Let's look at each one of them in turn.

- Make sure you have at least a few objects on your screen with which to test object snapping. Turn off Grid Snap and set Direction Snap to None, so that they don't interfere in your understanding of object snapping. Then activate any of the 2D or 3D modeling tools to test the different Object Snap options.

- The first option is No Object Snap, indicated by the icon displaying None in the sixth window tool position. It's selected by default when you launch form•Z and means that no object snapping is activated.

- Select the second option, Point. Move the cursor near an object and watch it "snap" on to the nearest point of that object, highlighting it in green, which is the default color for snapping. Move the cursor around and snap it to a few other points until you get a feel for how it works.

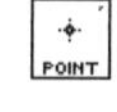

- Select the next option, Endpoint. This snaps the cursor to the endpoint of the nearest segment. For all practical purposes, it works the same way as Point, except that it also highlights the segment whose endpoint it's snapping to. Endpoint is one of the most frequently used object snaps in any kind of modeling.

- Try Midpoint next. This makes the cursor snap to the midpoint of the nearest segment, a facility that's often useful. In the case of a smooth arc, the cursor will snap by default to the midpoint of

its circumference. To modify this snapping behavior, double-click on the Midpoint snap tool to invoke the Object Snaps Options dialog (Figure 2.12), where you'll see two additional choices for how the Snap to Midpoint option should work with Smooth Arcs: Midpoint Of Arc Chord, which makes the cursor snap to the midpoint of the segment connecting the ends of the arc; or, Center Of Arc, which makes the cursor snap to the geometric center of the arc. Test out all three options on a smooth arc. The Object Snaps Options dialog contains options related to each one of the object snaps, and we'll be discussing it in more detail in the next section.

- The next object snap, Key Point, snaps to the key points of an object when their display is enabled. Key points are points that are critical to the shape of the object, and they're particularly relevant to nurbz and patch objects. You can ignore this snap for now, but be sure to come back to it once you learn about nurbz and patch objects in Workshop 6 (Going Organic).

- Move to the next option, Segment Part. This snaps not only to the endpoints but also to some intermediate points of a segment. Try it on a few segments and you'll find that, by default, it snaps to points located at 1/3rd and 2/3rd distances along the segment, i.e., it divides a segment into 3 parts and then snaps to the resulting points. Invoke the Object Snaps Options dialog by double-clicking on the Segment Part tool. Here, change the number of interval divisions in the Snap To Segment Part section to a value other than the default of 3, and test it out.

- The next object snap, Segment, snaps to *any* point of a segment nearest to the cursor position, not just the endpoint, midpoint, or a particular division, as with the preceding options. Although you'll have far less occasion to use this option compared to the other snaps, it can be useful sometimes, particularly when dimensional accuracy isn't a prime concern (as in the initial stages of design conceptualization).

- Move to the Line snapping option. It's similar to the Segment snap just before it, except that the cursor also snaps to points located *beyond* the endpoints of the segment. In essence, an imaginary line of infinite length is constructed in place of the fixed-length segment, and the cursor snaps to the point on this imaginary line closest to it. Experiment with this option and see how it can be very effectively used for creating objects that are aligned with existing objects but not necessarily touching them, as illustrated in Figure 2.10.

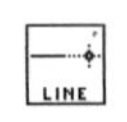

- With the Intersection option, you can locate and snap to the intersection point of any two segments. Try it. Then invoke the Object Snaps Options dialog through any one of the object snap tools, and check the Extended Intersections option. You'll find that you can now also locate intersection points lying *outside* the lengths of the segments, following the same principle as the Line snap tool. Such an intersection is illustrated in Figure 2.10. For Intersection, keep in mind that the two segments have to be in the same plane and should not be parallel to each other. In planar views, some segments might look as though they're in the same plane, but they're actually not, so Intersection won't work. Watch out for such situations—it's often a source of great vexation!

- Next, select the Perpendicular/Angular snap tool. This is slightly confusing, since it initially snaps to any point of a segment rather than a specific point, and then constrains the cursor movement in a perpendicular direction. However, subsequent point selections work differently—the cursor snaps only to those points on other segments that make a 90° angle between the two segments, *if* any such points exist. To change the snapping angle from the default of 90°, access the Object Snaps Options dialog and specify any other angle value for the Angular Snap mode.

- The next option, Tangent, constrains the cursor movement along the tangent to a circle, ellipse, arc, or curve. Try it, and note that it only works for smooth objects.

Figure 2.11

Using Face snap to create 3D objects on inclined surfaces. The right option for generating an extrusion perpendicular to the inclined surface has to be selected first.

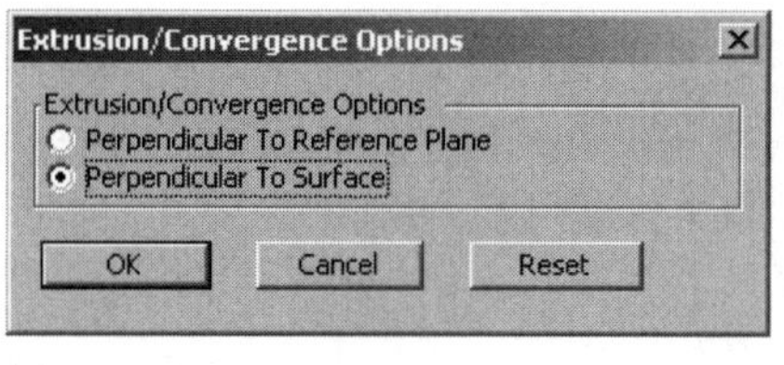

(a)

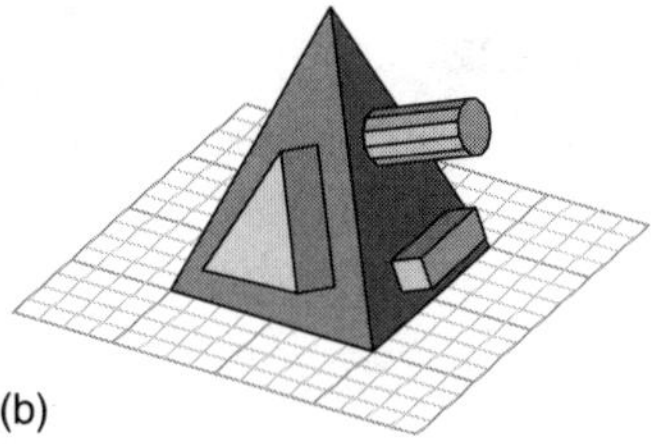

(b)

- Move to the option after it, Center Of Face, which is used for locating and snapping to the centroid of any closed 2D shape or any face of a 3D object. Try it, and notice that in a 3D view, you cannot use it on those 3D object faces that are hidden from you, even though you may be in the Wire Frame display mode.

- Try out also the Face option, which locates points that are within a closed 2D shape or a 3D face not hidden from you. It's similar to Center Of Face, except that it snaps to *all* points within the face and not just the centroid. It's particularly useful when you have to create an object on a surface that's not parallel to any of the three predefined reference planes, XY, YZ, and ZX. This is illustrated in Figure 2.11, where a number of 3D objects are constructed on the inclined faces of a pyramid rather than on the current reference plane. Note that to generate the extrusion perpendicular to the inclined surface using the 3D object generation modes on Row 2, say the 3D Extrusion mode, you *must* select the Perpendicular To Surface option instead of the default Perpendicular To Ref Plane option in its dialog (Figure 2.11-a). Recall that you learned about this option in Section 1.10 of Workshop 1 (Letting Yourself Go).

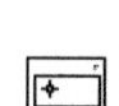

- Finally, move to the last option, Combination (phew!). This allows you to simultaneously use more than one of the twelve object snap modes that you just covered. The choice of these snaps is made in the dialog of the Combination snap tool. Here, you'll find the icons of all the snaps; simply highlight the ones you want to activate in your combination. The default selections are Point, Endpoint, and Midpoint. All the other options in the Object Snaps Options dialog are also given here, which is what we'll be looking at next.

2.5 Options for Object Snapping

- Double-click on any one of the Object Snap tools. This will bring up the Object Snaps Options dialog, which contains options that apply to all the tools as well as options that apply only to specific tools (Figure 2.12). Let's see what these options are.

- The Show Snap Preview and Tolerance options apply to all the tools. You can turn the snap preview off, if required, but it's generally useful to keep it turned on so that you can see what the cursor is snapping to. The tolerance value in pixels controls how close the cursor has to be to an entity to snap on to it. You can change the default tolerance value of 10 pixels to suit your requirements.

- The Extended Intersections option affects not only the Intersection snap as you saw in the last section, but also the Perpendicular/Angular snap. Since infinite lines are superimposed on finite segments when this option is selected, the Perpendicular/Angular snap will now *always* find locations for subsequent points—which could lie beyond the endpoints of existing segments—that would create the specified angle between the two segments.

Figure 2.12

The Object Snaps Options dialog.

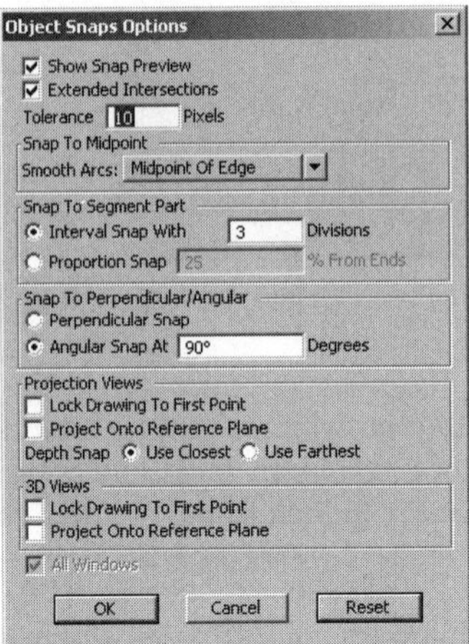

- The next three groups in the Object Snaps Options dialog are relevant only to specific snap options. We already studied the Snap To Midpoint and Snap To Perpendicular/Angular options in the last section. We also saw how the Interval Snap option for Snap To Segment Part allows you to change the number of interval divisions that the segment will be divided and snapped to. Alternately, you can choose the Proportion Snap method for the Segment Part snap, where you specify a proportionate distance from either endpoint at which the snapping will occur.

The next two sections in the Object Snaps Options dialog apply to all the snaps. They're extremely important and you should take care to understand them well. Object snapping isn't always straightforward, particularly in planar views such as Top, Front, etc., since you could have many points of 3D objects overlapping with one another. Moreover, points selected without snapping will always lie on the current reference plane, which further complicates matters. Try it.

Figure 2.13 illustrates such a scenario of erroneous object snapping. Item (a) shows the original set of 3D objects in 30-60 Axonometric view. In (b), the view is switched to Right, and Endpoint snap is used to create two 2D enclosures, spanning across the original objects. The intention was to create these in a single plane, and it seems as though the objective has been achieved. However, switching back to the 30-60 view shown in (c), the result is obviously erroneous. This is because the points selected without snapping lie on the YZ plane with an x coordinate of 0, as opposed to the snapped points that lie on a different plane.

- Coming back to the Object Snaps Options dialog, the Projection Views section gives you some options that let you control better how snapping will take place in planar views, thereby avoiding the problem we just saw. (Recall that a planar view is technically referred to as a *projection* view.) Turn to the Depth Snap option first. This determines which point will be snapped to in a planar view when there are overlapping points. You can simply choose to locate the point closest to you in the current view (which is the default and which is what happened in Figure 2.13), or the farthest.

- To avoid the problem shown in Figure 2.13, you can select either of the two remaining options under Projection Views. The Lock Drawing To First Point option will ensure that all the subsequent points selected for an operation lie on the same plane as the first point selected. As shown in Figure 2.13-d, this achieves the desired result. Alternately, you can choose the Project Onto Reference Plane option, which projects all the points that are selected, by snapping or otherwise, on to the current reference plane, thereby ensuring that the object created lies on one plane. You can then switch to a non-planar view and move the object to where it should have been located.

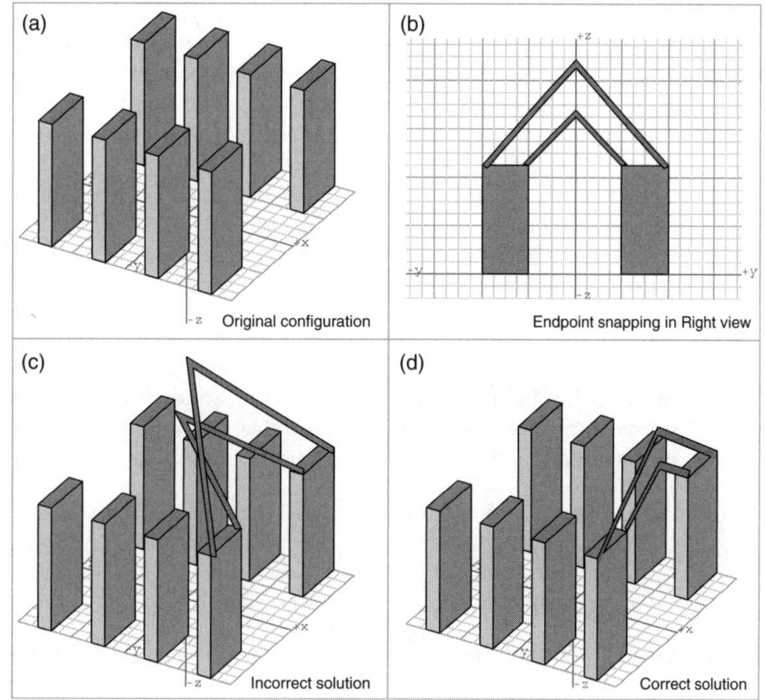

Figure 2.13

An example showing how endpoint snapping, which looks correct in a planar view, turns out to be erroneous when seen in a 3D view. The correct solution, achieved by checking the Lock Drawing To First Point option, is shown in (d).

- The Lock Drawing To First Point and Project Onto Reference Plane options also appear separately under the 3D Views section of the Object Snaps Options dialog. They work identically to those under Projection Views, but are listed separately so that you can have different settings for planar and non-planar views, if necessary.

This marks the end of Exercise 2, by which time you should have mastered the art of snapping to perfection! Let's move on to learn how to work at levels both above and below that of the individual object.

Exercise 3

Transcending Objects: Working at Multiple Levels

So far, we've been working entirely at the level of the objects themselves—moving them around, coloring them, deleting them, and so on. As far as facetted objects are concerned, however, you can select and modify not just the objects, but also individual object parts such as points, segments, faces, and so on. The level with which you choose to work is referred to as the *topological level.* The ability to work with multiple topological levels provides us with enormous flexibility in modeling and shaping facetted objects, as we shall see in the course of this exercise. We'll also work with groups, a topological level higher than that of the individual object.

For smooth objects, transformation operations such as Move don't work with topological levels lower than object. If you attempt to do so, you'll receive a warning message.

3.1 Working with Points, Segments, Outlines, and Faces

- Open up the left column of Row 4 of the modeling tool palette, from where you can choose between eight different kinds of topological levels. You'll work with all these levels now except the Hole/Volume level, which will be covered in Exercise 6. A topological level is made active by clicking on it, and it remains active until a new level is selected.
- Start by setting the topological level to Point. Then apply the Pick tool (M-Tool:4a,1) to any facetted object and you'll find that you can select the endpoints of the individual segments that make up the object. (While you can *snap* on to midpoints and other points along segments, as you learned in Section 2.4, you cannot *select* them with the Pick tool because such points are calculated on-the-fly rather than stored in the form•Z project database.) POINT
- Now activate the Move tool and move the selected points. If the object to which these points belong is a parametric object, you'll be warned that the object will be converted to a plain object before the operation can be applied. Click OK in response. This will happen anytime you try to modify a parametric object by manipulating its individual points, segments, outlines, and faces.
- Once the Move operation is completed, you'll find that you've distorted the shape of the object itself to which the points belong. While this gives you enormous capability, make sure you use it wisely, or else you might end up with objects having non-planar faces, as shown in Figure 2.14-a. (There's a way to fix this non-planarity problem, and we'll look at it in Exercise 6.)

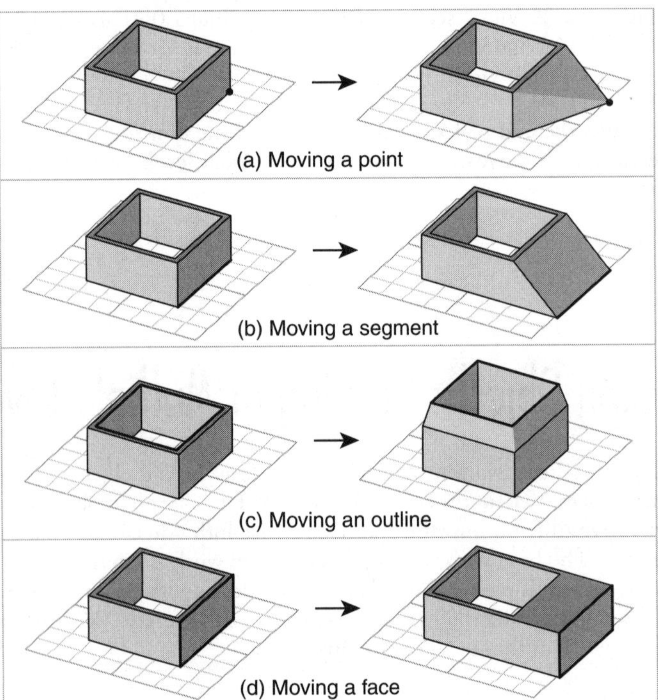

Figure 2.14

Modifying a facetted object by moving a point, segment, outline, and face, shown in (a), (b), (c), and (d) respectively. The original object is shown on the left, highlighting in bold the entities that were subsequently moved.

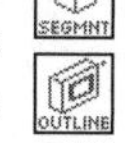

- Repeat the process by setting the topological level to Segment, Outline, and thereafter to Face, and see how easily you can modify the size and shape of an object in any desired manner by moving its constituent parts (Figure 2.14). An outline, as you can see, is one level below a face—a face can have one or more outlines.

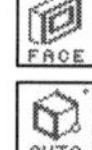

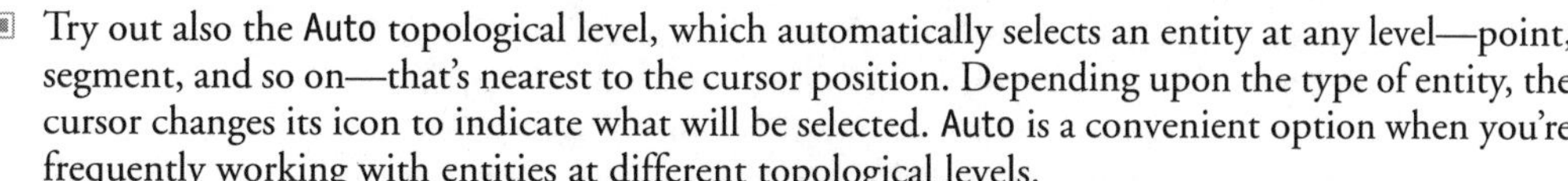

- Try out also the Auto topological level, which automatically selects an entity at any level—point, segment, and so on—that's nearest to the cursor position. Depending upon the type of entity, the cursor changes its icon to indicate what will be selected. Auto is a convenient option when you're frequently working with entities at different topological levels.

- By default, an outline or face is selected by clicking on any two of its edges. If you prefer to also be able to select the outline or face by clicking inside its boundary, invoke the Pick Options dialog by double-clicking on the Pick tool, and activate the Inside Boundaries box under the first Clicking option. You'll find that you can now deactivate the On Edges box. However, it is better to keep this mode of selection active as well since the Inside Boundaries mode doesn't work for hidden faces, i.e., faces that are not in the line of sight from the current viewpoint. Try it.

- It's also possible to apply the same transformation to many entities at different topological levels in one step. To do so, you have to resort to the *prepicking* method. Select some entities at one topological level, say Point, then switch to another level, say Segment, and make some more selections. Alternately, use the Auto level to select both the points and segments. Now apply the Move tool to the selection. All the entities—points as well as segments—are moved by the same distance and in the same direction.

- The topological level specified on Row 4 determines what is selected even when you use *area picking* (as you learned in Section 3.5 of Workshop 1, Letting Yourself Go). Thus, if the topological level has been set to Point, only the points within the bounding frame or lasso will be selected. Try this out.

- All of the topological levels have a dialog associated with them, as you can see from the red marks on their icons. Invoke this dialog through any of the tools, and you'll find that it's the same Pick Options dialog that's associated with the Pick tool. This shows how closely the Pick tool and the topological levels are related. We've already explored the first option in this dialog, and will explore the other options in more detail in Exercise 4.

Although you'll be using the Object level for most of your modeling activity, the other topological levels will come in very useful when you need to edit existing facetted objects, as you can see. You should always keep an eye on Row 4 and make sure that the topological level is set correctly, depending upon the operation you wish to perform. A very common mistake is to forget this, and then wonder why some operations are not being performed at all. For instance, the 3D Extrusion operation (M-Tool:5a,4) won't work with the topological level set to Point, since a point cannot, by its very nature, be extruded. Similarly, it makes no sense to color a point or a segment. Different faces of an object, however, can have different colors, as you saw in Section 4.5 of Workshop 1 (Letting Yourself Go).

3.2 Inserting Points and Segments

You saw in Figure 2.14 how facetted objects can be modified by moving constituent parts such as points, segments, and so on. To provide you with further flexibility in modeling, form•Z also lets you *insert* points and segments on existing objects, which can then be manipulated to transform the object in a desired manner. There are other kinds of insertions as well, which work as a convenient alternative to the boolean operations, and we'll explore these later in Exercise 6. For now, let's focus on the Insert Point and Insert Segment tools, located in the left column of Row 11 of the modeling tool palette.

- Select the Insert Point operator (M-Tool:11a,7) and apply it to any segment of a 2D or 3D facetted object. The change won't be visible unless you activate the Show Points option in the Wire Frame Options dialog, which you'll study in Section 2.1 of Workshop 3 (Personalizing Your Environment). However, you can snap to the inserted point using the Point or Endpoint snap tools. Then, with the topological level set to Point, you can apply the Move tool to it, or select it with the Pick tool for some other operation. Essentially, you can manipulate it just like any other existing point to modify the object it belongs to.

Figure 2.15

Use of the Insert Segment tool.

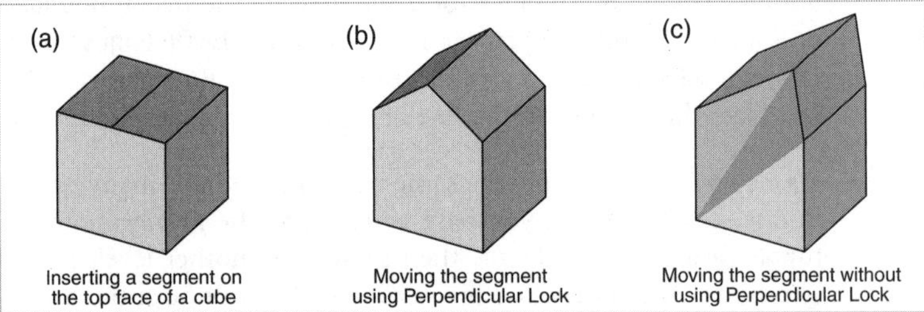

- Move on to the Insert Segment operator (M-Tool:11a,8), which works in a similar fashion. Use it to insert a segment on a surface, which can either be a closed 2D facetted object or the face of a 3D facetted object; you cannot insert a segment on an open 2D shape. The endpoints of the inserted segment must lie on the edges or points of the surface. The various point and segment snapping options can come in useful here. Inserting a segment on a surface effectively divides it up into two parts, and you can manipulate the inserted segment or the new faces to modify the object. An example is illustrated in Figure 2.15. As always, be careful when you move the segments you insert, so that you don't end up with non-planar faces and undesired results (as in Figure 2.15-c).

Points and segments can also be inserted on smooth objects, but since they cannot be subsequently moved, such insertions serve no purpose.

3.3 Deleting Topological and Geometrical Entities

So far, you've deleted entities only at the object level. However, form•Z allows you to delete facetted entities at all topological levels, ranging from points to groups. Objects and groups are deleted by using the familiar Delete tool (M-Tool:15a,1). But in order to delete entities at topological levels lower than Object, you must use either the Delete Topology or the Delete Geometry tool, depending upon the result you want to achieve. Both these tools are located in the right column of Row 15, just next to the Delete tool.

- Set the topological level to Point. Select the Delete Topology tool and apply it to any point of a facetted object. You'll find that all the segments connected to that point get deleted. If the faces connected to these segments are not coplanar, the object will acquire non-planar faces. Apply the same tool to a segment and then to a face by setting the topological level appropriately. You'll find that deleting a segment again results in non-planar faces if the faces on both sides of the segment are not coplanar, while deleting a face simply removes it from the object it belongs to. All these Delete Topology operations are illustrated in Figure 2.16.

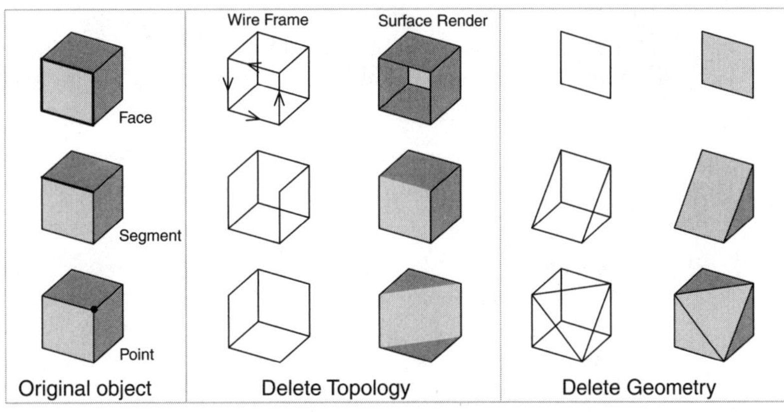

Figure 2.16

Applying the Delete Topology and Delete Geometry tools at different topological levels. The results are shown in Wire Frame as well as Surface Render.

- Now switch to the Delete Geometry tool and apply it to a point, a segment, and a face in the same manner. It operates very differently from the Delete Topology tool, as you can see in Figure 2.16. Deleting a point once again deletes all the segments connected to that point, but a new face is added to the object, ensuring planarity. Deletion of segments and faces operates on the same principle, sometimes leading to very interesting and unexpected results. In general, you'll find yourself using the Delete Geometry tool a lot more than the Delete Topology tool.

For smooth objects, the Delete Topology operation can only be applied at the face level, while the Delete Geometry tool cannot be applied at all.

3.4 Working with Groups

A group is a topological level higher than an individual object in the sense that multiple objects can be brought together into groups. It's also possible to have *multiple levels of hierarchy*, with several groups themselves forming a larger group. Any kind of operation can then be performed on the entire group rather than on individual objects. The concept of groups applies to facetted as well as smooth objects in the same manner. Let's see how groups work.

- Create some additional objects in the current project so that you have a total of at least five objects. Use Pick (M-Tool:4b,1) with the topological level set to Object (M-Tool:4a,5) to select any three of these objects. Then select the Group tool (M-Tool:9b,3) and following the instructions in the Prompts palette, click anywhere in the window. The selected objects will be collected together into a single group.

- However, there's no visible change in the window, so how do we know what really happened? Let's see if we can apply some operation to the entire group. Set the topological level to Group (M-Tool:4a,6) and choose a different color from the Surface Styles palette. Then activate the Color tool and select any one of the three objects that you had grouped. You'll find that all the three objects in the group acquire the new color. In the same manner, you can apply any other transformation in one step to the entire group.

- Form a second group of the remaining objects in your project. Then set the topological level to Group and use the Pick tool to select both the groups. Finally, select the Group tool (M-Tool:9b,3) again and, as prompted, click anywhere in the graphics window. What you just did was create a higher-level group containing the existing two groups, as illustrated in Figure 2.17. Any transformation such as Move or Color will now be applied at the level of the highest group (provided, of course, that the topological level is set to Group). Try it. You'll find that all objects in both groups undergo the operation you apply.

But now, how can a transformation be applied to only a lower-level group, if necessary? This requires the use of the Objects palette, which we'll look at in the next section. For now, let's see how to ungroup objects once they have been grouped.

- Select the Ungroup tool, located immediately after the Group tool in the right column of the ninth row. Make sure the topological level is still set to Group. Click on any one of the objects that was grouped. There's no visible change, but if you now use the Pick tool to select a group, you'll find that you can select and transform the two original groups independently of each other. What you just did was break the highest level of the grouping hierarchy. Apply the Ungroup tool once again to each of the two remaining groups—this will break down all the groups and return you to your original modeling world, devoid of any groupings whatsoever.

- Undo all the ungrouping operations you just performed so that you get back to the state where you had two groups forming a larger group. This state can be used to explore some of the other options of the Ungroup tool. Open its dialog by double-clicking on it. The default selection is Dismantle One Level, which is why you were ungrouping only one level of grouping at a time (Figure 2.17-a).

- Choose the second option, Dismantle All Levels, and reapply the Ungroup tool to one of the grouped objects. You'll find that you've now broken down not only the higher-level group but also all the groups contained within it—in a single step. This option thus destroys the grouping links at *all* levels, for the selected group and those below it (Figure 2.17-b).

- Once again, undo what you just did to get back to the grouped state. Now activate the third option in the dialog of the Ungroup tool, Remove Object From Group. Set the topological level to Object and apply the Ungroup tool to one of the grouped objects. You'll find that the selected object is now removed from all the groups to which it belongs (Figure 2.17-c). This option is useful when you wish to extract only one or a few objects from a large group—it saves you from the tedious process of ungrouping the whole group and having to reassemble it.

Working with groups can be very useful and convenient. For instance, in architectural modeling, you can group together similar elements of a building such as columns, beams, floor slabs, doors, windows, and so on in different categories, i.e., groups. At a higher level in the hierarchy could be a floor, so that all objects and groups on one floor could be part of that floor group. At a still higher level in the hierarchy could be the entire building, useful if the project consisted of a cluster of buildings. In this way, a hierarchical grouping relating the model to the real world scenario could be established. Thereafter, any geometric transformation could be applied to an entire group at any level, modifying all its objects as well as objects in the lower-level groups contained within it.

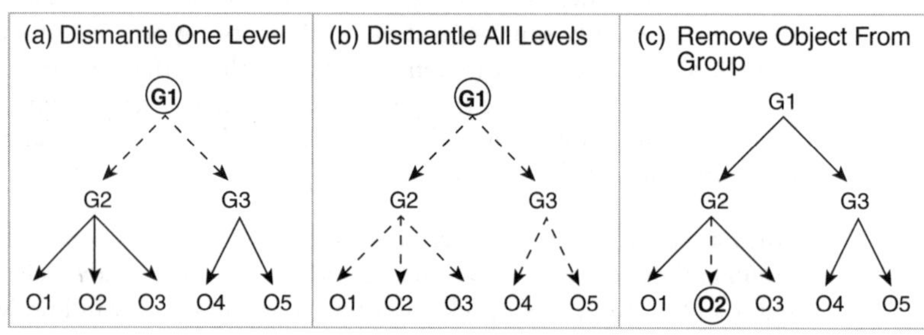

Figure 2.17

The three different options of the Ungroup tool and how they work. The broken group links are indicated by dotted lines.

Figure 2.18

Working with the Objects palette. (a) All the entries for the objects and groups created in Section 3.4. (b) Selecting all the objects in a lower-level group. (c) Ghosting an entire group of objects.

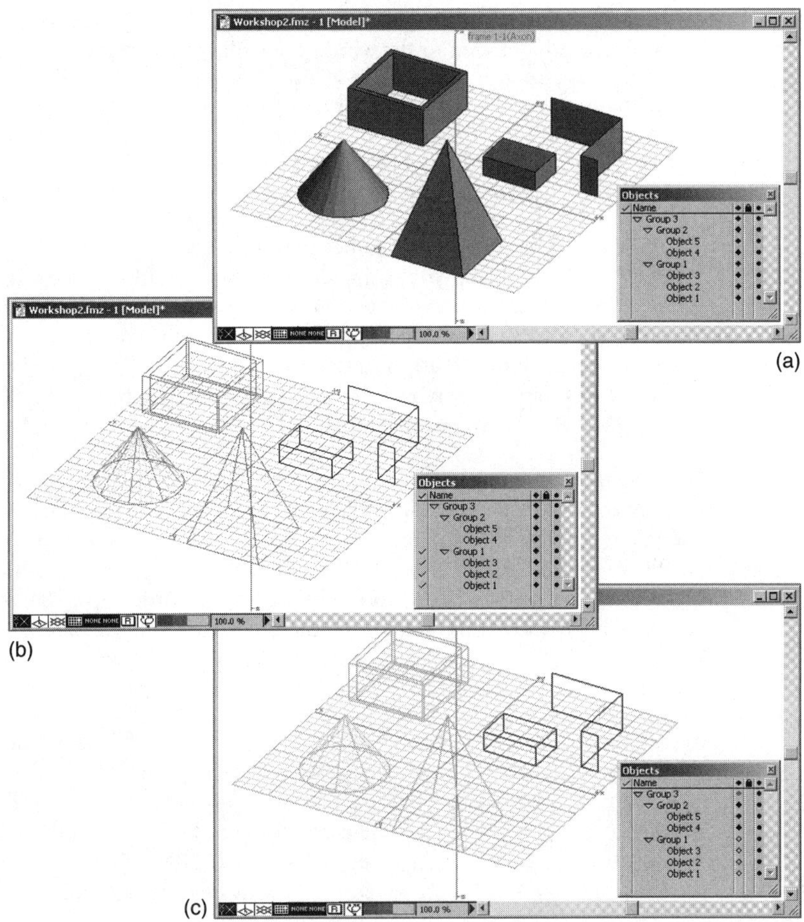

3.5 Using the Objects Palette

- form•Z automatically makes an entry in the Objects palette for each object that's created in the project. Since you had closed this palette at the beginning of the workshop, go to the Palettes menu and select the Objects palette to open it. Resize it so that you can see all the entries it contains. Based on the last section on groups, your palette should be similar to that shown in Figure 2.18-a.

- Notice that there are entries for objects as well as for groups. All the entries are automatically named in the sequence in which the corresponding objects and groups were created. Generate some new objects and use the Group and Ungroup tools on them; watch the changes being reflected in the Objects palette. The concept of groups within a larger group is really simple to comprehend by seeing the manner in which the group entries are listed in this palette.

- Let's now solve the problem of selecting a lower-level group for an operation, once it has been made part of a larger group. Simply click in the first column of the Objects palette, next to the name of that group. A √ mark will appear beside the name of the group and the names of all the objects contained in it, as shown in Figure 2.18-b. At the same time, all these objects will be automatically selected in the window, enabling you to apply any desired operation to them.

- In the same manner, if you click beside the name of the highest level group, all the groups it contains and the objects within these groups get selected. You can even select individual objects using the same method. The Objects palette is thus a convenient shortcut for making various kinds of selections.

- You can change the default names that have been assigned to objects and groups in the Objects palette. This will help you easily identify a specific object or group when required, which would be a difficult task otherwise, particularly as the number of new objects and groups continues to increase. To change a name, simply click on it in the palette. It gets highlighted, and you can now write over it. Press Return or enter after you finish typing. It's best to assign a new name to an object or group as soon as it's created, allowing you to use the Objects palette more efficiently. Figure 2.18-c illustrates the same Objects palette shown earlier, but with modified object names.

Be warned, however, that as the size of your project expands by ever-increasing numbers of objects, keeping track of each one of them through the Objects palette by renaming them can get very tedious, and you might just abandon it after some time. Lots of form•Z users get by without using the Objects palette at all. So use it if it suits your style of working, but remember that it's not mandatory. In particular, once you learn to work with layers in Workshop 3 (Personalizing Your Environment), you'll find that what you can do using the Group tool and the Object palette, you can just as easily do using layers. Still, it's important to be cognizant of these features of the program, should you need to use them at some point.

- Let's look at the other functionalities afforded by the Objects palette. Click on the shaded diamond icon in the third column of the palette, next to the name of an object. This icon, which indicates the attribute of *visibility*, gets unshaded. At the same time, the object will become ghosted in the window (Figure 2.18-c). You'll see the ghosted object only if you're in the Wire Frame display mode and the Hide Ghosted option in its dialog isn't selected. This technique is thus a convenient shortcut to the Ghost tool (M-Tool:14b,1) you learned about in Section 3.7 of Workshop 1 (Letting Yourself Go). GHOST

- Click once more on the same spot—in the third column next to the name. The object will become invisible. A third click restores it to its original state of visibility, and the diamond icon too will be shaded as before. Again, this is a convenient shortcut for the Unghost tool (M-Tool:14b,2); it can even be applied to retrieve ghosted objects that are created as a result of modeling operations such as 3D Extrusion, Union, Difference, and so on, that you covered in Workshop 1. UNGHOST

- There are two more object attributes that can be manipulated using the Objects palette—*pickability* and *snapability*—indicated by the lock icon and the shaded circle respectively. Click next to an object name in the column to the right of visibility; a lock icon will appear there. Now try and select the object or perform any other operation on it, and you'll find that you cannot. It's effectively "locked" against any possible action. This is useful when you're no longer working on an object and want to prevent any operation from accidentally being applied to it.

- Repeat the same process with the last column of the Objects palette. When you click on the shaded circle in the same line as an object, the circle disappears. Now try snapping on to that object using any of the Object Snap tools, and you'll find that you cannot. This ability is useful when there are many objects spaced closely together, making it difficult to snap to the objects you need. You can turn off the snapability attribute of the other objects so that snapping to the required objects is made easier.

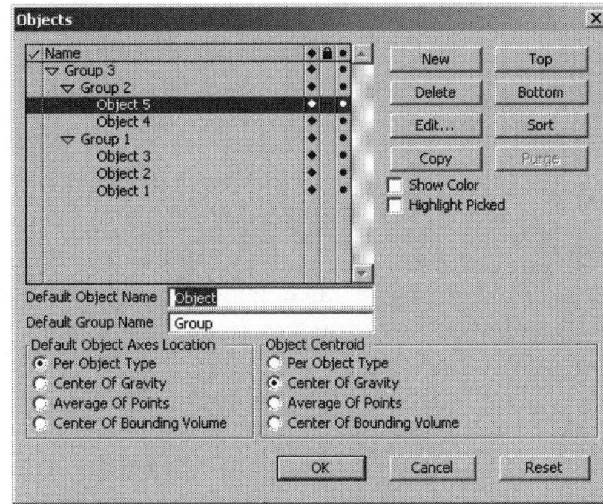

Figure 2.19

The Objects dialog that's associated with the Objects palette.

- You can also manipulate the visibility, pickability and snapability attributes of all the objects within a group simultaneously by using the corresponding icons next to the name of the group, as in Figure 2.18-c. Try it.

- The listing of object and group names in the Objects palette behaves in a manner similar to the listing of files and folders in the navigation windows of most operating systems, which should be familiar to you. Thus, if you click on the downward-pointing arrow next to a group name, the arrow will point sideways and the object listing for that group will be suppressed. Clicking on a sideways-pointing arrow has the reverse effect. The arrows thus work as toggle switches, allowing you to expand or compress the listing of names as desired.

- You can create new groups directly in the Objects palette by clicking in the blank space under the last name entry—such groups are empty to begin with. You can move an object to a group, or transfer it from one group to another, by simply "dragging and dropping" it in the targeted group. An object can be dropped out of all groups in a similar fashion. The same technique can also be used for rearranging the order in which the entries are listed in the palette. To select multiple consecutive entries, click and drag across their names. The Objects palette thus provides you with many convenient shortcuts, particularly for the Group and Ungroup tool operations.

- Let's conclude this section by looking at the Objects dialog (shown in Figure 2.19) that's associated with the Objects palette. There are three ways to invoke this dialog: one, go to Options > Objects; two, click anywhere in the Objects palette while holding down the option key (Mac) or Ctrl+Shift keys (PC); three, simply click in the top row of the Objects palette where the column title Name appears. Go ahead and open the dialog using one of these methods.

- In the Objects dialog, you can create new groups and sort all the existing entries. An individual object or group is selected by clicking on it (as shown in Figure 2.19), after which a variety of operations can be applied to it such as Delete, Copy, Edit, or moving it to the top or bottom of its list. Clicking on the Edit button will open up the Query Object Attributes dialog for an object, which will be covered in Section 5.4 of Workshop 5 (Illuminating, Texturing, and Rendering Your World), or the Query Group dialog for a group, which you'll learn about in the next section. (Double-clicking on the object or group name in the Objects palette itself also has the same effect.) The Purge button, if active, indicates that there are "empty" groups, i.e., groups without objects, which you can choose to delete from the project by clicking on this button. You can also choose to change the default object and group names, if you prefer something else. The options,

Show Color and Highlight Picked, are also available for layers and will be discussed when we do layers in Section 3.6 of Workshop 3 (Personalizing Your Environment).

You may not have realized that every object in form•Z comes with its own local origin and coordinate system, centroid, and bounding volume, all of which are stored along with the object. They can be displayed by setting the appropriate options in the Wire Frame Options dialog, which we'll look at in Section 2.1 of Workshop 3. When displayed, it's possible to *snap* to the origin and centroid of an object using the point snapping options. The location of these points is determined when the object is created, based on choices made in the Objects dialog. These locations can subsequently be changed by using the Query tool, coming up in the next section.

- Turn your attention to the two groups of options located in the lower half of the Objects dialog. There are four choices for the Default Object Axes Location, which determines the initial placement and orientation of an object's axes when the object is created. The same choices are available for also locating the Object Centroid. All the options are self-explanatory, except Per Object Type; this locates the origin and axes, or centroid, according to the type of object. It's the default option for axes location, which means the origin of a cube or a cylinder, for instance, will be placed at the center of its base, while that of a sphere will be placed at its center.

When you use the Preset option for generating primitives, the single point in the window you click on is actually the origin of the object. The complete object gets positioned according to the selection for Default Object Axes Location in the Objects dialog.

3.6 Querying at Different Levels

In the course of modeling, you'll often need to obtain various kinds of information about an entity, such as the exact coordinate position of a point, the length of a segment, the circumference and area of a face, the volume of a solid object, the number of objects in a group, and so on. You can obtain all this information and more by using the Query tool.

Figure 2.20

The Query dialog for a point, a segment, and an object.

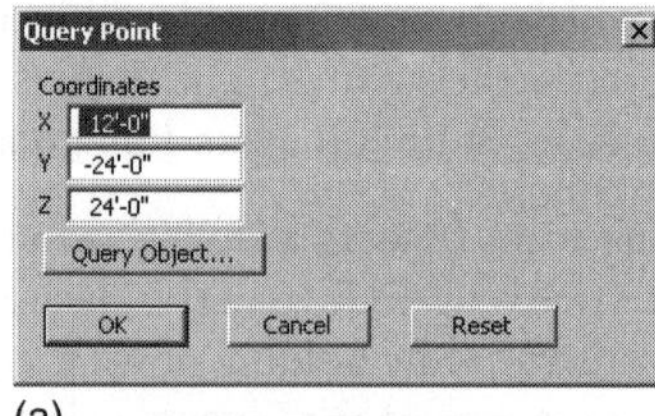

(a)

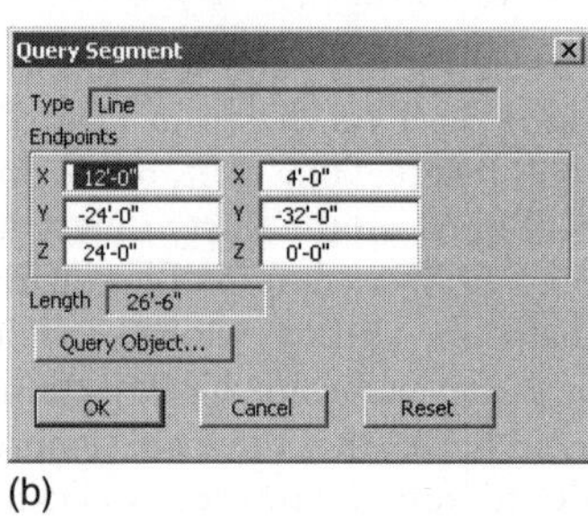

(b)

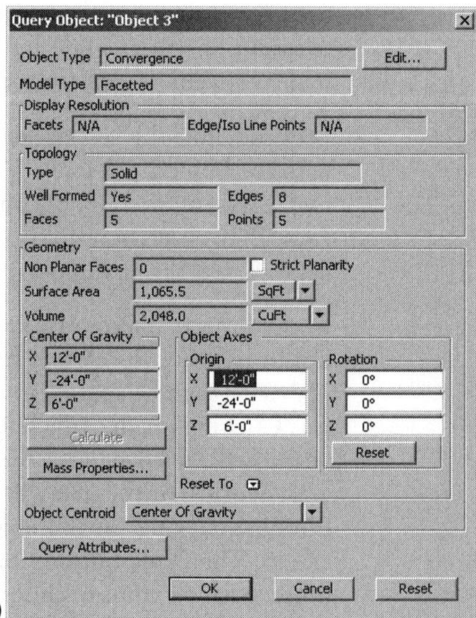

(c)

- Set the topological level on Row 4 to Point. Then activate the Query tool (M-Tool:12b,1) and apply it to any point of an object. This invokes a dialog that lists the coordinate values of the selected point. For a facetted object, these values are also editable, enabling the position of the point to be changed by keying in different values (Figure 2.20-a). This technique is often useful for fixing a point precisely in an exact location when it cannot be done so graphically. QUERY

- Next, apply the Query tool to a segment by setting the topological level to Segment. A different dialog is now presented, showing the coordinate values of the endpoints of the segment. For a facetted object, these can once again be edited. The length of the segment is also calculated and displayed (Figure 2.20-b).

- Apply the Query tool to an object in a similar fashion. The dialog that's invoked contains extensive information about the object type, model type, topology, and geometry of the object (Figure 2.20-c). It tells you whether the object is well formed or not, and how many non-planar faces it has, if any. The surface area is calculated and displayed, as well as the volume if it's a solid object. Keep in mind that the level of Numeric Accuracy you specified in your Working Units dialog (in Section 1.1) will be reflected in the calculation, so set this appropriately. The locations of the Center Of Gravity and the Object Axes are also given, of which the latter can be modified, if required.

- For a parametric object, the Edit button at the top of the Query Object dialog is active, leading you to a second dialog. Here, various changes can be made to the creation parameters of the object, so the dialog will be different depending upon its type. The dialog for a conical primitive is shown in Figure 2.21—you can see that the options are identical to the Cone Options dialog that we saw while creating a cone in Section 2.3 of Workshop 1 (Letting Yourself Go). Any modifications to the cone are made with respect to its local origin and axes orientation, which can also be changed in the same dialog. Make some changes, and you'll find them reflected in the preview window on the left. The set of tool icons located at the base of this window lets you change the view and display type. From left to right, these tools are: Top, Right, Back, and Axonometric views; Fit; Zoom In/Out (use the option or Ctrl+Shift keys for zooming out); Scroll; and finally, Interactive Rotation of View. The single icon on the right lets you choose from the seven different kinds of displays in form•Z.

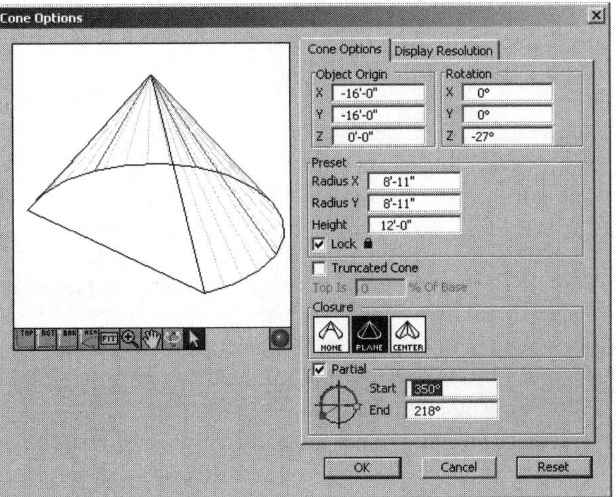

Figure 2.21

Accessing the Edit dialog for a primitive cone from the Query Object dialog.

- After exploring all aspects of the Query Object dialog, proceed to apply the Query tool to a face, an outline, and then to a group. The Query dialogs for a face and an outline provide information about these entities in a format similar to that provided for an object, although the scale of this information is much less. The Query dialog for a group, which you may have explored in the last section, gives you some additional information about a group that might come in useful.

There's an Attributes tool located immediately after the Query tool on Row 12, which can only be applied to objects and faces. It provides information about various attributes of these entities such as color, smooth shading, and so on. You'll be learning about most of these attributes in the next three workshops, so we'll postpone working with the Attributes tool till the end of Workshop 5 (Illuminating, Texturing, and Rendering Your World). However, we can work now with the Measure tool, which follows right after the Attributes tool.

3.7 Measuring Distances Using Different Topological Levels

- Invoke the dialog of the Measure tool (Figure 2.22-a). Here, you'll find seven distance-calculating options that are crucial in the process of creating scaled models. Let's select each one of them in turn and see what they do.

- Activate the first option, Length Of Vector/Boundary Line. You can now apply the Measure tool to any segment, outline, face, open 2D object, or closed 2D object containing a single outline, and it will calculate and display the total length of all the segments that make up the selected entity. You can also select multiple entities, at the same or at different topological levels, to obtain the combined segment length. Thus, it goes one step further than the Query tool, which provides these calculations for a single entity only.

- With the Interactive Point To Point option, you first select a point. Then, as you move the cursor around in the window, the distance between the first point and the current position of the cursor gets interactively displayed in the Prompts palette (Figure 2.22-b). The T box must be checked to enable tracking. You can use the relevant Object Snap tools if you need to measure distances between specific points of objects. Keep in mind that if you're using object snapping, you can measure distances in 3D, e.g., across the diagonals of a box; but if you're not, you'll only be measuring distances in 2D, along the current reference plane. If this is confusing, open up the Coordinates palette and keep track of the actual X, Y, and Z values of the cursor as you move it in the window.

- Move on to the next option, Point/Segment To Point/Segment. The Measure tool now gives you the distance between any two points, two parallel segments, or a point and a segment. What is really convenient is that you don't have to bother with setting the topological level to Point or Segment—it just finds the nearest point or segment automatically.

- The remaining four options are similar to the ones you just explored. Point To Surface lets you select first a point and then a face on an object, and gives you the shortest distance between them. Point To Reference Plane requires you to select just a point, and it will tell you its distance from the current reference plane. (Keep this in mind when you work with reference planes in Workshop 3, Personalizing Your Environment.) Surface To Parallel Surface gives you the distance between any two parallel faces, belonging to the same object or to different objects. And finally, Angle Between Segments lets you measure the angle enclosed between two selected segments.

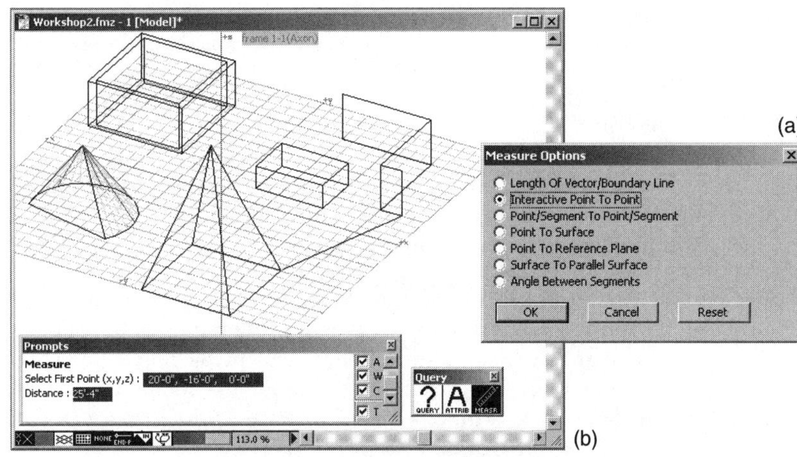

Figure 2.22

The dialog of the Measure tool, and using its Interactive Point To Point option to measure the distance between two points.

Exercise 4

Executing Transformations and Making Copies

So far, we've worked with just one kind of geometric transformation—Move. In this exercise, we'll work with the other elementary transformation tools located in the left column of Row 13 of the modeling tool palette. These are closely related to the Self/Copy modes on Row 12 that allow you to make copies of objects in various ways, so it will be a good time to study these as well. We'll then explore alternative ways of executing transformations and learn to define and execute composite transformations in the form of macros.

4.1 Elementary Geometric Transformations

- Open a new project or clear the window of all its contents. Create some objects using the tools you're familiar with by now. You'll apply some elementary transformations to these objects. Make sure that the left column of Row 12 of the tool palette is set to Self, so that all transformations at this stage are applied to the targeted object itself.

- You've already worked with the Move tool, but not with its options. Invoke its dialog, and notice that, by default, the movement happens relative to the current Reference Plane. You could, instead, choose to move the object along any of the three planes of the Object Coordinate System. Try out all of them, but first set the display to Interactive Shaded, so that you can see the movement better. Ignore the Copy Options tab in the Move Options dialog for now; it's related to the Self/Copy modes that we'll look at in the next section.

- Now proceed to activate the Rotate tool, used for rotating any entity about a point, in the left column of Row 13 and follow the instructions in the Prompts palette. Select the object to be rotated; then enter a *center of rotation*, either by keying in its coordinates or by selecting a point graphically with the mouse. You can also select a point on the object itself or on any other object

by using the appropriate Object Snap tool. The point selected as the center of rotation will affect the positioning of the rotated object, as demonstrated in Figure 2.23, so pick it carefully.

- Next, you'll be prompted for the *angle of rotation*. You can enter this value numerically in degrees—a positive value for the anticlockwise direction; a negative value for clockwise rotation (unless you changed the default Angle Options in the Working Units dialog, in which case you should follow that specification). Alternately, you can indicate the angle graphically by selecting, first, a reference point, and second, a new position for that reference point. Direction snapping can be useful in doing this precisely. Switching to a planar view also helps in performing rotation more accurately.

- Just like the Move tool, the Rotate tool can be applied to the individual points, segments, outlines, or faces of a facetted object to produce interesting deformations. Try it. You can also apply the same rotation to many entities at a time by prepicking them with the Pick tool and then selecting the Rotate tool. However, a transformation like rotation, unlike translation, is usually applied to a single entity at a time because it's relative to the center of rotation, which would usually be different for different entities.

- Invoke the dialog of the Rotate tool, and explore its main options. Just as for Move, the rotation happens with respect to the current Reference Plane, but you could choose the X, Y, or Z axis of the Object Coordinate System instead. Try out all three. Notice also that the default Reference Plane option lets you indicate the axis of rotation, not just through clicking, but also through the origin or centroid of the object, when required. If you choose either of these options, you only need to specify the rotation angle after selecting the object.

- Proceed to select the next transformation tool on Row 13, Scale. This tool is used to scale an entity *independently* in the X, Y, and Z directions. Select an object for scaling and then establish a *base of scale*—this can be any point selected, as in Rotate. Most often, you'd choose either a vertex of the object or the center of one of its faces as the base of scale, using object snapping to pick the point accurately (see Figure 2.24-a). Just like the center of rotation for the Rotate tool, the base of scale for the Scale tool affects the position of the resultant object, so select it with care.

- After selecting the base of scale, you need to specify three *scaling factors* to indicate the amount of scaling along the X, Y, and Z axes. For instance, if you want to scale an object such that it's half the original size in the X direction, twice the original size in the Y direction, and unchanged in the Z direction, your scaling factors would be [0.5,2,1]. Figure 2.24-b shows an example of scaling with these factors. It's most common to key in these values in the Prompts palette, but you could also specify them graphically by selecting a reference point and dragging it until the desired scaling is achieved.

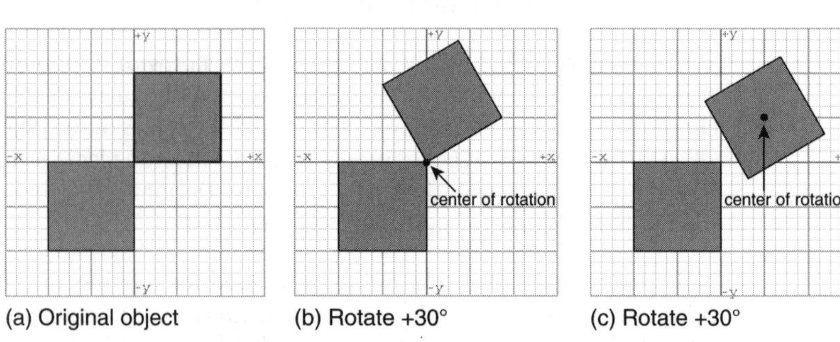

Figure 2.23

Applying the Rotate transformation to an object. The rotated object is positioned differently (b and c), depending upon where the center of rotation is picked.

Figure 2.24

Applying the Scale and Uniform Scale tools to an object. The scaling factors were [0.5,2,1] for scaling and [1.5] for uniform scaling.

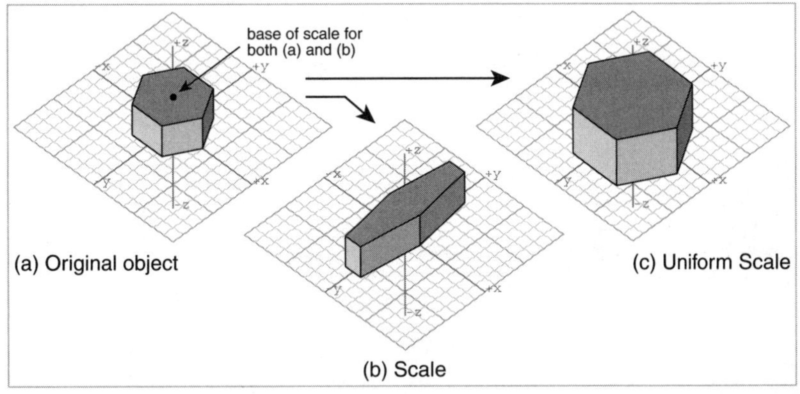

- Move to the next tool, Uniform Scale, which is identical to Scale in all respects except that it applies a uniform scaling factor along the three axes (as shown in Figure 2.24-c). Thus, after you specify the base of scale, you're prompted for a single value rather than three separate values. Again, you can specify this through the keyboard or indicate it graphically with the mouse.

- Both the Scale and Uniform Scale tools have the same dialog associated with them. Invoke it, and you'll find that the default option is Scale By Percentage, which is the dynamic scaling you've been doing so far. This has suboptions similar to those of the Rotate tool you've already explored, so skip those for now. Instead, select the main alternate option, Scale By Absolute Value. You'll find that when you now apply either of the Scale tools to a segment, face, outline, or object, a new dialog is invoked in which you can conveniently modify the actual dimensions of the selected entity. For Scale, you can modify all three direction values independently, whereas for Uniform Scale, you can modify only a single value which will be applied to all three directions. Although you can apply this scaling technique to multiple selections, it works best when applied to a single entity at a time.

- Proceed to select the fifth transformation tool, Mirror. This tool mirrors the selected object or objects about an *axis of reflection*, indicated by two successive mouse clicks. Note that the axis of reflection is the perpendicular bisector of the line that connects the two selected points, rather than the line itself. For this transformation, it usually helps to have an existing object whose points can be used as reference points (as shown in Figure 2.25-a). If such an object doesn't exist, create one.

- Mirroring an object by specifying the perpendicular bisector of the mirror line rather than the mirror line itself might seem counterintuitive. In that case, you can choose to apply this transformation in a different way. Invoke the dialog of the Mirror tool and you'll find that you can also choose to mirror about a point, segment, or surface, instead of specifying the axis of reflection dynamically as you just did. Explore all of these options. The most intuitive one seems to be About A Segment, in which you simply select an existing segment as the axis of reflection. The About A Surface option makes it possible to perform the Mirror operation in actual 3D space (as shown in Figure 2.25-b) rather than only along a plane (as shown in Figure 2.25-a). The three About Local Plane options work with respect to the specified plane of the object coordinate system, and don't require you to select an axis. Try them out.

- The next tool in the left column of Row 13, Repeat Last Transformation, repeats the most recently executed geometric transformation on a different object of your choice. In addition to the object,

the base point for the transformation also has to specified. The remaining factors, such as the translation distance, or the angle of rotation, or the scaling factor, will be taken from the previous transformation. Try it out.

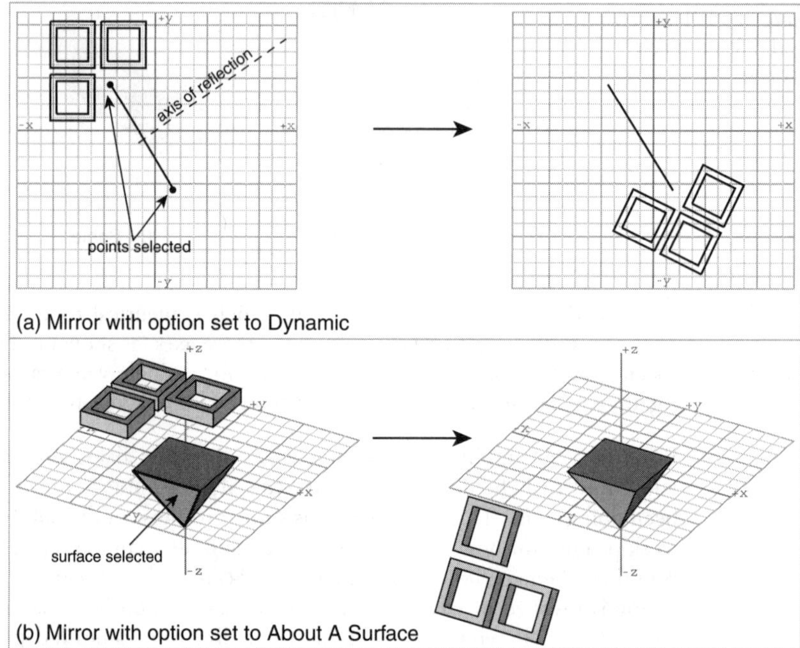

(a) Mirror with option set to Dynamic

(b) Mirror with option set to About A Surface

Figure 2.25

Two ways of applying the Mirror tool. (a) Dynamic option. The selected points and the resulting axis of reflection are indicated. (b) About A Surface option. The surface of reflection is indicated.

4.2 The Self-Copy Modifiers

All the transformations you executed in the last section were applied to the selected entity directly, i.e., you were moving the object itself, or rotating it, or scaling it. Even while using Mirror, you were relocating the object itself to its mirror image position. You must have found this quite annoying, since you'd usually expect a Mirror command to produce a mirror image *copy* of an object while still retaining the original.

What controls the behavior of the transformation tools on Row 13 is the row of teal-colored tools located just above it. These tools are referred to as the *self-copy modifiers*, and they determine whether a transformation is applied to the object itself or in making copies of it. Let's look at each of them in turn.

- The Self mode (M-Tool:12a,1) is the default option to which the self-copy modifier is set, the mode you were working in all this time. It determines that any transformation executed is performed on the object itself. That's why even a transformation such as Mirror in Self mode didn't make a copy of the object, but simply changed its position.

- Switch to the One Copy mode (M-Tool:12a,2) and apply one of the transformation tools, say Move, to an object. You'll find that a copy of the object is now produced in the transformed state, leaving the original as it is.

Figure 2.26

A repetitive configuration generated by rotating an object about the indicated point in the Repeat Copy mode. After the first rotated copy, five more identically rotated copies were generated using five mouse clicks.

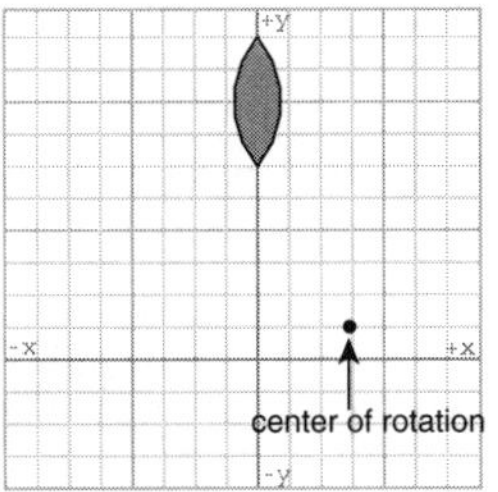

(a) Original object

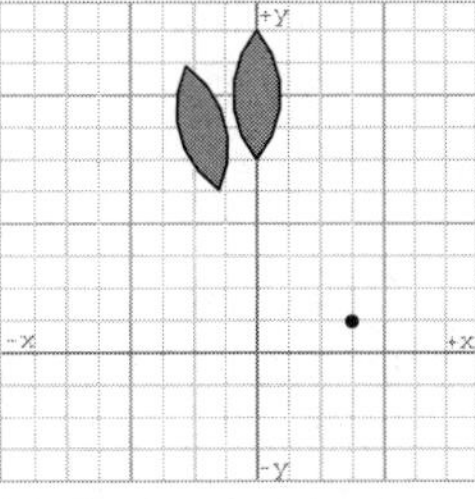

(b) Single rotated copy

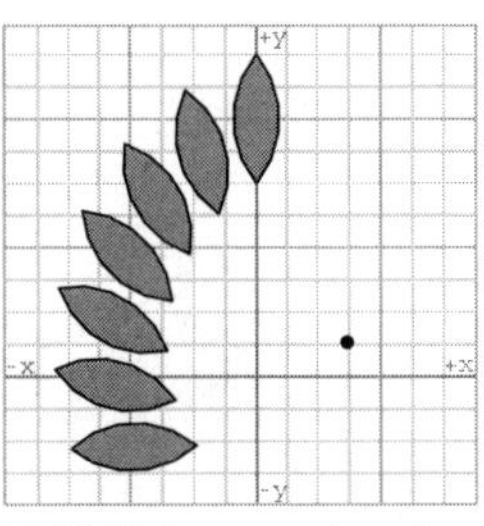

(c) Multiple rotated copies

- The next mode, Continuous Copy, is practically the same as the Copy mode, except that the copy-making process doesn't terminate after a single copy is made. You can make multiple copies of the object one after another, simply by selecting additional transformation points. To terminate the making of copies, double-click with the mouse in the graphics window or type an "e" in the Prompts palette. The copy-making process will also stop if you select another tool from the modeling palette.

- Try out the next self-copy mode, Repeat Copy, in the same manner. You can now make multiple copies of the object using the *same* transformation parameters that were established by the first execution of the operation, simply by clicking the mouse repeatedly. You don't have to specify new transformation values for additional copies, as you did for Continuous Copy. Thus, if you're using the Move tool in Repeat Copy mode, once you specify the distance of the first move, subsequent copies *at the same distance* can be generated by continuing to click the mouse anywhere in the window. The copy-making process is terminated in the same manner—double-click or type an "e." Figure 2.26 shows how a repetitive configuration is created by using the Rotate tool in Repeat Copy mode.

- Move on to the Multi Copy mode. It's similar to Repeat Copy except that it lets you make the desired number of copies in one step, rather than having to click for each additional copy. The number of copies needed is specified in the Copy Options dialog accessible from the Multi Copy tool; the default number is 6. The transformation values from one copy to the next are identical and are established by the first execution of the operation, just as for Repeat Copy. Thus, the configuration shown in Figure 2.26 could have been generated in one step by using the Multi Copy mode, with the number of copies specified as 6.

- Invoke the Copy Options dialog from any one of the Copy modes, and look at the Multi-Copy section. In addition to the # Of Copies, there are two alternate options that determine how the multi-copying operation is performed. You've been working with the default of Even Increment, in which you specified the first copy, and the remaining were generated based on its transformation parameters. For the Divide Distance option, on the other hand, you specify the *last* copy instead of the first. The desired number of copies is then evenly distributed between the original object and the last copy. Experiment with this mode of multi-copying as well. You might find it more useful than the default mode, since design is usually done from the "outside in"—a basic framework is first established which is then filled in.

- The Copy Options dialog contains one more option, Return To Self After Copy, which applies to all the Copy modes. When selected, it automatically reverts the self-copy mode back to Self each time a Copy mode is used. It can be helpful if you keep forgetting to switch back to Self for applying transformations to objects without making copies. Basically, it ensures that Self is always selected by default.

- Finally, try changing the topological level in Row 4 to Point, Segment, Outline, or Face, and watch what happens when you apply a transformation using a Copy mode to a facetted object. You'll find that the transformation doesn't result in multiple copies of the selected point, segment, outline, or face. Essentially, you cannot make copies of object parts, but only of entire objects, groups, holes, and volumes (the last two will be covered in Exercise 6).

4.3 Copying and Duplicating

form•Z has two additional ways of making copies of objects. These involve the use of the Copy and Duplicate commands under the Edit menu.

- You must be familiar with the Cut, Copy, and Paste commands found under the Edit menu of virtually any program. In form•Z, you can use these commands to transfer or copy objects from one project to another, as well as to transfer or copy objects from one layer to another *within* the same project. (Keep this in mind when you work with layers in Workshop 3, Personalizing Your Environment.) Objects that are cut or copied are temporarily stored in the clipboard, the contents of which can be viewed by going to Edit > form•Z Clipboard.

- If you Copy an object and simply Paste it (without changing layers), it will be pasted exactly on top of the original object. Thus, you'll not be able to see the copy unless you apply a transformation such as Move to the object, in which case you'll have the object in its original position and a copy of it in the transformed position. It's thus the equivalent of a Move using the Copy mode, but in a more roundabout manner; so there's no reason why you should ever use this option, except on the rare occasion when you want to make a copy of an object in exactly the same position.

- The Duplicate command, however, is a viable alternative to the Move and Copy combination. Select an object using the Pick tool. Then go to Duplicate in the Edit menu. A copy of the selected object will be made at some distance away from the original, allowing you to see and work easily with both the original as well as the duplicated copy. Notice also that the duplicated copy remains highlighted, allowing you to continue the duplication process by simply selecting Duplicate again. Thus, you have the convenient equivalent of the Repeat Copy and Multi Copy modes as well.

- Naturally, you'd like to control the distance by which the duplication takes place. This distance is known as the *duplication offset*, and it can be specified by going to the Duplication Offset command, located just below Duplicate in the Edit menu. A dialog is invoked in which you can specify the required translation along all three axes.

- Note that the Duplicate command can only be applied to objects and groups, not to entities at any other topological level. But you can, of course, apply it to multiple selections of objects and groups, just as you did for a single object.

4.4 Defining and Using Macro Transformations

Coming back to the geometric transformations, form•Z allows you to record a sequence of frequently used transformations into a *macro*. Thereafter, the recorded macro can be applied to any entity to execute the entire sequence of transformations on it directly in one step, doing away with the tedium of performing each transformation individually. Such composite transformations are known as *macro transformations*, and they can save you a lot of time and effort in modeling. Let's see how macro transformations are recorded and executed.

- With the Pick tool, select an object on which you'll carry out a certain sequence of transformations, say Move, Rotate, and Scale. Set the self-copy modifier on Row 12 to Define Macro. As soon as you select this mode, a dialog will be invoked asking you to name the macro transformation. Give it an appropriate name.

- You're now ready to begin recording your macro. Select the Move tool and translate the selected object by a certain distance. Since you used the Pick tool to select the object, it will remain selected even after the execution of the Move tool. Go ahead and apply a Rotate operation to it, and then a Scale or Uniform Scale operation. Let's assume that this is all we want to record in our macro. To stop the recording, simply go to the left column of Row 12 and select any one of the other self-copy modifiers instead of Define Macro; the macro definition will be automatically completed.

- You'll now apply the macro you just recorded to another object. First, set the self-copy mode to Self. Then go to 1-Macro-T (M-Tool:13a,7), the first of the three Macro-T tools, and watch the message in the Prompts palette. It gives you the name of the macro you just recorded and asks you to select an object for applying the macro to (assuming the topological level is still set to Object). Do so. You'll then be prompted for the *macro origin*, which is the point relative to which the entire sequence of recorded transformations will take place. Select an appropriate point and watch the object being transformed according to all the operations you had previously recorded, but this time in a single step.

- Repeat the application of the macro on another object, this time in Multi Copy mode, and see how you can model complex configurations such as the one shown in Figure 2.27 in just one step.

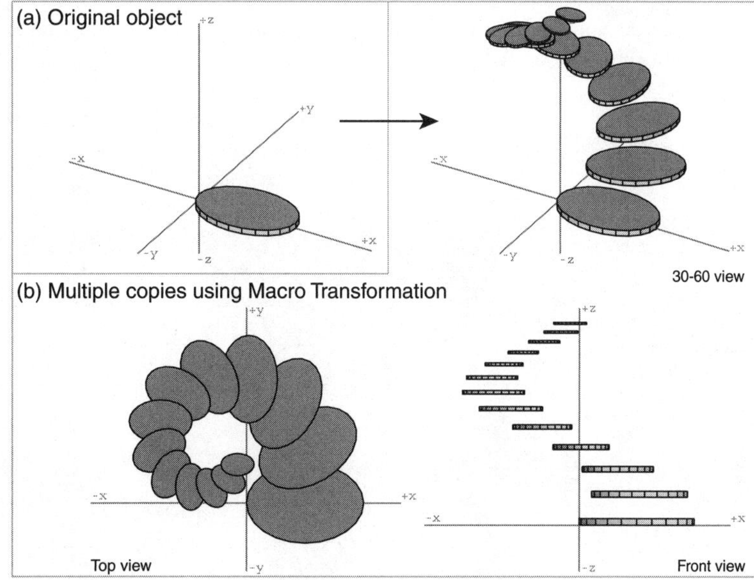

Figure 2.27

Using a macro transformation comprising Move, Rotate, and Uniform Scale in Multi Copy mode. The actual macro is shown in Figure 2.29.

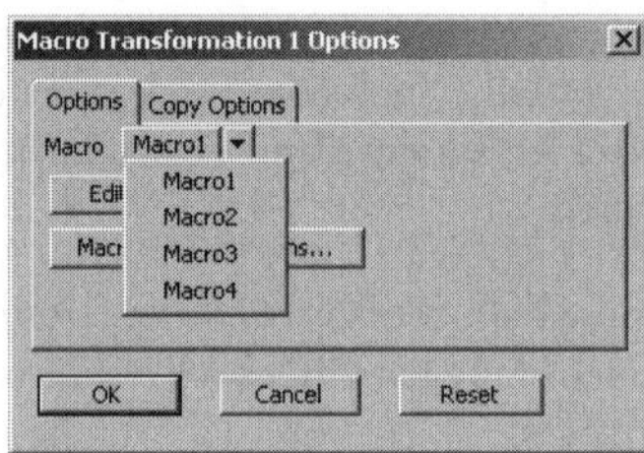

Figure 2.28

Assigning a specific macro to one of the three Macro-T tools.

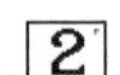

- Define at least three more macros using the Define Macro mode as you did earlier. How do you now choose from among the four macros you've defined so far? Notice that in the left column of Row 13, there are two more Macro-T tools labeled 2-Macro-T and 3-Macro-T, following 1-Macro-T. Select each one of these tools in turn. You'll find that the first three recorded macros are stored sequentially in these three tools—you can apply them to an object by simply selecting the corresponding tool. Try it.

- What about the fourth macro—or the fifth, sixth, and so on, if you've defined more? How do you access these for applying to other objects? For this, invoke the dialog of any of the Macro-T tools, and select the macro to be assigned to that tool from the Macro popup menu (see Figure 2.28). The Macro Transformations button in this dialog takes you to another dialog where you can manage all the recorded macros: assign them to specific tools, delete them, rename them, and so on.

- Click on the Edit button in the dialog of the Macro-T tool. This invokes a dialog displaying all the transformations recorded in the macro assigned to that tool, along with their respective numeric values. To edit a value, highlight it and type over it, as shown in Figure 2.29. This facility is useful when you want to make precise adjustments to a macro definition. You can also delete a particular transformation from the macro, completely change its type (for instance, change Move to Rotate), or add a new transformation and numerically specify the corresponding values.

- To end this section, define a new macro using an *existing* macro as one of the component transformations. To do this, simply use one of the Macro-T tools while recording the new macro, just as you'd use Move, Rotate, etc. Needless to say, you can have multiple macros recorded in another macro—try it!

Macro transformations are independent of the topological level of the entity used for their definition. Thus, you can define a macro using an object, but you can apply it just as well to points, segments, faces, groups, etc.

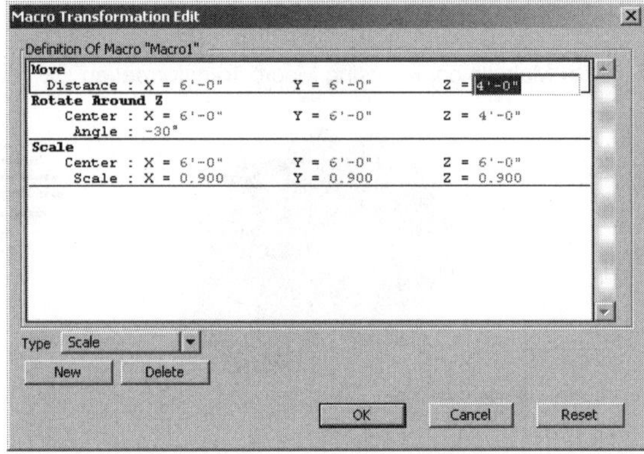

Figure 2.29

The Macro Definition dialog for the macro used in the example illustrated in Figure 2.27.

4.5 Transformations Using the Pick Tool

In form•Z, basic transformations like translation, rotation, and scaling can also be carried out using the Pick tool, making it a convenient alternative at times to the dedicated transformation tools on Row 13. Exploring how this works involves taking a comprehensive look at the Pick Options dialog you first encountered in Section 3.5 of Workshop 1 (Letting Yourself Go). In the process, let's also look at the other Pick tool options, in addition to those related to transformations, that we haven't yet covered.

- Double-click on the Pick tool, or on any one of the topological levels on Row 4. The Pick Options dialog will be invoked (Figure 2.30). The first and last sets of options in this dialog are already familiar to you from Workshop 1.

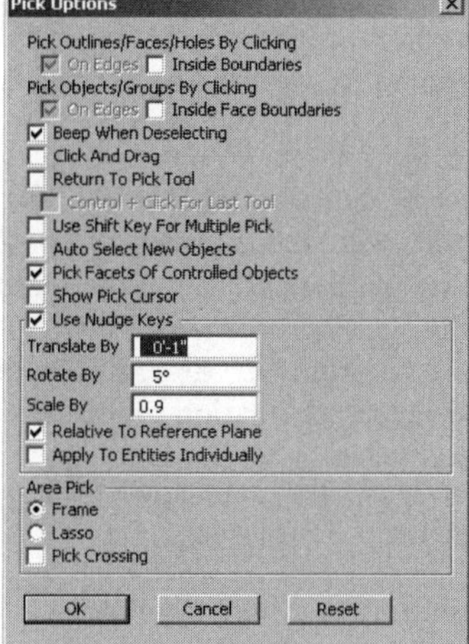

Figure 2.30

The Pick Options dialog.

- Let's quickly browse through the non-transformation related options first. You can turn off the Beep When Deselecting option if you find the beep annoying. If you're used to other programs in which the Shift key *has* to be pressed to make multiple selections, you have the option of retaining the habit by checking the Use Shift Key For Multiple Pick box. You can also choose to Auto Select New Objects, which can be useful in some specific modeling situations, as you'll see in the next workshop. The Pick Facets Of Controlled Objects option lets you select and modify the points, segments, faces, etc. of facetted parametric objects; you'll use this ability often, so leave this option turned on. To make the cursor behave for all topological levels like it does for Auto, turn on the Show Pick Cursor option—it will now change to a different icon when brought near a selectable entity, depending upon the active topological level.

- Turn your attention to the Return To Pick Tool option. By default, form•Z retains the selection of a tool until another tool is selected. However, if you usually don't apply the same operation repeatedly and find this aspect of the interface hindering your speed, you can check this option to automatically shift the selection to the Pick tool after the execution of an operation by another tool. Within this option, you can also, if necessary, choose to reselect the last tool applied by clicking in the window while holding down the control key (Mac) or Ctrl+Alt keys (PC).

- The first of two options that gives the Pick tool the ability to carry out geometric transformations is Click And Drag. Select this option by checking the box and exit the Pick Options dialog. You'll find that you can now use the Pick tool to transform an entity in various ways. For moving, simply click on the entity (which can be at any topological level) and drag. To rotate with respect to the active reference plane, click and drag while pressing the control key (Mac) or Ctrl+Alt keys (PC). To rotate with respect to the plane of the screen, use the command key (Mac) or Ctrl key (PC). To scale, click and drag while pressing the option key (Mac) or Ctrl+Shift keys (PC). Try out all these transformations.

- If you keep the Shift key pressed down during any of these operations, some additional constraints such as orthogonal movement, 45° rotation, and 5% scaling only are applied to the transformation. Check this out as well.

The Click And Drag method can be convenient, particularly if it's another interface characteristic you're used to. However, keep in mind that this method doesn't guarantee preciseness and accuracy since you cannot use direct numeric input—you have to rely only on the mouse. Also, you can transform only one entity at a time, not multiple entities. When you use Click And Drag therefore, keep Grid Snap (W-Tool:4,1) turned on for at least some degree of accuracy.

The last group of options we have to explore in the Pick Options dialog are grouped under the Use Nudge Keys section. This feature is active by default. It lets you use the arrow keys on your keyboard, in combination with the Pick tool, to carry out the same transformations—move, rotate, and scale—you just saw. The difference between this and the Click And Drag method is that you can specify the *exact* values by which the transformation will occur, thereby guaranteeing accuracy. Also, you can apply the Nudge Keys method to multiple selections at a time. This makes it equivalent, both in scope as well as accuracy, to the actual geometric transformation tools. Let's see how it works.

- Make sure the Use Nudge Keys option is selected. Take note of the values specified for Translate By, Rotate By, and Scale By, and change them if necessary.

- Back on the screen, select multiple entities at different topological levels with the Pick tool. Then keep pressing one of the four arrow keys on your keyboard, and watch your selection respond by moving along an axis by the amount specified in the Translate By field. For instance, the left arrow key ← will move the selection left with respect to the active reference plane. Experiment with all the arrow keys in this manner, and note the direction of movement. Then use the Shift key combined with the up ↑ or down ↓ arrow keys and watch the selection move in a direction perpendicular to the reference plane.

- Similarly, explore other key combinations for executing transformations. These are: control (Mac) or Ctrl+Alt (PC) for rotation, option (Mac) or Ctrl+Shift (PC) for uniform scale, and command (Mac) or Ctrl (PC) for independent scale. The extent of rotation and scaling will be determined by the Rotate By and Scale By values specified in the Pick Options dialog. When working with multiple selections, if the rotation and scaling needs to be applied for each element about its individual centroid rather than about the collective centroid of the entire selection, simply check the Apply To Each Selected Entity Individually option in the Use Nudge Keys section.

- By default, nudge key transformations are executed with respect to the active reference plane, which, as you'll learn in Workshop 3 (Personalizing Your Environment), can also be user-defined. To always execute the transformations with respect to the original reference plane (referred to as the *world coordinate system*), deselect the Relative To Reference Plane option in the Pick Options dialog.

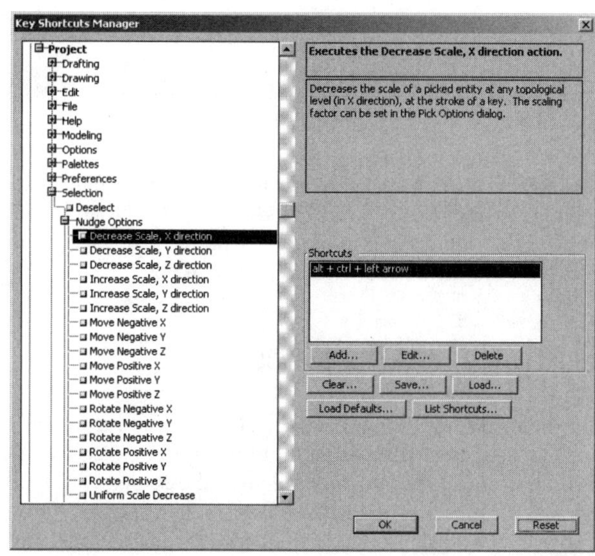

Figure 2.31

Finding the exact Nudge Key shortcut for a particular transformation in the Key Shortcuts dialog.

- To find out the exact nudge key combination for any transformation along a specific direction, go to Edit > Key Shortcuts. You're familiar with this dialog from Section 6 of the Introduction. Expand the Selection item under the Project section, and within it, the Nudge Keys item, as shown in Figure 2.31. You can now highlight any of the direction-specific transformations contained in the list to see its shortcut key combination.

We'll end this section by looking at a feature of the Pick tool that doesn't appear in its dialog, but is nevertheless very important. This is the *pick parade* feature, used for selecting entities that overlap or lie directly on top of other entities, making it difficult to select them in the regular fashion.

- Set the object generation mode on Row 2 to 2D Surface Object and create a 2D shape that coincides exactly with the face of a 3D object. Use Endpoint snapping for accuracy. Then activate the Pick tool and the Object topological level, and click on an edge of the newly created shape. As you'd expect, the 2D shape gets selected since it was created more recently, not the 3D object overlapping with it.

- You could, of course, select the 3D object by clicking on one of its other edges. But suppose that, for some reason, all its edges were lying behind other objects. To go about selecting the object in such a situation (which isn't uncommon, as you'll discover in the course of your modeling), this is what you need to do: Click on the overlapping edge with the Pick tool while holding down the Shift key. The first object found at that point gets highlighted in black. Click again, still holding down the Shift key, and the next object found at that point gets highlighted. In this manner, all overlapping objects at that point get highlighted in turn (or "paraded") with each click. When the entity you're interested in gets highlighted, release the Shift key and click one last time—this will select it, highlighting it in the usual selection color, which is red.

Experiment with the pick parade feature a little more before moving on to the next exercise.

EXERCISE 5

Editing Elements

In this exercise, we'll explore the different ways in which elements can be edited in form•Z, starting with how to change their object type and model type. We'll then look at two editing tools that can be used to manipulate the creation parameters of parametric objects graphically. Finally, we'll work with the set of tools that's exclusively devoted to editing lines.

5.1 Changing Object Types and Model Types

In Section 1 of the Introduction, you learned about the two different object types in form•Z—plain and parametric—as well as the two different model types—facetted and smooth. You've encountered objects of all these various types in the modeling operations you've performed so far, and have seen how some operations convert parametric objects to plain objects, for instance, moving the point of an object. Let's now look at a dedicated tool that's used to perform both kinds of conversions when required.

- Use the 3D Extrusion object generation mode on Row 2, in conjunction with the Rectangle and Circle tools on Row 3, to create a cubical and cylindrical extrusion respectively.
- Select the Convert tool (M-Tool:11b,6) and apply it to the cubical extrusion. A Convert Options dialog is invoked, where you can see the current object type and model type of the object, and the options to convert to a different object type and model type. Note that for the cubical extrusion, you can convert its object type from Extrusion to Plain Object, but you cannot convert its model type from Facetted to Smooth (Figure 2.32-a).

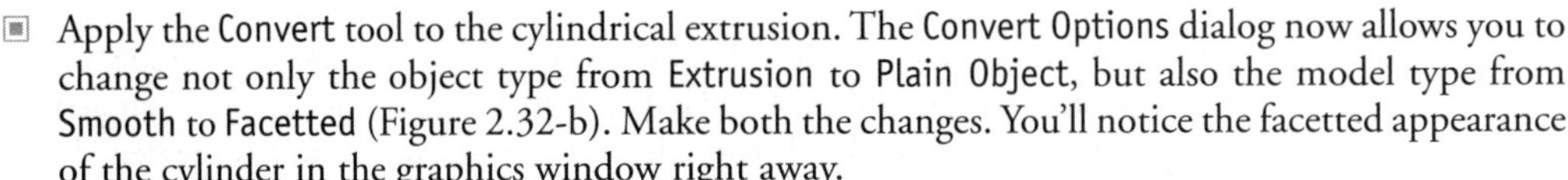

- Apply the Convert tool to the cylindrical extrusion. The Convert Options dialog now allows you to change not only the object type from Extrusion to Plain Object, but also the model type from Smooth to Facetted (Figure 2.32-b). Make both the changes. You'll notice the facetted appearance of the cylinder in the graphics window right away.

Facetted objects cannot be converted to smooth objects, but smooth objects can easily be converted to facetted objects.

- Apply the Query tool to the cylindrical extrusion that you converted to plain. You'll find that the Edit button in the Query Object dialog is deactivated, since the object is no longer parametric.

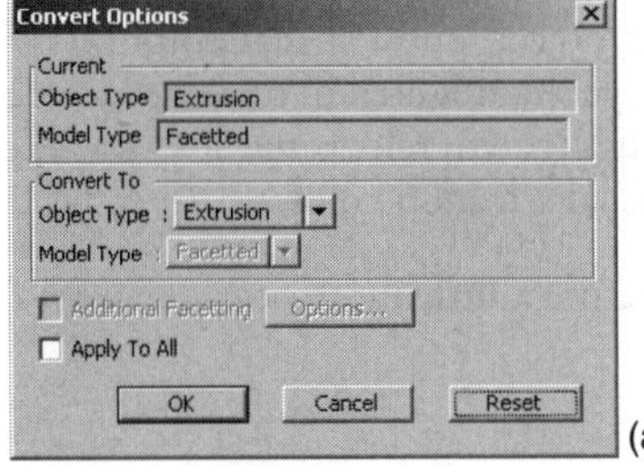

(a)

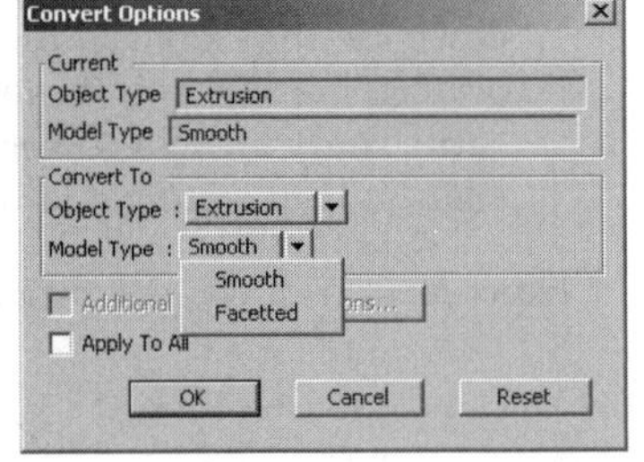

(b)

Figure 2.32

The Convert Options dialog, for a cubical extrusion and for a cylindrical extrusion.

- Now use the primitive Cube and Cylinder tools on Row 1 to create a cube and a cylinder. Apply the Convert tool to each of these in turn. You'll find that for both these objects, there are now two additional options under Object Type, apart from Plain Object, to which they can be converted: Nurbz Object and Patch Object. You'll learn more about such objects in Workshop 6 (Going Organic), so you can ignore those two options for now.

5.2 Editing Parametric Objects Graphically

In Section 3.6, you saw how the creation parameters of a parametric object could be changed using the Query tool, through the Edit button in its dialog. That method let you change the creation parameters numerically. Sometimes, it's more convenient to edit the parameters graphically. The Edit Controls tool, located immediately after the Pick tool on Row 4, can be used to do this.

- Create any parametric object, either by using the primitive tools on Row 1, or by using the drawing tools on Row 3 in conjunction with the object generation modes on Row 2. The object can be a 2D or a 3D object.

- Select the Edit Controls tool (M-Tool:4b,2) and apply it to the object. Depending upon the type of object, various *controls* that govern its shape will be displayed. In the case of an arc, for instance, there are controls for modifying its radius, center point, and the start and end points—in short, everything that went into defining the arc when it was created (Figure 2.33-a). In the case of a cylinder created with the Cylinder tool, there are controls for manipulating its radius, height, revolution angle, location, orientation, and tilt (Figure 2.33-b).

- Click and drag on any one of the displayed controls to move it, and click again to reposition it. See how the shape of the object changes in response. Manipulate other controls in a similar fashion to completely reshape the object (Figures 2.33-c and 2.33-d). Multiple controls can be selected for manipulation at the same time by using the Shift key.

Figure 2.33

Modifying the creation parameters of an arc and a cylinder with the Edit Controls tool.

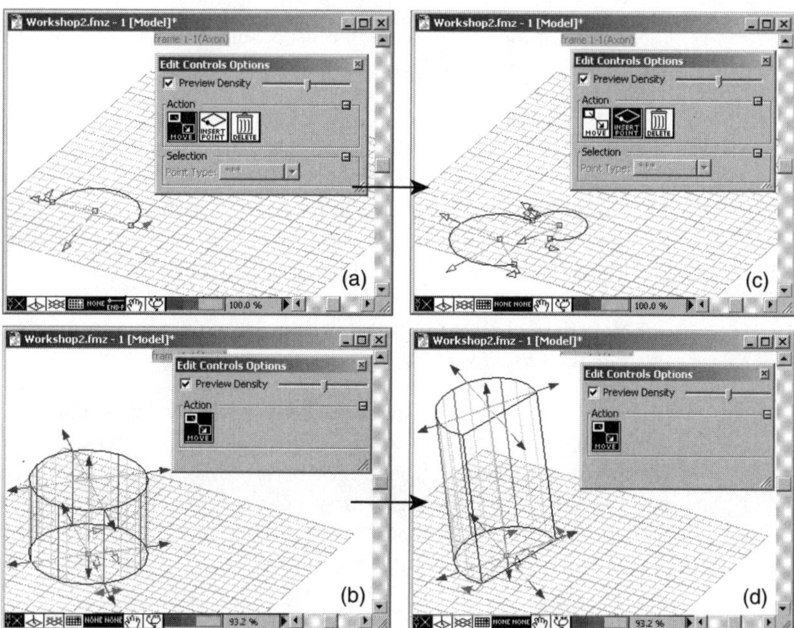

- Notice that when the Edit Controls tool is active, it automatically invokes a dialog containing some editing options. The Preview Density is relevant to smooth objects only, and can be used to control how smoothly the object is displayed as it's being edited. Unless the object is very complex, you should have little reason to change this setting. The Action section lets you choose from a number of editing operations that can be applied to the object; these will vary depending upon its type. As you can see in Figure 2.33, only a move action can be applied to edit the controls of a cylinder, whereas for an arc, you can also insert and delete control points, as needed, to reshape the object.

- Objects created with the primitive tools on Row 1 also can be graphically manipulated using the Edit Surface tool, located immediately after the Edit Controls tool on Row 4. Try it. You'll find that this tool allows you to move the *surface* of the object at the selection point, rather than its controls. The little arrow that appears on the surface at the point you click on represents the normal to the surface at that point.

Both the Edit Controls and Edit Surface tools are used to modify nurbz and patch objects as well, and have a number of options associated with these editing functions. We'll study these in detail in Workshop 6 (Going Organic). For now, explore the use of these tools, particularly the Edit Controls tool, on different kinds of objects.

5.3 Editing Lines

We'll now look at a set of tools that are used for carrying out specific transformations on segments, vector lines, arcs, splines, and other line objects, which we'll collectively refer to as *lines* in this section. Very often, such lines are created as the base elements for generating 3D solids and they need to be manipulated in ways that 3D solids don't. The first six tools in the left column of Row 11 bundle together a large number of line-manipulation functions that you'll find extremely helpful in certain situations. Let's see how they work.

- Clear the graphics window of all objects and switch to the Top view. Select the 2D Surface mode and create a number of open and closed shapes. Let some of the shapes intersect with each other.

- Let's start with the first tool, Break (M-Tool:11a,1), which is used for breaking a continuous line into two parts. Select this tool and apply it to a line, keeping track of where you click on the line to select it. There appears to be no visible change. But if you now apply the Move tool to the line, you'll find that it has been broken into two parts at the point where you clicked on it. Thus, you can move one part of the line away from the other. Object snapping can be used to locate the break point more precisely—for instance, Intersection for breaking a segment or arc at the point where it intersects with another line, Endpoint for breaking up a rectangle at its endpoints, and so on. Note that you need to break at least two points in a closed shape like a rectangle to be able to separate the two broken parts.

- Let's now explore the options of the Break tool. Invoke its dialog (Figure 2.34) and you'll find that the default option you were just using was At Click. It's accompanied by a tolerance distance, which you can change. If you click within this distance from a point, the break happens at the point rather than at the segment you clicked on. The second option, With Line, is used to break one or more lines at their points of intersection with another line. You can preselect any number of lines with the Pick tool, then select the break line after activating the Break tool. Try it.

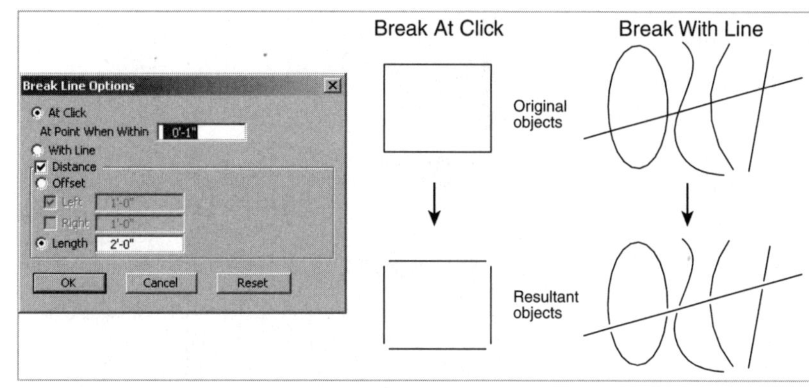

Figure 2.34

The two main operations of the Break tool, along with its dialog.

- It's also possible to create a space before and after the break, which will make the break more visible. This can be done by activating the Distance option and choosing one of two methods. Try out both of them. The Offset method lets you specify a left and right offset distance independently, while the Length method requires you to specify a single value that's equally distributed on both sides of the break. Figure 2.34 illustrates both the At Click and With Line break operations, applied with a break distance.

- Move on to select the next line-editing tool, Close. This is used for converting an open line shape to a closed shape. It has three options in its dialog: Trim, Join, and Connect. Work with all three in turn. Trim connects the two end segments of the line by extending or trimming them at their point of intersection. In contrast, Join deletes the last point of the line and connects the point before it to the first point; thus, the direction of the line is important here. The last option, Connect, simply adds a new segment that connects the first and last points of the line. All three methods of closing lines are illustrated in Figure 2.35. Of all three options, only Join maintains the curvature of a curved line object. CLOSE

To see the direction of a line object in the Wire Frame mode, select Display > Wire Frame while holding down the option key (Mac) or Ctrl+Shift keys (PC). Go to the Interactive tab of the Wire Frame Options dialog that opens up, and check the Show Direction option under 2D Surface Objects. You'll study this dialog in detail in Workshop 3 (Personalizing Your Environment).

- Select the next tool, Trim. This lets you trim segments of lines against each other, either by extending them or trimming them at their point of intersection. Obviously, the selected segments should not be parallel and must lie on the same plane. With this tool, only the individual segments of 2D shapes get selected, irrespective of what the currently active topological level is. Try it on some segment pairs until you understand how it works. TRIM

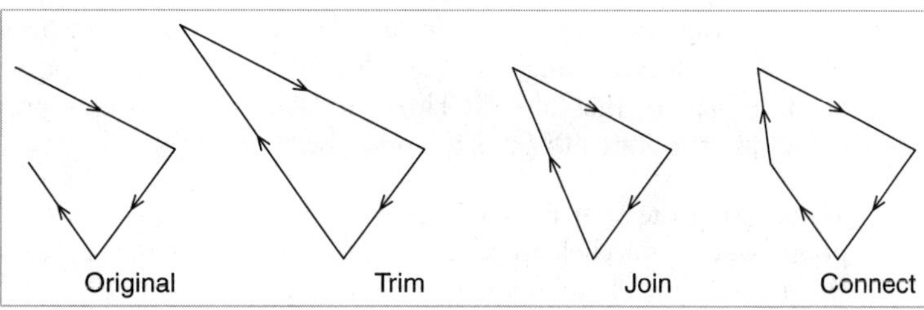

Figure 2.35

The three options of the Close tool. The directions of the lines are also indicated.

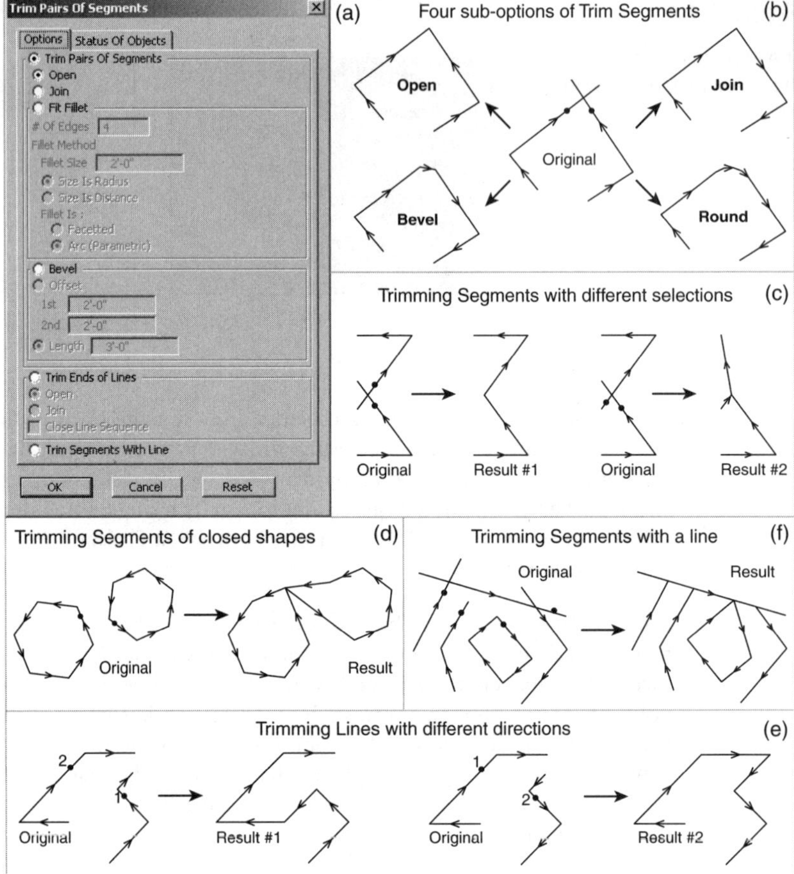

Figure 2.36

The various operations of the Trim tool, along with its dialog. The points where the selections for trimming were made are also indicated.

- Invoke the dialog of the Trim tool (Figure 2.36-a), and you'll find that it has three main options. The default is Trim Pairs Of Segments, which is the operation you just performed. This has four additional sub-options—Open, Join, Fit Fillet, and Bevel. Explore each one of them. The default of Open ensures that the trimmed elements are retained as separate entities. Thus, after trimming them, you can select and transform them independently of each other. Join, on the other hand, not only trims the segments against each other but also joins the separate lines into one continuous line. This could involve a change in the direction of one of the lines, as shown in Figure 2.36-b. Fit Fillet goes a step further—not only does it join the lines into one object, it also rounds the point of intersection by the values listed for the # Of Edges and Fillet Size fields. The fillet is Parametric by default, but you can opt for it to be Facetted instead. The last sub-option, Bevel, works on the same principle, beveling the intersection point by a distance specified in terms of two Offset values or a single Length value. All these four sub-options are illustrated in Figure 2.36-b. Note that for the Join, Fit Fillet, and Bevel sub-options, the original lines are ghosted by default, so the Status Of Objects option becomes applicable.

- When using the Trim Pairs Of Segments option, if a segment extends beyond the intersection point, where you click to select it will determine which part of the segment will be retained (Figure 2.36-c). Therefore, make the selection carefully to get the desired results. Also, see how pairs of closed shapes can be transformed in interesting ways by trimming their segments against each other (Figure 2.36-d).

- Move to the second option of the Trim tool, Trim Ends Of Lines. This is very similar to the first option, except that the operation is applied to entire lines rather than to individual segments of lines. Because of this, the directions of the lines play an important role in determining how they get trimmed, as illustrated in Figure 2.36-e. Again, you have the choice of letting the trimmed lines remain as independent objects (the Open sub-option), or merging them into a single line object (the Join sub-option). Additionally, you can check the Close Line Sequence box if you want to close the resultant shape. The prepicking method can be used to advantage here if a large number of lines is to be trimmed or joined. Of course, you must first ensure that the lines have the appropriate directions, otherwise the operation will give you unexpected results.

- The last option of the Trim tool, Trim Segments With Line, is used to trim one or more segments against a trim line. The trim line itself doesn't get modified in any way. A large number of segments can be prepicked, using the Segment topological level, to be trimmed against the same line, as shown in Figure 2.36-f.

- Move to the fourth line-editing tool in the left column of Row 11, Connect. This has two options in its dialog, Segments and Lines. With the first option, the Connect tool can be used to join two segments by connecting their open ends with a new segment. One end of each segment, therefore, has to be open. The selected segments can belong to the same line or to different lines. In the first case, which is identical to the Connect sub-option of the Close tool, the open line will get transformed to a closed surface. In the second case, illustrated in Figure 2.37-a, the lines will be combined into one open surface. Notice that this may involve a change in the direction of the second line, as shown.

- The second Connect tool option, Lines, is similar to the first except that it operates on lines instead of segments. The line directions play an important part here. As you can see in Figure 2.37-b, the last point of the first line is connected to the first point of the second line. Additionally, if the Close Line Sequence box is checked, the first and last points of the combined line are also connected, resulting in a closed shape as shown. Unlike the Segments option, the directions of the lines being connected never change when the Lines option is used, and the point of selection *on* the line also doesn't matter. Using the prepick method, many lines can be connected at a time by selecting them in the desired sequence.

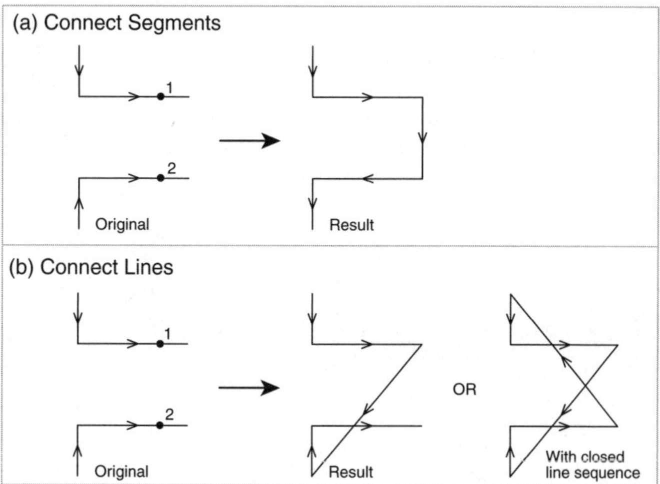

Figure 2.37

The two operations of the Connect tool.

Figure 2.38

Using the Join tool.

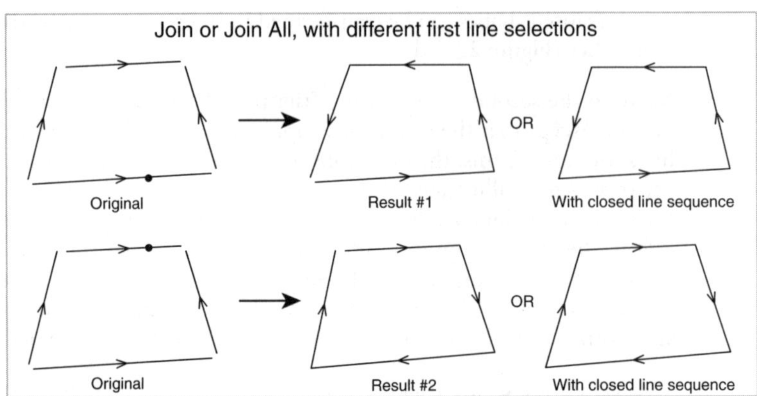

- Move on to the next tool, Join. This is used for joining lines whose endpoints coincide or are located closer than the distance specified in the accompanying Tolerance field. For arcs and splines, no tolerance can be used. More than two lines can be selected by prepicking. Needless to say, this is a very convenient tool because you'll often end up creating separate lines for what should have been a single line. Since you're dealing with lines, direction is again important. The direction of the first line will be applied to the joined object, as shown in Figure 2.38, so make sure you select the appropriate line first.
- Check the Close Line Sequence box in the dialog of the Join tool and reapply it to a set of lines. You'll find that if the distance between the first and last points of the joined line sequence is less than the specified Tolerance value, the line will be converted to a closed shape (Figure 2.38).
- The Join tool has an additional option, Join All. It's similar to Join except that you need to select just one line. This line will then automatically be joined to all the lines with compatible directions whose endpoints are coincident or closer than the Tolerance value. Alternately, just click in the graphics window, away from any object, and all the line sequences that can potentially be joined are done so in a single step. Once you learn about layers, you can choose to restrict the joining to visible layers only.

- The last of the line-editing tools, Fillet/Bevel, can be used to round and bevel the endpoints of a segment. The corresponding options in the dialog of the tool are Fit Fillet and Bevel respectively. You're already familiar with the fillet and bevel concepts from the Trim tool you saw earlier, including the parameters that control the extent of rounding and beveling. The topological level plays an important role for both functions. If Point is selected, a single point is rounded or beveled. If Segment is selected, the operation is applied to both endpoints of the segment. For the other topological levels, all points are affected, leading to potentially interesting shapes as shown in Figure 2.39. Watch out for segment lengths that are too small to permit a fillet of the specified radius, or a bevel of the specified distance.

Figure 2.39

The Fit Fillet and Bevel operations applied to a patterned polygon, with the topological level set to Object.

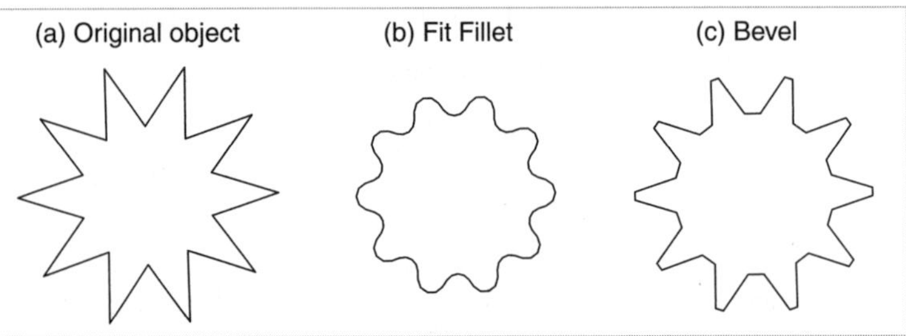

Exercise 6

Insertions: A Convenient Alternative to Booleans

In this exercise, you'll work with the four magenta-colored tools located in the right column of Row 2 of the modeling tool palette. These are the *insertion tools*, used for dividing surfaces and adding and subtracting volumes from existing objects. They can often be used as a convenient alternative to the boolean operations, Union and Difference. The four insertion tools represent four different types of insertion modes, and just like the five object generation tools you saw in Workshop 1 (Letting Yourself Go), they're used in conjunction with the drawing tools on Row 3 to create insertions of various shapes and sizes. Let's see how they work.

- Open a new project or clear the window of all its contents—both ghosted and unghosted—using the corresponding Clear commands in the Edit menu. Create a few 3D solids, both smooth and facetted. These will be used as the base objects on which the insertions will be performed.

Just like a boolean operation, if an insertion is applied to a parametric object, it gets converted to a plain object. If a smooth shape in inserted on a facetted object, the result will be a smooth object.

6.1 Inserting Outlines

- Select M-Tool:2b,1 to set the mode to Insert Outline. This is similar to the Insert Segment tool (M-Tool:11a,8) you used in Section 3.2, except that it can be used to insert not just a single segment, but an entire sequence of lines, a circle, a polygon, or any other desired 2D shape on the face of an object. Also, the face on which the insertion is to be made needs to be prepicked, otherwise an error message is displayed. So go ahead and select a face of any one of your objects by setting the topological level to Face and using the Pick tool.

- Once the face is selected, use one of the drawing tools on Row 3 to draw a shape on it. For an open shape, both endpoints must lie on the *edges* of the face (Figure 2.40-a), so use the appropriate object snapping option. A closed shape, on the other hand, must lie completely *inside* the face (Figure 2.40-b). Experiment with both types of shapes. Since you're in the Insert Outline mode, these shapes are being inserted on the selected face. It's possible to insert multiple outlines within a single face as shown in Figure 2.40-b, provided they don't overlap with each other.

- Just like an inserted segment, an inserted outline divides the face on which it's inserted into two parts. Thereafter, one part can be transformed independently of the other to modify the shape of the object. Again, watch out for non-planar faces, such as those shown in Figure 2.40-a. Also recall from Exercise 3 that object parts cannot be moved for smooth objects.

- The different faces resulting from the insertion of an outline can also be colored in different colors, as shown in Figure 2.40-b. A good application of this would be for façade design in architectural modeling in the early conceptualization phase, when it's too tedious and time-consuming to model the individual openings.

- Notice that an outline gets selected as soon as it's inserted, so it can be moved, or colored in a different color, or transformed in any other manner right away. If you need to do this at a later stage, remember to select the insertion with the topological level set to Face, not to Outline. When a closed shape is inserted on a face using Insert Outline, a new face is created by cutting a "hole" in the original face. Thus, the edges of the new face will coincide with the edges of the outline (i.e., the hole) of the original face. This might make it difficult to select the new face with the Pick tool in the usual fashion—you'll have to resort to the pick parade feature (Section 4.5), or use the Inside Boundaries option for the Pick tool (Section 3.1).

When the Inside Boundaries option for the Pick tool is activated, you don't even need to prepick a face for insertion—it's automatically detected when you start drawing the insertion shape. This applies to all the insertion modes, ranging from Insert Outline to Insert Opening, which otherwise require a face to be preselected.

Figure 2.40

Using the Insert Outline mode.

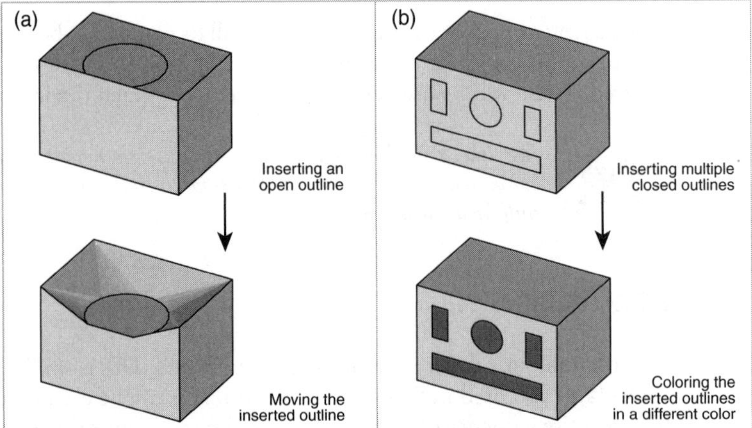

6.2 Inserting Faces

- ▣ Move on to select the next insertion mode, Insert Face. This works on the same principle as Insert Outline, except that a 3D extrusion is now inserted instead of a 2D shape. The height of the inserted extrusion can be preset in the Heights menu, or input interactively by setting Heights to Graphic/Keyed. Choose the latter option for now.

- ▣ Select a face of an object and with the appropriate tool from Row 3, draw any shape on it. For an open shape, remember that the start and end points must lie on the edges of the face.

- ▣ After the base insertion shape is defined, you'll be prompted for the height of the inserted volume. Since Heights is set to Graphic/Keyed, you can drag the volume either *into* the object, or *out* of it. The first action will subtract the volume from the object, and is therefore equivalent to the Difference operation (Figure 2.41-b); the second will add the volume to the object, and is thus equivalent to the Union operation (Figure 2.41-c). If you want to specify the height using the keyboard, use a negative height for subtraction and a positive height for addition.

- ▣ Work with the Insert Face mode some more, using different shapes on different surfaces. Experiment with closed shapes that are *larger* than the faces on which they're being inserted (Figure 2.41-d) and with insertions *within* insertions (Figure 2.41-e), and see how many unique and interesting objects can be generated using these techniques. Notice that when a larger base shape is dragged into the object, it adds to the object instead of subtracting a volume from it.

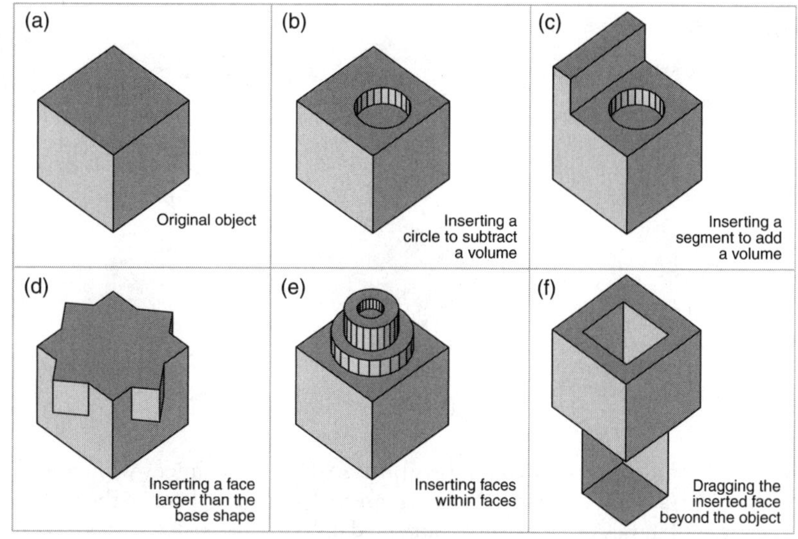

Figure 2.41

Various configurations created using the Insert Face mode.

- Finally, insert a facetted shape on the face of a facetted object and drag it all the way through, beyond the other side. You'll see that the insertion creates the expected hole within the solid where it encounters volume, but beyond the solid where it encounters a void, a volume is created and added. The resulting object isn't quite right, as you can see in Figure 2.41-f. You should, therefore, avoid using `Insert Face` in this manner for facetted objects, but use `Insert Hole` instead. This problem doesn't exist for smooth objects, or when a smooth shape is being inserted on a facetted object (as this operation converts it to a smooth object).

6.3 Inserting Holes

- Select the third insertion mode, `Insert Hole`. This is almost identical to the `Insert Face` mode except that it can only subtract volumes from objects and not add them. Depending upon the height of the insertion that's specified, the subtracted volume can be either a cavity or a hole that extends throughout the depth of the object (see Figure 2.42-a). Unlike the `Insert Face` mode, the inserted shape can be dragged all the way through the object and further beyond—the result will only create a hole without any ill-formed additions at the opposite end like you saw for facetted objects in Figure 2.41-f.

Make sure a preset positive height isn't selected in the Heights menu, otherwise Insert Hole as well as Insert Opening won't work, as they require that negative heights be specified.

- The `Insert Hole` mode provides a neat and efficient way of drilling identical holes on the opposite sides of a 3D enclosure. Try it out. Simply select one of the outer faces on one side of the enclosure and then drag the insertion beyond the corresponding face on the opposite side (Figure 2.42-b).

- Likewise, `Insert Hole` can also be used to drill holes on curved surfaces like that of a cylinder. Draw the insertion shape where the hole is required and drag it into the volume of the cylinder. A cavity or hole will be created, depending on the extrusion height specified (see Figure 2.42-c).

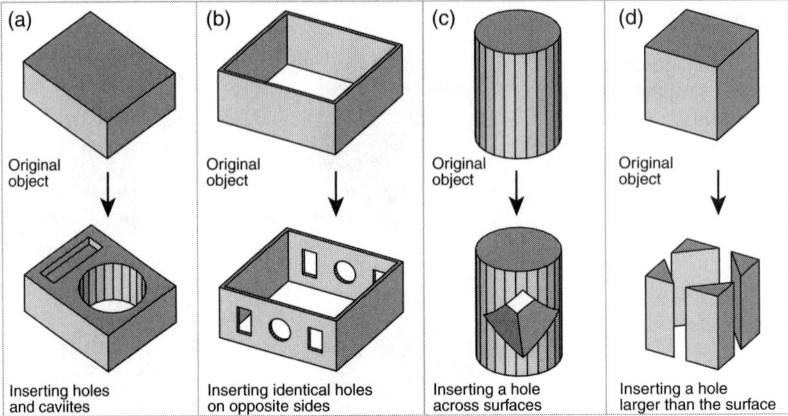

Figure 2.42

Various uses of the Insert Hole mode.

- Finally, just as you did with Insert Face, experiment with closed shapes that are *larger* than the faces on which they're being inserted, dragging them all the way beyond the volume of the object. Figure 2.42-d shows a four-sided polygon inserted diagonally on the top face of a cube, extending beyond its sides. You can see that such an insertion results in discontiguous volumes, similar to what you encountered when working with the Intersection and Difference tools in Workshop 1 (Letting Yourself Go). You already know from that workshop how to deal with such a situation.

6.4 Inserting Openings

- Proceed to select the last insertion mode, Insert Opening. This simply punches holes into objects through the selected face. The difference from the Insert Hole mode is that the height of the insertion doesn't have to be specified—it's simply taken to be the entire depth of the object from the selected face.

- Keep in mind that with the Insert Opening mode, the shape of the opening must lie completely *within* the face on which it's being inserted; it cannot spill over the edges of the face, as it can with the Insert Hole mode. The edge of the opening cannot even *overlap* with the edge of the face. This is demonstrated in Figure 2.43, where all the openings in the 3D enclosure were conveniently made using Insert Opening except the corner one, for which Insert Hole had to be used.

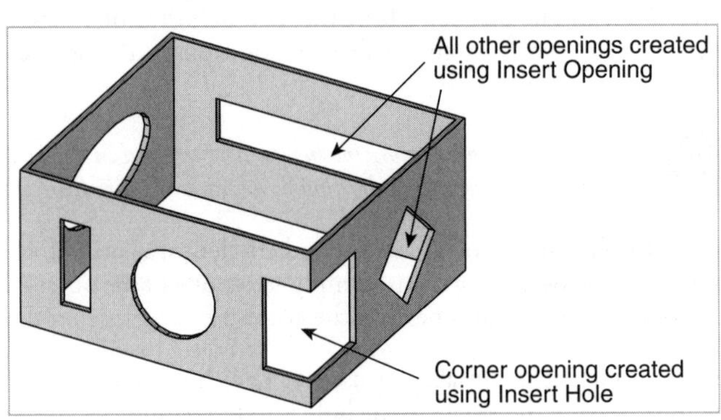

Figure 2.43

Insert Opening is the fastest mode for creating openings in objects, since the extrusion height doesn't have to be specified. However, it cannot be used to create a corner opening as shown.

6.5 Working with Holes and Volumes

Now that you've seen how to add and subtract volumes from objects using Insert Face, Insert Hole, and Insert Opening, let's work with the last topological level in the left column of Row 4, Hole/Volume, that we didn't cover in Exercise 3.

- Set the topological level to Hole/Volume (M-Tool:4a,7). Then use the Pick tool to select a volume that you've added to or subtracted from an object. You can select several of these *holes and volumes*, as they're called. Because the topological level is set appropriately, you'll be able to select just the holes and volumes without selecting the rest of the object.

In general, volumes that are added to an object are easier to select when the first Clicking option in the Pick tool dialog is set to Inside Boundaries rather than On Edges.

- You can now apply any kind of transformation on the selected holes and volumes, provided they remain on the same face. Try it. You'll be able to move, rotate, scale, or mirror them along the surface. You can also perform these transformations in the Copy mode to make additional insertions of the same type on the surface. You can even delete the holes and volumes with the Delete Geometry tool (M-Tool:15b,2), which will restore the object back to its original form. All these operations are illustrated in Figure 2.44. Essentially, inserted holes and volumes can be treated just like any other object in form•Z.

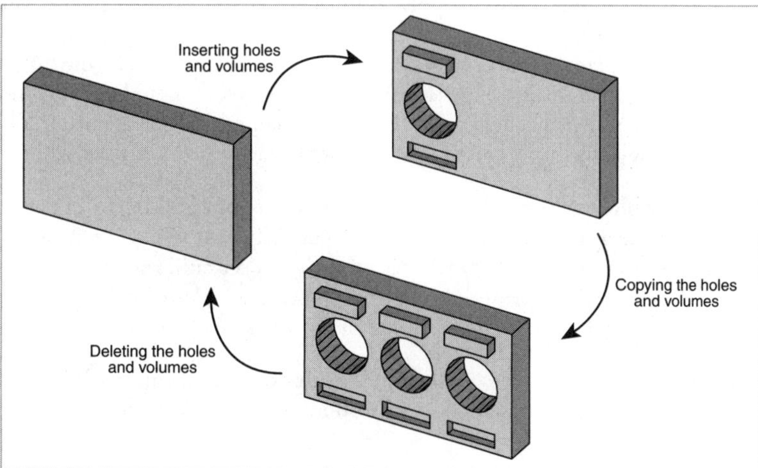

Figure 2.44

Working with the Hole/Volume topological level.

6.6 Triangulation: Getting Rid of Non-Planar Faces

You've seen how objects sometimes acquire non-planar faces when a part of the object such as a point or a segment is moved in a certain way. Examples of such objects were shown in Figures 2.14, 2.15, and 2.40. These objects had been deliberately created, but often, you'll inadvertently create an object with non-planar faces without even realizing it. Such objects are problematic because they may not render accurately in some display modes. Even worse, many operations such as the booleans (and others we haven't yet covered) cannot be applied to them. Let's learn how to recognize this problem when it exists, and then, how to fix it.

Figure 2.45

Working with the Triangulate tool.

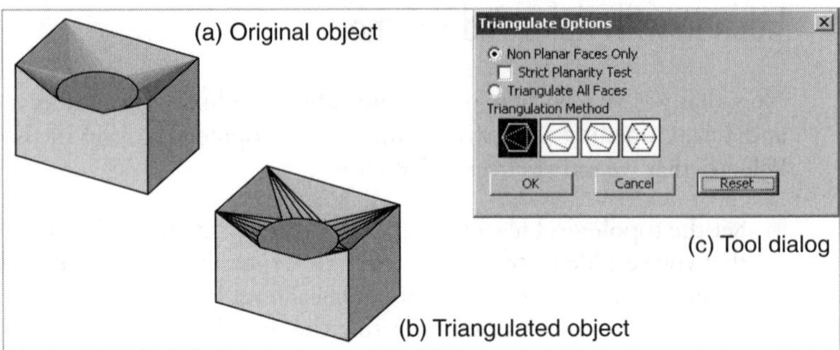

- Create an object with non-planar faces, if you don't have one, by simply moving a point, segment, outline, or face appropriately (Figure 2.45-a). Set the topological level to Object, and apply the Query tool (M-Tool:12b,1) to it. In the Query dialog, the number of non-planar faces that the object has is calculated and displayed, as you saw in Figure 2.20-c. This helps you to check an object for planarity. Normally, form•Z allows a certain tolerance while calculating planarity, but you can make the calculation more sensitive by checking the accompanying Strict Planarity box in the Query dialog.

- When the Query dialog reveals that an object does have non-planar faces (which is obvious for the object in Figure 2.45-a, but may not be in many other cases), and you must retain this object in your model, you can apply a tool to it that will convert the non-planar faces to planar faces. This is the Triangulate tool (M-Tool:6a,10). Select it and apply it to the object. You'll find that all the non-planar faces get subdivided into triangular parts (Figure 2.45-b). Recall from basic geometry that a minimum of three points is needed to define a plane, therefore a triangle is the only polygon that's always planar. The process of triangulation thus rids an object of any non-planar faces it might have. Of course, the number of faces the object has will now increase, as you can see.

- Explore the options of the Triangulate tool by invoking its dialog (Figure 2.45-c). You can choose, once again, to activate the Strict Planarity Test while executing the triangulation operation. You can opt to Triangulate All Faces of the object rather than just the non-planar faces, if you'd like to give it a uniformly triangulated appearance. And finally, you can select between four different triangulation methods for the use of the tool.

With this, we come to the end of the last exercise for this workshop. It's time to take on the challenge of modeling the basic blocks of a building in our Workshop Assignment.

An Architectural Block Model

- *Locate the drawings of any famous building of acclaimed visual composition. Break it down into volumes and model it directly in 3D using the correct proportions. Keep in mind that this is just a massing model, so you're not aiming for full detail or 100% accuracy. You would, however, like to convey an accurate impression of its form.*

The building selected here is the Guggenheim Museum by Frank Lloyd Wright. The process of modeling it will now be demonstrated step by step, accompanied by the graphic window snapshots at the end of each step. You can also refer to the form•Z files for this assignment in the Assignments > Workshop2 folder of the accompanying CD-ROM, if you get stuck at any stage. A color rendering of the project is in the Assignment2.tif file in the same folder.

Setup

Open a new form•Z project. In the **Project Working Units** dialog, select **Feet** as the base unit, set **Numeric Accuracy** to 1' and **Angle Accuracy** to 1°. Invoke the **Window Setup** dialog, and change the **Module** value for all three axes to 10' with 5 **Divisions**.

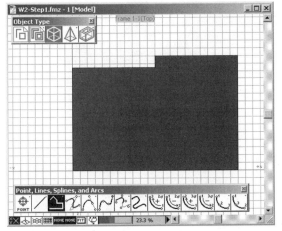

Step 1

We'll first model the base, i.e., the site, as a thin slab. Choose an appropriate color from the **Surface Styles** palette, switch to the **Top** view, and set **Heights** to a preset value of 1'. Set the object generation mode to **3D Extrusion**, and select the **Vector Line** tool from Row 3.

Using direct numeric input, specify the first point as [0,0,0] in the **Prompts** palette in absolute mode. Then change the mode to relative, and specify the remaining points as follows:

Pt #2: [220] (Since both the y and z coordinates are 0, they can be omitted from the input.)
Pt #3: [0,150] Pt #4: [-110]
Pt #5: [0,-15] Pt #6: [-110]
Pt #7: [c] (Type in a "c" for closing the line sequence)

Step 2

Change the object generation mode to **2D Surface**. We'll use it to draw some construction lines that will be deleted later. We can either draw them in the correct position to begin with, or draw them coinciding with the axes and then move them to where they should be. For example, for the first line, located 35' inside from the lower horizontal site line, input [-10, 35] as the absolute coordinates of the first point and [240] as the relative coordinates of the second point. The second point can also be specified graphically.

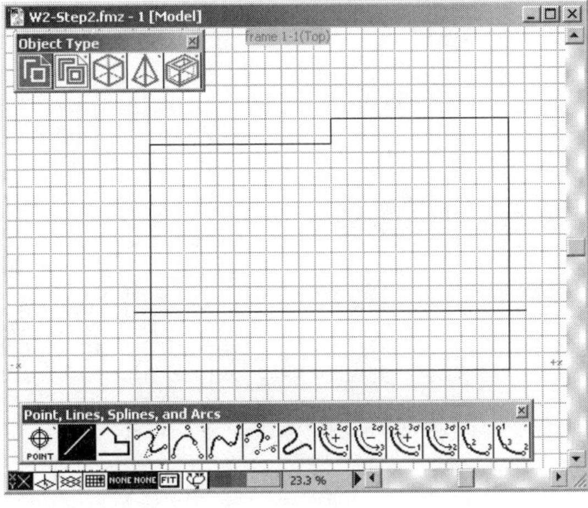

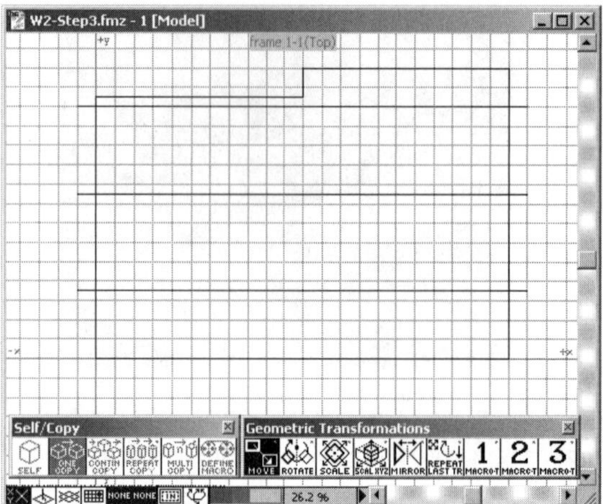

Step 3

Set the self-copy mode on Row 12 to **One Copy**. Select the line you just drew with the **Move** tool, and specify [0,50] as the relative coordinates of the move. Repeat the process with the same line, this time with relative coordinates of [0,95].

Step 4

Similarly, draw vertical construction lines 15' inside from the left end, and 25' inside from the right end. Notice how easy this is because you started with [0,0,0] as the first point. You can do all this graphically, by setting **Grid Snap** to 5'.

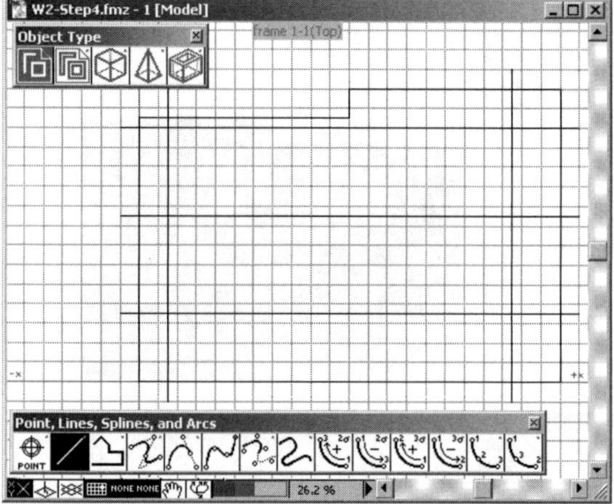

Step 5

Make copies of the left and right construction lines, 50' and 95' inside respectively.

Step 6

Select the Cylinder tool (M-Tool:1a,3), and set the construction option to 3 Points in its dialog. Use the construction lines to inscribe two cylinders with diameters of 50' and 95' and heights of 52' and 28' respectively. These will be referred to as Block1 and Block2 respectively. The blocks need to actually be a little smaller—the construction lines you've created are for drawing the second level later. To resize them, apply the Query tool (M-Tool:12ab,1) to each of them individually, click on the Edit button, and set the Radius X and Radius Y values to 20' for Block1 and 46' for Block2. The cylinders will be resized but their centers will remain in the same position.

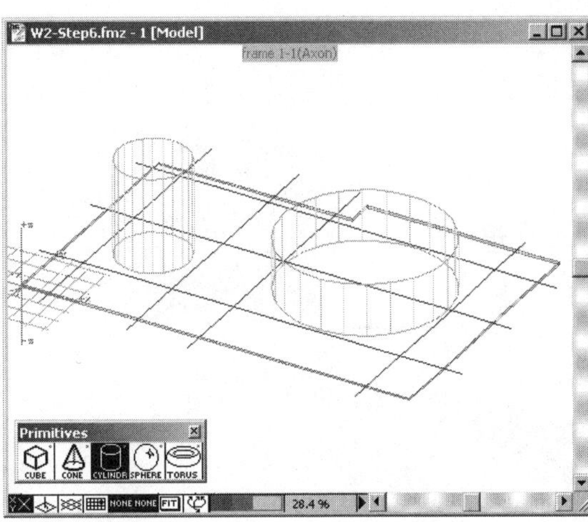

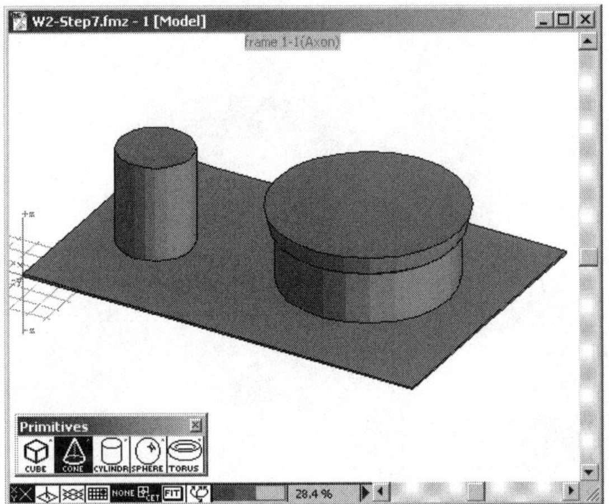

Step 7

We'll now start modeling the four landmark cylindrical blocks that sit on top of Block2. Since their sides are inclined, we'll be modeling them as truncated cones. Select the Cone tool (M-Tool:1a,3), and in its dialog, set the construction option to Preset and check the Truncated Cone option. Enter the following preset values in the dialog—Radius X as 49', Radius Y as 49', Height as 10', and Top Is 105% Of Base. Back in the graphics window, activate the Center Of Face snapping option, and click on the center of the top face of Block2 as the center point for positioning the cone.

Apply the Move tool to translate this cone by a distance of 2' in the +Z direction. This will create the required gap between Block2 and the cone.

Step 8

The second inclined block sitting on top of the first one is similar to it in all respects, except that it is larger along the X and Y directions. You could, of course, model it by following the same steps as the first block. However, it would be easier to simply make a copy of the first cone and then resize it. Set the topological level to Object, set the self-copy modifier to One Copy, and use the Move tool to make a copy of the cone exactly 12' above it. Then apply the Query tool to it. Click on the Edit button and change the Radius X and Radius Y values to 52' instead of 49'. Switch to the Front, Right, or any other elevation view to make sure you have the correct results.

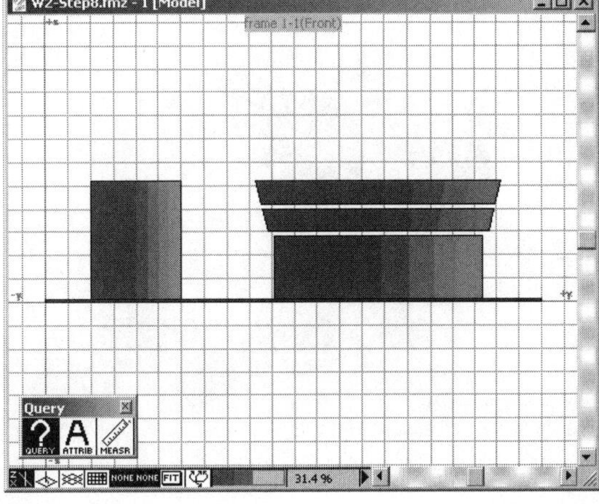

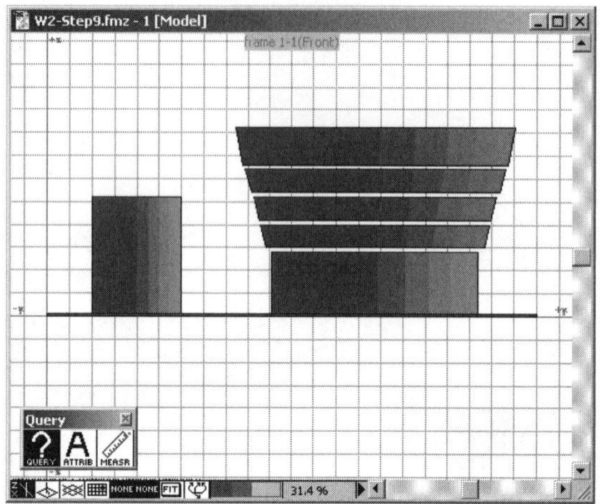

Step 9

Repeat Step 8 twice to create two more inclined blocks, sitting on top of the first two. Set the radius values of the third block to 56' and that of the fourth block to 60'. The last block is actually a little taller than the first three, so set its height value to 16' instead of 10'.

Step 10

To quickly fill in the gaps between all these blocks, apply the Query tool to the original base cylinder, Block2, and use the Edit option to change its height value to 86' instead of 28'. It'll now project beyond the top face of the last inclined block. This is a quick fix rather than an accurate solution for what are actually strips of glazing sitting between the stacked blocks. However, it's acceptable, since our aim at this stage is to create a massing model that can approximate the appearance of the building, rather than a fully accurate, detailed model.

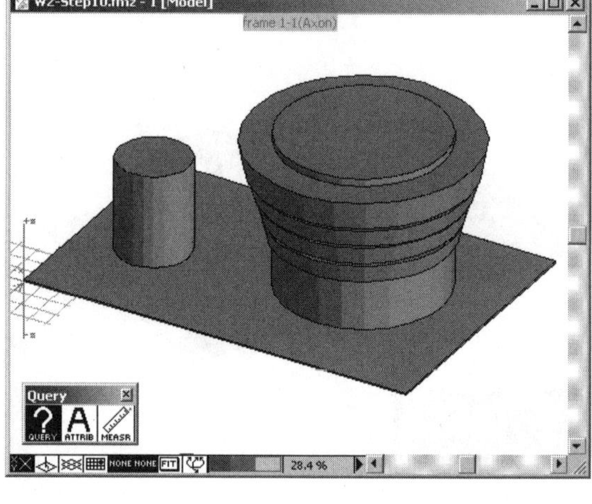

Step 11

Next, you'll create a conical skylight sitting on the top face of Block2. Choose a color from the Surface Styles palette that's appropriate to glass. Select the Cone tool again, but this time, set its construction option back to Radius and deselect the Truncated Cone option. Using the Center Of Face snap, select the center of the top face of Block2 for positioning the cone. In the Prompts palette, specify the radius of the cone as 46' and its height as 16'. Block2 will be crowned with a conical roof as required.

Use the Group tool to bring Block2 and all the objects sitting on top of it into one group.

Step 12

Now turn your attention to Block1, the smaller cylinder you created in Step 6. It should have a square block positioned about 8' below its top face. We'll tackle this next. Set object snapping to Intersection. Use the Cube tool (M-Tool:1a,1), and snap to the intersection of the construction lines to create a square block with a height of 8', sitting on the XY plane around Block1.

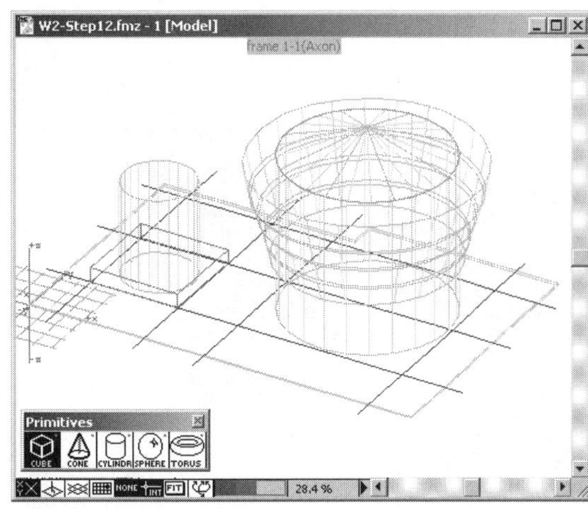

Step 13

The length of the side of the square block is currently 50'. This has to be changed to 45'. As with the earlier blocks, use the Query tool and its Edit option to change the width and depth values of the block to 45'.

Step 14

Two additional operations need to be performed on the square block before it's correct. First, move it vertically upwards by a distance of 36'. Then set the topological level on Row 4 to Face. Select the Scale tool (M-Tool:13a,3), set the option in its dialog to Scale By Absolute Value, and apply it to the top face of the block. Change both the X and the Y values from 45' to 47', and click OK in response to the message telling you that the object will be converted to Plain. The sides of the square block will now have the correct inclination.

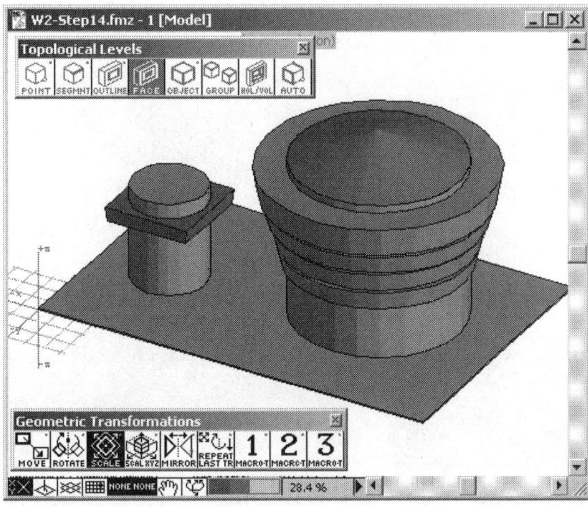

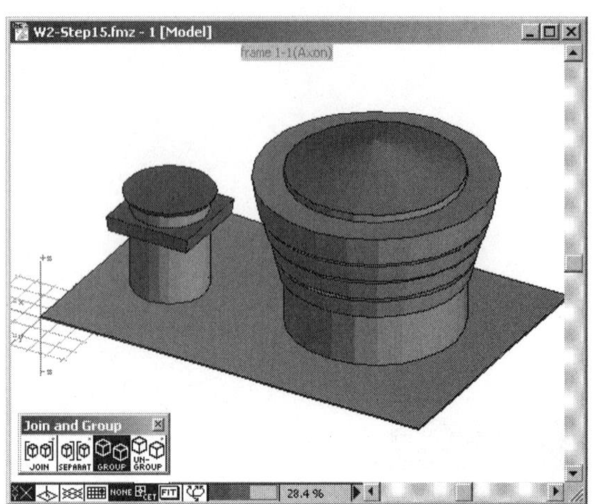

Step 15

The next step is to add an inclined cylindrical roof slab to the top of Block1. Select the Cone tool, and in its dialog, set the construction option to Preset and check the Truncated Cone option. Enter the following preset values—Radius X as 23', Radius Y as 23', Height as 2', and Top Is 103% Of Base. In the graphics window, activate the Center Of Face snapping option, and click on the center of the top face of Block1 as the center point for positioning the preset truncated cone.

This completes Block1. Just as you did for Block2, group Block1 and its related objects together using the Group tool.

Step 16

Next, we'll add the 100' tall rectangular block at the back of the building. Set object snapping to Endpoint and select the Cube tool. For the first point, snap to the upper left corner of the site, as shown. Then turn to the Prompts palette. Specify [45,-30,0] as the relative coordinates for the second point, and the height as 100'.

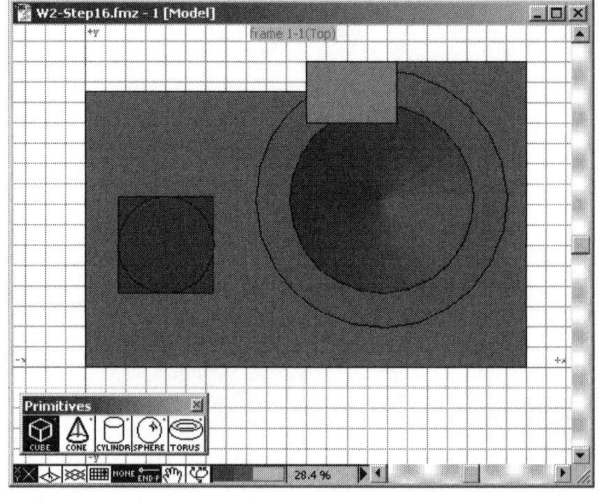

Step 17

Complete the back corner of the building by using the Cube tool to add a 27' high square block of side 65', starting from the upper right corner of the site as shown. Use Endpoint snap and relative coordinates of [-65,-65,0].

Step 18

Finally, we'll model the second level that projects beyond the first level, using the construction lines we drew earlier. Preset a height of 16' in the Heights menu. Invoke the Object Snaps Options dialog and select the option, Project Onto Reference Plane, in the Projection Views section. Also, open the Objects palette and make all the objects in the two groups you had created earlier invisible by clicking twice on the diamond icon.

Switch to the Top view, and set the object generation mode on Row 2 to 3D Extrusion. Using the Vector Line and Arc tools, and with the help of the construction lines and appropriate object snapping, model the extruded shape as shown. This will be created on the XY plane because of the Project Onto Reference Plane option active in the Object Snaps dialog.

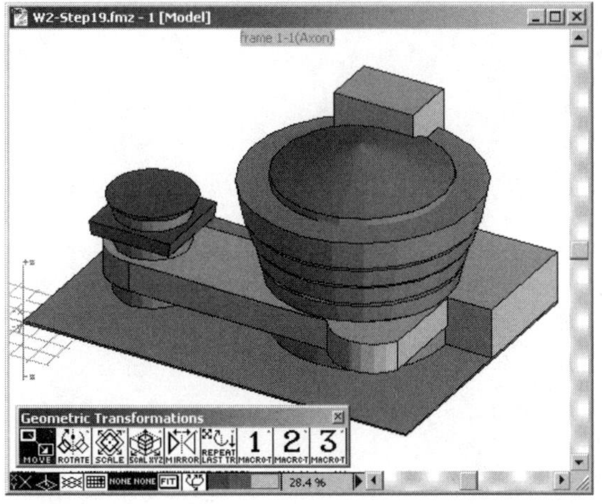

Step 19

Move the block you just created vertically upwards by a distance of 12'. Restore the visibility of the grouped cylindrical blocks by clicking in the third column of the Objects palette.

Step 20

Finish the model by deleting all the 2D construction lines you had created in the beginning.

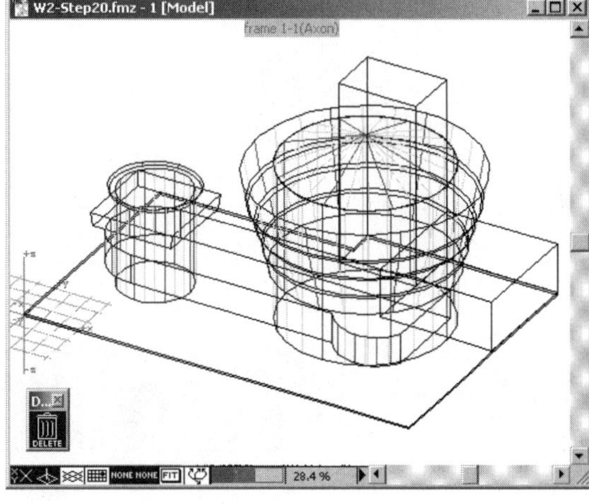

You now have the massing model of the world-famous Guggenheim Museum, which you were able to model quite accurately in form•Z with the knowledge gained from just two workshops. The process was long but relatively straightforward, as you've seen. It would've helped to make use of multiple layers and reference planes, as well as to be able to view the model from different angles. All these aspects of form•Z and more will be covered in Workshop 3, coming up next.

Personalizing Your Environment

You've covered a lot of the form•Z basics in the last two workshops and should be well equipped, by now, to model projects of some complexity. However, you've so far been confined to the default settings of form•Z. For instance, you've been working only with the predefined colors in the Surface Styles palette, the predefined views in the Views menu, the three predefined reference planes, and so on. Eventually, you'll need to go beyond these defaults and define your own settings, depending upon your style of working and the needs of the project at hand.

In Workshop 3, you'll accomplish precisely this—customizing your modeling environment to suit your requirements. You'll learn how to modify the default project colors and create new surface styles, as well as change the way the various display options work. You'll go on to see how you can enhance your efficiency using multiple layers, and create and save your own reference planes and views of the modeling world. Finally, you'll learn how to save the modified settings as preference files and template files, which you can then recall for use in other projects when needed.

EXERCISE 1

Your Own Colors and Styles

This exercise will briefly lead you through the process of defining your own surface styles, to add to the predefined ones you find in the Surface Styles palette. If you have the non-RenderZone version of form•Z, you'll have the Colors palette instead of the Surface Styles palette. However, the basic procedure for creating and managing your colors remains the same, so go through the complete exercise and make the appropriate inferences to work with the Colors palette.

Let's first look at how to change the default color settings of the form•Z interface.

1.1 Customizing Project Colors

form•Z makes use of certain colors for different components of its user interface by default. Thus, the background color of the graphics window that you see when you launch the program is white, the reference plane grid is in teal, the axes are in red, the highlight color to indicate selection is again red, ghosted objects are colored in gray, and so on. These are referred to as *project colors* because they can be different for different projects.

- Launch form•Z and save the default modeling window that appears as a new project using File > Save As. Close all palettes except Prompts and Surface Styles.
- To see the list of default color settings for the current project, select Project Colors from the first group of the Options menu. This will invoke the Project Colors dialog which lists all the display colors used in the project (Figure 3.1).
- To change any of these colors to suit your requirements, simply click on the associated box. Thus, for instance, to change the Highlight color to something other than red, click on the red-colored box next to it. You'll be presented with the standard color selection dialog for your operating system (Mac or PC), from which you can choose a different color (see Figure 3.4-b). If you now return to the graphics window, create an object, and select it with the Pick tool, you'll find that the selection color is the new one you specified rather than the original red color.
- Similarly, you can change any of the other colors as well. The most commonly changed project color is Background—usually set to black or dark gray instead of the default of white. It may be a little hard on the eyes but can make for nice presentations (Figure 3.2).

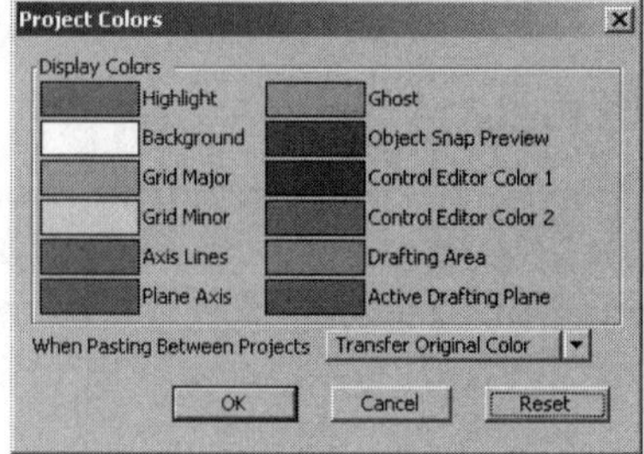

Figure 3.1

The Project Colors dialog, showing the display colors used for various components of the form•Z interface.

Figure 3.2

A different look to the graphics window, created by selecting a dark background color. form•Z automatically adjusts the object color in displays such as Hidden Line so that it contrasts with the background.

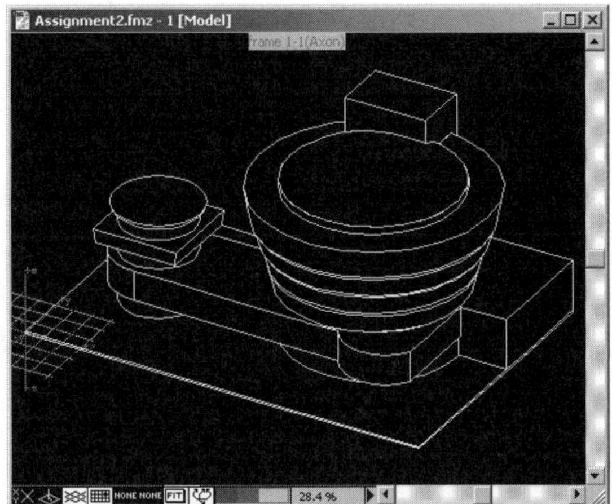

- The Project Colors dialog also gives you three options for dealing with the colors of objects created in other files that are pasted into the current project. The default is to transfer the original color of the object. If that color doesn't exist in the Surface Styles palette, it will be added to it as a new color. If you don't wish the color to be transferred, you can opt for using either the active color or the best matching color in the current palette.

1.2 Creating a New Surface Style

We have, so far, often been using the word *color* for what is actually a *surface style*. This is because, until now, we've worked only with the plain colors present in the Surface Styles palette; therefore, using the term *surface style* would have only led to confusion. A surface, however, can actually have various attributes in addition to color such as reflection, transparency, and bumps, which is why the more fancy term *surface style* is used instead of simply *color*. In this exercise, we'll take a brief look at how to define and use surface styles with different attributes. More complicated aspects such as sizing styles and mapping them accurately on an object will be covered in Workshop 5 (Illuminating, Texturing, and Rendering Your World).

- Turn your attention to the Surface Styles palette. Unless you've already modified it in some manner, you should see eight styles immediately visible in the palette. There are sixteen in all by default—scroll down the palette to see the rest. Alternately, you can increase the size of the palette window until all the styles are visible (Figure 3.3-a). As you can see, all of these are plain color styles without any other surface attributes.

Figure 3.3

Working with the Surface Styles palette. (a) Resizing it so that all the default styles are visible. (b) Scrolling down to the bottom to define a new style.

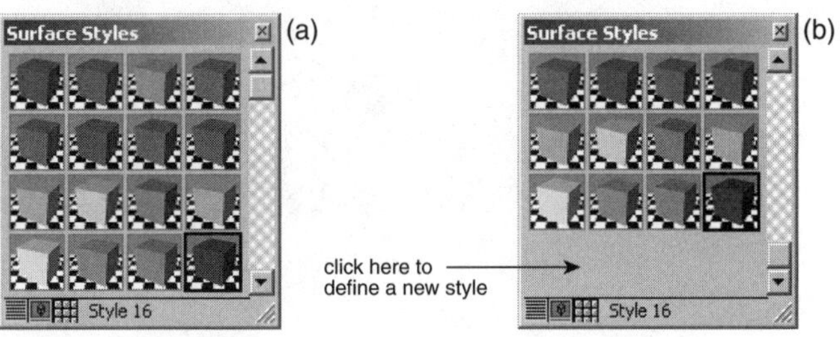

- Let's now add a new surface style to the default ones that exist in the Surface Styles palette. Scroll down to the bottom of the palette until you come to the blank white row (Figure 3.3-b). Click anywhere in this blank space. The Surface Style Parameters dialog is invoked for defining a new style (Figure 3.4-a). Here, you can change its default name and specify different *shaders* for the Color, Reflection, Transparency, and Bumps attributes from their respective pulldown menus. The large number of shaders allows you to create, literally, an infinite number of unique surface styles.

- By default, the Color attribute is set to Plain Color, as you can see from the dialog in Figure 3.4-a. If you want to create a plain style but of a different color, click on the Options button associated with the Plain Color shader. The standard color selection dialog for your operating system will be invoked (Figure 3.4-b shows the PC dialog), from which you can select the color you want for the new style. Exit the dialog after making your selection.

- On the other hand, you can create a *textured* surface style by choosing one of the other shaders for the Color attribute instead of Plain Color. Open up the Color attribute pulldown menu in the Surface Style Parameters dialog and select, for instance, the Brick, Simple shader. Click on the associated Options button, and you'll be presented with a new dialog where you can modify various parameters such as the color and proportions of the brick and the mortar (Figure 3.5). Experiment with changes in these parameters and see how they affect the resulting texture.

- Explore also the various shaders for Reflection, Transparency, and Bumps in the same manner. You can use the Copy From option in the dialog to copy the parameters of any existing surface style and apply them to the current one. Keep in mind that for a new surface style to be actually created with the selected or copied parameters, you've to exit the Surface Style Parameters dialog by clicking on the OK button. To create additional styles, invoke the dialog again by clicking on the blank space in the Surface Styles palette, as you did before.

Figure 3.4

The Surface Style Parameters dialog for defining a new surface style. A plain color is being selected for the Color attribute of the style.

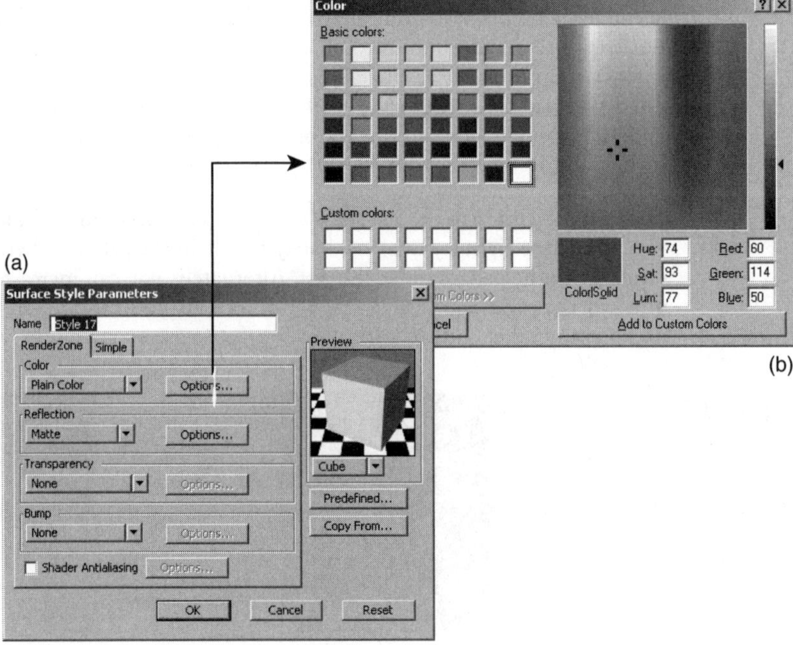

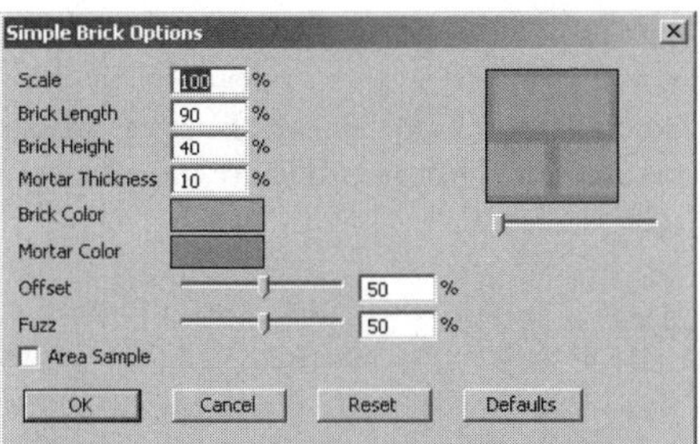

Figure 3.5

The parameters associated with the Simple Brick shader for the Color attribute of a surface style.

- form•Z also has a number of predefined textures for different types of surfaces. Click on the Predefined button in the Surface Style Parameters dialog to access these textures. You can choose from among ten different categories of materials available here (Figure 3.6). After you've finished making a selection, click on Apply Selected Material to return to the main dialog. You'll find that all four attributes in the Surface Style Parameters dialog will now have acquired shader options appropriate to the material selected. Additional modifications to these attributes can be made in the accompanying Options dialogs. For instance, you could select Glass as a predefined material and then simply change its Color attribute to obtain glass of a different color.

- Create at least three or four new textured surface styles with different attributes. Then get back to the graphics window and create some objects using these styles. Switch to the RenderZone display mode to see the fully rendered display. The proportion of a texture with respect to the size of the object might not be satisfactory, but don't worry about that for now. You'll learn how to map these textured styles precisely on the surfaces of objects in Workshop 5 (Illuminating, Texturing, and Rendering Your World).

- Switch to the other display modes in turn, and you'll find that even the textured objects are displayed in plain color only. Basically, RenderZone is the only display mode capable of showing *all* the attributes of a surface style that you just manipulated (which is why it's also the slowest).

- Double-click on any one of the textured surface styles you created in the Surface Styles palette to invoke its Surface Style Parameters dialog. Notice that the Color, Reflection, Transparency, and Bumps attributes are grouped together under the RenderZone tab (Figure 3.4-a), indicating that these are applicable only to the RenderZone display. There's an additional option here called Shader Antialiasing, which will be discussed in Workshop 5 (Illuminating, Texturing, and Rendering Your World).

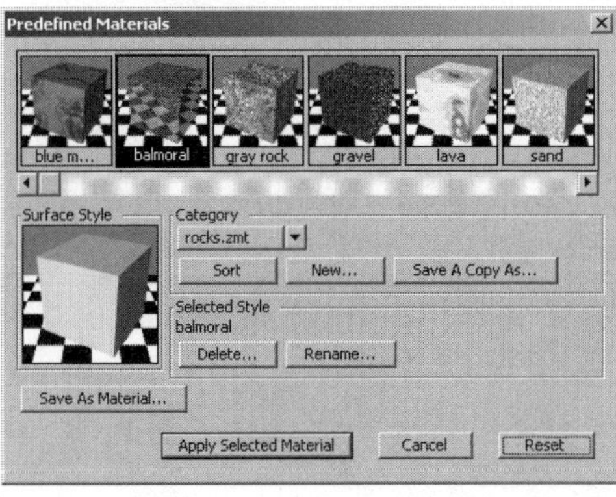

Figure 3.6

Selecting a predefined material for a surface style.

- Switch to the Simple tab in Surface Style Parameters dialog. This has options for specifying the color and transparency of a surface style as it appears in all the non-RenderZone displays. The default color is a RenderZone Average, but you can choose the Custom option instead, and specify the desired color and transparency. Different display modes deal with transparency in different ways, as we shall see in Exercise 2.

This is just the tip of the iceberg as far as creating and applying surface styles is concerned. As mentioned, we'll revisit this aspect of form•Z in more detail in Workshop 5. You'll then be able to carry out more precise and sophisticated texture mapping. For now, it's sufficient to have a basic understanding of how various surface styles can be created and applied to objects.

1.3 Editing and Managing Existing Surface Styles

- You've seen that to modify an existing surface style, you need to simply double-click on it in the Surface Styles palette. The same Surface Style Parameters dialog that you saw in Figure 3.4-a is invoked, allowing you to make the required modifications to the attributes of the style.

- All the surface styles in a project are managed through the Surface Styles dialog, which can be invoked in two ways: click anywhere inside the Surface Styles palette while holding down the option key (Mac) or Ctrl+Shift keys (PC), or go to Options > Surface Styles. The Surface Styles dialog is similar to the Objects dialog you saw in Section 3.5 of the last workshop, with identical options. You can highlight any style and move it to the top or the bottom of the palette, delete it, edit it (which will again invoke the Surface Style Parameters dialog), or make a copy of it. You can use New to create new styles to add to the palette, Sort to sort all the styles by name, and Purge to delete all the styles that haven't been used in the project. The last option, Load Surface Styles, can be conveniently used to import the styles you created in another project into the current one.

Now that we have our choice of project colors and surface styles up and running, we can proceed to learn how to modify the various displays through which these colors and styles are seen.

EXERCISE 2

Controlling the Displays

You were briefly introduced to the various display modes under the Display menu in Section 1.11 of Workshop 1 (Letting Yourself Go). Since then, you must have switched frequently between these different kinds of displays in the course of your work and must be well acquainted with each of them. However, you probably didn't realize that there's a lot more to each display than what meets the eye. Each comes with its own extensive set of options that can be adjusted to suit your requirements, thereby giving you greater control over how your modeling world appears in the graphics window. In this exercise, we'll explore the options for all display modes except RenderZone and the Sketch Render plug-in, which will be covered along with texture mapping and imaging in Workshop 5 (Illuminating, Texturing, and Rendering Your World).

- Continue working with the project you have from the last exercise, or open up any other project such as the Assignment from Workshop 2 (Bringing a Sense of Scale). In the course of the exercise, you'll see this project using different displays, modifying the options of each. To access these options, go to Display > Display Options. This will open up the Display Options dialog that has buttons leading to the options for each individual display mode. Alternately, you can bypass this dialog and go directly to the dialog of a particular display mode by selecting it from the Display menu while holding down the option key (Mac) or Ctrl+Shift keys (PC).

2.1 Wire Frame Options

- Invoke the dialog for the Wire Frame display mode using one of these two methods. You'll find that its options are categorized under two separate tabs: Wire Frame and Interactive.
- Try out each option in the Wire Frame tab first, and see how it affects the display (Figure 3.7-a). Show Back Faces, for instance, shows the back faces of objects in addition to their front faces. Deselecting this option will hide the back faces, useful for partially simulating a Hidden Line display in much less time. If the colors of some objects are so similar to the background color that they can hardly be seen, you can deselect the Show Color option; this will display all the objects in a single color that contrasts with the background. You're already familiar with the Hide Ghosted options from Section 3.7 of Workshop 1 (Letting Yourself Go).
- The display of smooth objects in wire frame mode comprises two separate components, facets and iso lines. You can control the color intensity of both these components separately using the options in the Smooth Objects section. You can also turn off the display of facets altogether, as demonstrated in Figure 3.7-b for a sphere.

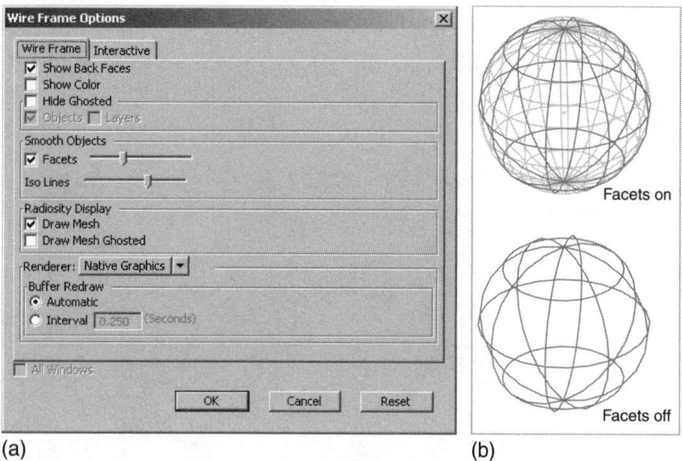

Figure 3.7

The Wire Frame tab of the Wire Frame Options dialog, and the result of deselecting the Facets display for Smooth Objects.

- With regard to the remaining options, ignore Radiosity Display for now. This will become clear once you do radiosity in Workshop 5 (Illuminating, Texturing, and Rendering Your World). The Renderer option lets you choose the renderer for the wire frame rendering. It currently has two options, Native Graphics and OpenGL, each with its own sub-options. Future plug-ins can provide more Renderer options. The OpenGL option is active only when it's installed on the system, and its performance depends upon the graphics card and memory—it can be faster than Native Graphics given a superior hardware configuration. The Buffer Redraw option for the Native Graphics renderer controls screen refresh rates. A window redraw buffer stores the window image information, which is used to refresh the screen almost instantaneously when a palette is moved or windows are switched. Stick with the default Automatic option, which lets the system determine how frequently to update the screen from the buffer.

Most often, the default options set for a display are the most common and useful ones.

- Now switch to the Interactive tab of the Wire Frame Options dialog (Figure 3.8-a). Most of the Show options in the beginning are quite self-explanatory. Try them all out.
- You're already acquainted with the Show Direction option under the 2D Surface Objects section, which you activated while working with the line-editing tools in Section 5.3 of Workshop 2 (Bringing a Sense of Scale). You can select the Show First Point option as well. Both options are useful in a variety of operations you'll work with in due course.
- Recall from Section 3.5 of Workshop 2 that the Objects dialog gives you various options for locating the object axes and centroid of an object. These can be actually displayed in the graphics window by selecting the Show Object Axes and Show Centroid options. Once displayed (see Figure 3.8-b), you can snap to them and use them as a reference for any further operation.
- The remaining options such as those dealing with marked points, lights, cameras, text objects, and symbols will become comprehensible as and when you cover these topics in later exercises and workshops. You can ignore them for now, but do come back and explore them once the corresponding topics are learned.
- As far as the All Windows option at the base of the Wire Frame Options dialog is concerned, recall from Section 2.1 of Workshop 2 (Bringing a Sense of Scale) that this will be activated if multiple windows are open for the project, allowing you to apply the modified display settings to all the windows. The same option exists for all the other display modes as well.

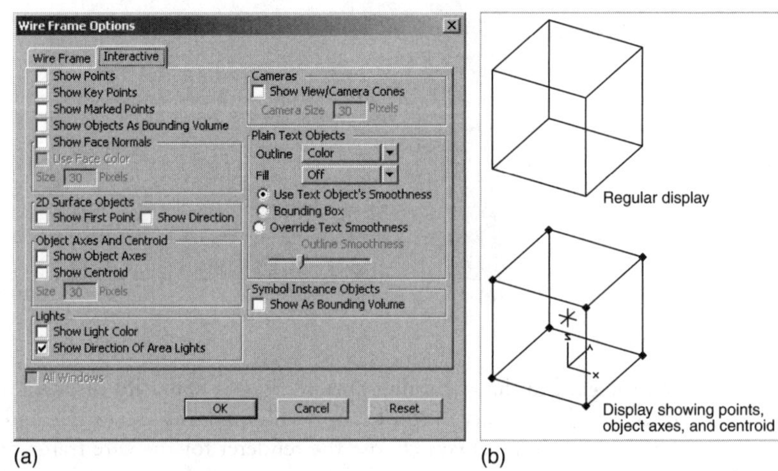

Figure 3.8

The Interactive tab of the Wire Frame Options dialog, and the result of activating the Show Point, Show Object Axes, and Show Centroid options for a cube.

2.2 Interactive Shaded Options

- Next, invoke the dialog of the Interactive Shaded display mode. Just like the Wire Frame display, you'll find that its options are categorized under two separate tabs. Of these, the Interactive tab is identical to the Interactive tab of the Wire Frame display we just covered. So we'll focus only on the options in the Shaded tab (see Figure 3.9-a). Recall that this display mode enables you to carry out interactive modeling of objects using shaded surfaces rather than lines.

- The Show Edges option, when activated, displays the edges of the object in addition to its surfaces. To display these edges in the color of the object, also select the sub-option, Show Object Color. To see the transparency attribute of objects with transparent surface styles in this display mode, check the Transparencies option. The Hide Ghosted options are already familiar to you.

- In Workshop 5 (Illuminating, Texturing, and Rendering Your World), you'll learn how to map images as textures to the faces of objects. Such textures are usually visible only in the RenderZone display mode. By activating the Textures option, such image-based textures can also be seen in Interactive Shaded. The subsequent Fog option allows you to give a fog-like effect to the scene, with sub-options for modifying the color of the fog and other settings. However, keep in mind that these two features don't help in the main purpose of this display mode, which is to enable shaded interactive modeling, so I recommend that you leave them turned off. Otherwise, they will needlessly slow down your modeling activity.

- The Lights options won't be comprehensible until we deal with lights in Workshop 5. So stick with the default options for now, but come back to explore the alternatives once lights are covered. The Project Rendering Options button at the base of the dialog leads you to some additional rendering options that are covered in Section 2.6.

- The last option, Highlight Edge Size, lets you specify a pixel width for object parts such as points, segments, faces, etc. when they're selected in this display mode. Figure 3.9-b shows an exaggerated width of 10 pixels for a face that has been selected. Complete objects and groups, when selected, get fully shaded in the highlight color.

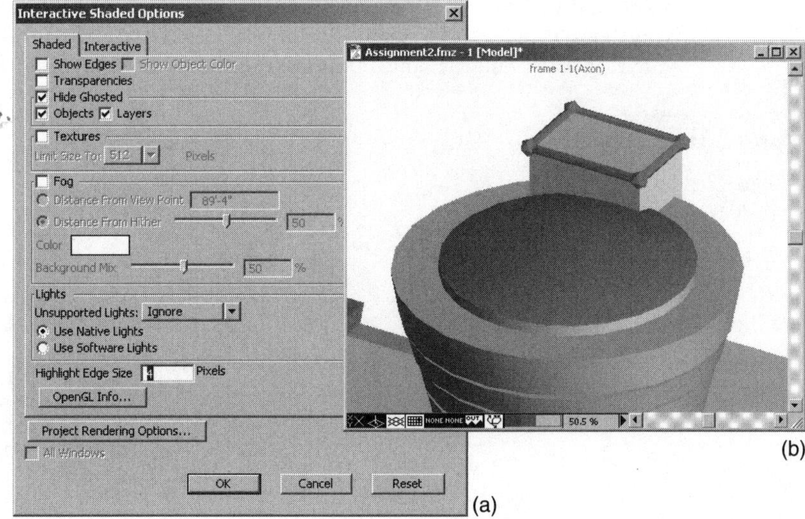

Figure 3.9

The Shaded tab of the Interactive Shaded dialog, and the effect of setting Highlight Edge Size to 10 pixels.

2.3 Quick Paint and Surface Render Options

- Next, invoke the dialogs of the Quick Paint and Surface Render display modes in turn and look at their options (Figure 3.10). These are similar and should, by now, be quite self-explanatory. One option that you can expect to activate quite frequently is Render With Shadows, particularly for Surface Render, and you'll begin doing so when you deal with lights and shadows in Workshop 5 (Illuminating, Texturing, and Rendering Your World). For transparent objects, you've the option of showing them As Wire Frame to distinguish them from other objects that are shown with shaded surfaces.

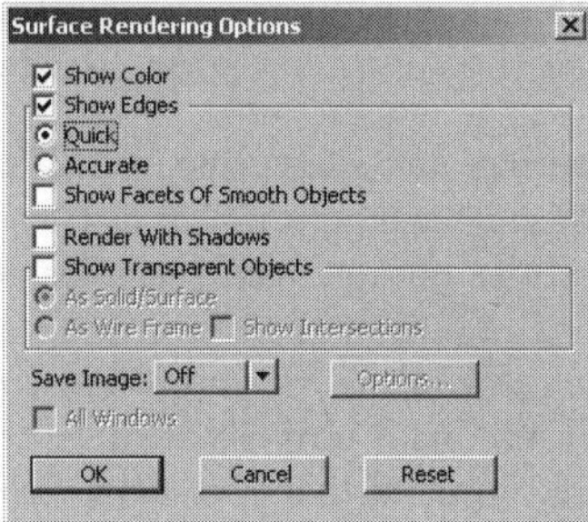

Figure 3.10

The dialog showing the options for the Surface Render display mode.

- For final renderings in Surface Render, it's a good idea to choose Accurate rather than Quick for the Show Edges option. Additionally, you could select the Show Facets Of Smooth Objects option, resulting in the effect shown in Figure 3.11. Try it. This option has been used quite frequently in the illustrations in this book.

- The dialog for Surface Render has an additional Save Image option, which is set to Off by default. If you set this to Manual, each time you select the Surface Render display, a Save Image As dialog will be invoked, allowing you to save the contents of the window in a variety of image file formats. If you set the Save Image option to Auto, the saving is done automatically, each time you select the Surface Render display, in a file format and folder location you specify. The defaults are BMP format and the project folder. You'll learn more about saving image files of your renderings in Workshops 5 and 7, and it's unlikely that you'll need to use the Save Image option described here. Note that you'll find the same option in the dialogs of some other display modes as well.

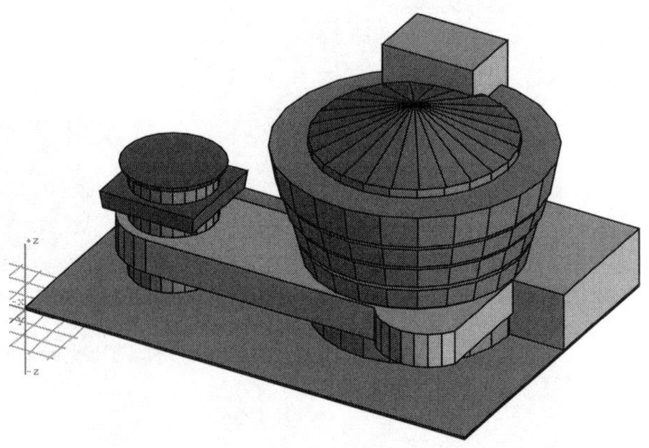

Figure 3.11

A Surface Render display of the building model project from Workshop 2, with Accurate edges and the Show Facets Of Smooth Objects option activated.

2.4 Hidden Line Options

- Invoke the dialog for the Hidden Line display, which has many options you've already explored in the other display dialogs. Check both the Show Object Color and the Include Open Shapes options and see the resultant display. Contrary to the defaults, it's often useful to have both these options selected: the first, if you've used colors to differentiate between different groupings of objects; the second, if open shapes are an integral part of the scene and must be visible. The Hide Edges With Angle Greater Than option is useful for hiding the display of edges in facetted objects whose adjoining surfaces meet at an angle greater than the specified value.

You already saw the default Hidden Line display of the building model project in Figure 3.2.

2.5 Shaded Render Options

- Move on to the Shaded Render display dialog, and select its first option, Set Image Size. You now have to select a *portion* of the graphics window to render; the entire window isn't rendered as it was before. This same option also exists for the RenderZone display where it's generally more useful, so we'll revisit it again when we study the RenderZone options in Workshop 5 (Illuminating, Texturing, and Rendering Your World).

- Most of the other options for Shaded Render are grouped under two separate tabs: Shading and Geometry (Figure 3.12-a). Let's explore the Shading options first. Antialiasing is an important option since it removes the jagged edges in your rendering, as shown in Figure 3.12-b. The effect may be hard to see in the illustration since that was generated as a high-resolution image for printing, but it should be readily apparent at the low screen resolution you're working in. Moreover, the Antialiasing option must be selected in order to activate the Transparencies option, which is used to render transparent all those objects created in transparent surface styles.

- The Shadows option will be familiar to you from the earlier displays. It has three sub-options, which are the same as in the RenderZone display, and we'll discuss them in detail in Workshop 5, along with the Unsupported Lights option. So you can ignore these options for now.

- By default, the display of grid and axes is turned off in a Shaded Render display, as you can see in Figure 3.12-b. Sometimes, however, you might want to display these to enhance a presentation or add a dramatic touch. In that case, select the Show Grid, Axes And Underlay option. (We'll cover underlays in Exercise 5.) For an added 3D effect to the grid and axes display, also check the Render Grid And Axes As 3D Lines sub-option.

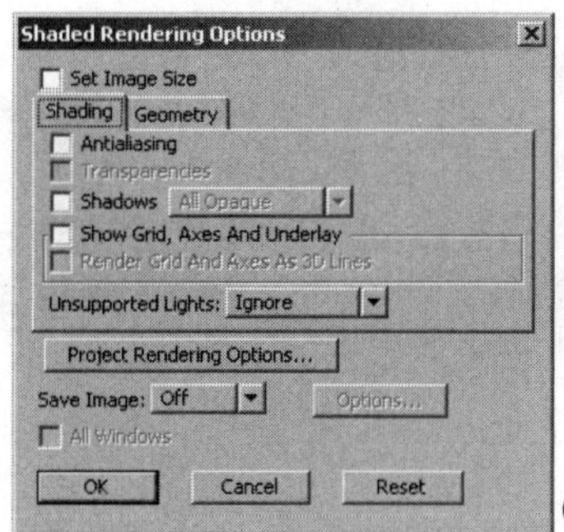

Figure 3.12

The Shaded Render Options dialog, and the rendering obtained by checking the Antialiasing option.

- Move on to the Geometry tab of the dialog. The first option here is Decompose Non Planar Faces, which is used to control how objects with non-planar faces will be rendered. When this option is checked, non-planar faces are first triangulated and then rendered. Note, however, that the triangulation is temporary, done for the purpose of rendering only, and not permanent as applied by the Triangulate tool you covered in Section 6.6 of the last workshop.

Ignore the Wireframe Width options—we'll look at them while working with the RenderZone display in Workshop 5 (Illuminating, Texturing, and Rendering Your World). You're already familiar with the Save Image option from Section 2.3. The Project Rendering Options section will be covered in the next section.

Since the Shaded Render display doesn't show textures, you'll probably not use it very much.

2.6 Project Rendering Options

You've seen that both the Interactive Shaded and Shaded Render displays have a Project Rendering Options button in their dialog. In Workshop 5 (Illuminating, Texturing, and Rendering Your World), you'll see that the RenderZone dialog also has the same button. Depending upon the display dialog you invoke it from, the Project Rendering Options dialog will have different tabs. In this section, we'll look at the Smooth Shading tab that's common to all displays, and the Geometry tab that's accessed from the Shaded Render display. Note that the Project Rendering Options dialog, with all its tabs, can also be accessed directly from the Display menu.

- In the Shaded Render display dialog, click on the Project Rendering Options button and explore the different sub-options under Smooth Shading, which is selected by default (see Figure 3.13-a) and causes the individual surfaces of curved facetted objects to display smoothly. You can select the first sub-option to specify that only objects for which the Smooth Shading attribute has been applied using M-Tool:14a,2 (which you'll learn about in Workshop 5) should be rendered smooth. The other sub-options will apply smooth shading to all the objects, with or without overriding the individual object smoothing attributes that have been specified using the same tool.

- Proceed to explore the Smooth Shade sub-section. Here, you can set the global smooth shading attributes that will be used for the rendering. Choose between smoothing all faces of an object, resulting in inaccurate but nevertheless interesting results (Figure 3.13-b), or smoothing only specific faces. For the second option, you can specify the smoothing criteria in two ways: edges with an angle greater than the accompanying value, or faces with a specified range of sides.

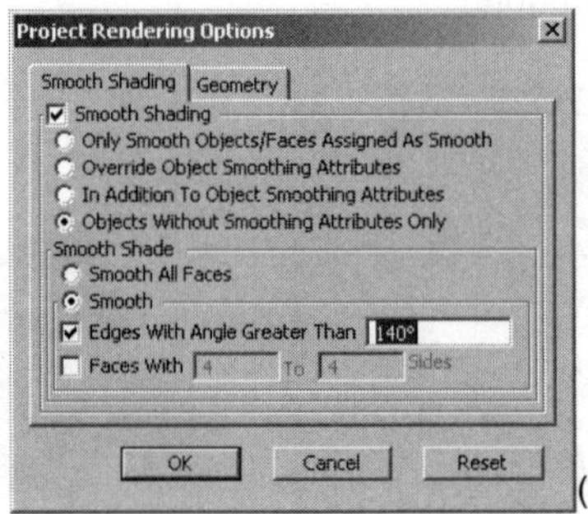

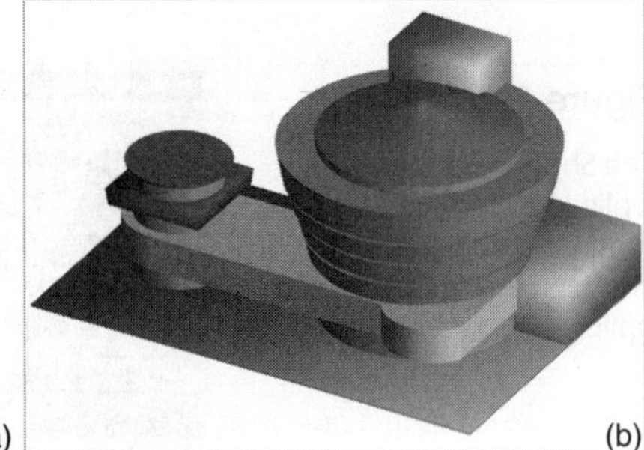

Figure 3.13

The Smooth Shading tab of the Project Rendering Options dialog, and the rendering obtained by checking the Smooth All Faces option.

- Switch to the Geometry tab of the Project Rendering Options dialog. Here, the Smooth Objects popup menu gives you three options for rendering smooth objects. By default, smooth objects are always rendered smoothly. Alternately, you can choose to apply to them the same smooth shading options you just specified in the Smooth Shading tab, or use their individual smoothing attributes as set by the Smooth Shade tool (M-Tool:14a,2), which we'll study in Workshop 5 (Illuminating, Texturing, and Rendering Your World). Additionally, you can set the Quality of the smoothing by using the accompanying slider bar.

EXERCISE 3

Working with Layers

A layer in a CAD program is like a transparent screen on which graphical entities are created. There can be many layers superimposed on top of each other and because they're transparent, all the entities drawn on them are visible. However, just as when writing or drawing takes place, it can only be on one of these transparent screens at a time, similarly, only one layer can be *active* at any given time. All the graphical entities being modeled then will be created on this active layer. form•Z allows you to define an unlimited number of layers in a project. When required, some of these layers can be made invisible, making it easier to work with the required entities on the visible layers only. The analogy with the transparent screens is to simply take away some of them from the pile and keep them aside.

Layers are indispensable as a means of segregating the various objects in your modeling world into different categories, so that they can be isolated when required. For instance, if you're modeling a chair, you can create the legs on one layer, the seat on a second, the back on a third, the arm-rests on a fourth, and so on. This makes the overall modeling process much easier, because you can make only the necessary layers visible at a time instead of having each and every object visible in the window. That can quickly get messy and chaotic, even for a project of only moderate complexity. Moreover, the time required for regenerating the display each time you zoom, scroll, or choose a different display mode increases proportionately with the number of objects visible in the window. In general, you should try and minimize the number of objects on a single layer, so that you can have a minimum number of objects visible in the window at a time.

Another important advantage of using layers is that it enables you to print different combinations or aspects of your model very easily. Let's say, for instance, that in a building model you judiciously use separate layers for different categories of related elements—slabs, beams, columns, exterior and interior walls along with their openings, furniture, lights, and so on. You can then easily isolate and print out various useful layer combinations: the structural components only; walls, slabs, and furniture only; walls, slabs, and lights only; and so on.

In short, *use layers as much as you can*! This cannot be emphasized enough. The payoffs are worth the effort of organizing all your objects into layers, many times over.

3.1 Creating New Layers

- Open a new project and create an object of any shape or size. Look for the Layers palette, through which layers are manipulated in form•Z. If it's closed, open it from the Palettes menu.

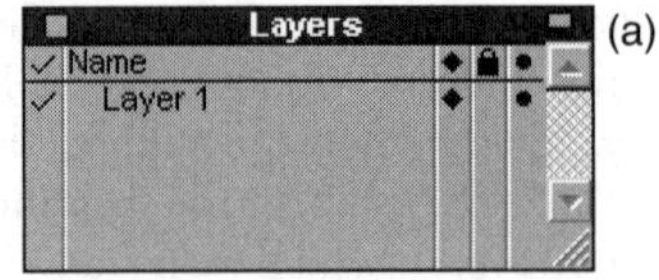

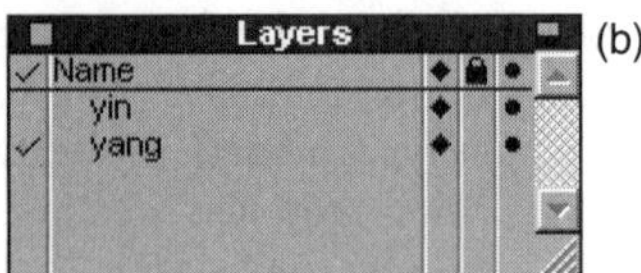

Figure 3.14

Working with the Layers palette. (a) The single default layer. (b) Creating and activating a new layer, and changing both layer names.

- Turn your attention to the Layers palette. It's almost identical to the Objects palette we saw in Section 3.5 of Workshop 2 (Bringing a Sense of Scale), so learning to work with it will be easy. Notice that the palette has a default layer called "Layer 1" with a √ mark beside it (Figure 3.14-a). This indicates that Layer 1 is the currently active layer. The single object you modeled was created on this layer. Change the default name of the layer by writing over it, just as you did for the entries in the Objects palette. Call it "yin."
- You'll now create a new layer. Click on the blank space under the yin layer name in the Layers palette; a new layer gets created with the default name "Layer 2." The name is highlighted, so you can give the layer a new name right away by typing over it. Call it "yang" to go with "yin."
- So you now have two layers, yin and yang. Notice that although you created a new layer yang, the active layer is still yin, as denoted by the √ mark. If you'd like to create new objects on the yang layer, you need to simply click in the first column of the Layers palette beside its name. The √ mark shifts to this position, indicating that yang is the active layer (Figure 3.14-b). Now create a new object, and it will be placed on the yang layer.

3.2 Attributes of a Layer

- To check that the second object has actually been created on the yang layer rather than on the yin layer, make the yin layer invisible. Just as with the Objects palette, the visibility of a layer can be turned off in the Layers palette by clicking on the shaded diamond icon in the first column to the right of the layer name. Try it. The icon will become unshaded, indicating that the layer is now ghosted. Correspondingly, the object that was created on the yin layer will appear ghosted, leaving the object created on the yang layer still visible.

Ghosting a layer is a property of the layer rather than of the objects on that layer. The basic notion of ghosting, however, remains the same—the objects on a ghosted layer are displayed in a light gray color and cannot be selected. Ghosting a layer is useful if you don't need to work with the objects it contains but would still like to use them for reference. This feature can also be used as an effective presentation technique, as illustrated in Figure 3.15, where a structural plan of columns is shown in visible mode while the floor that it supports above is shown in ghosted mode. The same image would have been hard to comprehend if the floor was fully visible or if it was not shown at all.

Ghosted layers will be hidden if the Layers sub-option of the Hide Ghosted option in the Wire Frame Options dialog is selected.

- Click on the diamond icon next to the yin layer once more. It will disappear, indicating that this layer is now totally invisible; the object on it will no longer be seen. What you just did was turn the layer off. Click once more in the same spot, and the diamond icon will reappear in its original state—fully shaded—restoring the visibility of the layer. Thus, the diamond icon in the Layers palette toggles between the three attributes of visibility, ghostedness, and invisibility, just like the corresponding icon in the Objects palette.

Figure 3.15

A structural plan of columns, demonstrating the usefulness of ghosting a layer.

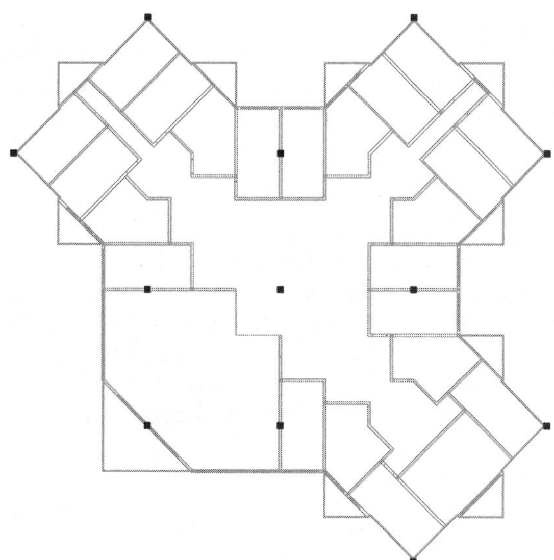

- Now try changing the visibility attribute of the yang layer. You'll find that you cannot do so—it must remain in visible mode. This is because it's the active layer, which, naturally, must always be visible. To make this layer invisible, you must first designate another layer as the active layer.
- Just like the Objects palette, the Layers palette has two more columns for the attributes of pickability and snapability, indicated by the lock icon and the shaded circle respectively (see Figure 3.16). These toggle-switch icons work identically to the corresponding icons in the Objects palette that you explored in the last workshop. Try them out. Lock one of the layers and you'll find that you can no longer select and modify the object on this layer. Click on the circular icon in the last column of the same layer, and none of the Object Snap tools will work any more on the object it contains.

The rationale for turning off the visibility, pickability, or snapability attributes of an entire layer is the same as that for a single object. In a large and complex project in which you've judiciously used many layers for segregating related groups of objects, the layers not being used at any particular time can be made totally invisible. If they need to be used as a reference, they can be made ghosted, so that you can still snap to the objects in them. If a layer needs to be visible but without the possibility of the objects in it being accidentally modified in any way, it can be locked and therefore effectively "frozen." Additionally, if the objects in such a layer don't need to be used for snapping, it's better to turn off the snapability attribute of the layer—this will make it easier to snap only to the desired objects.

Figure 3.16

Manipulating the pickability and snapability attributes of a layer.

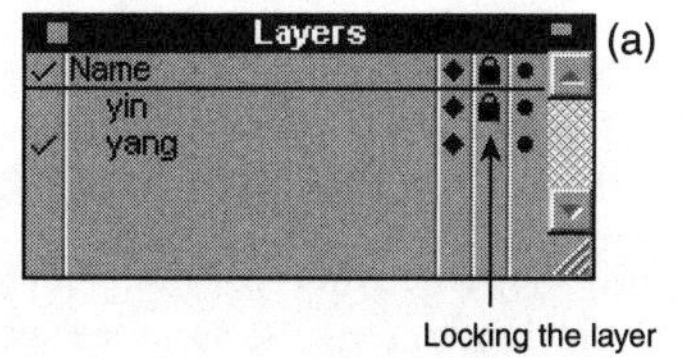

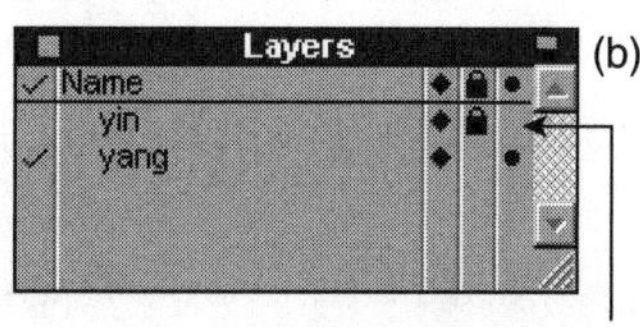

You've seen that you can also lock the active layer or turn off its snapability. This is in contrast to the visibility attribute, which cannot be turned off for the active layer. The ability to lock even the active layer can be useful, for instance, in a situation where you want to select all the objects in some specific layers for an operation such as Move, Color, Delete, etc. In that case, you'd simply lock all the other layers *including* the active one, and then go to Edit > Select All Unghosted to make the desired selection.

In general, manipulating the attributes of an entire layer is much more useful and convenient than manipulating the attributes of individual objects, which is why you'll find yourself using the Layers palette far more frequently than the Objects palette. The object listing in the Objects palette is unfortunately not sorted by layer, which makes it very difficult to keep track of which object is in which layer through it. Especially for large projects, this task is almost impossible. Therefore, until such a feature is introduced (hopefully!) in a future version of form•Z, focus on the Layers palette rather than on the Objects palette, and as mentioned earlier, aim for the minimum number of objects on a single layer.

3.3 Moving Objects Between Layers

You created the first object on the yin layer and the second on the yang layer. What if you realize later that the second object should really have been categorized with the first object and should therefore be on the yin layer? Basically, what we need to know is how to move objects from one layer to another *after* they have been created.

- The currently active layer is yang. Since you want to move the object to the yin layer, make the yin layer active.
- Now select the object on the yang layer that's to be transferred. If you've forgotten which of the two objects was in the yang layer, simply lock the yin layer. This will guarantee that the object you select is in the yang layer, which is the one you want.
- After selecting the object, go to the Set Layer tool (M-Tool:14b,3). Following the instructions in the Prompts palette, click anywhere in the window. The object gets moved to the active layer, which is yin. There's no visible change, but you can verify the move by making the yang layer invisible or ghosted. Both your objects will remain visible, since they're now in the yin layer. LAYER
- The method just described can be used to transfer many objects at a time to a different layer by prepicking them with the Pick tool. To change the layer of just a single object, you can also use the Attributes tool (M-Tool:12b,2). Simply apply this tool to an object and in the dialog that's invoked, use the On Layer popup menu to specify a different layer for it. We'll explore this tool in more detail in Workshop 5 (Illuminating, Texturing, and Rendering Your World). A ATTRIB

3.4 Global Manipulation of Layers

By default, layers are visible, unlocked and snapable when they're created (see Figure 3.17-a). Each of these attributes can then be modified for individual layers, as we've seen. You can also conveniently modify the attributes of *all* the layers in one step, when necessary.

- Create about three to four additional layers in the Layers palette. Don't bother changing their names. Having many layers will help you understand better how global manipulation of layers works. Make sure the visibility attribute of all the layers is turned on to start with.

- Click on the diamond icon that appears at the head of the visibility column, as indicated in Figure 3.17-a. You'll find that all the layers except the active layer become ghosted (Figure 3.17-b). A second click at the same spot will turn all the ghosted layers off (Figure 3.17-c). So basically, this works as a toggle switch for all the layers in one step, setting them to on, ghosted, or off repeatedly. Of course, the initial setting of a layer will determine how it's toggled. Thus, if some layers are ghosted, they will be made invisible, while invisible layers are toggled back to visibility (see Figures 3.17-d to 3.17-f).

Figure 3.17

Manipulating the visibility settings of all the layers at a time (except the active layer) by using the header visibility icon.

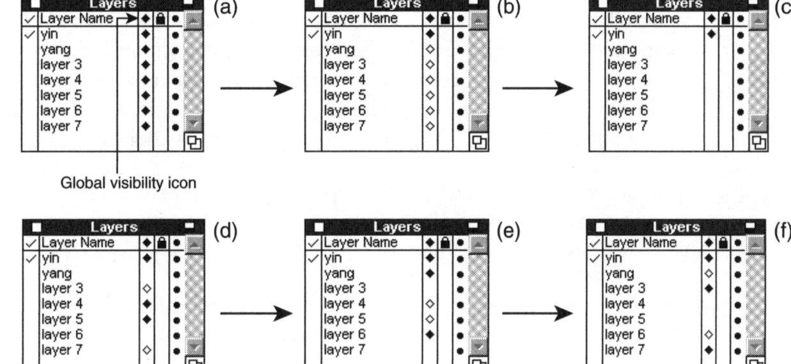

- Try out the same technique with the other two header icons for pickability and snapability. They work in an identical fashion.

- As you can see, this is a very convenient method for changing the attributes of all the layers at a time. However, what if, for instance, you want to change the attributes of only 5 or 6 layers in a project with a total of 12 layers? You cannot use the method just described. If you manipulate the layers individually, you'll find it tiresomely slow for a complex project (even in Wire Frame display), since the graphics window is regenerated each time the visibility attribute of a layer is changed. The solution to this problem is to hold down the Shift key as you change the visibility attribute of an individual layer. This will postpone the regeneration of the display until the Shift key is released, which you can do after manipulating all the required layers.

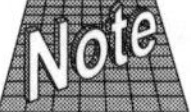

The Objects palette affords the same ability for global manipulation of attributes as the Layers palette, but it's not so useful there.

3.5 Working with Layer Groups

form•Z provides the ability to collate individual layers into layer groups, in a manner similar to how individual objects are collected together into object groups. Thus, you can create layer hierarchies in much the same way as you can create object hierarchies. The rationale for doing so is the same as that discussed in Section 3.4 of Workshop 2 (Bringing a Sense of Scale), where we worked with object groups. In fact, with the ability to group layers, you might find that you don't need to bother with grouping objects at all.

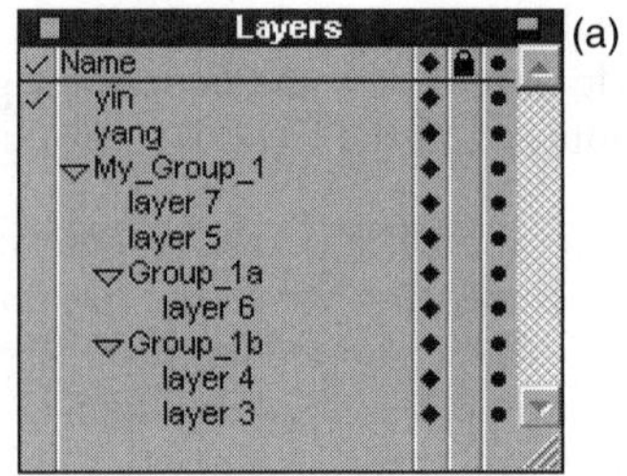

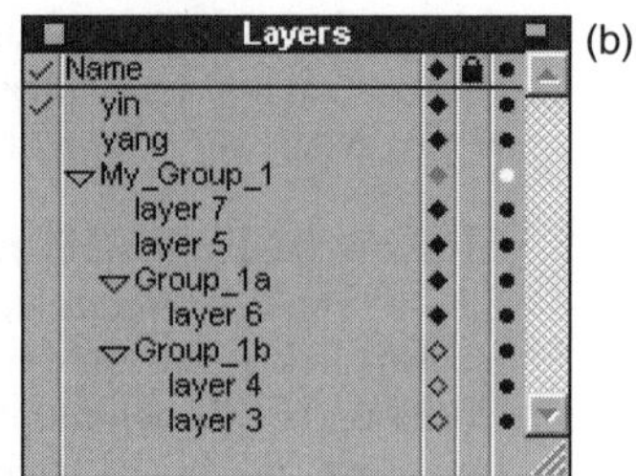

Figure 3.18

Working with layer groups. (a) Creating groups within groups. (b) Manipulating the visibility attribute of all the layers within a group simultaneously.

- Go to the Layers palette, and click on the blank space under the last layer name while pressing the control key (Mac) or Ctrl+Alt keys (PC). This will create a new layer group with a default name, which you can type over. Existing layers can now be moved into this layer group by the drag-and-drop method, identical to how you rearranged objects and groups in the Objects palette. You can create as many layer groups as you want, and move some of them within other layer groups, building up any desired hierarchy (Figure 3.18-a). Try it. Keep in mind that you can select multiple consecutive entries by clicking and dragging across their names in the palette.
- You can manipulate the attributes of all the layers within a layer group simultaneously by using the corresponding visibility, pickability, and snapability icons next to the name of the group (Figure 3.18-b). Recall that you tried this out for object groups in the Objects palette as well.
- Just as with the Objects palette, the arrows in front of a layer group name work as toggle switches, allowing you to show or hide the list of layers contained within the group.

3.6 The Layers Dialog

- The Layers dialog provides you with some more options for working with layers. It's like the Objects dialog you explored in Workshop 2 (Bringing a Sense of Scale) and is similarly invoked by one of three methods. The easiest way is to click in the header row of the Layers palette, where the column title Name appears. Alternately, click anywhere inside the Layers palette while holding down the option key (Mac) or Ctrl+Shift keys (PC), or go to Options > Layers.
- As you can see in Figure 3.19-a, the information about layers and layer groups displayed on the left side of the Layers dialog is in the same format as the Layers palette. The attributes of visibility, pickability, and snapability for the layers and groups can be manipulated through the same icons and in the same way as you did for the palette. You can create new layers and layer groups directly in the dialog by using the Layer and Group commands respectively. You can highlight a layer or group, and apply the usual operations to it such as Delete, Copy, Top, Bottom, and Sort. The Active option will make the selected layer active, while the Purge option will remove all the empty layers and layer groups—which contain no objects—from the project. Be careful about deleting layers or layer groups that are not empty using Delete, as this action cannot be undone. At the base of the Layers dialog are the options for changing the default layer and layer group names, if required.
- Select a layer and click on the Edit button. This will invoke the Layer Attributes dialog where you can specify various attributes for the selected layer. You can see that this dialog is very similar to the Object Attributes dialog you used in Section 3.3 to change the layer of an object. Thus, you can assign to a layer the same attributes that you can assign to individual objects. Keep in mind that the former override the latter. Thus, if you select a surface style for the layer by activating the

Surface Style box, as shown in Figure 3.19-b, *all* the objects on that layer will be rendered with the chosen surface style, regardless of the surface style assigned to them individually. We'll learn about all the other attributes shown in the dialog in Workshop 5 (Illuminating, Texturing, and Rendering Your World).

Figure 3.19

The Layers dialog, and the Layer Attributes dialog for the selected layer.

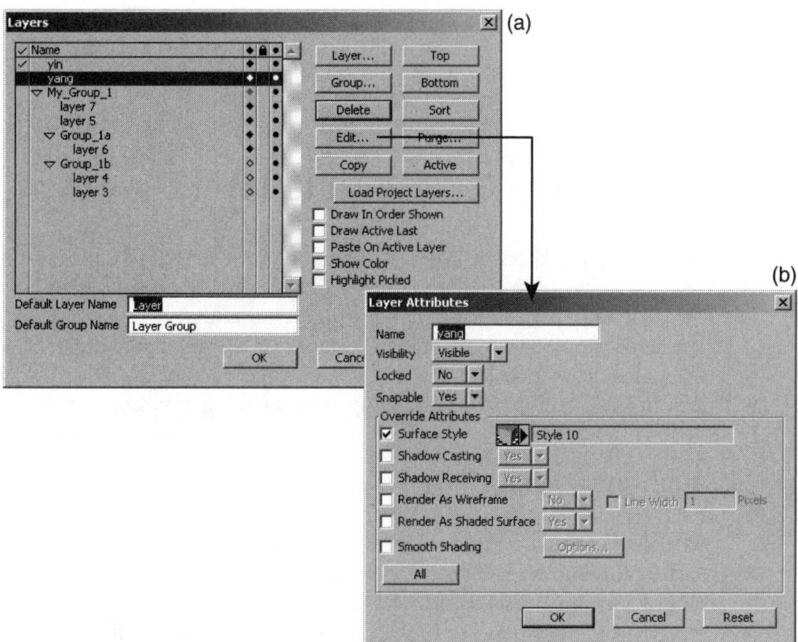

▣ The Load Project Layers option in the Layers dialog lets you import layers from another project into the current one and is thus similar to the Load Surface Styles option you saw in the Surface Styles dialog. For layers, this option comes in especially useful when you're working on similar projects, or working on parts of the same project in two or more separate files.

▣ Move on to the next three options. Draw In Order Shown and Draw Active Last are used to determine the order in which objects are drawn in the window. These are not very critical. Note, however, the Paste On Active Layer option—it's unchecked by default. This means that if you use Cut or Copy after making a selection in form•Z and then use Paste in the same project, the selected elements will be pasted on the layers they were originally in. However, if you want them to be pasted on a different layer, make that layer active and check the Paste On Active Layer option in the Layers dialog. Now the cut or copied objects will be pasted on the active layer, irrespective of which layer they came from. Apart from its obvious use of *duplicating* objects across layers (using Copy and Paste), this method can also be used to *transfer* objects between layers (using Cut and Paste) instead of the Set Layer or Attribute tools.

Thus, in form•Z, there invariably is more than one way of doing something. In time, you'll find out which works best for you.

▣ The remaining two options in the Layers dialog give layers some interesting abilities. If you activate the Show Color option, a layer will be displayed in the Layers palette in the color that was assigned to it in the Layer Attributes dialog you just saw. And if you activate the Highlight Picked option, selecting an object in the graphics window will highlight the name of the layer it's on in the Layers palette. Activate both these options and test them out. The Highlight Picked one is especially handy. Note that both these options are available in the Objects dialog as well.

Now that you know how to properly organize all your objects in multiple layers, let's proceed to learn to use multiple reference planes, which will further improve your modeling efficiency.

EXERCISE 4

Using Your Own Reference Planes

In Workshop 1 (Letting Yourself Go), you learned how to use the three predefined planes—XY, YZ, and ZX—that are available in form•Z. In this exercise, you'll learn how to define and work with your own reference planes that better suit the requirements of the objects you're modeling. For instance, a reference plane passing through a surface can be very convenient for positioning openings accurately on it. Just as you created your own surface styles and layers, defining your own planes is one more step in the direction of customizing your working environment.

4.1 Arbitrary Reference Planes

The three predefined planes may not be sufficient even for a relatively simple modeling situation such as that shown in Figure 3.20, where a 3D triangular enclosure needs to be created on an inclined face of a pyramid. You could, of course, use the Face object snap to create the enclosure on the desired face, as you learned in Section 2.4 of Workshop 2 (Bringing a Sense of Scale). But that method lacks preciseness. What if, for instance, the enclosure needs to be sized such that it's exactly 3' inside from all the edges of the face? How can this be done without getting into complex numeric calculations in 3D coordinate space?

What would be really useful to have here is the ability to treat the face itself on which the extrusion has to be created as the reference plane for the modeling. Then creating an extrusion on it in a precise location would be as simple as creating the same extrusion on the predefined XY plane, dimensionally accurate as you learned in Workshop 2.

Well, you *can* do exactly this—create a reference plane passing *through* the face on which you want to locate the extrusion. Such a plane is called an *arbitrary* plane, since it can be located anywhere in 3D space. Let's go through the process of modeling the required configuration using an arbitrary plane.

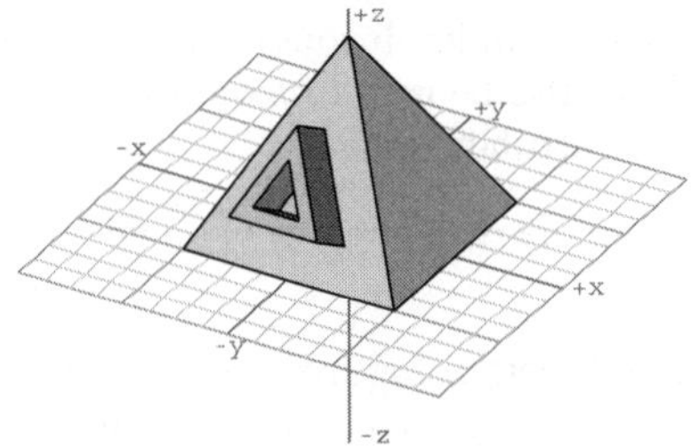

Figure 3.20

A simple example of a configuration to be modeled.

Figure 3.21

Different axes orientations depending upon the picking sequence of the face. The display of the world axes was temporarily turned off.

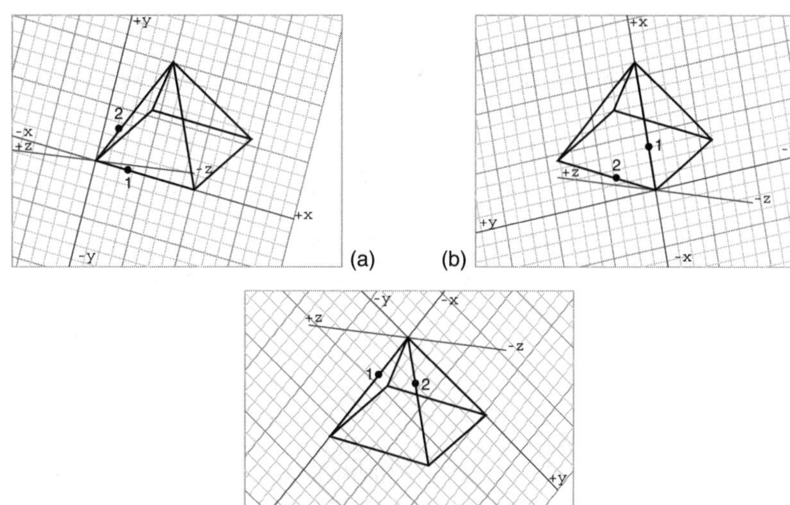

- Create and activate a new layer, now that you know how to do so, and make all the other layers invisible. Create a pyramid using the Rectangle tool in 3D Converged mode. Then select a face of the pyramid on which you'll situate the enclosure by setting the topological level to Face and using the Pick tool.

- Turn to the third column of window tools located at the base of the graphics window and select the first one, Define Arbitrary Plane (W-Tool:3,1). The Prompts palette will ask you to click to define an arbitrary plane, since a face has already been selected. Do so, and a new reference plane will be created passing through the selected face. It has its own axes—called *reference plane axes*—that are colored in teal to distinguish them from the original red-colored *world axes.*

- The orientation of the reference plane axes will depend upon the sequence in which the segments were picked to select the face. Try out different pick sequences, reapplying the Define Arbitrary Plane tool each time. You'll get the same plane but with different axes orientations. Figure 3.21 shows all possible variations of the pick sequences for the same face, and the resulting axes. As you can see, the X axis is always aligned with the segment that's selected first. For the purpose of modeling our target configuration, the axes orientation shown in Figure 3.21-a seems suitable.

- Try creating any object now, not necessarily the triangular extrusion. You'll find that all 2D and 3D objects are created with respect to this arbitrary reference plane. Notice that the dimensions of the new grid are the same as those for the predefined planes, and that if the Grid Snap switch is on, it's also active for the new plane. Arbitrary planes reflect the same grid settings as the regular planes.

Let's get back to the original problem of creating the extrusion so that it's exactly 3' inside the face from all sides. How would you do this? You can, of course, use the grid as a reference and draw the base triangle approximately 3' inside from the edges of the face. But what if you had to be absolutely precise? This is where the arbitrary reference plane you just defined will come in most useful. Execute the following sequence of steps exactly as described.

- Invoke the dialog of the Pick tool and select the option, Auto Select New Objects. (So there's some use for it after all!) Select the Vector Line tool in 2D Surface mode; with this, draw a triangle that coincides with the face on which the extrusion is to be located, by snapping to its segment endpoints. You now have a base triangle that's of the same size as the face, lying exactly on top of it. It gets highlighted as soon as it's created because of the Auto Select feature. The same base triangle could also have been obtained using the Derivative 2D Surface tool (M-Tool:5a,2), which you'll learn about in Section 6.1 of Workshop 4 (Enhancing Your Modeling Capabilities).

- You'll now scale the 2D triangle with respect to the arbitrary plane, so that it lies exactly 3' inside the face from all sides. Moreover, you'll do this graphically using the grid, rather than by typing in a scaling factor. Select the Uniform Scale tool (M-Tool:13a,4). The triangle is already selected, so the scaling will be applied to this object. For the base of scale, specify the center of the triangle by selecting it using the Center Of Face snap (W-Tool:6,12).

- Next, you need to specify the scaling factor. Activate Grid Snap and set the snapping module to 1'-0". Also, turn off object snapping by setting it to None. Click on any point at the bottom edge of the face which coincides with the plane's X axis; this will be the first point for the scaling factor. Since Grid Snap is on, you should easily be able to click at a point 3' inside from the first point along the same face. This will be the second point for determining the scaling factor. The 2D triangle gets resized according to this factor, and it should now be 3' inside from all edges of the face (Figure 3.22).

- Now simply use the 3D Enclosure tool (M-Tool:5a,6) to generate a 3D enclosure from this 2D triangle. By default, the enclosure is centered about the original 2D line, so you'll lose some of the 3' margin on all sides. To retain the exact margin, set the Justification option to Left in the dialog of the 3D Enclosure tool, and then apply it to generate the triangular enclosure.

Voila! You've finished creating the target configuration (shown in Figure 3.20) by defining and using your own reference plane.

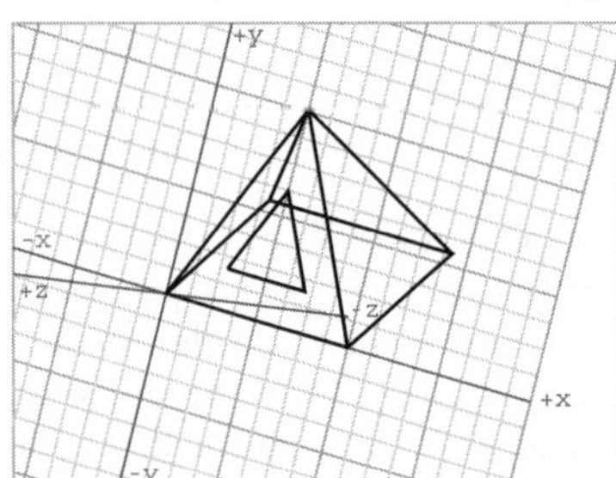

Figure 3.22

Creating the appropriately sized base triangle with the help of the new reference plane.

4.2 Switching Between Predefined and Arbitrary Planes

What if you want to switch to the XY plane for creating other objects, but would like to retain the option of returning to the newly created arbitrary plane whenever needed? Let's see how to do this.

- Turn your attention to the first window tool palette that contains the reference planes. You'll notice that the Arbitrary icon is highlighted, indicating that the currently active plane is a user-defined one. To switch to one of the predefined planes, simply select the corresponding icon from the palette. Create some object on the plane you switched to.

- Now select the Arbitrary icon again. The arbitrary plane you had created becomes active once more and can be used for further modeling activity.

- Keep switching between the four different kinds of planes in the palette and create various objects. It will give you a feel for the flexibility and convenience afforded by multiple planes, both predefined and arbitrary.

4.3 Using Arbitrary Plane Coordinates

You saw that only one plane can be active, and therefore visible in the window, at any given time. You're always modeling with respect to this currently active plane, which can be predefined or arbitrary.

- Switch back to the Arbitrary plane if it's not active. Your next task is to move the triangular extrusion you created earlier by a specific distance, up and away from the face it's located on in a perpendicular direction, as shown in Figure 3.23-a. Assume that the distance is a fractional number—say 16'-1/2"—so that the Move operation needs to be executed using direct numeric input rather than graphically with the mouse.
- You already know from Workshop 2 (Bringing a Sense of Scale) that you can use relative coordinates to carry out the move. Deselect the box marked A in the Prompts palette to set its mode to relative. Then activate the Move tool, select the enclosure as the object to be moved, and key in 0,0,16'-1/2" as the relative coordinates of the move. What you'll get (Figure 3.23-b) is obviously not what you had aimed for.

So what went wrong? Obviously, the coordinates you keyed in were not correct. If you look carefully, you'll find that the triangular enclosure *has* been moved by the distance [0',0',16'-1/2"] away from its original position, but with respect to the red-colored world axes rather than the teal-colored axes of the current reference plane. The solution to this problem is really very simple.

- Undo the Move operation you just performed. Then deselect the box marked W in the Prompts palette. Execute the Move again by keying in the same relative coordinates as before, and you'll find that it now gives the correct result (Figure 3.23-a). By deselecting the W box, you specified that all input should be with respect to the coordinate system of the current reference plane rather than that of the predefined planes. That's why the numeric input works correctly this time.

Each arbitrary reference plane that you create comes with its coordinate system, relative to its axes. Such coordinates are known as "reference plane coordinates." In contrast, the coordinates of the predefined planes, relative to the original X, Y, and Z axes, are known as "world coordinates." Just as the A checkbox in the Prompts palette switches between relative and absolute coordinates, similarly, the W checkbox switches between world and reference plane coordinates.

Figure 3.23

The next modeling goal, and the erroneous move that occurred at the first attempt.

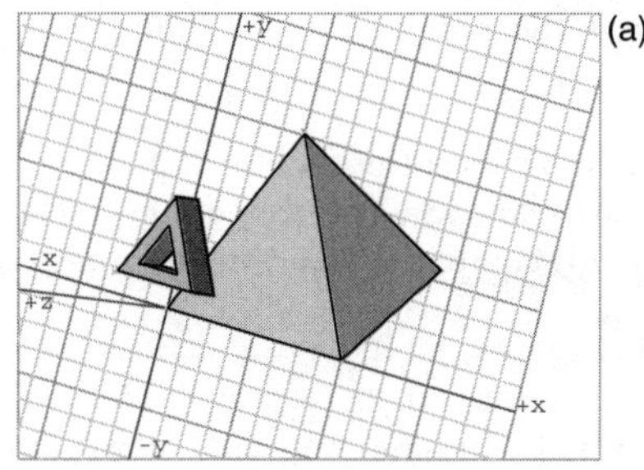

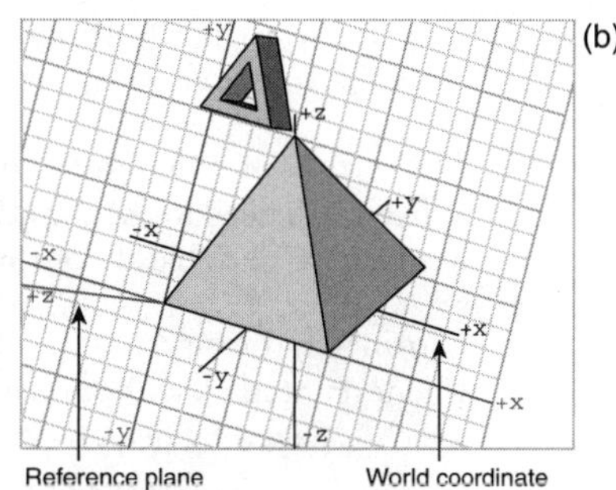

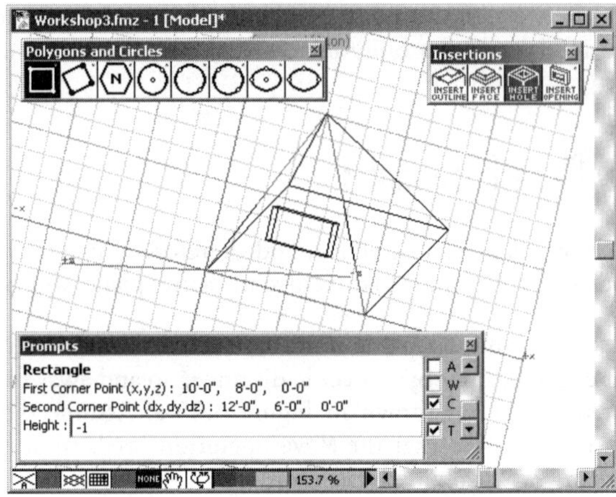

Figure 3.24

Inserting a hole on an inclined face precisely, using reference plane coordinates.

- Let's carry out another operation using reference plane coordinates. Delete the triangular enclosure you just moved. We'll insert an opening on the same face of the pyramid where the enclosure was initially located. The opening must be of specified dimensions, say 12' by 6' with a depth of 1', and located at a precise distance, say 10' by 8', from the lower left corner of the face (see Figure 3.24). Make sure the arbitrary plane is still active, and that the W box in the Prompts palette is deselected. Go ahead and check the A box, however, so that you can locate the first point of the opening correctly with respect to the plane origin using absolute coordinates.

- Set the Heights menu to Graphic/Keyed. Prepick the face of the pyramid with the Pick tool. Activate the Insert Hole mode on Row 2, and select the Rectangle tool on Row 3. Specify [10',8',0'] as the first corner point. Then deselect the A box to set the mode to relative, and specify [12',6',0'] as the second corner point. Finally, specify the height as [-1'], and the hole will be inserted, correctly located and sized. Practice this procedure some more until you can do it easily.

4.4 Using Multiple Arbitrary Planes

- Suppose that you now want to create a new object with reference to one of the *other* faces of the pyramid. Naturally, you'll have to create a new arbitrary plane passing though that face. Select the face and use Define Arbitrary Plane (W-Tool:3,1) as you did before to define a reference plane passing through it. Create any object on this new plane.

- Switch to one of the three predefined planes—XY, YZ, or ZX—using the first window tool palette. Then select the Arbitrary icon in the same palette. You'll find yourself going back to the arbitrary plane you *last* created.

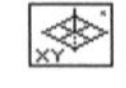

Thus, you can only return to the most recent user-defined plane using the Arbitrary window tool. What if you need to use the arbitrary plane you *first* created? Do you have to recreate it every time you need to use it? What if your model is complicated and you're using many such planes?

Fortunately, form•Z has the ability to store multiple user-defined planes, so that you can recall them whenever needed, without having to recreate them each time. This is done through the Planes palette, which is closed by default—that's why you never noticed it all this time.

- Go to Palettes > Planes to open the Planes palette. You can see that it's similar to the Objects and Layers palettes, which you've already worked with. In fact, it's simpler with three columns only: the first designates the active plane; the second lists the name of the plane; and the third indicates what kind of plane it is (see Figure 3.25). The palette is empty in the beginning, as no planes have been saved in it. We'll proceed to do this right away.

- Click on the palette in the space under Plane Name. A default name will appear which you can type over; click in the space below or press Return or enter to complete the definition of the new plane. It will be checked in the first column, indicating that it's the active plane. Also, a tag of ARB appears in the third column next to the name, indicating that it's an arbitrary plane (Figure 3.25-a). What you've effectively done is store the current user-defined plane in the Planes palette.

- Now create another arbitrary plane, passing through one of the other faces of the pyramid. Save it in the Planes palette in the same manner. See how easily you can now switch between these two arbitrary planes, simply by clicking in the first column next to their names in the palette. You can similarly create, store, and recall as many planes as needed. The active plane is indicated by a √ mark, just as for active layers.

- The Planes palette is so convenient for switching between planes that you might also want to store the three predefined planes in it. Activate the XY, YZ, and ZX planes in turn using the first window tool palette, and create a new entry for each of them in the Planes palette. As you can see in Figure 3.25-b, the tag in the third column changes to reflect the type of plane. You can now forget about the first window tool palette altogether, and use only the Planes palette for switching between planes—both predefined as well as arbitrary.

- Finally, click on the label Plane Name in the title row of the Planes palette, just as you did for the Layers palette. This will invoke the Reference Planes dialog which is similar to the dialogs for Layers, Objects, and Surface Styles, containing the same options for managing your planes such as Delete, Rename, Sort, and so on.

WORKSHOP 3

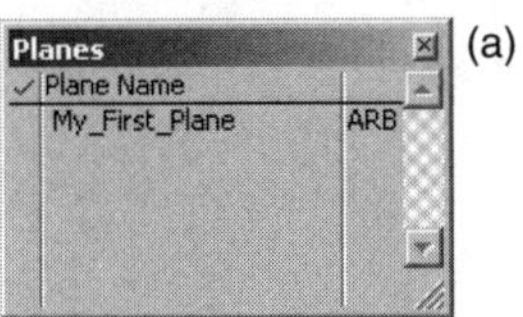

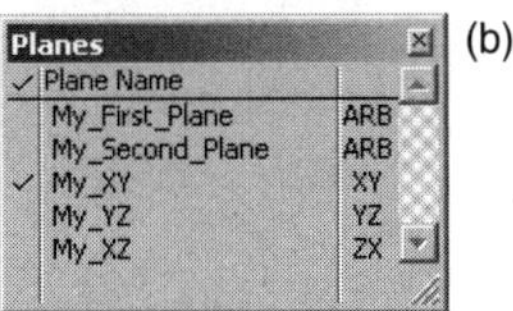

Figure 3.25

Working with the Planes palette. (a) Storing an arbitrary plane. (b) Storing predefined planes as well.

4.5 The Reference Plane Manipulation Tools

The third column of the window tool palette contains some other tools, in addition to Define Arbitrary Plane, that are used for manipulating the active reference plane, whether predefined or arbitrary. Let's briefly look at each one of them in turn.

- The second tool in the palette, Define Perpendicular Plane, lets you define a plane which is perpendicular to an existing plane. Try it for one of the arbitrary planes you've created; of course, you need to activate the plane first. Since there can be two planes perpendicular to a given plane (for instance, both the YZ and ZX planes are perpendicular to the XY plane) you'll be asked to specify the axis about which the new plane is to be created. 

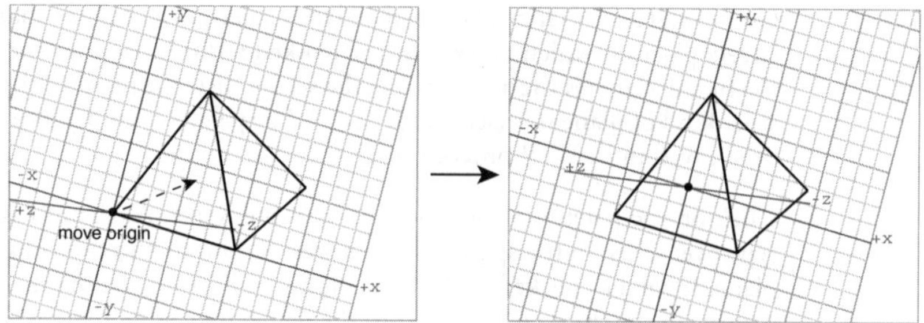

Figure 3.26

Moving the origin of an arbitrary plane from the vertex to the center of a face.

- Move Plane lets you move an existing plane to a different location. Try it for both an arbitrary plane as well as a predefined one. The distance of the move can be specified graphically or by direct numeric input, similar to how the Move tool is used for moving objects. The relocated plane can be saved as a new plane in the Planes palette, if required. The Move Plane tool has many applications; for instance, in architectural modeling, subsequent floors of a building can be constructed on XY planes that are "moved" up to the required floor heights.

- The next tool, Move Plane Origin, can be used to change the origin of a reference plane from its default location to any other point on the same plane. The plane itself won't be moved, just its origin. This tool is useful because very often, it's difficult to create a plane with the origin at the exact point that's needed. You can use Move Plane Origin, for example, to change the origin of your first arbitrary plane from a vertex of the pyramid to the center of one of its faces (Figure 3.26). The Endpoint and Center Of Face snapping options can be used to accomplish this precisely.

- Use the next tool, Rotate Plane, to rotate the active plane about its origin by a specified angle, which you can type in or indicate graphically. It's thus similar to the Rotate tool used for rotating objects, except that this tool works on planes. It's much more convenient than using the Angle direction snap (W-Tool:5,4) for working on parts of a project that are rotated at an angle with respect to the rest of the project. This is illustrated in the building model shown in Figure 3.27, where the XY plane is rotated by an angle of 45° to conveniently model the diagonal floor plan.

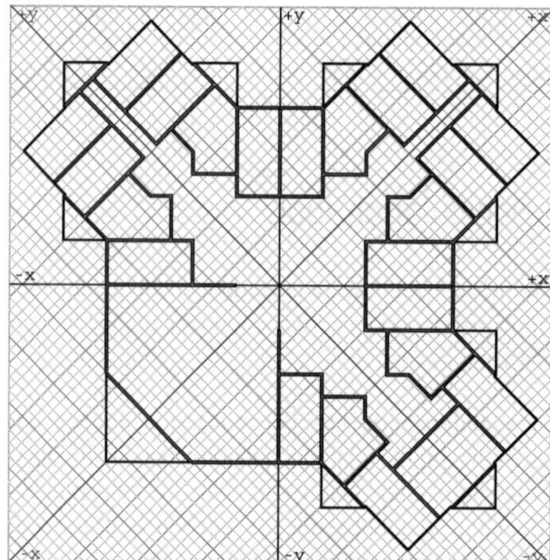

Figure 3.27

Rotating the XY plane to assist in the modeling of a floor, most of which is diagonally oriented with respect to the rest of the building.

- For those of you who have been yearning to change the size of the reference grid from Day 1, select the next tool, Extend Plane Grid, and use it to grab an edge of the plane and drag it outwards. The grid will increase automatically by the designated distance. You can also shrink the grid using the same technique. The Extend Plane Grid tool can be applied in turn to all the edges of the plane.

- Keep in mind that any plane you modify using these plane manipulation tools can be saved in the Planes palette as a new plane. What's more, you can retrieve the original plane itself with the last tool in the palette, Reset Plane. This tool discards any changes made to the active plane and restores it to its original configuration. Thus, you can modify a plane and save both the original *and* the modified versions in the Planes palette.

Now that you know how to create and manipulate your own reference planes, you can proceed to do the same with views.

Having Different Views

So far, you've used the Views menu in a very limited fashion, switching between the various predefined views it contains. In this exercise, you'll expand your visualization capabilities enormously by creating views from desired positions and angles. You'll also work with the Views palette, which lets you save and manage your views in a manner similar to the Objects, Surface Styles, Layers, and Planes palettes you've been working with.

5.1 Predefined Axonometric Views

form•Z has a large number of predefined views that you can use to visualize your modeling world in various ways. All of these are accessible from the Views pulldown menu (Figure 3.28), which you were briefly introduced to in Section 1.8 of Workshop 1 (Letting Yourself Go). We'll now study this menu in more detail.

- Recreate the configuration shown in Figure 3.20 of the last exercise—the pyramid with the 3D triangular enclosure located on one of its inclined faces. You'll be seeing these objects in a 30-60 axonometric view by default. Correspondingly, there's a √ mark against the z=30° x=60° item in the first group of the Views menu, which specifies the viewing angle from each one of the three axes; the y angle isn't given, indicating that it's 0°. There's also a √ mark against the Axonometric item in the third group of the menu, which denotes the kind of view.

- Switch to each one of the other viewing angle options in the first group of the Views menu, and see how they give you different axonometric views of your world. The last option in this group, Custom View Angles, lets you define your own viewing angles. Try keying in different values for X, Y, and Z, and see the resultant view. Notice that for the Z axis to be positioned vertically in the window, the Y angle *must* be 0°.

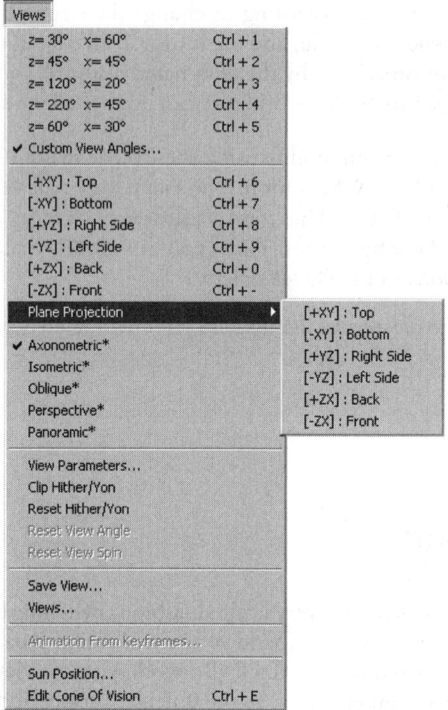

Figure 3.28

The Views menu, expanded to show the Plane Projection submenu.

- Move to the second group of the Views menu. The first six options in this group give you all the six planar (or projection) views possible—Top, Bottom, Right, Left, Back, and Front—with respect to the world axes. (Think of your modeling world as being inside a box; then you can look at it head-on from the six sides of the box.) Switch to one of the predefined reference planes, XY, YZ, or ZX; then try out the six planar views to see orthogonal views of your modeling world from all sides (Figure 3.29). For each view, go to the Custom View Angles option and note the angle values for X, Y, and Z. This will give you a better sense of how to define your own viewing angles when the need arises.

You'll find that planar views are particularly convenient for more precise and accurate work, as working directly in 3D can sometimes be misleading. Even if you prefer to work directly in 3D all the time, you should make it a habit to periodically switch to the planar views to check if the objects are indeed being created or modified as you intend them to be.

The planar views you've just used are with reference to the red-colored world axes. But you may not always be using the world coordinate system, as in the last exercise where you learned to create your own reference planes and use their respective coordinate systems. form•Z conveniently gives you the same six planar views for your customized reference planes as well. This is an incredibly useful feature.

- Activate any one of the non-planar views in the View menu. Then switch to an arbitrary plane coinciding with one of the inclined faces of the pyramid that you had created in the last exercise—it should be saved in the Planes palette. Re-create it if you don't have it anymore. Then switch to the Top view. You'll find that this still gives you a planar view of the *original* XY plane (shown in Figure 3.29), not of the arbitrary one you just activated.

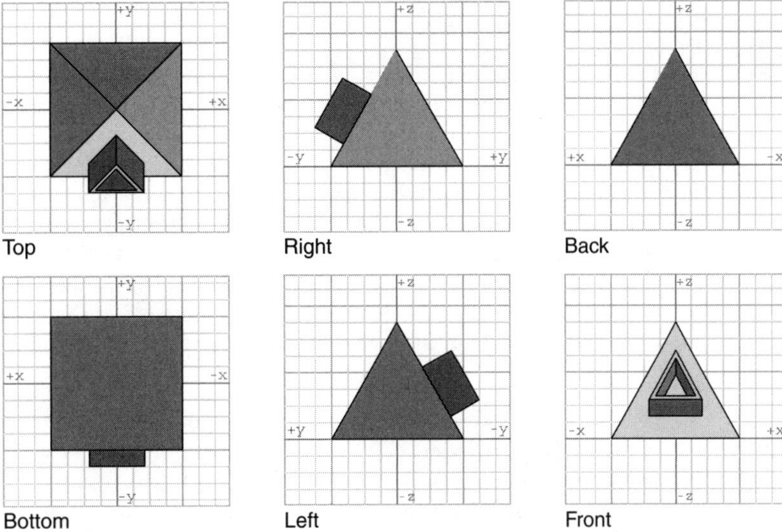

Figure 3.29

The six planar views of the 3D world shown in Figure 3.20, with respect to any of the three predefined planes.

- Go to the last command in the second group of the Views menu, called Plane Projection. It has a submenu with six options, as shown in Figure 3.28. If you're still in the Top view (or in any other planar view), all these options will be grayed out. Switch back to a non-planar view, and make sure the active plane is still the arbitrary one.
- The Plane Projection sub-options now get activated. Select Top—the first of these sub-options. This will show you the top planar view of your 3D world, but with respect to the *arbitrary reference plane* rather than the predefined XY plane. Try out the other five planar views in the Plane Projection submenu as well, all of which work with respect to the arbitrary plane (Figure 3.30). As you can see, these views will be extremely useful when you need to work accurately with the coordinate system of an arbitrary plane.

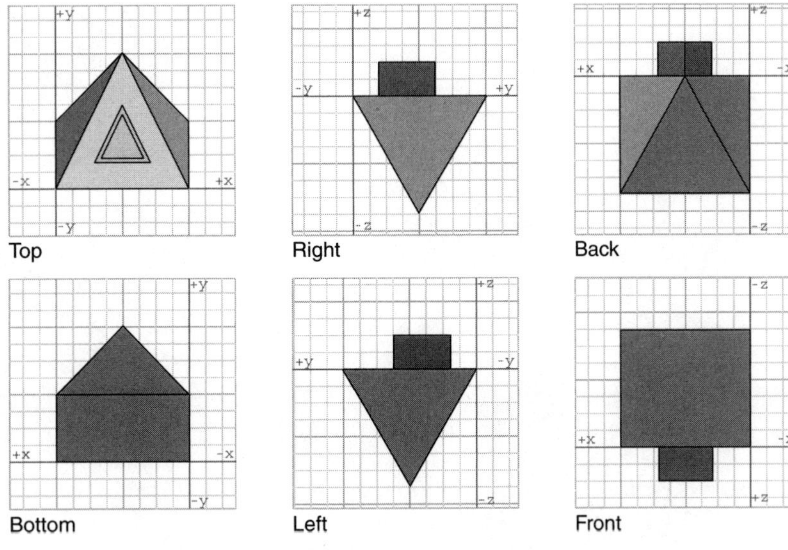

Figure 3.30

The six planar views of the same 3D world as in Figure 3.29, but with respect to the arbitrary plane shown in Figure 3.21-a rather than the predefined planes.

5.2 Other Types of 3D Views

For the rest of this exercise, use a completed project such as the building model you created in the Assignment for Workshop 2 (Bringing a Sense of Scale)—it should be fun viewing it in various ways. Turn your attention to the third group of the Views menu; this has four more types of views in addition to the default of Axonometric that we've been using predominantly so far. All these views have dialogs associated with them, as indicated by the * sign, which can be invoked in the usual fashion—selecting them while holding down the option key (Mac) or Ctrl+Shift keys (PC). You can also invoke the dialog of the *current* view by going to Views > View Parameters. Most of the options in this dialog can be graphically (and thus more conveniently) specified using the Edit Cone Of Vision command, which will be covered a little later in Section 5.4; therefore, we'll skip the dialog for now. However, let's browse through the remaining four types of views and see how they differ from each other.

- Switch from Axonometric to Isometric. This mode allows only non-planar views, so if you switch to any of the planar views in the second group of the Views menu, the mode will revert back to Axonometric. Look closely and you'll find that in the Isometric mode, the actual dimensions of objects, measured in directions parallel to the three orthogonal axes, are retained (see Figure 3.31-a). This is in contrast to the "natural" Axonometric views, in which non-planar views don't convey the real size of objects. The Isometric mode has different viewing angle combinations located in the first group of the Views menu, just like the Axonometric mode. Try out each one of these. There's no Custom option, but more isometric views can be generated interactively through the Edit Cone Of Vision command, which you'll soon work with.

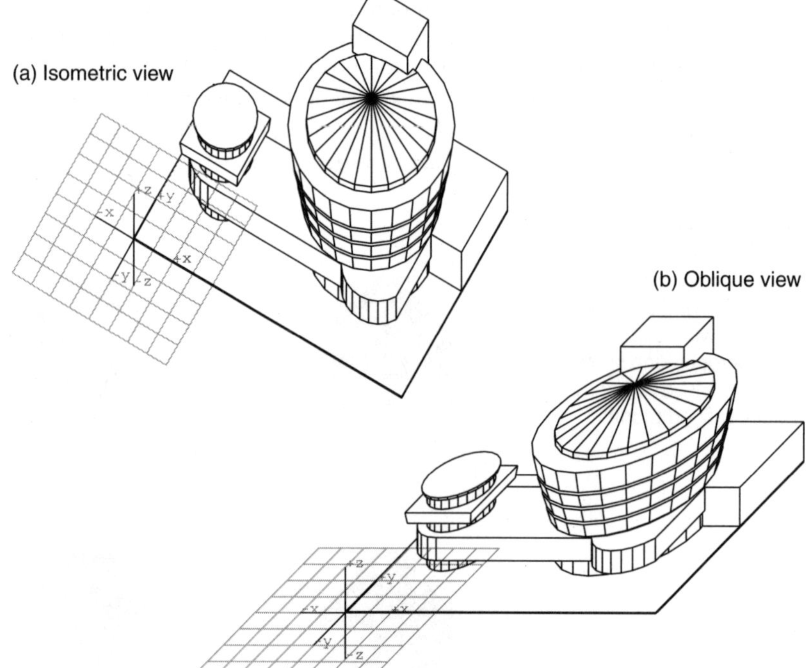

Figure 3.31

An Isometric view (x=30° y=60°) and an Oblique view (Inclination = 45°) of the building model created in Workshop 2. The display of facets in Hidden Line mode was turned on.

- Next, switch to Oblique, which is similar to the Isometric mode in preserving dimensions measured parallel to the axes and in not including planar views (see Figure 3.31-b). Browse through the different viewing angles in the first group of the Views menu for this mode. Again, you can generate various other oblique views using Edit Cone Of Vision.

Both the Isometric and Oblique modes are used only in specific cases when a presentation expressly calls for the use of such a mode. But for practical application during actual modeling, these modes can be safely ignored.

- Select the next viewing mode, Perspective. You'll find that this is identical to Axonometric except that it adds a perspective effect to the view. Try it out for different viewing angles, and see how you can quickly generate one-point perspectives by switching to the planar views with the Perspective mode activated (Figure 3.32). We'll look more closely at the Perspective mode and its options when we work with the Edit Cone Of Vision command.

Figure 3.32

A one-point perspective of the same building model, obtained by switching to the Front view in Perspective mode.

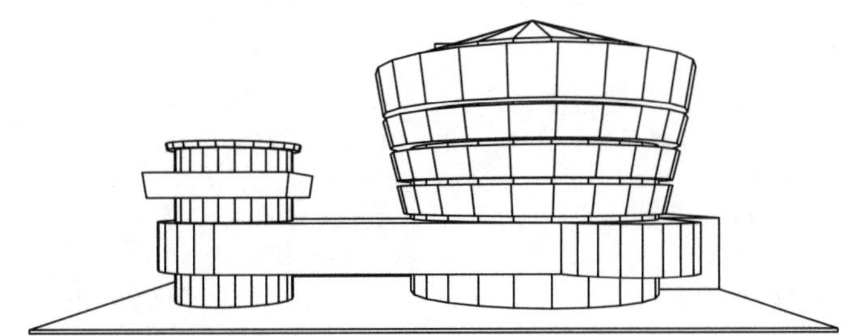

- Select the fifth and final viewing mode, Panoramic. This will display a panoramic view of the project, deactivating all the modeling and windows tools. A panoramic view is basically a 360° view of the world, and as you can see, it would be impossible to perform any modeling operations in this mode. It's meant for display only, and can be saved for presentation as an image file or used to generate QuickTime VR movies. We'll look at this feature in detail in Workshop 7 (Ending With More), along with the viewing parameters for panoramic views.

5.3 Using the Views Palette

As you get seriously under way with form•Z, speed will become an important consideration and you'll find yourself constantly searching for the fastest possible way to do something. One such operation you'd prefer to spend minimal time on is changing views, particularly since it's done so frequently. You'll often need to change views to see what you're doing from various angles, sometimes even in the middle of an operation. (Keep in mind that you *can* do that in form•Z.) Even if you're working only in a single view for an extended period of time, you'll still need to constantly zoom in and out of that view to see different parts of the project.

Having to constantly navigate through the Views menu to select the view you want can get very tiresome and time-consuming. A convenient shortcut is to store all the views you need in the Views palette, so that you can recall them with just a single mouse click when needed. form•Z lets you save as many views as you like in the Views palette. The views can be predefined, such as the ones you've seen so far, or customized, such as the ones you'll learn to create in just a short while.

- Go to the Palettes menu and open the Views palette if it's closed. It operates in a manner similar to the Objects and Layers palettes, so working with it should not present any problems. There are some differences, however, which we'll explore.

- The Views palette is currently empty since you haven't yet saved any views in it. Let's do that right away. First, switch to the view that you want to save. Then click on the Views palette in the blank space under View Name. Just as with layers and planes, the current view gets saved under a default name that you can change right away. An "eye" mark appears in the column to the left of the newly created view, indicating that it's the active view. The type of view—Perspective, Axonometric, Top, Right, and so on—is also indicated in the column to the right of the view name (see Figure 3.33).

- Switch to a different view using the Views menu. We'll save this view using another method. Go to the Save View option, located in the fifth group of the Views menu. A dialog will pop up, asking you for the name of the view. Write over the default name and click OK. This view will now appear in the Views palette by the specified name. To switch back to the first view, simply click in the eye-mark column to the left of its name.

- Any view that's saved in the Views palette can be actually displayed in the graphics window in Wire Frame mode by clicking in the column to the right of its type. A diamond icon will appear there, indicating that the view is visible. To see this graphical view display better, you should switch to another view. Figure 3.33 shows the representation of both an axonometric and a perspective view, seen from an altogether different viewpoint. As you'll notice, the representation is made up of various components that you'll learn about in the next section (see Figure 3.35). Once a view is made visible, it can also be selected by clicking in the left-most column of the palette. A selected view is indicated by a √ mark. While only one view can be *active* at a time, many can be *selected* at the same time. A selected view can be graphically manipulated using tools such as Move, Rotate, etc., unless it has been locked; you can do this by clicking in the last column beside its name.

- Just like the dialogs of other palettes, the dialog of the Views palette can be easily invoked by clicking on the header, View Name, in the title row of the palette. This dialog provides you with options for deleting, sorting, loading views from another project, and so on, like those you encountered in the dialogs of other palettes. The Edit option here will invoke the same dialog for the selected view as the View Parameters command in the Views menu. You'll be studying this dialog in detail in Section 5.6.

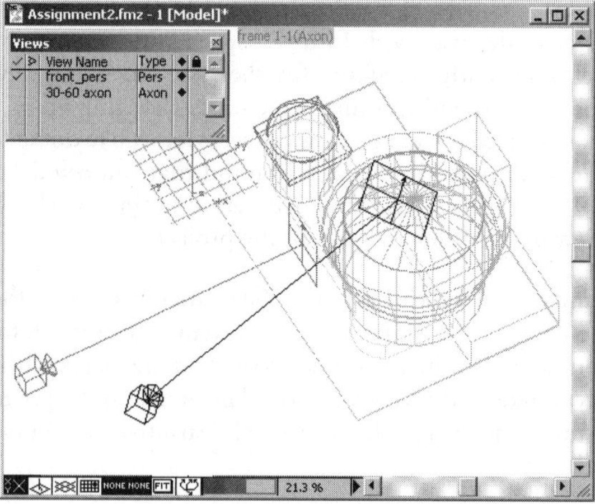

Figure 3.33

The Views palette, and the graphical representation of two views. One of the views has been selected.

Not only can you save different viewing types and viewing angles as separate views, you can also save zoomed in or zoomed out versions of the same view under separate names in the Views palette. In a Top view, for instance, you can fit the entire model in the window and save that as a view. You can then zoom in to various parts of the model and save each of them as a separate view. You'll quickly learn to appreciate both the convenience of switching between views by simply activating them in the Views palette and the substantial time savings that will accrue.

Make it a habit to save your most frequently used views in the Views palette, even if they're simple planar views such as Top, Front, and so on.

5.4 Creating Customized Views: The Cone of Vision

In Section 5.2, we saw what seemed to be a vast assortment of predefined viewing angles in different modes such as Axonometric, Isometric, and Oblique. However, even these might often seem to be insufficient or too limiting. You'd like to create your own views in which you have full control over where you are and what you're looking at in your modeling world. In a detailed building model, for instance, you'll almost certainly want to generate interior views of the building, which would be practically impossible to get using predefined views. Generating such customized views, which let you see your modeling world from any desired angle, is done in form•Z using the Cone Of Vision feature. Mentioned so often since the beginning of this exercise, we're going to be working with it at last!

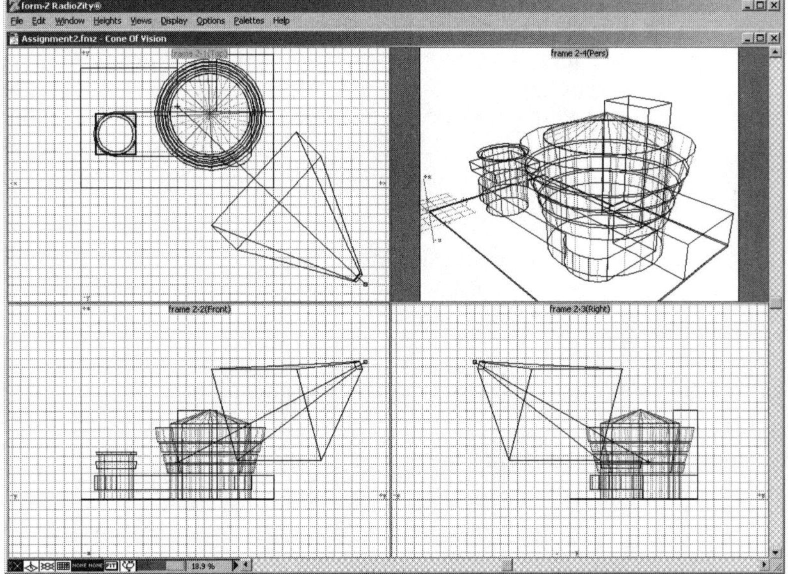

Figure 3.34

The Edit Cone Of Vision environment.

- Turn off the visibility of the views in the Views palette you had activated in the last section, and switch to any Perspective view. From the Views menu, select the very last option, Edit Cone Of Vision. This transports you to a new environment where the graphics window is divided into four smaller windows (see Figure 3.34). Three of these windows show the top, front, and right side planar views of the model and are used to manipulate the parameters of the view. They're referred to as the *modification windows*, and only one of them can be active at a time to modify the viewing parameters. The fourth window in the top right-hand corner redraws the actual view after each change of parameter, enabling the desired view to be generated interactively. This window is called the *preview area*.

- Notice the set of window tools in the lower left corner of the Cone Of Vision environment. These are the same window tools that you find in the modeling environment; here, they're used to control the graphic environment of the active modification window. You can zoom in or out, scroll, use the various kinds of snapping options, and so on. Similarly, you can use the options in the Window menu to make any desired adjustments to the settings of the active window.

The Cone Of Vision environment provides control over all the view parameters and lets them be graphically manipulated to obtain desired views. These parameters, which appear in all the three modification windows, are illustrated in Figure 3.35 in the top view window.

The parameters you'll most frequently manipulate are the *eye point* and the *center of interest*. The segment connecting the two is the *line of sight*. By default, the single light source in the model isn't visible, but you may have made it visible and created other light sources—as you'll see in the Lights exercise in Workshop 5 (Illuminating, Texturing, and Rendering Your World)—in which case these will be displayed as well. Make sure that you don't confuse them with the line of sight. The *view angle* and the *view spin* parameters respectively determine how much you see and in what angle from the vertical. Finally, the front and back clipping planes—referred to as the *hither* and *yon* planes respectively—can be adjusted to prevent objects in front of or beyond a certain plane from appearing in the view. They're especially useful in generating sections or sectional perspectives, as we'll see in the next section.

- To obtain a customized view, you need to make simultaneous adjustments to these parameters in all three modification windows. An example is shown in Figure 3.36. You'll find that certain adjustments can be more conveniently made in specific windows. Horizontal positions, for instance, are best adjusted in the top window, which is active by default. Simply move the eye point and the center of interest individually, by clicking and dragging, to the desired locations along the XY plane. Alternately, you can click and drag on the line of sight, which will move both the eye point and the center of interest.

- On the other hand, the heights of the eye point and the center of interest can be adjusted only in the two lower elevation windows. Activate either one of these by clicking on it. Then adjust the z coordinates of both points until you see the view you're aiming for in the preview area.

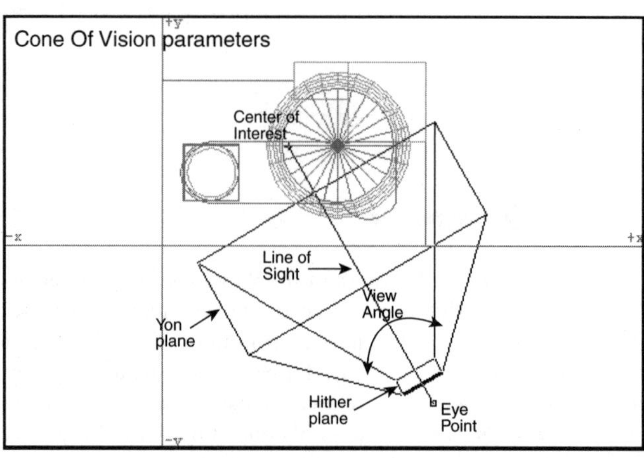

Figure 3.35

The Cone Of Vision parameters, illustrated in the top modification window.

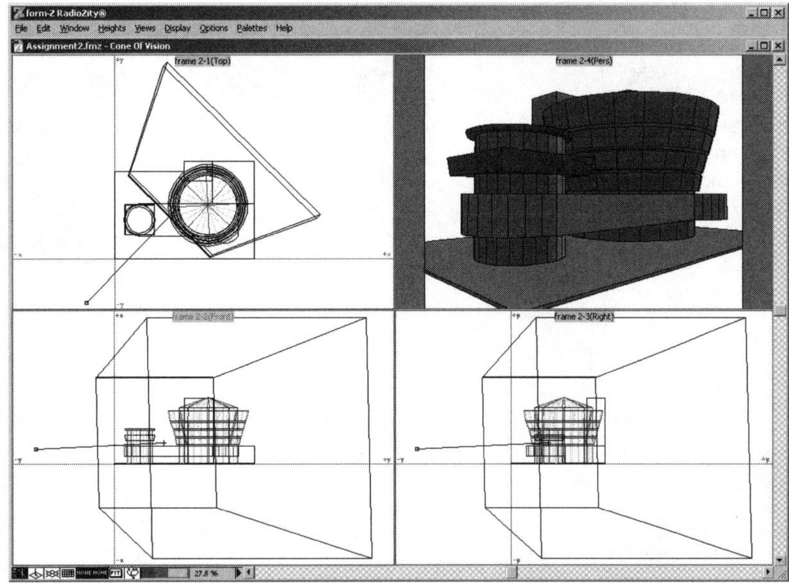

Figure 3.36

A customized view, generated by manipulating the appropriate parameters in all the three modification windows.

- Experiment with changes in the other parameters too—view angle, spin, and clipping planes—and observe the changes in the resulting view. The clipping planes can be pulled in or out by dragging them from their sides. Dragging their corners, on the other hand, changes the view spin but not the position of the plane. The view angle can be changed by dragging the lines connecting the front and back clipping planes, towards or away from the line of sight.

5.5 The Cone Of Vision Options

- The preview image in Figure 3.36 is in the Surface Render display mode, whereas what you're seeing in your window is probably a Wire Frame display. You can switch to any other kind of display mode by selecting it from the Display menu. Glance through this menu and the others, and you'll find that only those menu commands are activated which can be applied to either the preview window or the modification windows. The remaining commands are grayed out.

- Let's explore some of the other active commands to see how they work in the Cone Of Vision environment. Undo and Redo in the Edit menu allow you to undo and redo any changes you make to your viewing parameters in the modification windows.

- In the Views menu, activate the Clip Hither/Yon option. This will turn on the clipping action of the hither and yon planes. Now move the clipping planes in various ways, and you'll see how you can literally "chop off" parts of your model, preventing them from appearing in the view. For a building model in which the interior has been modeled, this is a great technique for generating sectional perspectives almost instantaneously, as shown in Figure 3.37.

- The three Reset commands in the Views menu allow you to reset the clipping plane parameters, view angle, and view spin, to the original values—the ones they had when you entered the Cone Of Vision environment. This is useful if changes made to these parameters prove to be unsatisfactory.

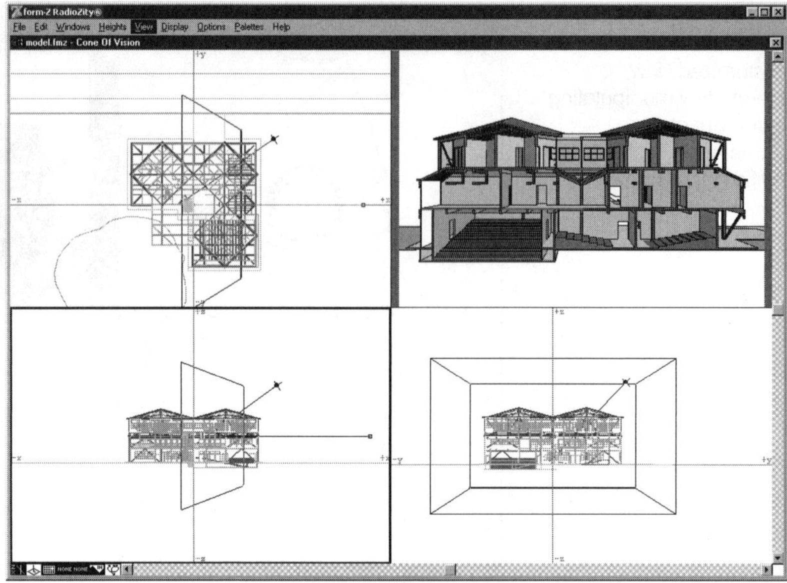

Figure 3.37

Generating a sectional perspective of a building model by appropriately positioning the clipping planes and activating the Clip Hither/Yon option.

- Align And Scale Frames in the Window menu is another very useful option. It will zoom in or out all three modification windows, such that the axes in all of them are aligned with one another, and all the objects fit in the windows and are displayed in the same scale. This is useful to do from time to time because the windows get desynchronized quite rapidly as you zoom in and out and scroll through them independently.

- The Window Setup command in the Window menu can be used to modify the settings of the modification windows, as you learned in Section 2.1 of Workshop 2 (Bringing a Sense of Scale). It's a good idea to use it for at least turning off the grid display, particularly if it's too dense, since it interferes with how well you can see and adjust the viewing parameters. This was done for all the Cone Of Vision illustrations so far, starting with Figure 3.35.

- Once you've generated a desired view, you can save it directly in the Views palette, if it's open, or use the Save View command from the Views menu that you encountered earlier in Section 5.3. You can then proceed to generate and save additional views, all *without* leaving the Cone Of Vision environment. The next command, Views, invokes the same Views dialog that's accessible through the Views palette. You can use it to delete or sort views, or to switch to another view while remaining in the Cone Of Vision environment, if your Views palette is closed.

- The only other command relevant to the Cone Of Vision environment is View Parameters from the Views menu. It is a crucial one and is discussed in detail in the next section. Before proceeding to it, however, familiarize yourself with all the Cone Of Vision options. Manipulate the various view parameters and generate some interesting views of your modeling world, saving them as you go along. When you're ready to exit the Cone Of Vision environment, click on the close button of the Cone Of Vision window. This will return you to the graphics window, and you'll see all the views you had saved within the Cone Of Vision environment listed in the Views palette. You can now switch to any of them by activating them in the usual manner.

5.6 The View Parameters Dialog

- There are various means of invoking the View Parameters dialog. You can select the View Parameters command from the Views menu in the Cone Of Vision or the regular modeling environment. You can also double-click on a view in the Views palette, click on the Edit button in the Views dialog for a selected view, or select any of the view types from the View menu with the option key (Mac) or Ctrl+Shift keys (PC) pressed. The View Parameters dialog lets you fine-tune your viewing parameters by numerical input, and is thus a good supplement to the graphical input you used in the Cone Of Vision mode. If this dialog is invoked for a saved view, the View Name will be displayed and all options will be active. For an unsaved view, the View Name and all the Camera View options are deactivated. Figure 3.38 shows the View Parameters dialog for a saved view.

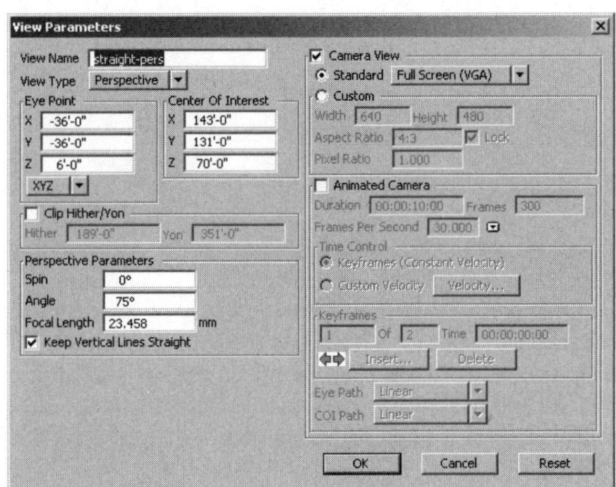

Figure 3.38

The View Parameters dialog, showing the parameters of the view depicted in Figure 3.39-a.

- Let's first explore the options on the left side of the dialog. The View Type shows the type of view, and also allows you to select a different type from the popup list. The Eye Point, Center Of Interest, and Clip Hither/Yon options are common to all view types and their exact values can be numerically specified. In the lower left part of the dialog, the parameters specific to the selected view type are displayed. Thus, for an axonometric view, the Spin and Angle values are listed, while a perspective view has an additional Focal Length value, along with an option to Keep Vertical Lines Straight. The focal length and viewing angle parameters are correlated, so a change in one will automatically update the other. Together, they represent the viewable area of a camera's lens. If the Keep Vertical Lines Straight option is selected, the perspective view will keep all the vertical lines parallel to the Z axis instead of converging them. The difference is illustrated in Figure 3.39.

- In the right half of the dialog is the Camera View option, which is activated only for a saved view. Go ahead and select this option. When you do this, the current view becomes a camera view instead of a regular view. The difference between the two can be only seen in a Shaded Render or RenderZone display. In a camera view, the resolution is determined by various parameters that simulate those in a real-life camera. In contrast, the resolution in a regular view is dependent upon the size of the graphics window and is set in the Image Options dialog, which we'll explore in Section 1.5 of Workshop 5 (Illuminating, Texturing, and Rendering Your World). To specify the camera settings for a camera view, use one of the standards available in the Standard popup list, or set the parameters individually using the Custom option. There is also a sizable Animated Camera sub-section, which we'll study when we work with animations in Workshop 7 (Ending With More), so ignore it for now.

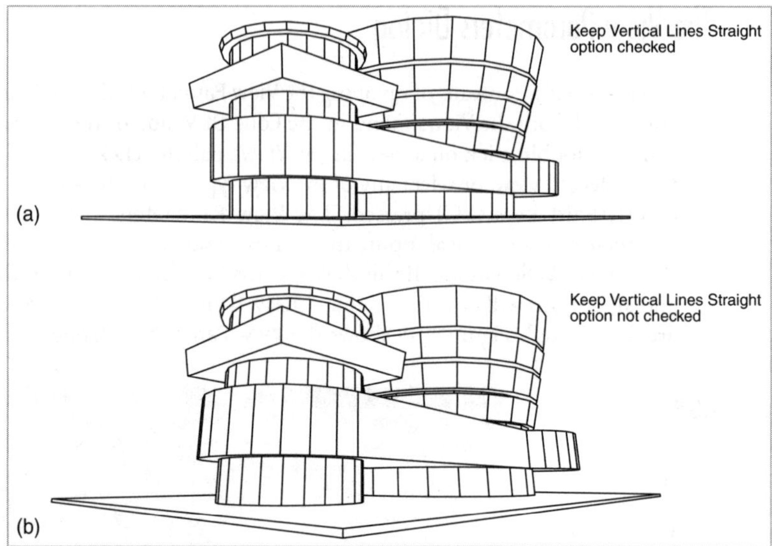

Figure 3.39

The same perspective view, shown with and without activating the Keep Vertical Lines Straight option.

- Make some modifications to various parameters in the View Parameters dialog for the current view, and see the resulting changes in the graphics window or in the Cone Of Vision environment, wherever you happen to be. One simple instance of where it can be useful to specify an exact numeric value for a parameter is in setting the Z value of the Eye Point to 6'-0" (as in the dialog in Figure 3.38), so as to position it at "human eye level" in a building model (as in the views in Figure 3.39). It's also usually easier to specify exact numeric values for Spin, Angle, Focal Length, etc., rather than set them graphically.

5.7 Setting, Navigating, and Walking Through Views

There are four more view-related tools located in the last window tool palette at the bottom of the graphics window. In this section, we'll work with three of these—Set View, Navigate View, and Walkthrough. The fourth tool—Match View—works best with a form•Z feature called Underlay, both of which will be covered together in the next section.

- Let's start with Set View, which is conceptually the simplest. Activate any of the views saved in your Views palette, then select the Set View tool (W-Tool:8,1). Click on any point in the graphics window. Now move the cursor and you'll find that the view gets rotated about its center, with the direction of rotation following that of the mouse movement. Clicking the mouse a second time stops the rotation of the view. 

- Notice that the Set View tool uses the same Continuous Window Tool Control feature as some of the Zoom tools you've seen—all other tools are grayed out when this tool is active, allowing you to apply it repeatedly for manipulating the current view. Thus, you can execute more view rotations with additional mouse clicks in the same fashion. To stop using the tool, simply click on it again or on any one of the deactivated tools, or press the Esc key, and the tool palette display will be restored to normal.

- The Set View tool can also be used with some modifier keys to move closer or further away from the center of the scene. The effect can be properly seen only in a perspective view, so switch to such a view if your current view isn't a perspective one. Then reapply the Set View tool, only this time keep the option key (Mac) or Ctrl+Shift keys (PC) pressed. You'll now find that as you move the cursor up, you're moving closer to the scene, and as you move the cursor down, you're moving further away from the scene. As soon as you release these modifier keys, the regular view rotations you saw earlier are performed.

- Perform some more view manipulations with the Set View tool until you get a sense of how it works. As you can see, it's very useful for quickly manipulating views without having to get into the Cone Of Vision mode. Keep in mind that you can save the new view as a separate entry in the Views palette—you'll then have instant access to both the original and the modified views.

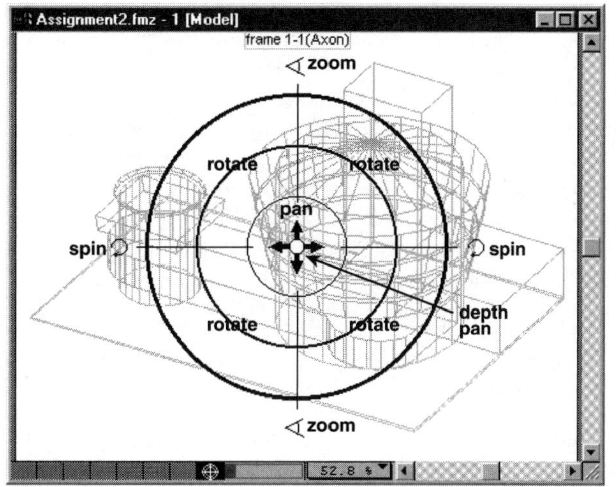

Figure 3.40

The navigation marquee invoked by the Navigate View tool, and its various controls.

WORKSHOP 3

For more complex manipulation of views outside the Cone Of Vision environment, you can use the next tool on the same tool palette, Navigate View. This lets you change many of the viewing parameters interactively, and not just rotate the view. The operation of this tool is again best seen in perspective mode, so switch to a perspective view before experimenting with it. Keep in mind, however, that it works for all types of views.

- As soon as you select the Navigate View tool, a navigation marquee appears in the center of the graphics window, as shown in Figure 3.40. The marquee is made up of four circles and a number of icons, the functionalities of which are also illustrated in the figure. Move the cursor near each one of the controls indicated, and see how it changes depending upon the control. Each of these controls represents a different view manipulation parameter.

- To activate a control, position the cursor on it and click. As you now drag the mouse, the view will change depending upon the type of control selected and the associated viewing parameter. Another click of the mouse will terminate the action of that control. The navigation marquee, however, is still displayed, allowing you to continue manipulating the view in different ways by selecting the appropriate controls. Thus the Navigate View tool also uses the Continuous Window Tool Control feature, just like the Set View tool, and its operation can be terminated in a similar fashion.

- Let's briefly review the five basic types of controls of the navigation marquee. The first is Depth Pan, active when the cursor is inside the innermost circle of the marquee. After the initial click, moving the cursor vertically upwards has the effect of moving you closer into the scene, while moving the cursor vertically downwards moves you away from the scene. Essentially, the eye point and the center of interest are being moved here *along* the line of sight.

- In contrast, the second control, Pan, moves the eye point and the center of interest *perpendicular* to the line of sight. This control is active when the cursor is positioned between the innermost and second circles. The panning is restricted to the horizontal direction if the cursor is close to the horizontal axis and to the vertical direction if it's close to the vertical axis; it's unrestricted if away from both the axes. The cursor icon changes, based on its position, to reflect the kind of panning.

- The third control, Rotate, is active when the cursor is positioned between the second and outermost circles. It has the effect of rotating the eye point, or the center of interest, or both, about the line of sight, depending upon whether the cursor is close to the outermost circle, the second circle, or between the outermost and second circles respectively. In the third situation, the relative rotation of the eye point and the center of interest depends upon the distance of the cursor from the bounding circles—clicking on the middle (third) circle between them will rotate both the eye point and the center of interest equally about the line of sight. The Rotate control of the Navigate View tool is thus a little more involved than the Set View tool, which is only capable of rotating the eye point about the center of interest. The rotation produced by the Rotate control can also be restricted to only the horizontal or vertical directions, if desired, by positioning the cursor close to the horizontal or vertical axes, just like the Pan control. The cursor icon changes to reflect the three kinds of directional rotations in a similar fashion.

- The fourth control, Spin, is activated by clicking on either one of the two Spin icons located outside the outermost circle along the horizontal axis of the marquee. Moving the mouse in a circular direction then causes the view to spin around the line of sight.

- The last control, Zoom, is similarly activated by clicking on either one of the two Zoom icons located outside the outermost circle along the vertical axis. Moving the cursor to the left then decreases the viewing angle, zooming the view in; in contrast, a rightward movement increases the viewing angle, zooming the view out.

You can see that Navigate View is quite a sophisticated view manipulation tool. Using it can be somewhat confusing at first, but persevere until you have a better understanding of how it works. It is, of course, no match for the simplicity and intuitiveness of the Cone Of Vision feature, but just like Set View, it lets you obtain a view without having to exit the modeling environment.

The next view-related tool in the eighth window tool palette is the Walkthrough tool. As is obvious from its name, this tool is used for obtaining an interactive walkthrough of the scene displayed in the modeling window. Such a walkthrough is often useful for getting a more realistic feel of the modeling project. Since perspective views are the only ones that can simulate the feeling of depth as perceived by the human eye, the Walkthrough tool is most effective when used with such views.

- Switch to a perspective view and activate the Walkthrough tool. This will invoke a small marquee made up of a central circle and horizontal and vertical arrows, as shown in Figure 3.41-a. You can see that it's far simpler than the marquee you encountered for the Navigate View tool. It also works a little differently. The movement of the cursor doesn't directly manipulate the view; instead, the position of the cursor with respect to the horizontal and vertical axes triggers a certain operation, the *speed* of which is determined by the distance of the cursor from the center of the marquee. The greater the distance, the faster the speed. Try it out. First click at the center or close to it, then move away. The view changes rapidly as you move further away from the center, and doesn't stop changing even if you stop moving the cursor. Move the cursor back to the center of the marquee, and the view stops changing. You can continue to change the view by moving the cursor out of the center again, or click to terminate the operation.

- Notice that bringing the cursor back to the center of the marquee doesn't restore the original view; it simply halts further modification of the view. Hopefully, you have the view saved in the Views palette from where you can restore it easily, if needed.
- So how does this tool enable you to walk through a scene? The answer to this lies in the various operations that can be triggered by moving the cursor, in combination with some modifier keys, horizontally or vertically away from the center of the marquee. These operations are illustrated in Figure 3.41-b. Experiment with each one of them until you get a sense of how the tool works.

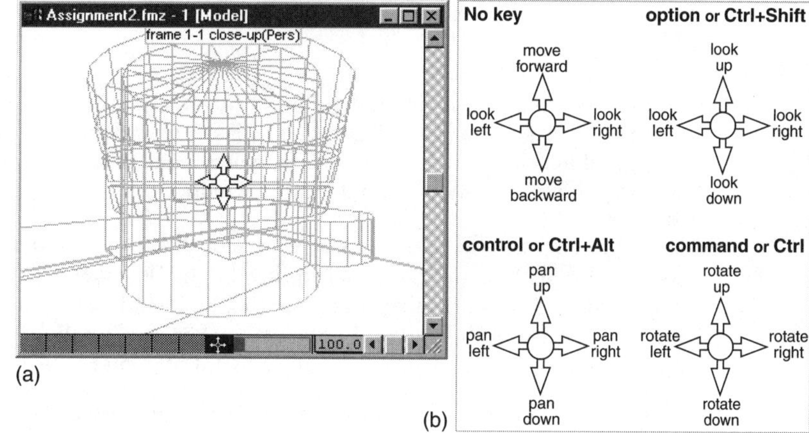

Figure 3.41

The marquee invoked by the Walkthrough tool, and the various operations that can be performed in combination with modifier keys on both the Mac and the PC.

5.8 Underlays and the Match View Tool

The last tool in the eighth window tool palette, Match View, is used in conjunction with a background image, letting you match a perspective view of the model with the perspective lines of the image. It's extremely useful when you want to situate your model in an appropriate background and then render it—you'd obviously want a realistic fit between the model and the background.

form•Z lets you place a background image in the graphics window in the form of an *underlay*. In this section, we'll first see how to place an underlay, and then how to use Match View to align a perspective view of the model with the underlay image.

- Open an existing project file for which you have a suitable background image. Otherwise, continue to use the building model project and locate any image to use as the background, even if it's unrelated to the building. Scan a photograph if you don't have access to any collection of image files. Use an image file format recognizable to form•Z: PICT, TIFF, JPEG, Targa, etc.
- Go to Window > Underlay. The Underlay dialog shown in Figure 3.42 will be invoked. Check the Show Underlay box to activate all the options in the dialog. Then click on the Select Underlay File button—this will invoke the standard File Open dialog for your operating system. Use it to locate and select the image file you want to use for the background. Leave the other options in the Underlay dialog as they are for now, and click on OK to exit the dialog.

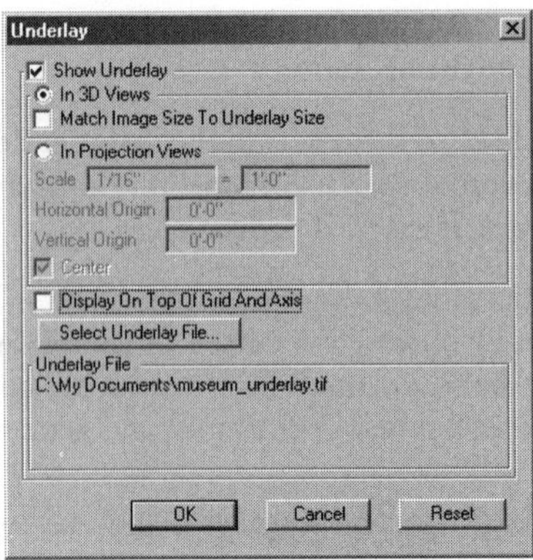

Figure 3.42

The Underlay dialog, with the Show Underlay option activated.

- Back in the window, you'll find that the selected image now appears in the background instead of the usual background color (Figure 3.43). Perform various operations such as zooming in and out, scrolling, changing the window size, switching to a different view, and so on, and you'll find that the underlay always fills up the entire window.

- If the proportions of your window happen to be different from those of the image, the image will look distorted. To avoid this problem, invoke the Underlay dialog again and select the option, Match Image Size To Underlay Size. Your graphics window will now be resized to match the size and proportions of the underlay image; thereafter, you'll only be able to reduce its size but not change its proportions. This is generally a useful option to leave turned on.

- Now switch to one of the planar views in the second group of the Views menu and select the Axonometric mode. You'll find that the underlay is no longer seen. If you have an image that you want to use as a reference in planar views—for instance, the site plan for a building—you'd naturally prefer to see the underlay in a planar view rather than in a 3D view. To do so, invoke the Underlay dialog again and switch from the default selection of In 3D Views to In Projection Views. Choose a different image file, if necessary. You can also specify the Scale at which the image should appear in the window, its Origin along both directions, and whether the specified origin should be placed in the center of the window or at the lower left corner. If you now return to the graphics window, the underlay will be visible in all the planar views following your scale and origin specifications, but not in any of the non-planar views.

- The only remaining option in the Underlay dialog, which applies to both 3D and planar views, determines whether the underlay should be displayed above or below the grid and axis. The default is below, which is fine as long as you continue to use the grid and axis for reference while you're modeling. However, when you want to generate renderings in which the underlay should be seen but not the grid and axis, you should activate the Display On Top Of Grid And Axis option.

Now that we've looked at underlays, let's see how the Match View tool comes in handy when a model needs to be aligned with an underlay image.

- Set the Underlay option back to In 3D Views and select its sub-option, Match Image Size To Underlay Size. Switch to a perspective view of your model, and select Edit Cone Of Vision from the Views menu. You'll find that the underlay now appears below the model in the preview area of the Cone Of Vision environment. You can try and align the model with the underlay by adjusting the various view parameters, as you learned to do in Section 5.4. While not impossible, this can be quite tedious. Fortunately, form•Z provides you with a convenient shortcut—the Match View tool.

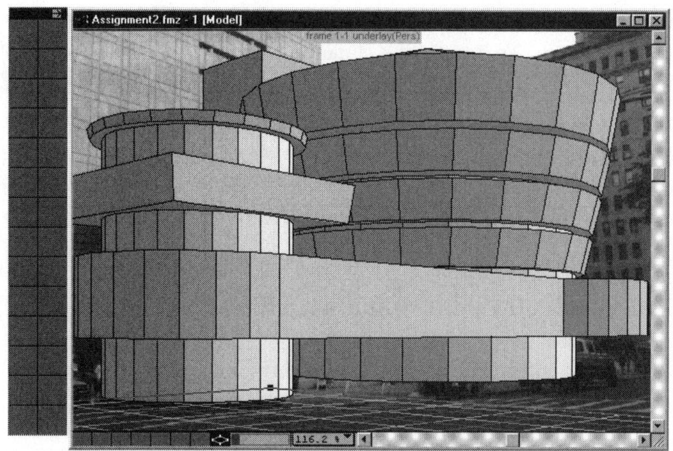

Figure 3.43

The Match View edit mode, with the selected underlay image in the background.

- Exit the Cone Of Vision environment, and make sure you're still in Perspective mode. Select the Match View tool (W-Tool:8,4). This will take you into the Match View *edit mode* in which all other tools in the modeling and window palettes are grayed out. At the same time, a *match rectangle* appears at the edges of the reference plane grid, with its vertices highlighted by little black boxes indicating that they can be edited (see Figure 3.43).

- Click on one of the vertices of the match rectangle and drag it to another position. This will change the shape of the rectangle, which in turn reshapes the reference grid and causes the perspective view to be changed. You can also click and drag the sides of the rectangle to reshape it—the perspective view is redrawn to match it. Keep moving the points and sides of the rectangle in this manner until the perspective view of your model seems aligned with that of the underlay image. When you're satisfied with the view, double-click to exit the Match View mode and save your new view in the Views palette.

- The Match View tool takes time getting used to, but it eventually gets easier and is more convenient than the Cone Of Vision method for generating a properly aligned view of the model with respect to an underlay image. It works best if the image has some rectangular shape that you can use as a reference for aligning the match rectangle. If you have such a shape in your image, create a new reference plane in the model which, in the final rendering, has to be positioned close to or on top of that shape. Make sure to activate *this* reference plane before selecting the Match View tool; you'll now find it much easier to properly align the model with the underlay image.

- You can modify the default behavior of the Match View tool by using it with the following keys: Shift to temporarily suspend the regeneration of the view that usually happens after each change, very useful for a complex model; control (Mac) or Ctrl+Alt (PC) to completely move the match rectangle; option (Mac) or Ctrl+Shift (PC) to move the view along the reference plane; and finally, control+shift (Mac) or Ctrl+Alt+Shift (PC) along with a mouse click to reset the match rectangle to coincide with the grid, if it has been displaced (which happens from time to time).

- By default, most of the display modes show the project background made up of the grid, axis, and underlay. For Shaded Render and RenderZone, however, the background isn't displayed by default—you need to actually go and activate this option in the dialogs of these displays. You already learned to do this for the Shaded Render display in Section 2.5; you'll study the RenderZone display options in Workshop 5 (Illuminating, Texturing, and Rendering Your World). If just the underlay is to be displayed in these modes, you can turn off the grid and axis displays from the Window menu, or invoke the Underlay dialog and check the Display On Top Of Grid And Axis option.

- You've seen how underlays can be useful for rendering and to provide reference points in modeling. When not in use, you should turn off the underlay display so that it doesn't distract you from the task at hand. To do this, simply deselect the Show Underlay option in the Underlay dialog, and your window background will be restored to its normal color.

5.9 Associated Windows, Tile Windows, and Window Frames

Now that you've learned how to create and use multiple views in many different ways, let's conclude this exercise by looking at three related utilities that can enhance your modeling speed and efficiency.

- Go to Window > New Model Window. A second window of the same project will open up, a status that's reflected by the name of the window in its title bar. You can change the view in this window to a different view of the project. Such a window is called an *associated window*, since it's a different window of the same project. You can open up several such associated windows and set them to different view angles or zoom levels, giving you the ability to quickly observe your model from different points of view or at different scales and levels of detail. You can also use different underlay files for different windows.

- Only one of such multiple associated windows can be the active window at a time, but the changes made to the model in the active window will be concurrently reflected in all the windows. All the associated windows of a project are listed in the last group of the Window menu. The active window is indicated by a √ mark. To switch from one window to another, simply select it from this menu or click on it if it's visible on the screen.

- There is a special type of associated windows called *tile windows*, which lie side by side instead of overlapping each other. Go to Window > Tile Windows > Open. Four smaller windows automatically open up and position themselves next to one another, each occupying a quarter of the default form•Z window size. The setup is similar to the Cone Of Vision environment. By default, three of the tile windows display planar views—Top, Right, and Back—while the fourth displays a 3D view. You can choose a different view for any window, either from the Views menu or the Views palette. Each tile window comes with its own set of window tools for manipulating its graphic environment, and can be resized, closed, etc., just like any regular window.

- The Tile Windows submenu has some other useful options. Arrange can rearrange the windows if you've resized or repositioned them. Align And Scale Views synchronizes the views in all the tile windows, in the same way as it was done for the three modification windows in the Cone Of Vision environment. And finally, the Close option closes all the open tile windows in one step.

Tile windows can be a great mode to work in if you have a large monitor. You can create or modify an object by seeing it simultaneously from many different angles, which is always a great help in visualizing a 3D world on an essentially 2D screen. Tile windows, however, doesn't allow you to continue a modeling operation started in one window in another window. form•Z, however, does have such a feature in the form of *window frames*. You were briefly introduced to the concept of frames in Section 3 of the Introduction. Let's now see how to work with them.

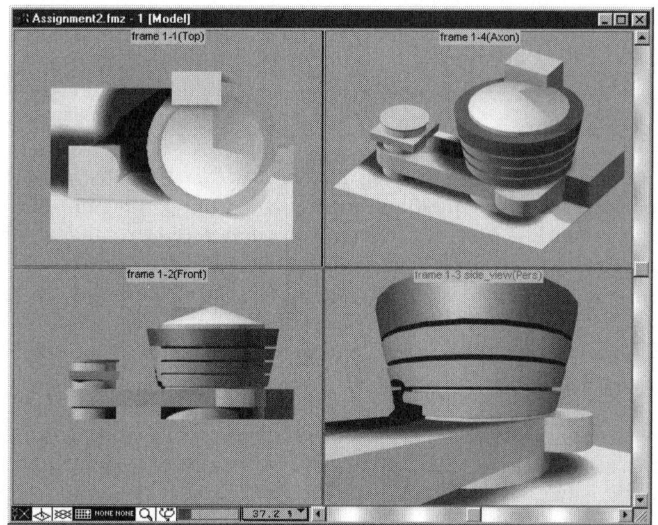

Figure 3.44

Working with window frames.

- Go to Window > Window Frames. This will invoke the Window Frame Options dialog, where you can specify the Layout of the frames and assign a specific View to each frame. Accept the default options by clicking on the OK button.
- You'll find that this divides the currently active graphics window into four parts or *frames*, each one of which is set to a different view, just like tile windows (see Figure 3.44). The number of a frame and the view it's set to is indicated at the top of each frame. The active frame is indicated by a red border; any other frame can be similarly activated by clicking on it. Once a frame is active, you can change its view or perform any part of a modeling operation in it. Go ahead and activate each frame in turn, setting them to views that you've saved in your Views palette.
- We'll now see how to continue a modeling operation from one frame to another. Activate a frame that's set to the Top view or to a 3D view, and use the Cube tool to draw the base of a cube in this frame. Don't specify the height of the cube just yet. Instead, take the mouse over to some of the other frames and see how a frame gets activated simply by positioning the mouse over it—you don't even have to click. Go to a frame with an elevation view—Front, Right, etc.—where you can now conveniently specify the height of the cube. Perform some more modeling operations using multiple frames in this manner, until you're comfortable with the technique.
- To change the frames layout, you can invoke the Window Frame Options dialog directly from the Window menu. Alternately, you can also make the necessary modifications graphically. To resize a frame, first make it active; then click on and drag any of its edges in the desired direction. To close a frame, drag one of its edges so that it touches the opposite edge. If you carry out this click-and-drag operation while pressing the option key (Mac) or Ctrl+Shift keys (PC), the frame will be split into two frames. You can continue to subdivide frames in this manner up to a maximum of 10, giving you plenty of views of your modeling world to work in simultaneously. To synchronize the views in all the frames, use the Align And Scale Frames command from the Window menu.
- When you no longer need the frames, go to Window > Window Frames once again. This option will be deselected and all the frames will disappear, returning you to your original graphics window.

EXERCISE 6

Specifying Your Preferences

Each one of you will end up working in form•Z with settings that *you* individually feel most comfortable with and which are best suited to the projects you're working on. These settings can be of two types: *system-related* such as icon style, the tools in the various tool palettes (which you may have customized as you learned in Section 4 of the Introduction), dialog options for various modeling and window tools and menu commands, open palettes and their positions on the screen at start-up, and so on; or *project-related*, such as working units, window setup, project colors for various interface components, default surface styles, layers, views, and so on. You've already learned how to modify all these settings to suit your modeling requirements.

However, you must have noticed that each time you open a new project, most of these settings revert back to the default form•Z values. It can be quite tedious having to reset these for every new project to the values that you prefer. form•Z, therefore, lets you store your preferred settings, which you can then apply when opening a new project. The system-related settings can be saved in a *preference file*, while the project-related settings can be saved in a *template file*. Let's see how to work with both file types.

6.1 Creating and Using Preference Files

- Quit form•Z if the application is still open and launch it again. You should see the interface shown in Figure I.4 of the Introduction. These are the default form•Z system settings for the interface.

- Make various changes to these system settings such as icon style and options in the various dialogs you've covered so far. Close the floating palettes you haven't covered, resize the others and move them around, and drag some frequently used tool palettes out and position them on in various locations of the application window. In short, make these settings visibly different from the default form•Z settings.

- You'll now save these system settings in a preference file. Go to Edit > Preferences. This will invoke the Preferences dialog. It contains a large number of options under various categories, which we'll look at in due course.

- For now, focus on the System:General category. Under the Preferences File section, select the Use Preference File option, as shown in Figure 3.45, instead of the Use Defaults option. Then click on the Save Preferences button, and specify a file name—say My_Pref1—and location in the Save Preferences As dialog. An extension of ".zpf" is automatically given to the file, indicating that it's a form•Z preference file.

- Quit form•Z again, and relaunch it. You'll find that the interface now reflects the system settings in the preference file you just saved.

You're not restricted to a single preference file only—any number of preference files incorporating different system settings can be created in the same manner. A preference file is just like any other regular file, form•Z or otherwise, which you can copy across disks, move, delete, and so on.

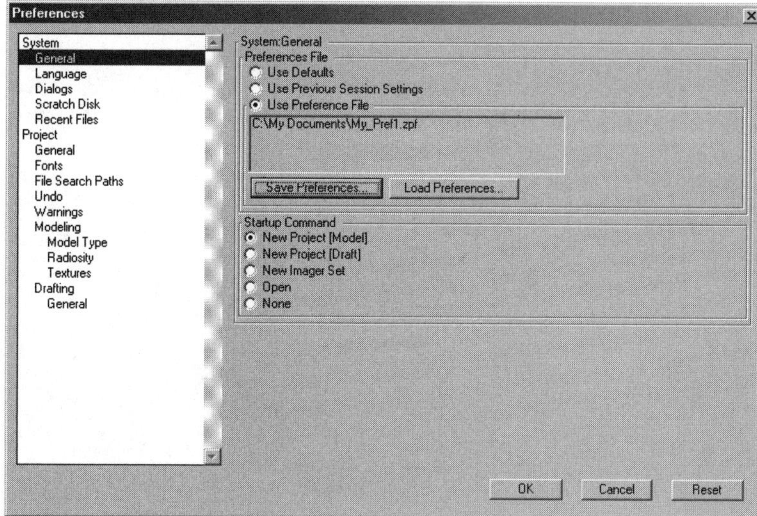

Figure 3.45

Instructing form•Z to use the system settings saved in the preference file, My_Pref1.zpf, instead of the defaults.

- To use a different preference file on the same computer, or to reference a preference file while using form•Z on a different computer, invoke the Preferences dialog from the Edit menu and select the Use Preference File option under the System:General category as before. Then simply click on the Load Preferences button and select the required preference file.

6.2 Creating and Using Template Files

You'll now see how to save and reuse project-related settings in a similar manner when required.

- In the open form•Z project you have right now, modify the default project colors and create additional surface styles as you learned in Exercise 1. Save a number of different views in the Views palette, and set the graphics window to one of them. Also, go through dialogs such as Working Units and Window Setup, and make some changes to the default settings they contain. The aim, again, is to make the project settings visibly different from the form•Z defaults.

- Go to File > Save and save the file in the form•Z format with a suitable name, say My_Template1. Then close it using File > Close.

- Open a new modeling project by going to File > New[Model]. You'll find that this has the system settings you specified in the preference file in the last section, but not the changes in project settings you just made.

- Invoke the Preferences dialog from the Edit menu as before, but this time, select the Project:General category from the hierarchical list to the left of the dialog. Under the New Projects section, select the Use Template Project option, as shown in Figure 3.46, instead of the Use Defaults option. Then click on the accompanying Choose Template File button and select the file you just saved with the desired project settings, My_Template1.fmz. Click on the OK button to exit the Preferences dialog.

- You'll find that the new settings won't be applied to the currently open project. But open a new modeling project, and you'll see that the project settings are identical to the ones you saved in My_Template1.fmz.

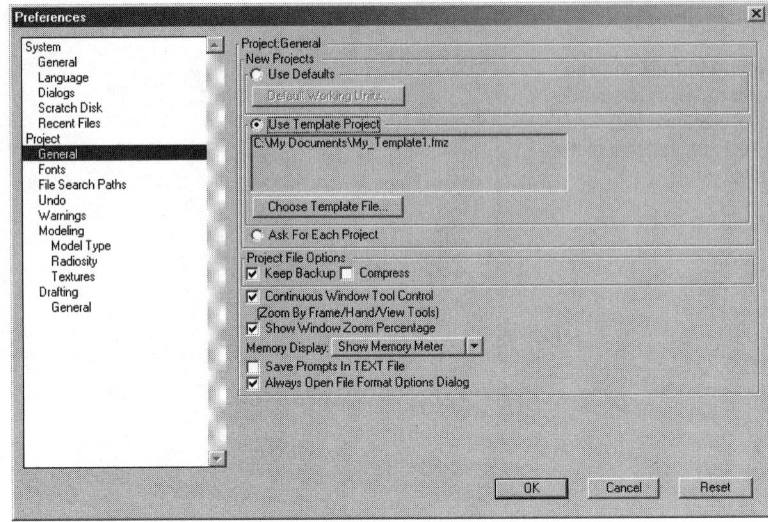

Figure 3.46

Instructing form•Z to use the project settings saved in the file, My_Template1.fmz, instead of the defaults.

Just as with preference files, you can create any number of template files for different categories of projects and load them when required.

6.3 Other Preferences

As you can see in Figures 3.45 and 3.46, the **Preferences** dialog contains a number of other options that determine how form•Z will operate. Most of these are self-explanatory, and you can explore them on your own at leisure. A few important options are described in detail here.

- Go back to the **Project:General** category, and notice that the **Keep Backup** option is checked by default for **Project File Options**. This accounts for the backup file, identified by the ".fzb" extension, that gets created for every form•Z file. It's useful to keep this option checked, so that if you inadvertently lose or delete the original project file, you can use the backup file instead.

- In the same category, you'll find the **Continuous Window Tool Control** option, which you'll recall from your encounters with the **Zoom** and **View** window tools. You can deselect this option if you're not comfortable with it. The next two options refer to the zoom percentage and memory availability values that are displayed at the end of the window tool palette by default; you can choose to turn these off if not required. The **Save Prompts In TEXT File** option, if checked, will save all the ongoing content of the **Prompts** palette to a text file called **form•Z Prompts** in the form•Z application folder; this can be useful for future reference. With regard to the **Always Open File Format Options Dialog** option, it's better to leave it turned on, unless you're repeatedly saving form•Z files into a different file format using the same settings.

- Next, go to the **Project:Auto Save** category and look at its options. Here you can activate the **Enable Auto Save** feature and specify how it should operate—how often the saving should happen, and whether it should be saved over the open project file or saved as a separate copy (Figure 3.47). The second option will take more disk space, but it's useful because it allows you to go back and undo any operations in the original file; this would not be possible if the project was saved automatically, unless you had activated the **Save Undos In Project** option in the **Undo Options** dialog, as you learned in Section 3.3 of Workshop 1 (Letting Yourself Go). You can even go one step further and select the Incremental File Names option in the Save As Copy section, which will create a separate project file for *each* automatic save. Do this only if you have plenty of disk space to spare!

- The next Preferences category under Project, Fonts, lets you specify the default fonts that will be used in form•Z. This will be relevant when you work with 2D and 3D text in Workshop 7 (Ending With More) and the drafting module in the Appendix, so you can skip it for now. The File Search Paths category lets you add folder locations that will be searched by the application. The Undo category lists the same options as the Undo Options dialog you worked with in Workshop 1 (Letting Yourself Go). The Warnings category lists several warning preferences, some of which you might like to turn off once you become proficient with the program and know what you're doing.
- The Model Type category under Modeling contains some options related to the smooth and facetted object types, and unless you have particular reasons to work with facetted objects, the default selections here should be fine. The Textures and Radiosity preferences, also under Modeling, and the Drafting preferences will become clear once you deal with these topics in Workshop 5 (Illuminating, Texturing, and Rendering Your World) and the Appendix respectively.
- You've already looked at the preferences in the System:General category. The Language category under System lets you choose from among the languages you opted to include when you installed the program.
- Look at the options for the next System category, Dialogs. Here, you can set the size of the Preview Dialogs, which are dialogs giving you a preview of how a particular operation will be performed. You came across such a dialog when working with the Query tool in Section 3.6 of Workshop 2 (Bringing a Sense of Scale), and will be encountering many more such dialogs in the next workshop. You can also choose the font settings for the dialog, specify how it will be centered, and choose a different button order.

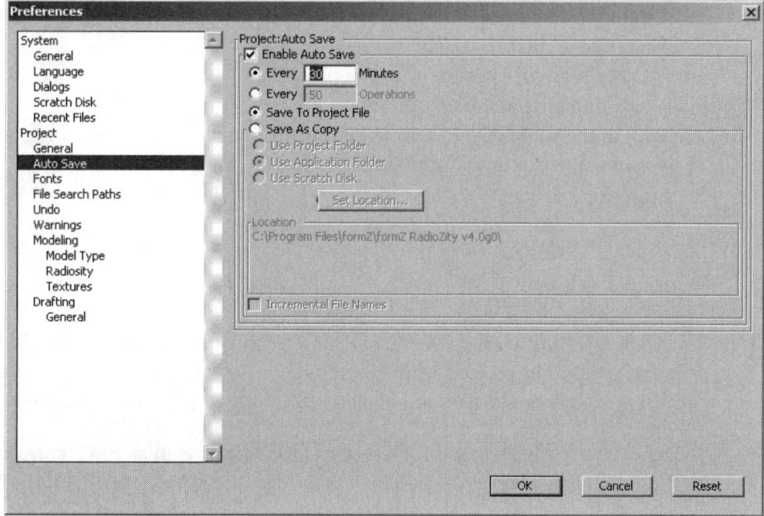

Figure 3.47

The Auto Save options in the Preferences dialog.

- The Scratch Disk options let you specify the location of the various temporary files that are automatically created by form•Z. These include files containing the Undo and Redo records, rendering information, and other calculations for an open project, as well as the scratch file that's created if the program crashes unexpectedly. It's a good idea to set a Custom location for these files, particularly if you're working in a networked environment, so that in the event of a crash, you know exactly where to locate the scratch file. When you find it, give it a ".fmz" extension if that's missing, and you should be able to open it like any other form•Z file.
- form•Z has an Open Recent option in the File menu that lists the last ten files opened by the program. It's a convenient shortcut for opening a file you've recently been working with. The final System category, Recent Files, is related to this option. Here, you can change the maximum number of files from the default value of 10. There are also a few other options related to how the file names are displayed and sorted.

Now that you've finished exploring all the Preferences options, it's time to move on to the assignment for this workshop.

ASSIGNMENT 3

An Item of Furniture

Model any piece of furniture, such as a table, chair, desk, cabinet, etc., in detail and to proper scale. Don't choose something that is too simple!

The actual exercise of modeling the chair shown here will now be demonstrated step by step. It's a variation of the famous "red and blue chair" by Gerrit Rietveld. You can refer to the form•Z files for this assignment in the Assignments > Workshop3 folder of the accompanying CD-ROM. A color rendering of the project is in the Assignment3.tif file in the same folder.

Setup

Open a new form•Z project. We first need to set its Working Units under the Options menu appropriate to the scale and type of the project, which is an item of furniture. Set the unit to Inches rather than Feet under the English measurement system, the Numeric Accuracy to 1/16", and the Angle Accuracy to 0.5°.

Change also the Window Setup. Have a grid module of 1' in all directions with 4 subdivisions. Finally, set the scale under the Display menu to 1" = 1' and select the Reset tool (W-Tool:7,9) from the Zoom tool palette.

Step 1

We'll start by constructing the front legs of the chair. Using the Cube tool (M-Tool:1a,1), create a block with dimensions of 7/8" along X, 3 1/2" along Y, and 23" along Z, starting from the origin [0,0,0] as shown.

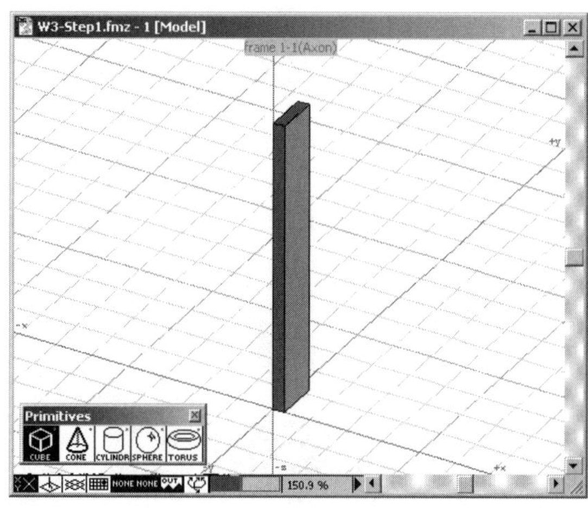

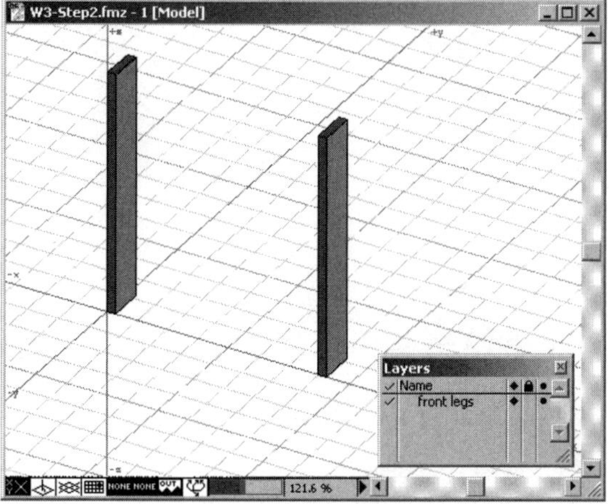

Step 2

With coordinate mode set to relative and self-copy modifier set to One Copy, apply the Move tool (M-Tool:13a,1) to the block and specify the Move coordinates as [20 7/8]. This will duplicate the block at a distance of 20" from the original block along the X axis.

Both the blocks have been created in the default layer. Change the name of this layer in the Layers palette to front legs.

Step 3

The next step is to model the front support. Create a new layer called front support and make it active. With the Cube tool, create a block of 22 1/2" by 7/8" and a height of 3 5/8" anywhere on the XY plane. This has to be positioned appropriately with respect to the legs.

Draw a temporary line connecting the facing points of the legs as shown.

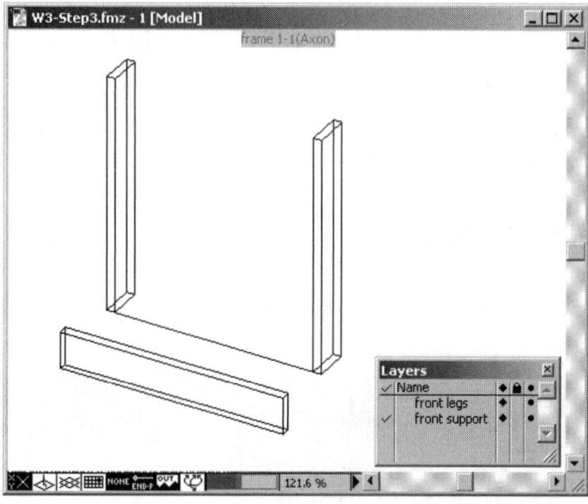

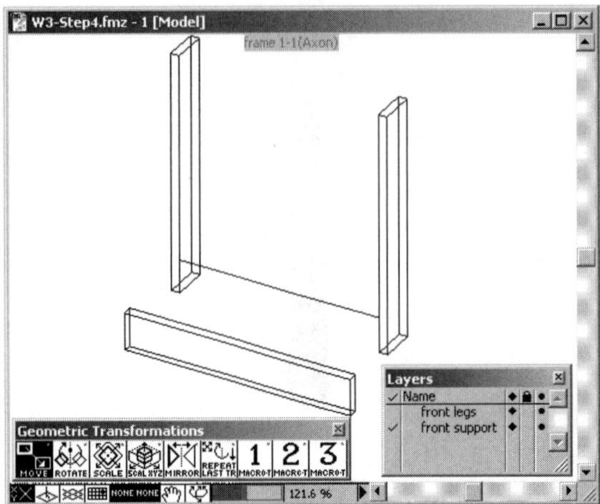

Step 4

Move the line vertically upwards by a distance of 3 1/4".

Step 5

Use Move again with Midpoint snap to position the front support on this line, centered between the two legs. Its front face should lie on the same plane as the front faces of the legs.

Use pick parade (as you learned in Section 4.5 of Workshop 2, Bringing a Sense of Scale) to select the temporary line coinciding with the front support and delete it.

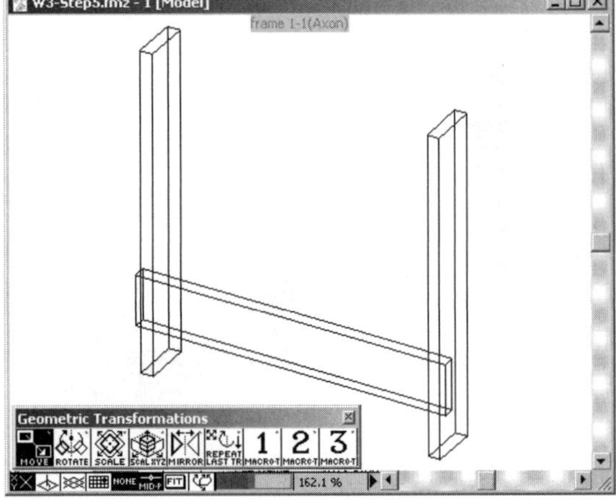

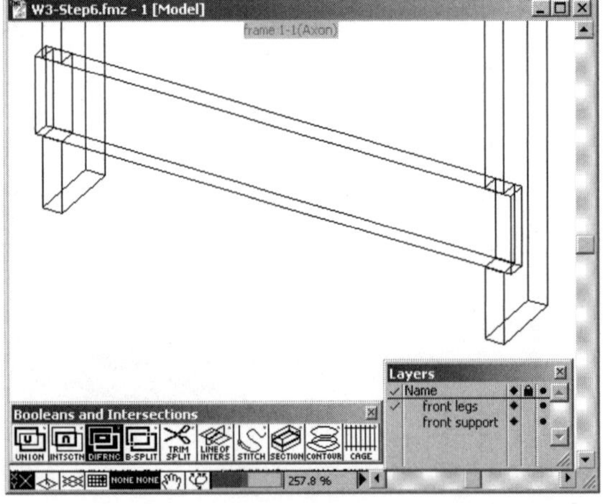

Step 6

You now have to create two notches in the front legs for the support you just modeled. Activate the front legs layer. Use the Difference tool (M-Tool:9a,3) with the Operand Status set to Keep so that the front support is retained. Difference the support from each of the legs in turn. Then delete the original, un-notched legs that are retained after the operation. These will overlap with the notched legs, so zoom in and select them carefully.

Step 7

The back legs are slightly more complicated and we'll model them using reference planes. Turn off the **front support** layer, and create and activate a new layer called **back legs**. Create an arbitrary reference plane on one of the inside faces of the front legs, oriented as shown. Deselect the **W** switch and activate the **A** switch in the **Prompts** palette. Set **Heights** to a custom value of 7/8". Then, with the **Vector Line** tool in **3D Extrusion** mode, create a polygonal slab on this plane by entering the following points:

Pt #1: [0] Pt #2: [26 3/8]

Pt #3: [26 3/8,2 7/8] Pt #4: [0,13 3/8]

Pt #5: [c] (for close) or triple-click

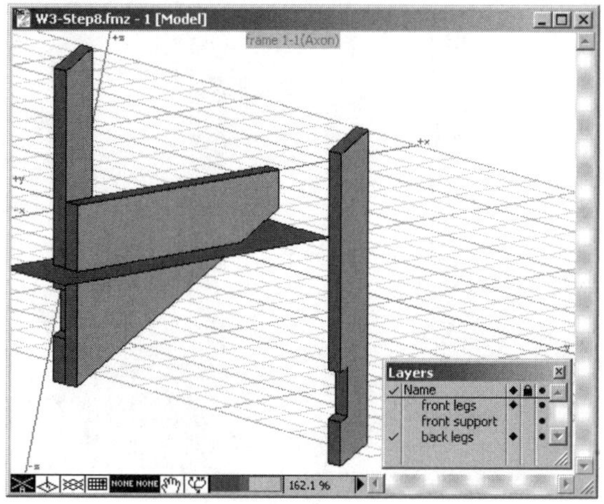

Step 8

Define a second arbitrary plane passing through the top, inclined face of the polygonal slab you just modeled. Create a 2D surface on this plane whose dimensions are larger than the inclined face on all sides. Then move this 2D surface in the Z direction so that it lies 4 1/2" below the face as shown.

Step 9

Set **Heights** to **Graphic/Keyed**. Extrude the 2D surface in the opposite direction from the top face of the polygonal slab, such that it extends beyond the lower face of the slab. Let's call this new block a *temporary block*.

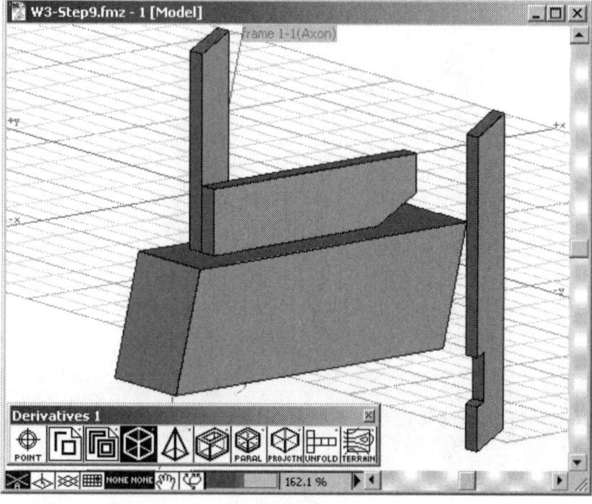

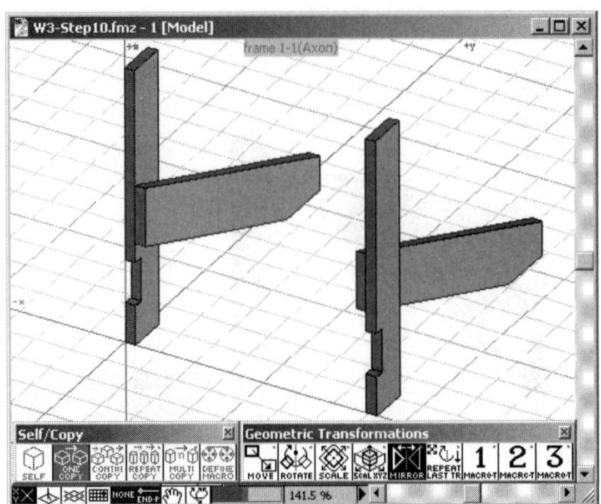

Step 10

Set the Operand Status in the dialog of the Difference tool back to Ghost. Use this tool to subtract the temporary block from the polygonal slab. This will yield one of the back legs in its final form. Delete the 2D surface you had created in Step 8, which served as the base of the temporary block.

Set the reference plane back to XY. Use the Mirror tool in One Copy mode to create another back leg touching the inside face of the second front leg. Use Endpoint snapping for accuracy.

WORKSHOP 3

Step 11

Next, we'll add the triangular side supports to the front legs. Create and activate a new layer called side supports. Turn off the back legs layer, so that you can see only the front legs now. Switch to the ZX plane. With the Prompts palette set to absolute world coordinate mode, use the Vector Line tool in 3D Extrusion mode to create a 3/4" thick slab with the following base point specification:

Pt #1: [0]

Pt #2: [0,0,-13 1/2]

Pt #3: [-6 5/8]

Pt #4: [c] (for close) or triple-click

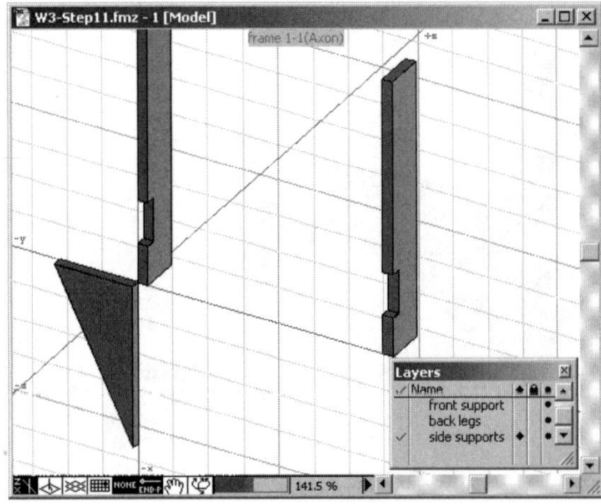

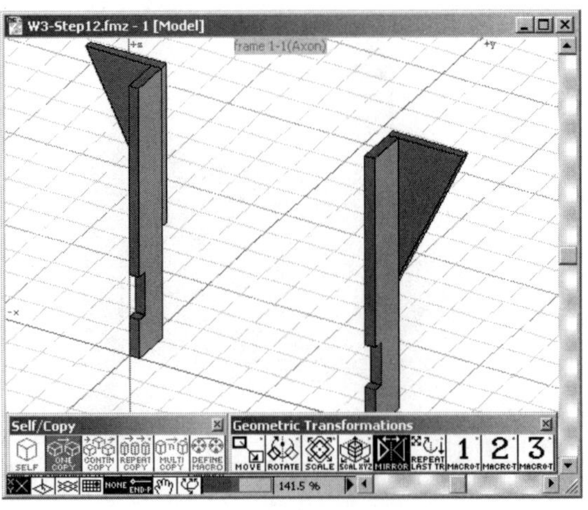

Step 12

Switch back to the XY plane. Use the Move tool in Self mode with Endpoint snap to move the newly created triangular block, such that it touches the top corner of the back face of the front leg as shown. Then use the Mirror tool in One Copy mode to make a mirror image copy of it for the other leg.

Step 13

Next, we'll move on to the seat. This is simply a 7/8" slab sitting on top of the inclined faces of the back legs. Turn off all layers except the **back legs** layer, and create and activate a new layer called **seat**. Create an arbitrary plane passing through the top face of one of the back legs as shown. Using reference plane coordinates and with the **Cube** tool, create a rectangular extrusion of base dimensions 20" by 18 1/8" and height 7/8", which fits exactly on top of the back legs as shown.

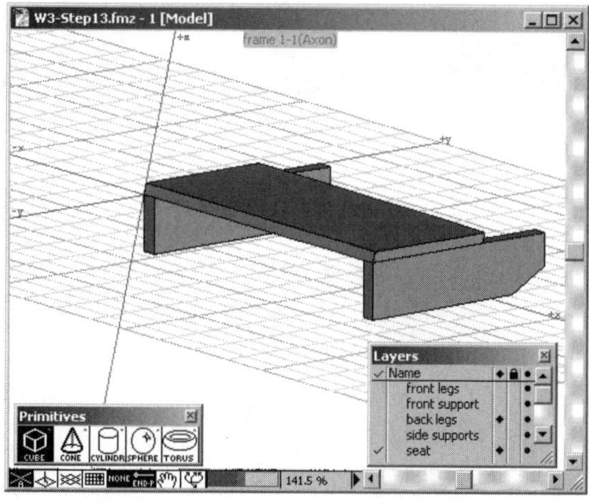

Step 14

The back of the chair relates to the seat, so we'll model that next. Turn off all layers except **seat**. Create and activate a new layer called **back**. In the dialog of the **2D Enclosure** tool, set the **Justification** option to **Right** and the **Wall Width** to 3/4". Switch to the **Right** view. Use the **Segment** tool (**M-Tool:3b,2**) to create a line, the first point of which must snap to the lower, right endpoint of the seat. The second point should be numerically specified as [32 3/4",60°,0] by setting the **Prompts** palette to relative, polar coordinate mode (deselect the **A** and **C** boxes).

Step 15

Switch to a non-planar view and extrude the double-line 2D object in a direction perpendicular to its surface by a height equal to the width of the seat, which is 20".

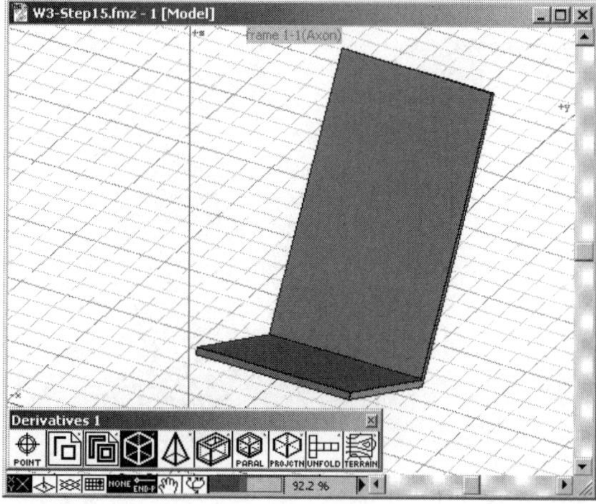

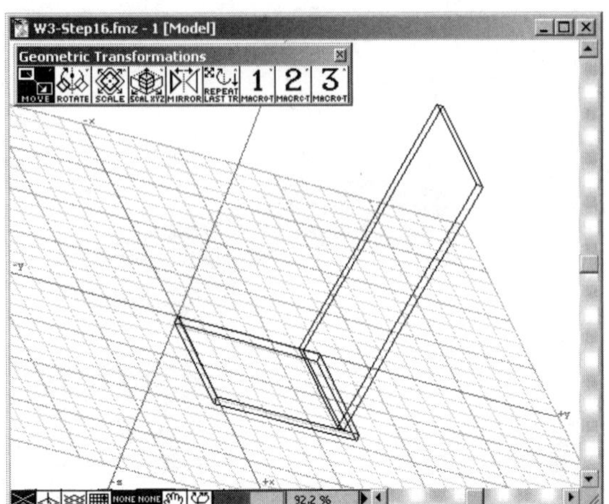

Step 16

Create a reference plane coinciding with the top face of the seat. Use reference plane coordinates to move the back by a distance of 2" towards the front of the chair along this plane. You can use the **Set View** tool to switch to a view where you can see the change more clearly.

Step 17

Turn off the **seat** layer, and create a reference plane passing through the front face of the chair back. The back is actually made up of three separate pieces: a central piece of width 10 1/2" and two side pieces of width 2 7/8", with a 3/4" gap between them. The side pieces are also 1 1/2" shorter than the central piece. With the help of the active arbitrary plane, create such a 2D pattern on the front face of the chair back, using a different color. You can switch to **View > Plane Projection > Top** to make this task easier.

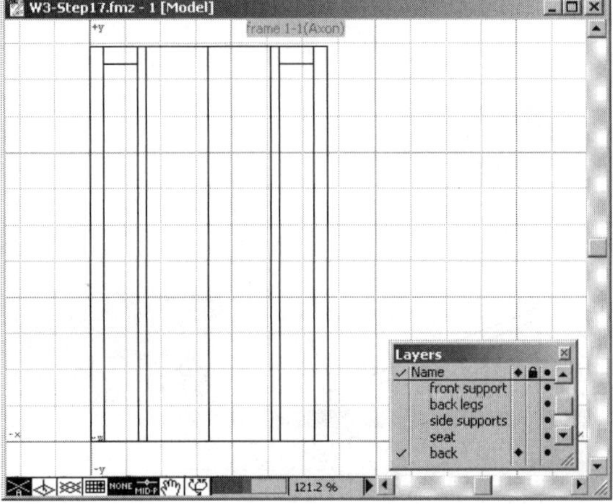

Step 18

Use the 2D pattern to recreate the 3D blocks for the back, with the **Cube** tool. The thickness of the blocks should be 3/4", oriented in the same direction as the original block. Delete the original block and 2D lines after you've finished creating the new blocks for the back. You can use **Edit > Select By** to easily select all the 2D lines that were created in a different color.

Step 19

Now that the back is complete, we can add the back support. This is a simple block measuring 25 1/2" by 4" by 1", attached to the back of the chair. Create and activate a new layer called **back support**. Using the same arbitrary plane you had created for the back, create a block of the required dimensions, starting at the origin.

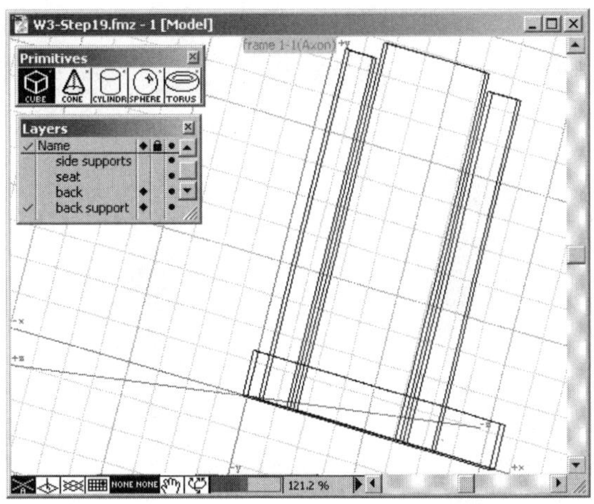

Step 20

Use **Midpoint** snap to move the support so that it's now centrally located with respect to the back. Its front face must touch the back faces of the blocks making up the back of the chair.

Step 21

Once this is done, simply move the back support by a relative distance of 14" upwards along the back surface of the chair. This would be along the +Y direction, if you have the same arbitrary reference plane shown in the previous illustration. Check the **Right** view to see if it's correctly positioned. The back support is now complete.

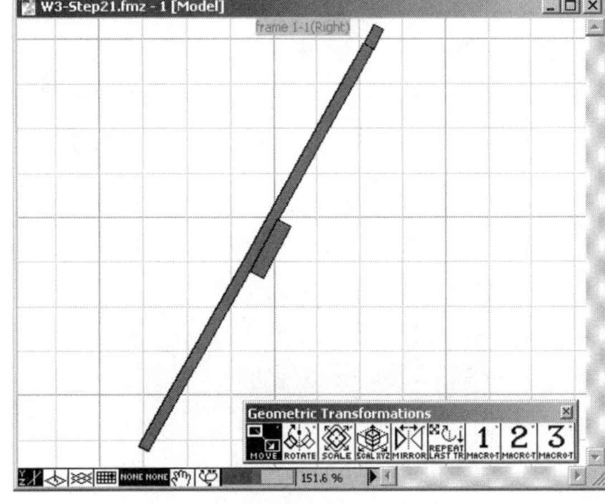

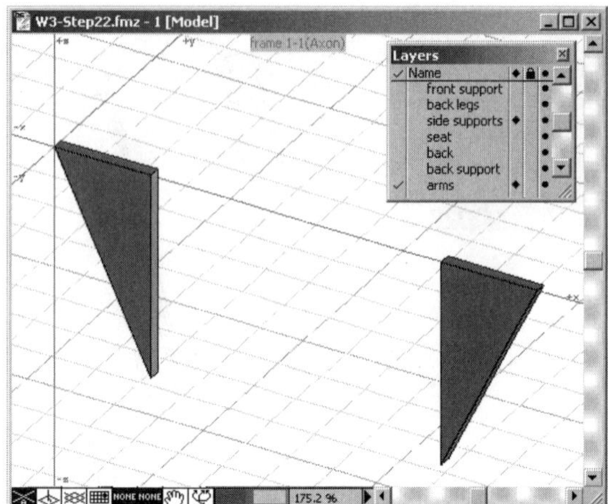

Step 22

Finally, we come to the most difficult part of the model—the arms. Turn off all the layers except side supports, and create and activate a new layer called arms. Define an arbitrary reference plane passing through the top face of the left side support as shown.

Step 23

Move the origin of the arbitrary reference plane by a distance of 1" along the –X direction and 8" along the –Y direction using the Move Plane Origin tool (W-Tool:3,4). Make sure the W box in the Prompts palette is deselected when you make this move. Save this plane in the Planes palette. Switch to View > Plane Projection > Top, and draw a 2D rectangle of size 8 3/4" by 30 7/8" positioned at the origin of the plane.

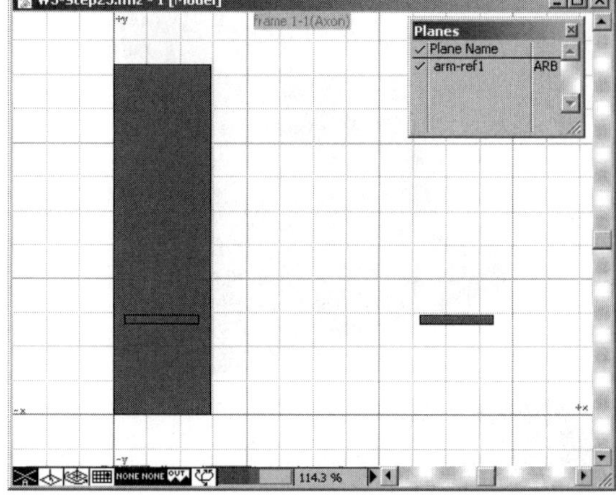

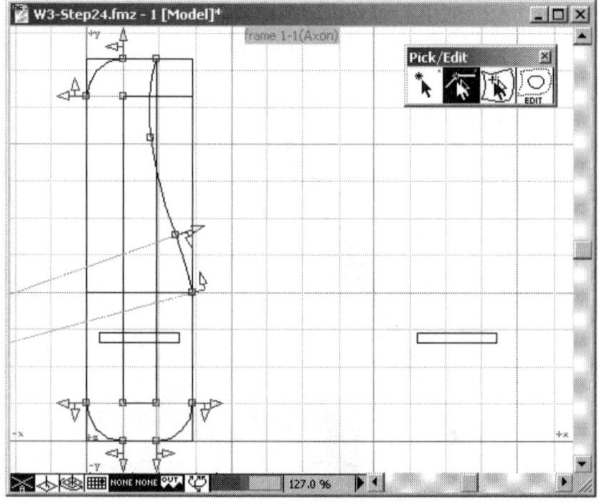

Step 24

Next, draw construction lines 3" inside from all the four sides of the rectangle. In addition, draw one construction line 12" inside from the side facing the front of the chair. Use these construction lines, and object snapping, to create a single 2D shape for the arm of the chair, combining lines, arcs, and B-splines. A certain amount of approximation can be used for the gradual curve at the back. Use the Edit Controls tool (M-Tool:4b,1) to reshape the curve if necessary.

Step 25

Delete the original rectangle and construction lines. Still in Top view, rotate the 2D arm surface by an angle of –11.5º, with the lower left corner of the side support selected as the center of rotation.

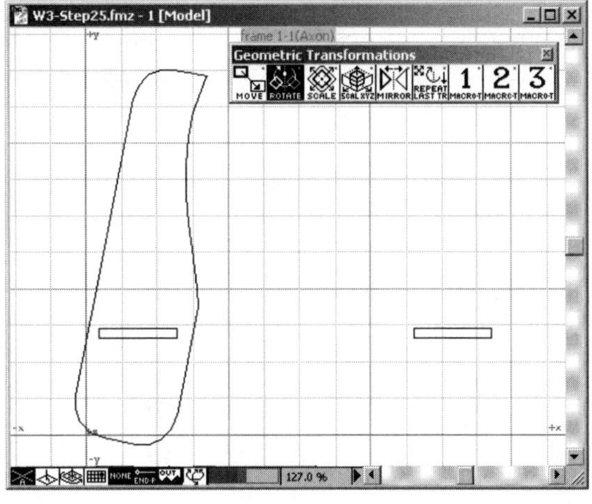

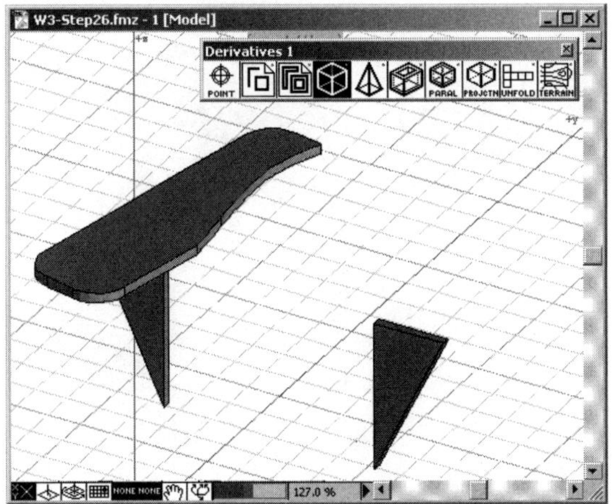

Step 26

Switch to a non-planar view and set the reference plane back to XY. Extrude the arm surface in the +Z direction by a distance of 7/8" to yield the 3D slab for the left arm.

Step 27

Make the back layer visible and use the Difference tool to create a notch in the arm where one of the back panels cuts into it. Turn on the display of ghosted objects in the Wire Frame Options dialog, and retrieve the back panel with the Unghost tool (M-Tool:14b,2). This completes one arm. Use the Mirror tool in One Copy mode to make a mirror image copy of it for the other arm. Switch to a different view to check if the result is accurate.

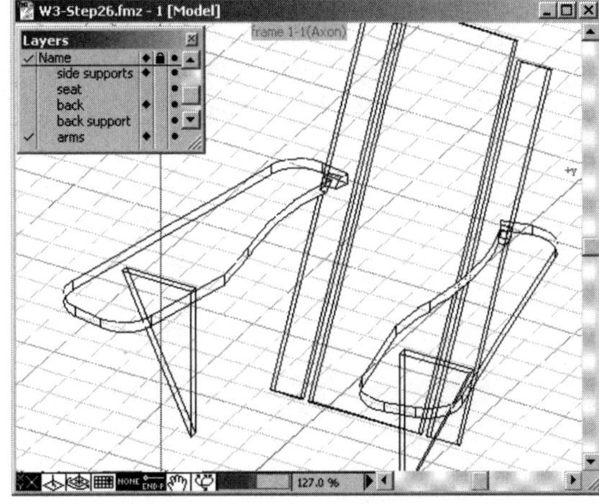

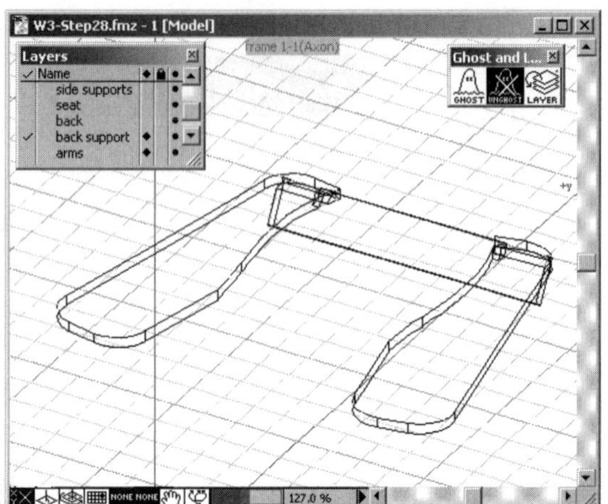

Step 28

Activate the back support layer, and turn off all other layers except arms. Use the Difference tool in the same manner to create a notch in the back support for each of the two arms where they cut into it. Unghost the arms to retrieve them.

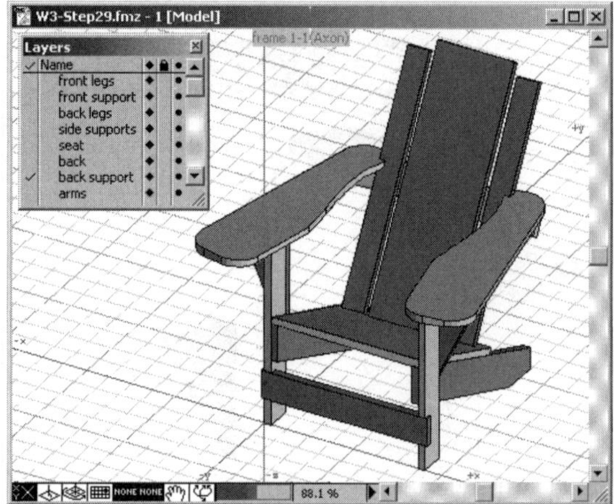

Step 29

With that, the chair is complete. Turn on all the layers to see it in its entirety. Many colors were used to make the modeling of different parts easier, but you can now change the colors to suit a desired color scheme.

The only additional embellishment needed for your chair is for some of the edges to be rounded off. You can leave this for Workshop 4, when you will learn to use the Round tool.

WORKSHOP 4

Enhancing Your Modeling Capabilities

In this workshop, you'll be introduced to several new modeling tools. Most of these are located in the left and right columns of Row 5; the remaining are scattered across Rows 6, 9, and 13.

You'll start by learning how to create complex objects from simple 2D shapes, first by revolving them about an axis, and then by sweeping, skinning, and lofting them along various paths. You'll then work with the powerful sectioning tools in form•Z, as well as model undulating landforms and terrains. The remaining derivative tools on Row 5 will also be covered. Next, you'll look at the processes of rounding object edges and corners, transforming objects using draft angles, and creating blends and fillets. Finally, you'll learn how to attach objects to each other in various ways to build up sophisticated configurations, align and distribute objects, extend and trim them with respect to other objects, and place them along a path to generate interesting forms.

EXERCISE 1

Going Round and Up and Down

In this exercise, we'll look at four different tools based on the same principle: deriving objects by the operation of revolution about an axis. These objects fall into four categories—generic objects of revolution, helixes, bolts and screws, and spiral staircases—and we'll explore the tools devoted to each one of them. Since we'll be working with spiral staircases, it is also a good time to look at the Stair From Path tool, which is used for creating regular staircases in building models.

1.1 Generic Objects of Revolution

- Begin a new project and close all palettes except Prompts and Surface Styles. Turn Grid Snap on (W-Tool:4,1) so that your modeling is more precise. Then draw a 2D circle on the XY plane, not too far from the Y axis, but not intersecting or touching it either (see Figure 4.1-a).
- Select the Revolve tool (M-Tool:5b,1). You'll be asked to first specify the *source shape*. This can be any 2D surface, 2D enclosure, or a segment, outline, or face of an existing 2D or 3D object. Select the 2D circle you just drew. Next, you'll be asked to specify the *axis of revolution*. Select the Y axis. This invokes the Revolve dialog, giving you a preview of the revolved object created by the operation, along with the options to make various modifications to it (see Figure 4.1-b). We'll briefly go through each one of these options and see how they affect the resultant object.

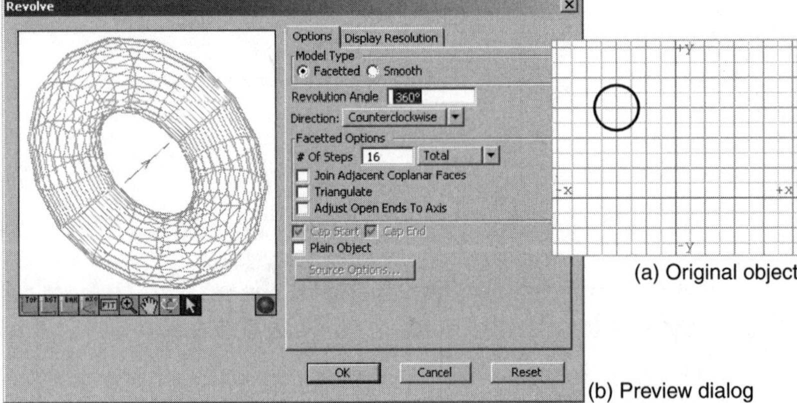

(a) Original object
(b) Preview dialog

Figure 4.1

Previewing an object of revolution in the Revolve dialog.

- The preview window to the left of the dialog shows how the circle gets revolved about the selected axis to generate a doughnut-like shape. At the base of the preview window are the same tool icons you encountered when working with the Query tool in Section 3.6 of Workshop 2 (Bringing a Sense of Scale). They let you see the object from different viewpoints and in different display modes, as well as zoom and scroll. Try them all out to familiarize yourself with them again. You'll encounter these icons in all the preview dialogs of various tools in form•Z.
- Let's move on to explore the options located on the right side of the dialog. Look under the open Options tab first. You can choose between the Facetted and Smooth model types for the revolved object; based on this choice, further options for that model type will appear in the dialog. There

are some options common to both types. These include the **Revolution Angle**, set to a full 360° by default. You can reduce this angle to create partial revolutions (see Figure 4.2-a). You can also specify whether the **Direction** should be **Clockwise** or **Counterclockwise**, a particularly important option for a partial revolution. The **Cap Start** and **Cap End** options lower down in the dialog are also relevant only to partially revolved objects. When checked, the corresponding ends of such objects are closed with a cap. Capping both ends creates a solid object.

- Select the **Facetted** model type and look at the options that appear in the **Facetted Options** section. To start with, you can specify the resolution of the revolved object in terms of the **# Of Steps** of the revolution, either for a full 360° angle, or for the specified angle. Thus, if the **Revolution Angle** is set to 180°, 16 steps specified using the **Total** sub-option will actually create only 8 steps; in contrast, if the **Per Angle** sub-option is used, the partial revolution will be made up of 16 facets.

- There are three additional options in the form of checkboxes that apply to a **Facetted** object of revolution. The first one, **Join Adjacent Coplanar Faces**, is relevant when the **Revolve** operation produces an object with separate end faces that touch each other and lie on the same plane. When this option is activated, such faces will be merged into a single larger face. An example of this is shown in Figure 4.2-a, where a 2D open shape is revolved about the Z axis with a revolution angle of 180°. The second option, **Triangulate**, works exactly like the **Triangulate** tool you saw in Section 6.6 of Workshop 2 (Bringing a Sense of Scale). When checked, it automatically triangulates any non-planar faces that might be created in the revolved object. This would happen if the source shape used for the **Revolve** operation did not lie on the same plane as the axis about which it was revolved. The last option, **Adjust Open Ends To Axis**, is relevant to a situation where the ends of an open source shape intersect the axis of revolution. When this option is checked, the object of revolution is generated by simply clipping off the parts of the shape that project beyond the axis. If the option is turned off, the parts projecting beyond the axis are also revolved (see Figure 4.2-b). The latter might sometimes lead to self-intersecting shapes, so be careful.

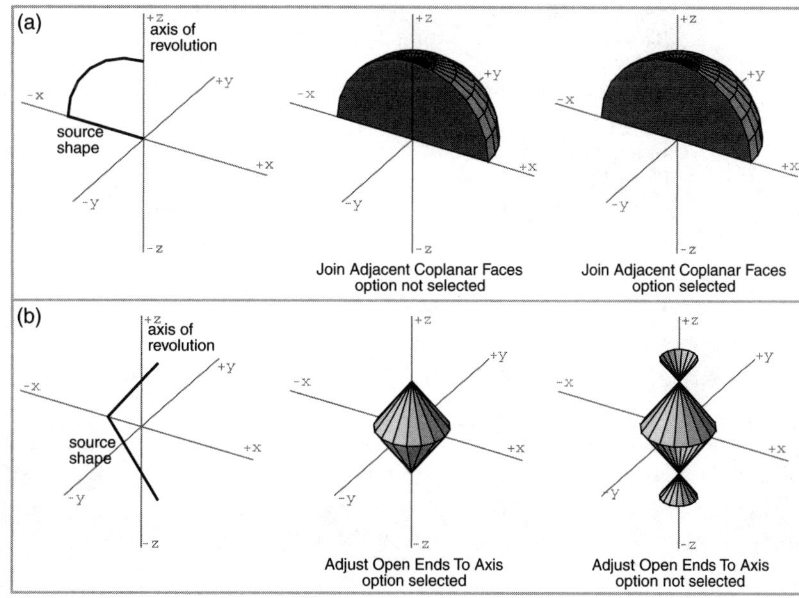

Figure 4.2

Various options of the Revolve tool. (a) Partial revolutions, with and without joining adjacent coplanar faces. (b) Adjusting open ends to the axis of revolution.

As far as a closed source shape is concerned, it is not allowed to cross the axis of revolution at all. In fact, it cannot even have a segment coinciding with the axis. It can, however, have a point that lies on the axis.

- Now switch to the Smooth model type and see how the Facetted Options section gets replaced by the Smooth Options section, which contains two main options. The first one, Construct as Smooth Revolve, creates the revolved object as a regular smooth object of the kind you've worked with so far. The second option, Construct as Nurbz, creates the revolved object as a *derivative nurbz* object. Nurbz in form•Z refers to a NURBS-based object. You'll be learning all about these objects in Workshop 6 (Going Organic), so ignore this option and its sub-option for now.

- By default, an object of revolution is a parametric object—it is stored along with the parameters that created it. So if you exit the revolution preview dialog, and reapply the Revolve tool to the object you just created, the same preview dialog will be invoked again, allowing you to modify various options to edit the object. Try it. If you are sure you won't need to change the creation parameters of a revolved object, select the Plain Object option at the base of the preview dialog. This will delete the creation parameters saved with it, reducing the size of the project file. You'll no longer be able to edit that object with the Revolve tool.

- An object of revolution that has *not* been converted to a plain object can also be graphically edited with the Edit Controls tool (M-Tool:4b,2), which you have already explored in Section 5.2 of Workshop 2 (Bringing a Sense of Scale). Apply this tool to the revolved object, and a small control arrow will be invoked, positioned near the object. Click and drag this arrow, and you'll find that the revolution angle changes, based on the direction of movement. The controls of the source shape are also shown, allowing you to edit them. Try it, and watch the revolved object change in response.

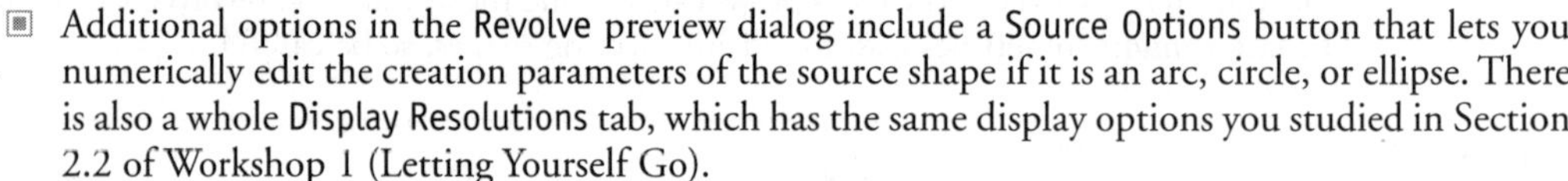

- Additional options in the Revolve preview dialog include a Source Options button that lets you numerically edit the creation parameters of the source shape if it is an arc, circle, or ellipse. There is also a whole Display Resolutions tab, which has the same display options you studied in Section 2.2 of Workshop 1 (Letting Yourself Go).

- Exit the Revolve preview dialog, and invoke the dialog of the Revolve tool by double-clicking on it. You'll find that all the options here are identical to the ones you explored in the Revolve preview dialog, except for the Edit and Adjust To New Parameters options located at the base of the dialog. The Edit option is active by default, which accounts for the preview dialog being invoked when the Revolve tool is applied to an object. The Edit option is deactivated, and cannot be turned off unless the Adjust To New Parameters option is selected. The effect of selecting this option is that if the Revolve tool is now applied to a previously created revolved object, the parameters *currently* set in the Revolve tool dialog will be applied to it, overriding its previous creation parameters. Try it.

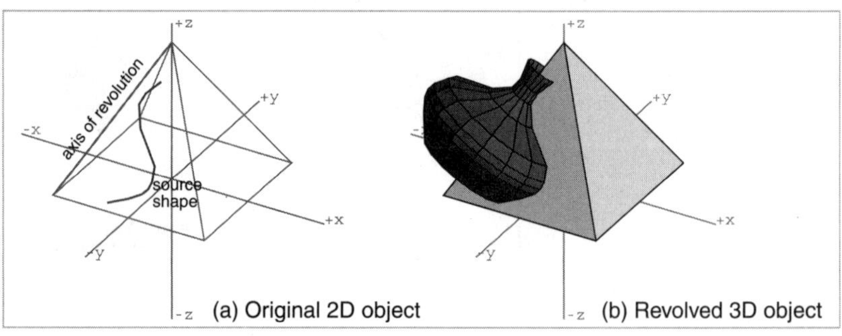

Figure 4.3

Using the segment of an existing object as the axis of revolution.

Now that we have finished exploring all the options of the Revolve tool, let's look at a few more aspects of the revolution operation.

- The form of an object of revolution is as much dependent upon the location of the source object in relation to the axis, as its shape. Thus, if you apply the Revolve tool to a semicircular arc whose open ends touch the axis of revolution, a solid sphere will be created, but if the same arc is moved away from the axis and then revolved, the resultant object will be a surface rather than a solid.
- The axis of revolution when using the Revolve tool can be any line segment—it is not restricted to the three coordinate axes. To see how this works, create a pyramid and draw a 2D shape on one of its faces using the Face object snap, as shown in Figure 4.3-a. You can now revolve this shape about any of the edges of the pyramid by simply selecting it as the axis of revolution—you don't even need to change the topological level to Segment before selecting the edge. You can see from Figure 4.3-b how this ability greatly enhances your modeling capabilities.
- Experiment further with the Revolve tool, using various kinds of source shapes and different axes of revolution. Keep in mind that you can also use *parts* of existing objects as source shapes—simply set the topological level to Face, Outline, or Segment in order to make the selection. When you revolve a part of an object, the original object will be ghosted, unless you specify otherwise in the Status Of Objects option associated with the Revolve tool.

We'll now proceed to look at the next four tools after Revolve in the right column of Row 5. All these tools work in a manner similar to the Revolve tool: a preview dialog is invoked when the tool is applied, and there are the Plain Object, Edit, and Adjust To New Parameters options in these tool dialogs, carrying out the same functions that you saw for the Revolve tool in this section.

1.2 Helixes

The Revolve tool you just used generates relatively simple objects of revolution, in which a source shape is revolved in a circular path about an axis. In contrast, the next tool, Helix, lets you create more complicated objects in which the source shape is revolved in a helical (i.e., spiral) path about an axis.

- Select the Helix tool (M-Tool:5b,2) and invoke its dialog. It contains a large number of options, most of which will appear in the preview dialog when the tool is applied. Concentrate only on the three Type options, which let you choose the type of helix you want to create. We'll go with the default option, Solid/Surface Helix, to start with.

- Exit the dialog and apply the Helix tool to a 2D shape, selecting an appropriate axis of revolution (Figure 4.4-a), just as you did for the Revolve tool. Instead of a simple object of revolution, you'll see a solid or a surface helix in the Helix preview dialog, depending upon whether the source shape was closed or open. Examples of both helixes are shown in Figures 4.4 and 4.5 respectively.
- There are several parameters that determine the shape and size of the resulting helix, which can be adjusted in the preview dialog (Figure 4.4-b). The actual revolution of the helix is determined by specifying the # Of Cycles or the total revolution Angle, while the Length can be given in terms of the total length or the length of a cycle. The Direction of revolution can be Clockwise or Counter Clockwise. The Facetted and Smooth options are similar to those you saw for the Revolve tool. Experiment with different values and combinations of these various parameters to get an idea of how they affect the configuration of the resultant object.

Figure 4.4

The preview dialog that is invoked when the Helix tool is applied to a source shape.

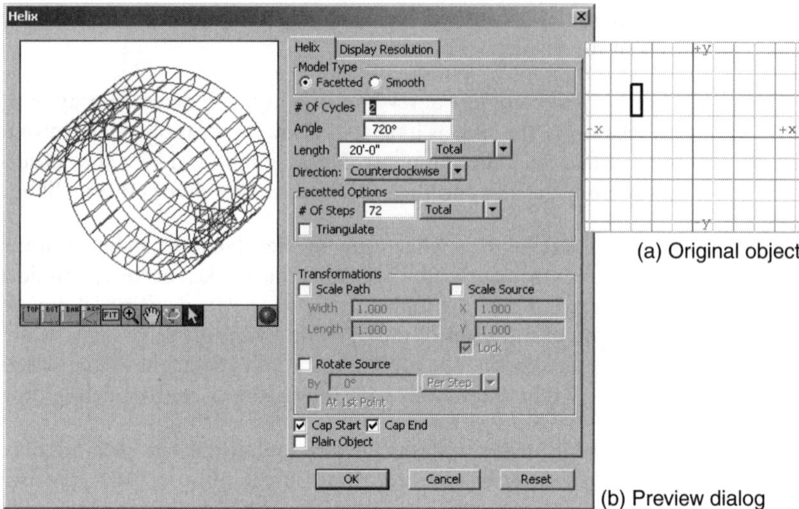

(a) Original object

(b) Preview dialog

▣ Additional parameters for creating helical objects, as seen in the preview dialog in Figure 4.4, include the ability to carry out various kinds of transformations. The path can be scaled along the width and length of the helix, and the source shape can be scaled as well as rotated in the course of its revolution about the path. Again, experiment with different values and combinations of transformations, some of which are demonstrated in Figure 4.5. (a) shows an open 2D shape which is revolved helically about the Z axis to generate the subsequent objects. The Facetted model type was selected, and the total Length of the helix was set at 40' with 6 Cycles. (b) shows the helix generated without applying any transformations. For (c), the Scale Path option was checked, and the Width value was set to 0.5. (d) resulted from scaling the Length of the path to 0.5 as well. For the tree-like object in (e), the Length of the path was reset to 1.0, and the Width was set to 0.05. Additionally, the Scale Source option was activated, and both the X and Y values were set to 0.5. Finally, (f) shows what happens if the Rotate Source option is also turned on with a value of 30°.

Figure 4.5

Different transformations yielding various types of helical objects with the Solid/Surface Helix option.

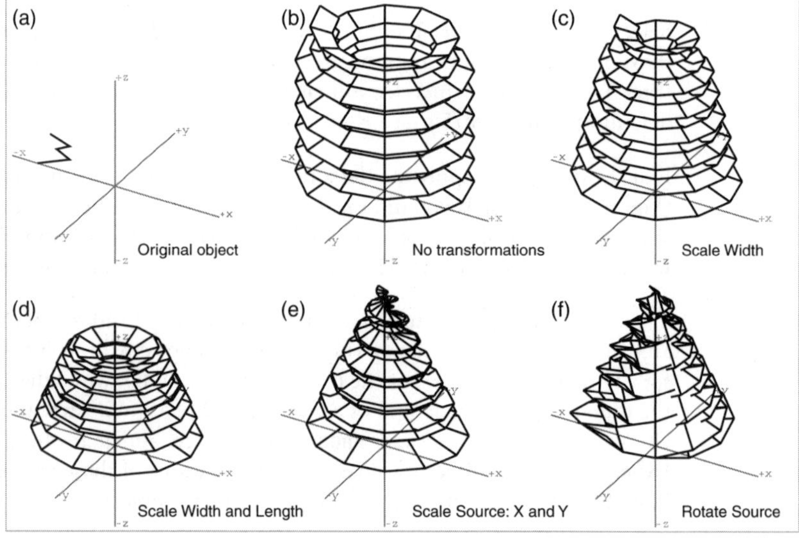

Figure 4.6

Generating simple wire helixes about an axis.

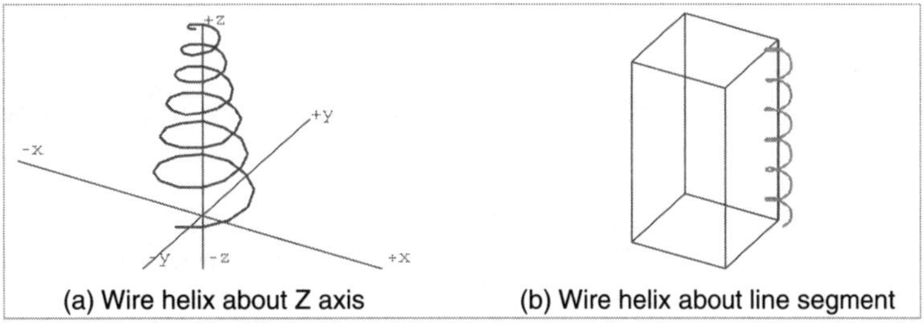

- Move on to select the next Type option in the Helix tool dialog, Wire Helix About Axis. Then simply click on one of the coordinate axes or on any line segment. The preview dialog will be invoked, showing a simple wire helix generated about that axis or segment, starting from the point you clicked on and running in the positive direction. The parameters that affect the shape and size of this helix are similar to the ones you just explored for the Solid/Surface Helix option. There is, however, an additional Radius value that determines the width of the helix, necessary because there is no source shape here that is revolved. Experiment with changes in these parameters. Two examples of wire helixes are shown in Figure 4.6. (a) was created by clicking on the Z axis, with the Width and Length of the path scaled by the values of 0.25 and 0.75 respectively. Contrast this with (b), in which the Scale Path option was deselected, a vertical segment of the block was selected as the axis of revolution, and the Length was set to the exact height of that segment.

- Proceed to select the third Helix tool option, Wire Helix Along Path. This is quite similar to the previous one, the only difference being that you can generate a helix along *any* path, not just about a straight axis. Figure 4.7 shows two variations of this type of helix, using the 2D curved path illustrated in (a). The # Of Cycles was set to 40. The version shown in (b) had no path scaling option, while in (c), the Scale Path option was checked and the Width value was set to 0.1. Notice that there is no Length value for path scaling, since the helix has to extend throughout the entire length of the selected path. Also see how the direction of scaling follows the direction of the path object. If you need to have the helix running in the opposite direction, simply reverse the direction of the path first. This can be done by using the Reverse Direction tool (M-Tool:11b,2). Try it.

WORKSHOP 4

Keep in mind that a helix object to which the Plain Object option has *not* been applied is a parametric object, just like the revolved object you saw in the last section. It is stored with its creation parameters, which can be edited by reapplying the Helix tool to it.

You must be wondering what can be done with the wire helixes you have created using the last two options of the Helix tool—after all, aren't most models made up of solid objects rather than lines and wires? Well, you'll soon learn about the Sweep tool in Exercise 2, with which you can generate coiled objects, such as a telephone cord, by simply sweeping a source shape along a wire helix.

Figure 4.7

Generating wire helixes about a path rather than about an axis.

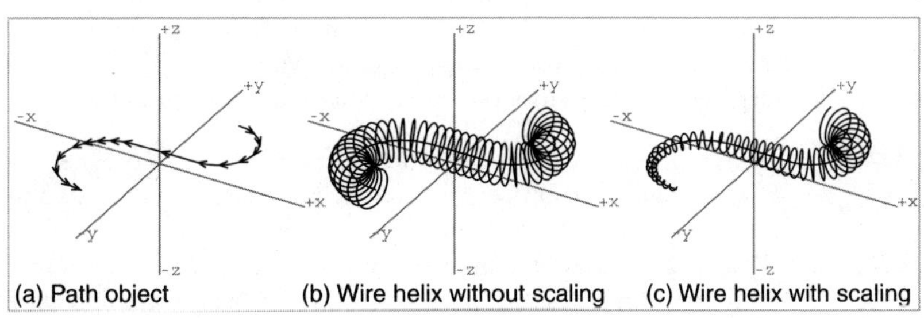

1.3 Screws and Bolts

■ If you belong to a field that deals with nuts and bolts in any manner, you'll find the next tool on Row 5, Screw/Bolt, really useful. As the name suggests, you can automatically generate screws and bolts by simply selecting an axis of revolution and then specifying a few key parameters in the preview dialog that is invoked. These are quite self-explanatory and you can explore them in detail. Figure 4.8 shows an example where a screw needs to be shown connecting two blocks. A line segment is first created in the required position, passing through both blocks. The screw is then generated by using this segment as the axis of revolution. The direction of the screw is determined by the direction of the segment, as you can see, so it has to be created accordingly.

Notice the lucid illustration of the resultant screw shown in Figure 4.8-b, in the Shaded Render display mode. It was generated by applying a surface style with a simple transparency attribute to the blocks, and then activating the Transparencies option in the Shaded Render Options dialog, as you learned in Section 2.5 of Workshop 3 (Personalizing Your Environment). You can see how transparency can be used as an effective presentation technique, even for those objects that are not actually transparent in real life.

Figure 4.8

Creating a screw about a line segment selected as the axis of revolution.

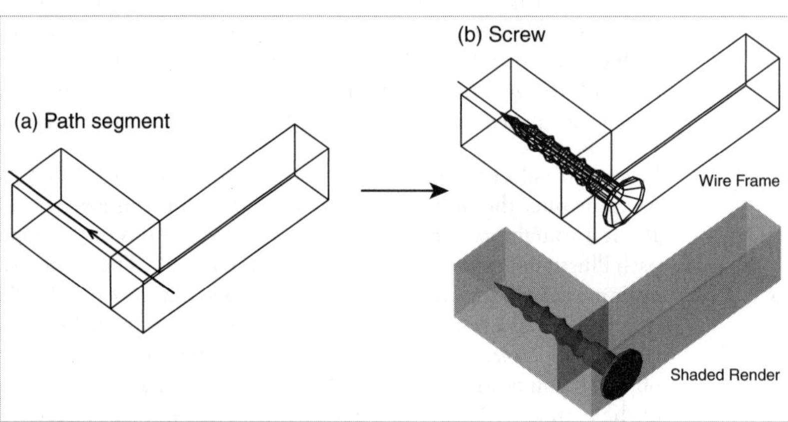

1.4 Spiral Staircases

If you are an architect, you'll fall in love with form•Z (if you haven't done so already!) the minute you see how it can generate, in one step, an object that is so tiresome and tedious to draft and model otherwise—a spiral staircase.

■ Draw a single vertical line segment, with direction from bottom to top, which you can use as the axis of revolution for your spiral staircase. Set object snapping to Endpoint, and select the Spiral Stair tool from Row 5. You'll be prompted for the axis of revolution. Select the segment you just drew by snapping to its lower endpoint. Voila! A spiral staircase is generated instantly around the segment, starting from the lower endpoint, as shown in the preview dialog in Figure 4.9.

■ You'll naturally want to manipulate the parameters in the preview dialog that determine the size and configuration of the staircase. The basic parameters, listed under the Options tab, include: the inside and outside radius, the difference of which is equal to the Width of the staircase; the total Height as well as related information such as the riser height or the number of steps, each of which will determine the value of the other since they have a reciprocal relationship; the total Length of the stair, given in terms of either the total angle, the angle of one step, or the width of one step; the # Of Segments Per Step, the default value for which is 3, as evident in the staircase shown in Figure 4.9; and finally, the Direction of the staircase. Experiment with changes in these parameters to create staircases of different configurations.

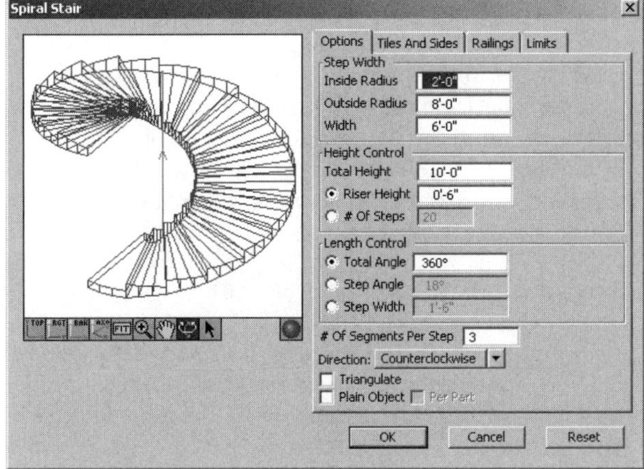

Figure 4.9

The preview dialog invoked by the Spiral Stair tool, showing the default options.

- In addition to the basic staircase, you can choose to incorporate various other features such as Tiles, Side Beams, and Railings, by activating them from the corresponding tabs in the spiral staircase preview dialog. Tiles are separate slabs that sit on top of each step of the staircase, extending beyond its sides if required. You can specify the height, as well as the front and side extensions of the tiles. Side beams are protective beams running along the two sides of the staircase. Their width, as well as their extensions above the top and under the bottom of the staircase, need to be specified. As far as railings are concerned, you can create a customized one by using the accompanying options. A staircase incorporating all these features is shown in Figure 4.10, along with the options used to generate the railing shown with it.

- There is only one more tab, Limits, in the spiral staircase preview dialog, which contains the Warn When Exceeding Limits option. You can activate this if you would like to be warned when certain limits related to the tread and riser dimensions of the staircase are exceeded. You can set these limits yourself in the dialog.

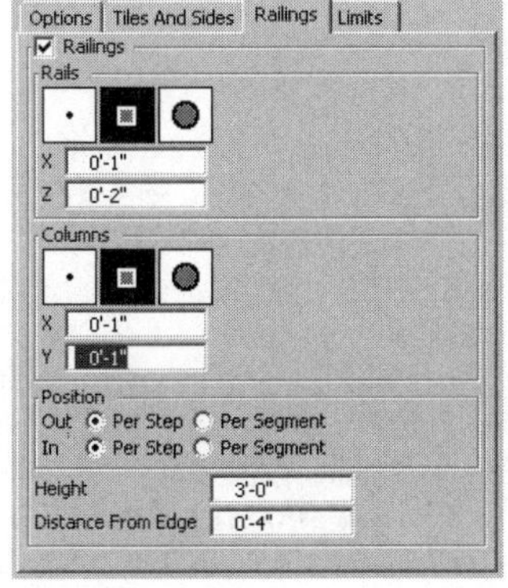

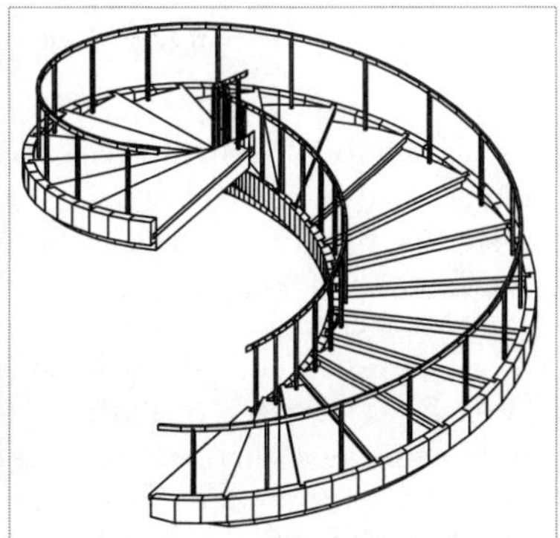

Figure 4.10

A spiral staircase modeled with tiles, side beams, and a railing, the options for which are also shown.

Finally, keep in mind that just like all the objects you have seen in this exercise so far, a spiral staircase to which the Plain Object option has not been applied is a parametric object. Thus, it can be edited by reapplying the Spiral Stair tool to it.

1.5 Regular Staircases

form•Z has a dedicated tool for modeling regular staircases, similar to the tool for generating spiral staircases. This is the Stair From Path tool, located immediately after the Spiral Stair tool in the right column of the fifth row. With this tool, regular staircases of a wide variety of shapes and configurations, complete with landings and railings, can be conveniently generated in one step. In architectural modeling, where such staircases are so common, this tool saves a lot of time and effort and is therefore a real boon to have. Let's see how it works.

- To generate a staircase with the Stair From Path tool, the path of the staircase has to be defined first. This can be either an open or closed 2D shape. Go ahead and create such a shape. Keep in mind that the staircase will be generated with respect to the plane of the path shape if it is made up of multiple segments, or with respect to the current reference plane if the path shape is made up of a single segment. Also note that if you want to create a staircase with multiple flights superimposed over the same 2D shape, the shape *has* to be closed. Examples of staircases created using both an open and a closed shape are shown in Figure 4.11.

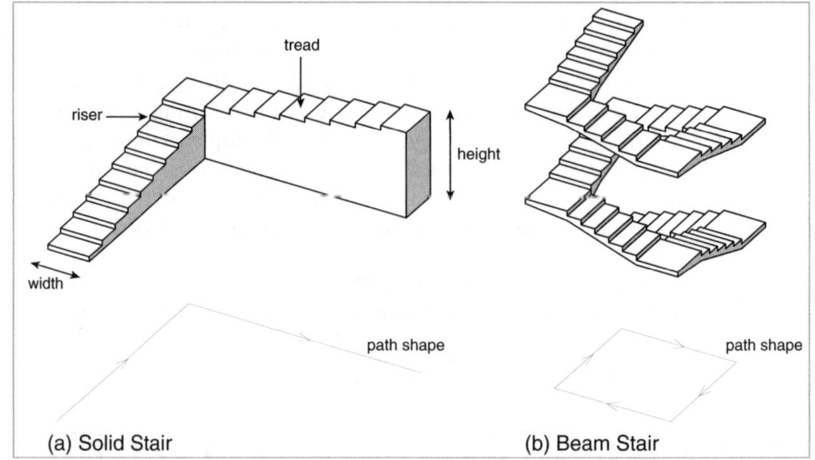

Figure 4.11

Staircases modeled with the Stair From Path tool. (a) A Solid Stair type single-flight staircase, created using an open shape. (b) A Beam Stair type multiple-flight staircase, created using a closed shape.

- Select the Stair From Path tool and apply it to the 2D path shape you have created. A preview dialog is invoked (Figure 4.12), containing an extensive set of options. Most of the options, including the ones related to Tiles, Side Beams, and Railings, will be already familiar to you from the Spiral Stair tool. Let's look at what is different.

- The Type popup menu lists six different types of staircases, the default selection for which is Solid Stair. Switch to each one of the other five types in turn, and watch the staircase display in the preview window change in response to your selection. After observing the differences between all the types, settle for one of your choice. Then explore the Align option, which has various methods for determining the alignment of the staircase with the line of the path shape.

Figure 4.12

The Stair From Path preview dialog for the single-flight staircase shown in Figure 4.11-a.

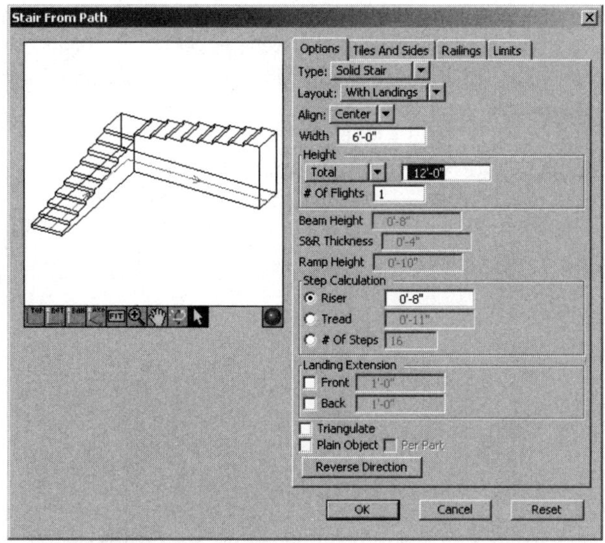

- Next, proceed to the **Layout** option, which is used to specify how the treads of the staircase are adjusted when the path shape is made up of multiple segments (see Figure 4.13). The default **Continuous** option places the total number of treads along the total length of the shape, without caring about breaks between consecutive segments. In contrast, the **Per Section** option adjusts the treads in such a manner that a complete number of treads is placed in every section of the staircase. The third option, **With Landings**, circumvents this problem altogether by placing a landing at every section break. When this sub-option is selected, you can also specify front and back **Landing Extensions** for your staircase, a little further down in the dialog.

- The **Width**, **Height**, and **Step Calculation** options in the preview dialog are the ones that determine the actual dimensions of the staircase (see Figure 4.11-a). The width is a single straightforward value. The height can be specified for the whole staircase or for a single flight. For a multiple-flight staircase generated from a closed path shape, the number of flights is also specified. And finally, the dimensions of each step are calculated by specifying either the height of the riser, the depth of the tread, or the total number of steps.

When a single-flight staircase is generated from a closed path shape, the starting point of the staircase is located at the "first point" of the shape. Turn on the Show First Point option in the Wire Frame Options dialog to see where the first point for your path is located. You can change the first point with the First Point tool (M-Tool:11b,1).

Figure 4.13

The three Layout options of the Stair From Path tool. Landing Extensions for the With Landings option are also shown.

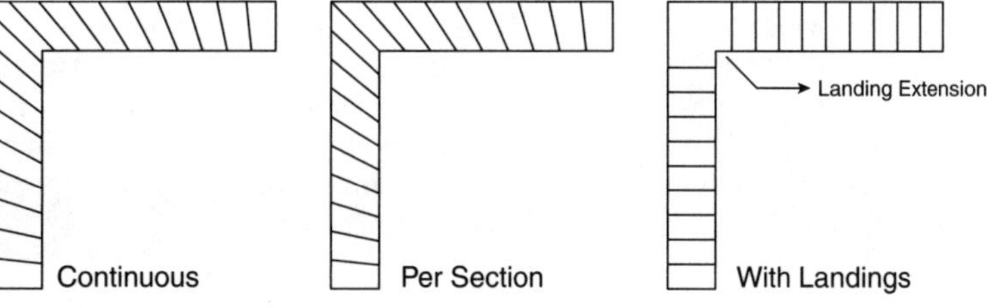

- There are only a few more options that are new to the Stair From Path preview dialog. The Beam Height and Ramp Height parameters get activated for the Beam Stair and Beam Ramp stair types respectively—they determine the vertical height of the associated beam or ramp. The S&R Thickness parameter similarly gets activated for the Steps & Risers stair type and is used to specify the thickness of the slabs from which this type of stair is constructed. The Triangulate option is not new, but note that it is especially relevant to the two Ramp types of stairs, as it will triangulate any non-planar faces that the staircase might have. Finally, keep in mind that a regular staircase is again a parametric object by default, so you can edit it by reapplying the Stair From Path tool to it.

EXERCISE 2

Sweeping Your Way Through

In this exercise, you'll learn about a simple yet extremely powerful tool in form•Z: the Sweep tool, which can generate complex 3D objects by tracing the profile of a 2D shape as it moves along a path. Unlike the Revolve or Helix tools, the path need not be circular or spiral but can be of any arbitrary shape that *you* define. Sounds intriguing, doesn't it? Let's see how it works.

2.1 Axial Sweep

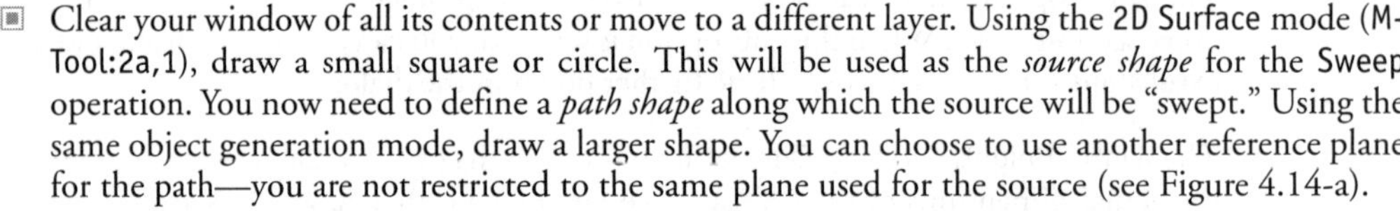

- Clear your window of all its contents or move to a different layer. Using the 2D Surface mode (M-Tool:2a,1), draw a small square or circle. This will be used as the *source shape* for the Sweep operation. You now need to define a *path shape* along which the source will be "swept." Using the same object generation mode, draw a larger shape. You can choose to use another reference plane for the path—you are not restricted to the same plane used for the source (see Figure 4.14-a).

- Make sure the topological level on Row 4 is set to Object. Now select the Sweep tool (M-Tool:5b,6) and follow the instructions in the Prompts palette. For the source, click on the smaller object; for the path, select the larger shape. This brings up the Sweep preview dialog (Figure 4.14-b), similar to what you encountered for the tools in Exercise 1. It shows you the resultant object, generated by sweeping the source shape along the path shape. Switch to one of the paint display modes to see the swept object more clearly.

- Let's look at the options in the preview dialog. The choice between Facetted and Smooth model types and their associated options are already familiar to you. Therefore, turn your attention to the options in the Source Shape section. Here, the source shape is shown in a smaller window, with a number of tool icons located under it. From left to right, these let you move, rotate, or scale the source shape, flip it horizontally or vertically, or reverse its direction. Each one of these transformations will modify the swept object in various ways. Try them out. You'll see how the transformation is always carried out with respect to the point that marks the crossing of the path shape through the source, graphically indicated in the source preview window by a red cross. It is placed by default at the centroid of the object.

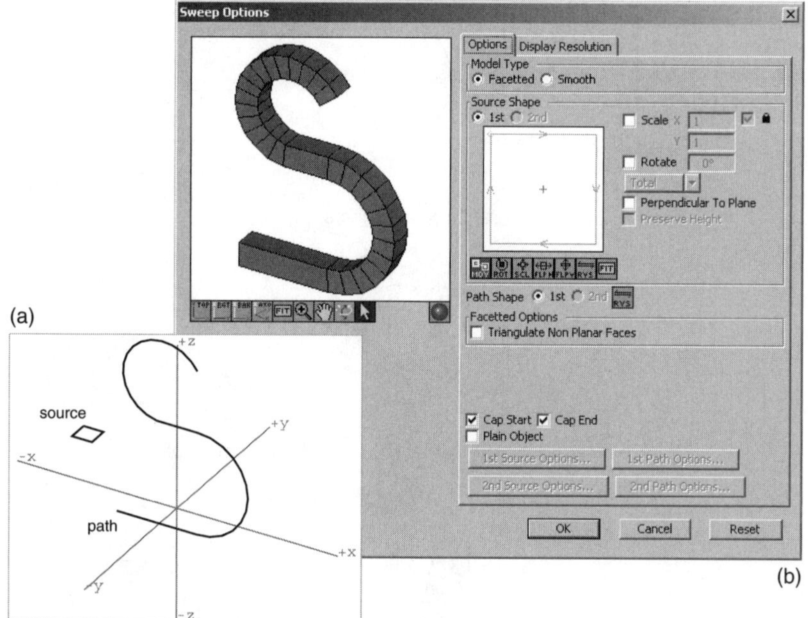

Figure 4.14

Using the Sweep tool. (a) The source and path shapes. (b) The preview dialog, showing the resultant object in Surface Render mode.

- The Sweep tool comes with another powerful feature that can greatly enhance your modeling capabilities. This is the ability to scale as well as rotate the source shape from one end to the other end of the path. By default, both options are off. Check the Scale option in the preview dialog and specify a scaling factor, which can be different along the X and Y directions. See how the resultant object changes in shape. Then check the Rotate option as well and explore the changes for different angle values. To flip the direction along which the scaling and rotation occurs, click on the Reverse icon that is located *below* the Source Shape section, alongside the Path Shape option. This will flip the direction of the path, and consequently, the direction in which the transformation will occur.

Figure 4.15 shows the variations in the resultant object, generated by sweeping the same source along the same path shown in Figure 4.14-a, but with different transformations. In (a), Scale was turned on with a factor of 3.0 for X and 1.0 for Y. In (b), Y was also set to 3.0. In (c), the Rotate option was selected with a total angle of 180°, in addition to Scale. Finally, (d) had the same transformations as (c), except that the path was reversed, so the transformations were applied in the opposite direction.

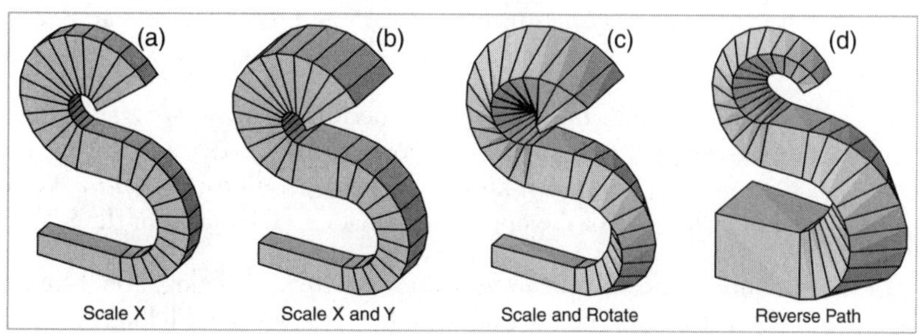

Figure 4.15

Different configurations generated by applying various transformations to the source in the Sweep preview dialog.

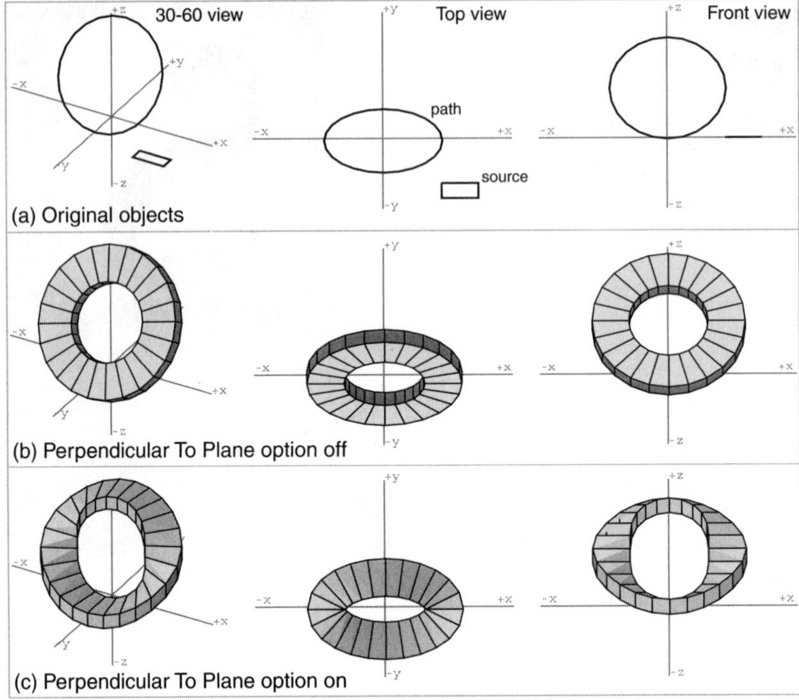

Figure 4.16

The effect of the Perpendicular To Plane option available in the Sweep preview dialog.

- Next, turn to the Perpendicular To Plane option located in the Source Shape section, the use of which is illustrated in Figure 4.16. (a) shows the 30-60, top and front views of the source and path shapes created for the Sweep operation. The circular path shape, as you can see, is not parallel to any of the predefined planes—it was created using an arbitrary plane. The XY plane, however, was activated when the Sweep tool was applied. (b) and (c) show the results of the operation with the Perpendicular To Plane option turned off and on respectively. You can see that when the option is off, the source shape keeps adjusting its orientation to be perpendicular to the path as it is swept along it. In contrast, if you turn the option on, the source always remains perpendicular to the active reference plane. You can make the choice depending upon the desired end result.

The remaining options in the Sweep preview dialog should be familiar to you from the preview dialogs of the tools you covered in Exercise 1. Keep in mind that the source and the path shapes for the Sweep operation you've been executing can be either open or closed. A closed source produces a solid, as in the examples in Figures 4.15 and 4.16, whereas an open source results in a surface. 2D enclosures can also be used as source shapes to produce 3D enclosures of various configurations.

The kind of Sweep operation you've performed so far—sweeping a source object along a single axis determined by a path object—is known as *axial sweep*, and it is the default mode for the Sweep tool. There are three additional kinds of Sweep operations: *two source sweep*, *two path sweep*, and *boundary sweep*. The choice of the operation is made in the dialog of the Sweep tool.

- Double-click on the Sweep tool to invoke its dialog. You'll find that Axial Sweep is the default Type selected. There are three more types, which we'll look at in subsequent sections. All the other options in this dialog are identical to those in the preview dialog, except for the Alignment option in the Source Shape section. This is used to determine the cross section alignment of the path shape with respect to the source shape. Centroid is selected by default, which is why the axis of the path shape has been passing through the center of the source shape all this time. Alternately, you can choose the Origin of the current reference plane, or the First Point of the source for the alignment. Also remember that you can always change the axis alignment by moving the source in the source shape window of the preview dialog, if required.

2.2 Two Source Sweep

- Select the Two Source Sweep option in the dialog of the Sweep tool. This kind of sweep, as the name suggests, expects two source shapes and one path shape. Back in the graphics window, create any two 2D objects to function as source shapes. Both can be either open or closed, but you cannot have one open and one closed. Also create a path object, open or closed (Figure 4.17-a). Then select the Sweep tool and follow the instructions in the Prompts palette to select, in turn, the first source, the second source, and the path. The preview dialog will be invoked, showing how the resultant object has a form which changes from the source shape selected first to the source shape selected second, as it is swept along the specified path (Figure 4.17-b).
- You should be familiar with most of the options in the preview dialog, which are similar to those for Axial Sweep. There are just a couple of additional options to note. In the Source Shape section, you'll now see two source objects instead of one. You can make either one active by selecting the 1st or 2nd options. The active source is shown in color while the other is shown in gray. Only the active source can be graphically manipulated using the accompanying transformation icons.
- In a Two Source Sweep operation, what's especially important is the location of the first point and the direction of one source with respect to the other. Preferably, the first points should be aligned and the directions should be the same, otherwise the swept object will be twisted. You can synchronize the sources in the preview dialog itself, using the Rotate tool to adjust the first point and the Reverse tool to adjust the direction of the active source.

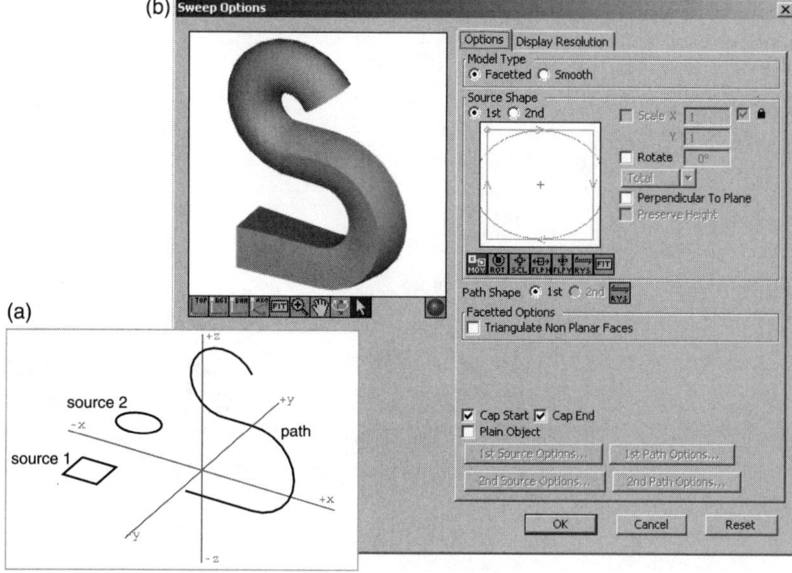

Figure 4.17

A Two Source Sweep operation. (a) The two source shapes and one path shape. (b) The Sweep preview dialog, showing the resultant object in RenderZone mode.

- Notice, also, that the first source is placed at the location of the first point of the path. Thus, if the path object is closed, you have to take care to create it correctly in order to achieve the effect you want. You cannot modify the location of the first point of the path object in the preview dialog, but you can reverse its direction, if necessary, using the Reverse tool in the Path Shape section.

- Just as with Axial Sweep, the Rotate transformation can be applied in the preview dialog for Two Source Sweep to achieve interesting twisted effects in the resultant object. The Scale option, however, is not available since there are two shapes that determine the two extremities of this type of Sweep.

2.3 Two Path Sweep

- Move on to select the next mode in the dialog of the Sweep tool, Two Path Sweep. As you can guess from its name, this Sweep type generates an object by sweeping one source along two paths. Go ahead and create these shapes. The only thing to keep in mind is that both the path shapes must either be closed or open—you cannot have one closed and one open path. And at least for now, ensure that the starting points and directions of these paths are aligned, as in the examples demonstrated in Figure 4.18. Later, once you learn how the operation actually works, you can deviate from these guidelines to create unusual objects with desired shapes.

- Perform the Sweep operation by selecting sequentially, as prompted, the source shape and the two path shapes. You should be able to deal with the preview dialog that opens up like an old hand now! The only new option that you'll see in this dialog is Preserve Height. Select it and then deselect it to see how it affects the resultant object. You'll find that when this option is not selected, the aspect ratio of the source is maintained as it is swept between the two paths. In other words, the source is uniformly scaled, resulting in an object with a constantly varying height. On the other hand, if you select the Preserve Height option, the resultant object has a constant height that is equal to the height of the source. The source is thus scaled only in one direction as it is swept between the two paths. Both scenarios are illustrated in Figure 4.18.

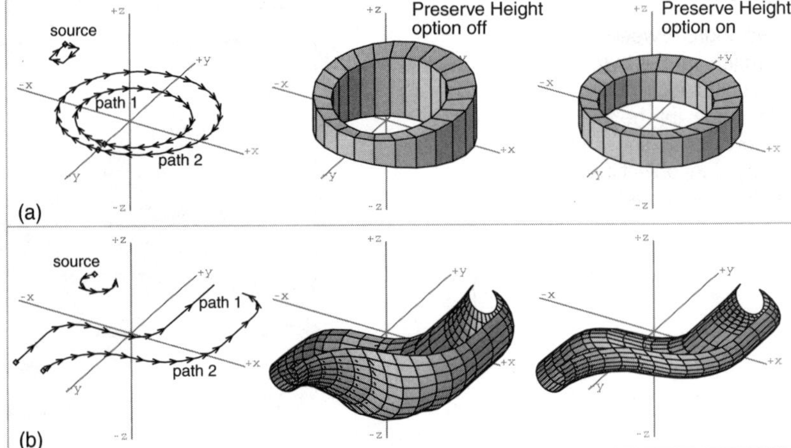

Figure 4.18

Two examples of the Two Path Sweep operation. The First Point and Direction displays were turned for the Wire Frame display of the original 2D shapes.

2.4 Boundary Sweep

- Proceed to activate the last **Sweep** tool mode, **Boundary Sweep**. This is similar to **Axial Sweep** in the sense that it requires only one source shape and one path shape. However, it works a little differently. Not only does it sweep the source shape along the specified path, it also goes on to add faces at the ends to *close* the form. Thus, it will always produce a solid object and requires the source shape to be open, as illustrated in Figure 4.19.
- Draw an open shape to function as the source, making sure it does not self-intersect. Stick to a fairly simple one for now. Then create a larger closed shape for the path (Figure 4.19-a). Select the **Sweep** tool and pick the two objects in the correct sequence. You'll see that what would have been a surface object in **Axial Sweep** is a solid object in **Boundary Sweep** because the open ends are closed up. Also, note that the **Scale** and **Rotate** transformations are not available, as they could interfere with the ability to create well-formed closures.

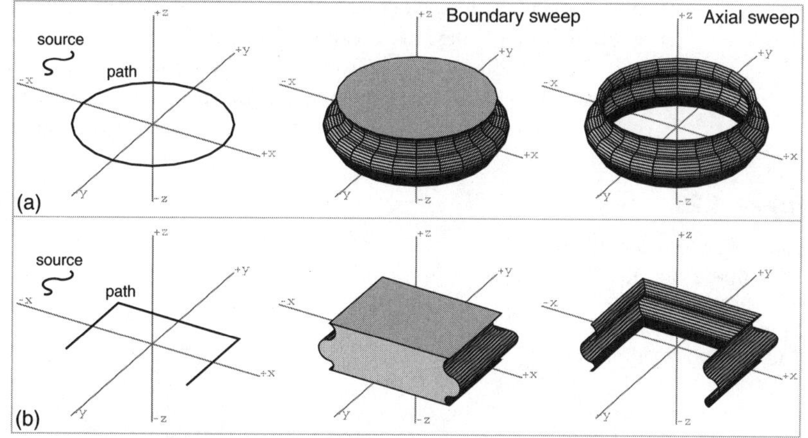

Figure 4.19

Two examples of Boundary Sweep, using a closed and an open path. The contrast with Axial Sweep is also shown.

- Now repeat the same **Sweep** operation, but with an open path shape instead of closed (Figure 4.19-b). For the **Boundary Sweep** to generate a well-formed object using an open path, the path has to meet two requirements: it must have at least two segments, and the "virtual" segment connecting the two open ends of the path must not intersect any of its other segments. If your path shape does not meet these conditions, you'll be issued a warning message. Once again, note the contrast between the results obtained by using **Boundary Sweep** and **Axial Sweep** for this source and path.

Exercise 3
Skinning and Lofting Your Forms

In this exercise, we'll work with the last two tools located in the right column of Row 5, the **Skin** and **Loft** tools. We'll start with the **Skin** tool, which is similar in concept to the **Sweep** tool you just covered but operates quite differently, producing different results. The **Sweep** operation is relatively simple—all it requires is one or two source shapes and one or two path shapes. You don't have to worry about the relative locations of the source and path shapes, as you just saw. The Skin tool also produces 3D objects by sweeping 2D sources along 2D paths, but the difference is that the sources and the paths have to be properly positioned such that they *describe the profile* of the 3D object that is to be created. In addition, there are some other conditions that need to be satisfied. Let's see how to use the Skin tool and explore the conditions involved.

3.1 Skinning Along a Path

- Clear everything in your window or move to a different layer. Invoke the Wire Frame Options dialog (as you learned in Section 2.1, Wire Frame Options, of Workshop 3, Personalizing Your Environment), and select the Show Points option, the first one in the Interactive tab. It's important to always activate this option before using the Skin tool, since the operation works better when the points of source and path shapes are properly matched.
- Turn Grid Snap on and create four path objects as shown in Figure 4.20-a, with the model type set as Facetted. Two of these are on the ZX plane; the other two are on the YZ plane. They can be created with precision by going to the Front/Back and Right/Left views respectively. Ensure that you create them in the same general direction. If you like, turn on also the Show Direction option in the Wire Frame Options dialog, so that there's no confusion about direction.

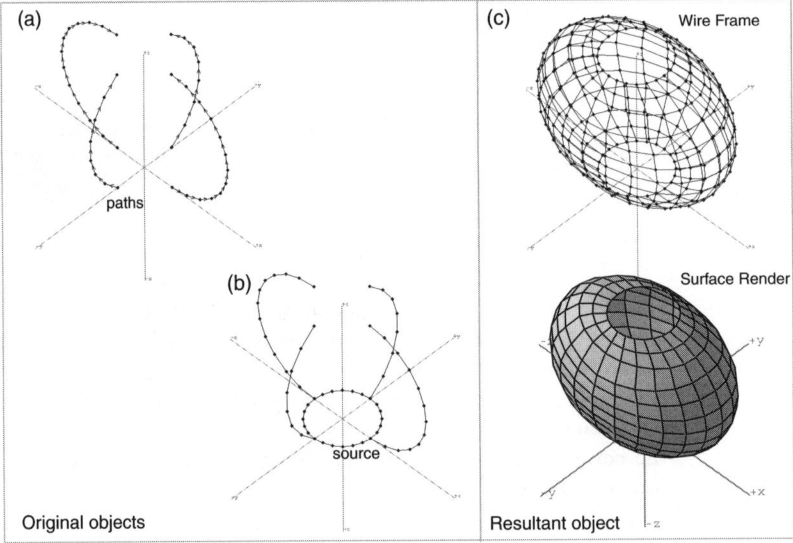

Figure 4.20

Executing a Skinning Along Paths operation. The original source and path shapes are shown with the display of points turned on.

WORKSHOP 4

- Next, create a source shape, also of the Facetted model type, on the XY plane such that it has points touching one end of each of the four path shapes, as shown in Figure 4.20-b. You'll execute your first Skin operation with this single source shape. Zoom in closer to ensure that points on the source actually touch points on the paths. You can see how important it is to turn on the point display in the Wire Frame mode, without which you would not be able to tell if the points coincided or not.
- You now have to tell the Skin tool (M-Tool:5b,7) exactly how many source and path shapes you'll be using for the operation, and change other settings if necessary. Select it and invoke its dialog

(Figure 4.21). It has a large number of options, many of which will be familiar to you from the tools you covered in the first two exercises. Stick with the default model type of Facetted for now, and focus on the two skinning modes listed in the dialog. The one selected by default is Skinning Along Paths, which is what you'll be executing first. Change the # Sources value to 1, since you have a single source. Leave the # Paths to the default value of 4, since you have four path shapes. Keep in mind that Skinning Along Paths requires at least 3 paths, so you won't be able to set # Paths to a value less than 3.

- Look further down in the Skin Options dialog and notice that the Placement Type is set to Current Position, which is fine for now. There is an associated Tolerance value, useful in case there are points on the source shapes that do not coincide exactly with points on the path shapes. You can change this value as necessary, so that the tool is able to relate the sources to the paths.
- Having set all the appropriate options, exit the Skin Options dialog and apply the tool. Following the instructions in the Prompts palette, select the source object first. Then select each of the four path shapes, taking care to pick them in the right sequence. You'll find that the source shape is swept between the four path shapes, resulting in a 3D surface object as shown in Figure 4.20-c.
- If you get any error messages at this stage and the operation is not performed, check to see if the directions of the path shapes are synchronized. If they're not, apply the Reverse Direction tool (M-Tool:11b,2) to the path shapes whose directions need to be corrected. If the Skin operation still doesn't work, increase the Tolerance value in the dialog. That should take care of the problem.

Since the Skin operation relies heavily on point matching, always use the Facetted model type to create the source and path shapes.

- Notice from Figure 4.20-c that the resultant object is a surface with open ends. Go back to the Skin Options dialog and check the Cap Start and Cap End options. Undo and reapply the Skin operation. If the source shape is closed, such as the one used in Figure 4.20, the resultant object will now be a solid with closed ends.

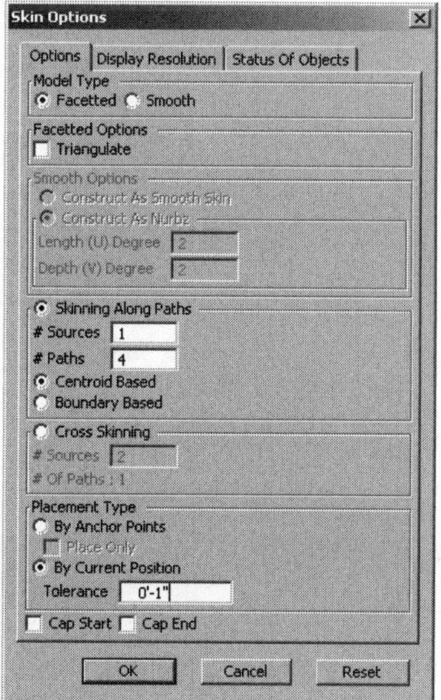

Figure 4.21

The dialog of the Skin tool, with the options set to perform the Skin operation illustrated in Figure 4.20.

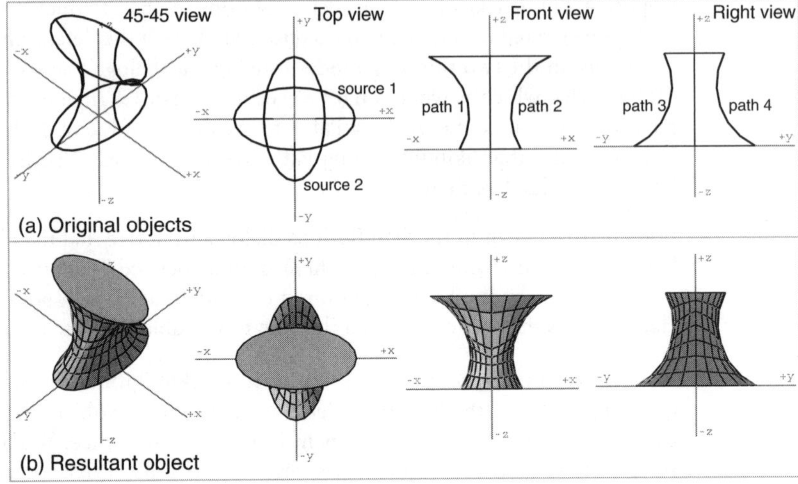

Figure 4.22

Applying the Skinning Along Paths operation to a configuration of two sources and four paths.

- Let's do another example of Skinning Along Paths in which there are two source shapes. Create the configuration of sources and paths shown in Figure 4.22-a. Invoke the Skin Options dialog and set the # Sources value to 2. Also, check the Cap Start and Cap End options. The other options should be the same as in the previous example. Apply the Skin tool to this configuration and you should get the result shown in Figure 4.22-b. You can see the ability to sculpt shapes precisely that is afforded by the Skin tool.

- We'll perform a final example of Skinning Along Paths, this time using closed rather than open paths. Create the paths as shown in Figure 4.23-a in Top view, and move them along the Z axis to space them out vertically. Then create a closed source as shown in Figure 4.23-b, making sure that it has points coinciding with points on all the three paths. As you can see, doing this is much easier when the configuration is centered about the origin; so it is a good idea to always do it this way, even if it means creating the configuration on a separate layer.

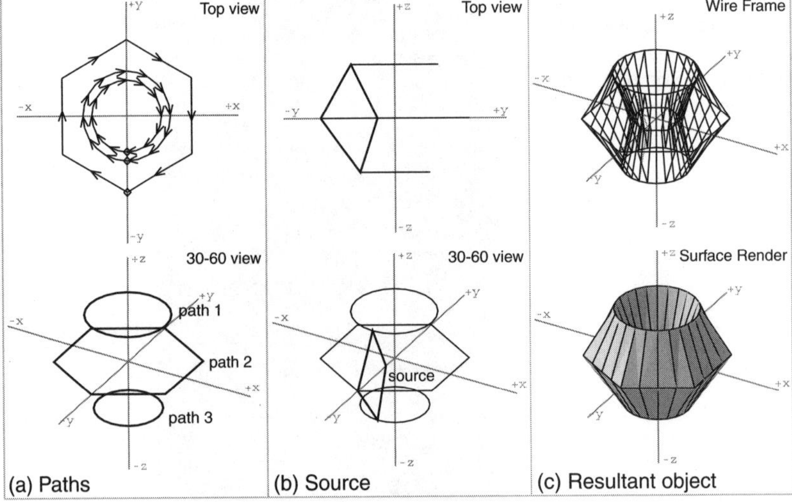

Figure 4.23

Applying the Skinning Along Paths operation to a closed source, using three closed paths.

- Make the appropriate changes to the values for # Sources and # Paths in the dialog of the Skin tool and then apply it to the configuration. You should have the result shown in Figure 4.23-c. Notice that the result is a solid object, since both the source and the paths were closed.

- Get back to the Skin Options dialog (Figure 4.21), and notice that there are two sub-options for Skinning Along Paths—Centroid Based and Boundary Based—that we didn't touch upon at all. The reason is that in most cases they will produce identical results, so it isn't necessary to get into the mathematical explanation of how they differ. Simply keep in mind that the default selection, Centroid Based, is better for curved shapes, whereas the alternative, Boundary Based, is better for angular shapes. You can select the sub-option appropriate to the modeling task at hand.

3.2 Skinning Using Anchor Points

At times, it might be difficult to create a source of the precise shape that is required, in the correct position, touching all the path shapes at the desired points. In such a situation, form•Z gives you the option of creating the source shape in a different, more convenient location, and then telling the Skin tool exactly how it is to be placed. This is done by positioning *anchor points*—which are specially marked points—along both the source and path shapes. Let's do an example of this type of skinning.

- Create three path shapes having the same direction, correctly positioned with respect to each other. Then create a properly dimensioned source shape, *not* in the position it should be for skinning, but somewhere else on the plane, as shown in Figure 4.24-a. "Properly dimensioned" means ensuring that *if* the source was drawn in the correct location, it would have points that correctly matched with points on each of the paths. This is very important, so do it carefully.

- You now have to indicate to the Skin tool the points on the source that need to be matched with the corresponding points on the paths. As mentioned, you'll use anchor points to do this. But first, invoke the Wire Frame Options dialog once more and select the option Show Marked Points, located under the Interactive tab. This will show the anchor points when you mark them. Since you haven't yet marked any points, there is no change in the display in the graphics window yet.

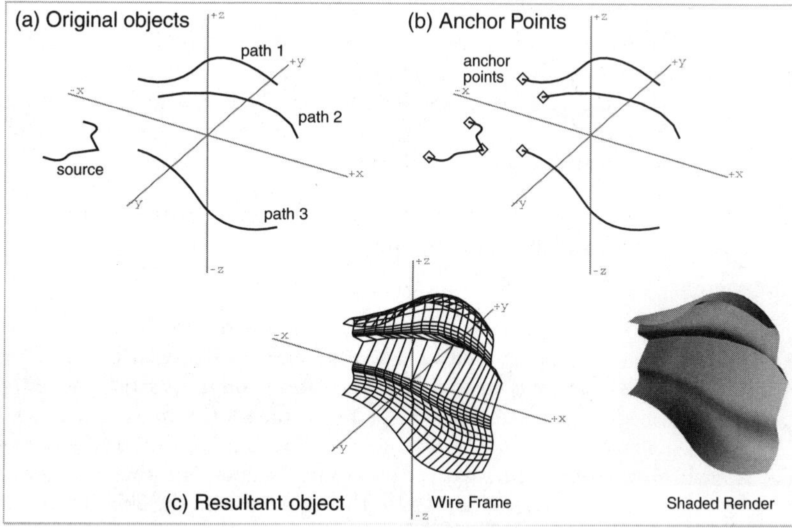

Figure 4.24

Performing a Skin operation using anchor points.

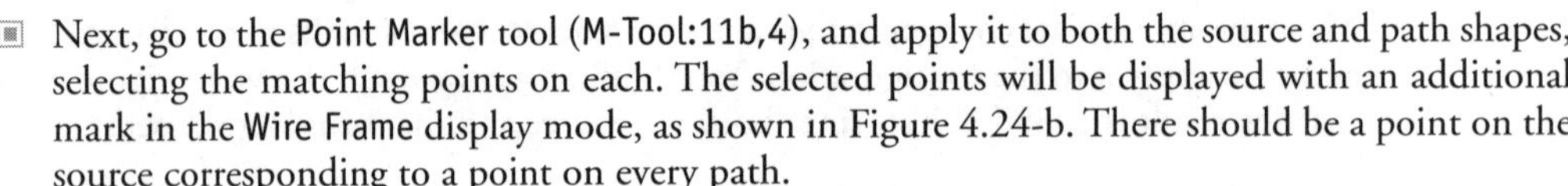

- Next, go to the Point Marker tool (M-Tool:11b,4), and apply it to both the source and path shapes, selecting the matching points on each. The selected points will be displayed with an additional mark in the Wire Frame display mode, as shown in Figure 4.24-b. There should be a point on the source corresponding to a point on every path.

- All that remains is to specify the appropriate options for the Skin tool. Invoke its dialog and set the values for # Sources and # Paths as 1 and 3 respectively. In the Placement Type section, activate the By Anchor Points option. Then exit the dialog and apply the Skin tool, following the instructions in the Prompts palette. You should achieve a result similar to that shown in Figure 4.24-c.

- If you weren't able to execute the operation successfully, reverse the direction of the source. If it still doesn't work, do the following: In the Skin Options dialog, check the Place Only sub-option that appears next to the By Anchor Points option; then reapply the Skin tool. This time, the source shape will only be placed in the correct position based on the anchor points, rather than swept along the paths. If you marked the points correctly, this should get done without any error messages. Then set the Placement Type option back to By Current Position in the dialog, specify an appropriate tolerance value, and reapply the Skin tool. This time, the operation should be executed without any problems, giving you the correct result.

3.3 Cross Skinning

So far, all the skinning operations we've executed were of the type, *skinning along paths*. The Skin tool provides us with a second type of skinning operation, referred to as *cross skinning*. While the former is similar to the Sweep tool, the latter is similar to the Revolve tool in the sense that one or more sources are revolved about a single path. The path has to be a closed shape, but need not necessarily be circular as with the Revolve tool. We'll carry out a few examples of cross skinning in this section.

- On a new layer, create a closed path of any shape and a single source, both facetted as noted earlier. If the source shape is open, as in Figure 4.25-a, make sure that one of its points coincides with a point on the path shape. For a closed source, two points on the source must match two points on the path, as in Figure 4.25-b.

- Invoke the dialog of the Skin tool and select the Cross Skinning option. Change the # Sources value to 1. Notice that you can't change the # Paths value, which is always 1 for this kind of skinning. Make sure that the Placement Type is set to By Current Position with a suitable tolerance. Exit the dialog, and as prompted, select first the source object and then the path object. You'll be rewarded with a beautifully skinned form, as shown in Figure 4.25-a.

- Repeat the operation with a different source shape, ensuring the correct matching of points. Figure 4.25-b shows the cross skinning of a closed source about the same path used in Figure 4.25-a.

- Let's now try a cross skinning operation with more than one source. You can continue using the same path; simply create a second source shape that is open or closed, to match with the first source. There is an additional condition you must satisfy when there are multiple source objects: in addition to touching the paths, all the sources must touch each other at two additional points, referred to as *apex points*, one on either side of the path. Figure 4.25-c shows an example with these points indicated for two source shapes, and the resultant cross skinning operation. Don't forget to change # Sources to the right value in the Skin Options dialog before applying the tool.

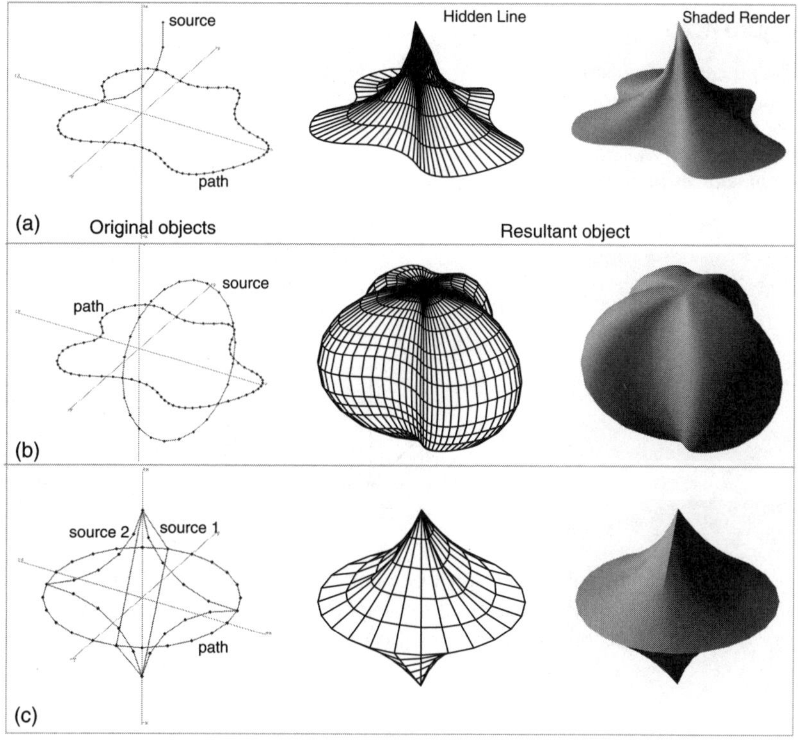

Figure 4.25

Performing Cross Skinning operations using various sources. (a) An open source. (b) A closed source. (c) Multiple sources.

- It might seem tricky to create multiple source shapes for cross skinning, all of which meet each other at the same two points, as well as touch the path object at distinct points. Figure 4.26 illustrates how this task can be accomplished more easily, using the source and path shapes from the last example. After creating the path shape, create single segments going across it at the positions where the sources are to be located, as shown in (a). Use Endpoint snap for accuracy. All these segments should pass through the same point located inside the path shape.

- Next, extrude these segments by the same distance on one side of the path, as shown in (b), using the 3D Extrusion tool (M-Tool:5a,4). Then apply the Move tool, with the topological level set to Segment and the Perpendicular Lock turned on, to move the lower segment of each extrusion by the same distance on the opposite side of the path. As shown in (c), this will give you a rectangular surface for each source, correctly positioned, and intersecting the surface of every other source at two apex points, one above and one below the path.

- Next, create an arbitrary plane for each of these rectangular surfaces using Define Arbitrary Plane (W-Tool:3,1). Thereafter, for each plane, go to Views > Plane Projection > Top and create the source shape for that plane, ensuring that it touches a point on the path (using Endpoint snap) as well as the two apex points (using Intersection snap). This is shown in (d) and (e). Delete the temporary rectangular surfaces after creating the sources. You should finally have your source and path shapes correctly positioned as shown in (f).

- You can also use the By Anchor Points method for cross skinning when the source objects are closed, or if they are open but touch the path at both ends. Note that you have to mark the apex points in the sources as well, in addition to the points where they touch the path. Do an example of this, following the same procedure you used in the last section.

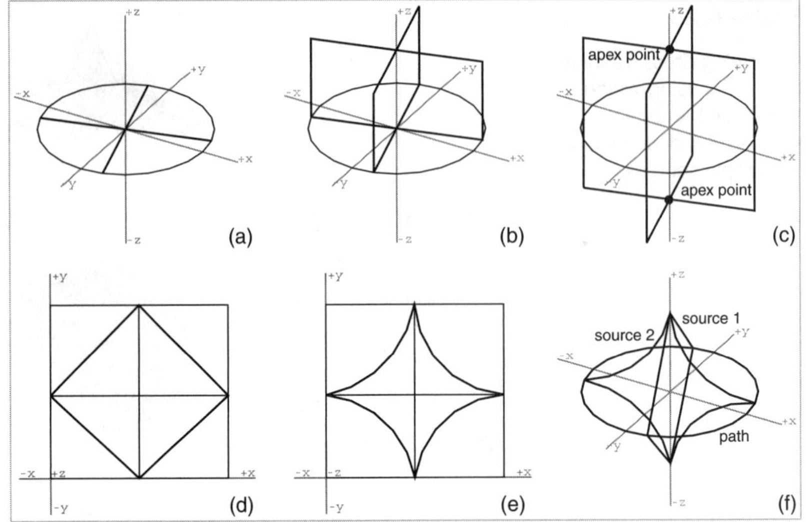

Figure 4.26

The process of creating source objects for cross skinning that touch the path object as well as other sources at apex points.

The Skin tool is a complex one and it's beyond the scope of this book to cover all its ramifications. The best way to master it is to experiment with different sources and paths and observe the results. Therefore, take some time to execute more skinning operations before proceeding to the next section.

3.4 Lofting

The concept of the Loft tool is similar to that of the Skin tool, except that lofting does not require a path object, which makes it a lot simpler to use. Instead, the Loft tool creates a new object from a sequence of source shapes by using a bulge factor and a direction setting for each source. Just as with the Skin tool, the sources have to be properly positioned such that they describe the desired profile of the object. We'll look at one lofting example in this section.

- On a new layer, create a sequence of shapes that defines the surface profile of an object, as shown in Figure 4.27-a. Make sure the first points and directions of the shapes are synchronized, otherwise you might get erroneous results. Since point matching is not involved as with the Skin tool, the source shapes for lofting can be smooth objects,

- Use the Pick tool to prepick these shapes in the correct sequence. Then select the Loft tool (M-Tool:5b,8) and click anywhere in the graphics window. The Loft preview dialog will open up, showing the resulting object in the preview window. You can see how its surface smoothly passes through the boundaries of each one of the source shapes (see Figure 4.27-b). 

- Experiment with the different lofting parameters in the preview dialog and see how they affect the shape of the resultant object. The most visible changes can be made by manipulating the Bulge factor, which determines how much the surface curves as it passes through the sources. You can use the Custom rather than the Automatic option to specify a desired value for the bulge; to activate this, set Direction to an option other than Automatic. Notice that the higher the bulge value, the more the lofting and the smoother the transition from one source to the next.

Figure 4.27

Applying the Loft tool to a sequence of source shapes that defines the desired surface profile.

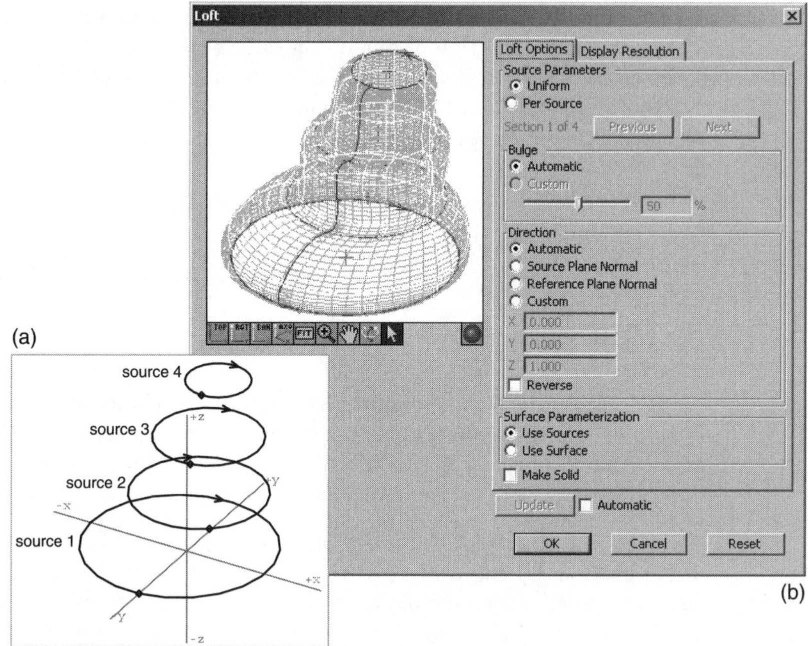

- To specify a bulge factor for each source separately, select the Per Source option under Source Parameters. You can now activate each source in turn and manipulate its settings individually. Figure 4.28 shows the same lofted object as in Figure 4.27, but with different custom bulge values for each source shape.

Figure 4.28

Reshaping the lofted object by specifying custom bulge values separately for each source.

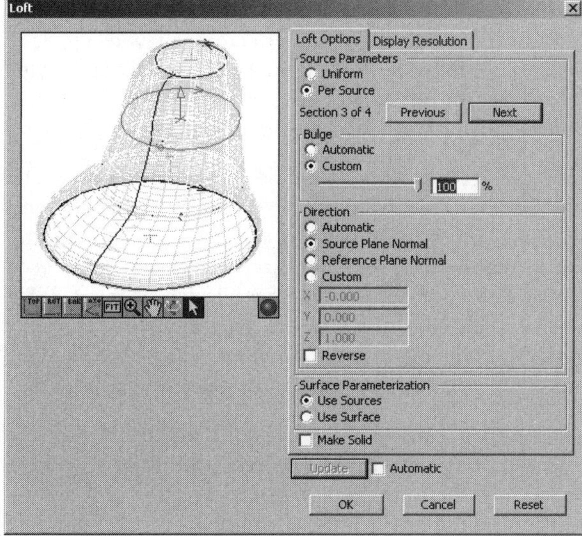

- The other lofting parameters are relevant to more complex lofting examples. The Direction options determine the direction of the lofting surface as it passes through the sources, while the Surface Parameterization options determine how the surface control points are positioned along its depth. Note also the Make Solid option, which you can use to construct a solid lofted object—instead of a surface—out of closed source shapes.

EXERCISE 4

Cutting Your Sections

In this exercise, you'll work with the Section tool, located in the left column of Row 9, which can be used to slice up one or more objects with a cutting plane. Alternately, it can be used to derive the 2D intersection of the cutting plane with the objects. You'll also look at the Contour tool, located immediately after the Section tool, which is used to create a sequence of 2D cuts through an object.

The Section tool is especially useful from a design presentation standpoint, as it lets you automatically derive plans and sections of your 3D models. All that is needed is a *cutting plane* created in the position through which the model is to be sectioned. Moreover, this cutting plane does not have to actually cut through (i.e., intersect) the objects. It can exist anywhere in the model provided that, in an infinitely extended position, it would intersect the objects along the plane of the desired section. In fact, you can even use a *cutting line* from which the cutting plane is automatically derived by extruding the line perpendicular to the active reference plane. Let's see how it works.

4.1 2D Sections

- Move to a new layer and create a few 3D objects of various shapes and sizes. Then use the Rectangle tool (M-Tool:3a,1) in 2D Surface mode to create a few rectangles in different positions such that, when extended infinitely, they would intersect your 3D objects in different ways. Some rectangles can be created on arbitrary planes or one of their segments can be moved, so as to incline them with respect to the objects. This will generate more interesting sections.

- Use the Pick tool to select all the 3D objects, but not the rectangles you created as cutting planes. Activate the Section tool (M-Tool:9a,8), access its dialog, and ensure that both the 2D and Plane options are active. Back in the graphics window, you'll be prompted to select a cutting plane—this can be an outline, face, or 2D object. Select one of the rectangles you had created (Figure 4.29-a), and watch your objects disappear, leaving behind 2D sections of the solids where the plane of the rectangle cut through them (Figure 4.29-b). You can change the Status Of Objects in the Section Options dialog from the default of Ghosted to Keep or Delete, if you want the original objects and cutting plane to be retained or deleted respectively.
- Undo and repeat with any of the other cutting planes you had created. You can also apply the Section tool without prepicking the objects. In that case, you would first select the object to be sectioned, and then the cutting plane. You can section only a single object in this manner. Use the prepick method when you want to section many objects at a time with the same cutting plane.

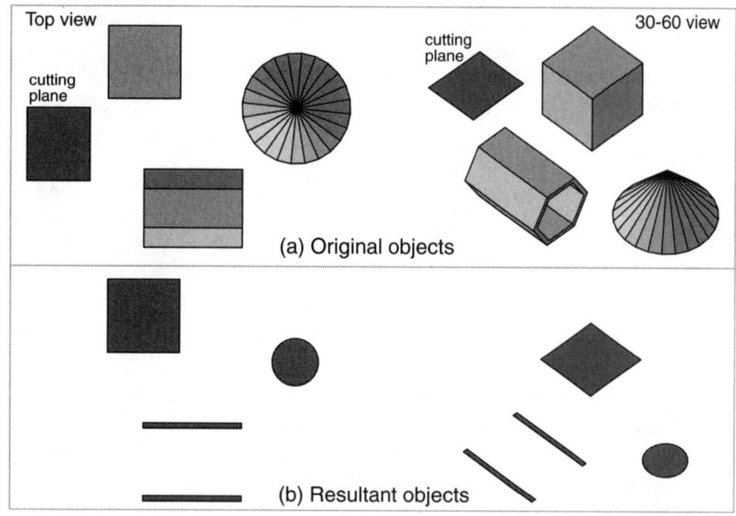

Figure 4.29

Using the Section tool to generate 2D sections using a cutting plane.

- Create a fresh set of 3D objects. This time, draw a single line segment running across them, such that if extruded perpendicular to the current reference plane, it would cut through the objects. In the dialog of the Section tool, set the Cut Objects With option to Line instead of Plane. Then apply the Section tool as you did earlier, this time selecting the cutting line after prepicking the objects. You'll have 2D sections of your solids as before. The Line option is thus useful when simple cuts perpendicular to a plane are required.

Only a single line segment can be used as the cutting line with the Section tool. To cut an object with a polyline, polycurve, arc, or any other shape, you have to use the With Line option of the Trim/Split tool, which will be covered in Exercise 6 of Workshop 6 (Going Organic).

The new objects created by the Section tool are regular objects and can be used for any other operation. You can also copy them across to the drafting module, where you can then proceed to annotate and dimension them if you need to produce plans and sections of your model. This process is described in the Appendix, which takes a brief look at drafting in form•Z.

4.2 3D Sections

Normally, when you draw plans and sections of your designs, you show not just the cut portion but also what's left beyond the cut, in order to give a clearer picture of what the various objects are. For instance, the 2D section of the cone in Figure 4.29 is a circle, but it could just as well have been the section of a cylinder. In this situation, it would've been useful to leave the lower half of the cut intact—that would clearly be the section of a cone. This is where 3D sections come in useful.

- Invoke the dialog of the Section tool, and set the options to 3D and Plane. Create a new set of objects and cutting plane. Perform the Section operation as before. You'll find that all the selected objects now get sliced into separate parts along the cutting plane. The cut is indicated by a line that appears on the surface of the objects (Figure 4.30-a). The sliced parts can be selected, moved, deleted, etc., independent of each other (Figure 4.30-b).

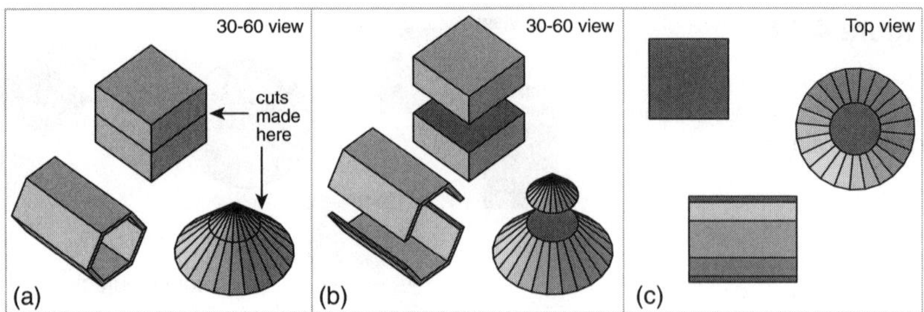

Figure 4.30

Applying the Section tool in 3D mode to the same set of objects shown in Figure 4.29-a, with the same cutting plane. The cut portions can be moved (b), or deleted (c), independently of each other.

- For generating a plan or section, simply delete those sectioned parts that should not be there, and then switch to the appropriate view. You now have your plan or section, not only cut in the right place but with all the portions beyond the cut also visible, making it more lucid (Figure 4.30-c). You can copy this view across to the drafting module, or save it in the appropriate file format for another 2D drafting program. Remember to Undo the Section operation if you had performed it for the purpose of generating plans and sections only, because you would, of course, want your original modeling objects back.

- The Section tool in 3D mode, as you can see, is useful not just for generating plans and sections of the model, but also for conveniently trimming away unwanted parts of objects. Remember that you can also use a cutting line instead of a cutting plane by setting the Cut Objects With option to Line, just as you did for 2D sections.

4.3 Contour Cuts

- Select the Contour tool, located immediately after the Section tool in the left column of Row 9, and apply it to any 3D object. You'll find that a number of 2D sections of the object are created at regular intervals, parallel to the currently active reference plane (see Figure 4.31-a). Each one of these sections is called a *contour*, and the distance between them is referred to as the *contour increment*. The Contour tool is thus similar to the Section tool in the sense that it makes 2D sections of the selected object; however, no cutting plane or line is needed here.

- Create an inclined arbitrary reference plane, then reapply the Contour tool to another object. Notice how the contours of the object are now created differently since they are parallel to the new plane. Needless to say, this method of deriving several parallel 2D surfaces from a single 3D object can come in very handy at times.

- Invoke the dialog of the Contour tool and look at its options (Figure 4.31-b). You can see that you have two basic choices: Use Contour Increment, where you specify the distance between two contours; or Use # Of Increments, where you specify the total number of cuts that should be made to the object. You have already worked with the first option, which is active by default. Switch to the second one and see how it works.

- For each of the two main options of the Contour tool, there are additional choices that determine where the *first* contour will be located. Try them all out. For the Use Contour Increment mode, you can specify the starting position relative to the reference plane (Start At), or a value that will be added to the lowest point of the object (Start At Min Plus), or simply opt for the lowest position that is a multiple of the contour increment (Start At Increment Multiple). For the # Of Increments mode, you can choose between Start At Min Plus or End At Max Minus, where the specified value will be subtracted from the highest point of the object to fix the position of the final contour.

- There are two additional options lower down in the dialog that apply to both modes of the Contour tool. By default, two discontiguous contours of an object created at the same level are treated as one object. This situation occurs with the 3D enclosure shown sectioned in Figure 4.31-a. By checking the One Object Per Contour option, such discontiguous same-level contours get created as separate objects. Keep in mind that you can always use the Separate tool (M-Tool:9b,2) to separate them later, if you forget to select this option.

- The last option for the Contour tool is Zero Heights. When this is checked, all the contours will be projected on the current reference plane and will lie on top of each other. You could use this option to quickly create, for instance, a set of concentric circles by applying it to a cone. Try it.

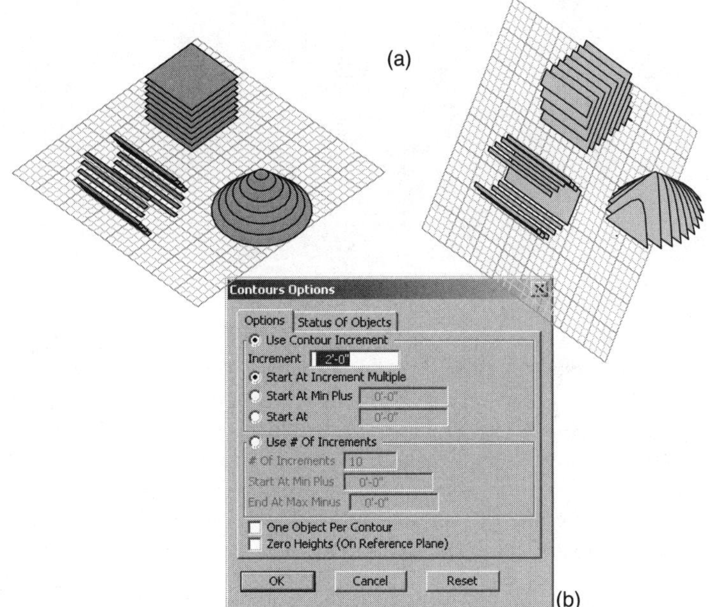

Figure 4.31

Applying the Contour tool to the same set of objects shown in Figure 4.29-a, using two different planes. The tool dialog is also shown.

EXERCISE 5

Moving Over Rugged Terrains

In this exercise, you'll learn how to create undulating landforms, i.e., sites for architecture and urban planning that are not flat. form•Z provides you with a dedicated tool for creating such undulating terrains: the Terrain Model tool, located at the end of the left column on Row 5. This tool lets you create sloping sites in the manner in which such sites are normally represented and illustrated outside CAD—using contour lines and contour intervals. This makes the Terrain Model tool very easy and intuitive to use, as you'll see in the course of this exercise.

5.1 Meshed Terrain Model

- On a new project or fresh layer, use the drawing tools in 2D mode to draw a site outline and some contour lines, all on the same reference plane. You can switch to the Top view in order to do this more accurately. The site *must* be a closed surface. Take care to ensure that those contour lines that do not form a closed loop within the site cross the boundary of the site. And, of course, you should not create contour lines that cross each other—a basic requirement of the contour concept, in CAD or outside of it.

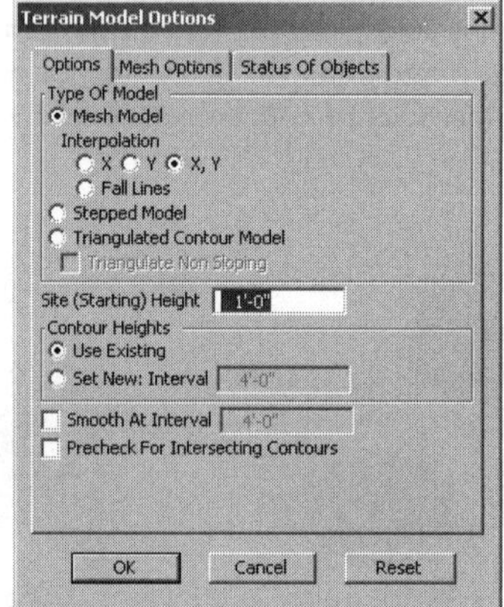

Figure 4.32

The Terrain Model Options dialog.

- Select the Terrain Model tool (M-Tool:5a,10) and invoke its dialog (Figure 4.32). Notice that there are three types of terrain models, of which Mesh Model is selected by default. This is the terrain type we'll work with first. Leave all the options selected the way they are, except for those in the Contour Heights section. Here, Use Existing is selected by default. Switch instead to the alternative, Set New: Interval, and change the associated contour interval value, if required. What this option lets you do is draw contour lines on the same level as the site (which is what you have done), and then use the specified contour interval to automatically space them out perpendicular to the site plane. Exit the Terrain Model Options dialog after making this change.

- Back in the graphics window, use the Pick tool to select each one of the contour lines in the correct height sequence, starting with the lowermost contour. The selection sequence is very important for the Contour Heights mode you just activated, since it will determine the height of each contour.

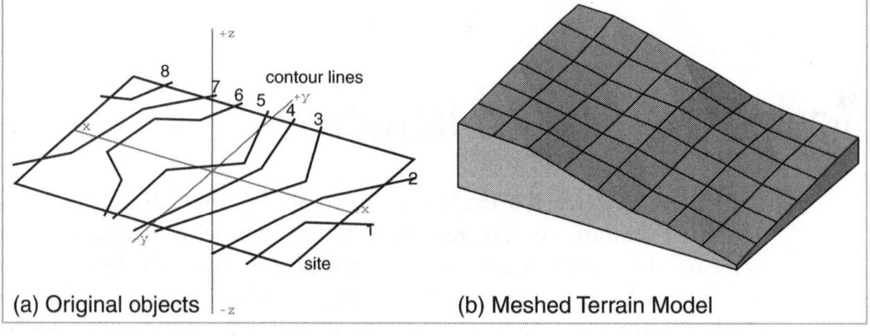

Figure 4.33

Creating a meshed terrain model using the Set New: Interval option for Contour Heights. The picking sequence of the contour lines is indicated.

If some contours need to be at the same height, group them first using the Group tool. Then pick all the contours with the topological level set to Group rather than Object.

- After prepicking all the contour lines, select the Terrain Model tool and watch the Prompts palette. You'll be asked to select a 2D object or the face of a 3D object to serve as the site for the landform. Click on the shape you created for the site. A meshed terrain model of your site will be created, following the shape, heights, and sequence of your contour lines (Figure 4.33).

- Return to the Terrain Model Options dialog and set the Contour Heights option back to the default of Use Existing. Undo the Terrain Model operation you just performed; you'll redo it using the new option. Since you'll now be using the actual heights of the contour lines, apply the Move tool with the Perpendicular Lock turned on to move each contour line to the desired height (Figure 4.34-a). As you can see, the advantage of this method is that you can have variable heights between contours rather than a uniform contour interval. After you have finished rearranging the contour lines, prepick them—the sequence of selection will not matter now—and apply the Terrain Model tool as before. You should see a different landform based on the new heights of your contour lines (Figure 4.34-b).

- You might wish to have a smoother terrain, which requires having a denser mesh with smaller subdivisions. This can be done by invoking the Terrain Model Options dialog and going to the Mesh Options tab, where you can change the dimensions of the mesh. These are the same options associated with the Mesh tool (M-Tool:6a,1) which we'll be exploring in detail in Workshop 6 (Going Organic). For now, simply change the X, Y, and Z values of the mesh, deselecting the XYZ Lock option if you require them to be different from each other. Then get back to the graphics window, Undo the Terrain Model operation, and reapply it with the new settings. The meshed terrain should now be denser, and therefore smoother, than before (Figure 4.34-c).

- Get back to the Terrain Model Options dialog and you'll see that there are four Interpolation options for the Mesh Model type. These options determine how the elevations of each point of the mesh are related to the heights of the contour lines you create. The four different options lead to very minor changes, so we won't get into the technical details of how the interpolation is actually done. All that you really need to know is that the Fall Lines method is considered to be more accurate (and therefore more time consuming), but the default of X,Y works reasonably well and you can leave it as such.

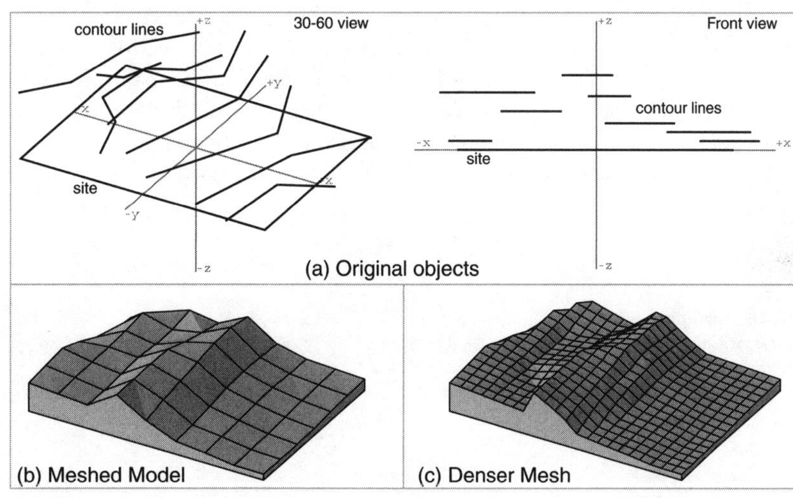

Figure 4.34

Using the Terrain Model tool with the option set to Use Existing for Contour Heights. Two versions of the resultant model are shown, each with different mesh settings.

- The Terrain Model Options dialog contains a number of other options that apply to all the three types of models. The value of the Site (Starting) Height determines the elevation of the base of the site when it is a 2D object, as in the examples used so far. It has no effect when the face of a solid object is selected as the site. Test it with a height that is different from the default value.
- The Smooth At Interval option is more relevant to the Stepped Model, so we'll look at it later. Turn to the last option, Precheck For Intersecting Contours. This will warn you if it finds intersecting contours before attempting to carry out the Terrain Model operation. As already mentioned, contours should not intersect, but if you have a large site and many closely spaced contours (which you may have entered through a digitizing tablet), you might inadvertently have some of them intersecting each other. Therefore, for modeling large sites and complicated terrains, it is advisable to turn this option on; otherwise it is not necessary.

A very common error when working with terrain models is to leave contour lines drawn on the same plane as the site, and then neglect to change the Contour Heights option from the default of Use Existing to Set New: Interval. This will result in a flat landform since the actual contour heights will be used, which are the same height as the site. Watch out for this error, and correct it by selecting the appropriate height option.

5.2 Stepped Terrain Model

- It's time to move on to the other types of terrain models. Get back to the Terrain Model Options dialog and select the second type, Stepped Model. Undo the Terrain Model operation you last performed and redo it using the new mode. You'll see that instead of a smooth mesh, the landform now has actual steps between the contour lines (Figure 4.35-a).
- Since the individual contours are now actually visible, these might need to be curvilinear to give a better appearance to the stepped site. You could, of course, create them as curved to begin with. An easy alternative is to activate the Smooth At Interval option in the Terrain Model Options dialog, and specify the desired smoothing distance in the associated box. If you now Undo and reapply the Terrain Model tool, the steps of the terrain will be smoothly curved (Figure 4.35-b).
- The Stepped Model terrain type can be used to create a simple staircase very quickly with minimal effort. And unlike the Stair From Path tool, the steps can be of any shape. Draw the outline of the staircase, and the individual steps as contours projecting beyond the outline, as shown in Figure 4.36-a. You could simply draw one contour and then transform it in Multi Copy mode to generate the rest. Activate the Set New: Interval option and specify the required riser height as the contour interval. Apply the Terrain Model tool to this configuration in the usual manner, and you have your staircase ready in a jiffy! The result is shown in Figure 4.36-b.

Figure 4.35

Creating a stepped terrain model, using the same site and contours as in Figure 4.33. The result of activating the Smooth At Interval option is also shown.

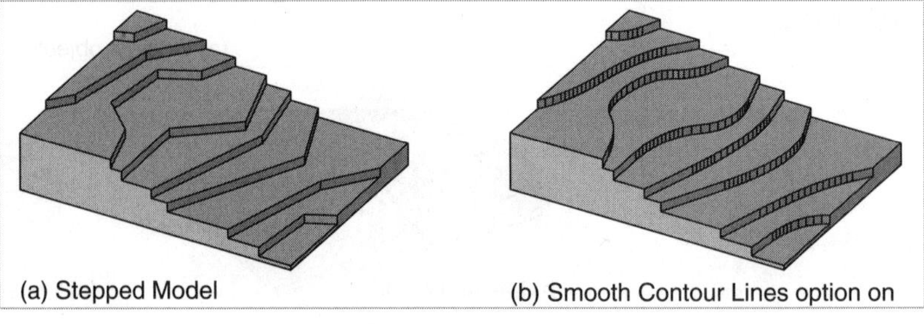

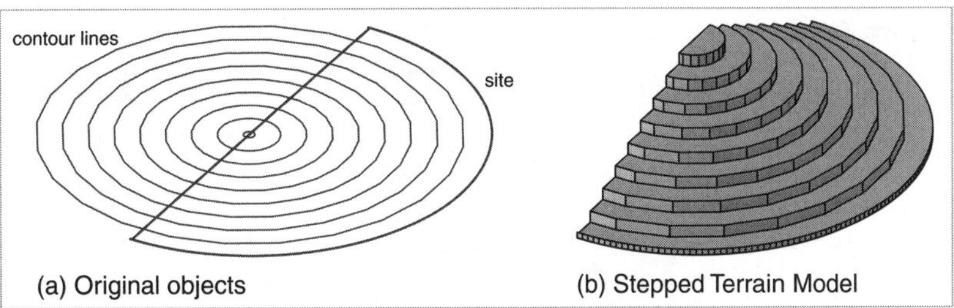

Figure 4.36

Creating a semicircular staircase quickly using the Stepped Terrain Model.

5.3 Triangulated Terrain Model

- Move on to select the third type of terrain, Triangulated Contour Model, in the dialog of the Terrain Model tool. Apply it to a new set of contour lines and site. This time, use a 3D slab rather than a 2D surface as your site (Figure 4.37-a). This means that after you finish prepicking your contour lines, you'll have to set the topological level to Face and apply the Terrain Model tool to the top face of the slab. Note that the contour lines themselves can be created at the level of the lower face, which coincides with the reference plane and is therefore more convenient.
- You'll find that the resultant terrain model is derived by preserving the shape and height of the contours and triangulating the resulting faces (Figure 4.37-b). Since the shape of the contour lines is preserved, it might be useful to check the Smooth At Interval option to smooth them out.

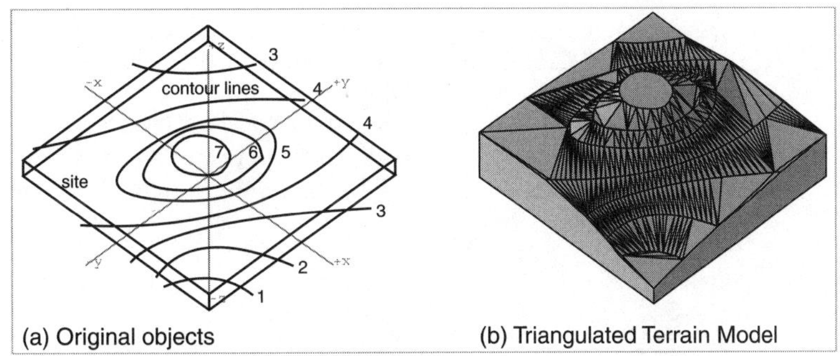

Figure 4.37

Creating a Triangulated Terrain Model, using the top face of a 3D slab as the site. The sequence of contour selection is also indicated. The same height contours were first grouped.

- You can increase the level of triangulation by selecting the Triangulate Non Sloping sub-option for the Triangulated Contour Model in the dialog. This will give you a more accurate terrain. Try it.

5.4 Combining Terrain Model Types

It is possible to combine different terrain model types on the same site. Let's end this exercise by executing one such combination example, which will show you how versatile the Terrain Model tool is.

- Create a horizontal slab with a thickness and then draw a single contour line such that it coincides with the top face of the slab, as shown in Figure 4.38-a. This contour will serve as the divider between the two different types of terrains that you'll create on the top face.

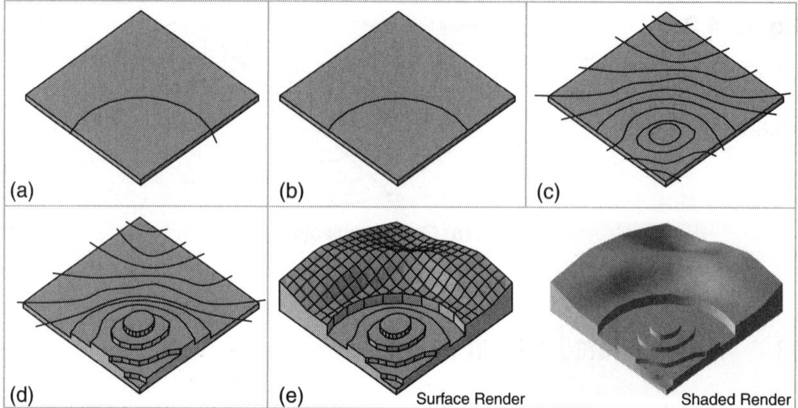

Figure 4.38

Creating a Terrain Model with two types of terrains on the same site.

- Invoke the Terrain Model Options dialog, and select the Stepped Model type with the Use Existing option. Select the single contour and apply the Terrain Model tool to the top face of the site, as you did in the previous section. Since the contour is at the same level as the top face, the result of the Terrain Model operation will simply be to divide the top face into two separate faces, as shown in Figure 4.38-b.
- Now create two separate sets of contour lines for each of the two faces, as shown in Figure 4.38-c. You can move these contour lines to the appropriate heights, or set the Contour Heights option in the Terrain Model Options dialog to Set New: Interval, with a suitable interval value.
- Preselect one set of contours and apply the Terrain Model tool to the corresponding face by setting the topological level to Face. That part of the site will become a stepped terrain (Figure 4.38-d).
- Choose another terrain type in the Terrain Model Options dialog, say Mesh Model. Change the value of the contour interval if necessary. Then apply the Terrain Model tool to the other set of contour lines and face. The final result will be a landform with both types of terrains (Figure 4.38-e).

EXERCISE 6

The Remaining Derivatives

The left column of Row 5 of the modeling tool palette contains all the *derivative object tools* that are used to derive new objects from existing ones in various ways. In Workshop 1 (Letting Yourself Go), you worked with three of these tools, 3D Extrusion, 3D Convergence, and 3D Enclosure, while in the last exercise, you worked with one more, the Terrain Model tool. In this exercise, we'll explore the remaining derivative object tools and see what they can do for us.

6.1 Deriving Points, 2D Objects, and 2D Enclosures

- Make sure the topological level is set to Object. Select the first tool in the left column of Row 5, Point Cloud, and apply it to any 2D or 3D object. This derives a *point cloud*—an unstructured

collection of points existing as a single object—from all the points of the object, ghosting it (see Figure 4.39-a). You can, of course, retrieve the original object with the Ghost tool.

- Apply the Pick tool to one of the points, and you'll find that all the other points also get selected. Apply the Separate tool (M-Tool:9b,2) to the point cloud, and you'll find that you can now select and manipulate the points independently of each other.

- Next, select the 2D Surface (M-Tool:5a,2) tool and apply it to any 3D object. There is no visible change. However, apply the Move tool to the object and you'll find that you can select each one of its faces separately and move them away, leaving behind the original object in ghosted mode (Figure 4.39-b). What this tool does is derive 2D shapes from a 3D object by literally splitting it up into independent faces. The original object can, of course, be retained by setting the Status Of Objects option to Keep.

Figure 4.39

Using the first three tools in the left column of Row 5 to derive points, 2D surfaces, and 2D enclosures from existing objects.

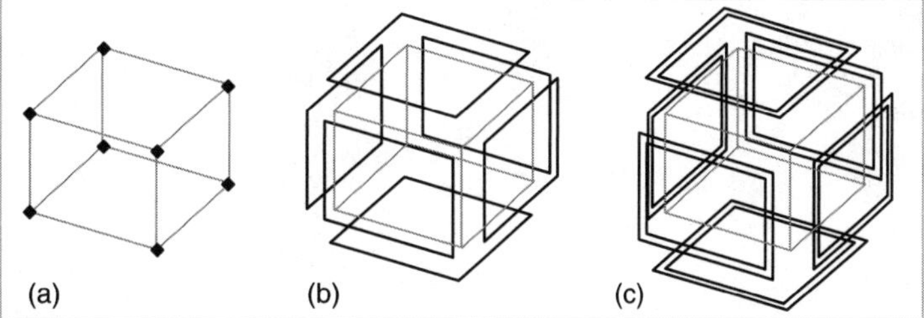

- The 2D Surface tool becomes especially useful when you want to use the face of an object for performing some operation—extrusion, for example—but need to retain the original object as it is. This tool can also be used to derive segments and faces from other 3D and 2D objects by setting the topological level appropriately. The dialog of this tool has some additional options that you should explore—for instance, the Boundary Of Surface Object option transforms a 2D enclosure into a 2D surface object by extracting only its outermost boundary.

- The next tool, 2D Enclosure (M-Tool:5a,3), functions identically to the 2D Surface tool, except that it generates enclosures instead of single lines or faces (see Figure 4.39-c). The wall width and justification options for the enclosure can be set in the tool dialog in the usual manner. Use it for various 2D and 3D objects and observe the results.

6.2 Creating Parallel Objects

- Create a few 2D and 3D objects on a fresh layer. Select the Parallel tool (M-Tool:5a,7) and apply it to each one of these objects. What this tool essentially does is create offsets of existing objects at a specified distance. For surface objects, you'll find that the object is moved parallel to itself in a positive direction with respect to the coordinate axes. For solid objects, all the faces are moved out parallel to the original faces, resulting in the entire object being enlarged by a certain factor. Thus, the Parallel tool always creates parallel surfaces, an operation which can often come in handy. As you can see from the examples illustrated in Figure 4.40-a, you can also apply the Parallel tool repeatedly to the same object to progressively increase the offset distance.

- Invoke the dialog of the Parallel tool and experiment with the options available. Here, you can change the direction as well as the distance of the offsets, both for surface and solid objects. While thc In and Out options are obvious for a solid object, for a surface object they relate to the direction in which the parallel surface gets created. The default is Out, which means that the surface object will be moved in the positive direction of the axes. Change this to In for moving in the opposite direction.

- You can also see that the default option is Single Parallel (Surface), which is why the Parallel tool has so far been creating a single surface parallel to the original face. Switch to the alternate option, Double Parallel (Solid), and you'll find that the Parallel tool now converts every single surface to a pair of surfaces with solid between them. Thus, 2D surfaces get transformed to 3D extrusions, while 3D objects themselves get transformed to hollow enclosures (Figure 4.40-b). The offset distances apply in the usual manner, and there is an additional option, Center, which will offset the pair of surfaces equally about the center of the original surface.

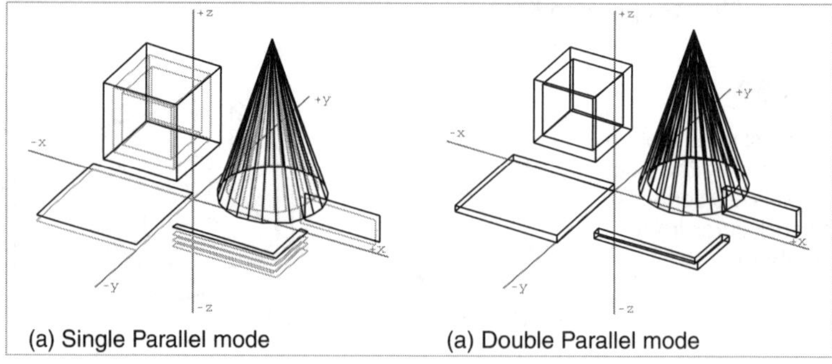

Figure 4.40

Applying the Parallel tool to a set of objects. The original objects are in ghosted mode.

- For surface objects, parallel surfaces are created in a direction perpendicular to the plane of the surface by default, as you can see in Figure 4.40. To create parallel surfaces on the *same* plane as the object, simply activate the On Same Plane option in the dialog of the Parallel tool. The surface will now be reduced or enlarged (depending on whether the In or Out option is activated), instead of simply being moved parallel to itself. Try it.

- You can also apply the Parallel tool with the topological level set to Face or Segment. This is useful if you are trying to create faces or segments parallel to existing objects, an operation that is sometimes necessary. You can set Status Of Objects to Keep to retain the original object.

There is an additional Nurbz Control Points section in the Parallel tool dialog, which contains options controlling how the Parallel operation gets applied to nurbz objects. You can come back to explore this section after you have worked with nurbz objects in Workshop 6 (Going Organic).

6.3 Making Projections

- Move on to the Projection tool (M-Tool:5a,8) which is used to derive 2D projections of 3D objects. There are two different kinds of projections that can be obtained. The default type is Projection Of View, as you can verify in the dialog of the Projection tool. 

- Create a 3D block and make multiple copies of it. Make sure you're in a non-planar view; then apply the Projection tool to one of the copies. Switch to a different non-planar view and apply the tool to another copy. Repeat this for a few other views. Finally, use the Top view for the last copy. Still in the Top view, look at the results of all the projections (Figure 4.41-a). Then see them in a non-planar view (Figure 4.41-b). You'll find that in each case, the current view of the object was projected onto the current reference plane, transforming the 3D object to a flat 2D object. To put it in simpler terms, the way you see the object on the screen is mapped and then placed on the active reference plane. Because the views kept changing, the projections kept changing as well. The projections would also be different for the same view but a different reference plane.

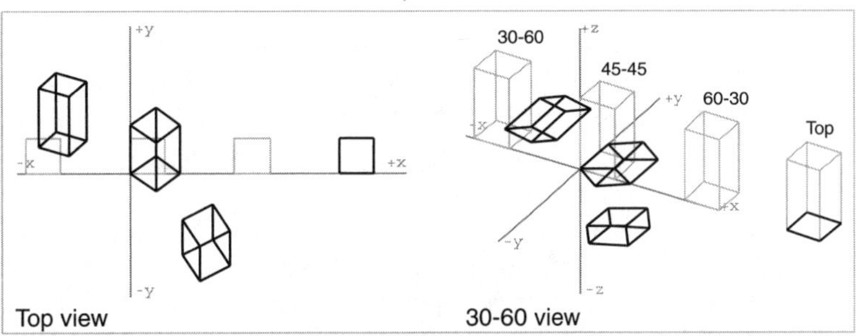

Figure 4.41

Using the Projection Of View mode to derive projections of the same object on the XY plane using four different views: 30-60, 45-45, 60-30, and Top. The original objects are seen in ghosted mode.

- Switch to the alternate option, Orthographic Projection, in the dialog of the Projection tool and apply it to some objects. You'll find that this kind of projection is derived by simply projecting the object straight onto the current reference plane, irrespective of the current view. Not only is this less confusing, it has greater utility in modeling as well. It can be used to derive plans and elevations, of sorts, from a model, which can then be reworked into more accurate drawings. This is illustrated in Figure 4.42, using the example of the chair modeled in the Assignment for Workshop 3 (Personalizing Your Environment). Its orthographic projection was derived on both the XY and YZ planes to give a plan and side elevation respectively. The Status Of Objects was set to Keep the first time, and both planes were moved some distance away from the chair prior to projection.

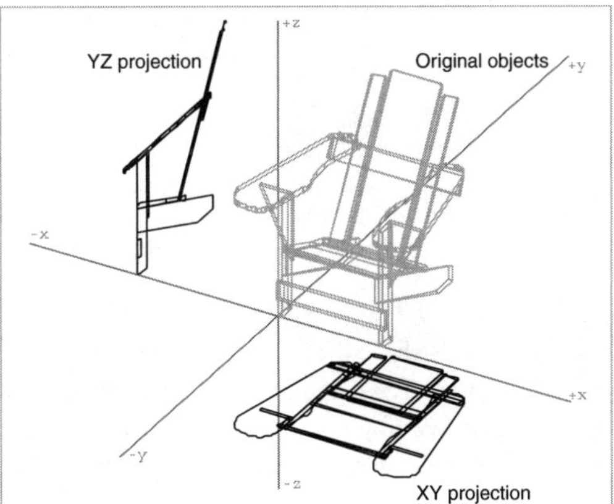

Figure 4.42

Using the Orthographic Projection mode to derive a rudimentary plan and elevation of a model.

6.4 Unfolding Objects

- Select the next derivative object tool, Unfold (M-Tool:5a,9), and try it on some objects. You'll find that, true to its name, this tool unfolds the object completely and lays out all its surfaces on the current reference plane, retaining some, but not all, of the surface adjacencies. (Needless to say, some connections have to be broken in order to "unfold" the object.) You can easily see the analogy of this to dismantling a box in real life by cutting along a few of its edges until all the faces are laid out flat on the ground. In the case of the Unfold tool, where the cut is made is determined

by where you click on the object to apply the operation to it. Also, the unfolded object is always located at the origin of the current reference plane relative to how the object was selected, and oriented in the positive axes direction. Figure 4.43 shows two examples of the Unfold operation.

The Unfold tool can be used to create the 2D layout of a 3D object that is to be constructed manually, for instance, the physical "block models" of cardboard or wood that so many design professionals build for design conceptualization. Needless to say, this tool is most useful when applied to a preliminary massing model of an object or a design rather than a detailed model. For curved objects, the unfolded entity is more useful when the objects are facetted rather than when they're smooth.

- The Unfold tool has a number of options in its dialog that you should explore. The Reposition Overlapping Parts option, which is selected by default, moves any overlapping parts in the original object to a new position in the unfolded object, where they do not overlap. Triangulate Non-Planar Faces has the usual meaning. When the Unfold tool is used for constructing the physical model of a design, it is helpful to activate the Generate Connectors option. This will create a connector on each edge of the unfolded object, which can be used to attach adjacent faces to each other in the physical model. You can also set the width and other specifications for these connectors.

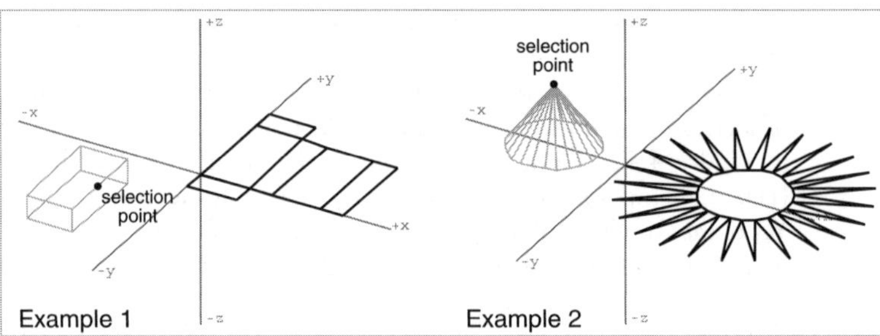

Figure 4.43

Two examples of the Unfold operation applied to facetted objects. The original objects are seen in ghosted mode.

6.5 Deriving Objects from Other Objects

There are no more derivative tools left on Row 5 to work with. But there's still one more option that we haven't yet explored, which is *deriving objects from complete objects*. Let's do one example of this.

- Create any extruded or converged solid (Figure 4.44-a). Let's suppose that you want to derive other solids from all the faces of this object simultaneously. Instead of tediously carrying out the operation for each face separately, use this simple shortcut. First, set the topological level to Object. Then, select any of the derivative object tools from Row 5, say the 3D Enclosure tool. Invoke its dialog and set the extrusion direction as Perpendicular To Surface. Also, preselect a height from the Heights menu.

Figure 4.44

Deriving 3D enclosures of a predefined height simultaneously from all the faces of an object.

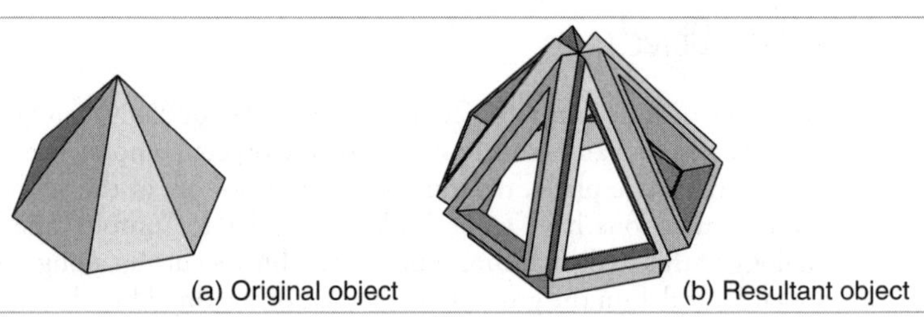

- Now apply the 3D Enclosure tool to the object. You'll find that all its faces are simultaneously converted to 3D enclosures of the same height and thickness, completely transforming the original object (Figure 4.44-b). Explore other interesting forms that can be generated using this method.

Rounding, Blending, Fillets, and Draft Angles

In this exercise, we'll work with all the tools located in the right column of Row 6 that can be used to manipulate existing objects in various ways, starting with the rounding tools. form•Z offers three different types of rounding—plain, controlled, and stitch—for which there are three separate tools. All the rounding operations can be applied to both facetted and smooth objects. The rounding itself can also be facetted or smooth, depending upon the object it is applied to and the tool options specified.

7.1 Plain Rounding

- Create a facetted 3D object as shown in Figure 4.45-a, and apply the Plain Rounding tool (M-Tool:6b,1) to it, with the topological level set to Object. Click OK in response to the message telling you that the object type will be converted to Plain. You'll find that all the edges and points of the object get smoothly rounded, as shown in Figure 4.45-b.

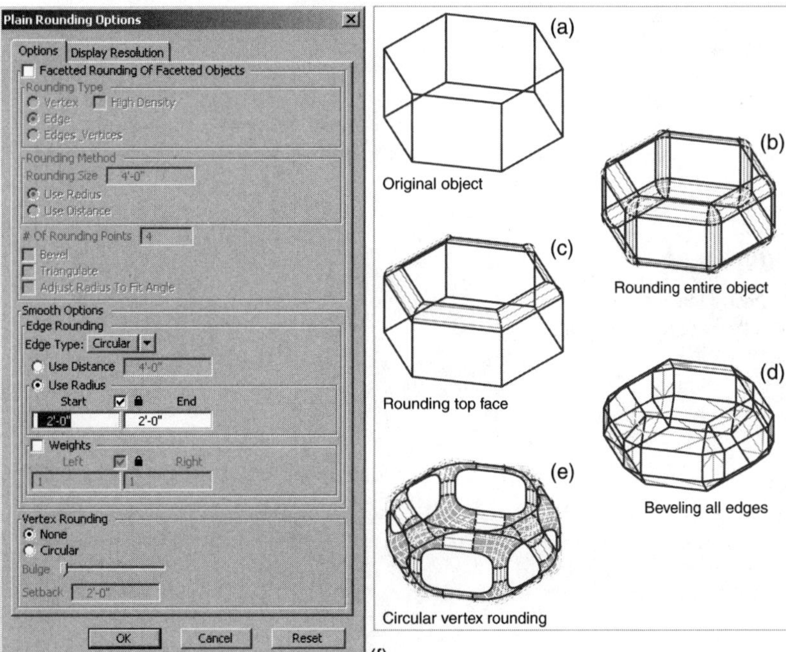

Figure 4.45

The Plain Rounding dialog, and the different options for smooth rounding it provides.

- The object created with the Plain Rounding tool is a plain object, so you cannot modify the rounding parameters after creating it. Undo the operation you just performed, and reapply the Plain Rounding tool to the object at different topological levels—Point, Segment, and so on. Notice how different parts of the object get rounded based on the topological level selected, as shown in Figure 4.45-c.

- Invoke the dialog of the Plain Rounding tool to explore its options (Figure 4.45-f). You'll see that the Facetted Rounding section is off by default, leaving the settings in the Smooth Options section to determine the type and nature of rounding. Explore the three different Edge Type options along with their associated sub-options and see how they affect the rounding. In particular, see how you can apply beveling instead of rounding with the Bevel edge type (Figure 4.45-d).

- By default, the Vertex Rounding option at the base of the Plain Rounding dialog is set to None, which means that the individual vertices don't get rounded. To turn vertex rounding on, select the alternate Circular option, and explore with different values for its Bulge and Setback parameters. One example is shown in Figure 4.45-e.

- After applying the Plain Rounding tool to the object, apply the Query tool (M-Tool:12b,1) to it. You'll find that the Model Type of the object is now listed as smooth. Thus, applying smooth rounding to facetted objects transforms them to smooth objects. You can, instead, choose to apply facetted rounding to facetted objects, which is what you'll explore next.

- Create a new facetted object, such as a cube (see Figure 4.46-a), and make sure the topological level is set to Object. In the dialog of the Plain Rounding tool, activate the Facetted Rounding Of Facetted Objects section, and apply it to the cube. You'll find that the rounding is now facetted rather than smooth. Apply the Query tool to the rounded object, and you'll see that it remains a facetted object.

- You can also see that this type of rounding takes place with four facets by default. To increase the resolution of the rounding, get back to the Facetted Rounding section of the Plain Rounding dialog and increase the value of # Of Rounding Points. You can also change the Rounding Size value to increase or decrease the distance that is to be rounded. Undo the previous operation and reapply the Plain Rounding tool with the new settings to the cube. You'll find that the rounding is now smoother (Figure 4.46-b).

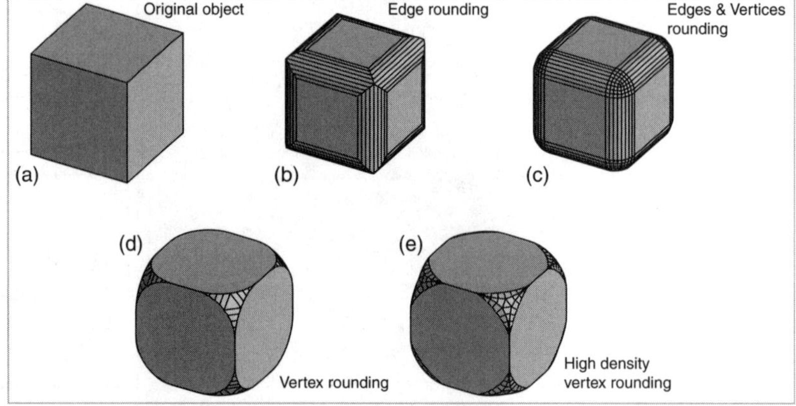

Figure 4.46

Applying the various Facetted Rounding options of the Plain Rounding tool to a facetted object.

Figure 4.47

Repeated rounding applied to a plain object. (a) Original object. (b) Rounding an edge with a large rounding value. (c) Rounding the vertices of the resulting edges with a much smaller rounding value.

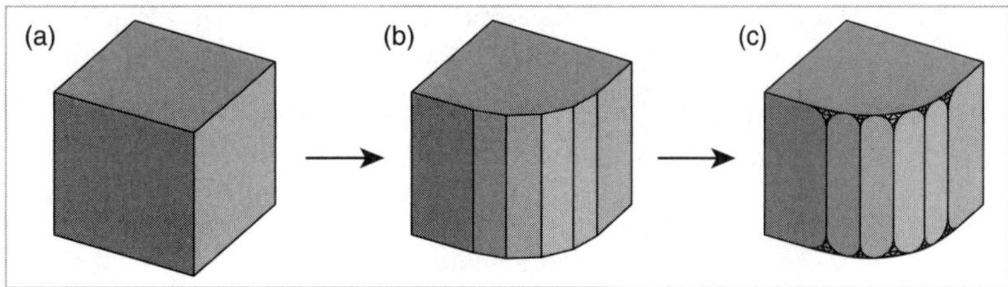

- By default, facetted rounding is applied to the edges only, as Figure 4.46-b shows. In the Plain Rounding tool, set the Rounding Type to Edges & Vertices and Vertex in turn and apply it to a fresh set of cubes. The results are shown in Figures 4.46-c and 4.46-d respectively. Note the High Density option associated with the Vertex rounding type. If this is checked, it increases the rounding resolution by generating additional faces for the rounding operation, as shown in Figure 4.46-e.

- Just like smooth rounding, facetted rounding can also be applied at different topological levels to round only specific points, segments, outlines, and faces. Try it.

- Proceed to explore the three options at the end of the Facetted Rounding section of the Plain Rounding dialog. When the Bevel option is selected, the edges and points will be beveled rather than rounded. The Triangulate option, as usual, triangulates any non-planar faces that are produced by a rounding operation. The last option, Adjust Radius To Fit Angle, is useful when the rounding value specified is too large for rounding an edge or a vertex. When this option is checked, the rounding value gets adjusted automatically (up to a maximum of 25%) and the rounding operation is reapplied. If the rounding still can't take place, an error message is issued.

- Since the object created with the Plain Rounding tool is a plain object rather than a parametric one, it lends itself to repeated facetted rounding, with appropriate rounding values. Try it. An example is shown in Figure 4.47, where an edge was first rounded with large rounding values, and the subsequent vertices were then rounded with much smaller rounding values.

7.2 Controlled Rounding

In contrast to the Plain Rounding tool, the next tool on Row 6, Controlled Rounding, creates a parametric object in which the rounding parameters are stored along with the object and can be edited later by applying the same tool.

- Create a simple 3D object, and apply the Controlled Rounding tool to it. This invokes the Smooth Round Edit dialog (see Figure 4.48-a), which is very similar to all the preview dialogs you've seen so far. The object is shown in a preview window on the left, with the familiar tool icons at the base of the window. There is only one additional tool, Pointer, which we'll soon explore. On the right side of the dialog are a variety of options for controlling the rounding, most of which are similar to the smooth rounding options for Plain Rounding you explored in the last section.

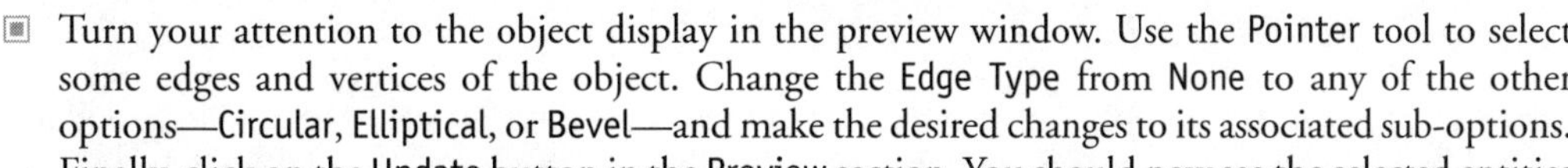

- Turn your attention to the object display in the preview window. Use the Pointer tool to select some edges and vertices of the object. Change the Edge Type from None to any of the other options—Circular, Elliptical, or Bevel—and make the desired changes to its associated sub-options. Finally, click on the Update button in the Preview section. You should now see the selected entities rounded according to the values specified in the dialog (Figure 4.48-a). Exit the preview dialog by clicking OK, and see your rounded object in the graphics window.

You could, of course, have achieved an identical result by applying the same smooth rounding options of the Plain Rounding tool. The difference, however, is that you have now created a controlled object rather than a plain one, and you can come back and modify it at any time. You'll do this next.

- Reapply the Controlled Rounding tool to the object, and the same preview dialog will be invoked, showing the original shape of the object, along with the rounded shape. You can now modify the rounding settings of any rounded edge or vertex by selecting it with the Pointer tool. You can choose to remove the rounding, if required, by setting the Edge Type back to None. Other edges and vertices can also be selected and have rounding parameters applied. All this would not have been possible with Plain Rounding.

- Just as with Plain Rounding, the Controlled Rounding tool gives you the option to apply facetted rounding to facetted objects instead of the default smooth rounding you just performed. Access the dialog of the Controlled Rounding tool and check the Keep Facetted option instead of the Make Smooth option. Now apply the Controlled Rounding tool to a new facetted object. A similar preview dialog is invoked, but with options relevant to facetted rounding (Figure 4.48-b).

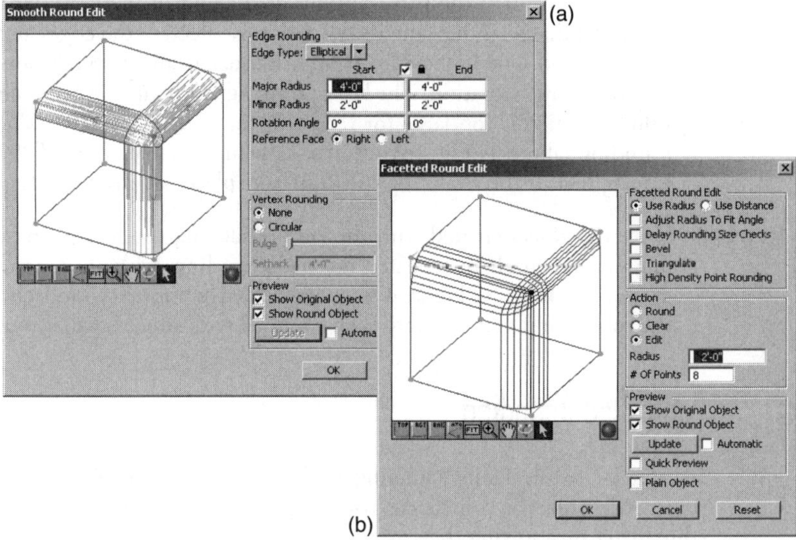

Figure 4.48

Applying the Controlled Rounding tool. (a) With the default Make Smooth option. (b) With the Keep Facetted option.

- Most of the options in the Facetted Round Edit dialog are identical to the facetted rounding options for Plain Rounding you explored in the last section. One new set of options is related to the type of action that needs to be performed in the preview dialog. The default Action is Round for applying the active rounding settings to a selected edge or vertex. To modify any previously rounded entity, you would activate the Edit option, select the rounded edge or vertex with the Pointer tool, and specify the new settings, as shown in Figure 4.48-b. To remove the rounding, use the Clear option.

- Another new option that is relevant only to controlled facetted rounding is Delay Rounding Size Checks. This is a useful option to activate when many adjacent entities are to be rounded, because rounding values can sometimes conflict when the rounding is done sequentially but not when done collectively. Having this option selected will postpone the rounding calculation until you complete the selection of entities and click on the Preview button or the OK button to exit the dialog.

- The Quick Preview option in the Facetted Round Edit dialog, when checked, will display the rounding in the preview window at a low resolution of 2 points, irrespective of the actual # Of Points value. This is useful when complex objects are being rounded. The last option, Make Plain, can be used to convert the rounded controlled object to a plain one, when you're sure you no longer need to modify its rounding parameters.

7.3 Stitch Rounding

The third type of rounding tool on Row 6 is Stitch Rounding. A *stitch* in a facetted object is a continuous, closed sequence of segments with the angles between adjacent segments equal to or greater than 100º. In a smooth object, a stitch is a continuous sequence of curves meeting at 180º. The Stitch Rounding tool enables you to conveniently round such stitches. Let's see how it works.

- Model an object with a polygonal and a circular insertion, created using the Insert Face mode (M-Tool:2b,2), as shown in Figure 4.49-a.

- Select the Stitch Rounding tool (M-Tool:6b,3), and apply it to the junctions of the insertions with the original object, as shown in Figure 4.49-b. Both junctions meet the conditions of a stitch, and get rounded as a result of the operation. You could, of course, have achieved the same result by using the Plain Rounding tool at the Outline topological level. The Stitch Rounding tool saves you from the bother of changing the topological level—it can remain as Object.

S-ROUND

WORKSHOP 4

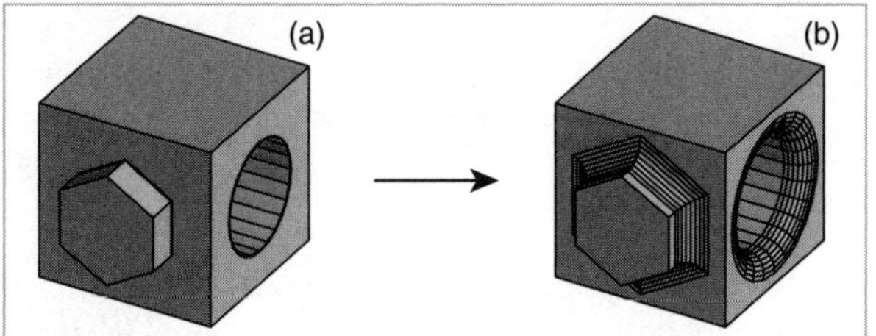

Figure 4.49

Applying the Stitch Rounding tool to an object to round off insertion junctions.

- Invoke the dialog of the Stitch Rounding tool and explore its options. You'll find that the rounding parameters are practically identical to those of the Plain Rounding and Controlled Rounding tools covered in the preceding sections. The only difference is that both the Facetted Options and Smooth Options are active simultaneously; these get automatically applied to facetted and smooth objects respectively.

7.4 Blending Objects

The next tool on Row 6, Blend, can be used to automatically create smooth transitions between two objects, and is thus very convenient. It works by connecting the objects through their ends that face each other, as you'll see in this exercise.

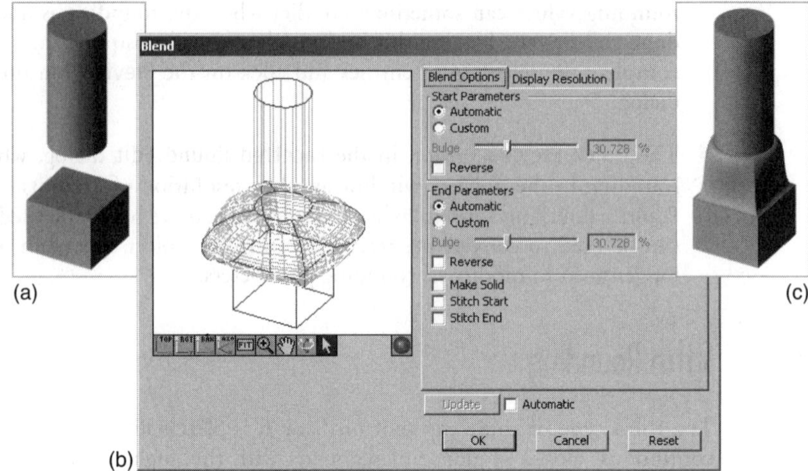

Figure 4.50

Applying the Blend tool to create a smooth transition between two solid objects. (a) Original objects. (b) The Blend Preview dialog showing the default settings. (c) The blended object obtained with custom settings, and united with the original objects,

- Create two solid objects positioned slightly apart, as shown in Figure 4.50-a. Select the Blend tool (M-Tool:6b,4), and follow the instructions in the Prompts palette to select the first and second objects. Make these selections by clicking on those faces of the objects that have to be blended.

- The Blend preview dialog will be invoked, displaying the blended object in the preview window, and allowing you to change the blending options (Figure 4.50-b). Both the Start Parameters and End Parameters are set to Automatic by default. Switch each to Custom and experiment with different Bulge values to see how they affect the blending. Use the Update button to see the result after each change in setting. Also try out the Reverse option, which directs the blending away from the blending edge.

- By default, the blending object is created as a surface. Check the Make Solid option to create it as a solid, since our two original objects are solids. Then exit the dialog. Back in the graphics window, you'll find that the blended object has been created as a solid. You can verify this with the Query tool (M-Tool:12b,1).

- Since the Status of Objects for the Blend tool is set to Ghosted by default, you'll find that the two original objects have been ghosted. Use the Unghost tool (M-Tool:14b,2) to retrieve them. If you like, you can now apply the Union tool (M-Tool:9a,1) to combine all three objects into one object (as shown in Figure 4.50-c).

- The Blend tool can be applied to surface objects in a similar manner. Try it. When the open edges of surface objects are being blended, you can use the Stitch Start and Stitch End options to stitch the blend to the edges and make the whole configuration a single object. The use of the Union tool is not required in this case.

7.5 Creating Fillets

The next tool on the same row, Fillet, has similarities with the Rounding tools as well as the Blend tool. It can be used to create rounded edges between faces of the same object or between the faces of different objects. Let's see an example of each.

- Create a simple cube. Select the Fillet tool (M-Tool:6b,5), and in response to the instructions in the Prompts palette, select two adjacent faces of the cube. A preview dialog will open up, showing how the common edge between the two faces gets rounded (see Figure 4.51-a). As you can see, the result is identical to what you could have achieved by applying the Plain or Controlled Rounding tools.

- Notice that the Fillet Type option in the preview dialog is set to Convex, which can also be verified from the direction of the fillet. Try switching to the Concave option, and you'll find that the operation doesn't work. For this particular situation, only a convex fillet can be created.

- By default, a Basic fillet is created based on a simple radius value. Switch to the Advanced option, and explore its various sub-options. You'll find that these are identical to the smooth rounding options of the Rounding tools you explored earlier.

- Go ahead and exit the preview dialog. Let's do a slightly more complex example. Undo the Fillet operation you just performed, and create a cylinder that slightly overlaps with the cube, as shown in Figure 4.51-b.

- Since the fillet between these two objects will be concave rather than convex, we need to specify that up front. Invoke the dialog of the Fillet tool and choose the Concave option for Fillet Type.

- Now apply the Fillet tool, selecting in turn, the faces of the cylinder and the cube that overlap with each other. In the preview dialog, you'll see that the junction between the two objects has been nicely rounded up by a fillet (see Figure 4.51-b). Again, explore the various Advanced sub-options to see how they affect this fillet. Applied in this manner, the effect of the Fillet tool is similar to that of the Blend tool you worked with in the preceding section.

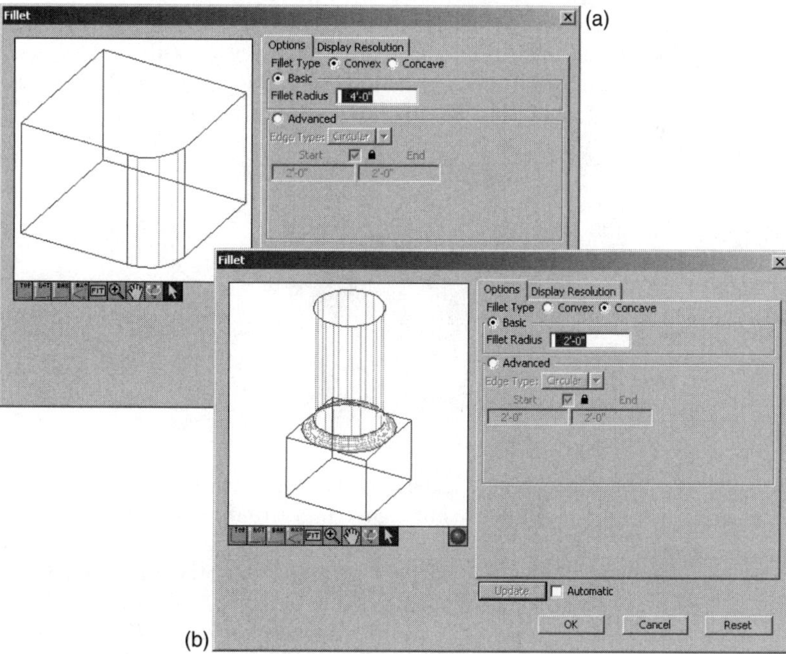

Figure 4.51

Applying the Fillet tool. (a) Between faces of the same object. (b) Between faces of different objects.

7.6 Applying Draft Angles

The last tool in the right column of Row 6, **Draft Angle**, is a nifty little tool that can be used to quickly incline a surface object, or one or more faces of a solid object, to the desired extent. The inclination takes place with respect to a specified reference plane. Let's see how it is done.

- Create a solid extrusion on the XY plane, as shown in Figure 4.52-a. Set the topological level to **Object**. With the XY plane still active, select the **Draft Angle** tool (**M-Tool:6b,6**) and apply it to the solid. You'll find that all the faces of the solid perpendicular to the XY plane are splayed inwards, changing the shape of the solid (Figure 4.52-b). **Undo** the operation, switch to a different plane, and reapply the **Draft Angle** tool to the solid. The same transformation happens, but now with respect to the new plane (Figure 4.52-c).

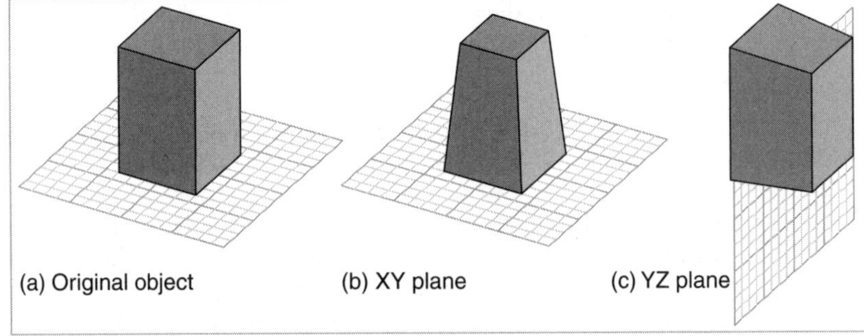

Figure 4.52

Applying the Draft Angle tool to the same object, but with respect to two different planes.

- The **Draft Angle** tool comes with a number of options in its dialog (Figure 4.53), which we'll explore next. The first option is **Base Reference Plane**, which is set to **Active Plane** by default. This is why all inclinations have been taking place with respect to the current plane. You can also choose to specify one of the three predefined planes as the base plane for executing the operation, irrespective of the currently active plane.

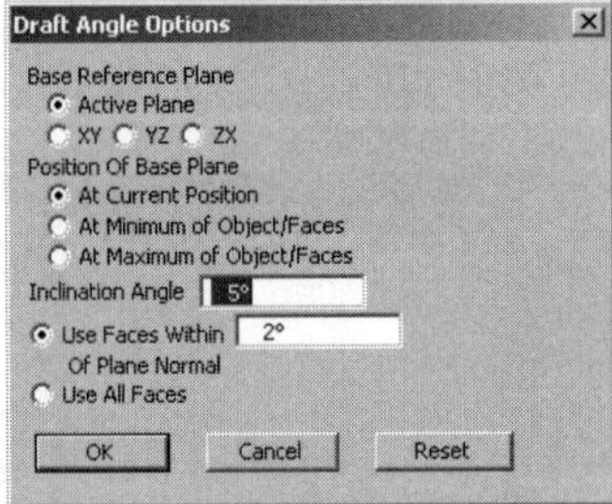

Figure 4.53

The dialog of the Draft Angle tool.

- The **Position Of Base Plane** option determines where the inclination calculation will begin. Consider the example illustrated in Figure 4.54-a of three identical objects whose lowest and highest points are 20' and 50' above the reference plane respectively. The draft angle calculation can be applied in three different ways depending upon where the base plane is located, leading to different results as shown in Figure 4.54-b. Try out all three. **At Current Position** uses the current location of the base plane, which is 0' in the example. For the **At Minimum Of Object/Faces** method, the base plane is moved to the lowest point of the object and then the inclination is calculated, leading to a larger object size. For the third method, **At Maximum Of Object/Faces**, the base plane is moved to the highest point for calculating the inclination, leading to the largest object size, even bigger than the original object.

- The next option in the Draft Angle Options dialog is Inclination Angle, which lets you specify the required inclination value. The default is 5°. Try higher values and watch your object, at some point, end up with surfaces crossing each other. Avoid creating such self-intersecting objects as they are mathematically not well formed and may cause problems later.

Figure 4.54

The effect of different Position Of Base Plane options for the same set of objects, while applying the Draft Angle operation.

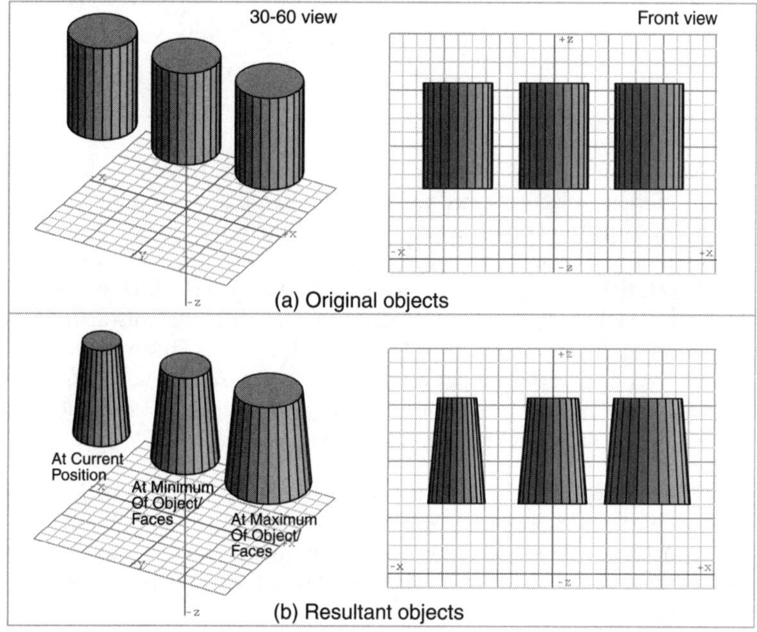

- The last two options in the dialog let you decide which faces of an object will be affected by the Draft Angle operation. The Use Faces Within option, which is selected by default, lets you specify an angle; only faces which are at an inclination of less than this angle with respect to the base plane will be affected by the operation. Going by the default value of 2°, a pyramid, for instance, will not be affected at all, unless its height is so large compared to its base that its sides are almost vertical. On the other hand, choosing the Use All Faces option will apply the Draft Angle operation to all the faces, irrespective of what their inclinations are.

EXERCISE 8

Cultivating Attachments

The remaining two exercises of this workshop will cover the Attach, Align/Distribute, Extend, and Place tools, located in the right column of Row 13 of the modeling tool palette. The operations executed by these tools are special types of geometric transformations in which the positions of selected entities can be transformed *relative* to other entities.

Figure 4.55

The dialog of the Attach tool.

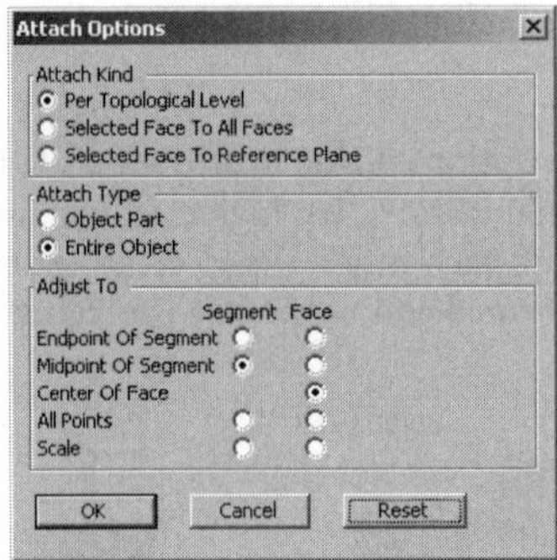

We'll begin by exploring the Attach tool in this exercise, which gives us the ability to move and position an object (referred to as the *source*) relative to another object (referred to as the *destination*), by attaching one of its parts to a part of the other object. The attachment can even be applied to another part of the same object. There are two basic types of attachments, Object Part and Entire Object, the choice of which is made in the dialog of the Attach tool (see Figure 4.55). In the first type, only the selected part of the source object gets displaced, distorting its shape; in the second, the entire object itself gets repositioned. The default mode is Entire Object. Additionally, attachments can be carried out at various topological levels: points, segments, faces, and entire objects. The Attach tool can also be used to reposition an object with respect to a reference plane. We'll explore each of these options in turn, after making some basic preparations.

- Clear your window of all its contents or move to a different layer. On the XY plane, create two 3D objects of substantially different sizes, not touching each other, as shown in Figure 4.56-a. The Attach tool, as pointed out, works in many different ways, so you can create multiple copies of these two objects—this will let you explore all the various permutations of the tool in relation to the same set of objects.

8.1 Point-to-Point Attachments

- In a point-to-point attachment, the selected point of one object is moved to coincide with the selected point of another object (or of itself). Set the topological level to Point and the self-copy mode to Self. Then select the Attach tool (M-Tool:13b,1), and verify that the Entire Object option is the one that is active in its dialog (as in Figure 4.55). Also, the Attach Kind option must be set to Per Topological Level. Don't worry about the other options in this dialog for now—they are not relevant to this kind of attachment.

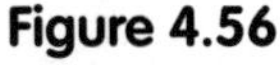

Figure 4.56

A point-to-point attachment, executed using both the Entire Object and Object Part options.

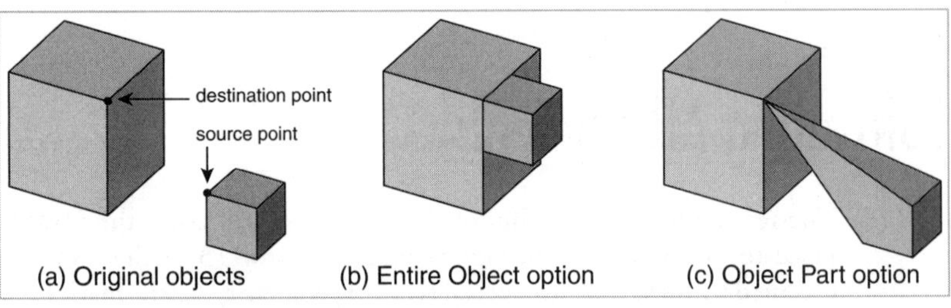

- Turn your attention to the Prompts palette and follow the instructions. For the *source point* (the point that will be displaced), select a point of the smaller object. For the *destination point* (the point to which the source point will be attached), select a point of the larger object. As soon as you do this, the smaller object is moved to reposition itself so that the selected source point coincides with the selected destination point (Figure 4.56-b). Undo the operation and repeat it with different combinations of source and destination points; this will give you a better understanding of how the tool operates.

- Now repeat the operation with the option set to Object Part in the dialog of the Attach tool. Switch to the Surface Render mode for a more accurate display of the result. You'll see that the source object gets completely deformed in the process of being *attached* to the destination object through the selected points (Figure 4.56-c). Such an object will often have non-planar faces, so watch out for these. In general, you'll find yourself using the Entire Object option for the most part.

- Another variation you should try is to set the self-copy mode on Row 12 to one of the Copy modes rather than Self. The Attach operation will now produce a copy of the source object in the attached position, retaining the original object.

Only actual points can be selected for attachments. You cannot, for instance, choose to attach the midpoint of a segment of an object to another object. This is because the midpoint is calculated interactively, it is not actually stored as part of the object description; so it cannot be selected. If there is any confusion, invoke the Wire Frame Options dialog and turn on the Show Points option so that all the points of an object are highlighted and clearly visible.

- The versatility of the Attach tool is greatly enhanced by its ability to attach a part of an object to another part of the *same* object. This can be done with the Object Part attachment type and the self-copy mode set to Self, which will result in transforming the shape of the object itself, as shown in Figure 4.57-a. Alternately, use the Entire Object attachment type with the self-copy mode set to One Copy to attach additional copies of the object to itself, as shown in Figures 4.57-b and 4.57-c. This involves selecting two different points of the same object as the source and destination points. You can see how easy it is to build any kind of repetitive 3D configuration or 2D pattern using this option of the Attach tool.

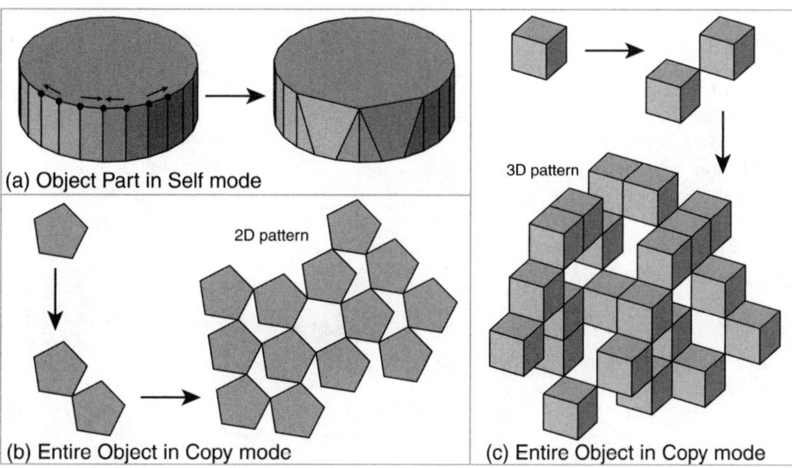

Figure 4.57

Examples of a point-to-point attachment of an object with itself.

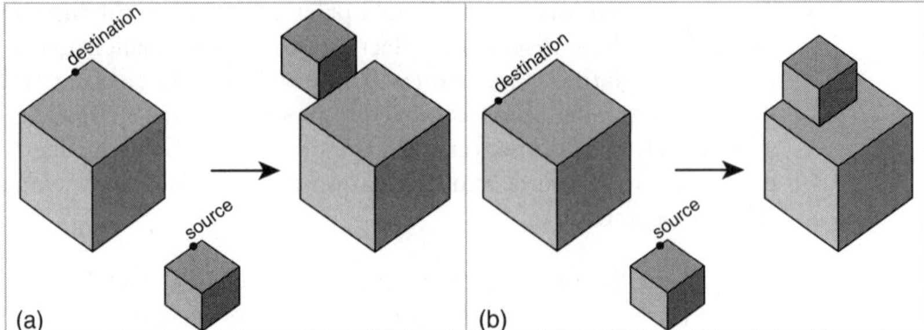

Figure 4.58

Illustration of how point mapping affects a segment-to-segment attachment. Two different results are obtained, depending upon how the source and destination segments are selected.

8.2 Segment-to-Segment Attachments

- Let's move on to segment-to-segment attachments. Use a fresh set of solids, as shown in Figure 4.58. Set the topological level to Segment, and repeat the entire sequence of operations you performed in the last section. The only difference is that you are now attaching objects through segments rather than through points. Try out a few variations of source and destination segments, using both types of attachments, Entire Object and Object Part. You might find it necessary to change to the Wire Frame display mode to be able to choose your segments correctly.

- You'll soon find yourself getting very unpredictable results with this type of attachment. This is because the operation is affected by *where* you click on the source and destination segments to select them—the ends must correspond according to the result you wish to achieve. Thus, if you are clicking near the endpoint of a source segment, you must click on the destination segment closer to the end to which the source segment is to be mapped. Figure 4.58 illustrates two different results of attaching the same source segment to the same destination segment, but selected in different ways. The attachment type was Entire Object.

- Notice also that the attached objects are being aligned according to the midpoints of the selected segments, which might not always be what is required. To specify a different segment alignment, invoke the dialog of the Attach tool and choose a different option for Adjust To under the Segment column. The default Midpoint Of Segment option attaches objects through segment midpoints.

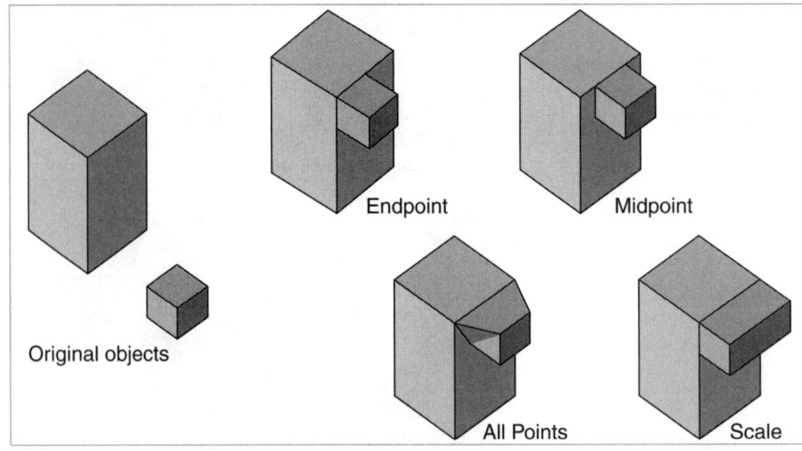

Figure 4.59

Segment-to-segment attachments with various Adjust To options. The attachment type was Entire Object throughout.

- Select each one of the other options in turn, and repeat the Attach operation to see how the results differ. Figure 4.59 illustrates all four adjustment options. Notice how the All Points option scales only the selected source segment so that it matches the size of the destination segment, while the Scale option scales the entire object so that it matches the destination segment.
- As with point-to-point attachments, the source and destination segments in a segment-to-segment attachment can belong to the same object, transforming it (Self mode) or attaching identical copies to it (one of the Copy modes). The results would be similar to those illustrated in Figure 4.57. Carry out a few such attachment operations before moving on to the next section.

8.3 Face-to-Face Attachments

- The next type of attachment is through the faces of objects. Use a fresh set of objects and with the topological level set to Face, explore the Attach tool in both modes, Object Part and Entire Object. Notice that here again, the order in which you select the segments that delineate a face affects the resultant operation—the segment picked first on the source face is mapped to the segment picked first on the destination face. Therefore, make the selection carefully.
- Experiment also with all the Adjust To modes for Face that are available in the Attach dialog. These are illustrated in Figure 4.60. You'll find that for face-to-face attachments, the Object Part option becomes a very convenient way to extend or trim an object with respect to the face of another object. Notice also that the first two Adjust To options for Face, in Entire Object mode, work identically to the corresponding options for Segment, and are, in fact, easier to carry out using segment-to-segment attachments rather than face-to-face attachments.
- The face-to-face attachment is a great technique for stacking solids on top of each other to create interesting configurations. Consider the generation of a column, for instance. You can create all the various elements—the base, pedestal, shaft, cornice, etc., separately (and thus more conveniently) on one plane, as in Figure 4.61-a. Then you can simply use the Attach tool to stack them up to create the final column, as shown in Figure 4.61-b. Try it out. Make sure that your attachment type is set to Entire Object and the adjustment option to Center Of Face.

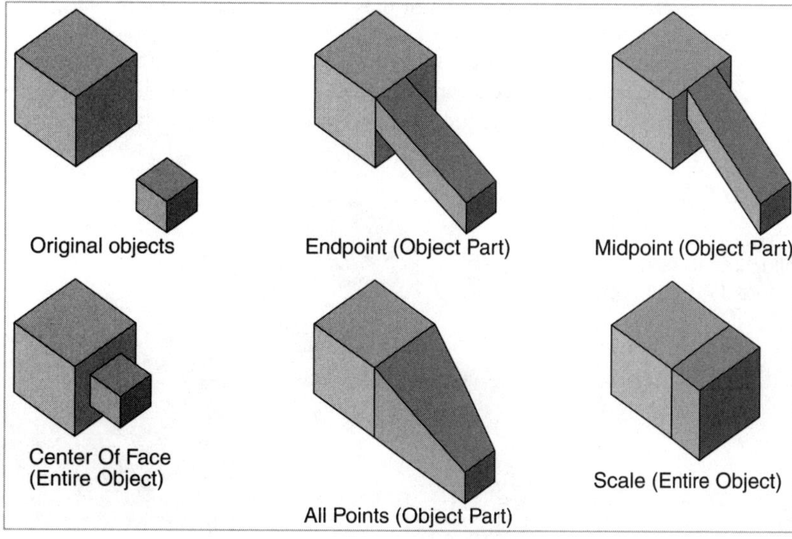

Figure 4.60

Face-to-face attachments in various modes with various adjustment options.

Figure 4.61

A good application of face-to-face attachments: stacking objects on top of each other about the same central axis.

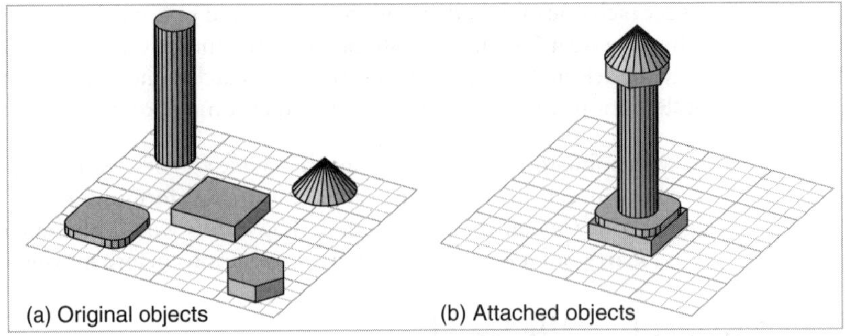

8.4 Object-to-Object Attachments

- You can also use the Attach tool for attaching one object *simultaneously to all faces* of another object. Create two solid objects, one relatively smaller than the other. You'll be attaching the smaller object to all the faces of the larger object. Set the topological level to Object, and the attachment type to Entire Object. (The self-copy modifier setting has no effect here, as it is always executed in Copy mode.) If you now perform the Attach operation, copies of the source object will be attached to every face of the destination object in one step, as shown in Figure 4.62. The attachment happens through the first face of the source object, which in turn is determined by how the object was created.
- To perform an object-to-object attachment through *any* desired face of the source object, without being restricted to the first face, activate the second Attach Kind option in the dialog of the Attach tool, Selected Face To All Faces. You can now use the Attach tool to select first a face and then an object; copies of the first object will be attached to all faces of the second object through the *selected* face. Try it out.
- Object-to-object attachments are affected by the same Adjust To option that is active for Face in the Attach Options dialog. Different results will be obtained depending upon the option selected—check them all out. Two of these are illustrated in Figure 4.62.
- Carry out some more examples of object-to-object attachments. You'll soon discover how some of the freakiest objects can be created with this mode! But also, be careful—it's very easy to make a mistake by picking the wrong objects or the wrong faces.

Figure 4.62

Object-to-object attachments using two different Adjust To options.

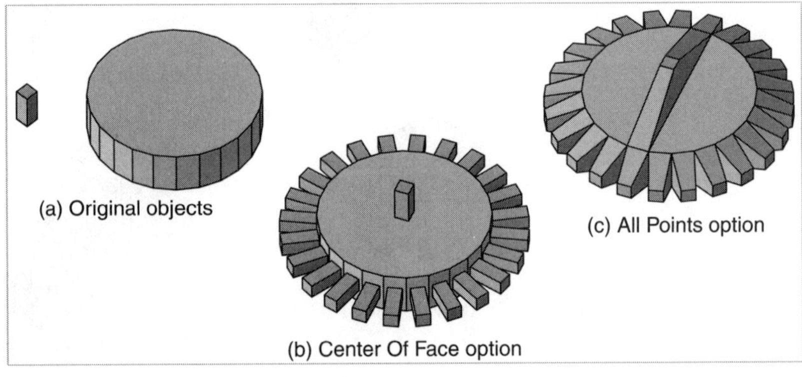

8.5 Repositioning Objects Using Attach

- We have worked with all the options of the Attach tool, except the third Attach Kind option, Selected Face To Reference Plane. Go ahead and activate this option. Then select any face of an object and click somewhere on the active reference plane. You'll find that the selected face gets placed exactly on the plane, repositioning the object to which it belongs. Try this out for different face selections. Also, keep in mind that this repositioning operation is governed by the same Adjust To option that is active for Face in the Attach Options dialog.

EXERCISE 9

Alignments, Distributions, Extensions, and Placements

This final exercise will cover the Align/Distribute, Extend, and Place tools, located immediately after the Attach tool in the right column of Row 13 of the modeling tool palette.

9.1 Aligning and Distributing Objects

The Align tool can be used to align objects located anywhere in 3D space along the X, Y, or Z directions, relative to each other. It can also be used to distribute selected objects at equal distances. Let's see how it works.

- Create a number of objects scattered randomly in 3D space, and prepick them with the Pick tool. Then select the Align tool (M-Tool:13b,2) and click anywhere in the window. As soon as you do this, the Align/Distribute Options dialog is invoked, showing the selected objects in the preview window and providing you with options for aligning and distributing them in various ways (see Figure 4.63-a).

- First, explore the Align and Distribute sections located to the right of the preview window. These are in the form of icons, spread out in a row and column format. Each section has three columns for each of the three axes, X, Y, and Z, and four rows indicating different alignment and distribution options. To begin with, the Off option is activated for all three axes in the Align section, as you can see in Figure 4.63-a. Choose one of the other three options—Min, Center, or Max—for one or more axes and see how the objects in the preview window line up accordingly, along the minimum, center, or maximum of the chosen directions respectively (Figure 4.63-b). Switch to the Top view to see the results more clearly.
- Explore also the four Distribute options in the same manner. The icons do a good job of explaining how the respective operations work. Thus, the Min option will distribute the selected objects equally between the minimum point of the first object and the minimum point of the last object, along the chosen axis. In contrast, the last option, Between, will distribute the objects between the maximum point of the first object and the minimum point of the last object. Note that for a given axis, you can activate either one of the Align or one of the Distribute options, but not both (see Figure 4.63-b).

Figure 4.63

Aligning and distributing objects with the Align tool. (a) The Align/Distribute Options dialog, when first invoked. (b) Specifying Align and Distribute options along the X and Y axes respectively.

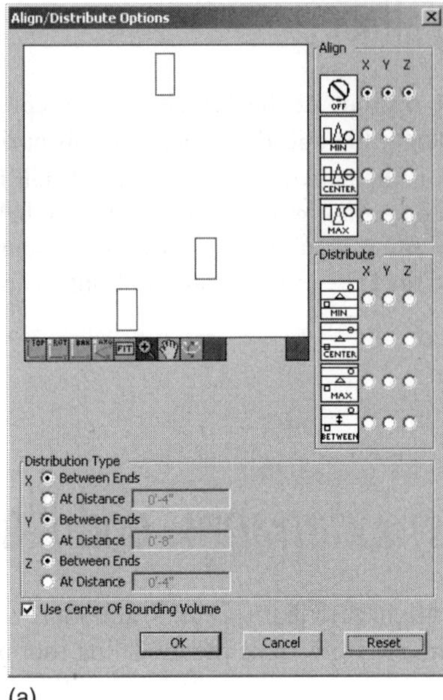

(a)

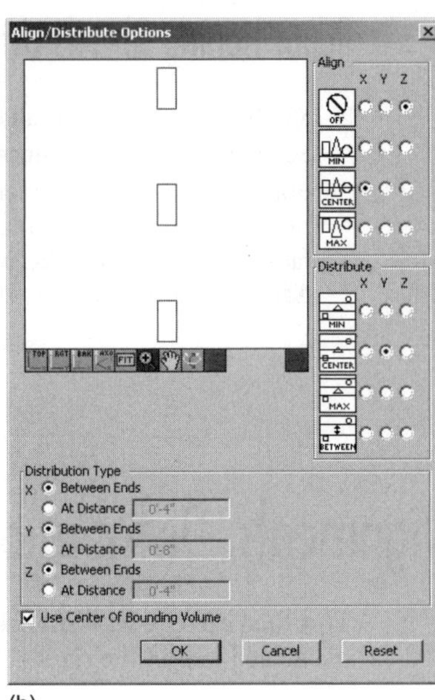

(b)

- Now proceed to explore the remaining options located in the lower half of the Align/Distribute Options dialog. By default, the Between Ends option is activated for all three axes, X, Y, and Z, which makes the distribution operation work as explained earlier—the first and last objects along the axes are determined, and the remaining objects are distributed between them at equal distances. In contrast, when the At Distance option is activated, the first, central, or last object along the axes is determined (depending upon whether the Min, Center, or Max distribution option is selected), and the remaining objects are placed sequentially at the distance specified in the accompanying box. The objects are placed in the order in which they were selected. If the fourth distribution option, Between, is selected, objects are distributed at the specified distance about the point which is the average of the maximum point of the first object and the minimum point of the last object. It might sound confusing, but will be clear once you try it out.

9.2 Extending Segments and Faces

Let's move on to look at the next tool, Extend. It is used for extending a segment, or the face on which a number of segments end, in various ways. The extension happens in such a manner that the "directionality" of the segment is maintained. Thus, the Move tool, for instance, cannot be used instead of the Extend tool, as it is not always possible to confine the direction of movement. The Extend tool is indispensable for extending and trimming objects accurately with respect to each other.

- Create any two 3D objects, located close to each other, but not touching or overlapping. Activate the Extend tool (M-Tool:13b,3) and watch the Prompts palette for instructions. For the *segment to extend*, select any segment of one of the objects. You'll then be prompted for the *face to extend to.* Select any face of the other object that is not parallel to the segment. As a result of the operation, the selected segment is stretched out to meet the selected face, distorting the object it belongs to in the process (Figure 4.64-a).

Figure 4.64

The default operation of the Extend tool, along with the tool dialog.

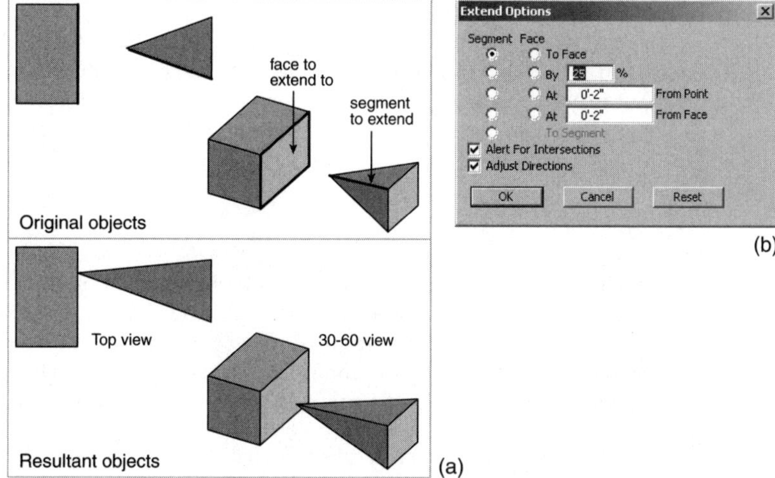

- Invoke the dialog of the Extend tool and examine its options (Figure 4.64-b). There are five methods for extending a Segment and four for extending a Face. By default, the Segment option is active using the To Face method, which is why you were asked to select a face for extending the segment in the last step. Explore all the other methods for extending segments as well. You can extend the segment by a percentage of its original length, or by a specified distance from its endpoint or the face at which it ends. These three methods only require the segment to be selected. For the remaining method, To Segment, you have to select a second segment for extending the first segment to.

- It'll often be more convenient to extend the face on which a number of segments end, rather than each individual segment, as in the example illustrated in Figure 4.65 where the corners of two walls in a building model need to be "flushed." Activate the To Face method for the Face entity in the Extend Options dialog. Then select the end face of one wall and extend it to the appropriate face of the other wall, as shown. Repeat the process for the second wall to trim it up to the first wall. Choose the further surface of the wall this time, so that the walls are properly flushed against each other.

Figure 4.65

Extending a face to another face with the Extend tool to flush two walls with each other.

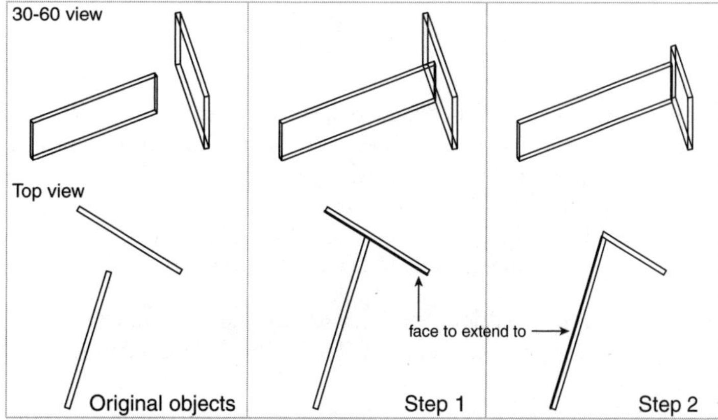

- Explore the other three methods for extending a face, which work in the same manner as for a segment. Also, note the remaining two options at the base of the Extend Options dialog, which are selected by default. When using the To Face extension method, occasionally a self-intersecting object may be produced, or the directions of a solid may get reversed. It helps to be alerted when either of these two situations occur, so it's advisable to leave both options turned on.

9.3 Placing Objects

Place, the last tool in the right column of Row 13, is used to place an object, called the *source*, on an edge or a corner point of another object, called the *destination*. Both the source and destination objects can be 2D or 3D. Multiple copies can be placed, if desired, in one step. The Place tool can also generate a nurbz object out of multiple 2D placements, as well as apply a macro transformation while making a placement. We'll explore these capabilities in the remainder of this workshop.

- Clear the window or move to a different layer. Create one large 2D shape and a smaller 3D object. Set the topological level to Object, and the self-copy modifier to Self. Then activate the Place tool (M-Tool:13b,4), and following the instructions in the Prompts palette, select the smaller object as the source and the larger shape as the destination (Figure 4.66-a). The source now gets placed on the destination at the point where you clicked on it to select it (Figure 4.66-b). This is the basic operation of the Place tool.

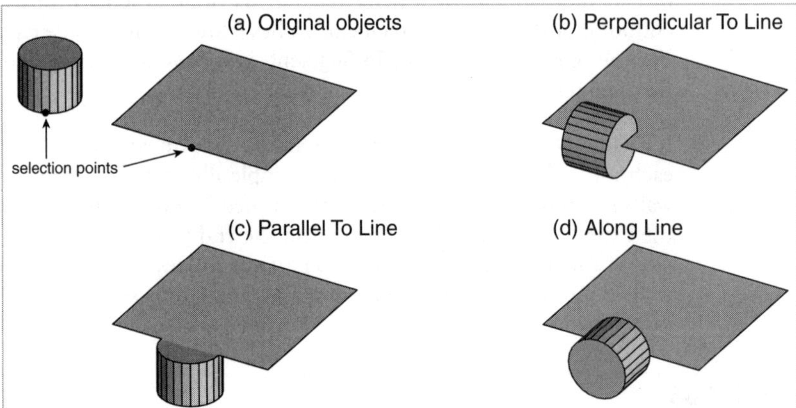

Figure 4.66

The basic operation of the Place tool, using different Orientation options.

- Invoke the dialog of the Place tool, shown in the next section in Figure 4.68. It has an extensive set of options, which we'll now study. Let's start with Orientation, which determines how the source object will be oriented when it is placed on the destination object. The default option is Perpendicular To Line, which accounts for the result you obtained in the last step. Explore all the other options (see Figure 4.66). You'll find that some options produce the same result, depending upon the location and orientation of the destination object.

- Next, turn to the Alignment options. You can see from Figure 4.66 that the source is placed by aligning it through its Centroid. This is the default alignment, but there are four other options. Explore each one in turn. You can mark any point of the source with the Point Marker tool (M-Tool:11b,4), and then use the Reference Point alignment option to place the source through that point. Using the First Point of the source is another option. The Middle Of Open Ends option is

applicable only to an open 2D source object—the placement happens through the midpoint of the imaginary segment joining the first and last points of the shape. And finally, the World Origin option places the source through the origin [0,0,0] of the world coordinate system. To use this option effectively, you must create the source in such a way that the origin passes through the point you want for the alignment.

Figure 4.67

The effect of the Snap To Points Within Distance Of option, when placing objects on endpoints.

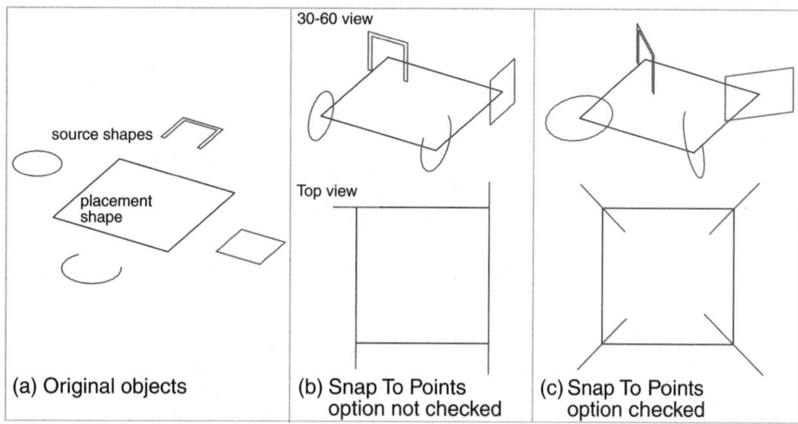

- Next, try placing a few objects on the endpoints of various segments of the destination object, using Endpoint snap, rather than on the edges (Figure 4.67-a). You'll find that in all cases, the source is oriented perpendicular to the line of the segment ending at the selected point (Figure 4.67-b). Go back to the Place tool dialog and check the Point Snap Within option. Undo all the Place operations you just did, and reapply the tool to place a source on an endpoint of the destination object. You'll find that the source is now oriented, not perpendicular to the segment as before, but on the angle *bisector* at the selected placement point (Figure 4.67-c). The default snapping distance of 2'-0" will make the Place tool snap to an endpoint rather than to a segment if you click within 2'-0" of the point.

9.4 Multiple Placements

- The real power of the Place tool is evident when it is used in one of the Copy modes. Set the self-copy modifier on Row 12 to Continuous Copy, then apply the Place tool to a different set of source and destination objects. You'll find that you can now place many copies of the source along the destination object by clicking on it at various points. In fact, you can even place multiple copies of the same source on *other* objects, without having to reselect the source and destination object combination each time.

- For placements at a uniform distance, set the mode to Repeat Copy. You can now place many copies of the source at regular intervals—determined by the first interval you specify—on the destination object, by simply clicking anywhere in the window after the first two placements. The source object will automatically wrap around all the individual segments of the destination object. For a 3D destination object, the face you click on is used for the placement. If the Point Snap Within option in the Place dialog is checked and a segment endpoint happens to become a placement location, the placement will automatically happen along the angle bisector, as you saw in Figure 4.67-c.

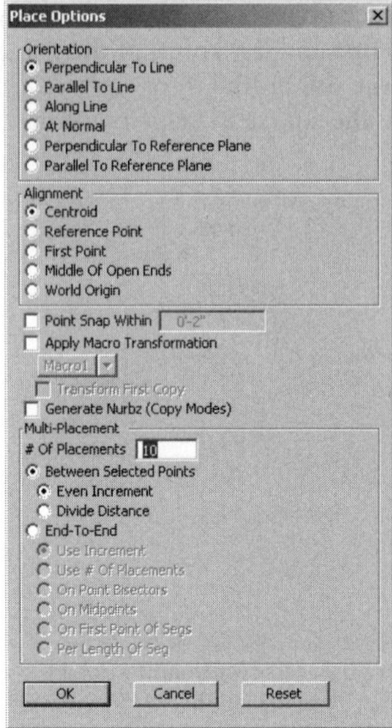

Figure 4.68

The dialog of the Place tool.

- Now switch to the Multi Copy mode. This lets you place the required number of copies of the source in one step. However, it works a little differently from the usual manner in which you use Multi Copy. Here, the number of copies made is determined not by the value set in the dialog of the Multi Copy tool, but by the value set in the dialog of the Place tool.

- Invoke the Place tool dialog and look at the Multi-Placement options in the lower half (Figure 4.68). The # Of Placements field is where you specify how many copies to place. You can also choose between two placement modes: Between Selected Points or End-To-End. The default is the first mode, for which you can choose between indicating the first two placements either by the placement increment or by the entire placement distance, which will then be divided into the specified number of placements. Experiment with both sub-options. The Divide Distance method is more convenient when you want to precisely locate the ending placement in addition to the starting placement. Figure 4.69-b shows a Multi-Placement using this method, with the # of Placements set to 14.

- Now activate the End-to-End method. This will automatically place the source along the entire length of the destination object, and it can do this in six different ways. Explore each one of them in turn. The only thing to note is that for all except the first option, only a single click on the destination object is needed to execute the placements. But for the Use Increment option, two clicks on the destination object are needed to specify the increment distance. Figure 4.69-c shows a Multi-Placement using the End-to-End method with the Use Increment option. A small increment distance was indicated.

- If your source object is a 2D shape, there is an additional option you can apply when you perform multiple placements. Go to the Place Options dialog and check the Generate Nurbz option. If you now apply the Place tool using a 2D source in the Multi Copy mode, a nurbz object will be generated instead of mere 2D placements (see Figure 4.69-d). We'll be learning more about nurbz objects in Workshop 6 (Going Organic).

Figure 4.69

Executing multiple placements in one step, using different options.

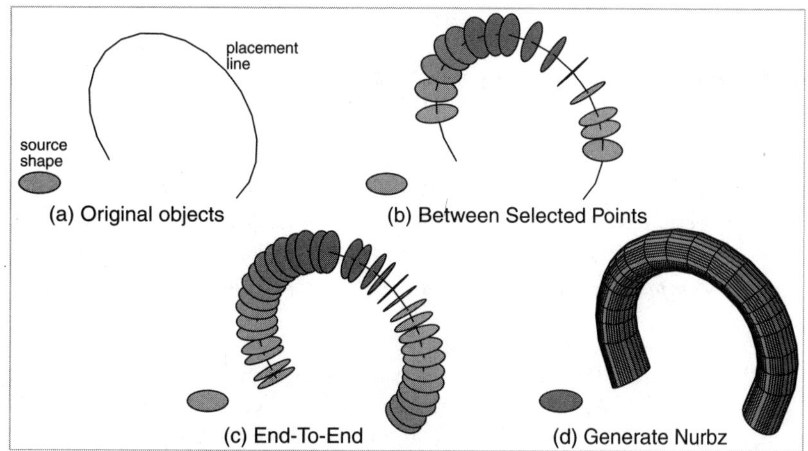

- The final word on the Place tool—you can also combine it with the use of macro transformations, which you learned about in Section 4.4 of Workshop 2 (Bringing A Sense Of Scale) to create some very interesting objects. Use Define Macro (M-Tool:12a,6) to create a simple macro transformation, for instance, Move and Scale, or Rotate and Scale. Then go to the Place dialog and check the option, Apply Macro Transformation. If you have defined more than one macro, you can select a specific one from the accompanying popup list, which shows all the macros in the project.

DEFINE MACRO

WORKSHOP 4

- Now apply the Place tool in Multi Copy mode to a different combination of source and destination objects. The source, in addition to being placed multiple times on the destination, also gets transformed according to the applied macro as it is placed, resulting in a potentially interesting configuration. A simple example is illustrated in Figure 4.70. As you can see, the versatility of the Place tool is greatly enhanced by combining it with macro transformations.

Figure 4.70

Combining macro transformations with the Place tool operation.

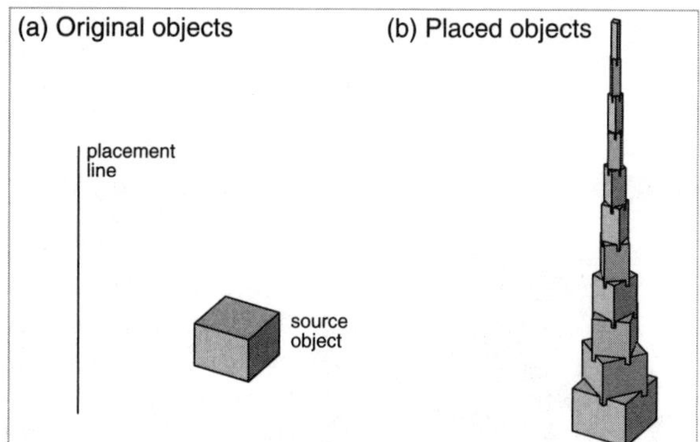

With that, we come to the end of the exercises for this workshop. Let's proceed to take up the challenge of the Workshop Assignment next.

ASSIGNMENT 4

Site Planning for Urban Design

Take any urban design project, preferably on a contoured site. Model the buildings that are to be placed within the site as blocks only. Model the blocks and the site separately first, and then concentrate on the placement of the building blocks within the site. The focus is not on complete accuracy, but on a preliminary layout for site planning at the conceptual design stage.

The actual exercise of modeling the site plan shown here will now be demonstrated step by step. You can refer to the form•Z files for each step of the assignment in the accompanying CD-ROM, under the folder Assignments > Workshop 4. A rendered image of the model is in the Assignment4.tif file in the same location. Working on this assignment will require the use of only a few of the new tools that have been covered in this workshop. The rest of the tools will be used in the assignment for the next workshop. So you can rest assured that you *will* get the opportunity to put into practice all the enhanced modeling capabilities you have recently acquired!

With all the experience gained from the previous workshop exercises and assignments, you should be very comfortable with the basic modeling operations of form•Z. Therefore, the instructions for this and subsequent assignments won't be as detailed compared to the instructions for previous assignments.

Setup

Open a new form•Z project. Let's first set up the Working Units under the Options menu appropriate to the scale of the project. Set the units to Feet under the English measurement system, the Numeric Accuracy to 1', and the Angle Accuracy to 1°. Change also the Window Setup under the Window menu to a grid module of 10' in all directions with 2 subdivisions, and set the Display Scale to 1/32"=1'. Select the Reset window tool (W-Tool:7,9) to set the window zoom level appropriate to the selected display scale.

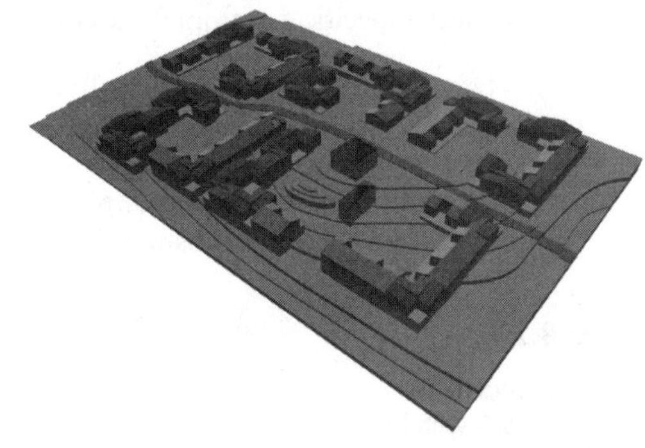

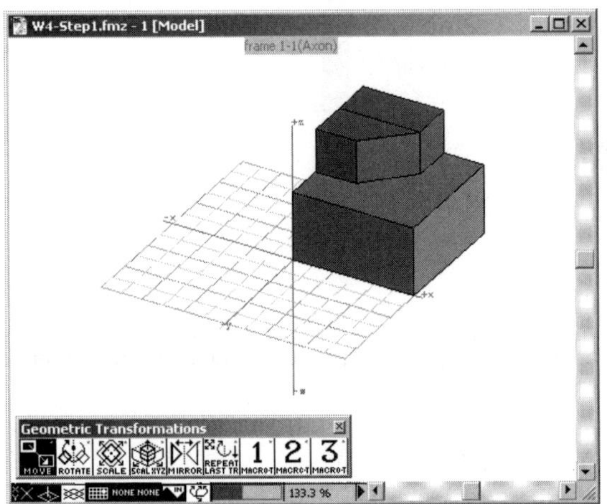

Step 1

Switch to the Top view, set the Heights menu to 16', turn Grid Snap on, and create a base block of 30' by 30'. We are making the height of the base deliberately this large so that we can adjust it at various positions within the contoured site.

Next, set the Heights menu to 10', and still in Top view, create two blocks within the base as shown. The exact size is not important. Then switch to a 3D view and move these blocks upwards by a distance of 16' so that they sit on top of the base.

Step 2

Give the top face of the blocks the required slope for the roofs, as shown, by moving the corresponding segments vertically upwards by a distance of 4'. Also select these top faces and Color them in a different color.

Use the Mirror tool to create a mirror image of the blocks on the base as shown.

Finally, select all these blocks and use the Join tool to combine them into one object. Change the layer name to unit1.

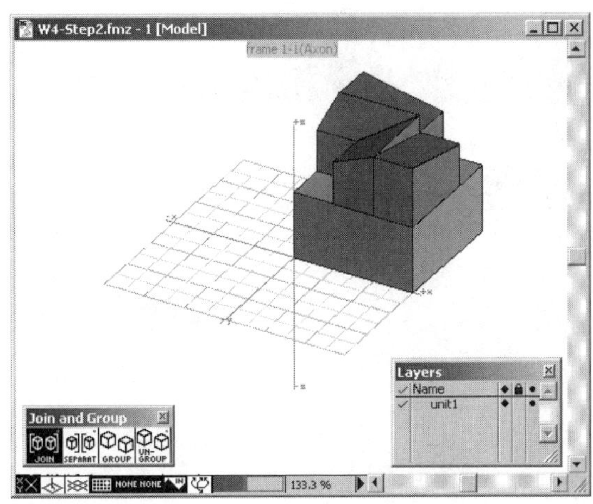

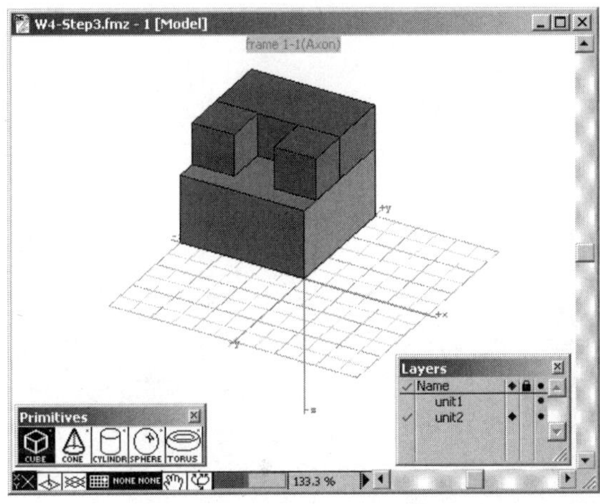

Step 3

Move to a new layer, unit2, and turn the unit1 layer off. Create the same base block of 30' by 30' with a height of 16'.

Create three 10' high blocks as shown, resting on top of the base as shown. Again, exact dimensions are not important.

Step 4

Give the roofs the required slope by moving the corresponding segments vertically upwards by 4'. Again, Color the top faces of the blocks in a different color.

Once again, use the Join tool to combine all the parts of this unit into one object.

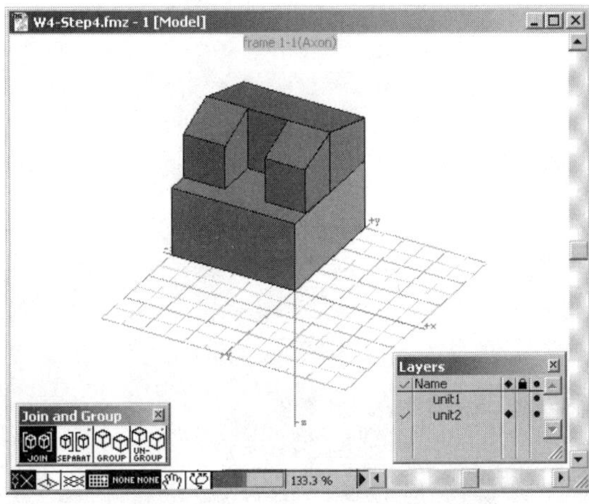

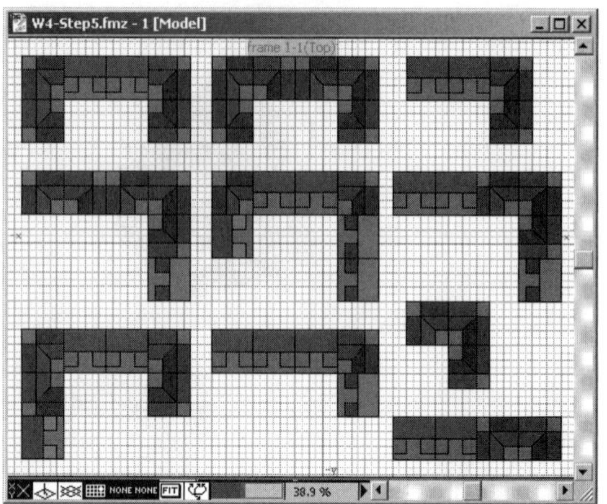

Step 5

Using these two unit types, create ten different clusters as shown. Each cluster should be created on a separate layer. To copy the units from their individual layers into the cluster layers, activate the Paste On Active Layer option in the Layers dialog. Then you can simply use the Copy and Paste commands to make copies of the units in the cluster layers.

After creating a cluster, select all its individual units and combine them into one object using the Join tool.

Step 6

We'll now model the contoured site. Activate a new layer, site, and turn off all the other layers. Switch to the Top view, and draw a 2D rectangle of dimensions 520' by 335'.

Then use the Vector Line tool to draw the contour lines as shown.

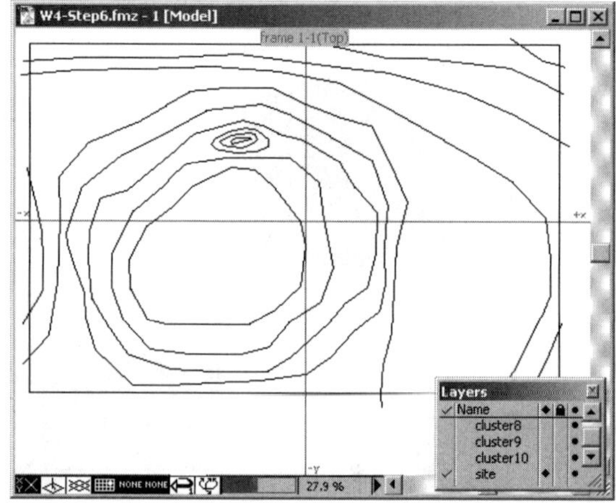

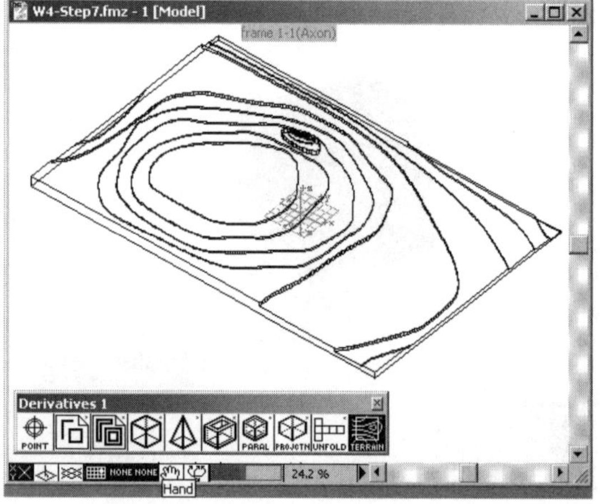

Step 7

Prepick the contour lines in the correct sequence using the Pick tool.

Select the Terrain Model tool and make the following specifications in its dialog: Select the Stepped Model type; set the Site Starting Height to 1'; for Contour Heights, choose the Set New: Interval option with a contour interval value of 2'; and check the Smooth At Interval option with a value of 5'.

Then apply the Terrain Model tool to your site rectangle. It'll be converted to a stepped terrain model.

Step 8

Switch back to the Top view and draw the road lines passing through the site. Connect their ends on either side using the Connect tool (M-Tool:11a,4), so that they form a closed shape.

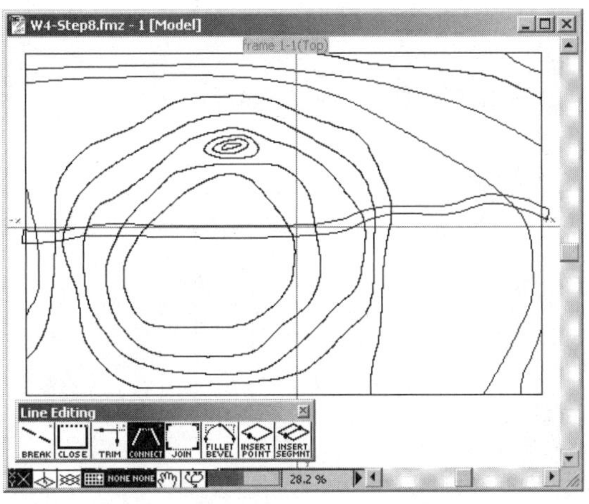

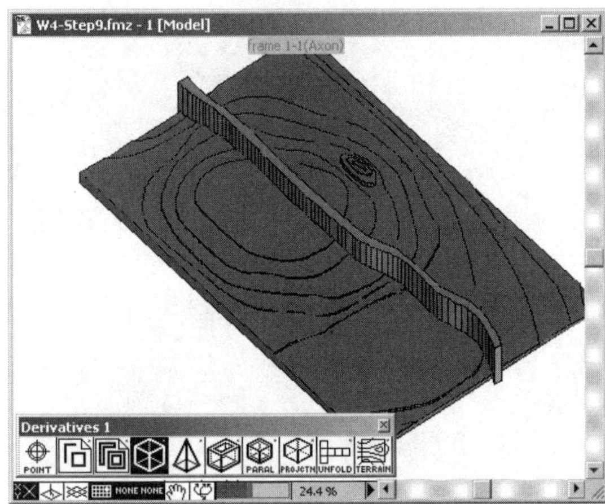

Step 9

In a non-planar view, move the closed shape for the road vertically downwards below the base of the site. Then extrude it so that its top face is higher than the highest point of the site.

Step 10

Use the road block to perform a One Way Split of the site, so that it's broken up into three separate pieces: one each for the two portions of the site, and the third for the road.

Move the separated road piece vertically upwards by 1' so that it's clearly distinguishable from the rest of the site. You can then move its base vertically downwards by 1' as well, so that it's aligned with the base of the site.

Apply appropriate colors to both the road and the site blocks. You'll have to set the option for the Color tool to Clear All Face Surface Styles in order to do this.

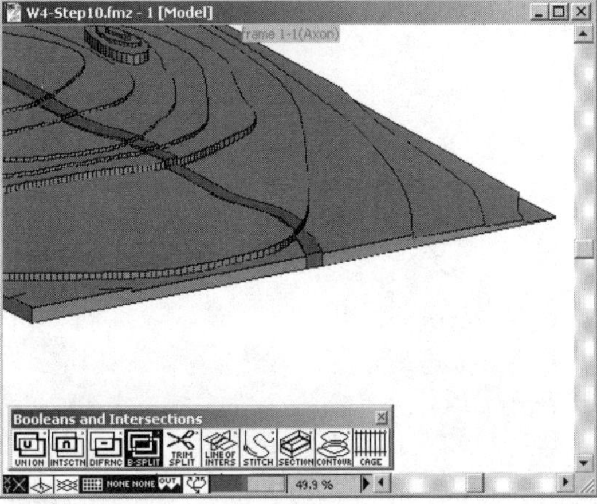

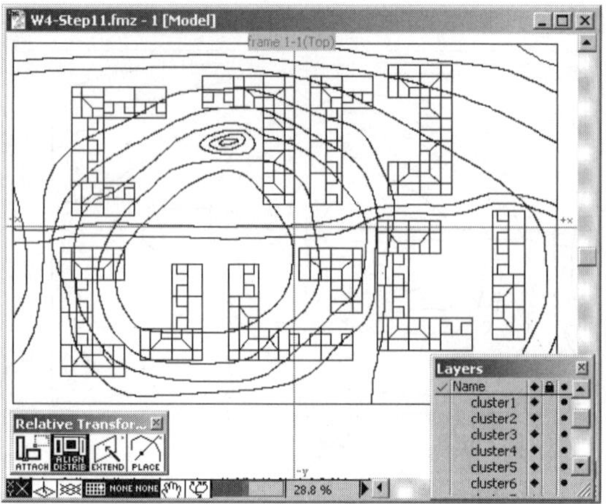

Step 11

Switch to the Top view. Turn on all the cluster layers and rearrange them on the site as shown, using the Move, Rotate, and Mirror tools. The location can be approximate rather than exact at this stage. You can use the Align tool to align the sides of the clusters wherever required.

Step 12

Switch to a paint display mode and you'll find that parts of the clusters are buried into the site, as shown here for the cluster in the lower left corner of the site. Obviously, the height of each cluster now has to be adjusted according to the slope of the terrain. A simple way to do this is to apply the Query tool at the Point topological level to a point of the highest contour passing through each cluster, and take note of its Z coordinate. Add 2'—the contour interval—to it for the next contour. So, for instance, for the cluster shown here, this value is 21'+2'=23'.

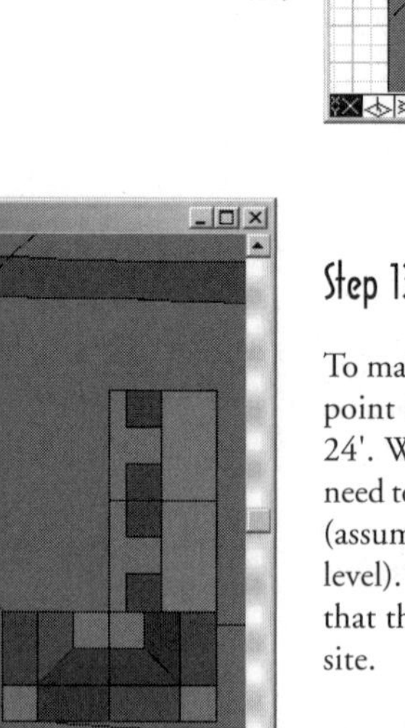

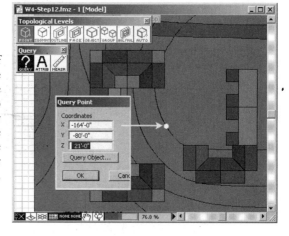

Step 13

To make the units in this cluster accessible from the highest point of the site, the base should be at a height of at least 24'. We modeled the base of each unit as 16' high. So we need to move this cluster upwards by a distance of 24'–16'=8' (assuming that all the units in a cluster are built at the same level). Do this and then check the paint display. You'll find that the cluster is now fully visible above the surface of the site.

Workshop 4

Step 14

Repeat this process for the other nine clusters as well. Some of the clusters located at lower contours will have to be moved downwards rather than upwards. Check the results for each cluster in a non-planar view.

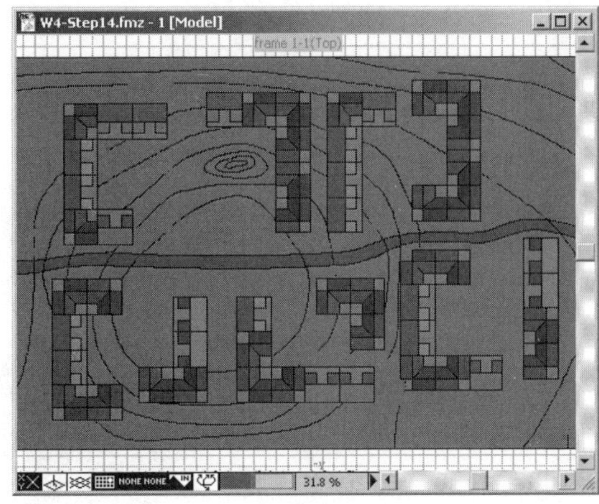

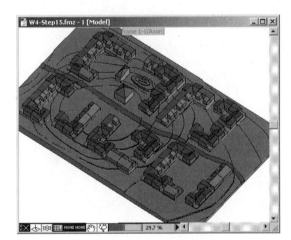

Step 15

Finally, model some community building blocks located in the open space between the clusters in the upper left corner of the site.

You now have your basic site plan design that you can build upon by adding pathways, community spaces, steps to the individual units, surrounding areas, and additional details.

WORKSHOP 5

Illuminating, Texturing, and Rendering Your World

This workshop is devoted to imaging, lights, and textures. You'll start by exploring the extensive set of options available to you for rendering your models in the RenderZone display mode, and use the Sketch Rendering plug-in to generate sketch-like renderings. You'll learn how to save these rendered images in files which can then be used in various other applications, work with the Imager Set that enables you to render a set of images efficiently in a batch mode, and explore various other rendering options.

You'll then move on to work with multiple lights, including the sun, and render your images realistically with shadows. Exercise 3 is devoted to exploring the radiosity-based rendering feature, which enhances lighting effects considerably. In Exercise 4, you'll see how to map textures to objects more precisely, and apply multiple textures to the same surface using decals. Finally, you'll study the remaining object properties you haven't yet covered, which can be modified to achieve various rendering effects.

Note that color versions of all the rendered images illustrated in this workshop are included in the CD-ROM accompanying this book.

EXERCISE 1

Imaging

A crucial component of any modeling activity is the generation of rendered images. The RenderZone display mode has an extensive set of options that let you create realistic images of your modeling world. There's also a Sketch Rendering plug-in that allows you to generate renderings that look more hand-drawn when required. Naturally, you'd like to be able to save some of these renderings, either for reference, or for printing, or for importing into an image-editing program, where you can make additional modifications. form•Z gives you the ability to save these renderings in various image file formats such as TIFF, Targa, JPEG, PICT (on Macs only), and BMP and Metafile (on PCs only). There are also many associated utilities such as viewing image files from within form•Z, specifying the size and resolution of these files, efficient management of rendering memory, and generating and saving renderings in a batch mode rather than individually. This exercise is devoted to exploring all these imaging capabilities.

1.1 RenderZone Options

- Open one of your completed projects; you'll be using it throughout this exercise. Choose a fairly simple one, so that you can explore various rendering techniques quickly.

- In Exercise 2 of Workshop 3 (Personalizing Your Environment), you explored the options accompanying the various display modes. Go ahead and invoke the dialog for the RenderZone display mode in the same fashion: select it from the Display menu while holding down the option key (Mac) or Ctrl+Shift keys (PC), or access it through the Display > Display Options command. There are a large number of options associated with the RenderZone display, divided into four tabs in its dialog, as shown in Figure 5.1.

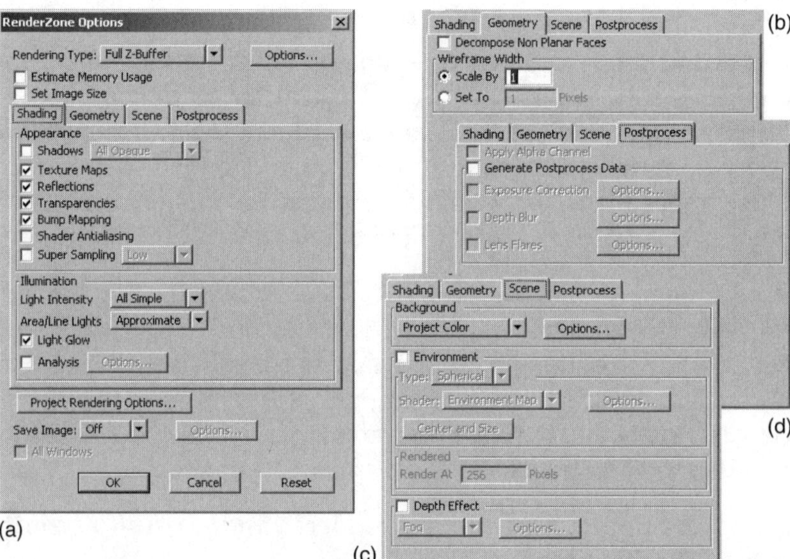

Figure 5.1

The RenderZone Options dialog, showing the options contained in each of its four tabs.

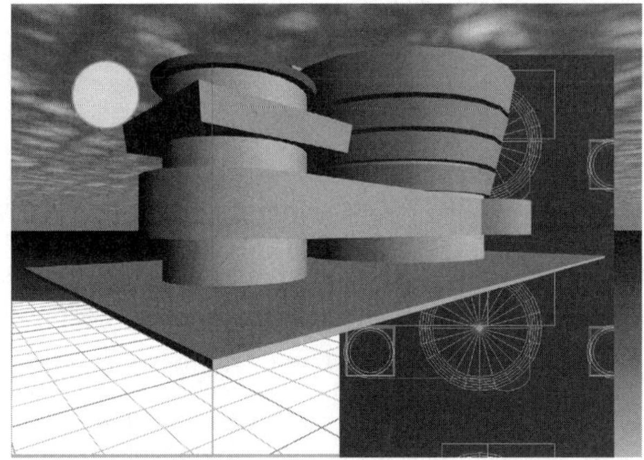

Figure 5.2

Some of the RenderZone display Background options, illustrated together in a single image.

- To start with, there are seven possible options for Rendering Type in the accompanying popup list, ranging from Flat to Full Raytrace, each one progressively more accurate and therefore more time-consuming. Test this out by trying each one in succession. The difference will be most obvious when you use complex surface styles with textures, reflections, transparencies, and so on. You can use the low-end rendering modes for drafts, and the high-end ones for final renderings. Most often, the default type of Full Z-Buffer should be sufficient. Use Full Raytrace only when the highest quality of rendering, with the maximum degree of realism, is required for an image.
- The Z-Buffer and Raytrace rendering types have some additional options that can be accessed by clicking on the associated Options button. These advanced options involve an in-depth understanding of the mathematics and technicalities of computer graphics and rendering, and we won't deal with them here. For most users, their default settings should work just fine.
- The next option, Estimate Memory Usage, is useful before executing a complex rendering to ensure that enough memory is available to finish the rendering with the specified options. It is followed by the Set Image Size option, which you have already encountered for Shaded Render. This is especially useful in RenderZone as it lets you render only selected parts of the image to check if textures, lighting, shadows, etc., are appropriate before doing a full rendering. You can also employ it, as shown in Figure 5.2, to make a collage of various RenderZone display options in a single image—which can be a potentially interesting presentation technique in itself.
- Let's now turn to the options in the Shading tab, shown in Figure 5.1-a. The Shadows option, when checked, displays the shadows cast by lights on the model. It has three sub-options that will be discussed in Section 2.1, so skip it for now. If you've applied image-based textures to any of your objects (as you'll learn to do towards the end of this workshop) and want them to be displayed in the rendering, the Texture Maps option should remain selected. Likewise, the Reflections, Transparencies, and Bump Mapping options should be selected if you have any textures with these attributes, so that they're rendered accurately.
- The next option, Shader Antialiasing, is relevant only to the Full Z-Buffer rendering type. When it's activated, the level of antialiasing in such a rendering is significantly improved, resulting in a greater clarity of the image, particularly when textured surface styles are used. (Recall from Workshop 3, Personalizing Your Environment, that the Surface Style Parameters dialog for an individual surface style also has a Shader Antialiasing option, which can be turned on or off for that style.) A still higher degree of antialiasing in the image can be obtained by activating the following Super

Sampling option. This is especially useful for reducing flickering while generating an animation. Keep in mind, however, that activating these options for a rendering will also consume more time and memory.

- The remaining Illumination section in the Shading tab relates to lighting that will be covered in Exercise 2, so you can skip it for now. Move on to the Geometry tab, shown in Figure 5.1-b. The Decompose Non Planar Faces option should already be familiar to you from the Shaded Render display options you explored in Section 2.5 of Workshop 3 (Personalizing Your Environment). The Wireframe Width option relates to the Render Attributes tool, which will be covered in Exercise 5 of this workshop.

- The next tab, Scene, contains several critical options related to the makeup of the rendered scene, and we'll be exploring these in detail. To start with, you can choose from an extensive array of Background options for the image, some of which are illustrated as a collage in Figure 5.2. The default option is the same Project Color you've set for the graphics window, but you can specify another Plain Color instead, if you want just a simple one-colored backdrop. For two colors, one fading into the other, use the Graduated option. If you choose Project Background—one of the options shown in Figure 5.2—the grid and axes are shown along with an underlay, if any. A number of other textures, similar to those in the Surface Styles dialog, are also available as options here, although their use as backgrounds is highly improbable.

- The Sky option is a useful one, providing a background with a base plane and sky, complete with clouds and the sun. Select this option, then click on the Options button associated with Background. This will bring up a dialog containing various parameters that define the selected background. For Sky, these include parameters such as the colors of all the individual components; the scale, coverage, and density of the clouds; the size and location of the sun; and the location of the horizon line. Experiment with different parameters to create different sky variations. The Sky options used to generate the background shown in Figure 5.2 are illustrated in Figure 5.3. Notice the Match Horizon With Perspective option in the Sky Options dialog that's checked by default. This automatically adjusts the horizon line for a perspective view, and lets you specify the exact distances of the clouds and the ground, above and below the selected reference plane respectively. For a non-perspective view, or if the Match Horizon With Perspective option is deselected, the Horizon slider bar can be used to specify the location of the horizon line from the lower margin of the image.

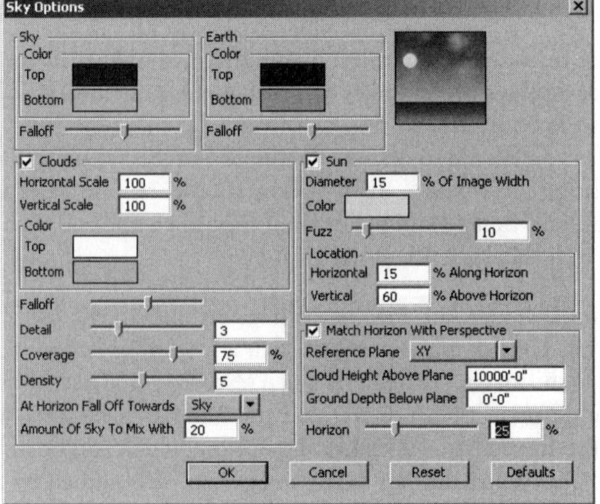

Figure 5.3

The Sky Options dialog, showing the settings used for generating the background in Figure 5.2.

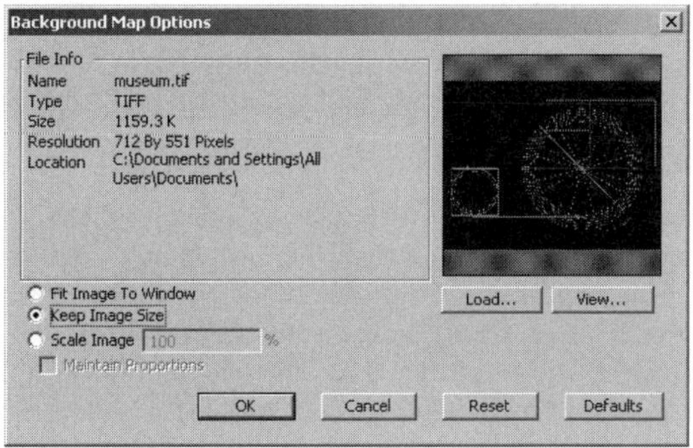

Figure 5.4

Specifying an image as the background for part of the RenderZone display shown in Figure 5.2.

If you use the Sky option for Background, make sure you adjust the view to suit the background. You've learned to do this in Exercise 5 of Workshop 3 (Personalizing Your Environment).

- Another useful background option is Background Map, which lets you load any image file to use as the backdrop for the scene. Select it, and explore the associated Options dialog (see Figure 5.4). Here, you can load another file to replace the default image (which is the logo of auto•des•sys Inc., the company that makes form•Z), and specify how it should be scaled with respect to the scene. If you choose to Keep Image Size rather than Fit Image To Window and the image size is smaller than the window size, the image will be "tiled" across the width and height of the window, creating an interesting effect. Figure 5.2 illustrates this technique, using a plan view of the same building project for the image file. You can also specify only a part of the image to be used for the background rather than the entire image, with the help of the View option. Note that none of these variations would have been possible if you had used the image as an Underlay. This shows that the two utilities are not interchangeable—each is important in its own right.

- The Environment option for Background is related to the Environment section further down in the dialog, which we'll be studying in a bit, so skip it for now. Instead, look at the last option, Alpha Channel. When this is selected, the background is rendered in black, but each pixel of the image stores an additional channel of information called the *alpha channel*, in addition to the three regular channels of color information—red, green, and blue. The alpha channel stores information on the level of transparency of each pixel relative to the background, and is used in image-composition programs to smoothly blend images into one another for photorealistic rendering effects. The Alpha Channel background in form•Z will capture the transparency information for those pixels in the image that belong to objects having a transparent surface style, or that lie on the antialiased edges of objects, or those that represent the glow of a light (coming up in the next exercise). For more information on how to work with alpha channels, refer to the manuals accompanying your image-editing program.

In form•Z, it's possible to surround your model with an "environment" to accurately simulate how it would be in real life. Objects in the modeling scene that have reflective surfaces will then reflect this environment in addition to reflecting other objects in the scene. This effect cannot be achieved by using a background only.

- To add an environment to your scene, activate the Environment section located just below the Background section. You can choose between two types of environments—Cubic and Spherical—which position an imaginary cube and sphere around the scene respectively. Apply reflective surface styles to some of the objects in your project, in order to explore how environments work. In addition to the Type, there is a Shader list that lets you choose from a variety of environments with which to surround the scene and produce reflections. Many of these are similar to the Background options. Explore some of these shaders and see what kind of reflections are produced.

- The Environment Shader can also be set to Environment Map, letting you specify image files with which to surround the scene. For a Spherical environment, only one image file is needed, but for a Cubic environment, six different image files can be specified for each of the six faces of the imaginary cube. Thus, it's possible to simulate the environment very precisely. A simple example of environment mapping for a Spherical environment is illustrated in Figure 5.5-a; the image file used for the map is shown in Figure 5.5-b. The background was also set to map the same image file using the Background Map option. For realistic effects, of course, you'd use actual photographs of the surroundings of your project for these environment and background maps.

- Now go back and set the Background to the Environment option you had skipped earlier. You'll find that the actual pattern of the current environment cube or sphere will be rendered as the background, in addition to being visible on reflective surfaces. This will most realistically simulate a real-life situation, more accurately than using Background Map, which simply positions the image as a backdrop in the rendering. Setting Background to Environment is especially useful when generating an animation, as you'll learn to do in Workshop 7 (Ending With More)—a different portion of the environment will be rendered as the background for each separate perspective view that makes up the animation. Thus, the impression of moving through the scene will be more vivid than it would be if the background remained the same for every view.

- There's an additional option in the Environment section, Rendered. This is relevant only when the scene contains objects whose surface styles have their Reflection attribute set to Environment in the Surface Style Parameters dialog. This setting is similar to the Mirror setting for Reflection, but is faster and less sharp. Also, an object with a Mirror reflection attribute reflects only the surrounding objects, not the project background; on the other hand, an object with the Environment reflection attribute will also reflect the project background when the Environment section has been activated. The resolution of the environment in pixels is specified in the accompanying Render At field, which determines the degree of sharpness of the reflections that will be produced. For sharper reflections, increase the resolution value.

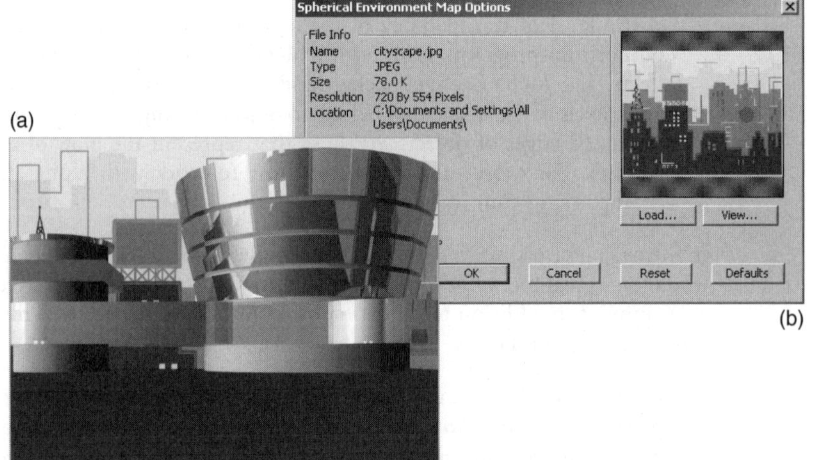

Figure 5.5

Rendering with the Spherical environment type, with reflective styles applied to some surfaces. Both the environment and background were set to map the same image file, shown in (b).

Figure 5.6

Rendering with various types of Depth Effects.

- Proceed to activate the last section in the Scene tab, Depth Effect, which lets you apply additional effects to your rendering (see Figure 5.6). You can choose from three effects: Depth Cue, Fog, and Snow. Switch to each one in turn and see how it affects the rendering. Depth Cue lets you merge the colors of your model with the color of a specified background to the desired extent. Fog, as is obvious from its name, creates a fog-like effect, while Snow is used to create simple snowflakes in the rendered image. Each effect is defined by several settings, which you can access and explore by clicking on the associated Options button.

- Move on to look at the options in the last tab of the RenderZone Options dialog, Postprocess. *Postprocessing* refers to the ability to manipulate the settings of an image after it has been rendered, and for this, certain data needs to generated and maintained after the rendering is complete. This is done by activating the Generate Postprocess Data option. Go ahead and do so, and exit the dialog. You'll find the rendering takes longer than before, as the postprocessing data is being generated. Also, the RenderZone Postprocess command in the Display menu is now active. Select it, and you'll find that you can choose among different kinds of postprocessing effects to be applied. We'll be looking more closely at these in the next section. For now, get back to the Postprocess tab of the RenderZone Options dialog, and notice that you can also activate postprocessing effects here, which will automatically be applied once the rendering is complete. In most cases, however, it's better to apply these effects later through the RenderZone Postprocess command, so that you can manipulate them interactively by seeing a preview of the image.

- Finally, let's look at the two remaining options at the base of the RenderZone Options dialog. The Project Rendering Options button takes you to the same dialog you studied in Section 2.6 of Workshop 3 (Personalizing Your Environment). The Save Image option can be used to save an image as soon as it is rendered, using one of two options: Manual, where you specify the file name, location, and format before each rendering; or Automatic, where the rendering is automatically saved with a unique file name in a location you specify in the associated Options dialog. The Save Image option is set to Off by default.

Let's move on to see how to postprocess a rendered image, the option for which we just activated in the RenderZone Options dialog.

1.2 Postprocessing a Rendered Image

▣ Go to the Display menu and select the RenderZone Postprocess command, which is active since you checked the Generate Postprocess Data option in the RenderZone Options dialog in the last section. This will invoke a dialog from which you can choose to apply a number of postprocessing effects to the image. Let's look at them one by one.

▣ The first option, Background, is a simple one. If you select it and click on the accompanying Options button, you can choose a different background for the scene from the popup menu. This is the same menu that is available in the Scene tab of the RenderZone Options dialog for choosing a background. You have already explored this menu in the last section. Select a different background option if required, and watch your image in the preview window show the new background. You can also adjust its settings using the associated Options button. Exit the Background Options dialog, and you will be returned back to the RenderZone Postprocess Options dialog.

▣ Activate the next option, Exposure Correction, and click on the accompanying Options button. You'll see your scene in the preview window on the left (see Figure 5.7-a), along with any background changes you applied using the Background option. On the right are settings for the Luminance and Brightness of the scene, which you can adjust either numerically or by moving the control points of the associated graph. You'll see the changes reflected in the preview window, allowing you to fine-tune the exposure settings of the image. Without this option, you would have to perform such corrections in an external image-editing application. Make the necessary changes and return to the main postprocessing dialog.

▣ The next postprocessing effect is Depth Blur. Activate it and access its options. Here, you'll find various settings for creating an "out of focus" effect in a rendering, similar to what you'd find in a photograph. You can specify the beginning and the end of the focussed area; the remaining area of the scene will be blurred. You can also alter the degree to which the blurring will take place. Explore different blurring options and values, and after you are done, return to the main postprocessing dialog as before.

▣ Move on to select the next effect, Lens Flares, and access its Options dialog. Lens flares—geometric patterns caused by the refraction of light rays—are common in photographs when the camera is pointing directly at a light source or at very bright spots in a scene. In form•Z, you can generate lens flares as a postprocessing effect to add to the scene from any active light source except distant lights, or from "hot spots" on glossy surfaces. In the image preview window in the Lens Flare Options dialog, yellow bullets indicate light sources whose Lens Flare option has been turned on in their respective Light Parameters dialogs (which you'll study in detail in Section 2.3), blue bullets indicate light sources whose Lens Flare option is off, and white bullets indicate potential hot spots on a reflective surface. Clicking on a yellow bullet turns it off, while clicking on a blue bullet turns it on. Since you have no light sources other than the default distant light in your scene yet, you won't see any blue or yellow bullets. If you don't see any white bullets indicating hot spots, decrease the Min Luminance value in the Range section until you do. If you have too many of them, increase the Min Luminance value, and some of the less illuminated hot spots will disappear. To find the luminance at any point of the image, move the cursor to it, and you'll see this value in the Sample Luminance field located below the preview window.

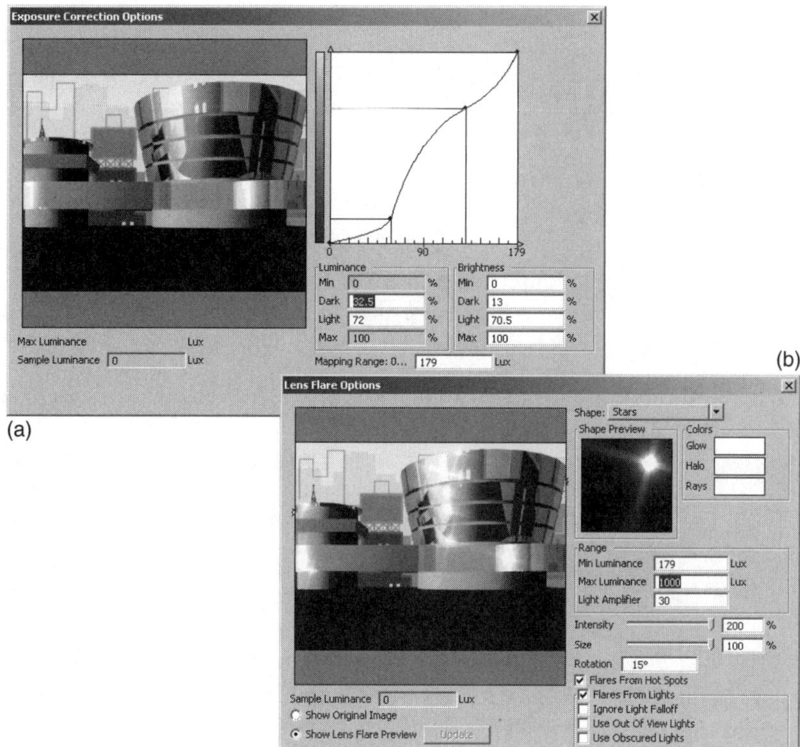

Figure 5.7

The postprocessing options dialogs for Exposure Correction and Lens Flares, applied to the rendering shown in Figure 5.5-a.

- Once you have your choice of yellow and white bullets in the preview window, you can create lens flares from them (see Figure 5.7-b). You can choose between different types of lens flares from the Shape popup menu; specify the Colors of the three parts of a lens flare; set the Intensity, Size, and Rotation values; and activate or deactivate Flares From Hot Spots and Flares From Lights with various sub-options as required. The Min Luminance and Max Luminance values set the luminance range for which lens flares are created from light sources and hot spots, as well as determine the size of the flare. The final setting, Light Amplifier, is used to amplify the intensity of light sources in the scene relative to hot spots. To see the lens flares created by the specified settings, select the Show Lens Flare Preview option located below the preview window. When you're satisfied with the results, click OK to return to the main postprocessing dialog.

- The last postprocessing effect, Apply Alpha Channel, will be activated only when the RenderZone background has been set to Alpha Channel. (Note that in this case, the Background postprocessing effect will be deactivated.) You saw earlier how the Alpha Channel background option produces images having an additional alpha channel in addition to the red, blue, and green channels. If the alpha channel is to be retained when the image is saved for use with other image-editing programs, leave this option turned off. On screen, however, the image will be displayed without the alpha channel and therefore will not be fully accurate. To view the image with the alpha channel within form•Z, turn on the Apply Alpha Channel postprocessing option. However, if the image is now saved, the alpha channel won't be exported.

- To apply all the activated postprocessing effects to the rendered scene, exit the RenderZone Postprocess Options dialog by clicking on the OK button. You will now see them rendered in the graphics window. You can save the resultant rendering as an image file, as you'll soon learn in

Section 1.4. Since the postprocessing options are active, they'll be applied every time you refresh the RenderZone display, which will slow you down considerably. Therefore, make sure you turn them off when they're not required. The settings you chose, however, will be preserved and can be easily reapplied the next time you activate postprocessing.

1.3 Performing Sketch Renderings

- Sketch Render is an additional rendering mode in form•Z that is installed as a separate plugin. If installed, it should be available under the Display menu under Shaded Render. If you don't see it, get back to your installation disk and look for it in the Plugins folder. Go ahead and install it, and restart form•Z. You should now see it in the Display menu.
- Continue working with the same project file you've been using so far. Switch to the Sketch Render display mode. You'll see that it is distinctly different from the other displays—it looks more hand-drawn than computer-generated. The intent of this display is to generate renderings that are more artistic and not photorealistic. Sketch Render has a number of such styles; what you're seeing in the graphics window is only one of them. Let's look at the others.
- Invoke the Sketch Render Options dialog in the usual manner: select it from the Display menu while holding down the option key (Mac) or Ctrl+Shift keys (PC), or access it through the Display > Display Options command. As you can see in Figure 5.8, you can choose from a variety of different styles contained in the Style popup menu. Switch to each one of them in turn, and click on the Update button below the preview window to see what the style looks like. If you like, check the Automatic button for the preview to be updated automatically whenever a setting is changed.
- After exploring all the styles, select one and then explore the other options in the dialog. Choose between the Full and Preview rendering types, based on whether you want the best quality or the fastest speed. The Base Rendering option, applicable to color styles only, lets you choose whether the base image for generating the sketch rendering is a Shaded Render or RenderZone rendering; if textures are important, you would, of course, choose RenderZone. The next set of options relates to the selected style, and can be used to customize its parameters. Explore them for your selected style. The Predefined button is similar to the Predefined button in the Surface Style Parameters dialog; it leads you to a number of additional predefined styles which you can choose from to apply to the rendering. The Save Image option works similarly to the other display dialogs.

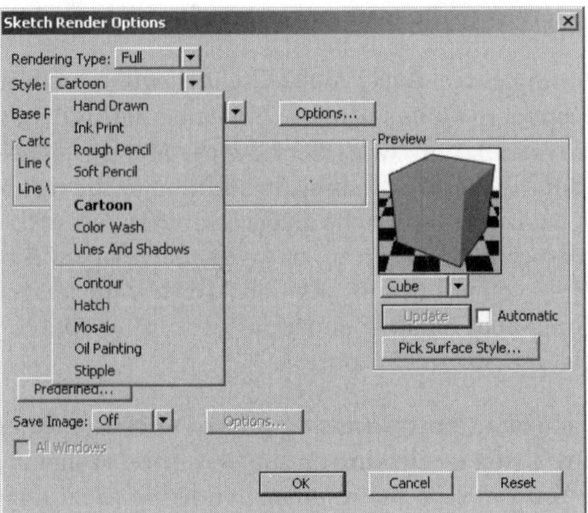

Figure 5.8

The Sketch Rendering Options dialog, showing the different styles available.

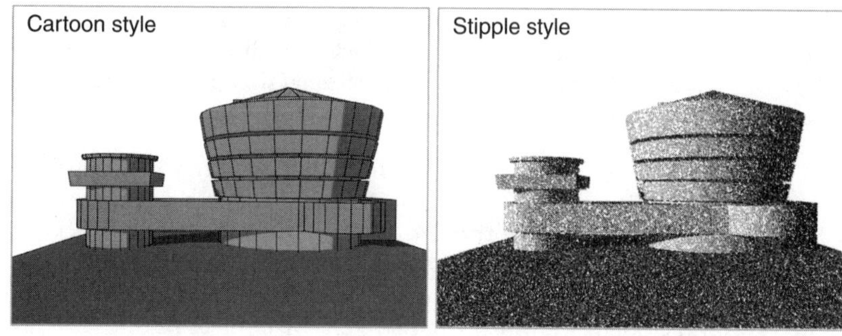

Figure 5.9

Two different sketch rendering styles applied to the same scene.

- To apply the selected settings, click OK to exit the Sketch Render Options dialog. You'll see the style you selected applied to the display in the graphics window (see Figure 5.9). Needless to say, you wouldn't use the Sketch Render display in the course of your modeling work, but only when you want to generate images of your model that look hand-drawn.

1.4 Saving and Viewing Image Files

You've already looked at the Save Image option in the RenderZone Options dialog that can be used to save an image as soon as it is rendered, either automatically or manually. In addition to RenderZone, the images from all the other display modes can also be saved in various 2D file formats. While all kinds of images can be saved to bitmapped file formats such as JPEG, TIFF, and Targa, line-based displays such as Wire Frame, Hidden Line, and Surface Render can also be saved as vector-based images in file formats such as HPGL and Illustrator. Vector-based images are resolution independent, and will therefore print faster and without the "jagged edges" of low-resolution bitmapped images.

Figure 5.10

Viewing an image file within form•Z.

- Generate a rendering of your project in any display mode. Then use File > Export Image to save the file in a common file format such as JPEG or TIFF. The file will automatically be given an extension, depending upon the file format selected. You'll learn about the export options associated with different file formats in Exercise 5 of Workshop 7 (Ending With More).

- Once you've exported an image file in this manner, you can open it in any program that recognizes that format to view, modify, or print it. You also have the option of viewing some specific image file formats within form•Z itself by going to File > View File. From the file selection dialog that's invoked, select the image file you just saved. A new window will open up, displaying the image, and giving you the ability to zoom and scroll (Figure 5.10). To zoom out, select the Zoom tool while holding down the option key (Mac) or Ctrl+Shift keys (PC). You can use the View File command to view even those image files that were not created in form•Z, but are in formats recognizable to it.

1.5 Setting Image Options

The image file you just saved was stored using the default form•Z settings for image size and resolution, set respectively to the current window size and the screen resolution of 72 pixels/inch. This resolution is adequate for screen displays of your bitmapped image files. But try printing the file, and you'll find that the image isn't very sharp. A much higher resolution is needed for acceptable printed images, depending upon the printer you'll use. You might also want to specify an image size that's different from the default value. form•Z gives you the ability to customize the image size and resolution for the images that you generate.

- Select the last item in the Display menu, Image Options. In the dialog that pops up, you can choose from among various options for Image Size. The default size is set to the current size of the window. Choose the alternate option, Use Custom Size. You can now specify the image size in two ways: By Number Of Pixels, or By Size And Resolution. The second method is more intuitive, allowing you to specify the exact size and resolution of the image (Figure 5.11). Since the Maintain Proportions option is checked by default, you need to specify either the width or the height—the other dimension will adjust itself appropriately. Also change the Resolution to a higher value.

- You'll now see the values for Width and Height in the By Number Of Pixels option change to reflect the actual number of pixels that will be contained in the specified image size at the specified resolution. A larger resolution increases the number of pixels—as seen in the Image Options dialog in Figure 5.11—which in turn means longer rendering times for the Shaded Render, Sketch Render, and RenderZone displays, since these are bitmapped rather than vector displays.

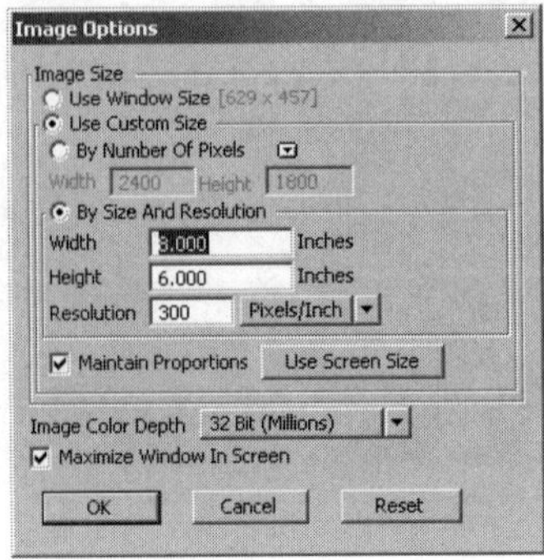

Figure 5.11

Specifying the Image Options for a rendering. An image size of 8 by 6 inches at a resolution of 300 pixels/inch is equivalent to 2400 by 1800 pixels.

- With the Use Custom Size option activated at a high resolution setting, exit the Image Options dialog and switch to a RenderZone display. You'll find that the rendering takes substantially longer, as there are many more pixels to render. Also notice that resizing the window doesn't change the proportions of the image, which are locked to the specified settings. If you go back and check the Maximize Window In Screen option in the Image Options dialog, the window will be automatically resized to fit on the entire screen. Note that any resizing of the window, whether automatic or manual, is for display purposes only; the actual number of pixels that will be rendered remains the same as was specified in the Use Custom Size option of the Image Options dialog.

- After you've generated your renderings at the specified size and resolution and want to resume regular modeling activity, you should go back to the Image Options dialog and select the Use Window Size option. This will revert the window settings to the default mode. At the very least, reduce the Resolution value back to 72 pixels/inch, so that your modeling work isn't slowed down.

- The Image Options dialog, as shown in Figure 5.11, also lets you specify the depth of color of your image. You can choose from among three options: 8 bits, 16 bits, and 32 bits. A larger color depth can capture more shades and hues of colors, but also results in larger files. You could settle for the lower color depth values for prefinal images, which will considerably reduce the time required for generating them. However, be sure to always use the highest color depth for final renderings.

1.6 Saving Incomplete Renderings

As a project gets larger and more complex and the number of textures and lights increases, a high-end RenderZone image will take an increasingly long time to render. form•Z therefore gives you the ability to interrupt a rendering, save the partial rendering in a file, and continue the rendering at a later time. Needless to say, this is an extremely useful option to have since a lot of time and effort is invariably invested in a high quality rendering, which would be a shame to waste.

- Open up your most complex project to date and switch to a perspective view. Invoke the RenderZone Options dialog, set the Rendering Type to Full Raytrace, and check the Shadows box. In the Image Options dialog, specify a high resolution value. In short, do whatever it takes to increase the rendering time for the image. If necessary, you can also increase the complexity of some of the surface styles applied to the objects in the scene.

- Activate the RenderZone display to begin the rendering. Wait until about half of the window has been rendered, then press the Shift key along with the command+period (Mac) or Ctrl+period (PC) or Esc (Mac or PC) keys. This will bring up a dialog in which you can choose to continue or cancel the rendering, or save it to a file. (Note that if the Shift key isn't pressed while pressing these other keys, the rendering will simply be cancelled.) Click on the Suspend Rendering To File button, which will invoke the usual File Save dialog for your operating system. Specify an appropriate name and location for the file. An extension of ".spd" is automatically given, indicating that it's a suspended rendering file. Once this is done, you're returned to a Wire Frame display of your project.

- A suspended rendering can be resumed at any time, even if the original project file isn't open. To test this, close the project file that you used for generating the partial rendering. Then go to File > Open and select the suspended rendering file you had saved. The partially rendered image opens up and the rendering is resumed from the point it left off.

- Let the rendering be fully completed this time. As soon as it's done, the standard File Save dialog will open up again, allowing you to save the completed rendering in any one of the image file formats you saw earlier. You're also conveniently given the option of deleting the suspended rendering file from disk, which you'd usually choose to do to reclaim your disk space.

1.7 Clearing Rendering Memory

As you can see, generating a full-blown RenderZone display for a complex project is a time-consuming and memory-intensive process, with a lot of calculations involved related to hidden faces, textures, lighting, shadows, and so on. All this information is referred to as the *rendering record*, and is, by default, stored in memory. This makes subsequent renderings of different views of the same project faster, but also takes up more memory. form•Z allows you to clear this rendering memory whenever required.

- When memory is running short, select the Clear Rendering Memory command from the Display menu. This will delete the rendering calculations from memory and free it up. Note that if you haven't generated a rendering yet, this command will be deactivated.

- When memory is really tight, you can select the following Always Clear Rendering Memory command, which will automatically erase the rendering record after each rendering and free up memory. Each new rendering will then be recalculated from the beginning, taking more time.

1.8 Using an Imager Set

form•Z has an extremely useful built-in utility called the *Imager* that allows you to render as well as print a set of form•Z images in a batch mode. With this utility, you can leave a whole set of renderings to be generated on the computer and come back when they're all done, instead of sitting at the computer throughout and attending to each one individually. This is particularly indispensable for rendering images in RenderZone mode that include a considerable amount of lighting, shadows, reflections, and image mapping. Let's take a detailed look at this useful feature.

- Start by creating additional views in your project if you don't have at least four or five—you'll render these in a batch mode in an *Imager Set*. Save the file so that these views are recorded and available for rendering. Then select New Imager Set from the File menu. (To open an existing Imager Set, you'd use File > Open.) This will invoke the Imager Set window shown in Figure 5.12.

- Once an Imager Set is created, it can be saved in the usual fashion using File > Save As. An Imager Set file is saved with a ".fis" extension. Although saving isn't mandatory for the rendering to take place, it can be very convenient for reasons we shall soon see. So go ahead and save it.

- The next step that you need to perform is to select the project file or files, along with the views from each file that are to be included in the Imager Set. To do this, click on the Add button in the Imager Set window. As soon as you select a form•Z file from the File Open dialog that's invoked, all the views saved for that project are loaded in a separate dialog, from which you can select those that you'd like to render. Just click on Select All for now. You can also choose to link the Image Options and Display Options specified in the file to the loaded views, but as we'll soon see, you can also specify these anew in the Imager Set, so leave these options unchecked for now. Click OK to exit the dialog. You'll see the views you loaded in the Imager Set window.

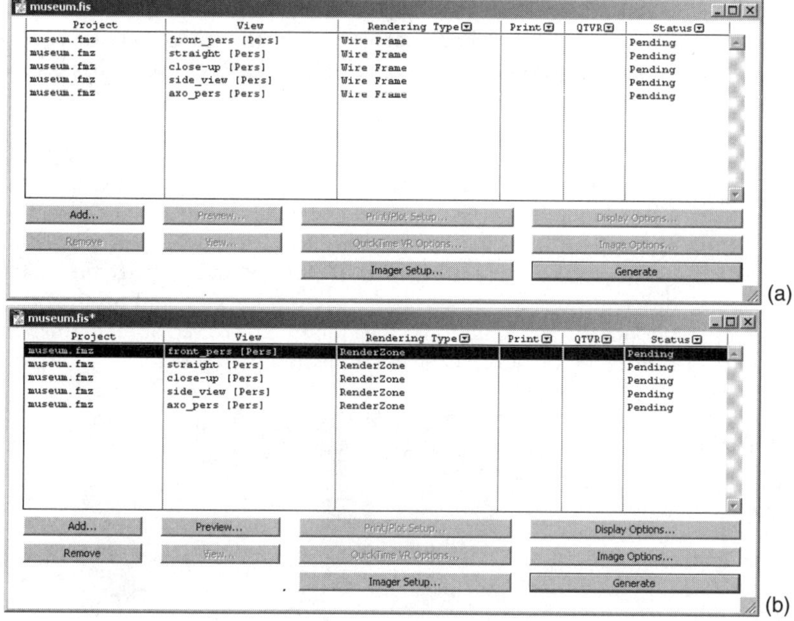

Figure 5.12

Working with the Imager Set. (a) Loading five views from a single project. (b) Activating one of the views to change its rendering parameters.

Keep in mind that you're not restricted to the views from a single project, but can use the Add button to load more project files and their views in a similar manner. It's advisable not to have more than 10 or 12 views in one Imager Set, however, so that if an error occurs, processing time isn't wasted on too many unusable images. Figure 5.12-a shows the Imager Set window, containing five views from a single project listed in the upper portion of the window.

- Each *view* in the Imager Set is an *image* that will be rendered. Along with the project file and the view that identifies it, an image is listed along with four other attributes—Rendering Type, Print, QuickTime VR (abbreviated to QTVR), and Status. Each attribute has a pulldown menu from which you can choose an option that applies to all the images in the list. Rendering Type sets the type of rendering that will be applied while generating an image. Change it from the default of Wire Frame to RenderZone from the pulldown menu. Print determines whether or not to print the images as they're being generated. You should leave this option turned off so that you can check if an image is satisfactory before it's printed. We'll be looking at QuickTime VR in Workshop 7 (Ending With More), so ignore the QTVR option for now. The last option, Status, can be used to change the status of all the images to Pending, if you need them to be regenerated for some reason after they have been rendered.

The images will be rendered in the order in which they appear in the list. You can click and drag them to rearrange their order in the list.

- Now click on one of the images in the list. It gets highlighted, activating some of the grayed out buttons in the lower half of the Imager Set window (Figure 5.12-b). The selected image becomes the *active image* on which these newly activated options can be applied. You can Remove it from the Imager Set, or Preview it to check that it's indeed the image that you want to render. Image Options lets you choose a different rendering type for the selected image—thus, all the renderings don't have to be of the same type—as well as change its size, resolution, and color depth settings, the way you learned to do earlier in Section 1.5. Display Options brings up Options dialog for the selected display type, letting you change those settings if required. Thus, if your Rendering Type is set to RenderZone, the RenderZone Options dialog you saw in Figure 5.1 will be invoked. The Print/Plot Setup button is active only if the Print option has been turned on, letting you modify the default printing parameters of the selected image.

- Next, deselect the active image by clicking on the blank space just below the last image in the list. No image is now active, and you'll find that all the buttons you just looked at get deactivated. Click on the Imager Setup button, which is still active. This brings up a dialog containing certain options that apply to the Imager Set as a whole (see Figure 5.13). Here, you can change the default image type as well as the default file formats of the image files that will be generated for the three different categories of displays—vector, polygon, and pixel. For each file format, the associated Options are accessible and can be modified. For vector renderings, it's also possible to save them as form•Z files that can be read by the drafting module.

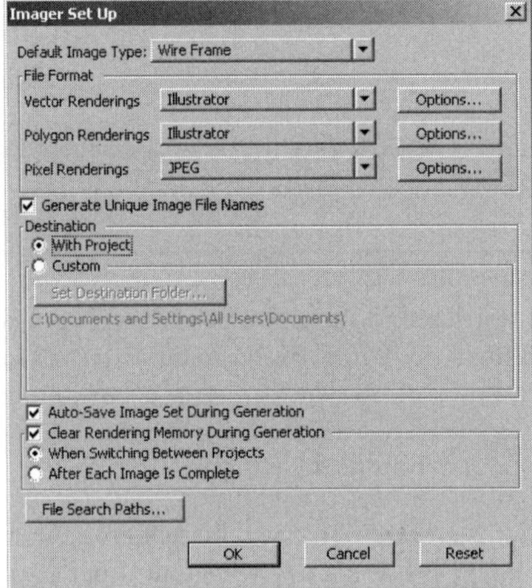

Figure 5.13

The Imager Set Up dialog contains options for the Imager Set as a whole.

- The Destination option in the Imager Setup dialog lets you choose between saving the generated images along with the project, or set up a custom folder. By default, the images will get saved with unique file names, which is a useful option to retain. Finally, there are some memory management options. If you choose to Clear Rendering Memory, which is on by default, it's better to opt for the second option, After Each Image Is Complete, when memory is tight. This will increase the time required for the generation of the Imager Set as a whole, but will make more memory available for the generation of each individual image.

- Now that you've finished setting all the necessary options, you're ready to begin the generation process. Return to the main Imager Set window and click on the Generate button. This will set the rendering process in motion. The Status of each image will change from Pending to Generating while it's being generated, Printing while it's being printed (if Print is on), and Complete when it's done. If an error occurs in the rendering, the error number will be displayed. A more detailed explanation of the error can be found by double-clicking in the Status column of the image.

- At any stage, the image generation can be interrupted by pressing the Command+period (Mac), Ctrl+period (PC), or Esc (Mac or PC) keys. This gives you the option of proceeding to the next image or of canceling all subsequent image generation. If the generation is canceled, it can be resumed from the point it left off rather than from the beginning the next time the Imager Set is opened and the Generate command is given. This is one compelling reason why it's desirable to save the Imager Set.

- Once the generation process is completed (which could take from a few minutes to several hours, depending upon the complexity of the renderings), any of the rendered images can be displayed by highlighting it and clicking on the View button. If the Imager Set is saved and reopened, the rendered images can be viewed in the same manner. Thus, you can also use the Imager Set as a presentation medium, where all your images are rendered and saved and can be displayed in a sequence at the touch of a button. This is another good reason for saving the Imager Set.
- As the final step in this exercise, go back to your desktop and locate the folder that was specified as the Destination in the Imager Set Up dialog. If you open this folder, you should see all the image files saved in it, with automatic file names assigned to them (see Figure 5.14). These files can now be used like any other image file—they can be opened and edited using other image-editing programs, as well as viewed within the regular form•Z environment using File > View File.

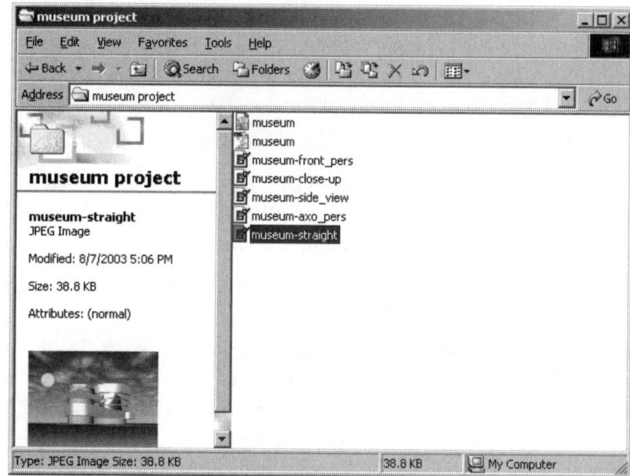

Figure 5.14

The five images in JPEG format generated automatically by the Imager Set, in the same folder as the project file.

EXERCISE 2

Lights Galore!

form•Z provides you with a vast array of light-related options, including both the type of light as well as how the lighting will be rendered. We'll explore all these options in this exercise, starting with a detailed look at how shadows are rendered in form•Z.

2.1 Rendering with Shadows

Shadows make a great difference in our perception of shapes and forms, so they're a crucial component of any rendered image. You've already learned how to activate the Shadows option for the various paint display modes. In this section, we'll see how the shadows are actually displayed in these modes.

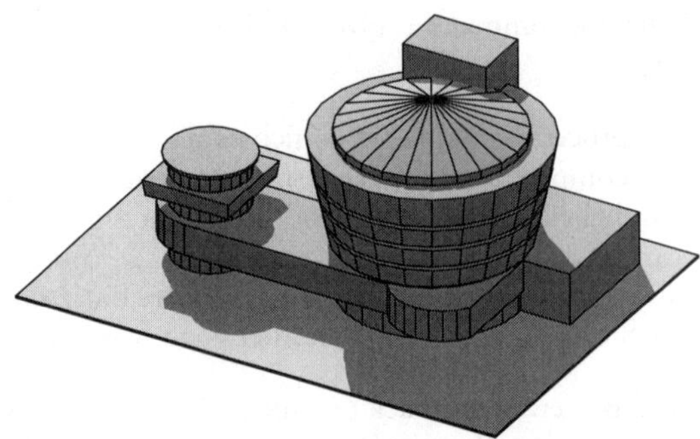

Figure 5.15

Displaying shadows in the Surface Render mode.

For now, we'll only deal with shadows cast by the "sun," which is the single light source existing in a modeling project by default. Shadow casting by additional light sources will be dealt with in later sections. Also, we'll focus simply on how the shadows are displayed, rather than on how their position is determined.

- Continue working with the same project you used in the last exercise. If it doesn't have some kind of base plane, add a large one so that you can capture the shadows of the objects on the ground (see Figure 5.15). For an existing base plane that isn't large enough, extend it by moving each one of its side faces outwards.
- Make sure that you're in a non-planar 3D view. Invoke the Quick Paint Options dialog and check the Render With Shadows option. Now watch how the rendering takes longer than usual, despite which the end result is even more inaccurate. Moral of the story—don't rely on the Quick Paint display when you want shadows! Use one of the other displays instead, even if they take more time.
- Move on to Surface Render and enable the Render With Shadows option for this display. The shadows have to be calculated, which takes time, particularly when you do it for the first time. Rendering information, including shadow calculations, is stored by default in memory, as you saw in Section 1.7, therefore subsequent renderings take less time to execute. The result of the rendering will be a nicely shaded image (Figure 5.15). Notice how the base plane is essential to capture the shadows of the building on the ground.
- Generate shadows for the RenderZone display as well in the same manner. Notice that the Shadows option in the RenderZone Options dialog has three sub-options: All Opaque, All Transparent, and Per Light. The default is All Opaque, and with this, even transparent objects will cast opaque, i.e., black shadows. By activating the All Transparent option, light passing through a transparent object will take on the color and transparency of that object. This will lead to more realistic renderings, but will also take more time to execute. Try it on an object with a transparent surface style, and you'll obtain transparent shadows, as shown in Figure 5.16. The third Shadows sub-option, Per Light, will make the shadows for each individual light opaque or transparent depending upon the settings of that light in its Light Parameters dialog, which we'll soon study in Section 2.3.
- Finally, generate shadows for the Shaded Render display as well. You'll find that its Shadows option has the same three sub-options we just saw, but in order to activate these, the Antialiasing option must be selected. To obtain transparent shadows in Shaded Render, you must also turn on the Transparencies option in its dialog.

Be careful to turn the Shadows feature off while you're in the early stages of modeling and don't really need it, as it will slow down the display process, and thus your work, considerably.

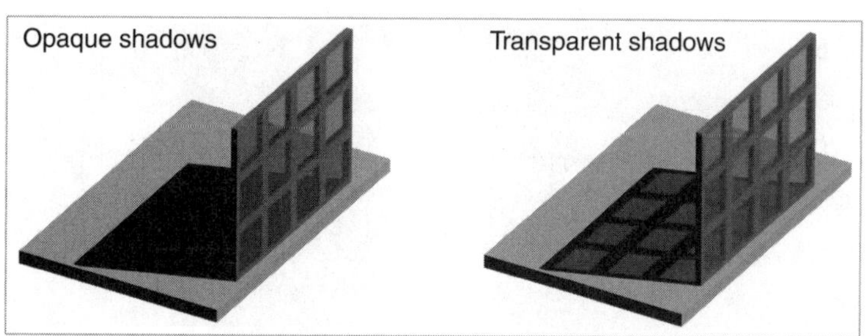

Figure 5.16

Opaque versus transparent shadows in the RenderZone display mode.

2.2 Positioning the Sun

- Switch to the Wire Frame display mode. Then turn your attention to the Lights palette. If it is closed, open it from the Palettes menu. It is almost identical to the Layers palette—except for one extra column we'll soon learn about—so working with it should be easy. The palette has a single default entry, Light1, which represents the sun by default.
- Naturally, you'd like to be able to specify the exact position of this sun and thereby control how the shadows are cast. The first step in doing this is to make the light display visible in the graphics window. To do this, click in the first column to the right of Light1. This will restore the shaded diamond icon and turn on the graphical representation of the light, which is a black arrowed line, as shown in Figure 5.17-a.
- Now switch to the Top view. The direction of the arrowed line represents the direction of the light. Verify this by doing a rendered display with shadows in the Top view, and see how the shadows are in accordance with the direction of the light (Figure 5.17-b). This light, Light1, in the absence of any other light source, represents the sun.
- You can apply the Move tool (M-Tool:13a,1) to the light just like any other object. Thus, you can graphically change the position of the sun by moving the entire light beam (the line), or just the light source (the shaded circle) or the light target (the arrow). The last two will result in the line being stretched or shrunk. You can switch between different planar views to fix the direction of the light more precisely. Do this a few times and see how the shadows change according to the orientation of the light. Make sure that none of the Copy modes are active when you apply the Move tool to the light, otherwise you'll be making new copies of the light rather than changing it. You can do this, however, once you learn to work with multiple lights in Section 2.4.

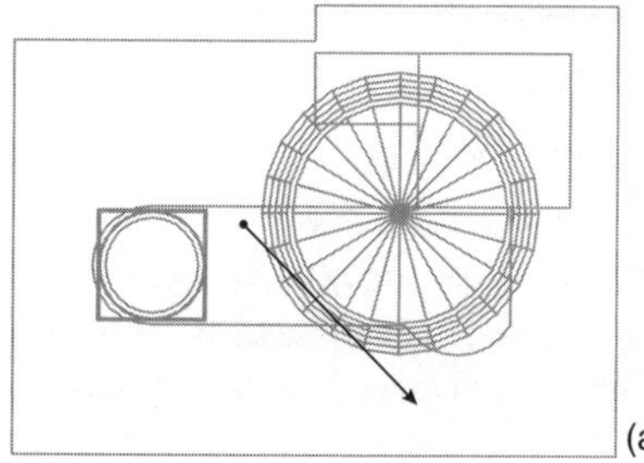

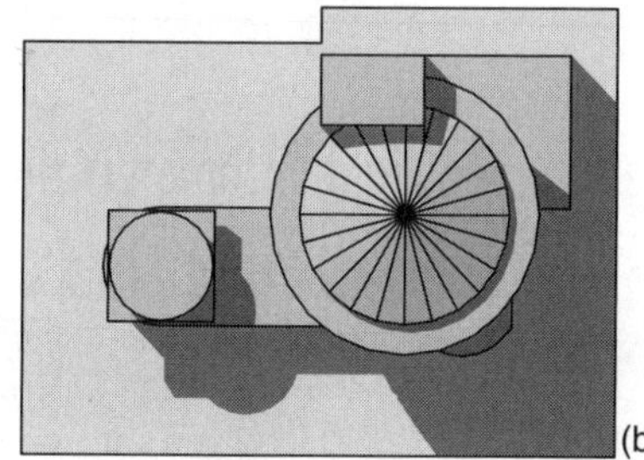

Figure 5.17

The sun in Wire Frame in Top view, and the corresponding shadows in Surface Render.

Figure 5.18

The Sun dialog, with the site, date, and time specifications, and the resultant rendering with shadows.

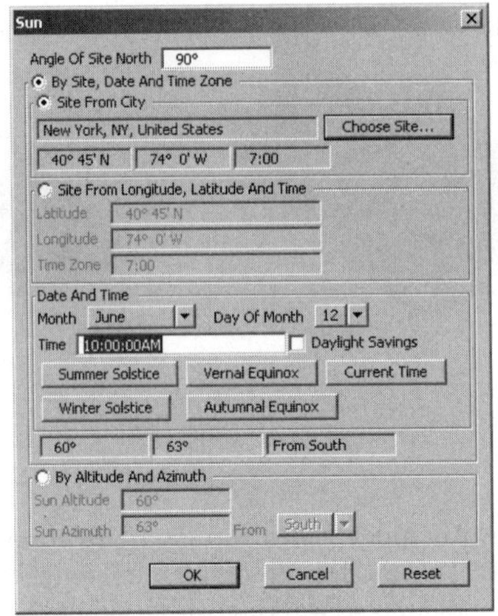

(a)

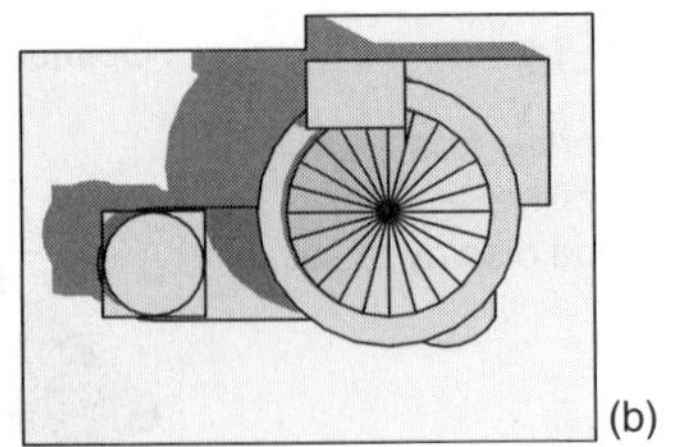

(b)

The capability to generate shadows for any specified direction of the sun might, in itself, seem more than adequate. But what if you want *real* shadows? In other words, what if you want to know *exactly* how various parts of your model (if it's a building) are going to be shaded at different times of the year, in a specific location in a specific country of the world? form•Z can do this as well.

- Go to Views > Sun Position. This will invoke a dialog in which you can specify the sun position in various ways: by city; by latitude, longitude, and time; or by altitude and azimuth. Let's explore the first method. Choose the By Site, Date And Time Zone option, and within it, the Site From City option. Then click on the Choose Site button. You'll be presented with the Geographic Position dialog containing an extensive list of cities around the world from which you can make your choice of location. You can also add your own location to this database, if it's not included, by specifying its latitude, longitude, and time zone.

- After selecting a location (or adding your own), you'll be returned to the Sun dialog (see Figure 5.18-a). Here, you can specify the date and time for which the shadows have to be determined. You should also specify the angle (measured, by default, as positive in the anticlockwise direction) that the North line of your site makes with the X axis. The default value for this angle is 90°, which means that North is in the +Y direction, following the usual convention in architectural practice. Try different variations of dates, times, and site angles, and watch the black line representing the sun reorient itself accordingly in the graphics window. Render the image to actually see the corresponding shadows that your model would have on the selected site, at the specified date and time (Figure 5.18-b).

2.3 The Light Parameters Dialog

- A light source is defined by a large number of attributes. In this section, you'll explore the attributes associated with the default light source, Light1, which represents the sun. Double-click on its name in the Lights palette. This will invoke the Light Parameters dialog for this light (Figure 5.19). Here, you can modify various parameters of the light, starting with its name. The Name field is highlighted and can be changed right away. Call it "The Sun" since you've assigned a sun position to it, and are treating it as such.

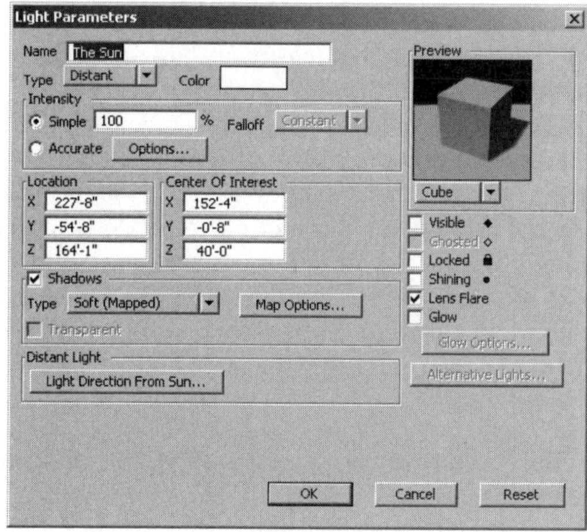

Figure 5.19

The Light Parameters dialog for the default light source.

- The Type of the light is automatically set to Distant. There are various other light types that you can create and position for achieving desired lighting effects in your renderings, and you'll be learning about these in subsequent sections. A *distant* type of light is located at an infinite distance away and emits parallel rays in a single direction. It is indicated by a single line with an arrow at the end, as you've seen for the sun. Try selecting another light type for the sun from the Type popup list, and you'll find that you're not allowed to do so. The light that is being used as the sun cannot be set to any type other than Distant.

- The color of the light is white by default. Click on the box beside Color and you'll be able to select a new color from the Color selection dialog of your operating system. Next, turn to the Intensity section, where you can choose to specify either with a simple value or accurately. Select Simple, set by default to 100%, and explore different values. Intensity values normally range from 0% to 100%, but you can go below 0% or above 100% to create effects of underexposure and overexposure respectively (see Figure 5.20). The changes in color and simple intensity are reflected in the little preview window, located in the top, right corner of the Light Parameters dialog. Here, you can verify the effects of the current light, applied to a white cube sitting on a white surface. A different object type can also be chosen from the accompanying popup list. Experiment with different colors and basic intensities and see the corresponding changes in the lighting effect. The Falloff menu accompanying the Simple intensity option is deactivated for a distant light, but we'll get the chance to explore it when we work with other light types.

100% Intensity

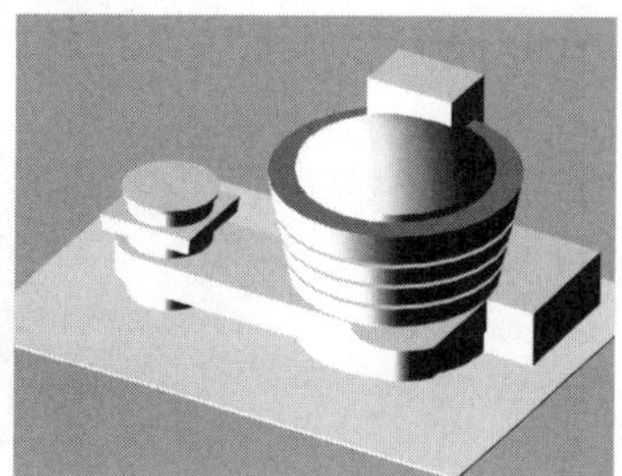

500% Intensity

Figure 5.20

Renderings obtained by using different simple Intensity values for the same light source.

- Now set the Intensity to Accurate, and click on the accompanying Options button. This takes you to a dialog where you can specify the intensity of the sun, which is a distant light, as it would be in real life. The Output Power value stands for the effect of such a light on a surface. The default value of 100 Watts Per SqFt is much too high—change this to 2 Watts Per SqFt for simulating sunlight on a bright sunny afternoon, with lower values for overcast days or evening light. You can also activate the Apply Atmospheric Light option, which will incorporate in your scene the indirect light reflected from the atmosphere that illuminates indoor spaces even when there's no direct light shining into them. Within this option, you can choose between three kinds of Cloud Coverage and three kinds of Sky Color, and specify the brightness of the sky in Candelas Per SqFt, all of which will affect the amount of atmospheric illumination calculated. Additionally, you can choose the level of quality of the solution. Applying atmospheric light is useful for generating realistic daytime interior renderings.

- To see the result of the Accurate intensity settings, exit the Light Parameters dialog and invoke the RenderZone Options dialog, shown earlier in Figure 5.1. Under the Illumination section in the Shading tab, change the Light Intensity option from All Simple to Per Light. This will apply the simple or accurate settings for each light depending upon its individual Intensity specifications. Exit the RenderZone Options dialog. You will now see the effect of the Accurate intensity settings you specified for the sun. The resultant rendering will be much more realistic, but will also take more time to render.

- In the last section, before you actually fixed the location of the light using Sun Position, you saw how you could change the location and direction of the sun graphically by using the Move tool. Get back to the Light Parameters dialog for the default light and see how you can perform the same operation by modifying the X, Y, and Z values of the Location and the Center Of Interest of the light. In most cases, however, it's far more convenient to manipulate these values graphically rather than by keying in coordinates, so you usually wouldn't worry about these values at all. In particular, if you've already set the light to a certain sun position, you absolutely should not change these values as that would render your sun settings inaccurate.

Figure 5.21

The renderings produced using different shadow options for the default distant light.

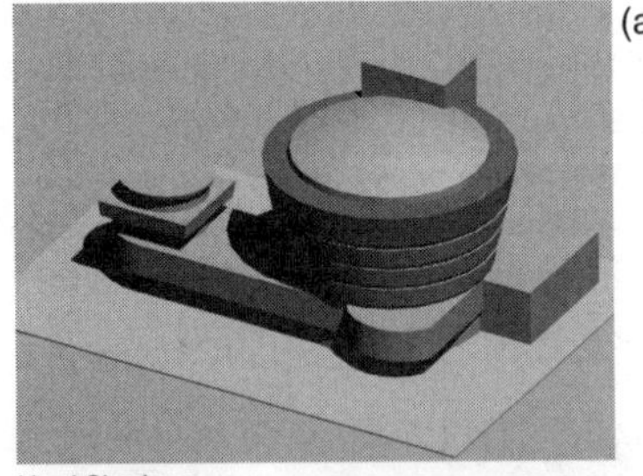

(a) Hard Shadows

(b) Soft Shadows with Softness = 50%

(c) Tolerance = 50%

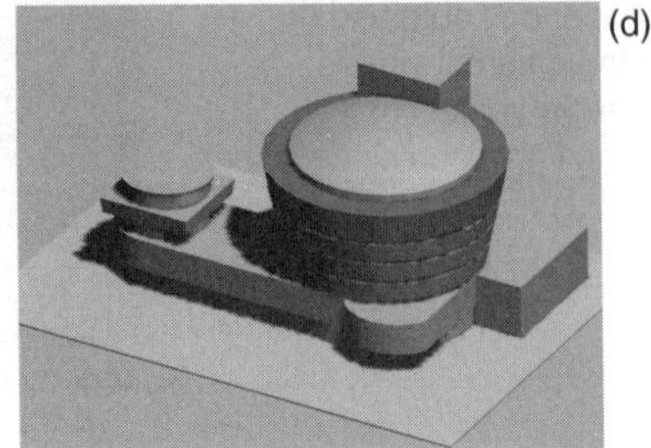

(d) Resolution = 0.25 Times Image Size

- The next facility that's available in the Light Parameters dialog is the ability to manipulate the quality and accuracy of the shadows that will be cast by the light. For shadows to be cast, the Shadows option must be checked. You can choose between three types using different techniques to create shadows: Soft (Mapped) uses shadow maps; Hard (Raytraced) uses raytracing; and Hard (Accelerated) uses a combination of shadow maps and raytracing. The shadow maps technique is faster, while raytracing produces shadows with crisper edges but requires more memory (see Figure 5.21-a). The Transparent option is available only when raytracing is used, and is thus active for the two Hard type shadows. When checked, transparent objects will produce transparent shadows, as you saw in Figure 5.16. The setting here will take effect only when the third Shadows sub-option, Per Light, is active in the RenderZone Options dialog. You should turn off the Transparent option if there are no transparent objects in the current scene, as it slows down the rendering.
- Both the Soft (Mapped) and Hard (Accelerated) types have the same additional parameters related to shadow maps that you can access by clicking on the accompanying Map Options button. The Quality of the shadows can be low, medium, or high, progressively requiring more time and memory. You can vary the degree of Softness of the shadows from 0 (hardest) to 100 (fuzziest). As the softness is increased, self-shadowing of objects also increases (Figure 5.21-b), which can be reduced by a proportionate increase in the Tolerance value (Figure 5.21-c). The Resolution option determines the resolution of the shadow map, relative to the image size, that's generated prior to rendering. For rough drafts, this can be reduced to less than 1 times the image size for faster but less accurate shadows (Figure 5.21-d). Alternately, you can specify an actual pixel value. The last option, Limit Map, applies to distant lights only and determines for which objects shadows are calculated. The default All Objects option calculates shadows for all the objects in the project, even if they're outside the current view. If you're rendering only a small portion of the model, choose one of the other two options, All Completely Visible Faces or All Completely Visible Objects, for crisper shadows.
- The next option in the Light Parameters dialog, Light Direction From Sun, allows you to set the position of any *distant* light to a specific site, date, and time, using the same Sun dialog you saw in Figure 5.18. You've already set this for the current light source in the last section. However, if you were to create more distant lights in your project (as you'll learn to do in the next section), you can use this option to conveniently set each one of them to a specific sun position, if required.
- Let's now proceed to explore the options located on the right side of the dialog, below the preview window. By default, a light is not visible. Check the Visible option to see it in the graphics window in the Wire Frame display mode. By checking the Ghosted option as well, the same light will be seen in ghosted mode and cannot be selected. This is useful when you don't want a light to be accidentally selected and operated upon by a modeling tool. Alternately, you can keep the light visible but check the Locked option, which will prevent it from being selected by a modeling tool.
- Keep in mind that making a light invisible doesn't mean that the light is inactive and doesn't illuminate the scene and cast shadows. The Visible option merely affects the *display* of the light in the graphics window. To actually deactivate the light, you need to deselect the Shining option. The light then still exists but doesn't contribute to the illumination of the scene. This feature is extremely useful, allowing you to create a large number of lights in various parts of your model and activate only a desired number of them at a time for different views and lighting effects.
- There are only two remaining active options in the Light Parameters dialog for the default distant light. The Lens Flare option, when checked, gives the light the ability to cause lens flares during postprocessing, but as you learned in Section 1.2, this option is more relevant to other light types. The Glow option makes the light source itself glow in a rendered scene. It is also more relevant to light types other than distant, so we'll explore its options in the next section.

2.4 Distant, Point, Cone, and Projector Lights

form•Z lets you create and position any number of different light sources in your model in addition to the single light source that exists in every project by default. You're already acquainted with a *distant* type of light such as the sun, located at an infinite distance away and emitting parallel rays in a single direction. There are six other types of lights. A *point* light is located at a specific finite point and emits rays equally in all directions about the source. A *cone* light is also located at a given point, but emits rays in all directions contained within a specified conical shape. A *projector* light projects a rectangular light in a given direction through a specified image, just like a slide projector. We'll be exploring all these light types in this section. There are three additional light types—*area*, *line* and *custom*—which will be covered in the next two sections.

Working with multiple lights is only possible in the Shaded Render and RenderZone display modes. Quick Paint and Surface Render use only the single distant light source that is designated as the sun. Moreover, the shades and shadows resulting from point, cone, projector, area, line, and custom lights can be seen accurately in the RenderZone display mode only.

- Let's actually get down to working with multiple lights. Continue to use the same model that you've been working with so far. Multiple lights in form•Z are created in the Lights palette. Currently, the palette has only one light, which you renamed as The Sun in the last section.

- To add a new light to your model, click on the blank space in the Lights palette below the last light name, The Sun. (The procedure is basically the same as creating a new layer or a new view in their respective palettes.) A new light will be created with a default name. Make it visible in the window by clicking in the first column to the right of the name. Then double-click on it to invoke its Light Parameters dialog where you can define the parameters of the new light. This time, select the Point option for the Type parameter of the light. You can also change its default name of "Light 2" to something more appropriate, such as "Point Source." Most of the parameters for this light type such as Color, Simple Intensity, Shadows, and so on, are the same as those you explored for the distant light in the last section. Let's concentrate on what's different.

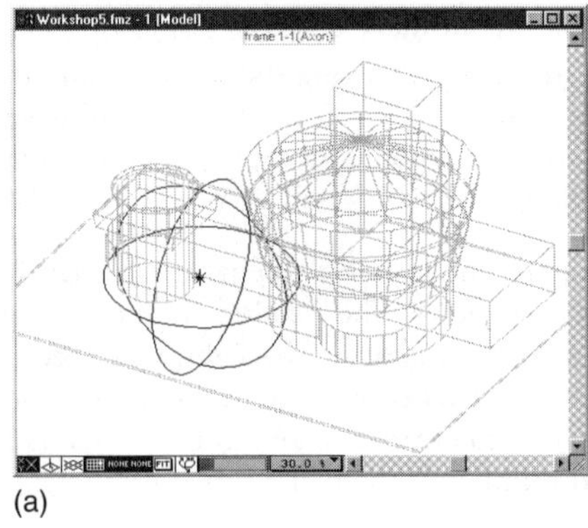

(a)

(b)

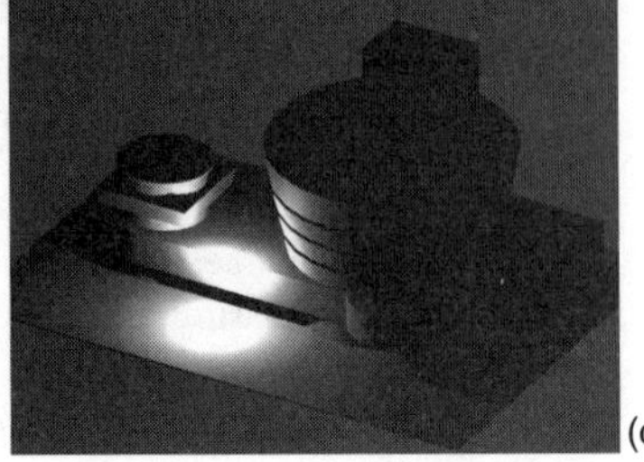
(c)

Figure 5.22

Adding a Point light to the model. (a) In Wire Frame display. (b) The resultant lighting in RenderZone, with default light settings. (c) Falloff set to Square.

- To accurately position the light in the model, you can modify the default coordinate values in the Location box, but as you saw for the sun in the last section, it's more convenient to do this graphically. (The Center Of Interest values are not relevant since a point light isn't restricted to one direction.) Exit the Light Parameters dialog by clicking on the OK button. You'll see the light in your window now represented graphically by a shaded circle for the location and 2D circles along all the three planes—XY, YZ, and ZX—indicating the radius of the light (Figure 5.22-a). Use the Move tool to position the light as desired, switching to some of the planar views for more accuracy. Note that you have to click on the *center* of the light to select it.

- To see the effect of the new light, turn off the Shining attribute for the first distant light, The Sun, in its Light Parameters dialog. (You'll soon see a shortcut for performing the same operation.) Then switch to the RenderZone display mode, making sure that its Shadows option is activated. Also set the Background to a dark color. You should see the unmistakable effect of the point source in the rendered image (Figure 5.22-b). To increase or decrease the light spread, invoke the Light Parameters dialog and change the Radius value, located in the lower half, accordingly.

- Switch to the Shaded Render display and you'll find that the image is completely blacked out, since the point light isn't recognized and the distant light is no longer shining. Get to the Shaded Render Options dialog and set the Unsupported Lights option to Approximate rather than Ignore. Refresh the display and you'll find that the point source is approximated by a distant source, resulting in the model being lighted this time.

- Get back to the Light Parameters dialog for the point light to explore its remaining parameters. Experiment with the three Falloff options in the Intensity section, which allow you to choose how the light intensity decreases with distance from the light source: Constant results in a constant intensity irrespective of distance and is the default; Linear decreases the intensity linearly with distance; and Square decreases the intensity exponentially with distance. Since the total intensity of the light has to remain the same, a larger falloff (i.e., lesser intensity at a greater distance) results in a higher light intensity in and around the center of the light. This is evident from Figure 5.22-c where the Falloff was set to Square, as opposed to the Constant option active for Figure 5.22-b.

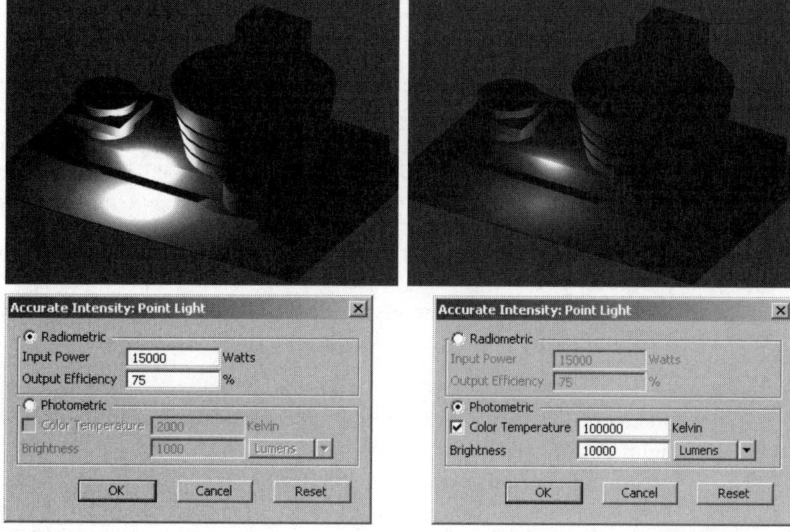

Figure 5.23

Specifying the Accurate Intensity for a point light. Two different specifications are shown, leading to two different lighting qualities in the rendering.

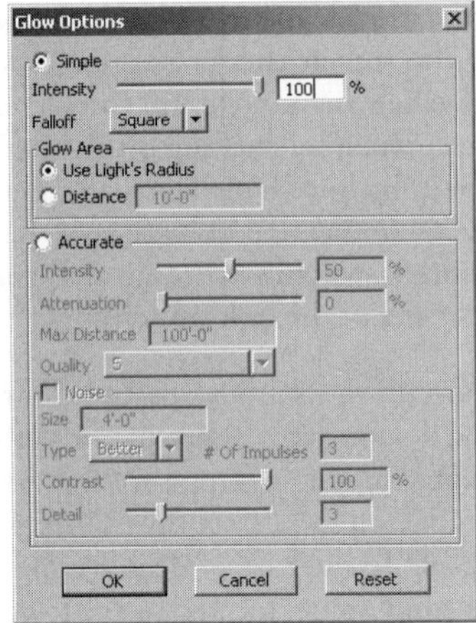

Figure 5.24

Activating the Glow option for a point light. The corresponding Glow Options dialog is also shown.

- Next, select the Accurate option for Intensity and click on its Options button. You'll find that the dialog invoked is different from the one you encountered for a distant light. Both point and cone lights use the same options for specifying the Accurate Intensity, using one of two methods: the Radiometric method, where the input power of a light in watts is given along with its output efficiency; and the Photometric method, where the brightness of the light is specified in lumens or candelas. Generate and compare renderings using both techniques, with different values for power and brightness (Figure 5.23). In the Photometric method, there's an additional option to specify the Color Temperature of the light: lower values give the light an orange color while higher values make it closer to white.

- The only remaining option left to explore is Glow, which is unchecked by default. This means that only the illumination from the light source is shown in renderings but not the light itself. By checking the Glow option, the light source will also be displayed as a glowing volume in a RenderZone display. Note that the rendering type in the RenderZone Options dialog has to be set to Preview Z-Buffer or above, and the Light Glow option under the Illumination section must be checked for the light glow to be rendered. If you don't achieve the glowing effect at the first attempt, click on the accompanying Glow Options button and increase the Intensity, Falloff, and Glow Area values under the Simple section until the glow is visible. You can also specify the Glow more accurately; explore these settings on your own. Figure 5.24 illustrates the glowing effect for a point light, along with the corresponding options. The Glow option is very useful in obtaining realistic rendering effects for a lamp, for instance, which can be created by enclosing a light source in a semi-transparent material. You'll work on such a project in the Assignment for this workshop.

- Let's move on to look at the other types of lights. Create two new lights following the same procedure you used to create the point light. Set one of them to Cone and the other to Projector. Open up the Light Parameters dialog for each of them and make the necessary adjustments to the attributes, most of which are identical to those for distant and point lights. Turn on their displays in the graphics window.

- The cone light is directional and has both a location and a center of interest, just like a distant light. Again, you'll find it easier to position it graphically using the Move tool rather than by specifying coordinate values in the Light Parameters dialog. Additionally, the spread of a cone light is controlled by two angles—the inner and the outer. Experiment with changes in these values, located at the base of the dialog, and see how they affect the resultant lighting. Figure

5.25-a shows a cone light rendering with all the other lights turned off. The Glow option was turned on in order to see the actual light.

- The projector light, as mentioned earlier, projects a specified image in a certain direction (Figure 5.25-b). The location and direction are, as usual, best modified graphically. Other attributes such as the angle and the spin of the light, as well as the image to be projected, can all be modified in the Light Parameters dialog (Figure 5.25-c). To change the image from the default logo, simply click on it and you'll be presented with a dialog through which you can select a new image.

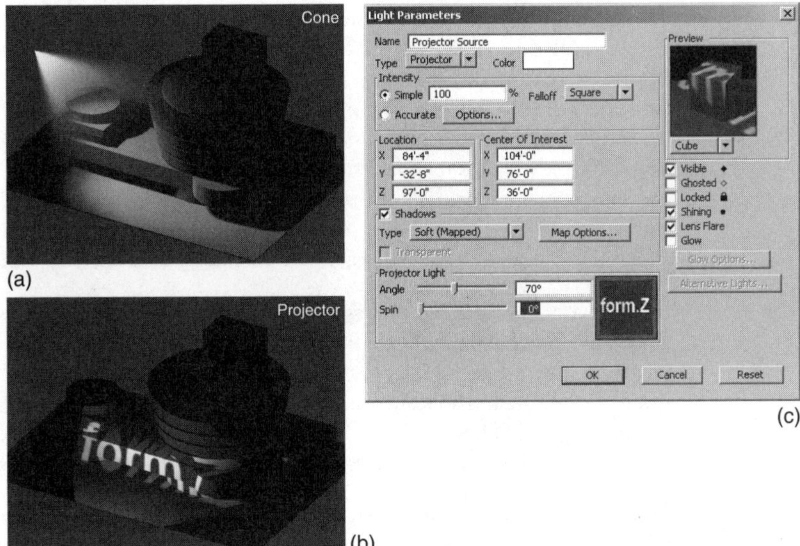

Figure 5.25

Rendering with a cone and a projector light. The Light Parameters dialog for the projector light used is also shown.

2.5 Area and Line Lights

form•Z lets you convert any physical object in the project into one of two types of primary light sources: an *area light*, where the entire solid or surface object becomes a light; or a *line light*, where the line object, or the line of the first face of a solid object, becomes a light of a specified radius. Such lights are extremely useful in different modeling situations. For instance, when modeling a lampshade, you can convert the lampshade itself into an area light and bypass the step of modeling a cone or point light to place inside the lampshade. You can convert a window pane into an area light to provide subtle nighttime lighting effects inside a space. A neon tube can be nicely simulated with a line light. Any object, of any shape and size, can be made to emit light. This provides enormous flexibility and versatility in creating interesting and unusual lighting effects.

The parameters of area and line lights are almost identical, and are similar to those of the light types you have already covered. We'll work with one area light in this section, and you can use that as the basis for experimenting with line lights as well.

- Select an object in your scene that you'd like to convert to a light source, or create a new object and then select it. With the object still selected, click in the Lights palette to create a new light. Double-click on the new entry to invoke its Light Parameters dialog, and select Area from the Type popup menu (Figure 5.26-a). Also check the Visible option, then click OK to exit the dialog and return to the graphics window. You'll notice that the selected object is now replaced by an area light symbol, depicted by surfaces with arrows pointing outwards to indicate the direction of the light (Figure 5.26-b).

- Turn off all the other lights to see the full impact of this light. Before you render, though, invoke the RenderZone Options dialog, and set the Area/Line Lights option under the Illumination section to Use rather than Approximate or Ignore. The RenderZone display will now show the illumination from the area light on nearby surfaces. You can control the intensity and spread of the light through the usual parameters in the Light Parameters dialog, such as Intensity, Falloff, and Radius.

- Notice that the area light itself isn't shown by default. To make the light visible in the rendering, check the Render Light Object option located in the Area Light section at the base of its Light Parameters dialog (as in Figure 5.26-a). Refresh the display after making this change, and you'll find that the area light itself now appears as a glowing object, in its original object color, in the scene (Figure 5.26-c). You can conveniently modify its surface style, if required, in the adjoining preview window. If you check the Ignore Light Object Color option in the Area Light section, only the color specified for the light in the Color box will be used to render it. Additionally, you can set the Quality of the illumination and shadows generated by the area light using the accompanying slider bar. A higher value will naturally also take more time to render.

- Since an area (or line) light takes a long time to render, you can choose to approximate it with an alternative point light, whose settings are accessed by clicking on the Alternative Lights button, located below the Glow Options button. In the dialog that opens up, you can specify the radius, intensity, falloff, and shadows options for the alternate light, just as you did for the point light in the last section. These settings will be used for rendering the light when the Area/Line Lights option in the RenderZone Options dialog is set to Approximate rather than Use.

- Once an object has been converted to an area light, modeling operations can no longer be applied to it since it's no longer regarded as an object. If you need to retrieve the object, simply change the light type from Area to something else in its Light Parameters dialog. Don't try to retrieve it by deleting the area light, since this will also delete the object that was converted to the light.

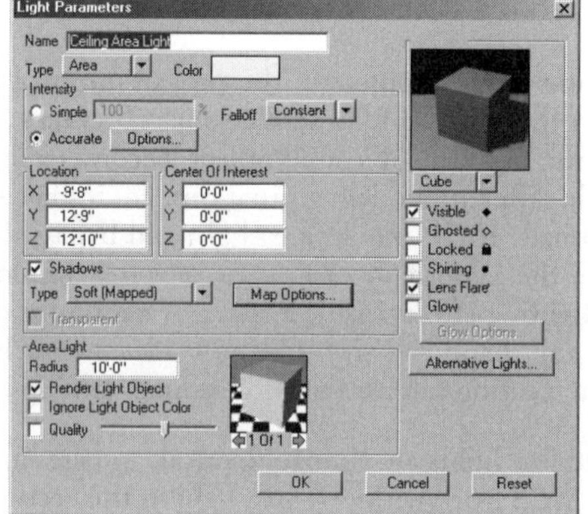

(a)

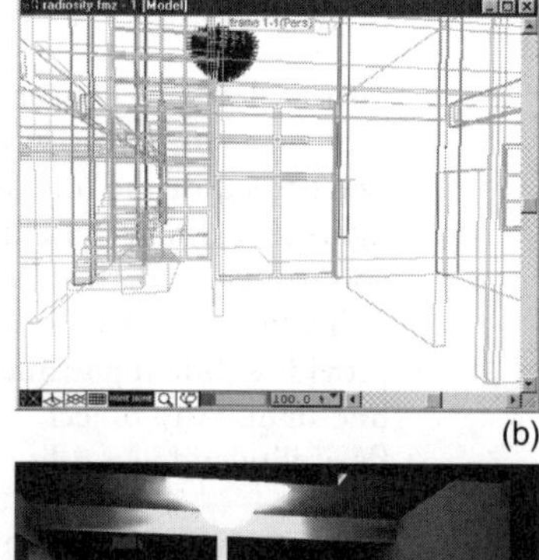

(b)

(c)

Figure 5.26

Working with an area light. (a) The Light Parameters dialog defining the light. (b) Wire Frame display of the scene, showing the area light. (c) RenderZone display of the scene, with the Render Light Object option turned on.

- After working with the area light, use a similar procedure to create a line light and explore its parameters before moving on to look at the last light type in the next section.

2.6 Custom Lights

The area and line lights you saw in the last section are one step towards customization of lights, enabling you to convert an object of any shape and size into a light, without being restricted to predefined light types such as point, cone, etc. form•Z goes a step further and allows you to create a light with a *customized spread* instead of a uniform spread. In other words, you can define what the light intensities should be in different directions about the light source, rather than settle for a uniform intensity in all directions. Such a light is called a *custom light* and it enables you to better simulate real-world lighting situations, which usually have varying light intensities in different directions about a source.

- Create a new light in the Lights palette. Open its Lights Parameters dialog, set the Type to Custom, and check the Visible option. Most of the options for this light are identical to those you've explored for the other light types. Modify some of these familiar options if you like, and exit the dialog.
- You should see your new light represented as a sphere in Wire Frame by three perpendicular circles, two of which intersect the *axis* of the light (Figure 5.27-a). The axis is the line that starts at the center of the spherical shape—the *origin*—and ends with the larger arrow—the *center of interest.* The other line starting from the center and ending with a smaller arrow is perpendicular to the axis and represents the *zero angle line*, with respect to which light intensities in different directions are defined. This line coincides with the 0° plane for light distribution, which you'll soon learn about. For now, adjust the position of the light so that it's visible in the scene you want to render.
- Generate a rendering with all other lights turned off except the custom light. With the default intensity settings, you'll find that the illumination from the custom light isn't very different from that of a point light.

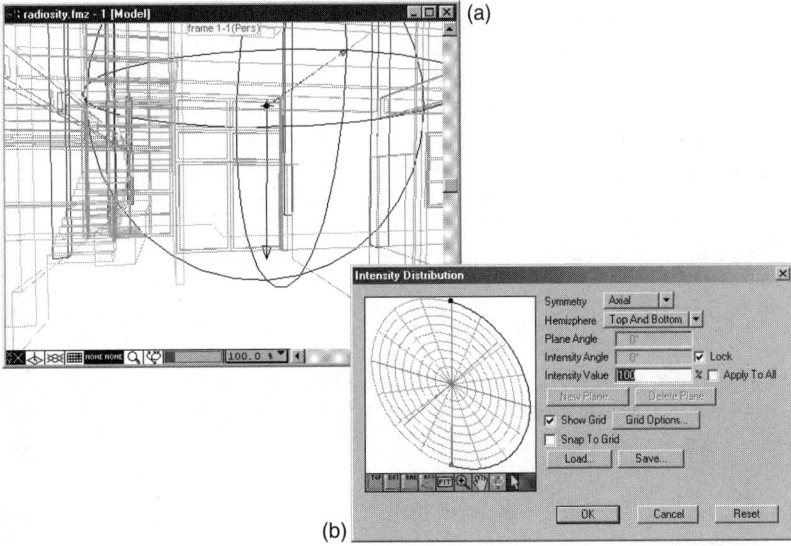

Figure 5.27

Adding a custom light to the scene. The Intensity Distribution dialog for this light, showing the default intensity spread, is also illustrated.

- We'll now proceed to customize the intensity spread of this light. Invoke its Light Parameters dialog once again and click on the Intensity Distribution button, located at the base. The dialog that opens up contains a preview window and a number of options (Figure 5.27-b). The preview window shows the current light distribution curve against a planar grid with radial subdivisions. (It is radial because light, by nature, travels radially outwards from a source.) The distance of each point on the curve from the central axis—which is the axis of the light you saw in the Wire Frame display—represents the intensity of light in that direction, at that position, and on that plane. The custom light will be completely defined by similar intensity curves for different planes, all of which pass through the axis. Only one of these planes is shown in the preview area to begin with.

- Use the tool icons located at the base of the preview window to switch to the planar view in which you can see the intensity curve head-on. Then select the Pointer tool and use it to move the active endpoint of the curve, which is colored in the highlight color. As you move the point, the shape of the curve changes. Notice that the Intensity Value field, located to the right of the preview window, also changes as you move the point. Try changing this value, which is expressed as a percentage, directly in this field and see the location of the active point change in response to the specified value.

- Activate the other point and move it as well. You're not limited to moving within the grid that's displayed; you can zoom out as much as you want to manipulate the spread of the light. Thus, you can have intensity values well over 100% if required.

- By default, there are only two points on the curve that you can move—the endpoints. To insert additional points on the curve so that you can further manipulate its shape, click on any part of the curve while pressing the option key (Mac) or Ctrl+Shift keys (PC). This will insert a new point at the location of the click, which can now be moved just like the earlier points (see Figure 5.28-a). Notice that the movement of this point seems constrained—this is because the angle that the point makes with respect to the origin is locked by default. To unlock it, deselect the Lock option next to the Intensity Angle box; now watch this value change in addition to the Intensity Value when you move the point. The intensity angles of the two endpoints of the curve remain constant and cannot be changed.

- Repeat the insertion and moving of points until you have a light distribution curve that's very different from what you had earlier (Figure 5.28-a). An inserted point can be deleted, if necessary, by selecting it with the control key (Mac) or Ctrl+Alt keys (PC). When you're satisfied with the curve, generate a rendering with this light to see what it looks like (Figure 5.28-b).

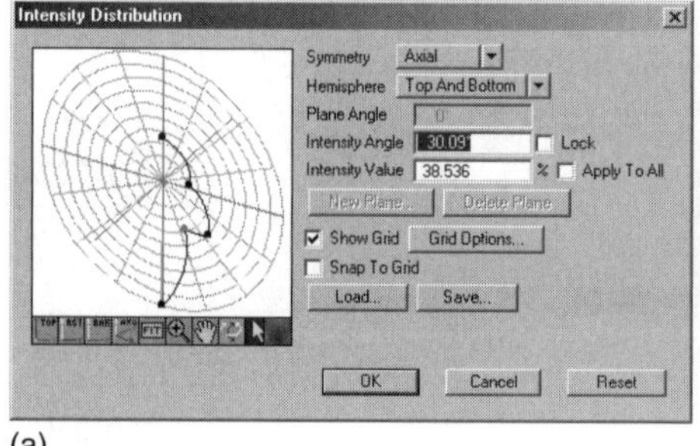

(a)

(b)

Figure 5.28

Modifying the light distribution curve of the custom light, and the resultant rendering.

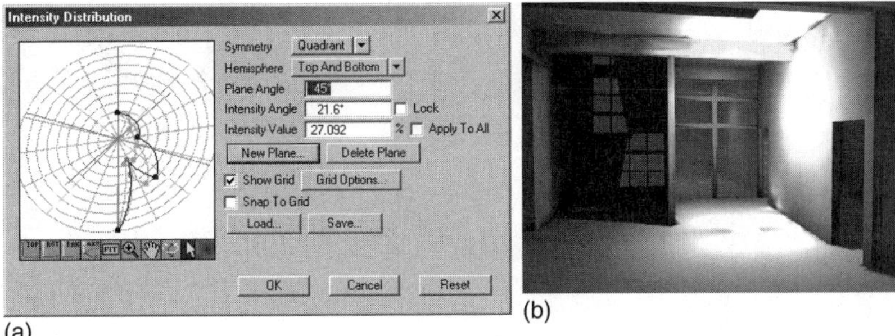

Figure 5.29

Working with Quadrant symmetry light distribution curves for the custom light, and the resultant rendering.

- Invoke the Intensity Distribution dialog for the custom light once again in order to explore the other available options. Start with the four options in the Symmetry popup menu. The default is the Axial option, which requires only one light distribution curve (i.e., a curve on one plane) as you just saw in the last step. The overall spread of the light is derived by revolving this single curve a full 360° about the axis of the light.

- Switch to the Quadrant type of symmetry and click OK in response to the query that pops up. Here, the light distribution is symmetrical in each quadrant. Therefore, at least two distribution curves are required to define the light spread within a single quadrant, one at the 0° plane and the other at the 90° plane. Curves at additional intermediate planes can be defined, if required, using the New Plane button.

- Switch to the Axo view in the preview window, and you'll see a second curve in ghosted mode, perpendicular to the first curve. Click on this curve with the Pointer tool to activate it; the first curve will now become ghosted. Notice also that the Plane Angle value has changed from 0° to 90°. The new curve is initially the same shape as the first curve and is placed on its own planar grid that is now visible. Use the Pointer tool to manipulate the shape of this curve, just as you did for the first curve, adding new points if necessary. You'll find that any changes you make to the second curve are also reflected in the first curve—new points are added, and if a point is moved on the active curve, corresponding points on the ghosted curve also get displaced slightly. This happens because the light spread ultimately has to be defined by smoothly blending all the curves, so they must have some correspondence with each other. If you want the changes made to the Intensity Value of the points on the active curve to be exactly duplicated in the ghosted curve, simply select the Apply To All option, located next to the Intensity Value field.

- Still in Quadrant symmetry, click on the New Plane button and specify an angle value between 0° and 90°. Modify the light distribution curve for this plane as well (Figure 5.29-a). You can modify the curves for any number of quadrant planes in this manner. After you're done, render the image to see what the resulting light spread looks like (Figure 5.29-b).

- Similarly, explore the remaining two Symmetry types as well. Plane is very similar to Quadrant except that the distribution is symmetrical in each of the two half-planes rather than the four quadrants. You can create any number of distribution curves between the 0° and 180° planes—the two extreme curves have to be specified as a minimum. The remaining option, None, as you can guess from its name, uses no symmetry in calculating the light distribution. It lets you specify the distribution curves for any number of planes. A minimum of three is required: the first at 0°, the second at any angle, and the third at any angle greater than 180°.

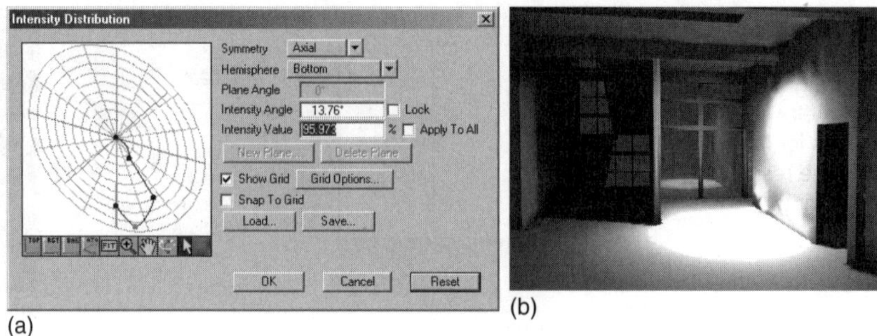

Figure 5.30

Changing the Hemisphere option of the custom light to Bottom, and the resultant rendering.

- Move on to explore the three Hemisphere options. By default, this option is set to Top And Bottom, which is why your light distribution curves so far could extend both above and below the origin of the light—represented by the center of the radial grid. Physically, this translates to a light source that provides illumination both above and below it, as you can see from the preceding illustrations. Change the Hemisphere option to Bottom for a downward pointing light, or to Top for an upward pointing light. The light distribution curves will be automatically adjusted, with points removed if necessary. Figure 5.30 shows the specifications of a downward pointing custom light and the resultant rendering.

- There are only a few more options left to explore in the Intensity Distribution dialog for the custom light. New Plane, as you have seen, lets you create a new plane at a specified angle for the symmetry types that allow multiple planes—which includes all except Axial symmetry. Delete Plane lets you delete the active plane; if a plane cannot be deleted such as the 0° plane, this option is dimmed. Show Grid and Snap To Grid are toggle switches for grid visibility and grid snapping respectively. You can also make changes to the distance and angle specifications of the grid by clicking on the Grid Options button and specifying the desired values in the dialog that's invoked.

- A custom light can be saved in a data file, by clicking on the Save button, in one of three standard light formats: IES (Illumination Engineering Society of North America), CIE (International Commission on Illumination), or the British CIBSE (Chartered Institution of Building Services Engineers). The parameters of a saved light can be recalled for a custom light in any project by clicking on the Load button. In addition to your own saved files, this is particularly useful for loading actual data files, supplied by the manufacturers, for commercially available lights that you plan to use in your project.

  We've covered all the options in the Intensity Distribution dialog, so go ahead and exit from it. Back in the Light Parameters dialog, notice that there's a Spin value below Radius for this light type that you haven't encountered before. You can use this to rotate the custom light about its axis—this angle is measured with respect to the zero angle line, i.e., the 0° plane orientation. Try it.

2.7 The Lights Palette, Light Groups, and the Lights Dialog

- It's time to take a closer look at the Lights palette and see the functionalities it affords. By this time, your palette should have seven entries, one for each of the light types you've created in your model so far. The name of each light is preceded by an icon, indicating what its type is (Figure 5.31-a).

Figure 5.31

Working with the Lights palette. (a) Entries for each of the seven light types. (b) Creating an additional distant light. (c) Designating the new distant light as the sun. (d) Manipulating various attributes of the lights.

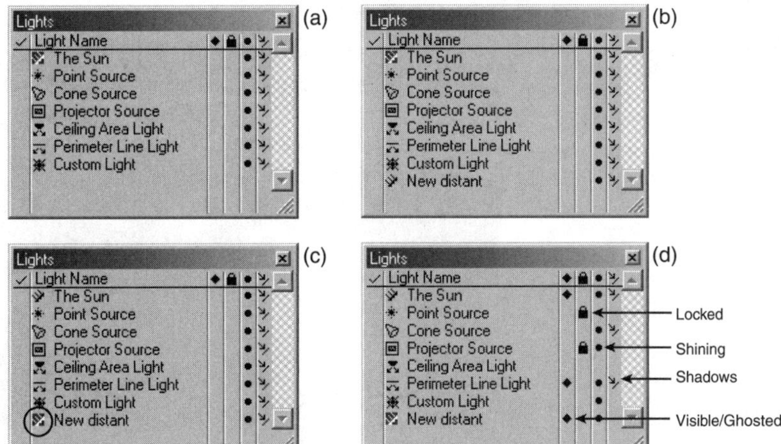

- Go ahead and create one more light in the usual fashion, and set its type to Distant. Make it visible and position it graphically in the desired location, or use the Light Direction From Sun option in the Light Parameters dialog to specify a sun position for it. Make sure its direction is sufficiently different from the first distant light you had.

- Deactivate all the other lights and switch the display to RenderZone. The scene will be rendered, as expected, according to the new light. But switch to Surface Render, and you'll find that it ignores the new distant light and works with the old light, even though the Shining attribute of that light has been turned off. Recall that the Surface Render and Quick Paint displays can only work with a single light source that is the sun. Obviously then, these displays are still regarding the first light as the sun.

- Look closely at the icon accompanying your first distant light, and you'll find that it's highlighted (Figure 5.31-b). This is why that light is considered to be the sun by the Surface Render and Quick Paint displays. To designate the *new* distant light as the sun, simply click on *its* icon. It will get highlighted, clearing the highlight from the icon of the first light (Figure 5.31-c). A Surface Render display will now give you the correct result, treating the new light as the sun. Thus, you can have many distant lights in your model, but only one of these can be designated as the sun at any given time by highlighting its icon.

The ability to create multiple distant lights but designate only one of them as the sun is very convenient for carrying out daylighting studies of an architectural or urban design model. Many lights can be created, each set to different dates and times for the same site by using the Light Direction From Sun option in its Light Parameters dialog. To render the model in Surface Render for different sun positions, simply highlight the corresponding icon in the Lights palette. To obtain the same renderings using Shaded Render or RenderZone, activate one light at a time by turning off the Shining attribute for all the others. This is how you can explore the variation in shades and shadows in a model at different times of the day or year, without needing to change the sun position every time.

- Now turn your attention to the various columns in the Lights palette. To the right of the Light Name are four columns—these provide a convenient way of manipulating some of the light attributes that you previously changed using the Light Parameters dialog. From left to right, these columns correspond with the Visible/Ghosted, Locked, Shining, and Shadows attributes respectively (see Figure 5.31-d). Just like the other palettes you've seen, icons in these columns work as toggle switches, reversing the corresponding attributes of the lights when selected. Try out each one of them.

Figure 5.32

Creating a light group, and using its Attributes dialog to override some attributes of the individual lights in that group.

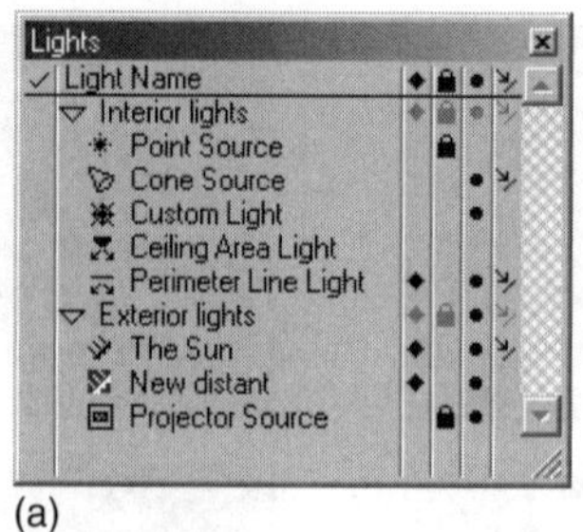

(a)

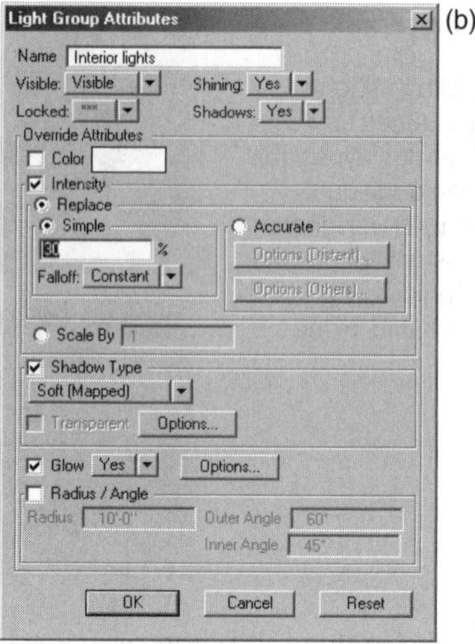

(b)

It's particularly useful to make lights ghosted or invisible before entering the Cone Of Vision mode, so that you have a less chaotic display and can concentrate on adjustments to the line of sight. Locking a light is always convenient to prevent accidental selections and transformations. As far as the Shining attribute is concerned, it should always be turned off for those lights that won't be contributing to the illumination of a particular scene. Thus, for daytime external renderings, the interior lights can be switched off, while for nighttime internal views, the external distant lights should be switched off.

- The column to the left of the Light Name is the familiar selection column. It can be used to conveniently select a light that's visible and not locked; for instance, when you want to move the light. Try it out. Very often in complex projects, lights get buried under mounds of modeling objects and are difficult to select using the Pick tool, so this is a really useful shortcut.

- form•Z gives you the ability to group lights in the Lights palette, similar to the manner in which layer groups are created in the Layers palette (see Section 3.5 of Workshop 3, Personalizing Your Environment). To create a light group, click on the blank space under the last light name in the Lights palette while pressing the control key (Mac) or Ctrl+Alt keys (PC). This will create a new light group with a default name, which you can type over. Existing lights can now be moved into this light group by the drag-and-drop method, just as you did for layers (see Figure 5.32-a). Creating a light group is particularly convenient for collating a series of related lights, for instance, a grid of ceiling lights of the same type within a room.

- Grouping lights lets you manipulate the attributes of all the lights within a group simultaneously by using the corresponding visibility, locked, shining, and shadows icons next to the group name. You can also override the lighting attributes of the individual lights with settings that apply to the entire group. To do this, double-click on the light group name in the Lights palette, select the individual attributes that you wish to override in the Override Attributes section, and specify the corresponding values (see Figure 5.32-b).

- Just like all the other palettes you've seen so far, the Lights palette has a dialog associated with it which you can access in the usual manner—click in the top bar of the Lights palette where the column title, Light Name, appears, or go to Options > Lights. Here, you have the usual options for creating, editing, deleting, copying and sorting lights and light groups (Figure 5.33-a). The Sun option is used to designate a particular distant light as the sun, and is the equivalent of graphically clicking on the light icon in the Lights palette. The Load Project Lights option can be used to load all the lights defined in another form•Z project into the current one—a useful option if you've divided up a complex modeling project into two or more smaller, more manageable projects and would like to synchronize them. The Show Color and Highlight Picked options show the light color and indicate if it is selected in the Lights palette respectively.

- The Ambient Light option in the Lights dialog will be new to you. It's important to remember that the sun, and any other lights that you create in a project, are in addition to the *ambient* light that is always present in a scene. The color and intensity of this ambient light is defined in the Lights dialog. The default is white light of 10% intensity. These attributes can be changed in the same way as you change the color and intensity of an individual light. Try it. You'll find that changes in the intensity of the ambient light affect all the display modes, while changes in the color are visible only in the rendered display modes. Figure 5.33-b shows the same lighting scene by the projector light as Figure 5.25-b, but with an ambient light of blue color and 80% intensity.

Figure 5.33

The Lights dialog, and the result of changing the ambient light settings from the defaults, for the scene using a projector light shown in Figure 5.25-b.

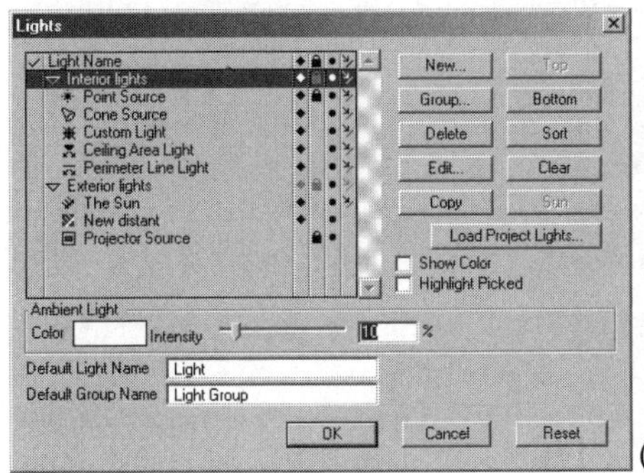

(a)

(b)

2.8 Performing an Illumination Analysis

We have, by now, already explored all the options under the Illumination section of the RenderZone Options dialog that we had skipped in Section 1.1, except one—the Analysis option. When this is activated, the current scene will be rendered, not with object colors as is usually done, but with a color coding scheme that shows the *light intensity* on every visible surface. Thus, you can analyze the illumination in any part of your model with this option. It is most useful in architecture and interior design for designing the lighting conditions inside a space.

- Open a building project you've modeled to a sufficient extent to be able to generate some internal views. If you don't have such a project, create a simple one: a 3D enclosure sitting on a base plan, its top enclosed by a flat or sloping slab, with a couple of openings in the walls. Generate a few interior views of the space with the openings in sight, using Edit Cone Of Vision. Add lights as appropriate. For a distant light, invoke its Light Parameters dialog, set the Intensity to Accurate, and set the Output Power in the corresponding Options dialog to 2 watts per sq. ft.

- Bring up the RenderZone Options dialog (shown earlier in Figure 5.1) and turn to the Illumination section. By default, the Analysis option is deactivated. Activate it and exit the dialog. You'll find that the rendered image now shows contour-like patches on all the surfaces in various colors, corresponding with different light intensities (Figure 5.34-a). All areas having the same intensity will be shown in the same color. Thus, you can visually get a quick estimate of the lighting conditions in the current scene.

- Go back to the RenderZone Options dialog, and click on the Options button accompanying the Analysis option. In the dialog that's invoked (Figure 5.34-b), you can modify the intensity values and their corresponding colors in the Value and Color fields, by selecting a particular color/value combination from the list on the left.
- You can also choose whether the rendering will show the Illuminance or the Luminance of a surface. The first option is selected by default. Illuminance is the amount of light intensity *received* by a surface, and can be used to determine if the lighting conditions in a space are proper. Luminance, on the other hand, is the amount of light intensity *reflected* by a surface, and is used to detect areas with a high degree of glare.
- The next option in the Illumination Analysis Options dialog is Blend Colors. When this is selected, the edges between adjacent color contours in the illumination rendering are blurred rather than sharp, caused by a smooth blending of colors from one contour to the next. Select or deselect it, based on your rendering requirements.
- Next, click on the Set Range button. This invokes a dialog where you can specify the Minimum and Maximum illuminance or luminance values that will appear in the Color/Value list. The other values in the list will then be divided into equal increments between the minimum and maximum values. Alternately, you could also specify the Increment value instead of the Maximum value.
- The remaining buttons in the Illumination Analysis Options dialog perform a variety of functions. Insert is used to insert a new color/value entry above the currently selected one, while Delete will remove the current one from the list. The Save, Load, and Default buttons can be used to save the analysis settings to a file, load a saved settings file, and restore the default settings respectively.

Having explored all the basic lighting options, let's move on to learn what radiosity is all about and how it affects the lighting in a rendered image.

Figure 5.34

Rendering the illumination analysis of a scene. The Illumination Analysis Options dialog is also shown.

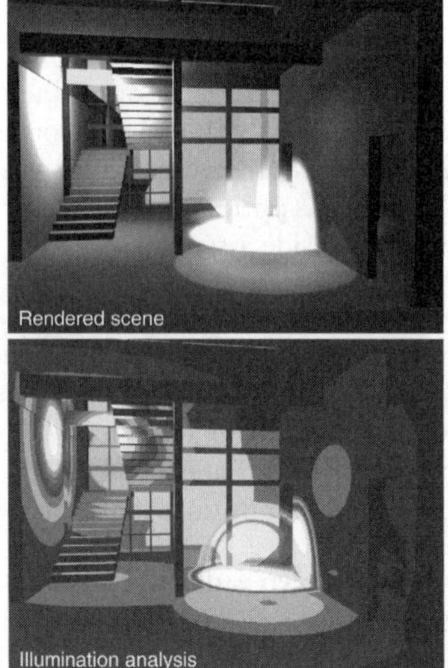

(a)

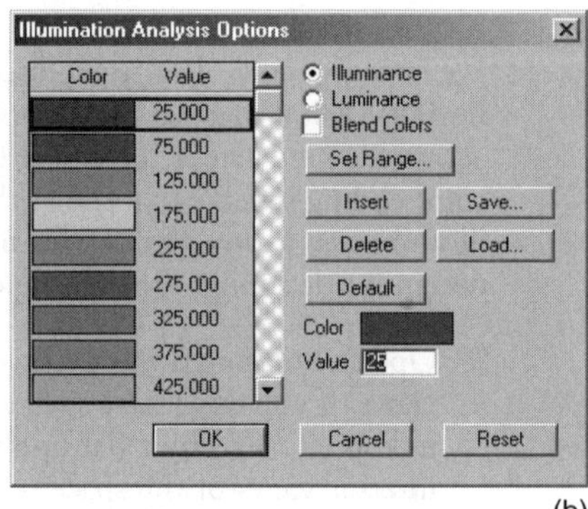

(b)

Exercise 3

Radiosity Based Rendering

Radiosity is a technique that enables the generation of very realistic renderings of the lighting conditions in a scene. The contrast is illustrated in Figure 5.35, which shows a RenderZone display of the interior of a space illuminated by a single distant light, with and without radiosity. You can see how much more real the radiosity rendering appears to be.

We'll not get into the technical details here of how radiosity works. It's sufficient to understand that radiosity simulates light very accurately—for instance, it takes into consideration the indirect light reflected off surfaces that are not directly illuminated, which is how light behaves in real life. Ordinary lighting calculations of the kind you've done so far don't account for such light. That's why the radiosity rendering of the scene in Figure 5.35 appears much brighter, and therefore more lifelike, than a non-radiosity rendering of the same scene.

Radiosity isn't a rendering technique like the various rendering types—Gourand, Phong, Z-Buffer, Raytrace, and so on—available in RenderZone. Rather, it's a description of the project model incorporating radiosity calculations. This description of the model is referred to as the *radiosity solution*, and its generation can be extremely memory-intensive and time-consuming, depending upon the complexity of the model. Once the radiosity solution has been generated, it can be displayed in RenderZone and other rendered display modes.

Radiosity rendering

Non-radiosity rendering

Figure 5.35

Radiosity and non-radiosity based renderings of the same scene, using a single distant light.

Radiosity based rendering in form•Z is executed by commands grouped in the fifth group of the Display menu. We'll start this exercise by going through one complete cycle of initializing, generating, and rendering a radiosity solution, using the default radiosity settings. Then, we'll look at some basic aspects of radiosity. Finally, we'll explore all the radiosity options and see how they can be manipulated to enhance the quality of the rendering, or reduce the time it takes to generate a solution.

3.1 Initializing, Generating, and Rendering a Radiosity Solution

As mentioned earlier, radiosity takes into account the indirect light reflected off surfaces, which accounts for the more realistic lighting effects it produces. This is done by meshing each surface of the model and treating each mesh subdivision as a *secondary* light source. *Primary* light sources, as opposed to secondary light sources, are the lights that you create and position in the model, which are listed in the Lights palette. There are three steps involved in the radiosity process: *initialization*, where the subdivisions on each surface are created; *generation*, where the radiosity calculations are performed; and *rendering*, where the radiosity solution is rendered. Let's see how the process works.

- Use the same building project that you used for exploring illumination analysis in the last section. Set the appropriate RenderZone parameters, render the image, and save it as an image file. This will help you compare the non-radiosity solution with the radiosity one.

- Invoke the Wire Frame Options dialog and make sure the Draw Mesh option under Radiosity Display is checked. Still in the Wire Frame display mode, go to Display > Initialize Radiosity. This will subdivide the surfaces of all the objects into a mesh (see Figure 5.36). At the same time, all the modeling tools and many of the window tools are grayed out, indicating that you're in the *radiosity mode*, within which no changes can be made to the model. The larger the number of initial subdivisions, the greater the number of secondary light sources, and the more physically accurate the lighting simulation becomes. We'll soon see how to increase the density of this initialization mesh.

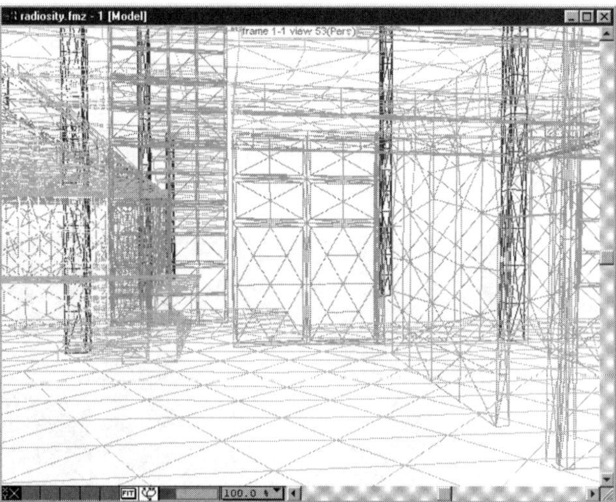

Figure 5.36

Initializing radiosity for the same model and view shown in Figure 5.35.

- Change the display mode to RenderZone. All the surfaces of the model will be fully blacked out—this is because the radiosity calculations haven't yet begun, let alone been completed. Switch back to Wire Frame and go to Display > Generate Radiosity Solution to set the process in motion. For a complex model, the calculations may take quite a bit of time. The slider bar shows the progress of the calculations, and periodically, all the windows get updated to reflect the lighting calculations. These would be visible to you if you were still in the RenderZone display mode, but refreshing the rendered display constantly consumes time and memory, so it's better to remain in the Wire Frame mode.

- Once the calculations are completed, switch the display to RenderZone to see the result. You'll find that the overall lighting is brighter and more realistic as compared to the non-radiosity rendering you saved earlier. You might, however, find some deficiencies in the radiosity rendering such as jagged edges, spots, and so on, which we'll soon learn to fix.

- Now switch to another view of the model and refresh the RenderZone display. You'll find that the new view takes hardly any time to render. This is because the radiosity calculations are, by default, performed for the whole model and are therefore view independent. Thus, once the solution is generated, any number of views can be rendered very quickly, taking even less time than a new view takes to render outside radiosity.

- To leave the radiosity mode, select Exit Radiosity from the Display menu. A dialog will pop up, asking you whether you want to save or discard the current radiosity solution. Choose the Discard Solution option for now, as we still want to explore various radiosity parameters. You'll be returned to the regular modeling environment in which all the tools are activated and accessible.

3.2 Other Radiosity Basics

We've gone through one complete radiosity cycle, comprising initialization, generation, rendering, and exit. Before moving on to look at the radiosity options in detail in the next section, it's important to understand a few other basic aspects of radiosity.

- Create and activate a point and a cone light in your model; at the same time, turn off any distant lights that are shining. Initialize and generate the radiosity solution, as you learned in the last section.

- After the radiosity solution has been generated, switch to the Shaded Render rather than the RenderZone display. You'll see that the lighting effects of the point and cone lights can also be seen in Shaded Render, which, outside of radiosity, works only with distant lights. This is a clear indication that radiosity effects are achieved by calculations incorporated in the model itself, rather than generated by any rendering technique.

- Now try generating a radiosity solution with a projector light in the scene and you'll find that a cone light is substituted instead of the projector light, and the lighting effects generated accordingly. So if a projector light is essential to your scene, you'll have to settle for a non-radiosity solution.

- Next, modify some of the surface styles of the objects or faces visible in the current radiosity solution, using the Surface Styles palette. As soon as you make a change, you'll be warned that the changes will only be reflected in the radiosity solution from that point on; click OK in response. Now refresh the display and you'll find that the surface style changes have been incorporated, *without* requiring the radiosity solution to be regenerated. This is of great advantage, letting you fine-tune your surface styles without going through the time-consuming process of regeneration after every minor change.

- With lights, however, it's a different story. Any changes made to the lights that are active for the current solution require the solution to be regenerated. Test this by deactivating a shining light in the Lights palette or changing its color or intensity, and you'll be warned that the solution will have to be discarded and regenerated. The regeneration won't take place automatically—you have to select the Generate Radiosity Solution command after you've finished making all the desired modifications.

- Recall from Workshop 3 (Personalizing Your Environment) that there are some radiosity options located in the Preferences dialog. To access these, go to Edit > Preferences and select Radiosity from the listing on the left. You'll see three radiosity preferences on the right, of which the first two are selected by default. You can deselect the first option if you don't wish to be warned before entering or exiting radiosity.

- Pay special attention to the second option, Save Solution In Project File. This will save the current radiosity solution when you save the file, *provided you're still in radiosity mode*. To test this, exit the Preferences dialog and while you're still in radiosity mode, go to File > Save A Copy As. This will let you save a copy of the current file under a different name. Then exit radiosity, thereby deleting the radiosity solution, and save the original file. Switch to the desktop and compare the file sizes of the original file and the copy you created. You'll find that the copy is substantially larger than the original, since it has the radiosity solution stored within it. Open up the copy in form•Z and select the Generate Radiosity Solution command. This will simply load the saved radiosity solution from the file, without needing it to be recalculated. It's convenient to do this once you've finalized both the project model and the radiosity solution, and don't anticipate making any more changes to either of them.

- Get back to the Preferences dialog and look at the third radiosity preference, Preserve Solution During Working Session, which is deselected by default. This explains why the radiosity solution gets deleted every time you exit the radiosity mode. If you want the solution to be preserved, simply check this option. However, considering that the radiosity solution has to be regenerated from scratch if any change is made to the model or to the lights, there's not much advantage to preserving the solution during a working session, considering the overhead of a larger file size.

3.3 Radiosity Options

Radiosity has a large number of options, both for the processes of initialization as well as generation, which, as you've seen, take place in two distinct stages. These options can be manipulated to reduce the time required to produce a solution in the initial stages, when you're still in the process of experimentation, and later, to increase the quality of the solution when you're ready to produce a final one. Let's get down to exploring these options.

- Go to Display > Radiosity Options. This opens up the Radiosity Options dialog, shown in Figure 5.37, which contains the Initialization and Generation parameters in separate tabs. Rather than plunging right away into an explanation of what each parameter stands for and exploring how it affects the quality of the solution, let's adopt a different, more convenient approach. Look at the Preset Parameters popup menu located in the lower half of the dialog, below the two tabs. This contains ten numbers, each corresponding with different preset values of the various radiosity parameters that will produce different qualities of the solution. It's set to 6 by default.

- Start by setting Preset Parameters to 1, which will produce the lowest quality solution in the least amount of time. Notice how this changes the default values of the various Initialization and Generation parameters. Then exit the dialog, generate a radiosity solution, and display it in RenderZone. Compare the quality of the solution, as well as the time taken to generate it, with the results you obtained in the last section. The quality might be so poor that it may never make sense to use this preset parameter, even if the solution is generated instantaneously.

- Repeat this process by setting Preset Parameters to increasingly higher values, and notice how all the Initialization and Generation parameters change in response. This will give you a good understanding of how they affect the quality of the solution. Generate and render the radiosity solution for each preset parameter to see the results visually. Preset parameters of 9 and 10 might take too long to complete, depending upon the complexity of your model and the capabilities of your computer. In that case, simply observe the maximum values acquired by each parameter and remember to stay below these numbers when you choose to specify your own parametric values.

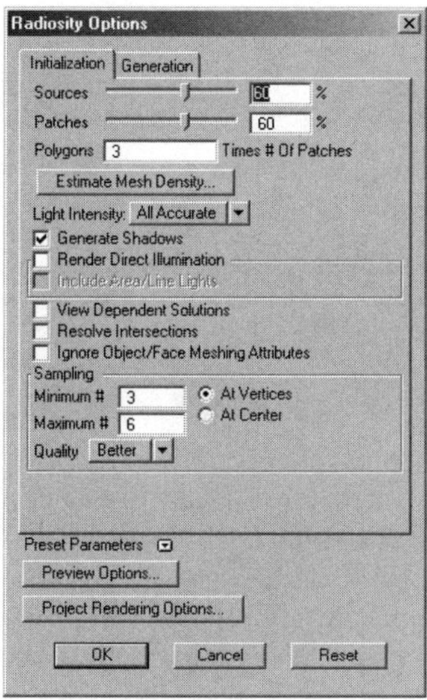

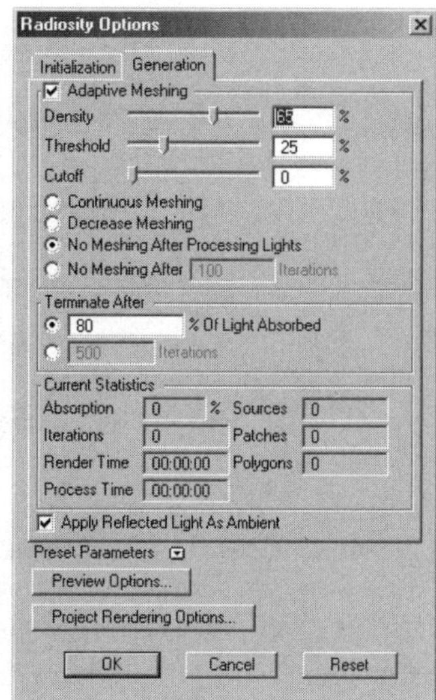

Figure 5.37

The Radiosity Options dialog, showing both the Initialization and Generation tabs.

In many cases, the preset parametric values will be sufficient to enable you to produce the kind of radiosity solution that you need, and you don't necessarily have to know what each individual parameter in the Radiosity Options dialog stands for. These will be discussed in the rest of this section, and you can just briefly skim through it for now if you want to get on with the rest of the workshop. Do come back to study it in detail, though, when you're ready for a better understanding of the radiosity parameters.

- Let's start with the Initialization parameters. There are two kinds of mesh density values you can modify. Sources deals with the subdivisions of the area light sources in the model, while Patches refers to the subdivisions of all object surfaces, which, as you've seen, are secondary light sources in radiosity. The level of subdivision for each of these two parameters can be modified by using the accompanying slider bar or numerically specifying a percentage value. The larger the number of subdivisions, the better the quality of the solution, but the greater the processing time.

- The subdivisions for both area lights and object surfaces can be further increased by using the next option. The value you enter for Polygons indicates how many more polygons will be generated on top of the initial source and patch subdivisions. To get an estimate of the number of sources, patches, and mesh polygons before the radiosity mesh is initialized, click on the Estimate Mesh Density button.

- The Light Intensity option should be familiar to you from the RenderZone Options dialog. Check the Generate Shadows if you want the radiosity solution to include shadows. The radiosity process, unlike the regular rendering methods, usually doesn't produce very crisp shadows, unless you use a high density initialization mesh. It's more suited to capturing the distribution of reflected light accurately. By selecting the next option, Render Direct Illumination, the computation of the direct illumination in a scene isn't done within radiosity, but is postponed until the solution is rendered using the Shaded Render or RenderZone displays. This combines the best of the radiosity and non-radiosity techniques, leading to crisper shadow boundaries in the final solution. The accompanying sub-option, Include Area/Line Lights, can be selected to specify that area and line lights be treated as direct illumination and rendered outside radiosity. However, since area and line lights don't usually cause sharp shadow boundaries, it's more efficient to leave this sub-option turned off.

(a) Original Solution

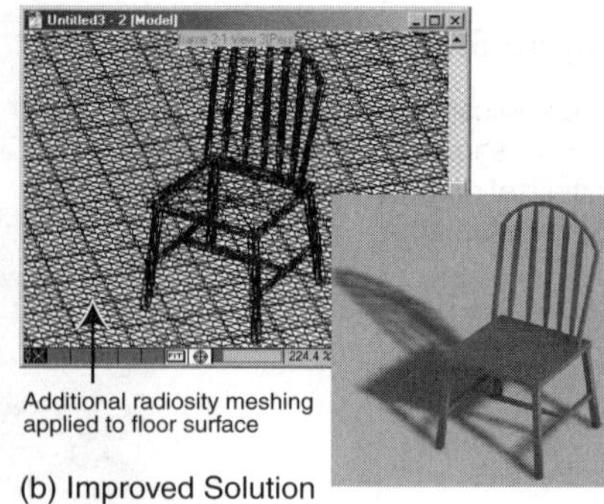

(b) Improved Solution

Figure 5.38

Improving the quality of the shadows in a radiosity solution by applying dense radiosity meshing only to the floor surface where the shadows will be cast.

- By default, a radiosity solution is calculated for an entire project, so it can be seen simultaneously in multiple views. In other words, it is view independent. One way of reducing the time required to produce a high quality solution, particularly when you're only interested in a single view, is to check the View Dependent Solution option. The solution will now be calculated only for the active view, and will take less time than if it were being calculated for the whole project.

- The Resolve Intersections option, when activated, improves the quality of the solution by splitting up patches that happen to intersect with other patches. This will lead to less jagged edges, cleaner shadow lines, and no shadow leaks in the solution. It will, however, increase the processing time considerably.

- One useful technique for improving the quality of a radiosity solution substantially, without adding exponentially to the time required to generate it, is to apply a highly dense mesh only to those surfaces on which shadows are expected to be cast (see Figure 5.38). This is done with the Rendering Attributes tool, which will be covered in Exercise 5. Low density specifications can be set in the Radiosity Options dialog for the remaining surfaces. The radiosity calculations will then proceed taking into account these different density values, unless you check the Ignore Object/ Face Meshing Attribute option, in which case all surfaces will be subdivided according to the same mesh density specified in this dialog.

- The final set of parameters for Initialization has to do with Sampling, which determines how the lighting calculations are performed with respect to each source or patch polygon. For each polygon, a number of randomly selected sample points is chosen for emitting the light that is supposed to leave that polygon. The Minimum # and Maximum # of these sample points has to be specified. In addition to how light leaves a polygon, you can also control how light is recorded when it arrives at a polygon. At Vertices will record the light intensity at each vertex of the polygon, while At Center records it only at the center. As you may have noticed when exploring the preset parameters, vertex sampling is more accurate and used when higher quality solutions are required. Under Sampling, you can also choose between three different levels of lighting quality available in the Quality popup menu: Simple will use the minimum number of sample points specified, while Best will use the maximum.

- Now move on to look at the Generation parameters, the first of which is Adaptive Meshing. When this option is turned on, the mesh produced by the initialization process is further subdivided during the generation process, leading to a better quality solution. The extent to which the subdivision occurs depends upon the values of the next three parameters. A higher Density value will create more subdivisions—a value of 80% is adequate for high quality images, and you should be wary of exceeding this limit. The Threshold parameter determines when a mesh polygon will be subdivided based on intensity differences with adjacent polygons—the lower this value, the greater the subdivision. The third parameter, Cutoff, is used to control mesh subdivision in poorly illuminated areas which don't need dense meshing—a higher value reduces the mesh density in such dark areas.

- The next set of four mutually exclusive options determines the sensitivity of the mesh subdivision as the generation process progresses. Continuous Meshing ensures the highest quality solution but may be inefficient and needlessly time-consuming, since it also leads to high mesh density in areas of small contrast where it's not necessary. Decrease Meshing, which reduces the meshing density as the solution progresses, is a better option, being a good compromise between speed and quality. No Meshing After Processing Lights takes even less time since meshing is stopped after all the area sources have emitted their light; the quality of the image might still be acceptable. The last option lets you stop the meshing process after a specified number of Iterations. A single iteration is defined by a single area source or secondary source patch emitting its light to all the other subdivisions of the radiosity mesh.
- The next two Terminate After conditions are very important since they're used to determine when the generation process will stop and the solution will be completed. You can choose to stop when a specified percentage of the total light in the scene has been absorbed—a value of around 85% will yield a high quality solution within a reasonable amount of time. Alternately, you can specify a desired number of iterations that the solution must go through before terminating.

During the actual process of generating a radiosity solution, the process can be terminated manually at any time by pressing the usual stop-processing keys—command+period (Mac), Ctrl+period (PC), or Esc (Mac or PC).

- The Current Statistics section displays several important aspects of the generation process of the previously executed solution. It's useful when the radiosity solution is being generated in an iterative manner. Based on the values displayed for one attempt, e.g., for Iterations, the termination conditions for the next attempt can be set to stop after a larger number of iterations, if a higher quality solution is desired.
- The last Generation parameter is Apply Reflected Light As Ambient. This option is turned on by default, causing reflected light which isn't yet recorded to be applied as ambient light to all the mesh subdivisions. This causes a scene to appear brighter in the initial stages of the generation process than it would be if the option was turned off. The difference between the two scenarios will reduce as the solution progresses and more and more of the light gets absorbed.
- You've already explored the Preset Parameters popup menu located below the Initialization and Generation tabs. Below this is the Preview Options button. This invokes a dialog where you can adjust the parameters that determine the quality of radiosity solution preview in the graphics window and the frequency with which its progress gets updated. And finally, the Project Rendering Options button takes you to the same dialog you studied in Section 2.6 of Workshop 3 (Personalizing Your Environment).

This marks the end of our exercise on radiosity. Keep in mind that a radiosity rendering isn't guaranteed to always be better than a non-radiosity rendering. For instance, textures with bumps don't render well in radiosity. Therefore, generate both radiosity and non-radiosity renderings for a scene, compare the results, and then pick the one that best captures the effect you wish to achieve. You can also simulate the effect of radiosity, without actually running it, by positioning low-intensity distant lights at strategic locations in a scene.

EXERCISE 4

A Closer Look at Textures

In Section 1.2 of Workshop 3 (Personalizing Your Environment), you briefly went through the process of creating a new surface style (which will here be referred to as a *texture*) using the Surface Styles Parameters dialog. You saw how you can create almost an infinite variety of textures by choosing different shaders for the Color, Reflection, Transparency, and Bump attributes, and making further modifications in the Options dialog for each shader. As you work with textures to produce realistic renderings of your models, you'll find that one of the biggest challenges is to scale and position a texture accurately on the surface of an object. Exercise 4 is devoted to understanding this and other texture-related issues, such as mapping an external image to an object as a texture, and applying multiple textures to the same surface.

4.1 Scaling Textures

- Open a new form•Z project. You'll start by creating a new surface style. Click on the blank space in the lower part of the Surface Styles palette to invoke the Surface Style Parameters dialog. For the Color attribute of the new style, choose the Checker shader from the third group of the pulldown menu. Make sure you don't choose the Checker option from the fourth group, which is a solid texture rather than a wrapped texture like the first Checker option. (You'll see the difference between the two types of textures later.) Leave Reflection, Transparency, and Bump to the default values. Give the new style an appropriate name, say "Checks."

- Click on the Options button for the Checker color shader to open its dialog (Figure 5.39-a). Examine the options and change the two checker colors to different ones if you like. Don't, however, change the Scale value for now. What you see in the preview area is referred to as a single *tile* of the texture.

Figure 5.39

Scaling a texture. The Checker Options dialog for the texture is also shown.

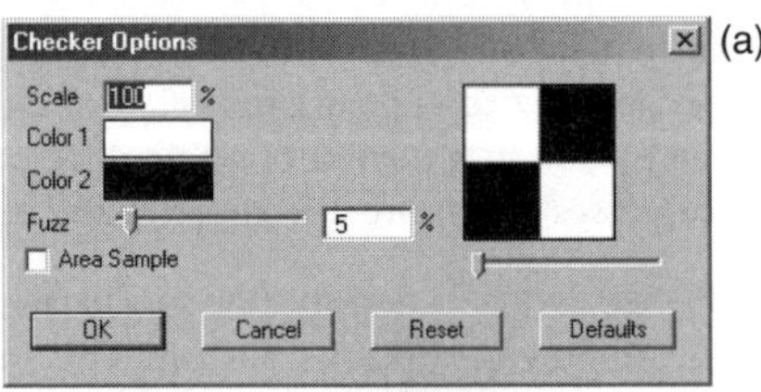

(a)

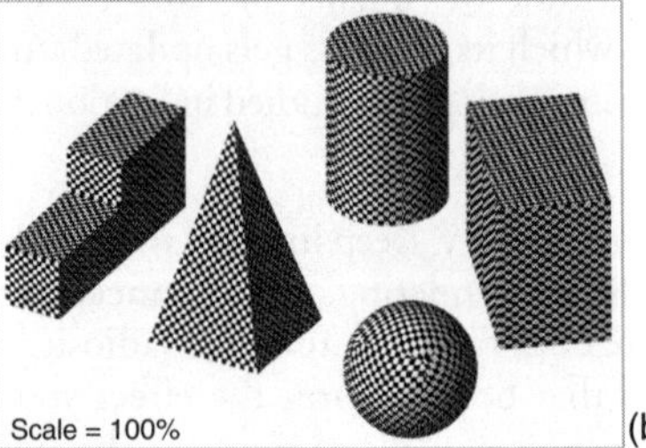

(b)

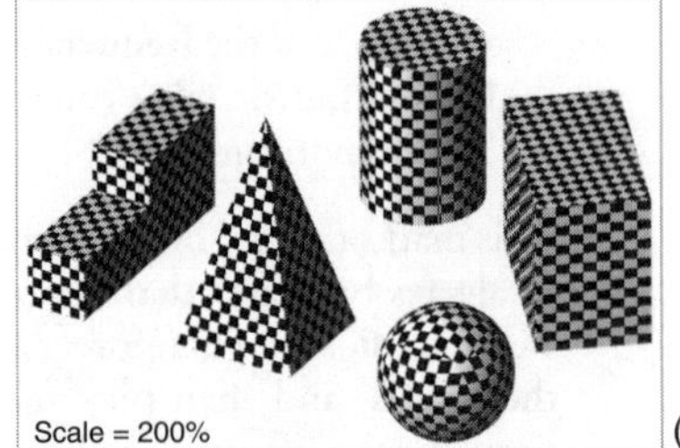

(c)

- Exit both the Checker Options dialog and then the Surface Styles Parameters dialog by clicking on their respective OK buttons. With this new surface style, create a few simple objects and switch to the RenderZone display mode (Figure 5.39-b). Notice that an individual tile of the texture is quite small in proportion to the size of the object. (Of course, you could have different results depending upon the size of the objects you create.)

- There's one simple and immediate method to increase the tile size. Double-click on the Checks style you just created in the Surface Styles palette and invoke the Checker Options dialog again. Change the Scale value to 200%, return to the graphics window, and regenerate the RenderZone display. You'll find that the tile size has doubled from what it was earlier (Figure 5.39-c).

As a quick fix, what we just did was fine. But what if we wanted to specify the exact size of a single tile of the texture? (And where is it coming from anyway?) What if we also wanted to orient the texture differently on different surfaces and on different objects? We can do all this and more by utilizing a special tool in the modeling tool palette devoted to this task, called the Texture Map tool.

4.2 Precise Texture Mapping

- First, go back and reset the Scale of the Checks style back to 100%. Then select the Texture Map tool (M-Tool:14a,4), and apply it to one of your objects. This will invoke the Texture Map Controls dialog for that object, containing various options for precisely adjusting how the texture is *mapped* on the faces of the object (Figure 5.40).

- At the top, left corner of the dialog is the preview window, showing the object along with the *shape* based on which the texture is mapped—referred to as the *mapping type*—and its origin. The mapping type will be explored in detail shortly. You're already familiar with all the tool icons located at the base of the preview window. Set the display of the preview window to Wire Frame, and check the Draw Tiles option below the window. This will display the actual tiles of the texture, which is convenient for its manipulation, as shown in Figure 5.40. You can occasionally switch the preview display to RenderZone to check how the texture mapping actually looks.

- Let's now see how to adjust the size of the tiles. Turn to the Wrapped Textures section to the right of the preview window. (Recall that you chose the *wrapped* Checker style rather than the *solid* Checker style when you defined the surface style, Checks.) Ignore Mapping Type for now. Instead, look at the Horizontal Tiling and Vertical Tiling options. Here, you can change both the horizontal and vertical sizes of a texture tile from the default values. Do so. To enable different horizontal and vertical values, change the Lock Size To option from Square Tile to None. The changes will be immediately reflected in the preview window (Figure 5.40-a). Ideally, you should choose tile sizes that are proportionate to the dimensions of your object.

- You might also like to change the orientation of the texture. As you can see from the axes display in the preview window, a texture map has its own coordinate system that determines how the texture will be mapped. The origin of this system, by default, lies at the center of the object, and its axes are parallel to the world coordinate axes. Thus, for an object not parallel to the axes, like the one shown in Figure 5.40, the tiles will be positioned non-orthogonally on some faces, such as the top and bottom faces of the sample object. This problem can be fixed by aligning the origin and axes of the texture map *with* the object: either numerically by changing the Origin and Rotation values located at the top of the dialog, or graphically by using the Pointer tool to move the origin and rotate the axes in the preview window. Try both methods, and observe the changes in how the texture gets mapped (Figure 5.40-b). You can always reset the Origin and Rotation values back to the defaults, if required, by using the associated Reset button.

- There are two points you should note when manipulating the origin and axes graphically. The Snap option below the preview window, which is checked by default, allows you to snap to the points, midpoints, and segments of the object, making the task of moving the origin and rotating the axes easier. Also, you cannot rotate the *current* axis of rotation that is shown in red in the preview window. Thus, if Y is the current axis, you can rotate only the X and Z axes about the Y axis. To change the current axis, go to the Axis/Plane popup menu, located just above the surface style preview window in the lower left corner of the dialog. Here, you can change the current axis, depending upon which one you'd like to rotate the other two axes about.

- Now that you know how to adjust the origin of the texture coordinate system according to your requirements, proceed to explore the Center and Mirror options for both Horizontal Tiling and Vertical Tiling. As is obvious from their names, Center will center the tile in one or both directions relative to the origin, while Mirror will mirror the tile in one or both directions. Both are off by default.

- Move on to look at the Mapping Type for Wrapped Textures, which determines how the texture will actually be wrapped around the object. As you saw in Figure 5.40, the default mapping type is Cubic. This is reflected by the shape of the mapping area in the preview window. You can deselect the Show Object option momentarily to have a better look at this shape.

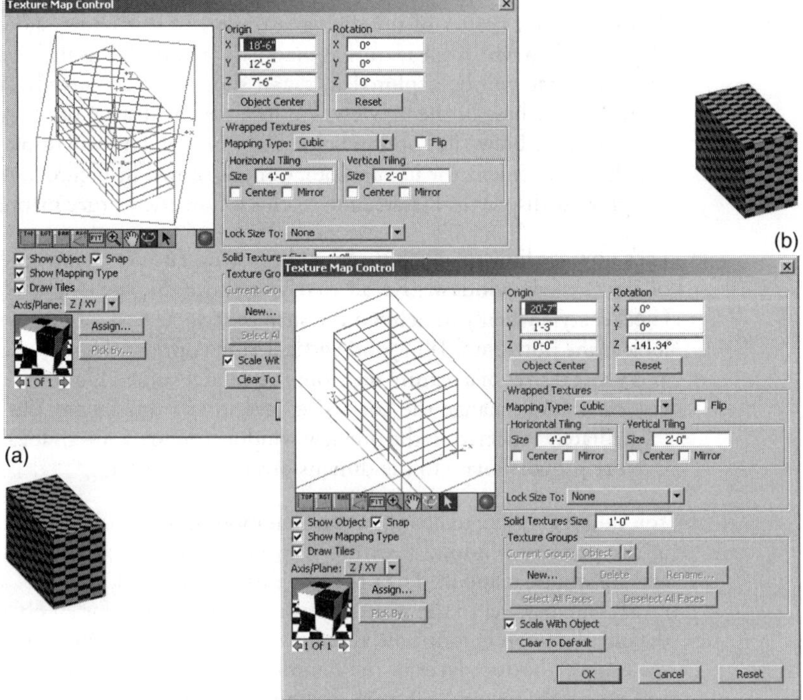

Figure 5.40

Working with the Texture Map Control dialog. (a) Changing the tile sizes from the defaults. (b) Aligning the origin and axes of the texture map with the object instead of the world coordinate system.

Figure 5.41

A comparison between Cubic and other mapping types for objects of various shapes.

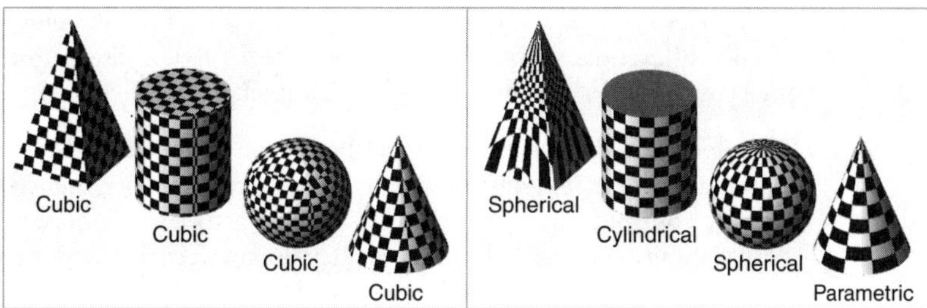

- Switch to the Flat, Cylindrical, and Spherical mapping types in turn by selecting them from the Mapping Type popup menu. For each mapping type, notice the change in the shape of the mapping area in the preview window. While the Cubic, Cylindrical, and Spherical mapping types wrap the texture around the object in the shape of a cube, cylinder, and sphere respectively, the Flat type places the texture along a single plane rather than wrapping it around the object. The default placement plane is XY, but you can reorient the texture map either numerically or graphically, as you learned a short while ago.

- Each mapping type also has different tiling options. For Flat and Cubic, the tile sizes are specified in terms of distance, for Spherical, they're measured in angles, while Cylindrical uses distance vertically and angles horizontally. The Flat, Cylindrical, and Spherical mapping types also give you the option of specifying the total number of tiles in one or both directions, rather than the tile sizes. Experiment with changes in these and see how they explore the resulting textures.

- The kind of mapping type you choose will usually depend upon the shape of the object to which the texture is being applied. Thus, cylindrical mapping is the obvious choice for cylindrical objects, spherical for spherical objects, and so on. Of course, you can also deliberately select a mapping type that's different from the shape of the object to get some interesting results, as illustrated in Figure 5.41. Flat mapping is most useful for mapping textures to individual faces rather than the entire object, a procedure that will be covered in Section 4.4.

- The next mapping type, Parametric, applies only to smooth objects. To explore it, create a smooth object—a cone for instance—in the same Checks surface style, and apply the Texture Map tool to it. Set the Mapping Type to Parametric. You'll find that the tile sizes are now specified as a percentage value, which indicates the extent to which a tile will wrap around the object surface. A size of 100% will wrap one tile around the surface for that direction, while a size of 50% will wrap two tiles, and so on. You can, of course, conveniently just specify the number of tiles required in both directions. The cone in Figure 5.41 with Parametric mapping has 5 tiles horizontally and vertically.

- There's only one remaining mapping type, UV Coordinates. This "freezes" the horizontal (U) and vertical (V) values of the current texture mapping on the object and stores them at the vertices. Thereafter, the scale of the texture on the object can be changed by simply expressing the two Size values as a percentage of the original values. This is useful once the texture mapping of an object has been finalized and you want to prevent it from being accidentally changed.

- Let's now look at solid textures and see how they differ from wrapped textures, whose options we've been exploring all this time. You can apply a solid texture to the current object without exiting the Texture Map Controls dialog—simply click on the Assign button located in the lower left corner. This will invoke the Surface Styles dialog you explored in Section 1.3 of Workshop 3 (Personalizing Your Environment). Click on the New button to create a new surface style, and this time, select the Checker shader in the fourth group for the Color attribute. Change its colors to visually differentiate it from the wrapped Checks style. Return to the Texture Map Controls dialog once your selection of the new style is complete.

- Your object now has a solid texture rather than a wrapped texture. It's not easy to tell the difference since the Wrapped Textures options are not grayed out. Also, the Tiled display option in the preview window continues to show the tiles according to the wrapped textures specifications. Change these settings, and you will find that they don't affect the rendering of the object. But now make a change to the Solid Textures Size value, located below the Wrapped Textures section, and it will be reflected in the Rendered display (Figure 5.42). You can see that a solid texture isn't wrapped two-dimensionally about an object but exists as a textured block in 3D space. It's almost as if the object is carved out of the material that the texture is made up of. A solid texture, unlike a wrapped texture, has a single tile dimension along all three axes, which you just changed. However, it does have a coordinate system that you can modify by making changes to the Origin and Rotation values, as you did before for wrapped textures.

- There are a few remaining options in the Texture Map Control dialog which we'll explore over the next three sections. For now, experiment further with all the options you've learned. When you're satisfied with the texture mapping of the object you see in the preview window, click OK to apply all the changes you've made and return to the modeling environment. Edit the texture maps of the remaining objects in a similar fashion, choosing different surface styles, mapping types for wrapped textures, coordinate systems of the texture maps, and tile sizes.

- Back in the graphics window, double-click on the Texture Map tool in the modeling tool palette. This will invoke a dialog containing essentially the same options as those you've just explored in the Texture Map Control dialog. The only difference is that in the Texture Map Options dialog, you are specifying the default mapping characteristics that will be applied to every newly created object. If you want the settings in this dialog to overwrite the texture map settings of existing objects when they are selected with the Texture Map tool, you would check the Adjust to New Parameters option. However, in most cases you wouldn't want this, so leave the option unchecked, as it is by default.

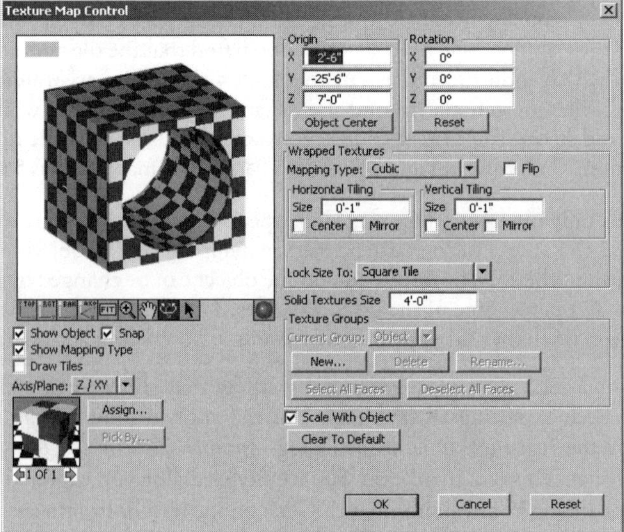

Figure 5.42

Applying a solid texture to an object.

4.3 Transformations to Textured Objects

- Textured objects retain their texture mapping for geometric transformations such as Move, Rotate, and Mirror, since these transformations don't change the shape of the object. But other operations such as scaling, moving a point or a face, creating a hole, and so on, which change the shape of the object, necessitate a change in the shape of the texture map as well. Apply some of these transformations to the textured objects you just created, and notice how, in most cases, the texture map reshapes itself appropriately without having to be reapplied.

- Look at the scaling operation in particular. Observe that if an object is scaled using either of the Scale tools on Row 13, the texture gets scaled with the object by default. If you'd like the object to always retain the original size of the texture, reapply the Texture Map tool to it and deselect the Scale With Object option that appears at the base of the Texture Map Control dialog. Scaling will now change the shape of the object but not the size of the texture. Notice that the Scale With Object option is grayed out for UV Coordinates because this mapping type will always scale the texture with respect to the object.

- If you transform the shape of a facetted object by moving a point, segment, or face, the results are not the same as those you'd get if you scaled the object. Figure 5.43 shows a comparison. The Scale With Object option was selected for the facetted cylindrical object, therefore when its height is reduced using the Scale tool (M-Tool:13a,3), the texture is scaled down in the Z direction. However, when its height is reduced by moving the top face down, the texture isn't scaled but retains its proportions, and also "spills" onto the top face. Watch out for results such as these and be aware of what is causing the difference.

SCALE

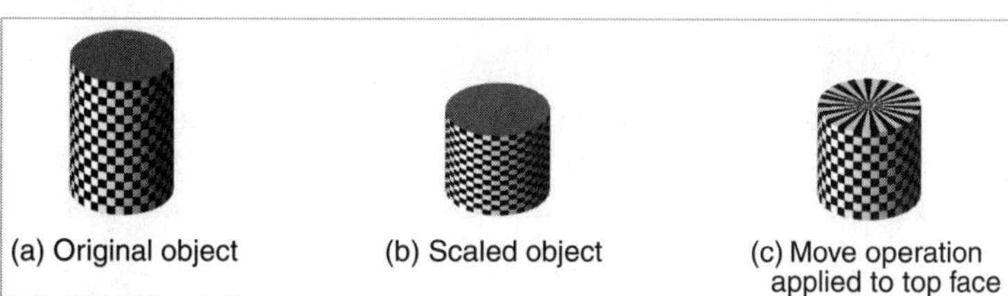

Figure 5.43

Different results in texture map scaling, depending upon the method used for transforming the object.

4.4 Mapping Textures to Individual Faces

So far, you've been making adjustments to the texture mapping of an object as a whole. But sometimes, different faces of an object have different textures applied to them that need to be adjusted individually. You could also have the same texture applied to all the faces of an object, but need different mapping for different faces. The Texture Map tool lets you map textures to the individual faces of an object as well.

- Create an object for which you need one or more faces to have a different texture map from the rest of the object. Use the Color tool, with the topological level set to Face, to change the surface style of these faces as required. You could also make such changes directly in the Texture Map Control dialog, as we will see.

- Select the object with the Texture Map tool, and change the display of the preview window to RenderZone. Since you have changed some of the individual face colors, you'll see the different textures of the object in the display (Figure 5.44). Notice also the surface style display at the lower left corner of the dialog. If the object has a total of two surface styles, it would say 1 Of 2 below the surface style display and give you the option to view the second one by clicking on the forward arrow button. Moreover, any of these surface styles can be edited directly by double-clicking on its display here. Keep in mind, though, that these changes will affect all the objects to which that style has been applied.

- You can make the usual changes to the mapping type, tile sizes, and the position and orientation of the coordinate system. These will affect the entire object, including the face or faces to which a different texture has been applied. Try it.

- What we would now like to do is manipulate the texture map only on the faces of the object that have a different texture. To do this, we need to create a new *texture group* that is comprised only of those faces. Turn to the section called Texture Groups in the lower right portion of the Texture Map Control dialog. We haven't created any groups yet, so the Current Group popup menu is deactivated. To create a new group, click on the New button. For a parametric object, you'll get a warning message telling you that the object type will be converted to plain. Click OK to proceed, and overwrite the default texture group name if you like.

- Change the display of the preview window to Wire Frame. You'll see that all the faces of the object are now grayed out, indicating that the newly created texture group is currently empty. You now need to add to this group all the faces whose texture is to be mapped separately. There are two ways to do this. Click on the Pick By button, located next to the surface style display at the base of the dialog. This lets you pick a surface style from all of those present in the object, and automatically selects the faces that have that style. Alternately, you can use the Pointer tool to select the required faces. Use either technique to select the faces with a different texture for the new texture group (Figure 5.45).

- Make some changes to the mapping type, tile sizes, and so on, and see the changes in the tiles in Wire Frame display, and in the RenderZone Display. You'll find that these changes affect only the faces that are contained in the new texture group.

Figure 5.44

The Texture Map Control dialog for an object that has two surface styles—one for the object, and the other for one of its faces.

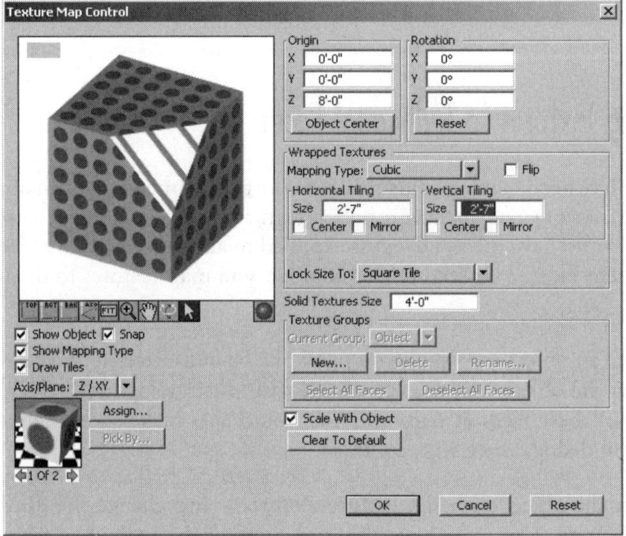

Figure 5.45

Applying the Flat mapping type to a texture group comprising only the face shown in Figure 5.44 that has a different texture. The origin and rotation of the axes were modified so as to be aligned with that face.

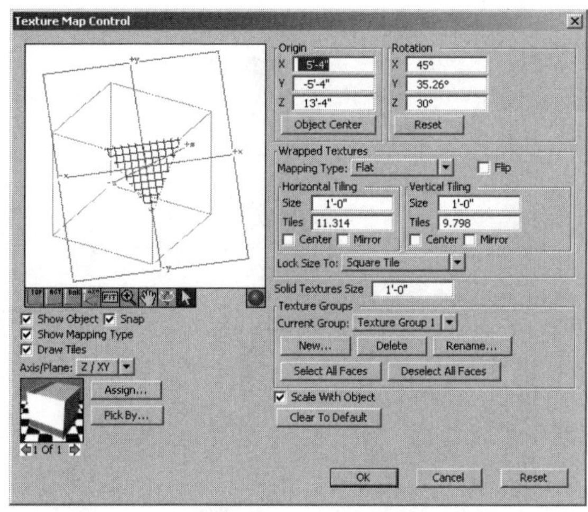

- Let's now see how to manipulate the texture map on an individual face, using the Flat mapping type. If there are multiple faces selected, use the Pointer tool to deselect them until you have only a single face in the texture group. Change the mapping type to Flat. It would help if the texture coordinate system were to be aligned with the selected face (as in Figure 5.45) instead of the complete object. Try to do this by moving the origin and rotating the axes—you'll find that it's not an easy task.

- Fortunately, there's a convenient shortcut. Deselect the face using the Pointer tool. Now holding down the option key (Mac) or Ctrl+Shift keys (PC), select the face. You'll find that the origin has shifted to the center of the face, the X and Y axes are on the face, and the Z axis is perpendicular to it (Figure 5.45). You may still want to modify the exact orientation of the X and Y axes, but this is much easier now since the Z axis doesn't have to be changed. (Remember to ensure that the Axis/Plane is set to Z/XY.) You can also simply move the origin to one of the corners of the face if necessary. Now that the texture coordinate system is aligned with the face, see how easy it is to control the mapping using the Flat mapping options.

- Continue to create different texture groups for different faces, or groups of faces, of the same object in this manner, and apply separate mapping techniques to them. Then switch back to the original texture group, Object, and see how all the faces assigned to other groups are no longer part of this group. Keep in mind also that the RenderZone display in the preview window will always show the complete object. Individual mapping and tiling of the different texture groups can be seen in the Wire Frame display with the Draw Tiles option turned on. Other options in the Texture Map Control dialog such as Assign, Scale With Object, and so on, work in the same manner for texture groups as they did for the entire object.

4.5 Image Mapping

In Workshop 3, you saw how the Surface Style Parameters dialog lets you create an enormous variety of surface styles using various permutations of the Color, Reflection, Transparency, and Bump attributes. For each one of these attributes, it's also possible to use an external image, adding infinitely to the numbers of textures you can create and apply to your objects. In this section, we'll explore image mapping for the four attributes of a surface style.

Figure 5.46

Preparing to model a picture frame. (a) The image that will be used. (b) The body of the frame.

- Let's start with a simple application of using an external image for the Color attribute—the modeling of a picture frame for a room interior. Locate an image that you can use for the picture frame, or scan a photograph to convert it to a digital file in a format that form•Z can read. Find out the dimensions of your image, either by viewing it in form•Z using File > View File or by using any image-editing program, and calculate the aspect ratio. Thus, for the example shown in Figure 5.46-a, the ratio of the width to the height would be 1200:1770, or 0.68:1.

- Model the body of the picture frame in form•Z, taking care to maintain the same aspect ratio as the image, so that the final mapping isn't distorted. The inset for the picture can be created using the Insert Hole mode (M-Tool:2b,3), as shown in Figure 5.46-b. For this object, use a surface style appropriate to the body of the frame.

- You'll now create a surface style that uses the image shown in Figure 5.46-a, instead of a plain color or any other texture. Invoke the Surface Styles Parameters dialog for defining a new style and select the Color Map shader for the Color attribute, the very last item in its popup menu. Click on the accompanying Options button and you'll see a Color Map Options dialog that's similar to the one you encountered when working with the RenderZone display options in Exercise 1. Click on the Load button to load your image file instead of the default logo image. In the Repetitions section, select 1 Times and the Center option, both Horizontally and Vertically. Then click OK to exit the dialog. In the preview window of the surface style, you'll see this image wrapped on all sides of the default cubical shape.

- The next step is to apply this style only to that face of the frame object where the image should appear. Use the Color tool at the Face topological level to do this. Check the effect by switching to the RenderZone display mode. As you'd expect, the image won't be correctly sized to fit exactly on the selected face, so you'll have to resort to the Texture Map tool to make the necessary adjustments.

- Select the frame object with the Texture Map tool, and create a new Texture Group consisting only of the face on which the image is being mapped, as you learned to do in the last section. Switch to the Flat mapping type for the new texture group, adjust the origin and orientation of the axes so that image map is correctly positioned on the face, and finally, specify a tile size that matches the face dimensions (see Figure 5.47). At the end of all these steps, you should have the image correctly mapped on the desired face, as shown.

Figure 5.47

Using the Texture Map Control dialog to accurately map an image on the inset face of the frame object.

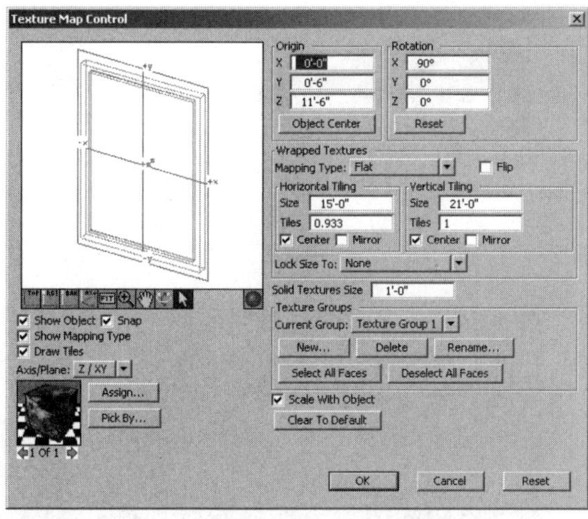

- Let's now see how to use an external image for the other attributes of a surface style, which enables you to create extremely interesting rendering effects. Locate a relatively simple image, or create one using a drawing or painting program, ensuring that it's in a recognizable file format.
- Create four new surface styles as described next, and illustrated in Figure 5.48. For `Style 1`, set the `Color` attribute to `Color Map` and load the selected image. The procedure is identical to what you just did for the picture frame example. Don't forget to select `1 Times` and the `Center` option both `Horizontally` and `Vertically` in the `Repetitions` section of the `Color Map Options` dialog.

Figure 5.48

Four different surface styles created using the same image, but for different attribute shaders.

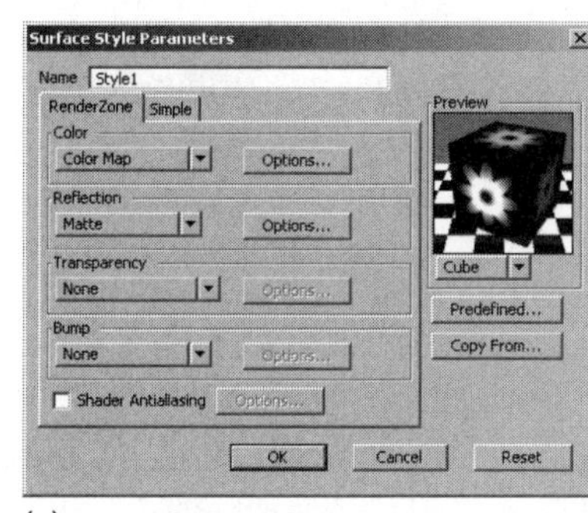

(a)

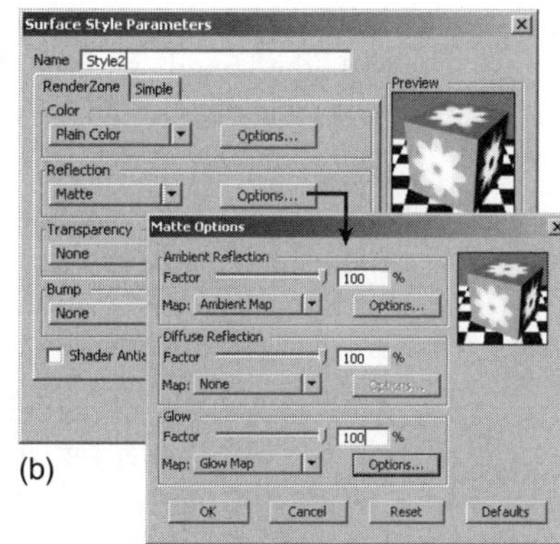

(b)

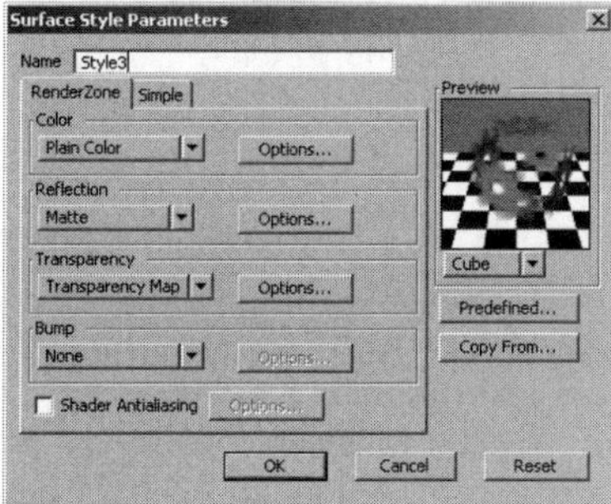

(c)

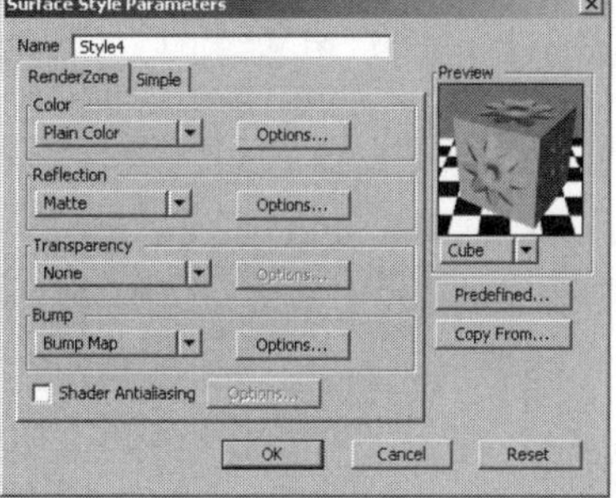

(d)

Figure 5.49

Applying the four different styles shown in Figure 5.48 to four identical boxes, using identical Texture Map settings. (a) With lights activated and project background set to white. (b) With lights deactivated and project background set to black.

- For Style 2, set the Color attribute to any Plain Color other than white. For the Reflection attribute, stick to the Matte shader, but click on the accompanying Options button to set some additional parameters. Set Ambient Reflection to Ambient Map and Glow to Glow Map. Click on the Options button for each, and load the same image with the same settings as you did for the Color image map in Style 1.
- For Style 3, set the Color attribute to any Plain Color other than white and leave Reflection as Matte with the default settings. Set the Transparency attribute to Transparency Map. Click on the accompanying Options button and load the same image.
- For Style 4, set the Color attribute to any Plain Color, the Reflection and Transparency attributes to default values, and the Bump attribute to Bump Map. Click on the Options button for Bump Map and load the same image. In the Repetitions section, select the usual 1 Times and Center options. Additionally, you can adjust the Amplitude to a desired value. A positive value will make the bump project *out* from the surface, while a negative value will project it *into* the surface of the object.
- After you've finished defining the four styles, invoke the dialog of the Texture Map tool, and set the tile size under Wrapped Textures to 8'-0". This will ensure that any new object to which the Texture Map tool is applied has a texture map with a tile size of 8'-0".
- Back in the graphics window, move to a new layer and create a cube with dimensions of 8' by 8' by 8'. Make three more copies of it. Then apply each one of the four styles you just created to the four boxes, and change the display to RenderZone. You can see the contrast in the four styles, all of which were created using the same image but in different ways (Figure 5.49-a).
- You must be wondering what the difference between Style 2 and Style 1 is—they seem identical, except that Style 2 seems to look brighter. To find the answer to this, move to the Lights palette and turn off all the lights in the model, including the sun. (Remember to click on the circular icon rather than on the diamond icon to turn off the Shining attribute of a light.) Change the project background to a dark color and refresh the RenderZone display. You'll find that the box with Style 2 is the most visible one since it's "glowing" in the dark; all the others are blacked out and cannot

be distinguished (see Figure 5.49-b). You can use this technique to create various kinds of glowing effects in your models.

- End this section by exploring various other combinations of predefined textures and external images for the four attributes of Color, Reflection, Transparency, and Bump. You can save all these new styles for use in future projects.

4.6 Decals

So far, you've learned to map predefined textures as well as external images to objects and their surfaces. You've also seen how to apply different textures to different faces of an object by creating texture groups comprising one or more faces. However, you might sometimes need to apply more than one texture to a single face. Rather than create faces within faces to apply different textures to—which can get very tedious—you can use the Decal tool, located immediately after the Texture Map tool, which lets you apply multiple styles to a single face. These styles can even overlap and if some of them are transparent, you'll be able to see the styles that lie underneath them as well! *Decals* is the term for additional styles that are applied to a face or to an object. In this section, we'll learn to work with decals by using two of the four surface styles that were created in the last section.

- Create a cube of size 8'-0", just like the one you used in the last section, in a plain surface style. Then apply the Decal tool (M-Tool:14a,5) to it. You'll be greeted with a message saying that the object has to have at least one texture map control, and asking if you'd like the default controls of the Texture Map tool to be applied to it. Click OK since you've used a plain surface style for the cube, so the kind of mapping won't matter. If you had used a textured style, you should have first ensured that the texture was mapped correctly to the object, before using the Decal tool.

- Applying the Decal tool to an object invokes the Decals dialog (Figure 5.50), which is very similar to the Texture Map Control dialog you've seen. When the dialog first opens up, most of its options are grayed out. This is because no decal has been created as yet for the object. To do so, click on the New button in the lower right part of the dialog. You'll be prompted for the New Decal Name. Stick with the default name if you like. As soon as you've created a new decal, all the options in the Decals dialog get activated. Check the Draw Tiles option, and you'll see the default tiling pattern of the decal. You cannot see the tile in the RenderZone display since it has the same surface style as the object.

- The next step is to select the desired style for this decal, replacing the default style applied to it. Click on the Set Style button in the lower left corner of the dialog and choose Style 4, the style with the bump map you had created earlier (shown in Figure 5.48-d). Set the mapping type to Cubic and the tile size to 8'-0". Also, select the Bumps option and deselect the Color option, both of which are located next to the style preview window. As you can see in Figure 5.50-a, this applies the bump of the texture but not its color to the rendering of the object.

- What you've got so far could easily have been achieved using the Texture Map tool. It's what we'll do next that can be done only with the Decal tool. Create a second decal by clicking again on the New button. For this decal, select Style 2, the style with the transparency map, and change the settings to those shown in Figure 5.50-b. The mapping type should be Cubic and the tile size should be slightly smaller than the size of the top face. In the rendered display, you'll see the transparent texture nicely superimposed on your first "bumped" decal.

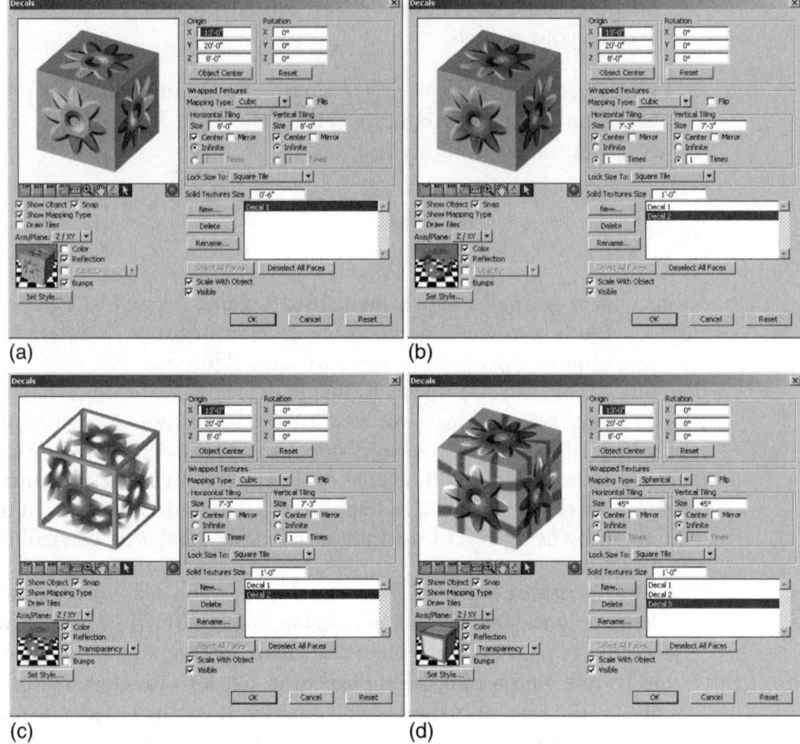

Figure 5.50

Using the Decal tool to apply multiple overlapping surface styles to an object.

- But that's not all you can do with transparent decals—there's more! For the same decal, click on the Opacity box to select it, and choose the Transparency option from the popup menu. The entire box except the edges will be rendered transparent as shown in Figure 5.50-c.

- Set the second decal back to Opacity, and create a third decal. This time, select a style with a predefined texture, such as Grid. If necessary, click on the Set Style button and create a new style in the Surface Styles dialog that's invoked. Apply a Spherical mapping for this decal, with the settings and tile sizes as shown. The final result will be an object with three overlapping decals, as shown in Figure 5.50-d.

- So far, you've been applying decals to the entire object, but keep in mind that you can also apply decals to selected faces. Each time a new decal is created, all the faces of the object are activated by default. Use the Pointer tool to deselect the faces you don't need, or deselect all the faces first and then select the ones you need. You can conveniently use the Select All Faces and Deselect All Faces buttons located below the decal list for selecting and deselecting all the faces respectively.

- To go back and modify the settings of any decal that is already created, simply highlight its name from the decal list. This makes it the active decal whose parameters are listed in the dialog and can be changed. You can Delete or Rename it, if required. You can choose whether or not to scale the decal with the object using the Scale With Object button, just like you did for a regular texture map. You can also choose to temporarily hide the decal, if necessary, by deselecting the Visible button.

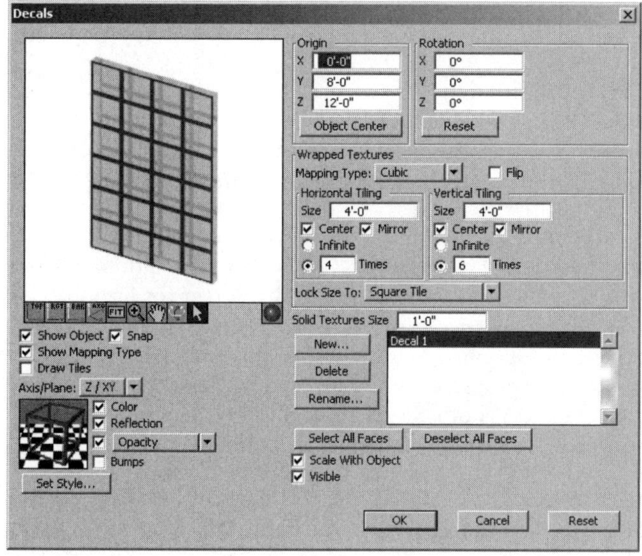

Figure 5.51

Using decals to simulate the appearance of window mullions on a glass pane.

- You can have as many as 32 decals for a single object. Overlapping decals of the kind you've created are rendered in the reverse order in which they appear in the list. Thus, for the object shown in Figure 5.50, Decal 3 will be applied first, followed by Decal 2, and finally Decal 1. You can change the order by dragging a decal to a new position in the list. Experiment with changes in the order and see what happens.

- Another simple application of the use of decals is demonstrated in Figure 5.51—creating mullions on a window pane. A glass surface style was first applied to the pane object. Then a decal was created, using a surface style with both the Color and Transparency attributes set to the Grid shader. It's a simple and fairly effective shortcut, useful when you don't have the time to model the mullions as separate objects.

This marks the end of the exercise on texture mapping. Let's end this workshop by looking at the remaining object properties that we haven't yet covered.

EXERCISE 5

Other Object Properties

We've already worked with most of the tools in both columns of Row 14 of the modeling tool palette—Color, Texture Map, Decal, Ghost, Unghost, and Set Layer—that manipulate various attributes of objects. In this exercise, we'll work with the remaining four attribute tools on this row, starting with Smooth Shade. We'll also look at the related Attributes tool, located after the Query tool on Row 12.

5.1 Smooth Shading

You already encountered the concept of smooth shading when you worked with the Project Rendering Options dialog in Section 2.6 of Workshop 3 (Personalizing Your Environment). Recall that you could limit the smooth shading effect only to those objects which had the "smooth shading attribute" assigned to them. This attribute can be applied to an object using the Smooth Shade tool.

- Select the Smooth Shade tool from the left column of Row 14. Invoke its dialog and select the option, Smooth Shade Object/Face. It has two sub-options, which should be familiar to you from the Project Rendering Options dialog. Recall that the Smooth All Faces option isn't very realistic but can be used for special effects, whereas the Smooth option will operate only on those edges or faces meeting a specified condition, smoothing curved surfaces in a realistic manner. The difference between the two options was illustrated in Figure 3.13 of Workshop 3. Activate one of these options for the Smooth Shade tool, and then apply it to an object. The object will acquire a smooth shading attribute, based on the selected options.

- Remember that to actually see the results of the Smooth Shade tool on an object in the Shaded Render or RenderZone displays, the Smooth Shading option in the Project Rendering Options dialog must be activated.

- To remove the smooth shading attribute from an object, i.e., to make it "flat shaded," simply deselect the Smooth Shade Object/Face option and then apply the Smooth Shade tool to it.

5.2 Rendering Attributes

The next tool in the left column of Row 14 is the Render Attributes tool, which groups together a number of attributes related to how an object will be rendered. You can make changes to these attributes in the dialog of this tool, and then apply the tool to the objects whose rendering attributes are to be changed. Let's see what these attributes are.

- Select the Render Attributes tool (M-Tool:14a,3) and invoke its dialog (Figure 5.52-a). Look at the Options tab. The first modification you can make is to turn on or off the shadow-casting ability of an object. For instance, the base plane in a building model has no other object to cast shadows on, so it would speed up rendering if its shadow-casting ability was turned off and its shadows were not calculated unnecessarily. There's an added advantage to doing this—the shadows *received* by an object which doesn't cast shadows are sharper and crisper.

- Similarly, you could turn off the ability of an object to receive shadows if it was not oriented to do so, or if you didn't want shadows to be displayed on an object for some reason.

- The next two options give you the ability to combine wireframe and shaded displays of objects in the same rendered image. An object can be rendered only in wireframe with the specified line width, or only as a shaded surface, or both in wireframe and with shaded surfaces. All three situations are shown in Figure 5.52-b. As you can see, this effect can be used to create very interesting, unusual, and informative renderings.

- Notice that if the Object Renders as Wireframe option isn't selected, the Object Renders as Shaded Surface option cannot be deselected, and vice versa. In other words, an object must have at least one of these two attributes, if not both.

Figure 5.52

Using the Render Attributes tool. (a) The tool dialog. (b) An image rendered with both wireframe and shaded surfaces.

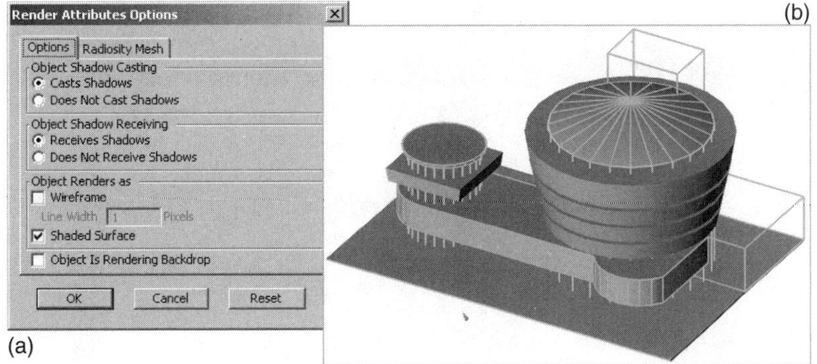

- Recall that the dialogs for both the Shaded Render and RenderZone displays have a Wireframe Width option that we ignored while working with them earlier. This option relates to the wireframe display activated for an object using the Render Attributes tool, for which you can specify different pixel widths, as you've seen. When the image is rendered, you can instruct the display to scale all the wireframes by a certain factor, using the Scale By option. This is useful, for instance, when you're generating the same image at different resolutions, and want to avoid the tedium of reapplying the Render Attributes tool each time to change the wireframe widths of the objects in proportion to the resolution. Alternately, you can instruct the display to ignore all the individual wireframe widths set for various objects and use a single width, by choosing the Set To option for Wireframe Width. Try out both options for an image with some wireframes in the rendering.
- The last option in the Options tab, Object is Rendering Backdrop, applies only when the RenderZone display rendering type is set to Raytrace. As you know, raytracing takes a long time to execute, and you may be able to reduce this time by applying the Object is Rendering Backdrop option to a few selected objects in the scene that do not obscure other objects. For this to work effectively, the number of faces of all objects to which it is applied should not exceed 20. A good candidate for the application of this option is the base plane of a building model that does not obscure any parts of the building and has few faces.
- The options in the Radiosity Mesh tab of the Render Attributes dialog let you apply radiosity meshing to specific objects and faces. These options are similar to what you had encountered in the Radiosity Options dialog in Section 3.3. As you learned in that exercise, you can improve the quality of your radiosity solution and reduce the time required to generate it by applying a dense radiosity mesh only to those surfaces where you expect large variations in light and shadow. A much less dense mesh can be specified in the Radiosity Options dialog for the remaining surfaces.

Remember that after making the desired changes in the Render Attributes dialog, you have to apply this tool to an object to make the specified changes in its attributes.

5.3 Setting and Getting Attributes

There are only two more tools remaining on Row 14 that we haven't yet covered—the related tools of Set Attributes and Get Attributes. Let's see what they can do for us.

Figure 5.53

The dialog of the Set Attributes tool.

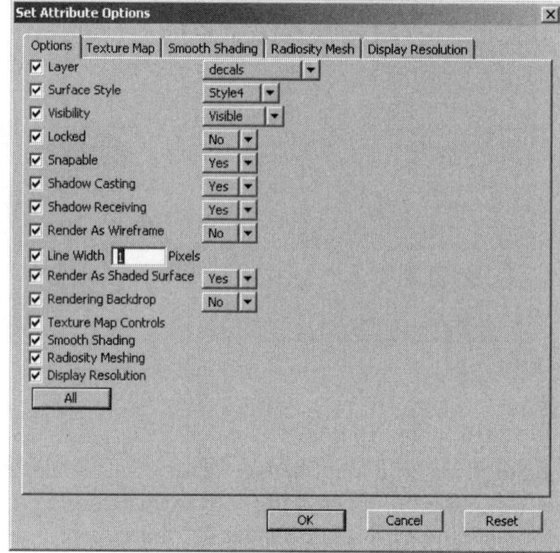

- The Set Attributes tool allows you to modify some or all attributes of an object in a single step. Select this tool and open its dialog. You'll find various options categorized in five different tabs related to different attributes of an object: layer, surface style, texture map, radiosity meshing, and so on. All the options are off by default. You can turn some of them on by clicking on their checkboxes. To turn them all on, click on the All button (Figure 5.53). For each attribute that's turned on, you can choose from among various options to set it to. Thus, for Layer, you can choose from among all the existing layers in the project. After making the desired attribute settings in this dialog, simply apply the Set Attribute tool to an object, and all its attributes will be modified as specified in the dialog.

- The Get Attributes tool works in conjunction with the Set Attributes tool. It can be applied to an object to retrieve some or all of its attributes, which are then recorded in the Set Attributes tool, where they can be easily applied to other objects. Thus, if you need to apply the attributes of one object to another object, all that you need to do is select the first object with the Get Attributes tool, then apply the Set Attributes tool to the second object. You can choose to retrieve only some, rather than all, attributes of the selected object by making the appropriate selections in the dialog of the Get Attributes tool.

5.4 Querying for Attributes

To modify the attributes of an object after looking at them first, you can use the Attributes tool, located immediately after the Query tool in the right column of Row 12.

- Select the Attributes tool and apply it to an object. This invokes a dialog that conveniently lists all the attributes of the object and allows them to be modified (see Figure 5.54). For instance, a different surface style can be applied to the object by simply selecting it from the Surface Style popup menu in the dialog.

- The Attributes tool can also be applied to faces to get information about their attributes. However, it cannot be applied to entities at other topological levels such as points, segments, and so on, since they don't have attributes as such, merely geometric information associated with them. You've seen in Workshop 2 (Bringing a Sense of Scale) how you can get such information about these entities using the Query tool.

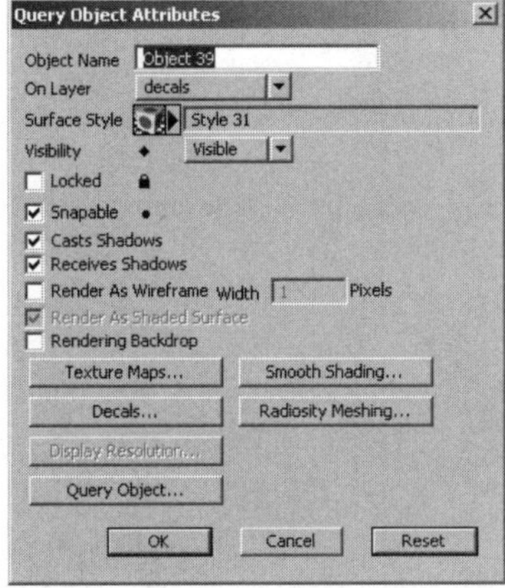

Figure 5.54

The dialog that's invoked when the Attributes tool is applied to an object.

This concludes the exercises for Workshop 5. Let's move on to tackle the Assignment for this workshop.

ASSIGNMENT 5

A Table Lamp

Model a standard table lamp in detail, with proper dimensions. Include the light bulb and actually position a light source inside it to complete the effect.

The actual exercise of modeling the table lamp shown here will now be demonstrated step by step. You can refer to the form•Z files for each step in the accompanying CD-ROM, under the folder Assignments > Workshop 5. A rendered image of the model is in the Assignment5.tif file in the same location.

Setup

Open a new form•Z project, and go to Options > Working Units to set them appropriate to the small scale of the project we're going to model. Set the Data Scale to Small (Lamp). Ensure that the unit is set to Inches under the English measurement system and that Numeric Display Options is set to Architectural. Change the Numeric Accuracy to 1/16" and the Angle Accuracy to 1°, since we won't need accuracy levels more precise than these values. Change also the Window Setup under the Window menu to a grid module of 1" in all directions with 4 subdivisions, and set the Display Scale to 6" = 1'-0". Select the Reset window tool (W-Tool:7,9) to set the window zoom level appropriate to the selected display scale.

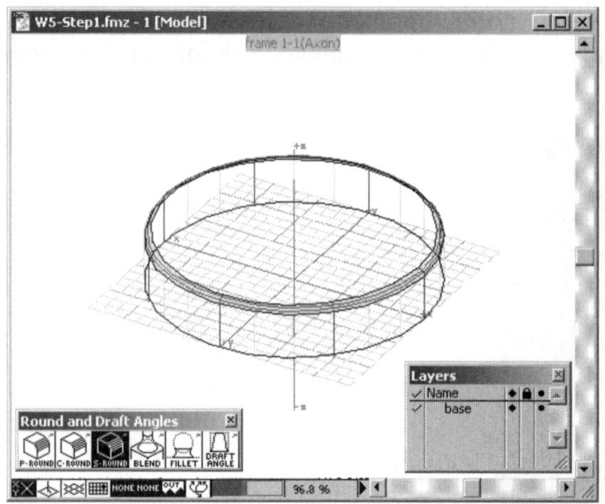

Step 1

Start by modeling the base of the lamp. Use the Cylinder tool to create a cylinder of radius 2 3/4" and height 1", centered at the origin [0,0,0]. After creating the extrusion, use one of the Round tools on Row 6 to round the edges of its top face by a radius value of 1/8". Also change the name of the layer in which this object has been created to base.

Step 2

Next, we'll move on to the striated cylindrical support that connects the head of the lamp to its base. Move to a new layer called support and switch to the Right view. Use the Vector Line tool in 2D Surface mode to draw a line with the following coordinates. (Remember that all dimensions entered are in inches.)

Pt #1: [0,0,1] Absolute, cartesian mode

Pt #2: [0,0,8 1/2] Relative, cartesian mode

Pt #3: [3 1/2,135,0] Relative, polar mode

Pt #4: [e] or double-click to end

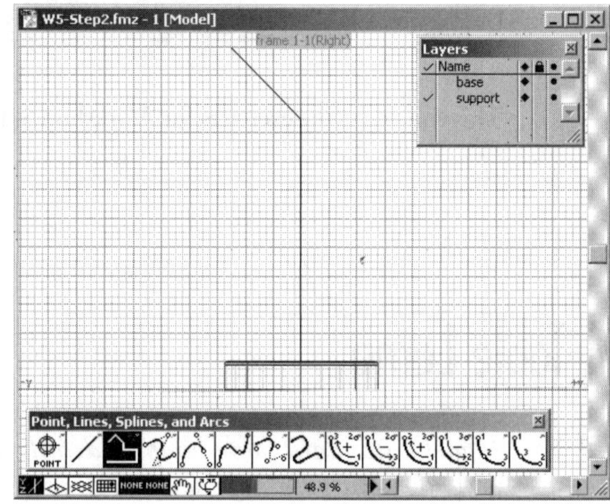

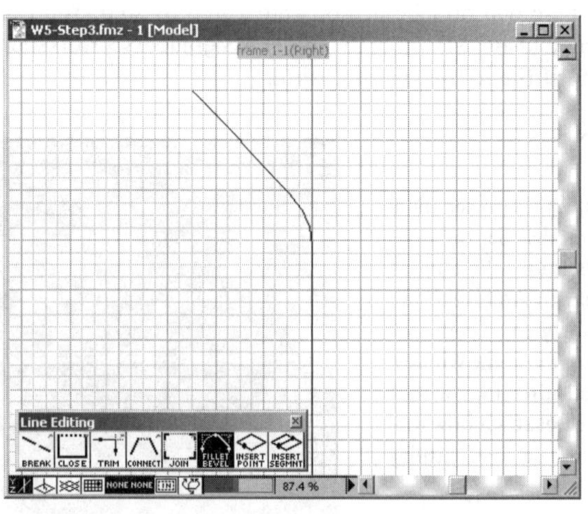

Step 3

Next, the angled point of this line needs to be rounded off. For this, select the Fillet/Bevel tool (M-Tool:11a,6), and set the # Of Edges and Fillet Size values in its dialog to 10 and 1 1/2" respectively. Apply the tool, with the topological level set to Point, to the angled point of the line and it will be nicely rounded off as shown.

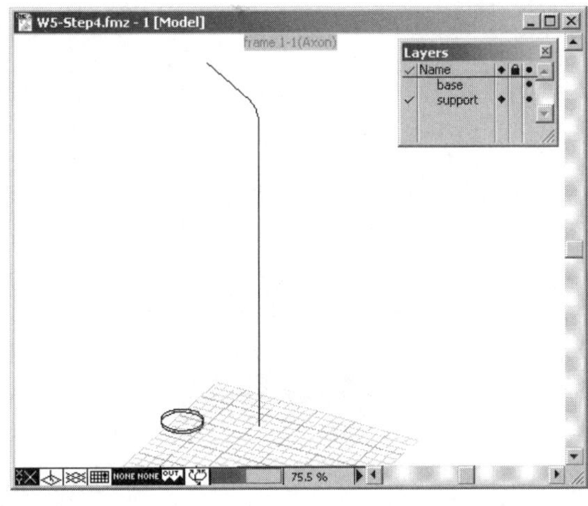

Step 4

We'll now proceed to model the striated support with the help of the 2D line we just rounded. Turn off the base layer so that only the 2D line is visible. Switch to a non-planar view, and create a cylinder of radius 1/2" and height 1/12" located anywhere in the window.

Step 5

Select the Place tool (M-Tool:13b,4) and set the Multi-Placement option in its dialog to End-To-End. Further, select the Use # Of Placements sub-option and set # Of Placements to 70. With the self-copy modifier set to Multi Copy, apply the Place tool by selecting the cylinder as the source object and the 2D line as the placement line. This should give you 70 copies of the cylinder placed along the line. Delete the original cylinder.

Select all the placed cylinders and use the Join tool (M-Tool:9b,1) to join them into one object. The Union tool cannot be used since the cylinders don't touch each other.

Step 6

Locate the 2D line that should still be there after the Place operation, and reposition it to the center of the joined cylinders, if necessary. Create a 2D circle of radius 7/16". Then use the Sweep tool (M-Tool:5b,6) to sweep the circle about the 2D line. Zoom in, if necessary, to perform the operation correctly.

Now perform a Union operation of the swept object with the joined cylinders. This will give you the completed cylindrical support following the shape of the line, and striated as required.

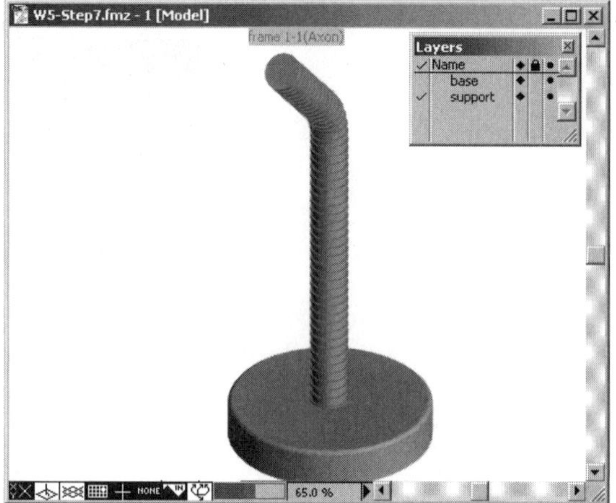

Step 7

Turn on the base layer, and move the support so that it is located at the center of the base, if the two objects are not aligned. This may have happened, depending upon how the Place operation was executed.

Step 8

Next, we'll proceed to model the little knob that connects the support to the bulb holder at the head of the lamp. Activate a new layer, knob, and switch to the Right view. Use the Rotate Plane tool (W-Tool:3,5) to rotate the current plane, YZ, by an angle of 45°. Then use Move Plane Origin (W-Tool:3,4) to move the origin of this plane to the center of the top face of the support. Turn off the display of the world axes from the Window menu to avoid confusion.

Zoom in to the top of the support. Use the coordinates of the new reference plane to draw a 2D square of side 1 1/2", attached to the top part of the support. Take care to see that it's centered about the support axis.

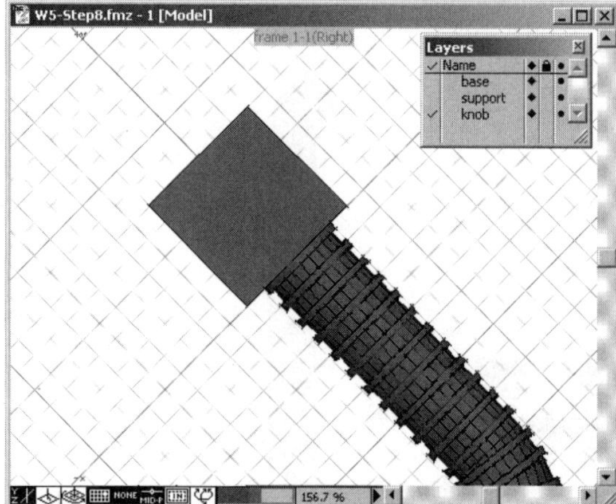

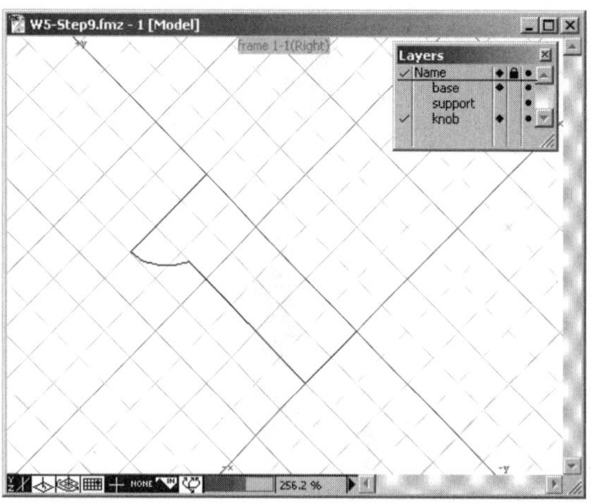

Step 9

Turn off the support layer so that you can see only the square. Zoom in close and use the square as a guideline for drawing the 2D open shape made up of lines and arcs on one half of the square as shown. Don't worry about the exact dimensions—just get the proportions right. This shape is going to be revolved about the Y axis of the plane, so make sure you don't cross the axis while drawing the shape. Use grid and object snapping for preciseness. Delete the square after you're done.

Step 10

Use the Revolve tool (M-Tool:5b,1) to revolve the open shape about the Y axis, choosing the Smooth model type in the preview dialog. The object of revolution that's created is the knob that will connect the support to the head of the lamp.

It's time to move on to the head itself. Activate a new layer, head. Create two rectangles of sizes 2 3/4" by 2 1/2", and 2 3/4" by 4"—the first dimension being along the X axis of the plane—and position them as shown.

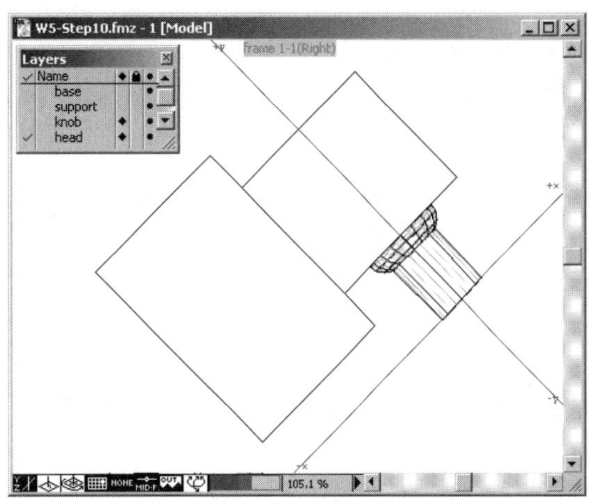

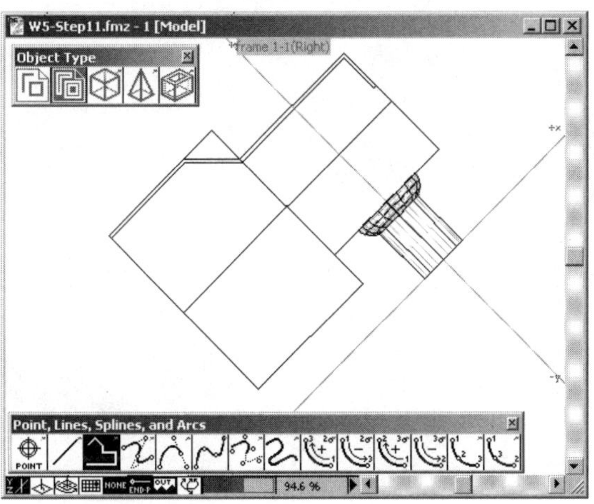

Step 11

Draw a line parallel to the X axis connecting the midpoints of the opposite sides of the two rectangles. This will function as the axis of revolution for the double-line shape we'll create to model the head. Activate the 2D Enclosure mode (M-Tool:2a,2), set its Wall Width to 1/16", and choose the Right justification option.

Using the rectangles as a guide, draw the double-line half-shape of the holder, moving from the top to the base. Use a combination of Endpoint and Segment object snapping and Ortho 45 direction snapping, the last two for the angled segment.

Step 12

Turn off the knob layer and delete the two rectangles you had created as guidelines. Use the Fillet/Bevel tool, as you did in Step 3, to round off the six intermediate points of the double-line shape, with # Of Edges and Fillet Size values of 4 and 1/16" respectively.

Now use the Revolve tool to revolve the double-line shape about the single line segment you created as the axis. Once again, choose the Smooth model type in the preview dialog. This will give you the head of the lamp.

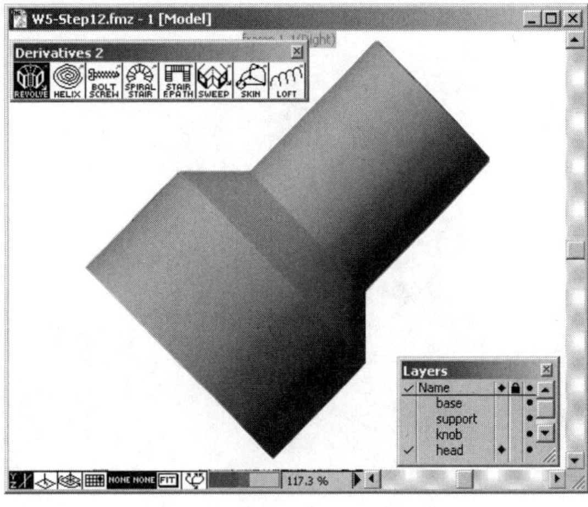

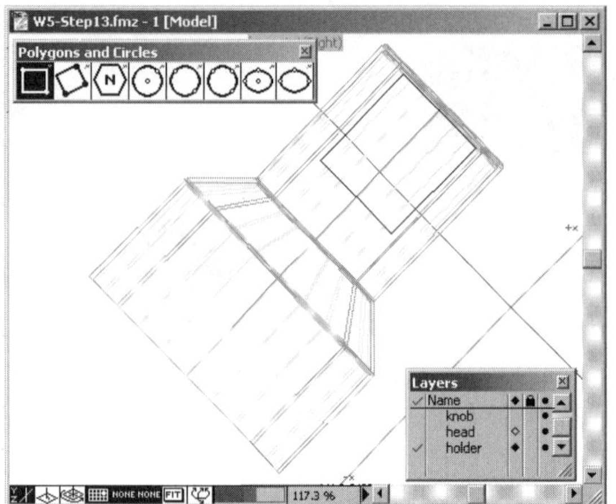

Step 13

The next task is to model the holder for the light bulb, located inside the head we just modeled. Activate a new layer, holder. Ghost the head layer rather than make it invisible, as you'll need it for reference. Create a rectangle of 1 3/4" by 1 1/2", centered within the head and touching its top inside surface. Use grid rather than object snapping, since the head object has too many overlapping points in a planar view for object snapping to work accurately.

Step 14

Make the head layer completely invisible, so that only the rectangle is visible. Draw a line connecting the midpoints of the two smaller sides of the rectangle. Use this line and the rectangle as guidelines for constructing the 2D shape as shown. Use the Fillet/Bevel tool with the appropriate radius for rounding the required points. This 2D shape will be revolved about the line in the usual fashion, so be careful to remain within the bounds of one half of the rectangle.

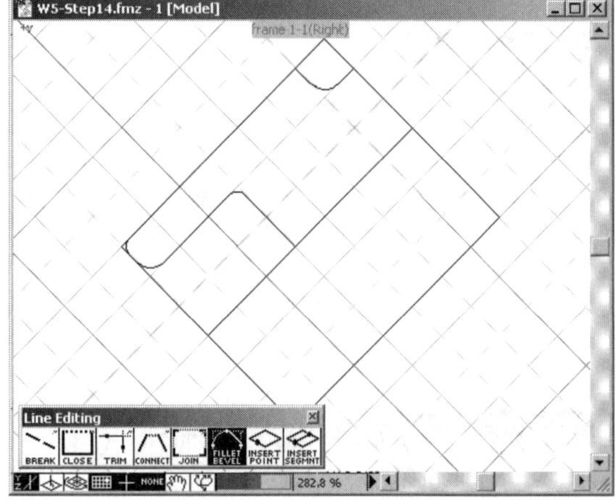

Step 15

Delete the rectangle. Use the Revolve tool to revolve the 2D rounded shape about the line, selecting the model type as Smooth. The revolved object will be the holder for the bulb.

Technically, we should also be modeling the screw plate inside the cavity of the holder where the bulb screws in, but we'll ignore that detail in this assignment since it won't be visible in the views of the lamp you're likely to generate.

Step 16

Let's move on to model the actual bulb. This consists of two parts: the head, which screws into the holder and is solid; and the body, which is hollow and contains the light source. We won't worry about modeling the filament and other internal details of the light bulb. Move to a new layer, **bulb**, and ghost the **holder** layer. Draw a 2D line along the axis of the holder. Use this line as the axis for generating a screw with the **Screw/Bolt** tool (**M-Tool:5b,3**), making the following specifications in the preview dialog: **Tip**, **Neck**, and **Head** options deselected; **Body Radius** value 7/16"; **Body Length** value 3/4"; **Threads** set to **By Distance** with value 1/8"; **Shaft** value 50%; **Depth** value 1/16"; **Direction** set to **Counterclockwise**. If required, move the screw object after creating it to correctly position it inside the cavity at the base of the holder.

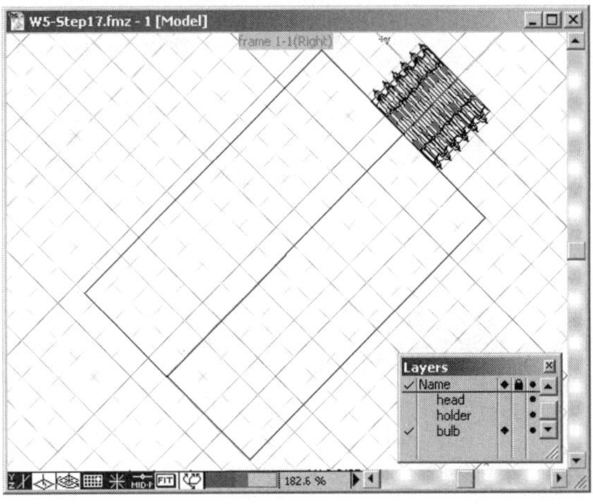
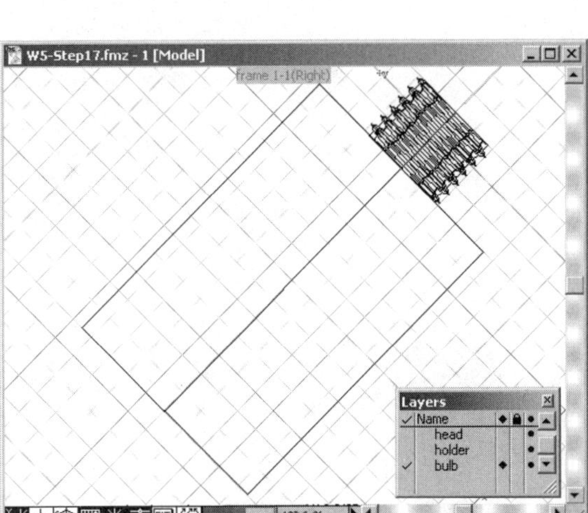

Step 17

Make the **holder** layer completely invisible. Draw a 3 1/4" by 2 1/4" rectangle and position it aligned with the center of the screw, as shown. Draw a 2D line connecting the opposite midpoints of the shorter side of the rectangle. This will function as the axis of revolution for the 2D half-shape that we'll create next for the light bulb.

Step 18

Activate the **2D Enclosure** object generation mode on Row 2, set the **Wall Width** to 1/16", and set the **Justification** option to **Left**. Use the **Arc** tools on Row 3 to inscribe a double-line curved shape for the bulb in one half of the rectangle as shown.

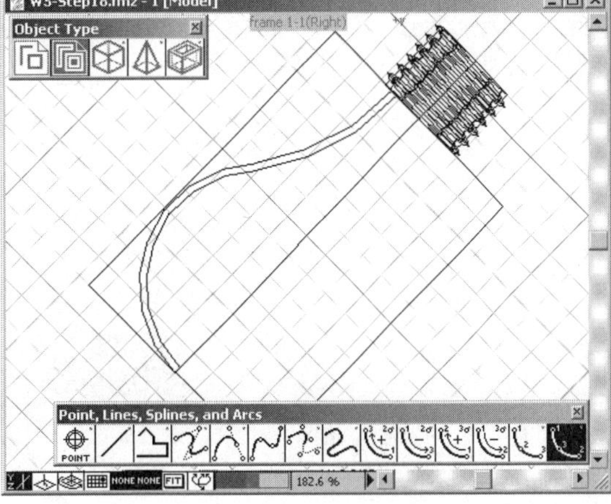

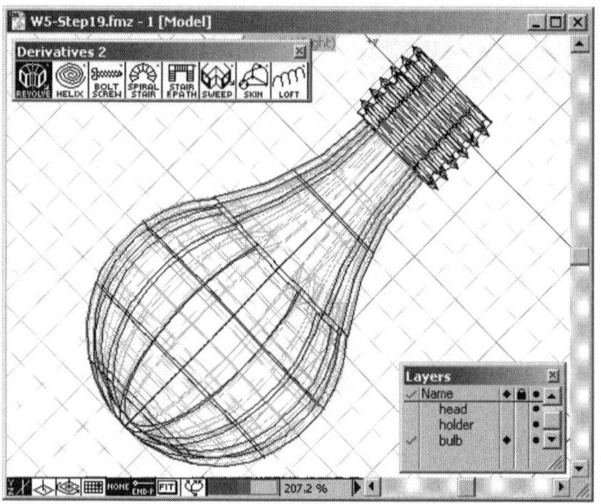

Step 19

Delete the rectangle you had drawn as a guide. Select the Revolve tool, and apply it to the curved shape to revolve it about the line, selecting the Smooth model type. This will give the curved, hollow object for the body of the light bulb.

Step 20

The final object to model is the switch located at the top of the head. Turn off the bulb layer, and make the head layer visible. Switch to the 120-20 Axonometric view, the third in the Views menu. Select the Define Arbitrary Plane tool (W-Tool:3,1), and click on a segment at the base of the holder. This will create the arbitrary plane passing through the base of the holder as shown.

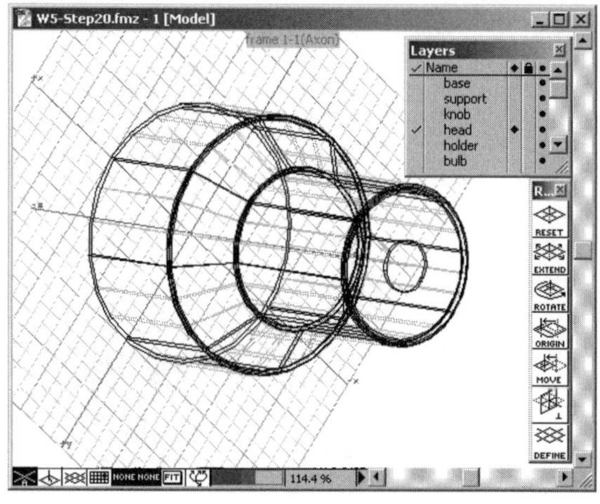

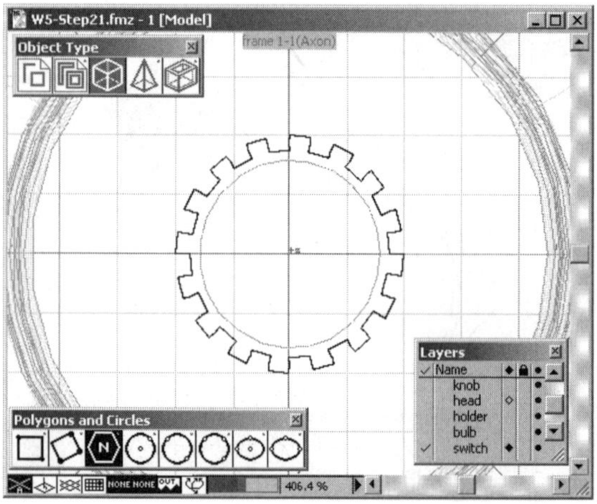

Step 21

Activate a new layer, switch. Change the view to Views > Plane Projection > Top. You should now be seeing the circular head of the lamp head-on from the top. Ghost the head layer. Set the object generation mode to 3D Extrusion and Heights to Graphic/Keyed. Select the Polygon tool and set the By # Of Segments in its dialog to 32. Also activate its Pattern option and select the fifth pattern—the middle one of the nine squares. Use this tool to create a patterned polygon, positioned at the origin of the arbitrary plane, having an outer radius of 1/2", an inner radius of 7/16", and a height of 1/4". It should completely cover the large circular hole located at the center of the head.

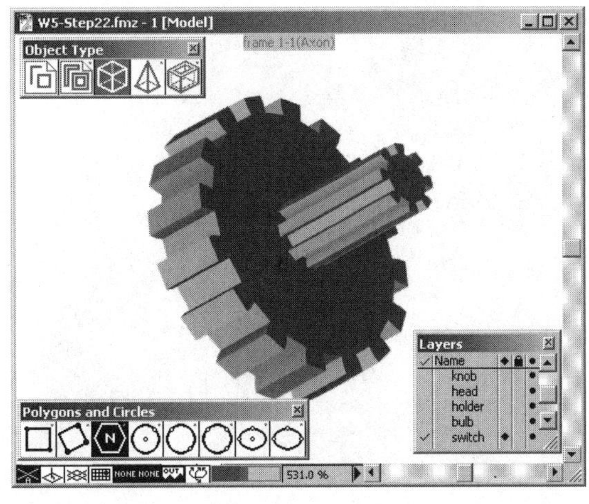

Step 22

Reduce the **By # Of Segments** in the **Polygon Options** dialog to 16, and reapply the tool to create a second polygon, also positioned at the center. The outer and inner radii are 1/8" and 1/16" respectively, and the height is 3/4". Turn off the **head** layer completely and switch to a non-planar view to check if the two extruded polygons have been created properly.

Step 23

Switch to the **Right** view, and turn the **head** layer back on. Fit the head and switch objects in the window using the **Fit** tool. Move the two extruded polygons comprising the switch from the base where they were created to the top of the head. Use the **Ortho 45** direction snapping for accuracy.

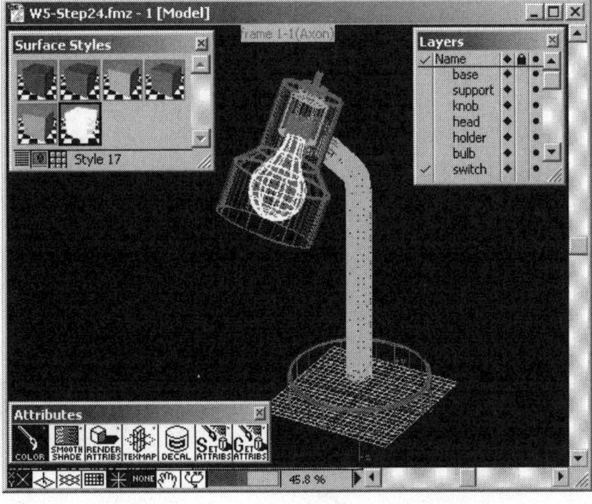

Step 24

With this, all the individual component parts of the lamp are complete. Turn on all the layers, and delete any extraneous objects that were created as guidelines. Apply surface styles to the objects as appropriate. Take care to apply a transparent surface style to the body of the bulb. Ideally, it should be reflective as well, but this will add to the rendering time considerably. A faster alternative is to make the bulb have a glowing effect. For this, set the **Reflection** attribute of its surface style to **Matte** and increase the **Glow Factor** in the **Matte Options** dialog to 75%. Switch the project background color to black by going to **Options > Project Colors**.

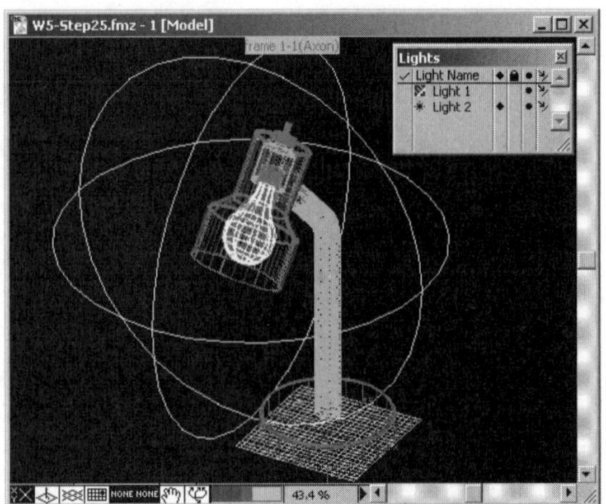

Step 25

Create a new light source in the Lights palette. Invoke its Light Parameters dialog, change its Type to Point, and specify a suitable value for the Radius, say 8". Also, change the Location value to [0,0,0] in the dialog, so that you can locate the light source easily in the graphics window. Exit the dialog, make the light source visible in the Lights palette, and apply the Move tool to position it accurately inside the light bulb.

Step 26

Your lamp is now ready to go. A RenderZone display of just the lamp won't be very effective. But put it on a flat, slightly reflective surface, and you should be able to see the effect of the lamp in lighting up this surface quite clearly. Remember to deactivate the Shining option of the default distant light first.

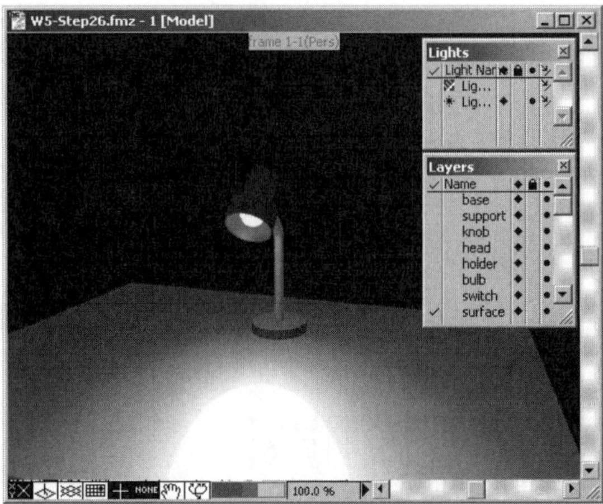

You can copy this lamp object, along with the point light, to any interior design project for use within a room. The cord for the lamp can be generated by using the Sweep tool so that it runs across the surface on which the lamp is placed. You can even connect it all the way to an electric outlet on a wall, for good measure!

Going Organic

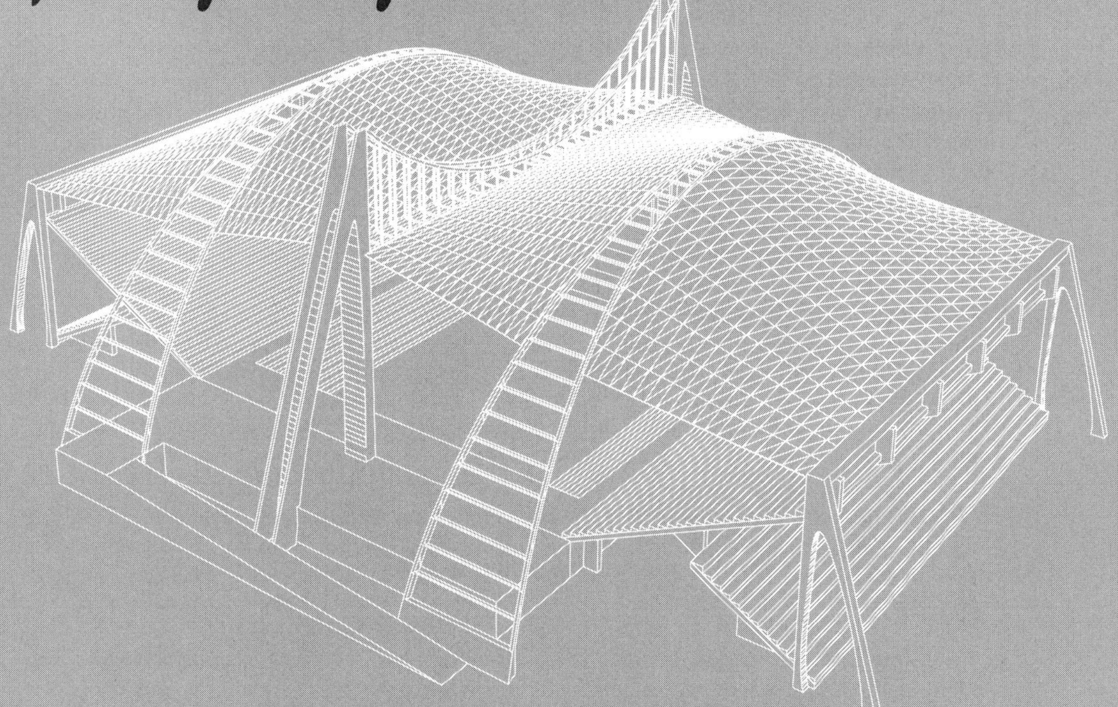

This exercise is devoted to exploring all those tools in form•Z designed for organic modeling, i.e., modeling of non-rectilinear forms. You'll start by creating meshes on the surfaces of objects in various ways. You'll then proceed to apply movements, disturbances, and various kinds of deformations to meshed objects, all of which can be used to mold the object as desired. A more sophisticated technique of sculpting an object is to use an image as the basis for displacing a meshed surface, which will be covered in Exercise 3. All these tools are located in the left column of the sixth row of the modeling tool palette.

In subsequent exercises, you'll enhance your freeform modeling capabilities further by learning to create and modify smooth curves, controlled curves and meshes, nurbz (NURBS-based) surfaces, and patches. You'll also learn how to carry out boolean operations on these kind of objects. In the final exercise, you'll work with metaformz, which are objects that have the ability to blend seamlessly with each other when they overlap.

EXERCISE 1

Plain Meshes and Subdivisions

In this exercise, we'll learn how to mesh the surface of an object, either plainly or by using two different kinds of subdivision algorithms. We'll also look at the reverse process—reducing the mesh density of an object that's already meshed. These operations involve the use of the first four tools in the left column of Row 6.

1.1 Plain Meshes

It's possible to transform a 2D closed shape or the face of a 3D object into a flat meshed surface. Such a mesh isn't a controlled object and cannot be edited after it has been created, so it's referred to as a *plain mesh*. Let's see how plain meshes are created and what they can be used for.

- Open a new form•Z project, and create a rectangular block with a base dimension of 40' by 56' and a height of 80'. Set the topological level to Face and use the Pick tool to select one of the vertical faces of the block (Figure 6.1-a). Then select the Mesh tool (M-Tool:6a,1) and watch the Prompts palette for instructions. Since you've already selected a face, you simply need to click anywhere in the window for the mesh operation to be executed. Click OK in the dialog telling you that the object type will be converted to Plain. The selected face will now be subdivided into many smaller faces, each measuring 8' by 8' (Figure 6.1-b). This is the default size of the mesh, set in its dialog. Since the original surface is an exact multiple of 8', the mesh will fit exactly within the surface.

- Now use the Pick tool to try and select the face you just meshed. You'll find that you can no longer select it, since it has been split up into many smaller faces. Essentially you've lost the original face. You can, however, retrieve it by using the Reduce Mesh tool, which we'll cover later on in this exercise.

So what can this meshed surface be used for? In Exercise 2, we'll work with sophisticated tools that can deform and displace meshed surfaces in various ways to yield non-rectilinear, "organic" forms. For now, let's apply some simpler transformations to the mesh.

- Using the Pick tool still at the Face level, select some of the mesh subdivisions, which are now basically faces in their own right. Apply a different color to them using the Color tool, making sure the default Keep Surface Style Of Faces option is active in its dialog, and switch to any of the paint display modes to see the result (Figure 6.1-c). The result is particularly impressive in the rendered displays, since the individual subdivisions of the mesh are not seen. Imagine how useful this would be, for instance, in quickly designing an architectural facade.

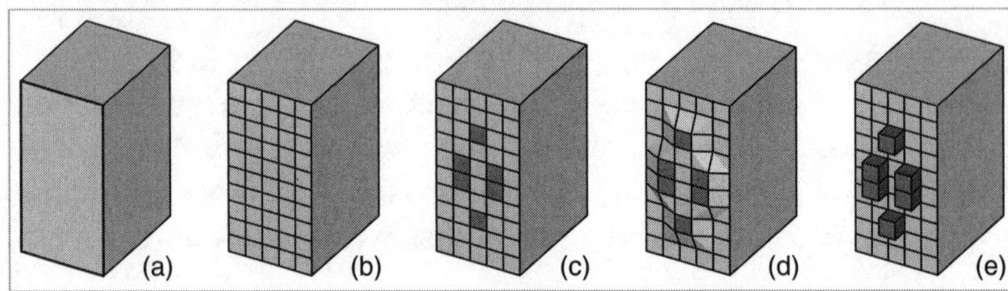

Figure 6.1

Creating and using plain meshes in various ways.

- Now select the mesh subdivisions you just colored (you can use Edit > Select Previous) and use the Move tool to drag them outside the surface of the block. You can create some interesting surface deformations in this manner (Figure 6.1-d).

- You could also use the mesh subdivisions for deriving various kinds of extruded objects. Undo the Move operation you just performed. The same faces will still be selected. In the dialog of the 3D Extrusion tool (M-Tool:5a,4), select the Perpendicular To Surface option and set Status Of Objects to Keep. From the Heights menu, preset a height, say 8'-0". Now apply the 3D Extrusion tool to the selected faces. You should have the extruded objects hanging off the meshed surface, as shown in Figure 6.1-e.

One useful application of the Mesh tool is creating a regular construction grid on a surface. This will facilitate the use of object snapping, enabling further operations on that surface or plane to be carried out more easily and accurately. In architectural modeling and urban design, for instance, you could use the Mesh tool to create a gridded base plane that the building or buildings will be located on. Since the individual mesh subdivisions are not seen in the rendered display modes, they won't affect your rendered images in any way.

1.2 Plain Mesh Options

- You will, of course, need to work with different mesh sizes and orientations from the defaults. Invoke the dialog of the Mesh tool to see what its options are (Figure 6.2). First of all, you can change the size of the mesh from the default values along the X, Y, and Z directions. Since the XYZ Lock option is selected, any change you make to one value is automatically made to the other two values as well. Try it and test the new mesh size on another face of the object.

- Note that the X, Y, and Z values that you specified don't stand for mesh divisions along the X, Y, and Z directions of the world or reference plane axes. To understand what they denote, create a new block of the same dimensions as before (Figure 6.3-a). Then invoke the Mesh Options dialog, deselect the XYZ Lock option, and key in sufficiently different mesh values for X, Y, and Z—say 4', 8', and 10' respectively. Also, deselect both the Y and the Z boxes to start with. This means that the mesh will be created only in the X direction, giving you the chance to see what it stands for.

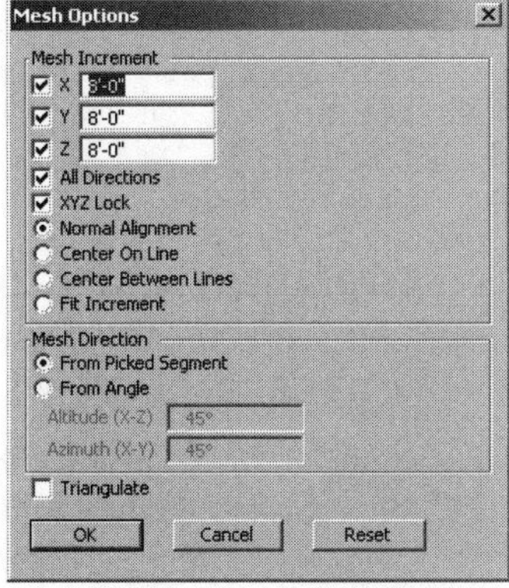

Figure 6.2

The dialog of the Mesh tool.

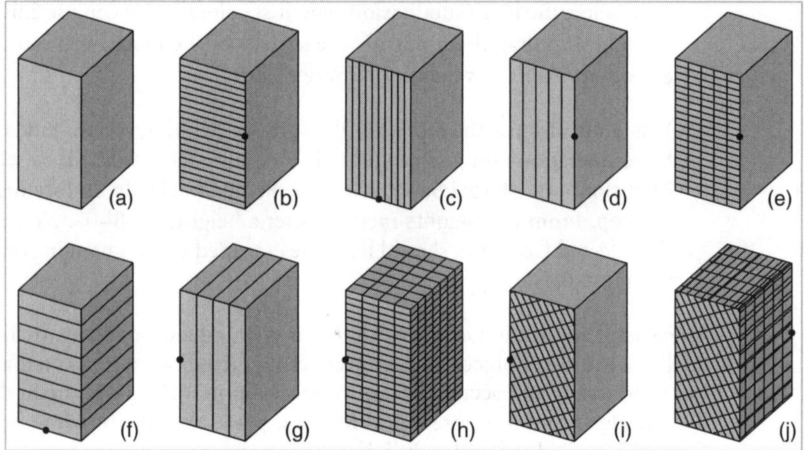

Figure 6.3

Different meshes produced by different direction settings. The segment selected first is indicated in each case.

- Use the Mesh tool to apply the new settings to one of the vertical faces of the block as before. You'll find that the mesh now runs only in one direction (Figure 6.3-b), perpendicular to the segment that's first selected (if you're using the Clicking On Edges picking method) or the segment that's closest to the pick point (if you're using the Clicking Inside Boundaries picking method). To test this, undo the operation and reapply the Mesh tool to the same face but by selecting it through a different segment (Figure 6.3-c). Then apply the tool with just the Y direction selected—the mesh now runs parallel to the segment that's picked (Figure 6.3-d). Use both X and Y, and the mesh will run in both directions, as expected (Figure 6.3-e).

- Apply the X and Y direction settings to the top face of the block, and you'll achieve the same mesh effect shown in Figure 6.3-e. This shows that the X, Y, and Z mesh directions aren't related to the X, Y, and Z axes of the active reference plane—they're relative only to the selected face and oriented according to how the face is picked. To verify this, change the mesh settings so that only the Z direction is activated. You'll find that applying the mesh tool now to a face produces no result, since the Z direction is perpendicular to the plane of that face, not lying on it.

- Why then have a Z direction at all? To find the answer to that, apply the Mesh tool to a new block with the topological level now set to Object. Only the Z option should be activated. You'll find that the mesh is applied in a direction perpendicular to the face that's picked, which in turn is determined by the segment used to select the object (Figures 6.3-f and 6.3-g). Thus, applying the Mesh tool at the Object level leads to a 3D rather than a 2D mesh, which is why all three directions are needed.

- Undo the operation, and check the All Directions option in the Mesh Options dialog. This will activate all three directions—X, Y, and Z—in one step. Reapply the Mesh tool to the block, and you'll see the full three-directional effect of the mesh (Figure 6.3-h).

- So far, all the meshes you created were parallel to the segments of the rectangular faces to which the Mesh tool was applied. But what if you want meshes that are oriented differently? Go to the Mesh Options dialog and under the Mesh Direction section, pick the From Angle option. This lets you specify a different orientation for the mesh by assigning two angle values for the X-Z and X-Y directions. Experiment with different values of these, both at the Face level (Figure 6.3-i) and at the Object level (Figure 6.3-j). Notice that at the Face level, it doesn't matter how the face is selected, but at the Object level, the alignment of the mesh does depend upon which segment is picked first. As you can see from Figure 6.3-j, the result of this method at the Object level isn't very "clean," and is therefore best avoided.

- Move on to the four mesh alignment options, located above the Mesh Direction section. Notice that the default is Normal Alignment. To see what this means, turn on the XYZ Lock option and specify a value for the mesh size, say 9', that's *not* a factor of the block size. Also, switch to the default From Picked Segment option under Mesh Direction. Undo any previous mesh operations and reapply the Mesh tool with the new settings to the top face of the block. Switch to the Top view to see the results better. You'll see that since the mesh dimensions are not synchronized with the face dimensions, there are smaller pieces of mesh left over after the mesh is placed relative to the segment first picked (Figure 6.4-a).
- Undo and repeat the operation with each one of the other three mesh alignment options, and observe the difference. The Center On Line option distributes the leftover pieces equally on all sides of the face, ensuring that the mesh lines pass through the center of the face (Figure 6.4-b). The Center Between Lines option also does an equal distribution of leftover pieces, but in such a way that a mesh subdivision lies exactly at the center of the face (Figure 6.4-c). And finally, the Fit Increment option nicely readjusts the mesh size so that it's uniformly distributed across the face (Figure 6.4-d), and is thus a very useful option.

Figure 6.4

Different mesh alignment options demonstrated on the top face of a block, seen in Top view.

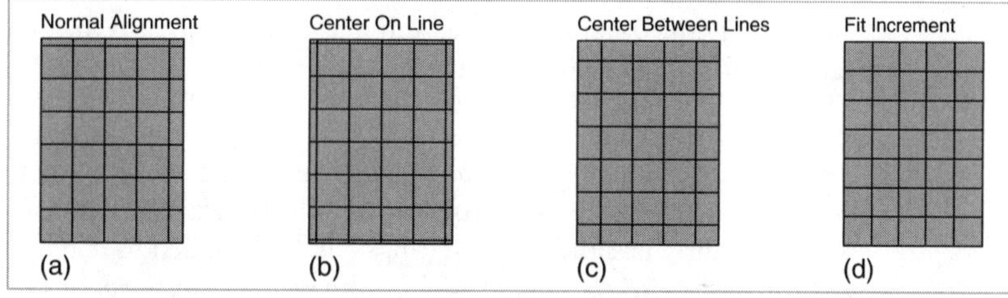

- The only remaining option in the Mesh Options dialog is the Triangulate option which, when checked, creates the mesh and then breaks it down into triangles.
- Since a mesh is actually breaking up a face into many smaller faces, you can also create meshes within meshes. First, create a mesh of a fairly large dimension on a face. Then reduce the mesh dimensions and apply the Mesh tool to one of the smaller meshed faces you just created. You could repeat this ad infinitum, creating fractal-like patterns on the face or other interesting variations (Figure 6.5).

Figure 6.5

Creating meshes within meshes on the top face of a block, seen in Top view.

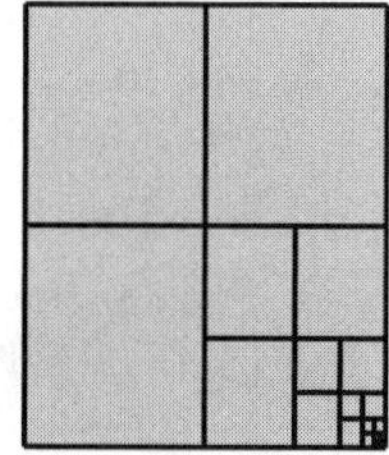

1.3 Quadratic Subdivisions

The next tool on Row 6, Q-Subz (short for Quadratic Subdivisions), also creates a mesh on the surface of an object in the same way as the Mesh tool you just saw. The difference, however, is that instead of uniformly subdividing the face of an object into a flat mesh, the Q-Subz tool subdivides a face non-uniformly into a pattern that matches the shape of that face. The mesh patterns would thus be different for rectangles, triangles, pentagons, hexagons, irregular polygons, and so on. Additionally, the Q-Subz tool can also smooth out the edges of the object by giving them a curvature.

- Clear everything you have in your project or move to a different layer. Create three extruded blocks with different base shapes—a rectangle, a hexagon, and an irregular polygon (Figure 6.6-a). Set the topological level to Object and apply the Q-Subz tool (M-Tool:6a,2) to the rectangular block first, and click OK to the subsequent message. A preview dialog will be invoked, containing various options for the Q-Subz operation.

- Don't worry about getting to know all these options right away. Instead, simply make the following changes to the dialog, as shown in Figure 6.6-b: reduce the Max # Of Subdivisions value from 4 to 2; deselect the Smoothing option; and finally, select the Show Meshed Object option rather than the Show Original Object option in the Preview section. This will update the image in the preview window to show you the mesh created on the object. Exit the dialog by clicking on the OK button.

- Next, apply the Q-Subz tool in exactly the same manner to the other two blocks, with exactly the same options. Notice how the mesh is different for each of the three blocks and is adapted to the shape of the face that's being meshed. (Figure 6.6-c).

- Apply the Q-Subz tool again to one of the objects you just meshed. Choose the one with the irregular base for more interesting results. The Q-Subz Edit dialog for the object opens up, allowing you to modify the subdivision settings you had applied to it. Thus, unlike the Mesh tool you saw a short while ago, the Q-Subz tool produces a *controlled object*, where the control parameters are stored and can be modified at a later stage.

- Click on the Deselect All Faces button in the dialog. This will deselect all the faces of the object in the preview window. Change the Preview to Show Meshed Object, and you'll find that you've retrieved the original unmeshed object by removing the meshes from all of its faces.

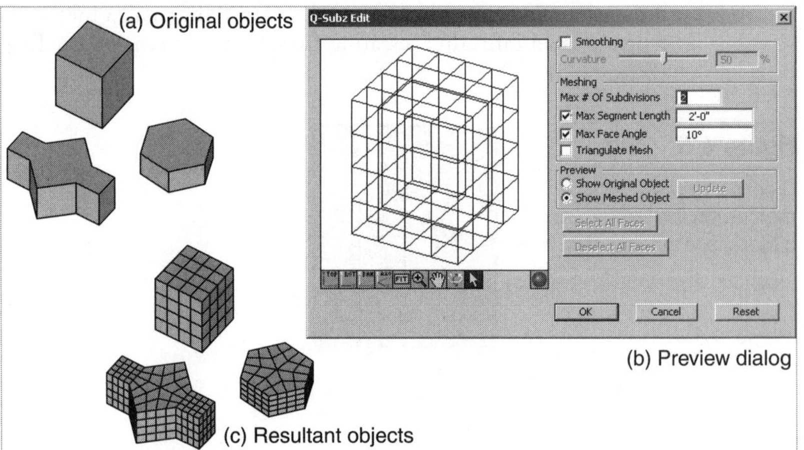

Figure 6.6

Using the Q-Subz tool on different objects with the Smoothing option deselected.

- Switch the Preview back to the default of Show Original Object. As you can see, the preview window on the left has the familiar tool icons at its base for changing views, zooming, scrolling, selecting, and changing display modes. Use the Pointer tool to select the top face of the object in the preview window, and activate the Show Meshed Object option to see the result. Rotate the object in the preview window so that you can see its top face clearly, or better still, switch to the Top view. We'll use this meshed face to explore some of the other options in the Q-Subz Edit dialog.

- The Smoothing option should still be deselected from the earlier settings, and keep it that way for now. Change the Max # Of Subdivisions value to 1. (A warning: Don't hit the return or Enter key for this value to be registered, or you'll unintentionally exit the dialog. Instead, click in the Max Segment Length field, located right below the subdivisions box, for the change to be registered.) The Update button, which was grayed out all this time, will now be activated, indicating that the mesh parameters have changed. Click on it to view the results of the change. You'll see that the mesh subdivisions have decreased. Do the same for the value of 2, then for 3, and finally for 4. Notice how the mesh subdivisions get finer each time (Figure 6.7-a). You can also clearly see the subdivision methodology at work—the mesh lines run from the midpoints of the boundary segments and end at the center of the face. For an irregular polygon like the one you have, it's first divided into regular polygons and then the subdivision begins.

You should settle for the lowest value of Max # Of Subdivisions that you can do with, as higher values correspondingly increase the complexity of the object.

- Notice in Figure 6.7 that for the Max # Of Subdivisions value of 4, a certain amount of non-uniformity exists in the subdivision. Try changing this value to 5, 6, and larger numbers. After a point, you'll find that further subdivisions are no longer being created. Obviously, some other parameter is at work here. This is the Max Segment Length option, which is currently set to 2'-0". Change it to 1'-0". Also switch to the highest subdivision value that gave you some different results. Compare the result now to the earlier mesh for the same subdivision value, and you'll find an increase in the number of subdivisions in certain areas of the mesh (Figure 6.7-b). Step down one subdivision value and you might still see some difference from the earlier result. Exit the dialog after you have explored all these settings.

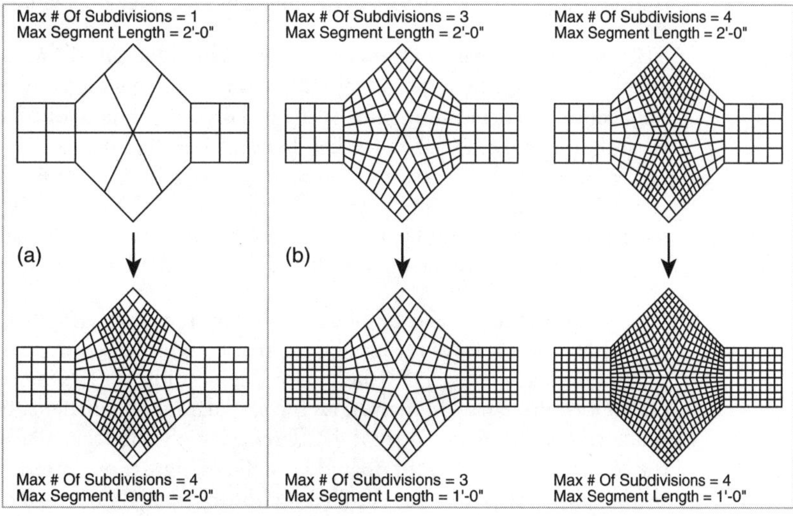

Figure 6.7

Exploring the Q-Subz subdivision options.

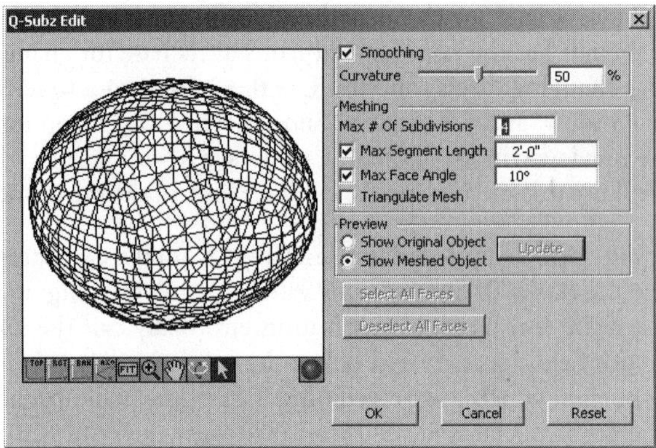

Figure 6.8

Activating the Smoothing option for the Q-Subz operation on the hexagonal object shown in Figure 6.6.

The Max Segment Length option basically ends the subdivision process as soon as all the individual mesh segments become smaller than the specified segment length. This accounts for the non-uniformity you saw in Figure 6.7-a, where the maximum segment length was specified as 2'-0". It's also due to the same option that an increase in the Max # Of Subdivisions value beyond a certain point doesn't actually increase the mesh subdivisions. The Max Segment Length option can be turned off altogether so that no check for segment length is made. However, it's recommended that you keep it selected with a reasonable value (depending upon the scale of the project) to avoid an unwieldy subdivision explosion.

- Let's move on to explore the Smoothing option that we had deactivated before. Apply the Q-Subz tool to the hexagonal object you had meshed earlier. In the Q-Subz Edit dialog, check the Smoothing option and click on Show Meshed Object to view the result. You'll find that the object is now not only meshed but smoothed out as well in the process (Figure 6.8).

- The Smoothing option includes a Curvature value that determines the amount of curvature of the mesh. The slider can go from 0% to 100%. Try out both extremes, as well as some intermediate values. You'll see that for a lower value, the object will be curved more around the edges and less at the face centers. It's exactly the opposite for a larger value. For the default value of 50%, the curvature is uniformly distributed between the edges and face centers. Figure 6.9-a shows all three scenarios.

- The options in the Meshing section apply to Smoothing as well. You've already explored the Max # Of Subdivisions and Max Segment Length options. Both these are, however, superseded by the Max Face Angle option in determining the level of subdivision of the mesh. The subdivision will stop as soon as all the angles between the meshed faces are less than the value specified for Max Face Angle. To understand how it works, keep increasing this value gradually and observe the changes in the configuration of the mesh. As you can see in Figure 6.9-b, a smaller value leads to a denser mesh, particularly in the areas of strong curvature, while a value of more than 90° doesn't mesh the object at all. The Max Face Angle option can also be turned off, which is the same as setting its value to 0°.

- Finally, there's the familiar Triangulate Mesh option that triangulates the resultant mesh. However, it's a little different from the usual triangulation option accompanying other tools that triangulates only non-planar faces. The Triangulate Mesh option for Q-Subz triangulates *all* faces uniformly, planar or non-planar. Moreover, each triangular face is further subdivided. The overall result is a much smoother mesh. To see the difference, apply the Triangulate tool (M-Tool:6a,10) to one of the objects you used Q-Subz on and note the triangulation pattern. Then Undo the operation, and reapply the Q-Subz tool to the object with the Triangulate Mesh option checked. The difference between the two operations should be clear (Figure 6.9-c).

Figure 6.9

Exploring different Smoothing options for the Q-Subz tool.

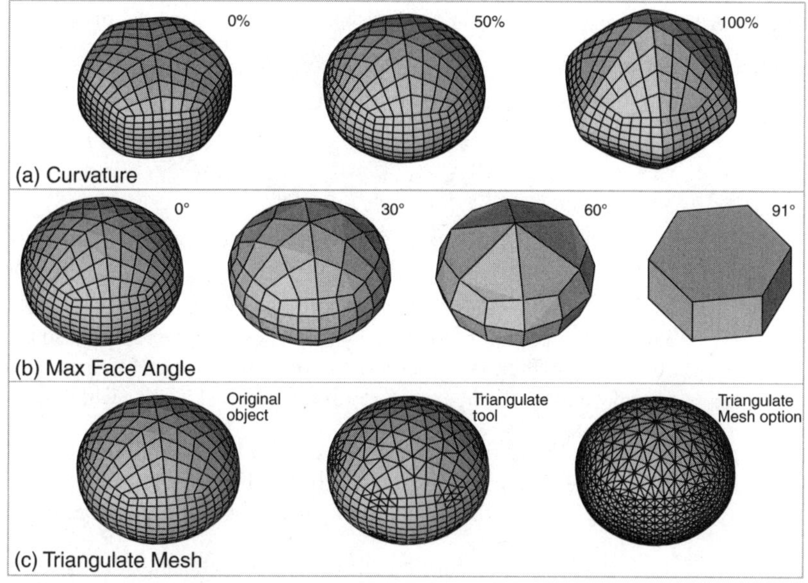

- Conclude this section on the Q-Subz tool by applying it in Smoothing mode to selected faces of the object rather than the entire object. You can see from the examples illustrated in Figure 6.10 how it's possible to achieve many interesting effects using the tool in this manner.

Figure 6.10

Applying the Q-Subz tool, with the Smoothing option on, only to selected faces of an object.

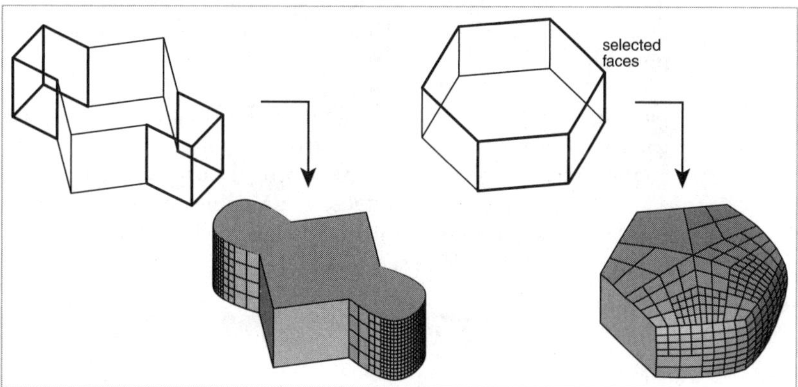

1.4 Triangular Subdivisions

The next tool on Row 6, T-Subz (short for Triangular Subdivisions), is very similar to the Q-Subz tool as it increases the resolution of an object by subdividing its faces. However, the T-Subz tool uses a different subdivision algorithm that creates triangular faces rather than the four-sided faces produced by the Q-Subz tool you saw in the last section. Just like the Q-Subz tool, the T-Subz tool can also smooth out the edges of the object by giving them a curvature, and can thus be used to shape curved forms out of regular objects.

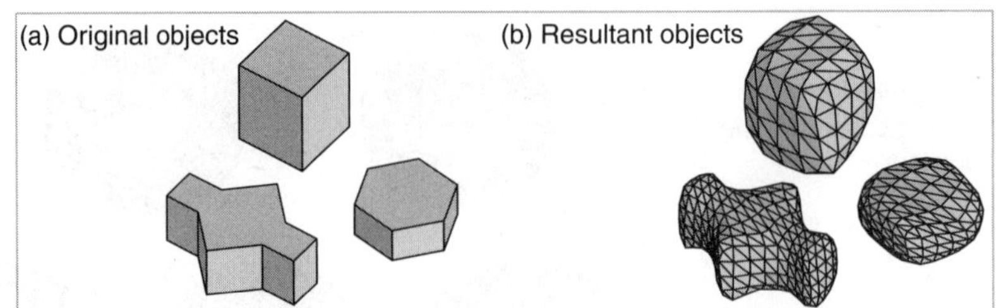

Figure 6.11

Applying the T-Subz tool to a group of objects with the default settings.

- Move to a different layer, and create three extruded blocks identical to those you created for the Q-Subz tool in the last section (6.11-a). Make sure the topological level is set to Object. Apply the T-Subz tool (M-Tool:6a,3) to each one of these blocks in turn, accepting the default settings in the preview dialog. Compare the results (Figure 6.11-b) to what you achieved using the Q-Subz tool.

- Apply the T-Subz tool again to one of the objects you just meshed, say the hexagonal block. Let's explore the options in the preview dialog (Figure 6.12). You can see that many of these are similar to the options for the Q-Subz tool you studied in the last section. Let's focus on what's different.

- To start with, the Smoothing option in the T-Subz Edit dialog cannot be deselected; also, it can be set to either In or Out. Try out both options, using different Meshing values and clicking on the Update button to see the changes. (If you like, turn on the Automatic option for automatically updating the preview after each change.) You'll find that the In option smoothes the object by moving its points inwards, making the resultant object noticeably smaller than the original. In contrast, the Out option smoothes by positioning the newly introduced points outwards while leaving the original points in their original locations, making the resultant object closer to the size of the original (see Figure 6.13-a). The Curvature slider bar lets you adjust the amount of curvature for both options.

- Now explore the effect of turning on the Triangulate By Center option. You'll find that the triangulation now happens by inserting a point in the center of every face rather than just by connecting existing edges, thus preserving the original shape of the face better (see Figure 6.13-b). The next option, Limit To Surface, is applicable only to the In type of smoothing. You'll find that checking this option is useful at higher subdivision levels as it prevents overmeshing, but it may lead to a rougher looking surface at lower subdivision levels.

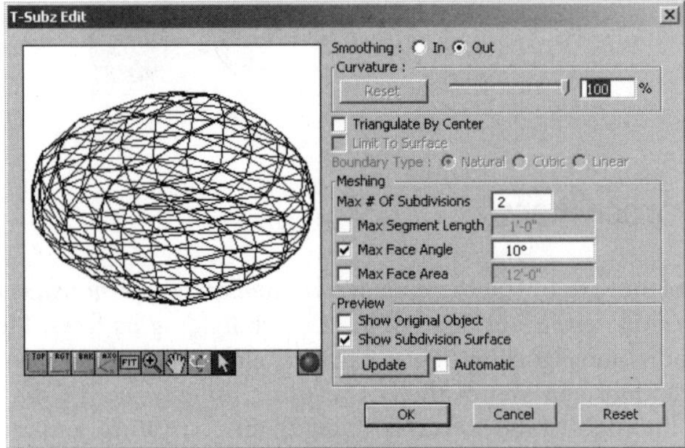

Figure 6.12

The options in the T-Subz Edit dialog.

- The three Boundary Type options will currently be deactivated as they apply only to surface objects, not to solid objects. When set to Natural, the boundary of the surface is naturally determined by the Smoothing and Curvature subdivision settings. The Cubic option, in contrast, constructs the boundaries as cubic b-spline curves, while the Linear option does not smooth the boundaries at all. Keep this explanation in mind for future use on a surface object.

- The remaining options in the T-Subz Edit dialog are identical to those in the Q-Subz Edit dialog except for the additional Max Face Area option under Meshing for controlling the level of subdivision of the mesh. When checked, this option stops the subdivision of a face as soon as its area is less than the specified value. It is a useful option to activate, as it automatically leads to a denser mesh in areas of strong curvature and a sparser mesh in flatter areas (see Figure 6.13-c).

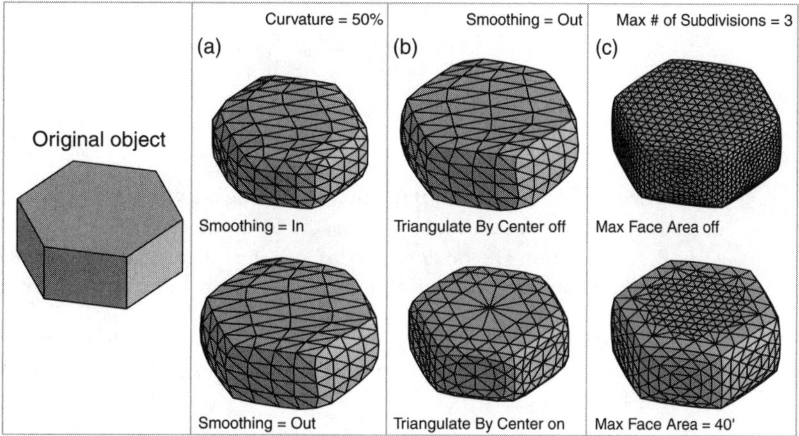

Figure 6.13

Exploring different options for the T-Subz tool.

- Notice that unlike the Q-Subz tool, the T-Subz tool cannot be applied to selected faces of the object. It must be applied to the entire object. Also, the object created by the T-Subz tool is a controlled object, so its subdivision settings are stored and can be modified at a later stage by applying the T-Subz tool to it. You can also apply the Edit Controls tool (M-Tool:4b,2) to it to modify some of the parameters graphically, as you learned to do in Section 5.2 of Workshop 2 (Bringing a Sense of Scale). Try it.

1.5 Reducing Mesh Density

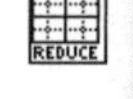

- Select the next tool in the left column of Row 6, Reduce Mesh, and apply it to one of the meshed objects you've created. A preview dialog, very similar to the ones you've just seen for the Q-Subz and T-Subz tools, is invoked (Figure 6.14-a). Here, you can specify the criteria that will be used to reduce the mesh density of the selected object.

- The Reduce Mesh tool works by merging the adjacent faces of an object and the adjacent segments of a face. The merging happens only when the angles enclosed by the faces or the segments are less than the values specified for the Face Angle and Edge Angle parameters respectively. Experiment with different values and see how they affect the reduction in mesh density of the object. One example is illustrated in Figure 6.14-b.

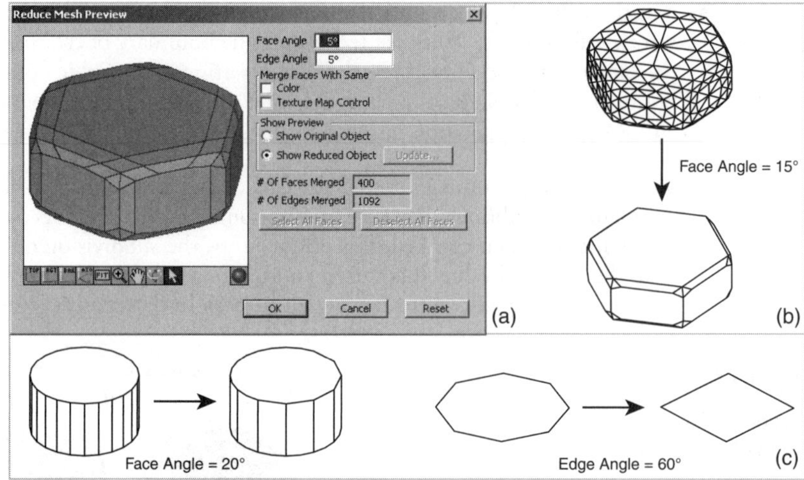

Figure 6.14

Applying the Reduce Mesh tool to meshed as well as unmeshed objects. The preview dialog for the meshed object is also shown.

- The remaining options in the preview dialog are very simple. You can choose to limit the merging only to those faces that have the same Color or Texture Map Control. The options under the Show Preview section are the same as those for the other meshing tools. And finally, information is given to you about the number of faces and edges that are merged, which you may find useful.

- The Reduce Mesh tool can also be used to reduce the number of segments in an unmeshed 2D object, and the number of faces in an unmeshed 3D object. This is demonstrated in Figure 6.14-c. Try it.

EXERCISE 2

Moving, Disturbing, and Deforming Meshes

You have, by now, worked with various types of meshed objects, flat as well as smooth. Often, you might not need to go beyond creating such meshes, using the different options that they afford—they might be the final forms of the objects you wish to model. However, at other times, these meshed objects might only be the intermediary objects on which further operations have to be performed to generate the forms you need. In this exercise, we'll look at three tools that are specifically targeted towards meshed objects, allowing you to further modify and sculpt them into forms you could not achieve with regular unmeshed objects.

2.1 Moving Meshes

- Move to a different layer and create an extruded slab—a solid whose base dimensions are much larger than its height. Select the top face of this slab, and apply the Mesh tool (M-Tool:6a,1) to it. The size of the mesh should be relatively small compared to the size of the slab (Figure 6.15-a).

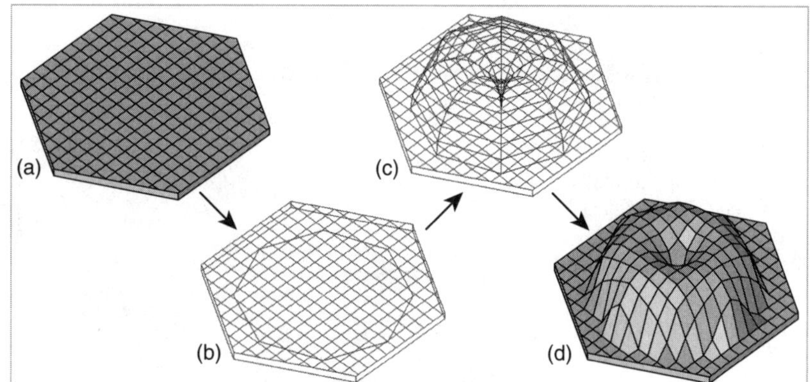

Figure 6.15

Moving a mesh with the Move Mesh tool. (a) Original object. (b) Defining the area to be moved. (c) Defining the movement height. (d) Resultant object.

- Select the Move Mesh tool (M-Tool:6a,6) and watch the instructions in the Prompts palette. The default behavior of this tool is to move parts of meshes in a radial fashion. Since the most logical movement direction for the flat mesh is perpendicular to its surface, turn on the Perpendicular Lock (W-Tool:2,1) to restrict the movement to that direction. Also, make sure that none of the Snap options are active so that the vertical movement is unhampered. 

- The Move Mesh tool is still active, prompting you to select the center of the mesh movement. Click on any point within the top meshed surface, preferably closer to the center. An octagonal shape will be rubber-banded as you move the mouse (Figure 6.15-b). This shape defines the area of the mesh to be moved. Click when you have a sufficiently large octagon, oriented as desired. You now have to indicate with the mouse how much movement you want. Drag the cursor upwards and as you do so, the meshed area you marked gets rubber-banded and moves following the shape of a certain *profile* (Figure 6.15-c). Position it at the desired height and click to freeze the mesh movement. You should have your mesh transformed as shown in Figure 6.15-d. You can see why it's important for the mesh to be relatively dense—the denser the mesh, the smoother the transformation.

- Undo what you just did and repeat the operation up to the point where you've defined the base octagon and are moving it in the vertical direction. While it's being rubber-banded in this manner, try manipulating it in other ways with the following key combinations: option key (Mac) or Ctrl+Shift keys (PC) for changing the radius of the octagonal area in addition to the height of the profile; control key (Mac) or Ctrl+Alt keys (PC) for changing the orientation of the octagon as the mouse is moved; and finally, option+control keys (Mac) or Ctrl+Shift+Alt keys (PC) for scaling the octagon independently in both directions. Thus, you can see that you're not limited to your initial shape definition of the movement area.

- Try applying repeated mesh movements to the same surface but in different directions—some upwards and some downwards. Interesting effects can also be obtained by partially extending the base octagon *beyond* the meshed surface. Play with it.

2.2 Creating and Using Profiles

The question that emerges based on what we just did is: Where does the shape of the profile that's used to move the mesh come from? The answer is simple: from the Profiles palette.

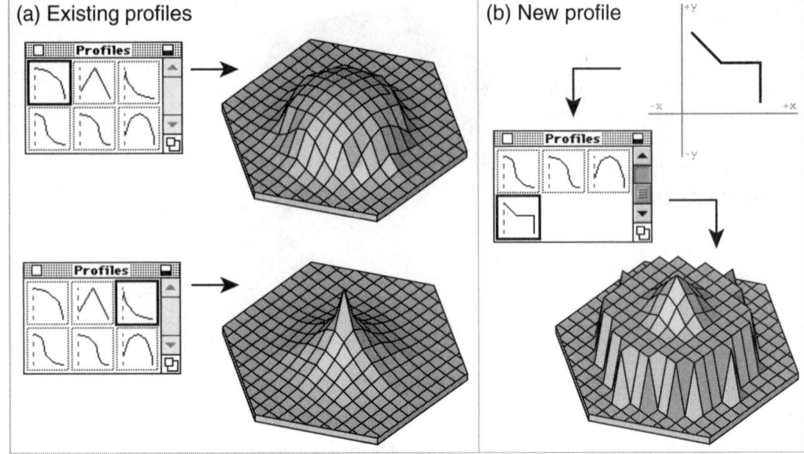

Figure 6.16

Working with the Profiles palette. (a) Choosing different profiles and the corresponding mesh movements, applied to the same original object shown in Figure 6.15-a. (b) Creating a new profile and applying it to transform the meshed object.

- Go to the Palettes menu and open the palette called Profiles. It contains a number of 2D profiles, of which one is highlighted. This is the currently active profile that is applied to the mesh movement. Choose some other profile from the palette. Then undo the previous mesh movement operation, and reapply the Move Mesh tool to the mesh. You'll find that it's now transformed differently, following the shape of the newly selected profile. Repeat with some other profiles and see the difference in the results (Figure 6.16-a).

The Profiles palette contains only six profiles by default. What if the profile you need to use for your mesh movement isn't there? In that case, you can create your own profiles and store them in the Profiles palette, just as you created your own surface styles and stored them in the Surface Styles palette.

- Create an open 2D object in the shape of your profile. (It obviously cannot be a closed shape, as you can see from the existing profiles in the palette.) Then select the Define Profiles tool, located just before the Move Mesh tool on Row 6, and apply it to the 2D object. It will immediately appear as a new profile in your Profiles palette (Figure 6.16-b). You can now use it just like any other profile for moving meshes, as shown in the illustration. The ability to create and use your own profiles gives you a lot of control over how to transform your meshed objects.

- Each profile in the Profiles palette can be further refined, if necessary, by clicking on it while pressing the option key (Mac) or Ctrl+Shift keys (PC). A dialog will open up in which you can change the width and the height of the profile. The proportions of the profile specified here will affect the shape of the mesh when it's moved using that profile. You can also delete the profile, if it's no longer needed, by clicking on the Delete button in the same dialog.

2.3 Mesh Movement Options

- Double-click on the Move Mesh tool to invoke its dialog. It contains a large number of options that determine how the mesh movement operation is executed (Figure 6.17). The first option, Movement Direction, is set to Relative To Reference Plane by default, but you should select the alternative, Perpendicular To Base Point, instead. This will ensure that the mesh is always moved perpendicular to the plane of the meshed surface, even if it's inclined. It will also save you from the hassle of turning on the Perpendicular Lock—which you'll find yourself invariably forgetting to do in the beginning—for meshed surfaces parallel to the reference plane, as in the last example. Unless, of course, you've set up a reference plane in such a way that you want to move relative to it rather than perpendicular to the meshed surface, in which case you should stick with the Relative To Reference Plane option.

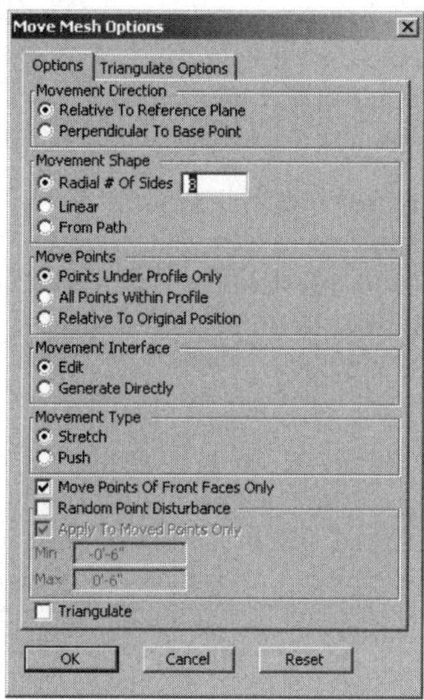

Figure 6.17

The Move Mesh Options dialog.

- The Movement Shape option lets you choose between different ways of specifying the base shape that defines the area of the mesh to be moved. Try them all out. The default, as you can see, is set to Radial # Of Sides with a value of 8, which is why your base shape was octagonal so far. This value can be changed to get a base polygon of a different size. The Linear option, on the other hand, lets you define a sequence of lines (i.e., a polyline) about which the mesh will be moved. The last option, From Path, lets you use any existing 2D shape as the base shape for the mesh movement. This is very convenient and flexible, as it lets you precisely define the part of the mesh you want to move. Figure 6.18 illustrates the From Path option using two shapes—an arc and an ellipse. The mesh movement was applied vertically upwards for the arc and vertically downwards for the ellipse.

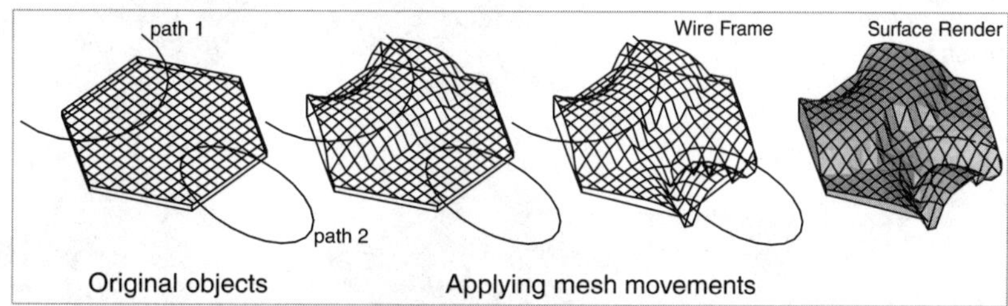

Figure 6.18

Using the From Path option for the Movement Shape of the mesh.

- The three options for Move Points come into play when a mesh move is applied on top of a previous mesh move. Undo all mesh movements you've done so far, and create two or more intersecting 2D shapes for moving the mesh using the From Path option (Figure 6.19-a). Apply the Move Mesh tool to the meshed surface using each one of your two path shapes. You'll find that the resultant mesh movement is like a *union* of the two individual mesh movements (Figure 6.19-b). This is with the Move Points option set to the default of Points Under Profile Only. Undo and reapply the same operation with the other two options in turn. You'll find that with the All Points Within Profile option, all points that fall within the move area are brought back to their original position first and then moved, resulting in the *partial loss* of the earlier movements (Figure 6.19-c). Finally, with the Relative To Original Position option, all points in the move area are still moved, but in relation to their previous height rather than in an absolute manner. In a sense, therefore, this *adds on* to any earlier mesh movements (Figure 6.19-d). The choice of which of these three options you use will depend upon what you wish to accomplish.

- Let's turn to the next two options in the Move Mesh Options dialog. The Movement Interface is set to Edit by default, which lets you define the movement dynamically. However, you can also set it to Generate Directly, in which case the movement will be applied automatically in a single step. For Movement Type, the default Stretch option, as you've seen, scales the mesh movement profile based on the specified height. The alternative Push option will retain the proportions of the profile, stretching the base of the mesh movement area if the specified height is greater than the height of the profile.

- There are only a few remaining options. Move Points Of Front Faces Only restricts the mesh movement to only those points on the surface to which the Move Mesh tool is applied, which will almost always be what is required. Deselecting this option will move *all* points of the object that lie within the profile, even if they lie on other surfaces. The Random Point Disturbance option can be selected to "disturb" the surface of the mesh by the specified values, in addition to moving it. You can also choose to apply it to the entire mesh rather than only to those points of the mesh that are moved. The final option, Triangulate, operates in its usual manner, and you can use it to triangulate only non-planar faces or all faces, based on the selection in the accompanying Triangulate Options tab.

All the mesh movements illustrated in this section were applied to plain meshes. However, they can be applied in the same manner to meshes created with the two subdivision tools, Q-Subz and T-Subz, the Terrain Model tool, and so on. This also applies to the remaining mesh manipulation tools we'll look at in this workshop.

Figure 6.19

Using the various Move Points options of the Move Mesh tool.

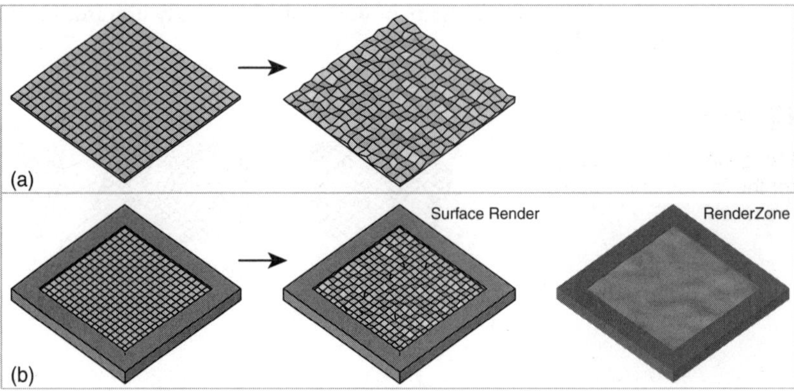

2.4 Disturbing Points

- Select the next tool in the left column of Row 6, Disturb, and invoke its dialog (Figure 6.20). Here, you can choose between two basic disturb operations, Random Disturbance and Wave Disturbance, each of which comes with its own set of options.

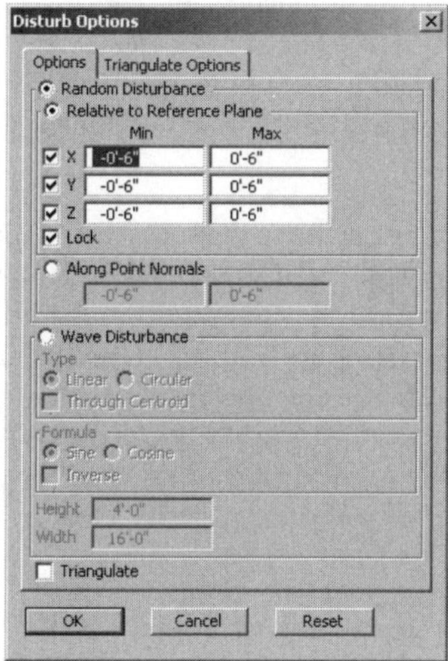

Figure 6.20

The Disturb Options dialog.

- Let's start by exploring the Random Disturbance option that is selected by default. Continue working with the same meshed slab you used in the last section, or create a new one and mesh its top face densely. Apply the Disturb tool to it. You'll find that each point of the object gets slightly displaced. Switch to the Top view and then to the Front view, and you'll see that the displacement has happened along all three directions—X, Y, and Z. The displacement value is quite small but because of the meshed surface, you can see the rippling effect quite clearly (Figure 6.21-a). The same operation applied to an unmeshed block would have been practically indiscernible.

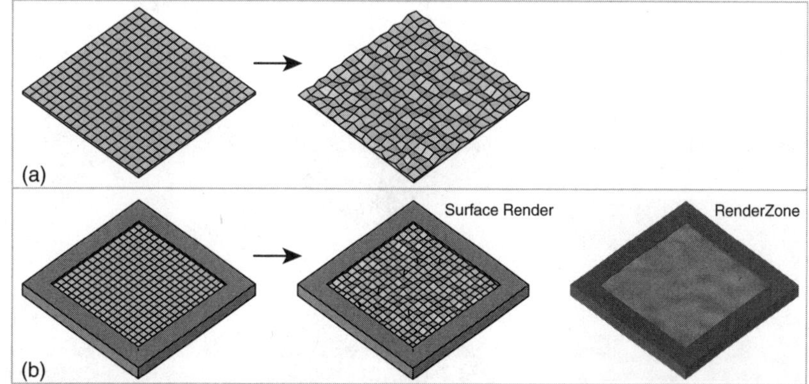

Figure 6.21

Applying Random Disturbances with the Disturb tool.
(a) Displacement in all directions.
(b) Displacement only along the Z direction.

- Move on to explore the parameters for Random Disturbance. There are two options, Relative To Reference Plane and Along Point Normals, which have the same meaning as the two Movement Direction options you saw earlier for the Move Mesh tool. To apply disturbances to inclined, curved, or any other non-orthogonal surfaces, use the Along Point Normals option to make sure that the disturbance always takes place perpendicular to the surface. For both options, you can specify the minimum and maximum values of the disturbance.

- For the Relative To Reference Plane option, deselecting the Lock box allows you to specify different values for the X, Y, and Z directions. On the other hand, you could choose to apply the disturbance only along a single direction by deactivating the other two options. Figure 6.21-b shows a random displacement only along the Z direction, applied to an object that's supposed to represent a pool of water bounded on the sides and bottom. The RenderZone image of the result shows how effective this technique is in realistically modeling a rippling effect such as that in water. (Of course, you have to add the appropriate reflection and transparency attributes to the surface style of the object for full realism.)

- Now activate the second Disturb option, Wave Disturbance. As it evident from its name, this option disturbs a meshed object in the form of waves. The default wave type is Linear. Apply the Disturb tool to a meshed object that has not been moved or disturbed (Figure 6.22-a), and you'll get the linear wave-like effect shown in Figure 6.22-b. The undulation of the wave is along the X axis of the current plane. Undo and repeat the operation a few more times, and you'll notice that the location of the wave with respect to the object is different each time, depending upon where you click on the object to select it. Go to the dialog and check the accompanying Through Centroid option. Now the wave is always located with respect to the centroid of the object, no matter where you click on it.

- Next, select Circular instead of Linear as the Type in the Disturb Options dialog—the waves will now be located in a circular fashion about a center. Again, this is affected by the Through Centroid option. If it's checked, the waves will automatically be centered about the center of the meshed surface. If not, the waves will be centered about the point that you click on to select the surface. The difference is illustrated in Figures 6.22-c and 6.22-d.

- If you're looking for mathematical precision, you can also choose between the Sine and Cosine wave formulas that are applied to generate the waves. Experiment with both types, keeping all other options the same, to see how they differ. Sine generates a wave that passes through the selection point, whereas Cosine generates a wave that peaks at the same point. You can also check the Inverse option, which will flip the *crests* (or peaks) and *troughs* (or valleys) of the wave.

Figure 6.22

Different options for Wave Disturbances, applied to a meshed surface.

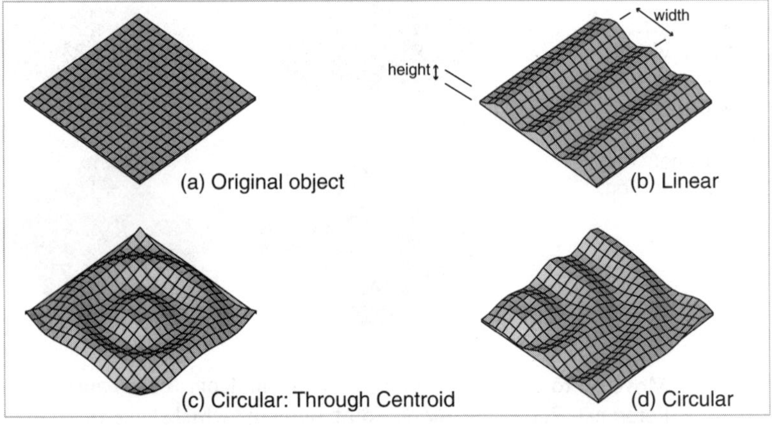

Figure 6.23

Applying a linear Wave Disturbance to an object that has all its faces meshed.

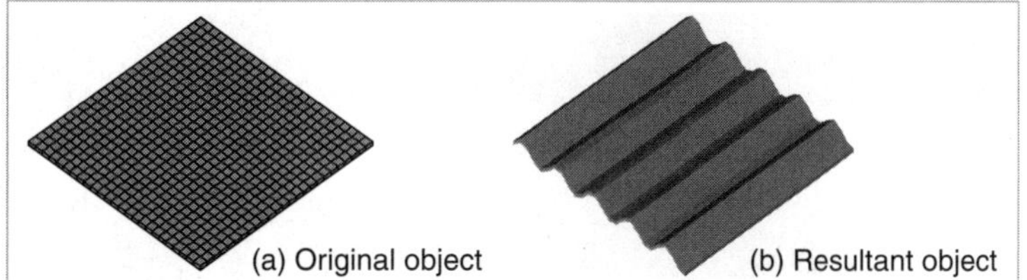

- Next, experiment with different values for the Width and Height of the waves. The width is the distance between two crests or two troughs, whereas the height is the distance between the highest point of a peak and the lowest point of a trough (see Figure 6.22-b).
- Finally, explore what happens if you apply the Wave Disturbance to an object that has all its faces meshed. Figure 6.23 shows an example of such a situation. The wave type was set to Linear and the Width was more than twice the Height. Also, both these values were relatively small compared to the dimensions of the slab. The result of the operation is a corrugated form that can be used for modeling roofing sheets and similar objects.

2.5 Deforming Objects

- We'll end this exercise by exploring the next mesh manipulation tool, Deform (M-Tool:6a,8). Invoke its dialog and you'll find that you have a choice of seven deformation types under the main Options tab, each of which can be used to deform a meshed object in different ways. Click on each one of these options—Shear, Taper, Twist, and so on—and notice the diagram in the preview window change to illustrate what the selected option does (Figure 6.24). Settle for the Twist option to begin with and exit the dialog. DEFORM
- On a new layer, create an extruded block such that its height is much larger compared to its base dimensions. Use the One Copy tool to make a copy of it. Mesh all the surfaces of one block using a relatively small mesh value; leave the other one as it is (Figure 6.25-a).

Figure 6.24

The Deform Options dialog, with the option set to Twist.

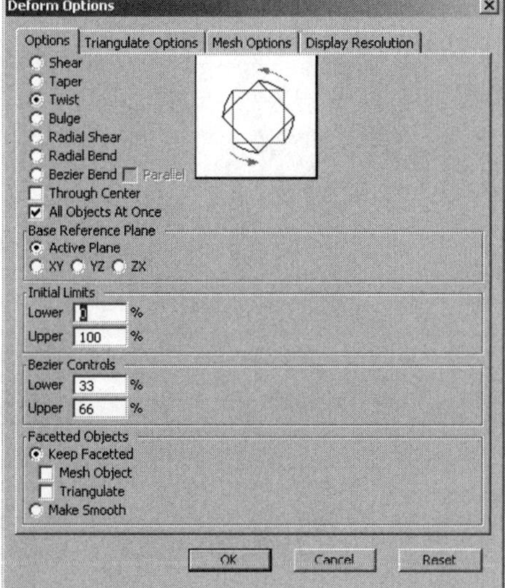

Figure 6.25

Applying the Twist operation to a meshed as well as an unmeshed object.

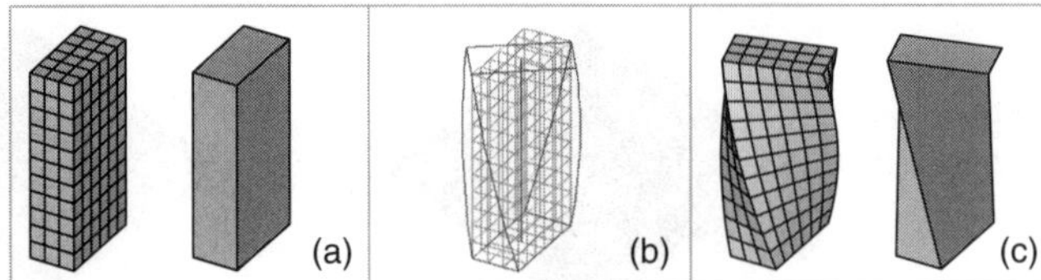

- Apply the Deform tool to the meshed block first. As soon as you click on the object, it gets highlighted and goes into an edit mode. Move the cursor around the object and you'll find that it changes in appearance when it detects a corner point or edge on the upper or lower surfaces of the block. Click on any one of these points and you'll find that as you move the mouse, a twisting motion is applied to the block about an axis (Figure 6.25-b). Click when you're satisfied with the amount of twist, and you'll be rewarded with a smoothly twisted block.

- Now apply the same operation to the other unmeshed block. You'll find that although it seems to work the same way, the end result isn't the same. The meshed block can be smoothly twisted since it's subdivided into many faces, whereas the unmeshed block is forced to retain its straight lines and cannot be properly deformed. The difference between the two is shown in Figure 6.25-c.

- Undo the Deform operation you just performed on the unmeshed block. Go back to the Deform Options dialog, and look at the Facetted Objects section at the base of the Options tab. Notice that the default selection here is Keep Facetted, which is why the extruded block continued to remain a facetted object after you applied the Deform tool to it. For the tool to work properly on unmeshed objects, you can choose the Mesh Object sub-option and set the desired meshing parameters, which are the same as those for the Mesh tool, in the accompanying Mesh Options tab, Now apply the Deform tool to the unmeshed block, and you'll find that it gets meshed and deformed just like the meshed block. You can also check the Triangulate sub-option to apply triangulation according to the settings in the Triangulate Options tab.

- On the other hand, if the Make Smooth option for Facetted Objects is selected, applying the Deform tool to the unmeshed block will make it smooth rather than meshed, as shown in Figure 6.25-d. The object display resolution is then controlled by the settings in the Display Resolution tab.

Figure 6.26

The other Deform operations applied to a meshed block.

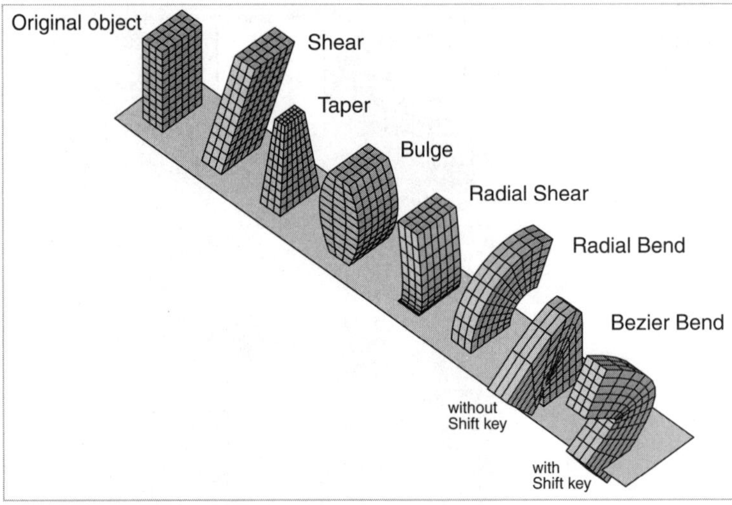

- Work with each of the remaining six Deform options, applying them to the same or to similar objects. Look at the accompanying illustration in the dialog before performing the operation to get an understanding of how it works. Figure 6.26 shows these six options applied to the same meshed block. Note that you can also numerically key in the amount of movement or rotation. The axis about which the deformation takes place is called the *deformation axis.*

- For the Bezier Bend operation, different effects can be achieved by using various combinations of the option, command, control, and shift keys (Mac) or the Ctrl, Shift, and alt keys (PC). The Shift key is particularly useful as it bends both the opposing sides of the object, rather than just the selected side. The contrast is illustrated in Figure 6.26. Be sure to explore this and the other key combinations before moving ahead.

- In addition to the seven basic operations, the Deform Options dialog contains a number of associated options that affect the way in which some or all of the operations work. Try them all out. The Through Center option affects the first six Deform operations. When checked, these operations are anchored about the midpoint of the deformation axis (Figure 6.27-a). The Parallel option, on the other hand, affects only the Bezier Bend operation, where it ensures that the top surface of the bent object continues to remain parallel to the top surface of the original object (Figure 6.27-b). The All Objects At Once option, active by default, is relevant when multiple objects are selected; it applies the Deform operation collectively to the whole group rather than to each object individually.

- Let's quickly go over the remaining options. The Base Reference Plane options let you select the reference plane based on which the deformation will happen. The values for Initial Limits define how much of the object is affected by the applied deformation. Change the Lower Limit to 25% and the Upper Limit to 75% and watch how only the middle half of the object gets deformed (Figure 6.27-c). The Bezier Controls option applies only to the Bezier Bend operation, and is used to locate the control points for the bending along the deformation axis. Bringing the points closer, for instance, by setting the Lower and Upper values to 45% and 55% respectively, will create a sharper bending at the center of the object (Figure 6.27-d).

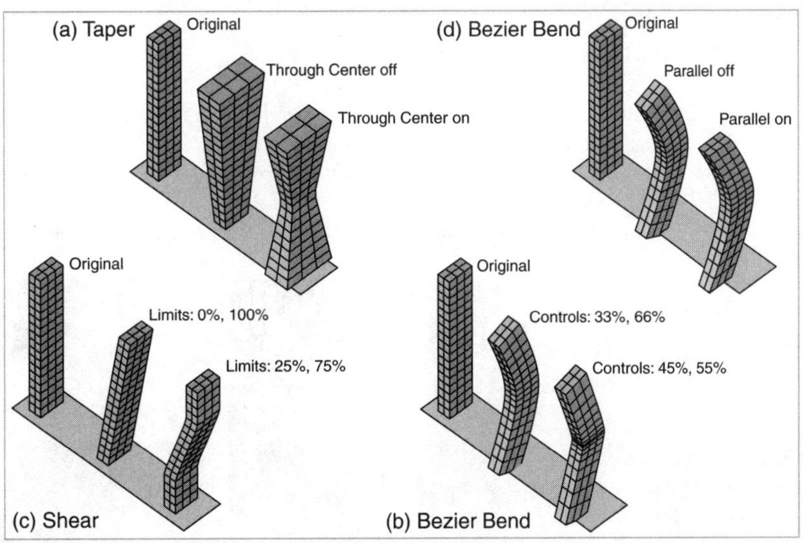

Figure 6.27

The effects of various other Deform options.

EXERCISE 3

Displacing Meshes

The next tool in the left column of Row 6, Displacement, uses a regular 2D image as the basis for the 3D movement of a meshed surface, sculpting it in the form of the image. The image has to be in grayscale rather than in color. Areas on the meshed surface that correspond to white on the image will have the maximum displacement, while areas that correspond to black will have the minimum displacement. Displacement in other areas is proportional to the corresponding shade of gray in the image. Sounds fascinating, doesn't it? Let's see how it works.

3.1 Image-Based Displacement

- The first step is to find or create an appropriate grayscale image for carrying out the displacement. You can easily create one using any paint program. The important thing to keep in mind about this image, apart from the fact that it must not have color, is to avoid sharp contrasts between black and white. A gradual gradation will produce a smoother displacement. If your paint program doesn't let you create such a gradation, you can use any photo-editing program for blurring the image. Figure 6.28 shows an image created using a paint program, which was then taken to Adobe Photoshop where the Blur filter was applied to it. This image will be used for illustrating how the Displacement tool works in this exercise.

- Get back to form•Z and create a simple 3D block. Apply a dense mesh to its top surface using the Mesh tool (M-Tool:6a,1) at the Face topological level.

- Set the topological level back to Object. Then select the Displacement tool (M-Tool:6a,9) and apply it to the block. A dialog will open up containing a large number of options for mapping the displacement. It's similar to the Texture Map Control and Decals dialogs you encountered in the last workshop—it has a preview window and various options to make the required adjustments to the displacement.

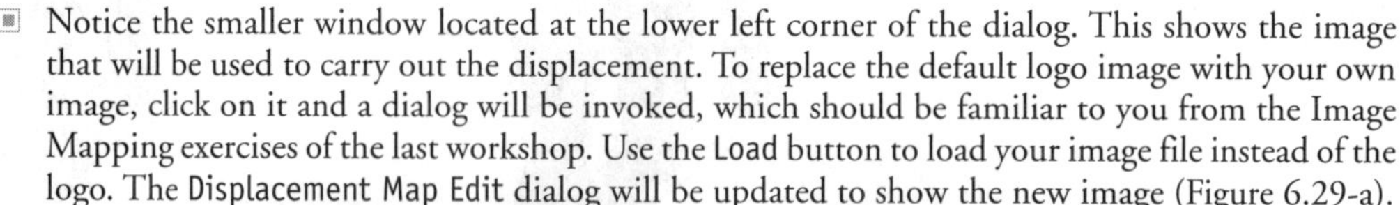

- Notice the smaller window located at the lower left corner of the dialog. This shows the image that will be used to carry out the displacement. To replace the default logo image with your own image, click on it and a dialog will be invoked, which should be familiar to you from the Image Mapping exercises of the last workshop. Use the Load button to load your image file instead of the logo. The Displacement Map Edit dialog will be updated to show the new image (Figure 6.29-a).

Figure 6.28

An image created for use with the Displacement tool. (a) The image as created using a paint program. (b) Blurring the image with an image-editing program to remove sharp contrasts.

(a)

(b)

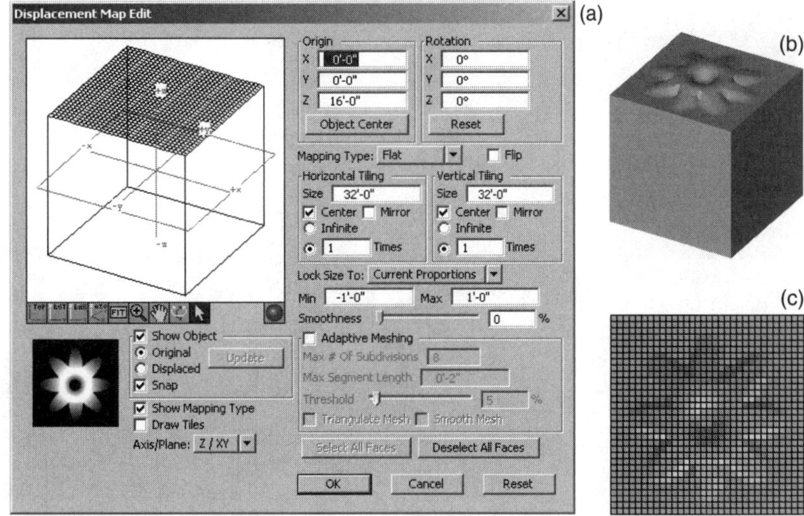

Figure 6.29

Using the Displacement tool. (a) The Displacement Map Edit dialog, showing the original object and the image that will be used for the displacement. (b) RenderZone display of the displaced object. (c) Top view of the displaced surface in the Surface Render mode.

- Now that the image has been chosen, we can attend to the actual business of displacement. Turn your attention to the preview window, where the object is shown in its original state. Click on the Displaced option in the Show Object section, located just below the window, to see the result of the displacement without modifying any of the settings. You'll see the meshed top face of the object take on a slight curvature that corresponds to the selected image. Set the display mode of the preview window to RenderZone, which should help you to visualize the displacement better (Figure 6.29-b). Exit the Displacement Map Edit dialog, change to Top view, and zoom in for a closer look at the displaced surface (Figure 6.29-c).

3.2 Basic Displacement Options

You can see that the meshed surface in Figure 6.29 does bear some semblance to the specified image, but the actual displacement seems to be of a rather low resolution. Obviously, further adjustments are necessary. We'll now explore how the options in the Displacement Map Edit dialog can be used to modify the displacement in various ways.

- Apply the Displacement tool to the same object once again, and you'll be back in the same Displacement Map Edit dialog shown in Figure 6.29-a. Thus, the object created by the Displacement tool is a controlled object—you can continue to reshape it with the Displacement tool, provided that it has not been modified by any other tool.

- The first task is to increase the resolution of the displaced surface. For this, check the Adaptive Meshing option that is located in the lower right part of the dialog. This option makes further subdivisions on all the necessary faces, thereby increasing the resolution of the surface for more accurate displacements. The amount of subdivision is controlled by two sub-options that you've already explored for the Q-Subz tool in Section 1.3. Leave the Max # Of Subdivisions to 8 for now, but keep reducing the Max Segment Length until you see a noticeable difference in the displacement resolution. Make sure the Displaced option under Show Object is selected, and keep clicking on the Update button to see the changes in the top meshed surface. You can switch the preview window to the Top view so that the changes are easier to see. Figure 6.30 shows the object in the preview window with a noticeably higher resolution than before. Notice how additional subdivisions have been made only in the necessary areas.

Don't reduce the Maximum Segment Length too much as you might run out of memory for the Displacement operation. As always, you should settle for the largest value you can get away with.

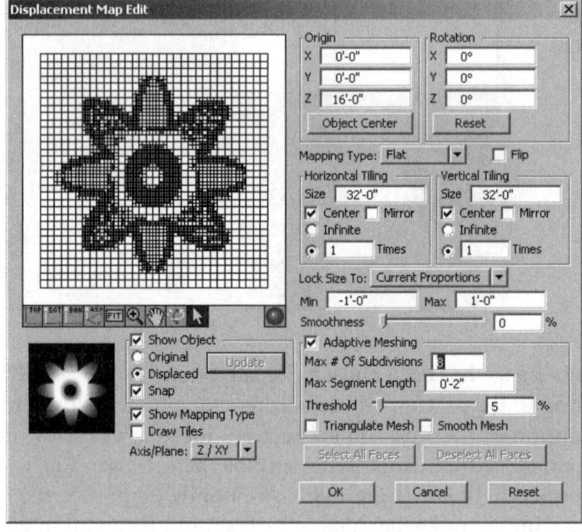

Figure 6.30

Increasing the resolution of the displacement by using the Adaptive Meshing option.

- The Adaptive Meshing section has a Threshold value that you can change as well. This is used to adjust the sensitivity of the displacement to the gradations in grayscale of the image. A lower value increases the sensitivity and vice versa. Test this by previewing the displacement for the two extreme Threshold values. There's also the usual Triangulate Mesh option that you can use when required. An additional Smooth Mesh option is available, which you can skip by for now. We'll learn how to apply it when the time comes.
- Next, turn off the Adaptive Meshing option and concentrate on the Smoothness slider bar located just above it. Try out different values for this option and Update to see the results. You'll find that larger smoothness values soften out areas of sharp contrast in the image, leading to a smoother displacement (Figure 6.31). At the same time, however, there's a loss of detail. If your original image has no sharp contrasts, the Smoothness can remain at the default value of 0%, since the displacement will already be fairly smooth.

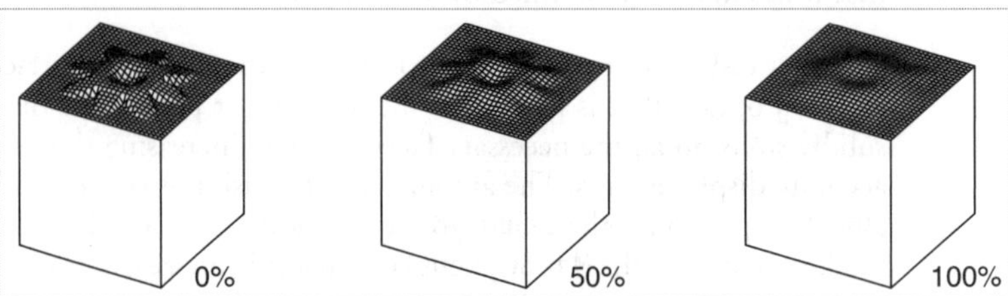

Figure 6.31

Increasing the Smoothness value of the displacement from 0% to 50% to 100%.

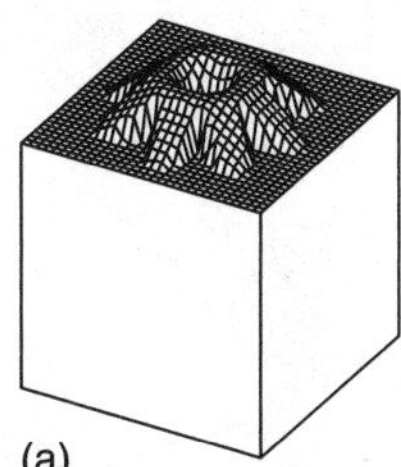
(a)

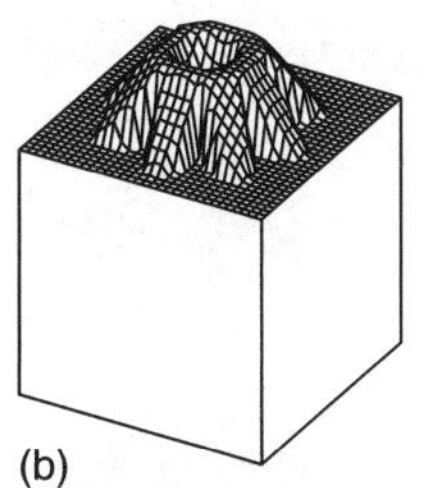
(b)

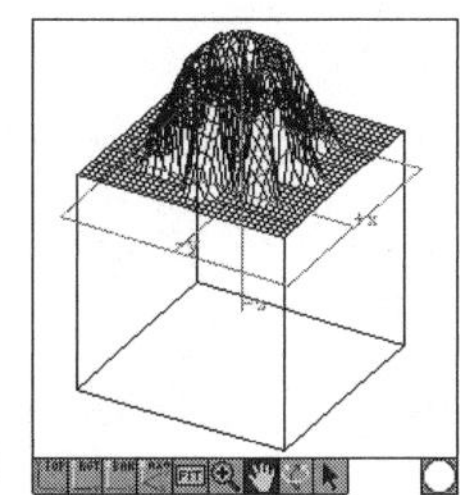
(c)

Figure 6.32

The effect of increasing Max and decreasing Min values on the displacement. The Displacement preview window as the Min value is reduced is also shown.

- Set Smoothing back to the default value of 0% and go up further to look at the Min and Max values. As mentioned earlier and as you can verify from the actual displacement, areas corresponding to white in the image have the most displacement, while those corresponding to black have the least. The actual *extents* of these displacements come from the Max and Min values respectively. Keep increasing the value of Max and watch the white areas project out of the original surface more considerably (Figure 6.32-a).
- Similarly, keep decreasing the value of Min to well below 0'-0". You'd expect the black areas to dig deeper into the surface of the object as a result of this change. That doesn't really happen, but the total projection of the displacement beyond the surface does increase proportionately to the difference between the Max and Min values (Figure 6.32-b). Look carefully at the object in the preview window as you further reduce the value of Min. You'll find that the distance between the top face and the XY plane running through the center of the object keeps decreasing, and this is what is causing the total projection to increase (Figure 6.32-c).

This XYZ coordinate system that you see in the preview window in Figure 6.32-c dictates how the displacement is mapped to the object. Not only can the displacement be mapped in a planar fashion, as it is by default, it can also be mapped in a cylindrical or spherical fashion, on the entire object or only on selected faces. We'll explore the different mapping types in the remaining sections of this exercise, as well as learn how to adjust the location and orientation of the coordinate system to achieve the desired displacement effect.

3.3 Flat Mapping

- Start afresh with a new object to explore the various mapping types. It can be just a simple 3D block like the one you had earlier. This time, however, don't mesh it, but apply the Displacement tool to it directly. Load your image as the displacement image in the Displacement Map Edit dialog as you did before. Notice that the Mapping Type, located below the Origin and Rotation sections, is currently set to Flat.
- Click on the Displaced option below the object preview window. Since the original object is unmeshed, there will be no displacement. Turn Adaptive Meshing on and adjust its values so that some displacement is obtained. You might also have to increase the level of Smoothing a little for the displacement to occur. Change the Min and Max values too if you like. You'll now find that both the top and bottom faces of the object get displaced this time (Figure 6.33).

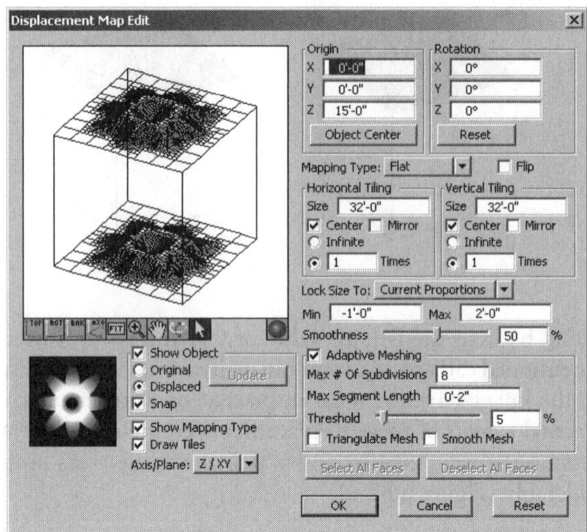

Figure 6.33

Applying the Displacement tool to an unmeshed object, with the mapping type set to Flat.

- Since the original object was not meshed, the displacement with adaptive meshing is applied to all its faces. Also, the mapping type is set to Flat which means that the displacement will occur in a planar fashion only along the +Z direction. This is why only the top and bottom faces of the block shown in Figure 6.33 get displaced, and in the +Z direction. Look closely at the axes in the preview window by setting it to the Original mode to verify this. Depending upon the default size of the mapping tile, some of the displacement might "spill over" to the vertical sides of the object. We'll see how to fix this problem later.

- The axes can be rotated in order to make the displacement happen in a different direction, and therefore to different surfaces. Turn to the Rotation section located in the top right corner of the Displacement Map Edit dialog, and change the rotation of Y to 90°. You'll now find that the displacement coordinate system flips and the displacement occurs along two of the vertical opposing faces of the object (Figure 6.34-a). A value of –90° for Y will displace the two same faces but in the reverse direction (Figure 6.34-b). A value of 90° for X will displace the other two sides of the block (Figure 6.34-c). Likewise, try out other values and see the changes in the axes orientation and the resultant displacement by switching between the Original and Displaced modes.

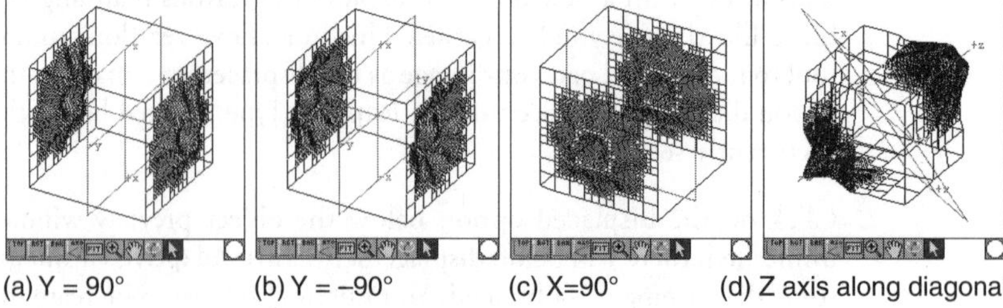

(a) Y = 90° (b) Y = –90° (c) X=90° (d) Z axis along diagonal

Figure 6.34

The effect of rotating the axes on the displacement.

- You know from working with the Texture Map and Decal tools in Workshop 5 that you can also rotate the axes graphically in the preview window. To do this, make sure the Show Object mode is set to Original, and use the Pointer tool to rotate the axes. Keep in mind the current Axis/Plane selection below the preview window, and recall that the current axis shown in red cannot be rotated. You can also switch to one of the planar views in the preview window to adjust the orientation better. After positioning the axes in a desired fashion, switch back to the Displaced mode to see the result. Figure 6.34-d shows the Z axis aligned along the diagonals of the block and the resultant displacement.

- Switch back to the Rotation value of 90º for Y to get the displacement along the two vertical faces of the block (6.35-a). If you want only one of these faces to be displaced without affecting the other, set the Show Object mode to Original and select that face which isn't to be displaced in the preview window using the Pointer tool. It gets grayed out, indicating that it's no longer available for displacement (Figure 6.35-b). Now switch to the Displaced mode and you'll find that the displacement is only restricted to the other face (Figure 6.35-c). Note that you could have achieved the same result by applying the Displacement tool at the Face topological level to only the face you wanted to displace.

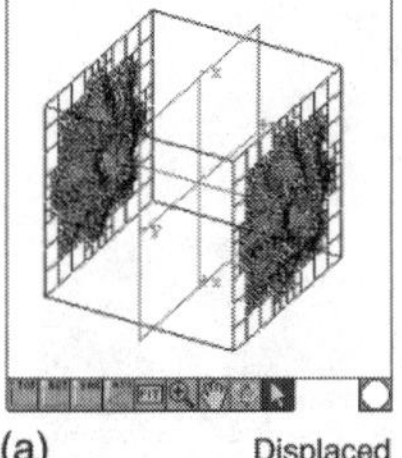

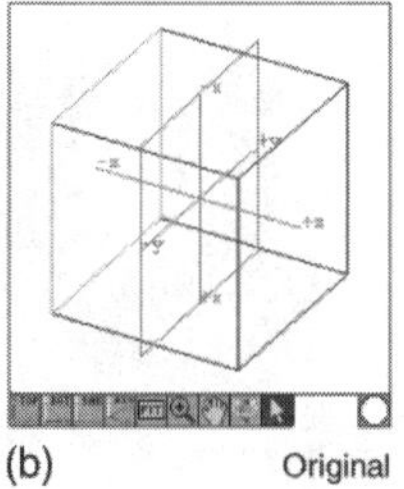

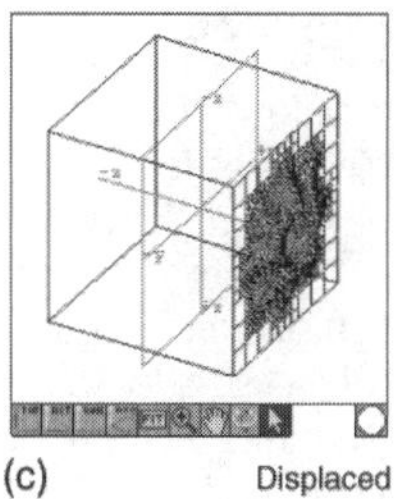

Figure 6.35

Manipulating faces for displacement. (a) Displacement of the entire object. (b) Deselecting one of the faces. (c) The resulting displacement.

- Switch back to the Original mode and click on the Deselect All Faces button. This will deselect all the faces in the preview window, with the result that no face of the object will now be displaced. Thus, you can retrieve your original, undisplaced object whenever required. To reselect all the faces of the object for displacement, use the Select All Faces button.

- Now turn to the Horizontal Tiling and Vertical Tiling sections in the Displacement Map Edit dialog, which should be familiar to you from the Texture Map and Decal tools. These let you fix the size of the displacement map and the frequency with which it's repeated across a surface. By default, the displacement map is first scaled according to the size of the object, so that the Size values for both Horizontal Tiling and Vertical Tiling take on the size of the face they're applied to. Larger or smaller areas can be displaced by increasing or decreasing the Size values; to prevent the displacement spilling over to other faces, decrease the Size value to the required extent. To change the two tiling Size values independently of the other, select None from the Lock Size To popup menu, in which case the displacement may no longer be in proportion to the image size. Figure 6.36-a shows an example of such a displacement, applied to all the faces of the object. Notice how the side faces are affected by the displacement spilling over the top and bottom faces of the block.

- You can also change the position of the displacement with respect to the object by moving the origin, placed by default in the center of the object. The move can be done numerically, by specifying the coordinates in the Origin section, or graphically with the Pointer tool. To use the graphical method, the Original option must be selected in the Show Object section. Since the Snap option in the same section is checked, you can readily snap to the points of the object. By default, the displacement is centered about the specified origin, as you can see from all the preceding illustrations. To position, instead, the lower left corner of the displacement at the origin (so that the displacement happens along the +X and +Y directions only), deselect the Center option in both the Tiling sections. Figure 6.36-b shows an example of such a displacement applied only to the top face of the block. All the faces were first deselected and only the top face was selected, after which the origin was moved to the lower left corner of the top face.

Here is a shortcut to move the origin from the center of the object to the collective center of only those faces that are selected for displacement—hold down the option key (Mac) or Ctrl+Shift keys (PC) when the preview window is in Original mode. The button in the Origin section will change to Center Of Faces instead of Object Center. Click on it to make the change in the origin position.

- If the specified tile size is much smaller than the face which is to be displaced, you can choose to have more than one tile along both directions by specifying the required number in the Times fields. Or else, you can choose the Infinite option that will repeat the tiles along the entire extent of the face, as shown in Figure 6.36-c.

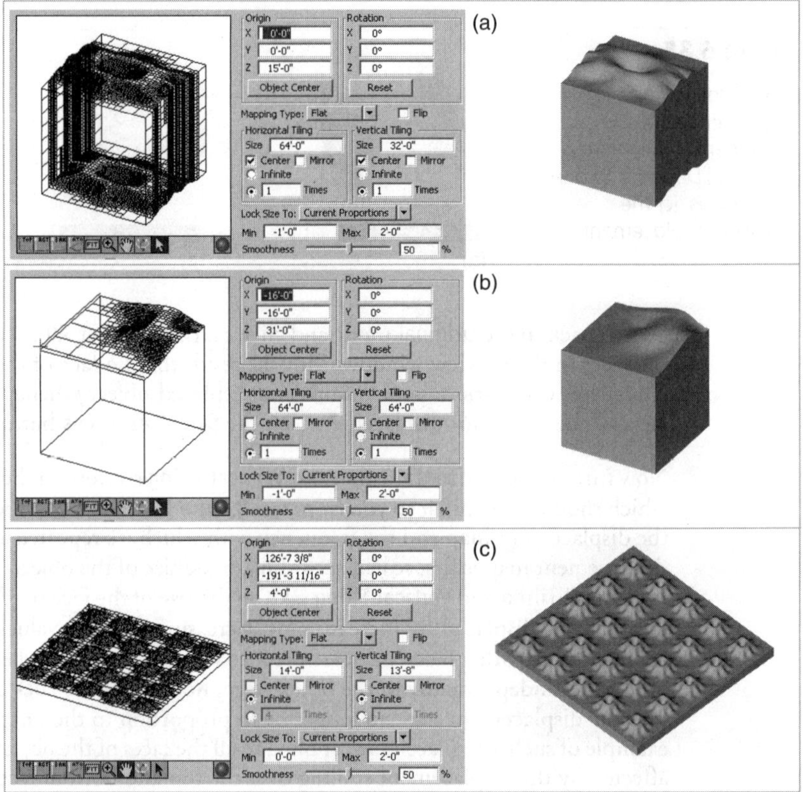

Figure 6.36

Manipulating the Tiling and Origin values for displacement. (a) Tile size disproportionate to the image size and larger than the object size. (b) Moving the Origin to a corner of the object and deselecting the Center option. (c) Tiling the displacement infinitely along both directions of a horizontal slab.

3.4 Cylindrical and Spherical Mapping

- To make a fresh start with the other displacement mapping types, Cylindrical and Spherical, create a new object similar to the one you used for Flat mapping. This will provide you with a good basis for comparison between the three mapping types. Don't mesh the object. Apply the Displacement tool to it directly, and choose your displacement image in the usual manner in the Displacement Map Edit dialog.

Figure 6.37

Using Cylindrical Mapping for image-based displacements. (a) Making some minor changes to the default parameters to displace one face. (b) Selecting the Infinite option and adjusting the Tiling sizes to displace all the vertical faces. (c) Activating the Smooth Mesh option to smooth out the object.

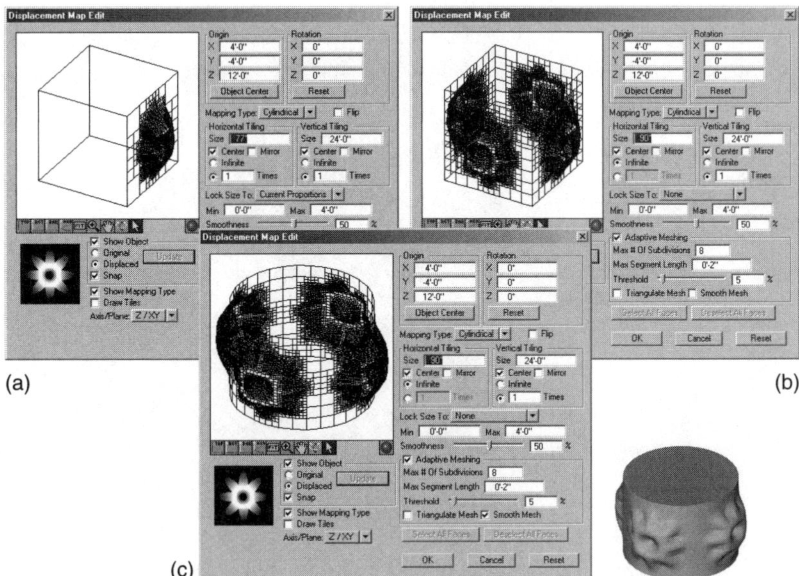

- Change the Mapping Type to Cylindrical and set the preview window to the Displaced mode. Turn Adaptive Meshing on, and adjust the values until you can see some displacement in the object. You might have to increase the Smoothness value. Change the Min and Max values if necessary. What you'll see is the use of a cylindrical shape as the displacement mapping boundary, with only a single displacement in the +X direction (Figure 6.37-a).

Of course, you could have easily obtained the same result using Flat mapping with the appropriate axes orientation. So why bother to use Cylindrical? In response to that question, make the following changes to the Tiling values and see what happens.

- First of all, set the Lock Size To option to None. Then change the horizontal tile Size value, so that it's equal to 360° divided by the number of vertical faces of the object. This is equal to 90° for the sample object shown in Figure 6.37. You can also adjust the vertical tile Size value if it doesn't match the aspect ratio of your image. Note that Vertical Tiling is specified in distances while Horizontal Tiling is specified in degrees for Cylindrical mapping. Finally, choose the Infinite option for Horizontal Tiling rather than 1 Times. You'll now see the displacement along all the vertical sides of the object, facing outwards (Figure 6.37-b). This was something you could not have achieved with Flat mapping.
- Take the additional step of selecting the Smooth Mesh option in the Adaptive Meshing section. Your object will now acquire a nice cylindrical curvature in addition to the displacement (Figure 6.37-c).
- Needless to say, there's a lot more that you can do. You can change the horizontal tile Size to 360° to wrap a single displacement around the entire object. You could change the orientation of the axes to change the direction of the cylinder and thereby displace different areas of the object. Explore these and more options until you're comfortable with the Cylindrical mapping type.

Figure 6.38

Displacing a cubical block using Spherical Mapping with the Infinite Tiling and Smooth Mesh options activated.

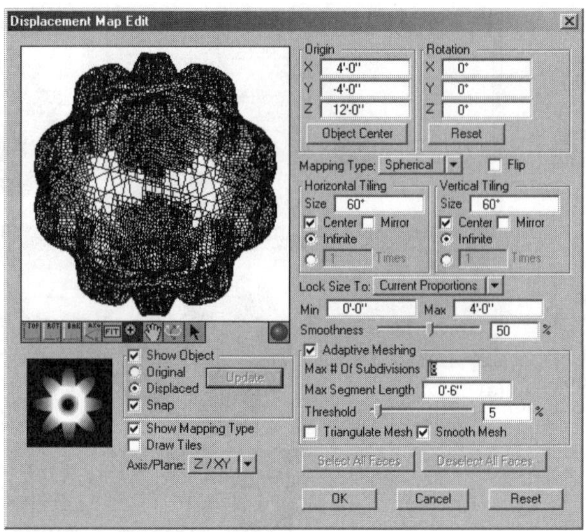

- Next, change the Mapping Type from Cylindrical to Spherical in the Displacement Map Edit dialog for the same object. The displacement mapping boundary is now spherical in shape, and if the Smooth Mesh option is still active, the displaced object will acquire a spherical curvature (Figure 6.38). The number of displacements will depend upon the Horizontal Tiling and Vertical Tiling values. Note that both are now specified in degrees. You might have to change them independently of each other, for which you need to set the Lock Size To option to None.
- Again, there are a lot of options that you can explore in detail, including different tile sizes, number of times the displacement is tiled both vertically and horizontally, different axes orientations, and so on. Do so before moving on to the next exercise.

EXERCISE 4

Smooth Curves, C-Curves, and C-Meshes

In Section 1.5 of Workshop 1 (Letting Yourself Go), you worked with the four Spline tools located in the right column of Row 3, which let you directly draw various kinds of spline curves. In this exercise, we'll first work with a tool that lets you create smooth curves from a source object, which can be an open or closed 2D shape. Located in the left column of Row 7, the Curve tool is accompanied by a number of other tools for editing and manipulating smooth curves. We'll see how these work. We'll also look at an alternate tool for creating curves, and a tool for creating a 3D mesh from a sequence of control lines.

4.1 Creating and Reconstructing Smooth Curves

- Move to a new layer, and change to the Top view. Set the object generation mode to 2D Surface and create two shapes using the Vector Line tool—one open and one closed (see Figure 6.39-a).

Then use one of the Copy modes to make two more copies of these objects. You'll use them to explore the three different types of smooth curves that are available in form•Z.

- Select the Curve tool (M-Tool:7a,1) and invoke its dialog (see Figure 6.39-b). It gives you the choice of three different types of smooth curves: Nurbs Curve, Tangent Curve, and Spline Curve. Select each type in turn and apply the Curve tool to the multiple copies of the open and closed linear shapes you have created. Each shape will be transformed to a curve, and each curve will be different depending upon the curve type. The original curve remains in ghosted mode by default. This allows you to easily compare the different curve types derived from the same source shape and see how they differ from each other.

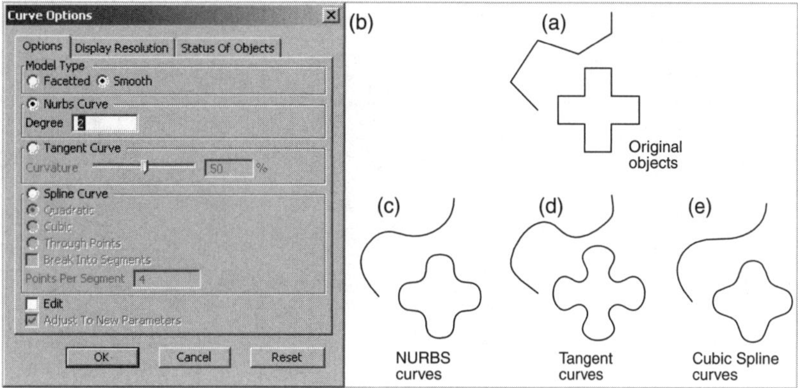

Figure 6.39

The dialog of the Curve tool, and the three different types of smooth curves generated from the same set of objects.

Here is a brief explanation of the different curve types. A *NURBS curve* is defined by a set of control points (which are the points of the original source shape), a weight factor for each control point that pushes the curve further away from or closer to it, and a degree that determines how flat the curve is. As you can see in Figure 6.39-c, this type of curve doesn't pass through the control points except for the first and last point. In contrast, a *tangent curve* passes through all the control points (see Figure 6.39-d), and has a curvature parameter that determines how sharply the curve bends at each point. And finally, a *spline curve* may or may not pass through the control points, depending upon the subtype selected (Figure 6.39-e). Quadratic and cubic splines don't pass through the control points. Spline curves can also be broken into segments (see the Curve Options dialog in Figure 6.39-b), representing several independent NURBS curves joined together. This is preferable for many modeling applications within form•Z as well as for exporting to other applications.

- Now that you have a basic understanding of the three different types of smooth curves, go back to the Curve Options dialog and experiment with different settings for each of the curves. An easy way to do this is to activate both the Edit and Adjust To New Parameters options located at the bottom of the Options tab. If you now apply the Curve tool to an existing smooth curve, the current settings in the Curve Options dialog will be applied to it, and an Edit dialog will be invoked allowing you to change its parameters. Being a controlled object, you can also graphically change the shape and parameters of the curve using the Edit Controls tool (M-Tool:4b,2), as you learned in Section 5.2 of Workshop 2 (Bringing a Sense of Scale).

- Notice that you can choose between the Facetted and Smooth model types for the curve in the Curve Options dialog as well as in the Edit dialog. Since these are meant to be smooth curves, you would rarely have reason to choose the Facetted option. The Curve Options dialog also has the

Display Resolution tab for setting the resolution of the curve if its model type is Smooth, as well as the Status Of Objects tab for specifying the status of the original object from which the curve is derived.

- Move on to the next tool in the left column of Row 7, Reconstruct Curve. Select it and apply it to one of the smooth curves you have created. This invokes the Curve Reconstruct preview dialog shown in Figure 6.40, where you can change the degree and number of control points of a curve while maintaining its shape as much as possible. Experiment with changes in these parameters, and click on the Reconstruct button to see the changes.

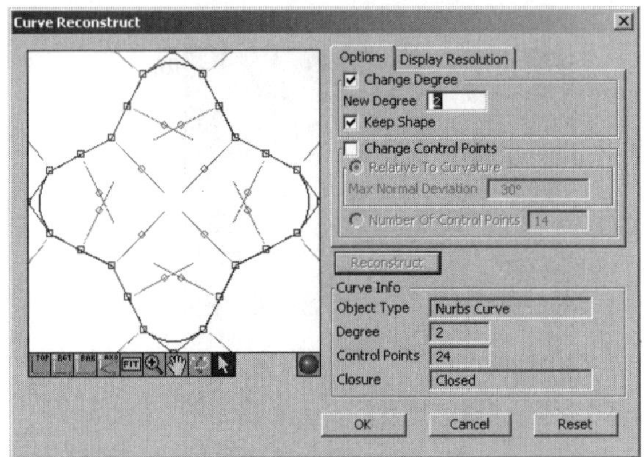

Figure 6.40

The Curve Reconstruct dialog for reconstructing the closed curve shown in Figure 6.39-e.

4.2 Other Smooth Curve Tools

Once created, smooth curves can be connected to other smooth curves in different ways, extended, as well as broken. These operations are similar to the line editing tools in the left column of Row 11, which we explored in Section 5.3 of Workshop 2 (Bringing a Sense of Scale).

- Create a set of two open smooth curves, as shown in Figure 6.41, and make two additional copies of them. We'll use these as the base objects for applying the remaining smooth curve tools.
- Select the Attach Curve tool (M-Tool:7a,3), and apply it to one pair of smooth curves. You'll find that the curve you picked first is stretched to be attached to the curve picked second. The selection points will affect how the curves get attached—all four scenarios are illustrated in Figure 6.41-a. The curves continue to remain separate entities, as you can verify by selecting them with the Pick tool.
- Invoke the dialog of the Attach Curve tool and explore its options. You'll find that under the default Stretch Curve operation you just performed, you can choose between four different Alignment methods, representing increasing levels of smoothness between the curves. Try them all out by undoing and reapplying the operation with different settings. Also check out the effect of selecting the Keep Opposite End option, which adds extra control points to ensure that the opposite edge to the edge being attached is not affected by the operation. Instead of stretching the curve, you can move it to attach itself to the second curve by choosing the Move Curve option. The last option, Merge, merges the two curves into one object after attaching them.

- Next, select the Blend Curve tool (M-Tool:7a,4), and apply it to another copy of the original smooth curve set. Compare the results, shown in Figure 6.41-b, to what you achieved using the Attach Curve tool. You'll find that this operation creates a new smooth curve blending the two original curves, giving you a total of three curves instead of two. Unlike Attach Curve, the order of selecting the original curves here does not affect the resultant curve.

- Move on to explore the options in the dialog of the Blend Curve tool, some of which are the same as those for the Attach Curve tool. The only new option is Degree, which determines the degree for the depth direction of the new curve. It can be the same as that of the picked curves, or you can specify a different value by choosing the New Degree option.

- The next curve tool, Merge Curve (M-Tool:7a,5), can only be used on two curves that touch each other at a point. To try it out, first use the Move tool with Endpoint snapping activated, and move one of the curves so that its endpoint touches the endpoint of the other curve. Then select the Merge Curve tool and apply it both these curves. You'll find that the two curves are seamlessly merged into one object; the point where they touched is nicely smoothed out (see Figure 6.41-c).

- You'll find two different merge options in the dialog of the Merge Curve tool. The Smooth Curves option works by smoothing out the point where the two curves touch. You can set the level of Smoothness using the accompanying slider bar. The alternate option, Align Curves, also merges the curves into one object, but it works by reshaping only the first curve at the merged point; the shape of the second curves remains intact. The difference is clear in Figure 6.41-c. The four different Alignment methods are the same as those for the Attach Curve and Blend Curve tools.

- The last two smooth curve tools are very straightforward. The Extend Curve tool (M-Tool:7a,6) can be applied to an endpoint of a curve to extend it, while the Break Curve tool (M-Tool:7a,7) can be used to break up a curve into two separate entities by clicking on the point where the break is required. Try out both of them. Also explore the options of the Extend Curve tool, which allow the curve to be extended in different ways: by interactively specifying a spline, an arc, or a segment; or by a specified distance. You can also use the Merge option to merge the extension with the original curve.

Figure 6.41

The Attach, Blend, and Merge Curve operations applied to a set of smooth curves. The selection points and order of picking the curves is indicated for the Attach and Blend operations.

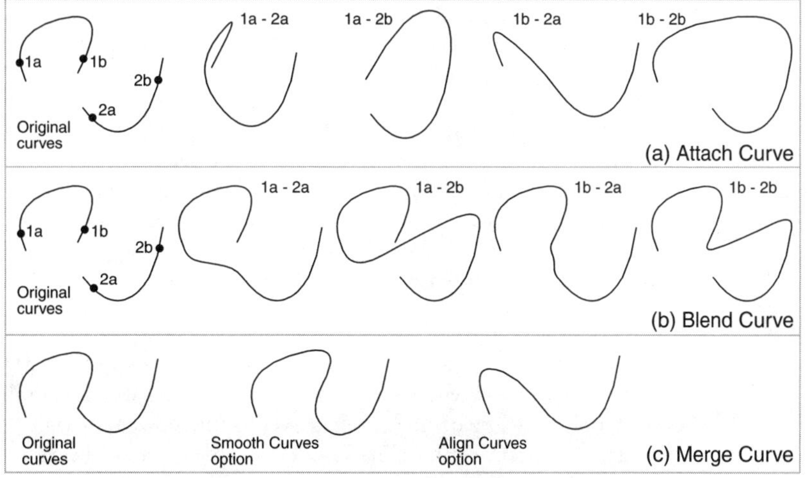

4.3 2D Controlled Curves

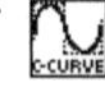

- Create a fresh 2D surface object with the Vector Line tool. Select the last tool in the left column of Row 7, C-Curve (M-Tool:7a,8), and apply it to this object. The object gets converted to a curve; at the same time, it takes you to an edit mode where the controls of the curve are displayed for editing and all other tools are grayed out (see Figure 6.42). That's why the curves generated by this tool are called *c-curves* or *controlled curves.*

- Move your mouse around the controls, and you'll find that the cursor changes its appearance depending upon the type of control—point, segment, or knot (which is the point at the middle of a segment). Move some controls and see how the shape of the curve changes interactively as you do so. Notice that a point or segment can be moved in any direction (provided direction snapping is off), but a knot can only be moved along the control segment that it is a part of. Once you're satisfied with the adjustments to the curve, exit the c-curve edit mode by double-clicking in the graphics window.

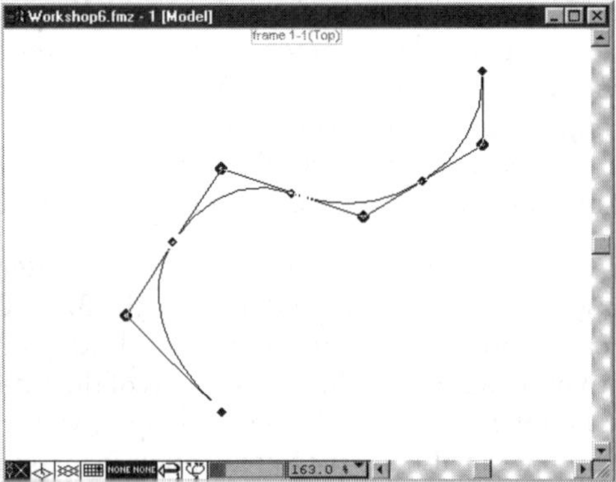

Figure 6.42

Applying the C-Curve tool to an object takes you to the c-curve edit mode.

- Reapply the C-Curve tool to the same curve and, once again, you'll be taken to the edit mode where you can directly make adjustments to its shape. Thus, you can see that the C-Curve tool is very convenient for fine-tuning the shape of a curve interactively after generating it from an initial configuration of control segments.

- Next, invoke the dialog of the C-Curve tool (see Figure 6.43). You'll find various options that decide how the curve will be generated. If you select the Construct Directly option instead of the default Edit option, the curve will be generated directly without entering the edit mode. The Construct Plain Curve option, when checked, creates a curve without storing its controls, which means it cannot be edited later. If you want to edit a curve while retaining its original settings rather than applying current settings to it, you should deselect the Adjust To New Parameters option.

- The other options in the dialog of the C-Curve tool are used to determine the shape of the curve. There are two basic types: Splines and Quick Curves. You are familiar with spline curves from the Curve tool you worked with earlier, as well as the tools in the right column of Row 3. Quick curves are mathematically simpler than splines, and are therefore faster and easier to use. Work with each curve type in both categories, and see how different shapes of curves are generated from the same base objects. Three of these are illustrated in Figure 6.44.

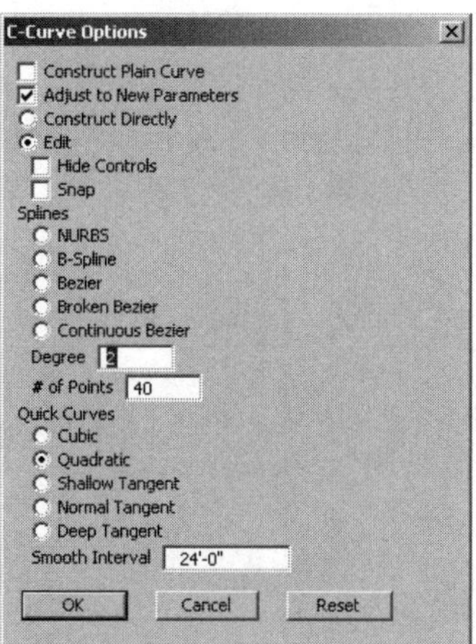

Figure 6.43

The dialog of the C-Curve tool.

- Look at the additional options under both curve types. Splines has the usual Degree parameter that determines the curvature of a spline curve. It also has an additional # of Points option, the value of which determines the resolution of the curve. Unlike the Curve tool, which can create both facetted and smooth curves, the C-Curve tool can only create facetted curves. For smoother c-curves created using any of the Splines, you would increase the # of Points value. For Quick Curves, on the other hand, the resolution is determined by the Smoothing Interval value; a smaller value leads to a higher resolution.

- Finally, look at the two options under the Edit mode that we haven't yet discussed. The Hide Controls option applies only to the Quick Curves group. When selected, all the controls in the Edit mode are hidden, allowing you to modify the curve seemingly by moving the curve itself rather than its controls. The Snap option, on the other hand, is useful when you're working with control points that need to be coincident. Turning this option on will facilitate the process of snapping to existing control points. The tolerance for this Snap is the same as that for object snapping and can be changed in the Object Snaps dialog. Try out both these options.

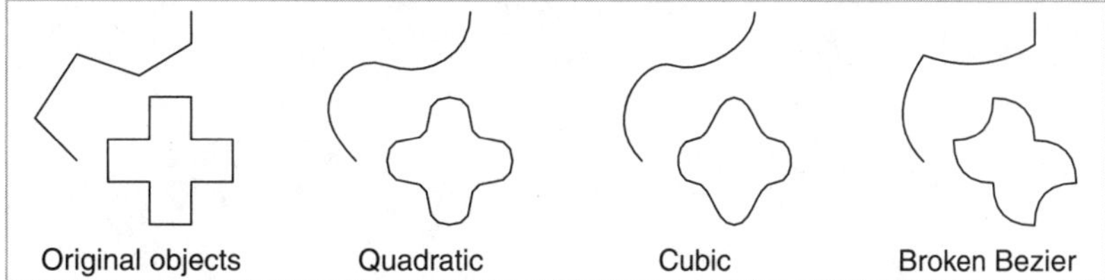

Figure 6.44

Three different types of c-curves generated from the same set of objects.

4.4 Deriving Other Objects from Curves

- You must have, by now, a number of curved objects in your window, created using the Curve and C-Curve tools. You can use these curves as the base shapes for deriving many different kinds of objects. Switch to a non-planar view and apply various kinds of derivative tools from Row 5 to these curves. Figure 6.45 shows a sampling. For some derivative tools, such as 3D Extrusion, a smooth curve will automatically yield a smooth object, while a facetted curve will automatically yield a facetted object. For other tools, such as **Revolve**, the smooth versus facetted choice is made in the tool dialog.

Keep in mind that once you derive another object from a curve, it loses its controls and cannot be reshaped.

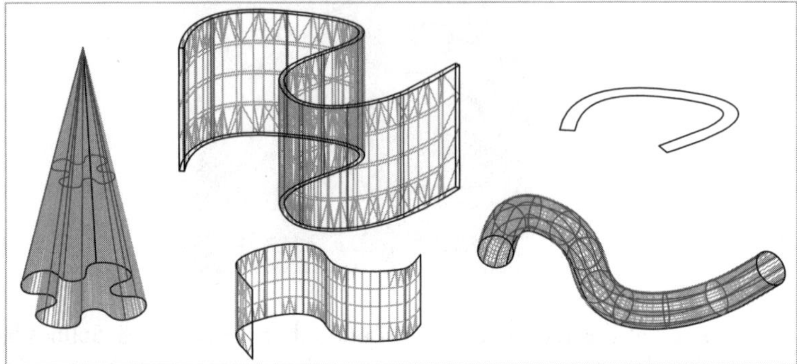

Figure 6.45

Using the curves created with the Curve and C-Curve tools to derive other 2D and 3D objects.

- So far, we've generated curves from 2D shapes that lie completely on one plane. It's also possible to generate curves from 2D shapes that are non-planar. To see how this works, create a closed 2D shape on the XY plane made up of at least 10 individual segments (Figure 6.46-a). Then set the topological level to **Segment**, turn on the **Perpendicular lock**, and move a few segments of this object in the Z direction. You now have a 2D object that's non-planar (Figure 6.46-b). Convert it to a curve using the **Curve** or **C-Curve** tool—you'll get a non-planar 3D curve (Figure 6.46-c). This can be treated like any other object, for instance, it can be extruded to create a 3D curved solid (Figure 6.46-d). It would have been difficult to create this object using other tools, but you saw how easy it was using this procedure.

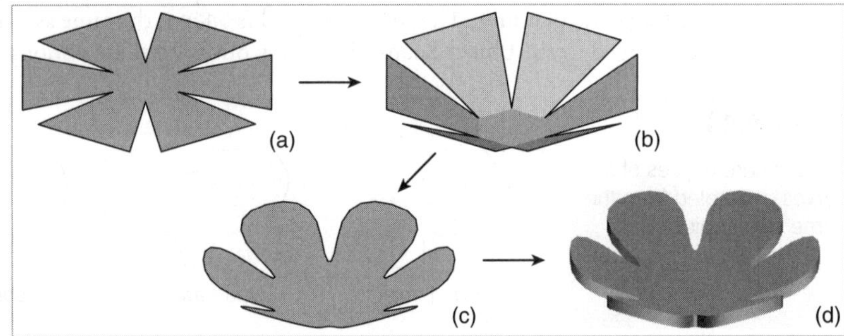

Figure 6.46

The sequence of steps for creating a non-planar curved object.

4.5 3D Controlled Meshes

Just as a controlled curve can be generated from a single control line, it's possible to generate a controlled mesh from a sequence of control lines positioned appropriately in 3D space. This provides enormous flexibility and precision in modeling curved surfaces. Just as with controlled curves, these meshed objects are stored along with their controls, enabling them to be modified later. They're called *c-meshes* for short, and they involve the use of the **C-Mesh** tool, the last tool in the right column of Row 7.

Figure 6.47

Creating a controlled mesh. (a) The control lines created on a plane. (b) Adjusting the heights of the control lines. (c) The resultant 3D mesh.

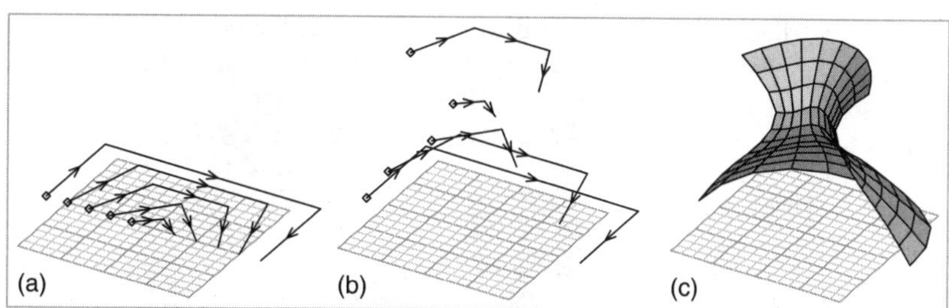

- Clear all the objects in your window or move to a different layer. Use the Vector Line tool in 2D Surface mode to draw a sequence of shapes on the XY plane. Ensure that their starting points and directions are synchronized, as shown in Figure 6.47-a. Then turn on the Perpendicular Lock and move each shape in the Z direction to a different height. Switch to the Front view, if necessary, to adjust the heights more precisely. The objective is to get a sequence of shapes at different heights, as shown in Figure 6.47-b. You'll use these shapes as control lines to generate a 3D mesh that spans across them.

- Next, activate the Pick tool and select all these lines sequentially, either from top to bottom or vice versa. It's important to pick them in the correct sequence. Finally, select the C-Mesh tool (M-Tool:7b,12), and click anywhere in the graphics window. A 3D mesh will be generated. At the same time, you'll enter the *c-mesh edit mode*, which is identical to the c-curve edit mode—the various control points and lines are indicated in a similar fashion. Move these around and observe the corresponding changes in the meshed object. Keep in mind that you're now moving in 3D, so depending upon whether the Perpendicular Lock is on or off, you'll move in a direction perpendicular to or on the reference plane itself. Double-click or select any other tool to exit the c-mesh edit mode after you've finished sculpting your mesh as desired (Figure 6.47-c)

To give a thickness to the meshed surface, you can use the Parallel tool (M-Tool:5a,7) in the Double Parallel (Solid) mode, as you learned in Section 6.2 of Workshop 4.

- The mesh shown in Figure 6.47 was generated with the default settings of the C-Mesh tool. Invoke its dialog to explore what the other options are (Figure 6.48). Rather than testing these on different sets of control lines, or undoing and reapplying the C-Mesh tool to the same set of lines but with different options, we'll make use of the Adjust To New Parameters option to regenerate the same mesh but with different settings. This option isn't activated by default, so go ahead and select it in the C-Mesh Options dialog. The other options at the top of the Options tab are the same as those in the C-Curve Options dialog, which were covered in Section 4.3.

- Skip the Length Of Net and Depth Of Net options for now, and turn your attention to the options for Mesh Length and Mesh Depth in the lower half of the Options tab. The *length* of the mesh is the direction along a control line, and the *depth* is the direction across the control lines, shown in Figure 6.49-a. This should also be clear from the mesh illustrated in Figure 6.49-d, which has different values for its length and depth. There are three options for determining both the length and the depth subdivision of the mesh. You can specify the actual mesh interval numerically by using the At Intervals option, or the # Of Segments into which the mesh should be divided. The third option, At Control Points, will use the actual control line intervals for the subdivision. For the Mesh Depth, there's an additional Per Segment sub-option for # Of Segments, which, when checked, will apply the number of segments specified between each pair of control lines rather than across the entire depth of the mesh. Experiment with all these options and with different values for the first two, applying the C-Mesh tool to the same object to see the resulting changes.

Figure 6.48

The dialog of the C-Mesh tool.

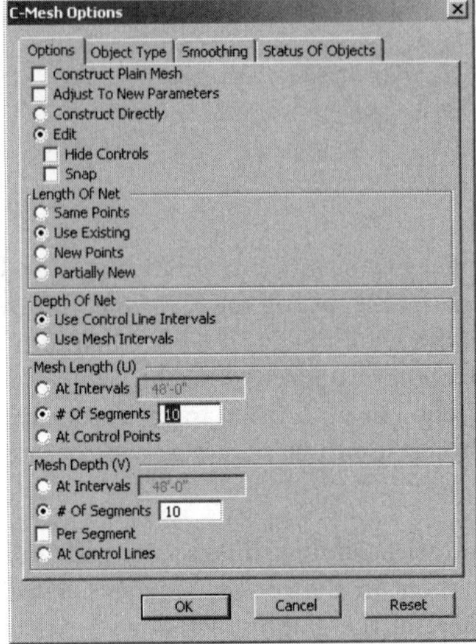

Figure 6.49 shows various length and depth variations for the same mesh shown earlier in Figure 6.47. Note that the length and depth options don't have to be the same. Notice also that a smaller mesh interval or a larger number of segments leads to a denser mesh, which will render more smoothly but take more time. So strive for the least density you can get away with.

Figure 6.49

Different mesh length and depth settings for the same mesh.

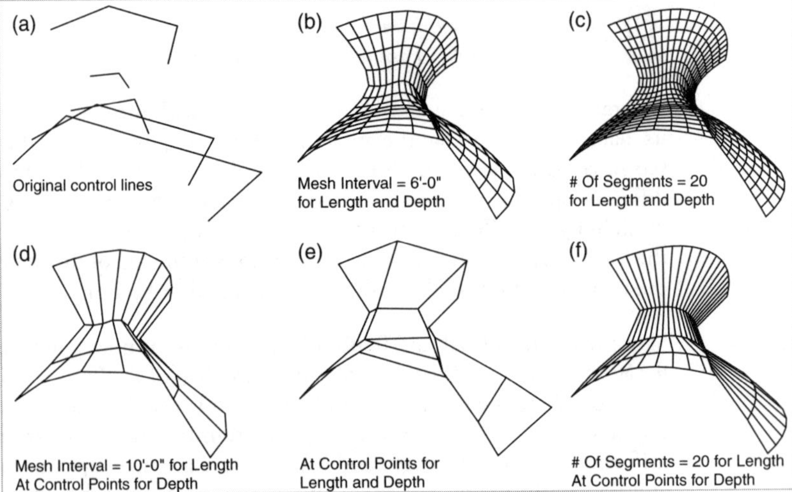

- Now turn to the Smoothing tab in the C-Mesh Options dialog. You'll find that smoothing is on by default for both the Length and Depth of the mesh, and the smoothing type is set to Quick Quadratic. This defines the type of curvature that will be applied to the control lines when they're smoothed. Set both the Length and Depth to None, and see how it affects the resultant mesh. You'll find that the mesh now strictly follows the contours of the control lines rather than being smoothed out. This is useful when you draw your control lines very precisely and want your mesh to pass exactly through them.

- Get back to the Smoothing tab. You'll find that the curve types here are essentially the same as those you encountered in the C-Curve Options dialog, with the same parameters. Experiment with a few different kinds of curves, both for Length and Depth, and see how they affect the curvature of the control lines and the resultant mesh.

Let's now turn to the Length Of Net and Depth Of Net options under the Options tab that we had skipped earlier. The *control net* here refers to the surface created by joining all the control lines, over which the mesh is then created. It's what you see in thick black lines when you're in the c-mesh edit mode. The difference between the control net and the mesh itself is illustrated in Figure 6.50.

- Start with the two Depth Of Net options that are contrasted in Figures 6.50-a and 6.50-b. The Use Control Line Intervals option, which is checked by default, gives you as many control lines along the depth of the net as there originally are, and in the same position. Try it on a set of control lines. Then undo the operation and apply the C-Mesh tool again, but with the Use Mesh Intervals option selected this time. You'll have a new set of control lines along the depth of the net that coincides with the Mesh Depth specification. This option is useful because you now have more control lines that you can manipulate for reshaping the mesh—assuming that your mesh depth specification is greater than your original control line specification.

- The Length Of Net options are related to the number of points in a set of control lines. The first option, Same Points, requires all the control lines to have the same number of points. This is the most accurate way of generating a c-mesh, so it's useful to have an option that carries out this check. For control lines that don't have the same number of points, such as those shown in Figure 6.51-a, the Same Points option won't work. The Use Existing option, which is the default selection, uses only the existing points of the control lines, both in the net and in the resultant mesh (Figure 6.51-b). The third option, New Points, automatically inserts new points on all the control lines until they're equal to the maximum number of points on any control line. Not only that, the points will be evenly distributed along the length of each control line, often changing its original shape by discarding its earlier points. The configuration of the mesh naturally changes as well (Figure 6.51-c). The last option, Partially New, inserts new points as well, but the original points are retained, preserving the shape of the original control lines to a greater extent (Figure 6.51-d).

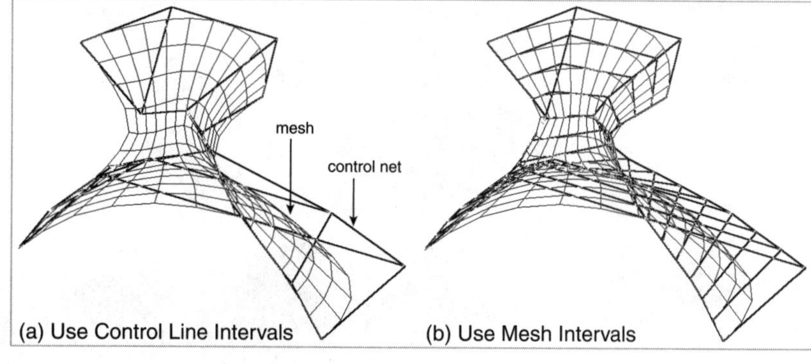

Figure 6.50

The same mesh of Figure 6.49-b in edit mode, but with different options for Depth of Net.

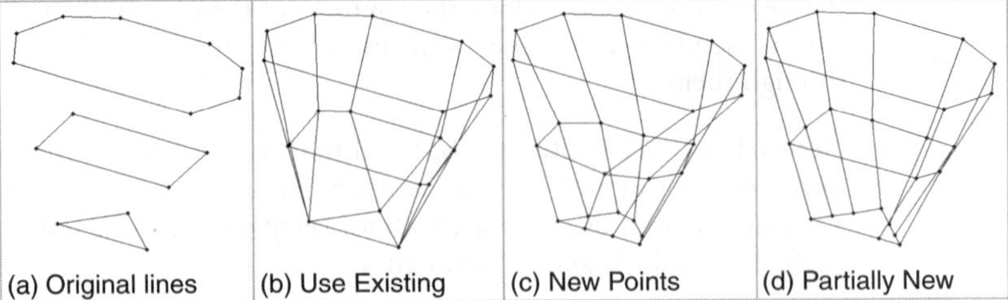

Figure 6.51

Exploring the various Length Of Net options. The Points display was turned on in the Wire Frame mode.

Let's move on to look at the final set of options for the C-Mesh tool. This involves defining the type of meshed object that will be created by the operation.

- In the C-Mesh Options dialog, turn to the Object Type tab. Here, you can specify the type of c-mesh object you want to generate (Figure 6.52-a). Explore all the available options using the same set of control lines (Figure 6.52-b) and compare the results. The Open Ends option creates a simple meshed surface (Figure 6.52-c). This is the default selection, which is why all the meshes you've created so far have been surfaces. The Closed Ends option closes the two ends of the mesh. For control lines that are closed, this will create a solid object (Figure 6.52-d), whereas for control lines that are open, this will close the ends by connecting the endpoints of the first and last lines, but still remain a surface. The All Closed option works in the same manner as Closed Ends for closed control lines, but for open control lines, it adds an additional face to completely close the object, converting it to a solid. Finally, the Ring option curves the mesh along its depth by connecting the first and last control lines. For closed lines, this will again produce a solid (Figure 6.52-e) while for open lines, the mesh remains a surface object.

- Try out also the additional options in the lower half of the Object Type tab, which can be used to make other adjustments to the meshed object. The Round Front and Round Back options can be checked to round the ends of all types of meshed objects except Ring (Figure 6.52-f). The size of the rounding is determined by the value specified in the Ratio box. The Two Sided option can be checked to make all surface meshed objects two-sided (i.e., surface solids) rather than one-sided (i.e., surface objects). The Triangulate option can be used to triangulate the resultant mesh so that all its faces are planar. The last Adjust Direction option, on by default, ensures that "inside-out meshes" are not created. It's advisable to keep this option always checked.

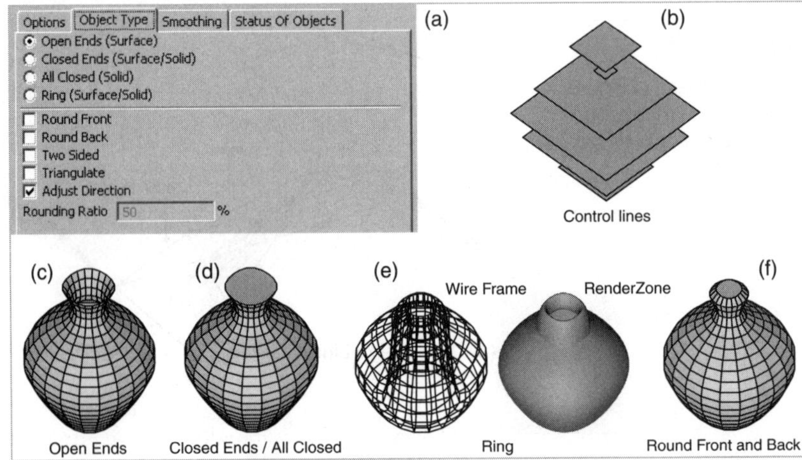

Figure 6.52

Exploring the various c-mesh object types.

EXERCISE 5

Nurbz and Patches

In Section 4.1, you saw that one of the three smooth curves type is a NURBS curve, which is defined by a set of control points, a weight factor for each control point that pushes the curve further away from or closer to it, and a degree that determines how flat the curve is. Extending this to three dimensions, a *NURBS surface* is a curved surface defined by a set of control lines with parameters such as degree, knots, and weights that can be modified to smoothly reshape it. Objects whose surfaces are NURBS surfaces are referred to as *nurbz* in form•Z. *NURBS* stands for Non-Uniform Rational B-Splines and is a standard term in the lexicon of computer graphics.

You've already encountered, albeit briefly, the nurbz object type in earlier workshops. In Section 5.1 of Workshop 2 (Bringing a Sense of Scale), you saw how the Convert tool (M-Tool:11b,6) can be used to transform 3D primitives to nurbz objects. In Exercise 1 of Workshop 4 (Enhancing Your Modeling Capabilities), you saw how derivative tools such as Revolve (M-Tool:5b,1) can create the revolved object as a derivative nurbz object.

In this exercise, we'll start by seeing how to create more generic objects with the nurbz personality from a set of open or closed control lines or points. We'll also look at several other tools for editing and manipulating nurbz objects. All these tools are located in the right column of Row 7 of the modeling tool palette.

Subsequently, we'll move on to work with objects that are internally represented by a set of *patches*. A single patch is a rectangular or triangular tile, whose sides are control lines from which curved surfaces can be generated. The patches that make up an object don't have to be all of the same size, enabling them to effectively model curved objects with widely varying surface detail. All the patch tools are located in the left column of Row 8 of the modeling tool palette.

5.1 Creating and Reconstructing Nurbz

- On a new layer, create a set of at least four appropriately spaced open or closed control lines (see Figure 6.53-a), just as you created for the C-Mesh tool. Take the usual precaution of ensuring that their first points and directions are synchronized. After creating the lines, prepick them in the correct sequence using the Pick tool.

- Select the Nurbz tool (M-Tool:7b,1) and click anywhere in the graphics window. A nurbz surface object will be generated from the selected controls (see Figure 6.53-b). Unlike the C-Mesh tool, you're not transported into an edit mode for reshaping the object immediately after creation. There are various means to edit this object later, both graphically and by changing the numeric parameters, which we will study soon. For now, verify that the object you've created is actually a nurbz object by applying the Query tool (M-Tool:12b,1) to it. The Object Type in the Query dialog will be listed as Nurbz Object.

NURBZ

- Let's now explore the options associated with the Nurbz tool, accessible through its dialog (Figure 6.53-c). The first set of items determines how the nurbz surface is constructed. The default option, By Loose Lofting, generates the nurbz surface from open or closed control lines connected in a given order. As you can see in Figure 6.53-b, the resulting surface does not strictly pass through all the control lines. Also, this method has some additional requirements for values of the Length and

Depth Degree parameters—which, as you have seen for c-meshes, determine the degree of curvature of the surface *along* and *across* the control lines respectively. The length must be less than the number of segments in the control lines, and the depth must be less than the number of control lines.

- Undo the Nurbz operation, and reapply it to the same set of control lines using the second Surface Construction option, By Tight Lofting. You'll find that the nurbz surface now passes through all the control lines (see Figure 6.53-d). There are no strict Length and Depth degree requirements for this method.

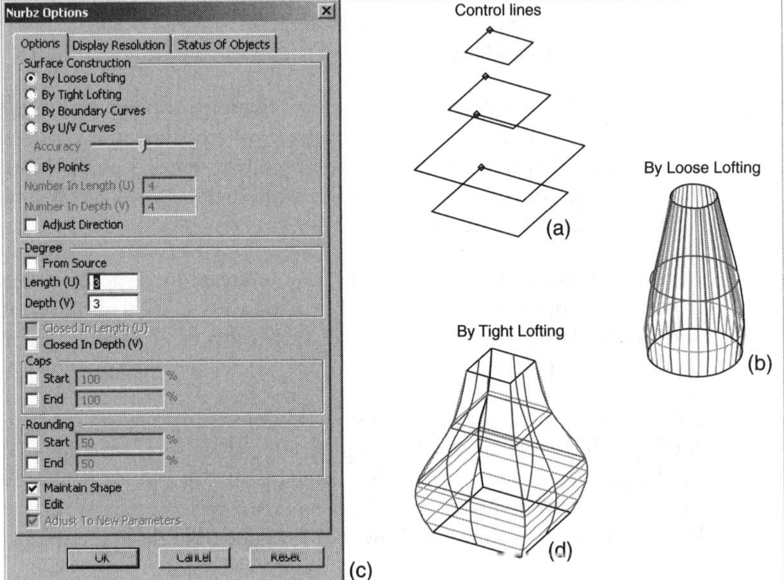

Figure 6.53

Creating nurbz objects using the Loose Lofting and Tight Lofting methods. The Nurbz Options dialog is also shown.

- To try out the remaining three Surface Construction options, you'll need different controls. The By Boundary Curves method needs two, three, or four open curves that define the boundary of a surface; it then constructs the nurbz surface to fill the area between the curves, as shown in Figure 6.54-a. The By U/V Curves method constructs a nurbz surface from a network of open curves, as shown in Figure 6.54-b. It includes an Accuracy slider that can be adjusted depending upon how closely you need to surface to pass through all the curves. The last method, By Points, needs a grid of points from which to create the nurbz surface, as shown in Figure 6.54-c.

- There are some additional options in the Surface Construction section. The Number In Length and Number In Depth values determine the number of curves or points along the length and depth of the nurbz surface for the By U/V Curves and By Points methods respectively. The Adjust Direction option applies only to the two Lofting methods. When checked, it corrects any inconsistent directions in the original control lines, thereby eliminating the twist in the nurbz surface that would otherwise result.

- There are various other options in the Nurbz Options dialog, apart from the construction type and degree, which determine the shape and type of the nurbz object. The Closed In Length and Closed In Depth options can be used to close the nurbz object along the length and depth respectively. The two Caps options can be selected to close one or both ends of the object. If both ends are capped, a solid nurbz object is created. You can also choose to round one or both ends of the object with the two Rounding options. Not all of these options are applicable to all the construction methods; the ones not applicable will be deactivated when a specific method is selected. The Maintain Shape option is relevant to all methods, and is used to preserve the shape of an existing nurbz object when the Nurbz tool is applied to it with higher degree values. The shape is maintained by adding more control points to the object. The remaining options in the Nurbz Options dialog are similar to those you've studied for the Curve and C-Mesh tools.

Figure 6.54

Creating nurbz objects using the other Surface Construction methods.

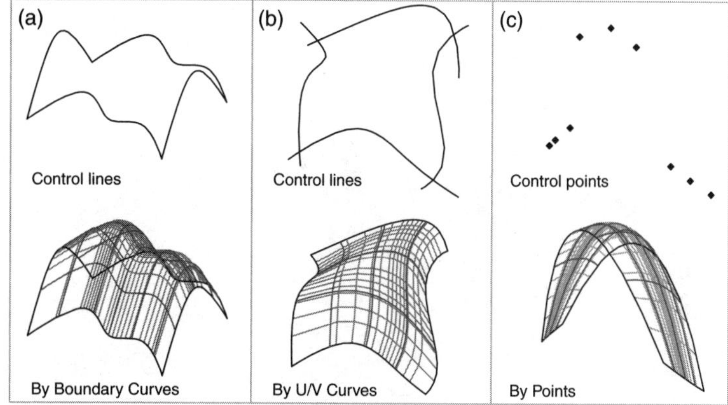

- The Nurbz tool can also be used to directly convert 3D primitives, as well as objects created with the Revolve, Helix, Sweep, and Skin tools to nurbz objects by simply clicking on them. Try it.

Often, it might be easier to draw out the profile curves of a desired nurbz object than to accurately define its control lines. In such a situation, the next tool on Row 7, Nurbz Cross Sections, comes in handy.

- Create a set of at least three profile curves, as shown in Figure 6.55-a. Select them in the correct sequence with the Pick tool. Then select the Nurbz Cross Sections tool (M-Tool:7b,2) and click anywhere in the graphics window. You'll find that 10 cross-sectional curves will be generated, spanning across each one of the selected profiles (see Figure 6.55-b). You can now use these as the control lines for generating a nurbz surface using the Nurbz tool (Figure 6.55-c).

- Look at the options in the dialog of the Nurbz Cross Sections tool. The default method is Place Along Curve, as in the operation you just performed. The alternate method, Use Reference Plane, is useful when planar cross-sectional curves are required, as shown in Figure 6.55-b. You would need to activate a reference plane that intersects the profile lines and is parallel to the required cross-sectional curves.

Figure 6.55

Using a set of profile curves to generate control lines for a nurbz surface with the Nurbz Cross Sections tool. The picking sequence of the curves is indicated.

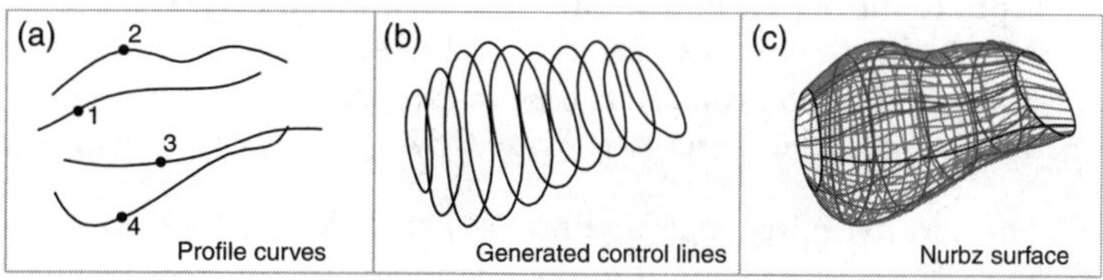

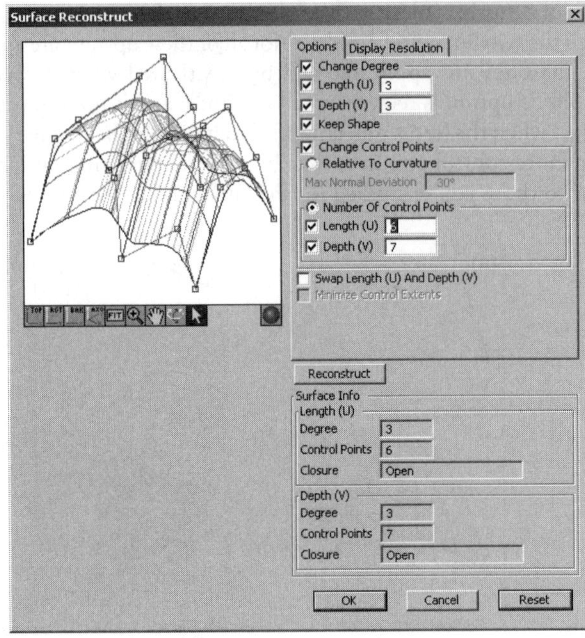

Figure 6.56

The Surface Reconstruct dialog for reconstructing the nurbz surface shown in Figure 6.54-a.

- The Nurbz Cross Sections tool also gives you a Create Surface option for directly creating the nurbz surface from the generated cross-sectional curves. The Degree, Caps, and Rounding parameters of the surface can be specified. The construction method used is By Tight Lofting.

- Move on to the next tool in the right column of Row 7, Reconstruct Nurbz. Select it and apply it to one of the nurbz objects you have created. This invokes the Surface Reconstruct preview dialog shown in Figure 6.56, where you can change the degree and number of control points of the nurbz surface while maintaining its shape as much as possible. Experiment with changes in these parameters, and click on the Reconstruct button to see the changes. The tool is very similar to the Reconstruct Curve tool you used to reconstruct smooth curves in the last exercise.

5.2 Other Nurbz Tools

Once created, you can apply a variety of operations to nurbz objects using a set of tools very similar to the smooth curve tools you worked with earlier in Section 4.2. Let's look at each one of these in turn.

- Select the Extract Curve tool (M-Tool:7b,4), and apply it to one of the nurbz objects you have created. You'll find that this gives you two curves, one along the length and the other along the depth of the object, intersecting at the point you clicked on. The original object gets ghosted by default. In a sense, this operation is the reverse of the nurbz creation operation. In the Options dialog of this tool, you can choose to extract multiple curves along one or both directions, across the extents of the object (see Figure 6.57-a), instead of curves at the click point only.

- The next five nurbz tools on Row 7—Attach Nurbz, Blend Nurbz, Merge Nurbz, Extend Nurbz, and Split Nurbz—are identical to their counterparts for smooth curves—Attach Curve, Blend Curve, Merge Curve, Extend Curve, and Break Curve—that we covered in Section 4.2, except that they operate on nurbz surfaces rather than curves. Even their options are very similar. Try them out to

WORKSHOP 6

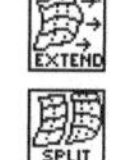

attach, blend, and merge a pair of nurbz objects, and extend and split a single nurbz object. These operations are illustrated in Figures 6.57-b through 6.57-d. Note that the Merge Nurbz tool will only work on nurbz surfaces that having a matching edge.

- The next tool on Row 7, Untrim Nurbz, is unique to nurbz objects. It is used to restore parts of nurbz surfaces that have been trimmed with the Curve On Nurbz tool (which is discussed next) or the Trim/Split tool (which we'll be covering in the next exercise). To carry out this operation, simply apply it to the trimming outline, and it will be removed, restoring that portion of the surface (see Figure 6.57-e). It can be repeatedly applied to restore specific trimmed portions. You can also check the Untrim All option in the tool dialog to remove all trimming outlines and restore the object to its untrimmed state in one step.

- The final nurbz tool on Row 7, Curve On Nurbz (M-Tool:7b,11), is also unique to nurbz objects. It is used to create a curve on a nurbz surface, which can stay on the surface or can be used to trim the surface. You can also map an existing curve on the surface instead of drawing it. To see how this works, access the tool dialog and choose the second drawing mode of the Sketch On Surface option as well as the Trimmed Nurbz option under Object Type, with the Curves Enclose Holes sub-option. Select a nurbz object by clicking on it. You'll find that you can now draw a curved shape directly on the surface. The drawing modes work similarly to the corresponding drawing tools on Row 3. After you finish the drawing by double-clicking or moving outside the surface, the shape you have drawn is used to create a hole in the object, as shown in Figure 6.57-f. You can also create more precise shapes on the active reference plane, and use the Map Existing Curve option to map these shapes on the surface of the nurbz object. The accompanying Max Pspace Size value can be used to control the size of the shape when it is mapped into the parameter space (or *pspace*) of the surface.

Now that we know how to create and manipulate nurbz objects, let's look at how to do the same for patch objects.

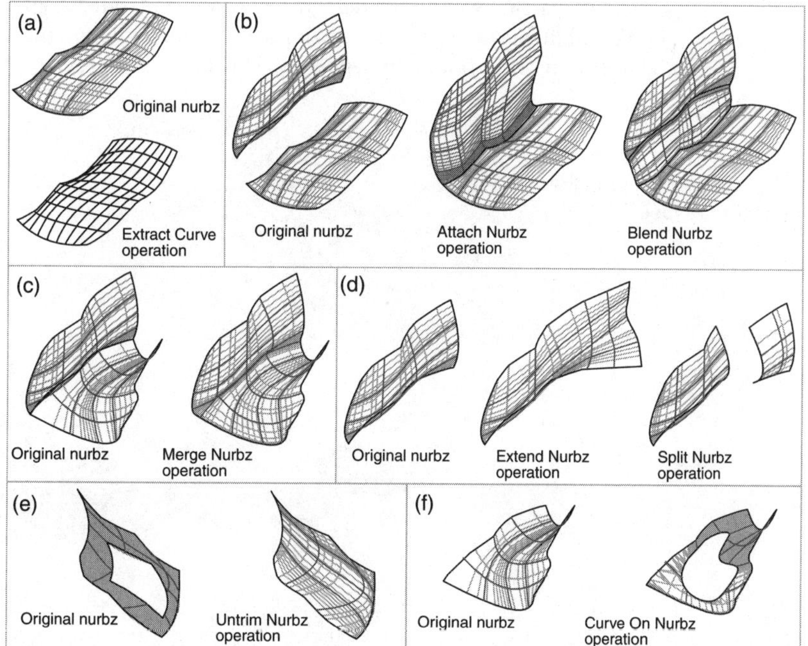

Figure 6.57

Various operations applied to nurbz objects.

5.3 Deriving and Growing Patches

The process for creating a patch object is different from creating a c-mesh or nurbz object, in the sense that no control shapes are drawn that define the shape of the desired object. Instead, create a solid object or a closed surface and simply apply the **Patch Derive** tool (**M-Tool:8a,1**) to it. The solid object will be transformed into a solid patch object, while the surface will be transformed into a surface patch object, as shown in Figure 6.58. When a surface patch is derived from the face of an object by applying the tool at the **Face** topological level, the original object is ghosted by default.

PATCH DERIVE

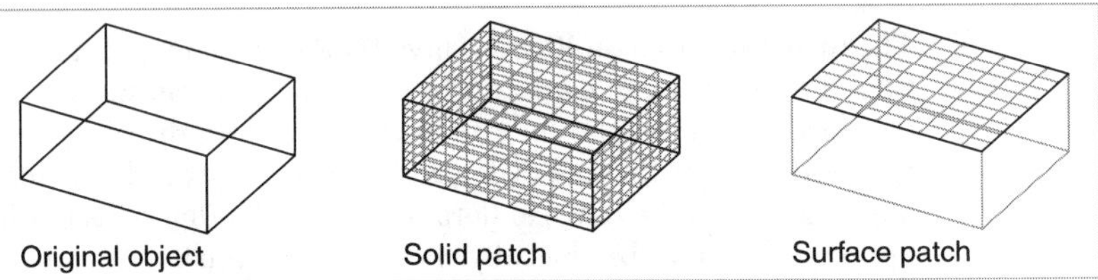

Figure 6.58

Applying the Patch Derive tool at the object and face topological level.

The **Patch Derive** tool has a number of options associated with it, as you can see in its dialog (Figure 6.59-a). The **Display Resolution** and **Status Of Objects** tabs will be familiar to you from the other tool dialogs, so focus on the **Options** tab. Two different types of patches can be created: **Bezier** and **Coons**. We'll not get into the mathematical differences between these two types here—it's sufficient to know that a **Bezier** patch has a larger number of control points with which the surface can be manipulated using the **Edit Controls** tool, as we'll see in Section 5.5.

There are some additional options that apply to both types of patches. The **Maintain 4-Sided Patches** option, when activated, ensures that only 4-sided shapes are used to construct the patches. Otherwise patches will be created with 4- as well as 3-sided shapes. The **Subdivide** option can be used to subdivide each patch at the time of creation with lines that start from its center and end at the midpoints of its boundary segments. This subdivision effect is demonstrated in Figure 6.59-b.

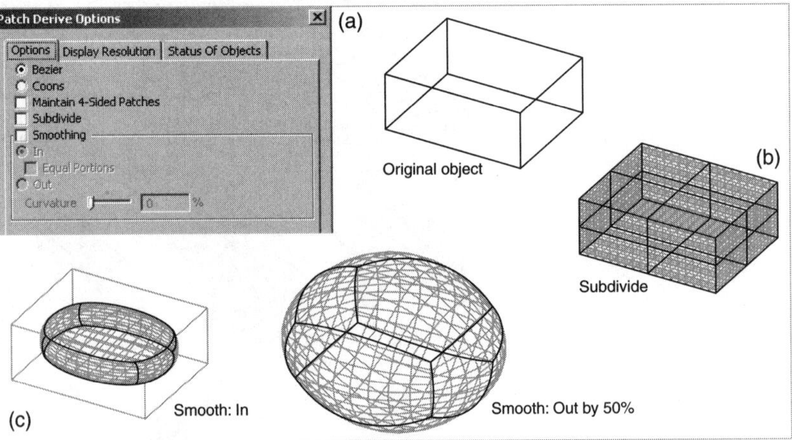

Figure 6.59

Exploring the options of the Patch Derive tool.

- By default, the flatness of a surface is maintained while constructing a patch on it. You can activate the Smoothing option if you want the object to be smoothed in addition to being converted to a patch. The In and Out sub-options apply the smoothing towards the inside and outside of the patch object respectively, as shown in Figure 6.59-c. The degree of curvature for the Out sub-option is set using the accompanying slider bar. Higher values will produce more curvature around the centers and edges of the original faces.

- Move on to the next tool on the same row, Patch Grow. Activate this tool, make sure that the topological level is set to Object, and click on an existing surface patch object like the ones shown in Figure 6.60. It's important for the selected patch to have at least one open edge, i.e., an edge that's not connected to another patch. The effect of the operation will be the construction of new patches on every *open* edge of the existing patch, with dimensions that match the corresponding edges.

- Explore the options in the dialog of the Patch Grow tool (Figure 6.60-a). The default option is From Edges, under which four different types of alignments are possible. All these are demonstrated in Figure 6.60-b, derived from the same patch object. Go ahead and explore each one of them—the difference should be quite obvious. The From Edges patch growing method can also be applied with the topological level set to Face or Segment. When a face is selected, a new patch is constructed using every open edge of the face. For a segment, the patch is constructed only if the segment is an open edge.

- The second patch growing method, Between Edges, can only be applied at the Segment topological level. It's used to construct patches *between* sets of two, three, or four segments, as shown in Figure 6.60-c. If the number of edges is three or four, the edges need to have coincident endpoints, otherwise the operation cannot be performed.

- The remaining Patch Grow options are fairly straightforward. The Construct Triangular Patches option creates 3-sided rather than 4-sided patches. The Stitch option stitches the new patches to the existing patch selected for the operation, connecting them into one object rather than letting them remain as separate entities. The Smooth sub-option under Stitch smoothes out the edges of the stitch. Finally, there are the usual Display Resolution and Status Of Objects tabs, as for the Patch Derive tool.

Figure 6.60

Exploring the options of the Patch Grow tool on a patch inclined with respect to the XY plane.

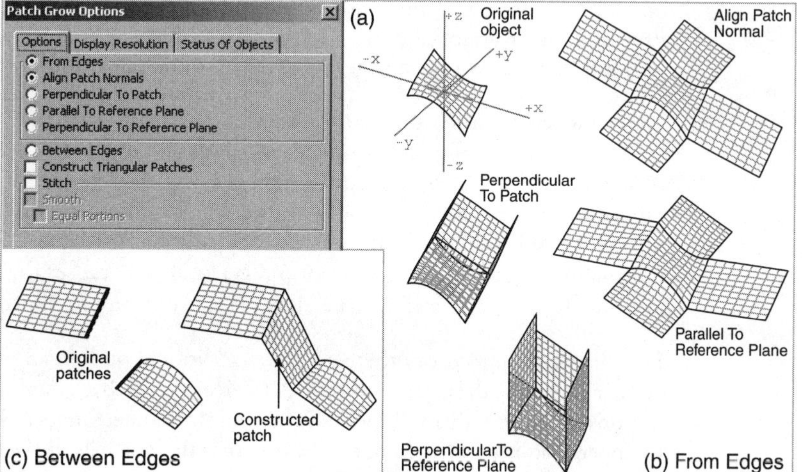

5.4 Dividing and Attaching Patches

- Activate the next patch tool, Patch Divide (M-Tool:8a,3), and apply it to a patch object with the topological level set to Object. You'll find that each patch of the object gets subdivided into smaller patches (see Figure 6.61). This subdivision can be useful when the object has to be graphically edited—a process we shall soon look at—as it increases the number of control points and the density of the surface. The greater the subdivision, the smoother the reshaping of the object. The Patch Divide tool can be repeatedly applied to the same object to increase the number of subdivisions.

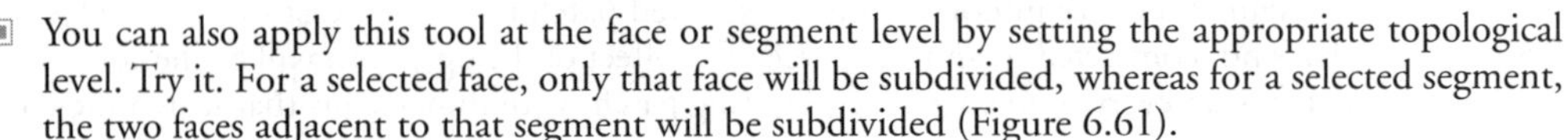

- You can also apply this tool at the face or segment level by setting the appropriate topological level. Try it. For a selected face, only that face will be subdivided, whereas for a selected segment, the two faces adjacent to that segment will be subdivided (Figure 6.61).

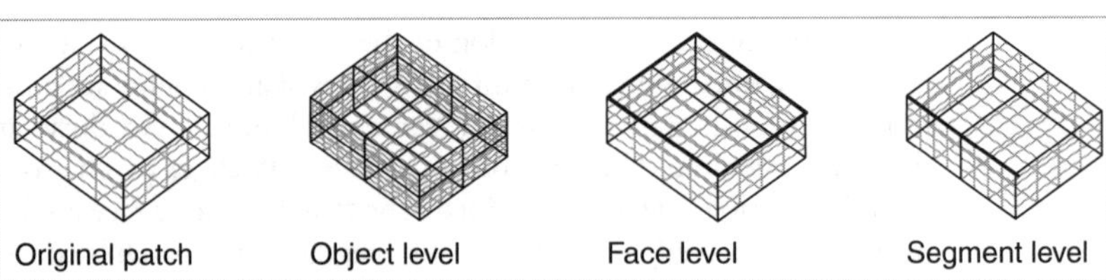

Figure 6.61

Using the Patch Divide tool at the object, face, and segment levels.

- The Patch Divide tool has a small number of associated options, which we'll quickly go over. By default, an existing patch is subdivided into 2 parts along both directions. The number of subdivisions can be changed to a higher value, if a greater degree of subdivision is required in one application of the tool. The Lock Edge Points option locks the control points on both sides of the edges that are subdivided, thereby preventing them from being moved when the object is graphically modified. This helps avoid fractures along the shared edges of a patch object. The last option, Undivide, can be activated to remove the subdivisions in a previously subdivided patch object or face.

- Move on to the last tool on the same row, Patch Attach. The function of this tool is to attach an open edge of one patch to the open edge of another patch. It's thus somewhat similar to the Attach tool (M-Tool:13b,1) but has more capabilities that are relevant to the patch objects on which it operates. For instance, the "source" patch object can get reshaped like a piece of paper in the process of being attached to the "destination" patch object, as shown in Figure 6.62. Try it. Keep in mind that the two open edges can belong to the same or to different objects.

- Let's now look at the options of the Patch Attach tool that are available in its dialog (Figure 6.62-a). There are four main operations possible, of which Attach is the default. Within the Attach mode, the Move Edge sub-option is active by default. This causes the source edge to be moved and scaled to correspond with the dimensions of the destination edge. The second sub-option, Move Patch, causes the patch face of the source edge to be moved to the location of the destination edge. The third sub-option, Move Object, causes the entire object to be moved and attached to the destination edge. All three sub-options are illustrated in Figure 6.62-b.

- For the Attach operation, there are three additional options in the form of checkboxes that are applicable to all these sub-options. All three are off by default. The Align Normals and Scale options are active only for the Move Patch and Move Object modes. When Align Normals is activated, the operation is performed in such a way that the normals of the source and destination patches get aligned. The Scale option is used to scale the source edge based on the dimensions of the destination edge. The final option, Stitch, is used to unite the two patches involved in the operation into one object. When necessary, it also modifies the geometry of the source edge according to the geometry of the destination edge in order to maintain continuity between the stitched patches.

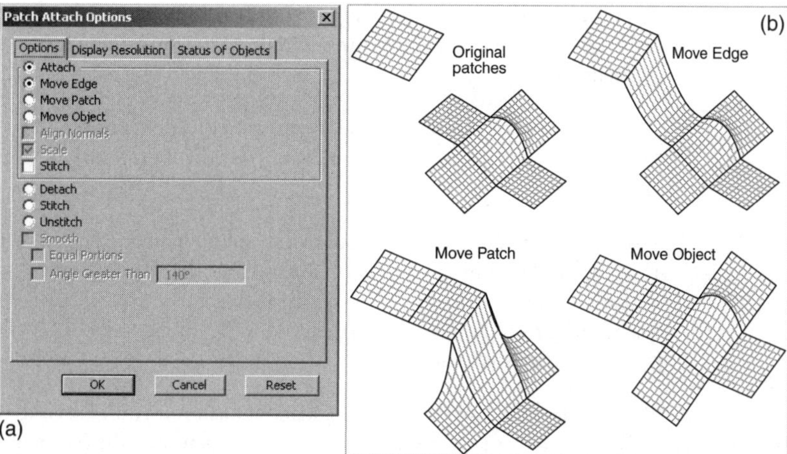

Figure 6.62

Using the Patch Attach tool in the Attach mode with each of its three sub-options. The dialog of the tool is also shown.

- Let's quickly look at the other three modes of the Patch Attach tool. The Detach operation is the reverse of the Attach operation—it separates all the patches of an object into separate objects. When applied at the face level, it detaches only the selected face or faces from the original object. The Stitch operation can be used to unite two patch edges that are lined up and coincident into one edge. The last operation, Unstitch, performs a partial detachment, breaking up stitched edges but making the control points at their ends remain coincident. Explore each one of these operations, applying them to various patch objects.

5.5 Editing Controls and Surfaces of Nurbz and Patches

In Section 5.2 of Workshop 2 (Bringing a Sense of Scale), you used both the Edit Controls and Edit Surface tools, located after the Pick tool in the right column of Row 4, to graphically edit the parameters of different kinds of parametric objects. However, these changes are limited only to the options afforded by the dialogs of the tools used to create those objects. Thus, the only settings that can be graphically modified for a primitive sphere are those that are available in the Sphere tool dialog, and they apply to the object as a whole. What if you want to reshape, for instance, only a portion of the sphere? For this, the sphere needs to be converted to a nurbz or patch object and then graphically manipulated using the same Edit Controls and Edit Surface tools. Let's actually go about doing this.

- Create a primitive sphere using the Sphere tool (M-Tool:1a,4) and make an additional copy of it. Convert one of these spheres into a nurbz object, and the other into a patch object. You already know from the previous sections that you can use the Nurbz and Patch Derive tools to perform this conversion. You could also use the Convert tool (M-Tool:11b,6) to do this, as you learned in Section 5.1 of Workshop 2.

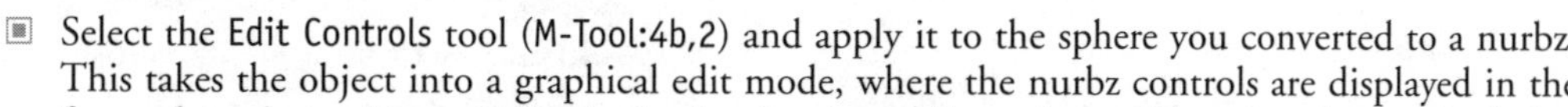

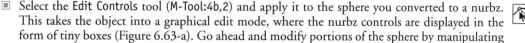

- Select the Edit Controls tool (M-Tool:4b,2) and apply it to the sphere you converted to a nurbz. This takes the object into a graphical edit mode, where the nurbz controls are displayed in the form of tiny boxes (Figure 6.63-a). Go ahead and modify portions of the sphere by manipulating these controls. A control is selected by clicking on it. Multiple controls can be selected by clicking on them individually while holding down the Shift key, or by holding the mouse down and enclosing them in a frame. All the selected controls are highlighted in the selection color. The shape of the object can now be changed by clicking on one of the selected controls and moving the mouse. All the selected controls get repositioned following the mouse movement, reshaping the object in the process (see Figure 6.63-b). Keep in mind that the setting of the Perpendicular Lock (W-Tool:2,1) will determine whether the movement takes place along the active plane or perpendicular to it.

- To deselect picked controls, click on an area of the window with no controls. A second click (after deselecting all controls) will terminate the editing operation. Pressing the Esc key will also have the same effect.

- Now apply the Edit Controls tool to the sphere you converted to a patch. It will once again enter the graphical edit mode where its controls are displayed (Figure 6.63-c). You can see that these are distinctly different from the controls of the nurbz sphere. Despite having different controls, the reshaping of the patch object proceeds in a similar fashion. Try it out. Figure 6.63-d shows one such shape modification.

- From your earlier work with the Edit Controls tool, you've seen that when it is applied to an object, a dialog is automatically invoked containing some editing options relevant to that object. This Edit Controls Options dialog is slightly different for nurbz and patch objects, as shown in Figure 6.64. Let's first look at the options common to both objects. The Preview Density, as you know, is used to control how smoothly the object is displayed as it is being edited. The Action section lets you choose from a number of transformations such as Move, Rotate, Scale, and Uniform Scale that determine the type of transformation applied to the selected controls when they're manipulated with the mouse. Additionally, there are three alternate options that determine how the cursor is mapped for the Move transformation. The default Reference Plane option, as is obvious from its name, maps the cursor to the current reference plane. The Local Normal option maps the cursor to the normal of the control that's nearest to where the mouse is clicked. And finally, the Average Normal option maps the cursor to the average normal of the selected controls.

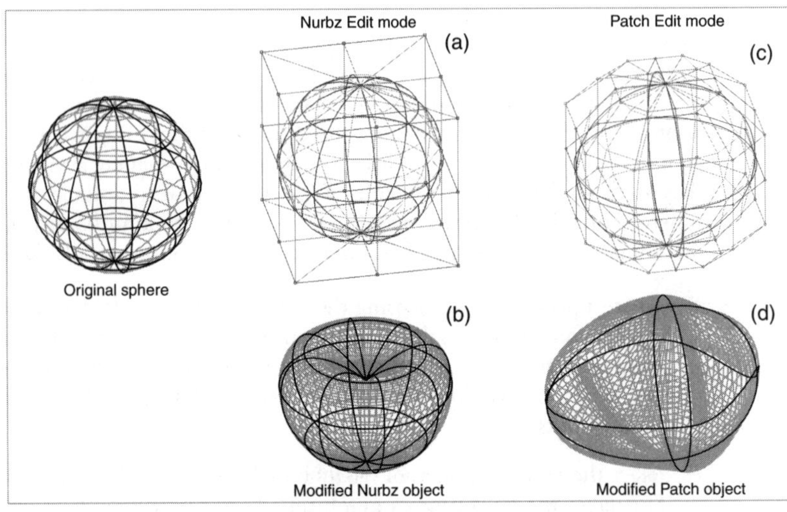

Figure 6.63

Converting two primitive spheres to nurbz and patch objects, and editing their controls to modify their shape.

Figure 6.64

The Edit Controls Options dialog for a nurbz object and for a patch object.

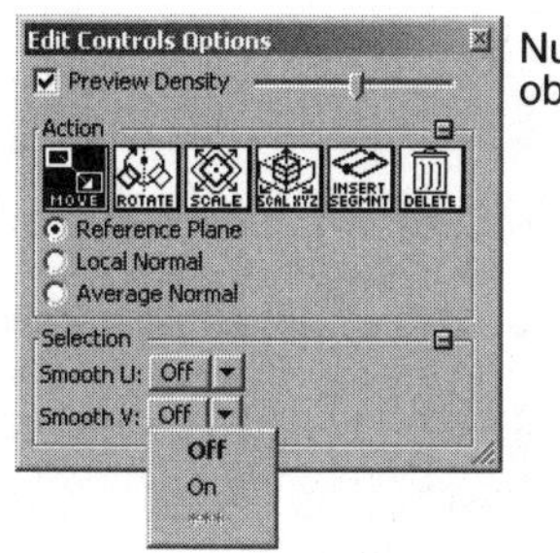

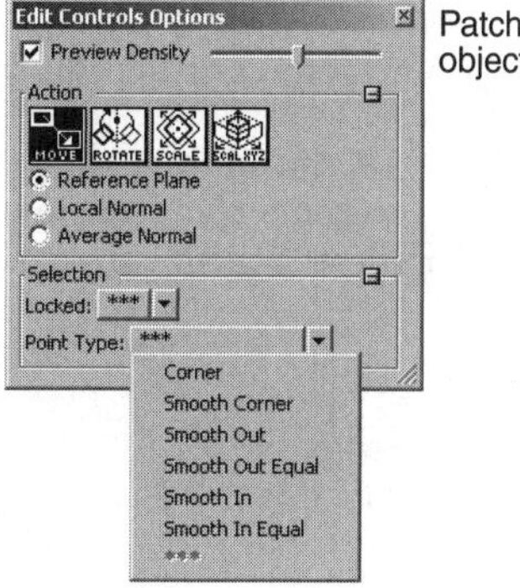

- For a nurbz object, the Edit Controls Options dialog has two more options in the Action section, which let you insert additional control segments and delete control points as necessary to reshape the object. Also, when a control point is selected, the two Smooth options get activated, and can be applied to smooth the surface in both directions at that point. For a patch object, the Edit Controls Options dialog has other options that can be applied to selected controls. The Locked option lets you lock the controls to prevent them from being moved, while the Point Type option lets you apply various kinds of smoothing at the selected controls. Try out all of them and see how they differ.

- Let's now turn to the Edit Surface tool, located immediately after the Edit Controls tool. You've applied this tool to 3D primitives in Workshop 2. Go ahead and apply it to the nurbz as well as the patch object. You'll find that you can now manipulate the object directly by clicking on its surface and moving the mouse in the desired direction. This might seem a more intuitive method of editing than having to activate and move individual controls. The Edit Surface tool is also accompanied by a dialog that automatically opens up when the tool is applied to an object. This Edit Surface Options is identical for both nurbz and patch objects, and contains few options, most of which are the same as those in the Edit Controls Options dialog. The only different option is Surface Normal, which maps the cursor to the surface normal at the click point instead of the current reference plane.

5.6 Editing Nurbz Curves in Parameter Space

We'll end this exercise by looking at one additional tool relevant to nurbz objects. Recall that in Section 5.2, you used the Curve On Nurbz tool to create a curve on a nurbz surface, which can stay on the surface or can be used to trim the surface. Such curves can be edited by using the Edit in Parameter Space tool, located right after the Edit Surface tool on Row 4.

- Create some curves on a nurbz surface with the Curve On Nurbz tool, as you learned to do in Section 5.2. Then select the Edit in Parameter Space tool (M-Tool:4b,4) and apply it to the surface. This will open up the preview dialog shown in Figure 6.65, which shows the surface in world space (that is, in 3D) on the left, and the same surface in parameter space (that is, flattened out in 2D) on the right.

- Select a curve on the nurbz surface in the Parameter Space window. Its control points are displayed. Select a control point and move it to reshape the curve. You'll see the change also reflected in 3D in the World Space window. Repeat with other control points, on this curve as well as on other curves and see the resulting changes in 3D. You'll also find other editing controls, which are the same as those in the Edit Controls Options dialog when applied to curves.

As you can see, by using the parameter space, you can specify the shape of the curve far more accurately than you could by relying on the world space alone. This is what makes the Edit in Parameter Space tool indispensable for any kind of organic modeling using nurbz objects.

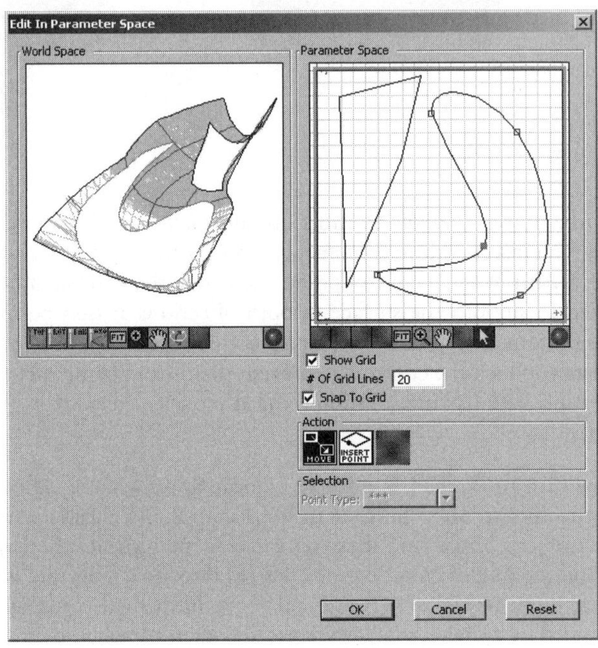

Figure 6.65

Editing the curves on a nurbz surface in parameter space.

EXERCISE 6

Cutting and Gluing Freeform Objects

The ability to create and modify individual meshed, nurbz, and patch objects, as you've done so far, might not always be sufficient for your modeling purposes. You might occasionally need to unite two or more such objects, subtract one from the other, split two of them against each other, and so on. In short, you might need to perform the same kind of boolean operations on these "freeform" objects that you performed on "regular" objects using the Union, Intersection, Difference, and Split tools in Workshop 1 (Letting Yourself Go). Since most freeform objects have non-planar faces, you cannot apply the regular boolean tools to them. This is why form•Z provides you with a special tool, the Trim/Split operator, to carry out boolean operations on such objects.

In this exercise, we'll apply the Trim/Split tool to meshed objects, but keep in mind that it works the same way for nurbz and patch objects as well.

6.1 Trimming and Splitting Objects

- On a new layer, create two meshed objects with non-planar faces, using the C-Mesh, Q-Subz, or T-Subz tools. You can also apply the Mesh tool to an unmeshed object and then deform or displace it in some manner. After creating the objects, position them so that they intersect each other. If the line of intersection is open, it should cut the surface of one object from end to end, otherwise the Trim/Split tool won't work. If there are two intersecting solids, as shown in Figure 6.66-a, the line of intersection will be closed, so the Trim/Split tool will always work.

- Try applying any of the four regular boolean tools—Union, Intersection, Difference, and Split—to these intersecting objects. As expected, you'll be greeted with an error message telling you that the boolean operation could not be carried out because the objects have non-planar faces. You can, of course, Triangulate the objects first, but this is an additional step, and you cannot "untriangulate" the objects after the boolean tool has been applied. Also, the process of triangulation introduces additional faces in an object, increasing its size—not physically, but in terms of the stored information needed to describe it—and slowing down operations. Thus, using the Triangulate tool might not always be desirable.

- Select the Trim/Split tool (M-Tool:9a,5) and look at the options in its dialog, which are arranged in a matrix-like fashion (Figure 6.66-b). The default selection is Trim under the First Object column, indicating that a trimming operation will be applied to the first of the two objects selected by the tool. Apply the tool with this option to your two meshed objects, following the instructions in the Prompts palette. Select the larger object first, and do so by clicking on that part of it which is to be retained. As a result of the operation, the second object will disappear, leaving behind the trimmed portion of the first object. (Figure 6.66-c).

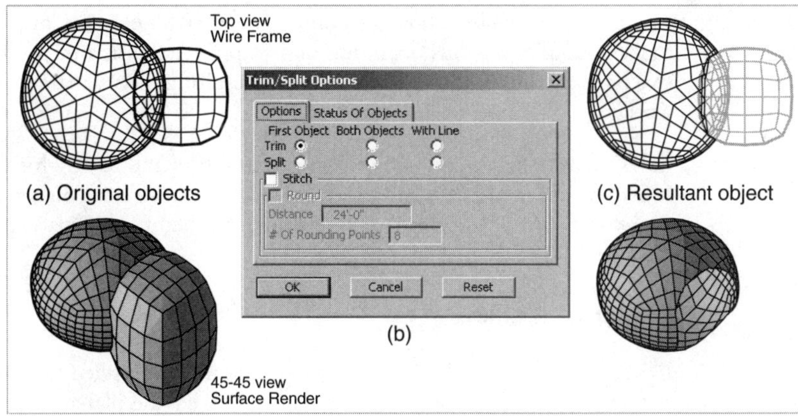

Figure 6.66

Trimming a meshed object with the Trim/Split tool. The tool dialog is also shown.

For all the Trim/Split operators, the part of the object you click on to select it will affect the result of the operation.

- The operation you just performed is equivalent to what the Difference tool does for regular objects, except that this leaves a "hole" in the object, making its insides visible. Thus, a solid object will get converted to a surface object by this operation. This might not be desirable, in which case you should select the Stitch option in the dialog of the Trim/Split tool. Undo and reapply the tool in this mode, and you'll find that not only is the second object subtracted from the first, it also "stitches" up the resulting hole that's created. Which part of the second object gets stitched depends upon where you click on it to select it, so do this carefully based on the result you want. Change to the front or side views, if necessary, to make the selection correctly. As you can see from Figure 6.67, different results are possible—equivalent to the Union, Difference, and Intersection operations—depending upon how both the objects are selected.

- Get back to the Trim/Split dialog and notice that the Stitch option has a Round sub-option. By selecting this, you can give a rounding effect to the stitch. You can also specify the distance and the resolution of the rounding. Activate this option and experiment with different rounding values for the same operation.

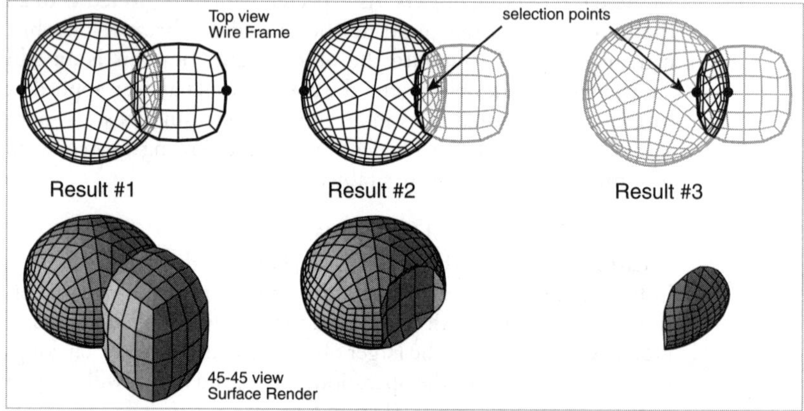

Figure 6.67

Activating the Stitch option for a Trim operation. Different results are obtained, depending upon where the two objects are selected.

- Next, select the Split mode, still under the First Object column, in the dialog of the Trim/Split tool. Undo the previous operation and reapply the tool, and you'll get the first object split into two parts by the second object. Move the resulting pieces apart to see how the operation actually worked.

- In a similar fashion, explore both operators—Trim and Split—for the Both Objects mode as well. Move parts of meshes around to see the results better when you're working in this mode. These are straightforward operations and very similar to their counterparts in the First Object mode.

6.2 Trimming with Lines

It might seem as though the Trim/Split tool can only be applied to freeform objects with non-planar faces. However, try and apply it to regular objects having planar faces, and you'll find that you can. The only condition is that the objects should not have overlapping faces that lie on the same plane, a condition easy enough to fulfil. But since there are the regular boolean tools for working with these objects, it's advisable to use them rather than the Trim/Split tool. There is, however, one exception to this rule, which has to do with the last Trim/Split mode, intriguingly called With Line. This is a fascinating concept in which you can use simple 2D shapes to perform boolean operations on all kinds of objects.

- On a new layer, create a meshed solid and a regular solid on the XY plane, positioned next to each other. Then switch to the Front view and draw two open shapes using the 2D Surface mode, in such a way that each of the two solids is completely cut through by a 2D shape (see Figure 6.68-a).

Figure 6.68

Applying the Trim operation in the With Line mode. The Stitch option was also activated.

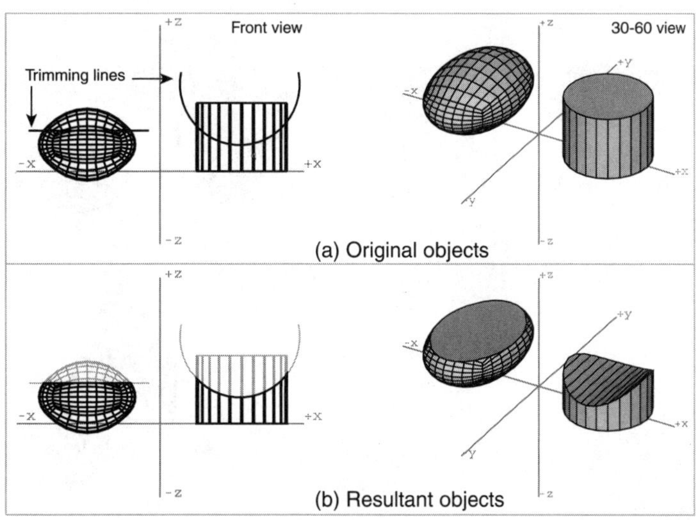

- In the dialog of the Trim/Split tool, select the Trim option under the With Line column, and also activate the Stitch option. Following the instructions in the Prompts palette, select one of the solid objects first, and then the 2D shape which intersects it as the trimming line, taking care to remain in the Front view. You'll find that your solid object has been trimmed along the line of the 2D shape, retaining the portion you clicked on while selecting it. The direction of the cut is perpendicular to the active plane, which is ZX in Front view. In a Wire Frame display with the Hide Ghosted option deselected, you should be able to see this clearly. Verify the result by switching to a non-planar view and a paint display (Figure 6.68-b). Then repeat the operation for the other object-line pair.

As you can see, this is an amazingly simple way to perform boolean operations on all kinds of objects. It's indispensable for freeform objects, of course, but is also useful for regular objects, as shown in Figure 6.68. Keep in mind that the Section tool (M-Tool:9a,8) can be used to cut a regular object with planar faces, but it can only do so along a straight line, not along a curve or any other non-linear shape. For that, the With Line option of the Trim/Split tool is the most convenient operator.

- Explore the With Line mode some more, trying out the Split option as well. The Stitch option can be used to connect the split parts back together, etching the lines of intersection on the surface of the object. Remember that the cutting action will always be executed with respect to the active reference plane, i.e., it's the projection of the 2D shape on the plane that's actually making the cut. You'll get unexpected results if a different plane is active instead of the one you intended to be. That's why it's always best to execute the operation in the same planar view as the one in which you draw the 2D cutting shape.

6.3 Deriving Lines of Intersection

- Proceed to select the next tool on Row 9, Line Of Intersection (M-Tool:9a,6). As is evident from its name, this simply gives you the line of intersection of any two intersecting objects. These can be any kind of objects—freeform or regular. Try it out on some object pairs.

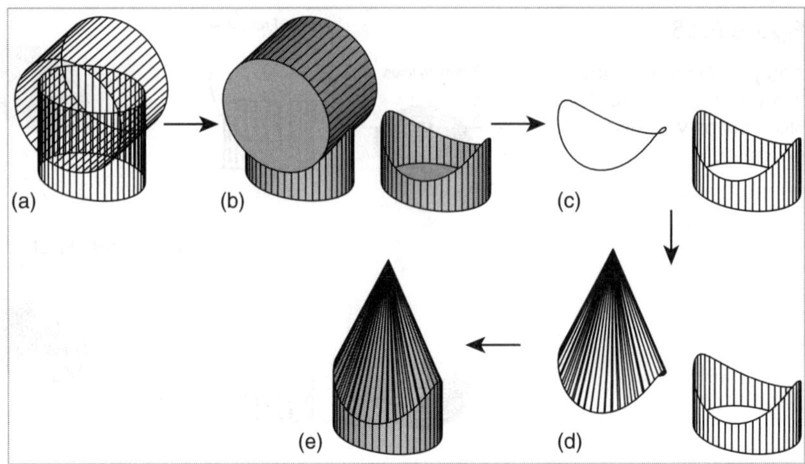

Figure 6.69

Demonstrating the use of the Line Of Intersection tool.

- Figure 6.69 shows a simple application of this option. From two intersecting objects (a), a trimmed portion of one object was derived using the Trim option of the Trim/Split tool (b). The Status Of Objects was set to Keep, so as to retain the original objects, whose line of intersection was then derived with the Status Of Objects set back to Ghost (c). The 3D Convergence tool was applied to the intersection shape, converting it to a 3D object (d). Finally, using Endpoint snap and the Move tool, the converged object was positioned on top of the trimmed half of the first object, where it's an exact fit (e).

6.4 Stitching Surface Objects

The next tool in the left column of Row 9, Stitch, allows you to create a number of surfaces individually and then "stitch" them together to create a solid object. Of course, you have to ensure that the ends of the surfaces indeed all match up and there are no gaps anywhere. The surfaces can be freeform or regular closed shapes. This is useful when the individual surfaces of an object are meaningful in their own right and need to be carefully and precisely shaped, which is difficult to achieve when the object itself is the focus of creation and is shaped first. Let's carry out one such Stitch operation.

- Create a square using the 2D Surface mode. Mesh it and then apply a mesh move operation to it, but in such a way that its boundary isn't disturbed, i.e., it should still be a square (Figure 6.70-a). Then, using the Rotate and Mirror tools in a Copy mode, make copies of this meshed surface until you have all six sides of a cube touching each other, with the same side facing outwards (see Figures 6.70-b and 6.70-c). It's important that the edges of adjacent faces should be completely coincident.

- Select all these six meshed surfaces with the Pick tool. Then activate the Stitch tool (M-Tool:9a,7) and click anywhere in the graphics window. The stitching operation will be applied, one surface at a time. As soon as the last surface is stitched and the object is closed, it automatically gets converted to a solid.

- To verify that the object is indeed a solid and not hollow inside, use the Query tool to check the status of the object. It should say Solid; if it continues to say Meshed Surface, it means that the surfaces were not positioned correctly. You can also triangulate the object and then apply the Section tool to it, as shown in Figure 6.70-d. The results will clearly indicate that the object is a solid.

- Invoke the dialog of the Stitch tool to examine its options. The default option is Stitch Multiple Parts, which is the operation you just applied. The alternate option, Stitch Object Parts, can be used to connect open ends within a single object. For both types of operations, the Round option can additionally be selected, allowing you to give a rounding effect to the stitched line. Try it.

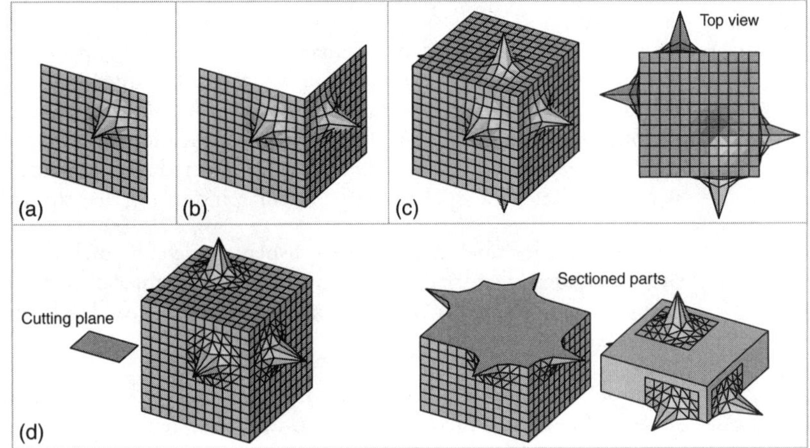

Figure 6.70

Using the Stitch tool to stitch six surfaces into a solid, and verifying the result with the Section tool.

EXERCISE 7

The Metaphysics of Metaformz

So far in this workshop, you've worked with various tools that greatly enhance your ability to do organic modeling. In this concluding exercise, we'll look at another set of tools that makes the task of organic modeling much easier. These are the three *metaformz* tools, located in Rows 1 and 8 of the modeling tool palette.

Metaformz are objects that have the ability to blend seamlessly with each other when they overlap. Each object has a *sphere of influence* that determines how much it merges with or repels another such object. The base objects for generating metaformz are of two kinds: *metaballs*, which are created directly by the Metaballs tool; and *metaforms*, which can be derived from regular form•Z objects by the Metaformz Derive/Edit tool. Both metaballs and metaforms can be converted to metaformz by the Metaformz Evaluate tool, so called because the process of conversion is referred to as *evaluation*. Thus, metaballs and metaforms can be regarded as *unevaluated metaformz.*

To generate smooth metaformz from a number of metaballs and metaforms, you need, first, to ensure they overlap with each other and, second, to collect them into a group. A metaformz is a controlled object in the sense that the original metaballs and metaforms are retained and can be modified to change the shape of the resultant metaformz. This enables you to very easily fine-tune the metaformz after creating it, until it takes on the desired form. Let's proceed to work with this fascinating concept.

7.1 Creating and Evaluating Metaballs

- Open a new form•Z project or move to a fresh layer, and set the display mode to Wire Frame. Select the Metaballs tool (M-Tool:1b,2) and follow the prompts. You'll be asked to select an *origin point* for the metaball. Click to select a point in the window or type in some coordinate value. You'll now be prompted for the *radius*. Move the cursor and you'll see a spherical shape being rubber-banded. Click to specify the radius, or type in a suitable value. You should have a spherical metaball, as shown in Figure 6.71-a.

- This metaball, as discussed, represents an unevaluated metaformz. Rather than an object of specified dimensions, it represents a *region of influence* that can interact with the regions of other objects of the same kind. This region is indicated by two sets of lines: the inner set in the active color, and the outer set in ghosted mode. (Make sure that the Hide Ghosted option in the Wire Frame Options dialog is not selected, so that you can see the ghosted lines.) Switch to each of the planar views and you'll find that both sets of lines are circular, indicating that this is a perfectly spherical metaball.

- Try to see the metaball in a different display mode and you'll find that you cannot. This gives us our first inkling that metaballs are not like regular objects. To confirm this, try to select a point, segment, or face of the metaball by setting the topological level appropriately, and you'll find that you cannot.

- Thus, an unevaluated metaformz such as the metaball you have created is of no practical use until it is evaluated into a metaformz object. Let us, therefore, do this right away. First, ensure that the topological level is set to Object. Then select the Metaformz Evaluate tool (M-Tool:8b,2) and apply it to the metaball. A dialog will be invoked showing various evaluation parameters (see Figure 6.74-a). We will look at these in detail later. For now, stick with the defaults and click OK to exit the dialog. Your metaball will be evaluated into a metaformz, as shown in Figure 6.71-b. This is a meshed spherical object following the shape of the metaball, and it behaves in a regular fashion—it can be rendered in different display modes and its individual points, segments, and faces can be selected for various operations.

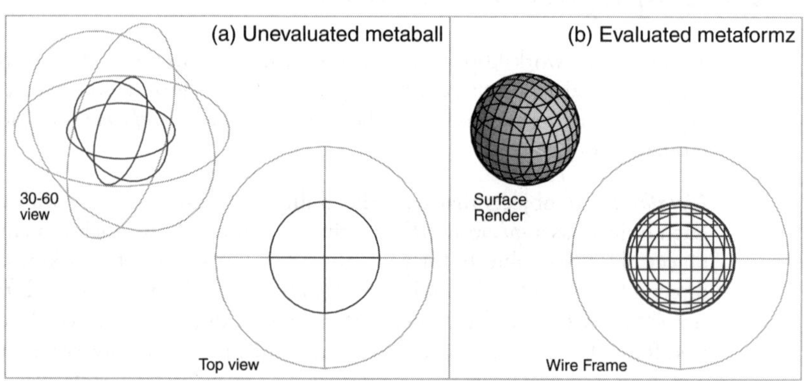

Figure 6.71

A metaball generated by the Metaballs tool with the default settings, and the resulting evaluated metaformz.

7.2 Metaballs and Metaformz Options

- It's possible to create three other kinds of metaballs—stretched ball, ellipsoid, and stretched ellipsoid—in addition to the perfectly spherical one you just created and evaluated. Double-click on the Metaballs tool to open its dialog (Figure 6.72). You will see these four types listed as options, with the default being Ball, the spherical metaball. Select each of the other three types in turn and apply the Metaballs tool. You should now have a metaball of each type. Notice that both the Ellipsoid and Stretched Ellipsoid types have two options that determine the way they are created. Experiment with both techniques.

Figure 6.72

The dialog of the Metaballs tool.

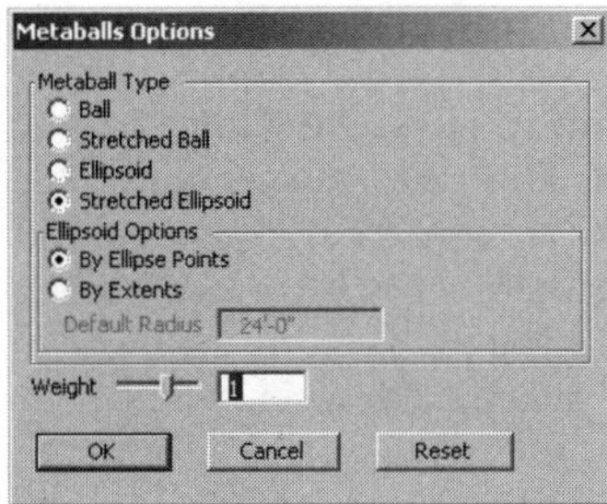

- Notice also that there is a Weight parameter associated with a metaball, which is set to 1 by default in the dialog of the Metaballs tool. This parameter controls the extent of a metaball that is converted to a metaformz. A weight of 0 would lead to a metaformz of zero volume, which would not be seen at all. Weight can also be negative, which is useful when a metaformz is derived from a group of metaballs. We'll look at this aspect more closely in the next section. For now, apply the Metaformz Evaluate tool to each unevaluated metaball as you did before, sticking with the default options. The differences between the various metaball types are much more evident now.

- Let's now try to create a blend of two or more metaballs. Clear the window and create a fresh set of metaballs, say one of each type. This time, take care to create them so that they overlap each other, as shown in Figure 6.73-a. Switch to a planar view to adjust the overlaps better, and use the Move tool if necessary.

- You would think that by prepicking all the metaballs with the Pick tool and then applying the Metaformz Evaluate tool to the whole selection, the desired blend should be produced. Try it. You will find that each metaball gets evaluated individually, leading to separate metaformz objects that are not aware of any overlaps (Figure 6.73-b). Obviously, this is not the way to go about blending metaballs with each other.

Figure 6.73

Evaluating a set of intersecting metaballs into metaformz, individually and collectively.

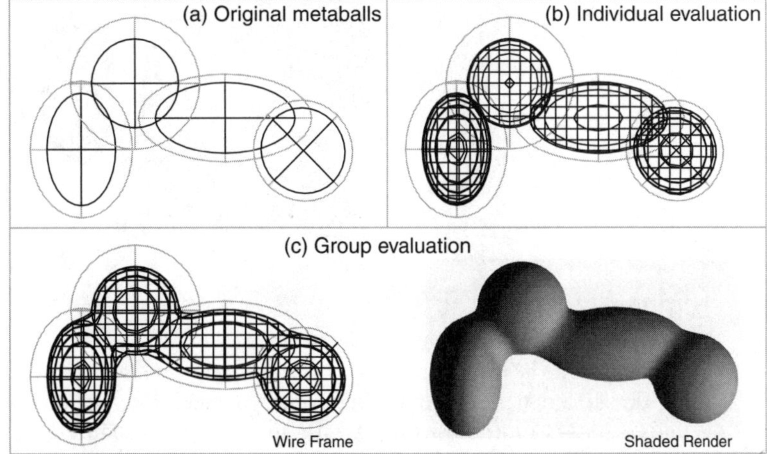

- Undo the Metaformz Evaluate operation you just performed to get back to the state shown in Figure 6.73-a. Prepick all the metaballs again with the Pick tool. Then select the Group tool (M-Tool:9b,3). This will automatically invoke the Metaformz Evaluation Parameters dialog you encountered earlier. The difference, however, is that this dialog is invoked only once for the entire group, and it determines the characteristics of the resultant metaformz. Stick with the defaults and exit the dialog, and you'll see a single metaformz blending across the individual metaballs (Figure 6.73-c).

- Let's now look at the options contained in the Metaformz Evaluation Parameters dialog (Figure 6.74-a) to see how they affect the metaformz you just created. Since the metaformz is a controlled object, there is no need to undo and reapply the operation with different settings. Simply select the final metaformz or any of the original metaballs with the Metaformz Evaluate tool, and the same dialog is invoked again, allowing you to change the settings. (Notice that the original metaballs do not get deleted or ghosted after the evaluation. There's a good reason for this, which we shall soon see.)

- The first parameter in the Metaformz Evaluation Parameters dialog is the Threshold value. This can range from 0.1 to 99% and determines the extent of the metaformz by controlling its region of influence. Experiment with both the highest and lowest values and watch the metaformz expand and shrink respectively. The next parameter, Metaform Operation, determines how the metaformz of the individual metaballs are joined. It has two options, Blend and Join. When Blend is selected, the metaformz will be blended even if the individual metaballs do not fully intersect. Join, on the other hand, will not blend or even touch the metaformz if the metaballs do not intersect. The difference is illustrated in Figure 6.74-b for a new set of metaballs. Finally, you can choose to generate the metaformz as a meshed object or as a nurbz object. You are already familiar with the creation options for both types of objects from the earlier exercises in this workshop.

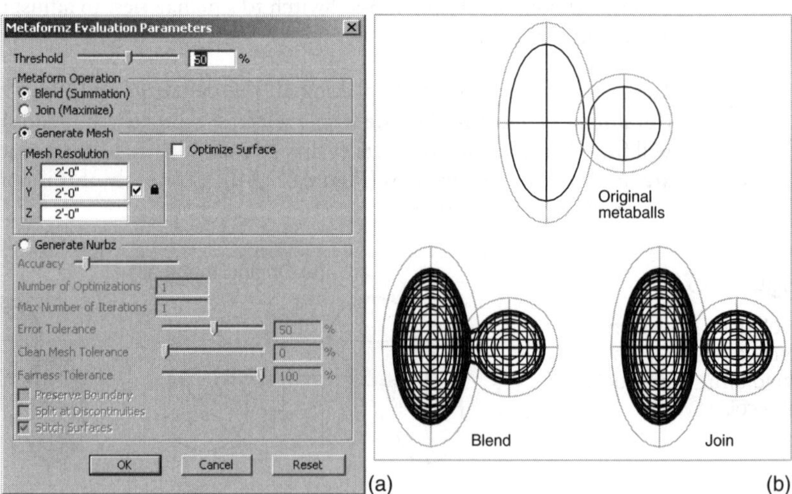

Figure 6.74

The Metaformz Evaluation Parameters dialog, and the difference between its Blend and Join operations.

7.3 Editing Metaballs

You've seen that the metaformz is a controlled object whose parameters can be modified at any time using the Metaformz Evaluate tool. You can go a step further and modify the *original* metaballs in various ways—the metaformz will be automatically recalculated. Let's see how.

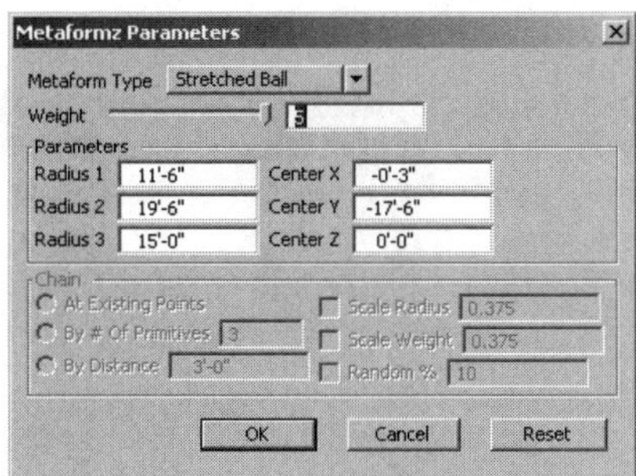

Figure 6.75

The dialog invoked when the Metaformz Derive/Edit tool is applied to a metaball.

- Use the Move tool to move any one of the original metaballs in the group to a different position. Ensure that it still overlaps one of the other metaballs in the group. You will find that the metaformz is automatically recalculated, blending the moved metaball in its new position with the others. In the same way, apply some of the other transformation tools to the metaballs, and see how you can fine-tune the shape of the resultant metaformz.

- If your metaformz is very complex, it's inefficient to automatically recalculate the metaformz for every slight change you make—it might be preferable to withhold the recalculation until you have made the desired changes to *all* the metaballs. In that case, double-click on the Metaformz Evaluate tool and select the third option, Evaluate Only When Selected, instead of the default, Automatic Evaluation. (The remaining option, Prompt For Evaluation, will prompt you each time a change is made, and is useful only when you want to prevent accidental modification of your metaformz.) Now you can make various modifications to the metaballs without affecting the metaformz. When you are ready to recalculate the metaformz, simply apply the Metaformz Evaluate tool to it.

- The original metaballs can be modified in another way in addition to using the transformation tools as you just did. This involves changing the parameters with which they were created. Select the Metaformz Derive/Edit tool (M-Tool:8b,1), which you haven't used so far, and apply it to one of the metaballs. This will invoke the Metaformz Parameters dialog, showing the original parameters of the metaball (Figure 6.75).

- At the top of the dialog, the Metaform Type shows the metaball as a Stretched Ball. You can change its position by entering different values for Center X, Center Y, and Center Z, although it is more convenient to do this graphically with the Move tool. You can set the size of the metaball more precisely by modifying the three radius values. You can go further and even change the Metaform Type itself to another type from the popup menu. In the case of Stretched Ball, all other options are grayed out except Ball. Switch to this type and see how the Radius 2 and Radius 3 values get deactivated, since the Ball type can have only a single radius. A Ball can similarly be changed to a Stretched Ball; however, the Ellipsoid and Stretched Ellipsoid types cannot be changed to any other type.

- Let's now examine the Weight parameter which we had bypassed earlier. Change this to 0, and then to the positive and negative extremes of 5 and –5 respectively, and see how the shape of the metaformz responds to the change. You'll find that decreasing the weight decreases the amount by which that metaball contributes to the metaform. Thus, a positive value has an additive effect, a weight of 0 is equivalent to the metaball not being there at all, and a negative value has a subtractive effect. All three are illustrated in Figure 6.76. Thus, you can adjust the weights of the metaballs depending upon the form you wish to achieve.

Figure 6.76

The effect of modifying the weight of a metaball from 5 to 0 to –5.

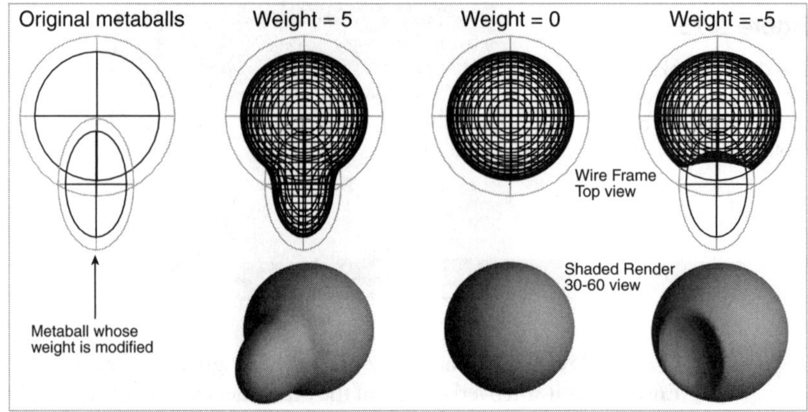

7.4 Deriving Metaforms from Regular Objects

So far, we've worked with only the four predefined metaball types available in the dialog of the `Create Metaball` tool. While you can group these four basic types in many different ways to achieve a large variety of metaformz shapes, form•Z goes a step further and lets you derive various kinds of metaforms from *regular* objects. These metaforms then behave just like metaballs and can be grouped to create metaformz.

- Move to a different layer and create a number of regular form•Z objects, as shown in Figure 6.77-a. Apply the `Metaformz Derive/Edit` tool to all of them, selecting a different type from the `Metaform Type` popup menu for each object. The choices available will depend upon what the original object is. Thus, a solid object can only be converted to a `Polyhedron` type of metaform, whereas a surface object has many other options that we will soon discuss. For now, notice that you can modify the weight, radius, and location values for each type of metaform, as you did before for the metaballs. 

Figure 6.77

Deriving metaforms from regular objects and then evaluating them to produce metaformz. If they are grouped and then evaluated, a single metaformz object is produced.

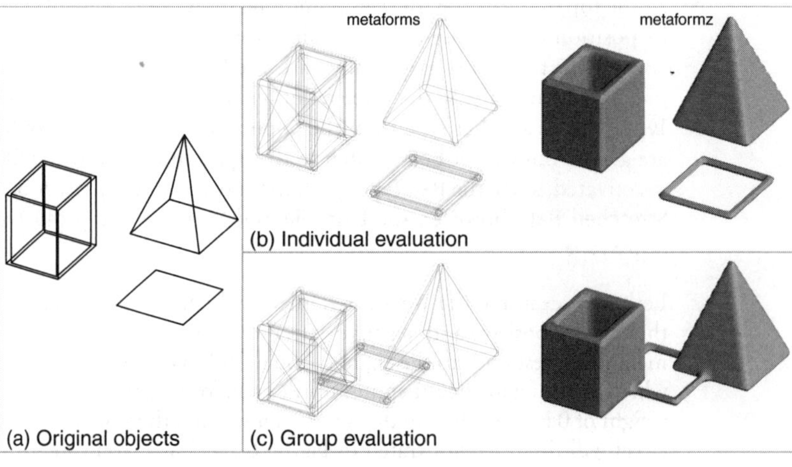

- After you have finished deriving different metaforms from all your objects, apply the Metaformz Evaluate tool to them in the usual manner (Figure 6.77-b). You can see that a much larger variety of metaformz can be created in this manner, giving you an enormous range of forms to play with. As before, you can group the metaforms before evaluating them to create the aggregated metaformz shape as desired (Figure 6.77-c).

- Apply the Metaformz Derive/Edit tool to a new open or closed 2D surface object (as shown in Figure 6.78) and look at the large number of choices you have for Metaform Type. Try out the Tube and Conic Tube options, as well as the Sheet option that applies to closed surfaces only. Remember to apply the Metaformz Evaluate tool to actually see the resultant metaformz.

- For the surface object, you can also choose from among the four familiar metaball options—Ball, Stretched Ball, Ellipsoid, and Stretched Ellipsoid—for the Metaform Type. Go ahead and select one of these. These four metaball options are generated as *chains* of metaballs when applied to a regular object. Notice that the Chain options in the Metaformz Parameters dialog (shown earlier in Figure 6.75) now get activated. You can specify the location of each ball of the chain in three ways: using the actual points of the object; the actual number of balls, which will then be uniformly distributed along the length of the object; or the distance between the balls. You can also uniformly vary the size and weight of the balls by applying a scaling factor, or else, specify a random percentage factor for applying to the radius, which will make all the balls look different in size. A couple of these options are illustrated in Figure 6.78.

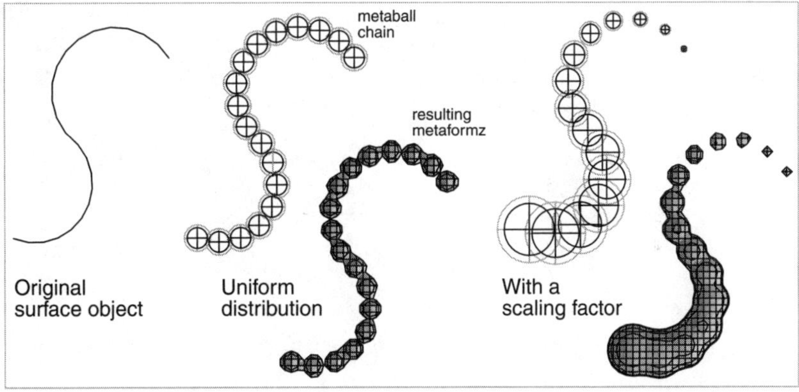

Figure 6.78

Creating chained metaformz, with and without changing the radius.

- A metaform, once created, can be modified in the same way as a metaball. You can apply any of the transformation tools such as Move, Rotate, and so on to it, or you can select it with the Metaformz Derive/Edit tool and modify its various parameters. If it has already been evaluated, the resulting metaformz can be updated either automatically or by selecting it, depending upon what option is active for the Metaformz Evaluate tool. A metaform can also be converted back to the original object from which it was derived by setting its Metaform Type to None in the Metaform Parameters dialog.

We've covered all the tools and options related to metaballs, metaforms, and metaformz. With this, we've also come to the end of the exercises for this workshop. You'll have the opportunity to test your newly acquired skills in organic modeling in the workshop assignment, coming up next.

ASSIGNMENT 6

A Curved Roof Structure for a Stadium

Model a roof covering for the stadium shown below. You need not go into full detail; it will be sufficient to model the basic components of the structure, conveying a good idea of its configuration and load distribution.

The steps for modeling the roof structure shown here will now be demonstrated step by step. You can refer to the form•Z files for each step of the assignment in the accompanying CD-ROM, under the folder Assignments > Workshop 6. A rendered image of the model is in the Assignment6.tif file in the same location.

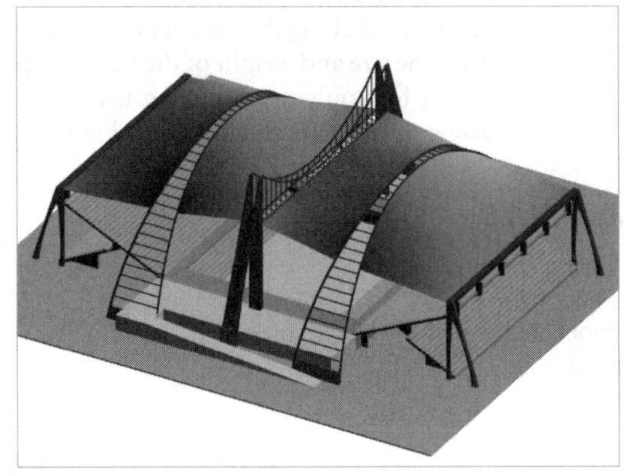

Setup

Open a new form•Z project, and go to Options > Working Units. Make sure the Data Scale is set to Medium (Building). Set the units to Feet under the English measurement system, Numeric Accuracy to 6", and Angle Accuracy to 1°. Change the Window Setup under the Window menu to a grid module of 10'-0" with 2 subdivisions, and set the Display Scale to 1/32" = 1'-0".

Step 1

In this exercise, only the roof of the stadium will be modeled, since it illustrates the use of some of the tools covered in this workshop. The body of the stadium is relatively straightforward and can be modeled with the basic modeling tools covered in the earlier workshops. You can copy the stadium body to your project from the "stadium-body.fmz" file, located in the Assignments > Workshop 6 folder on the accompanying CD-ROM. The layer stadium-body containing these objects will be added to your project as well.

Step 2

We need a base slab to situate the body as well as the roof of the stadium. Create a block with absolute coordinates of [-200,-100,0] and [200,280,0], and height [-1]. Rename the layer on which this is created as base plane. Then make the stadium-body layer invisible so that it doesn't interfere with the modeling of the roof.

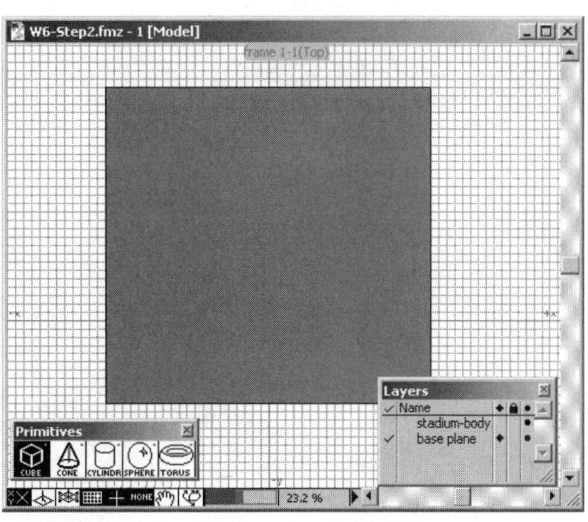

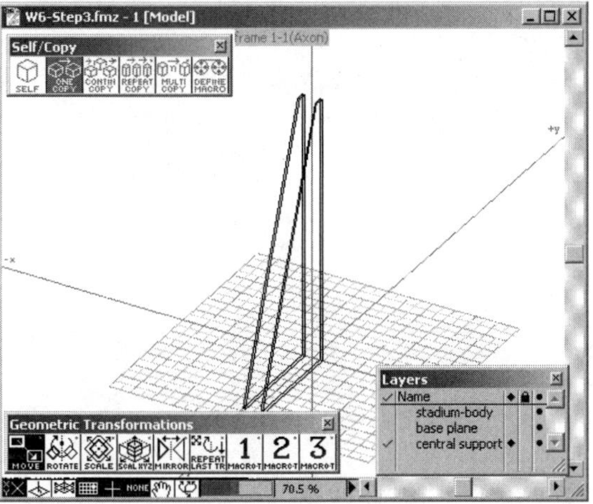

Step 3

We'll start by modeling the twin central supports located on one side of the roof. Activate a new layer, central support, and turn off the base plane layer. Use the Vector Line tool in 2D Surface mode to draw a closed shape at the origin with the following coordinates:

Pt #1: [0,-48,0] absolute
Pt #2: [0,0,0] absolute
Pt #3: [0,0,118] absolute
Pt #4: [0,-4,0] relative
Pt #5: [c] or triple-click to close

Extrude this 2D shape by a distance of 1' perpendicular to the surface. Create a copy of it and space out both objects so that they're located 7' apart, centered on either side of the origin.

Step 4

The next step is to model the curved shape cutting through these supports. Switch to the Right view. Use the Vector Line tool to create an approximate 2D open shape following the shape of the support, starting and ending at its base. Then use the Curve tool (M-Tool:7a,1) to convert it to a smoothly curved shape as shown. You can stick with the default curve settings of the Curve tool. Make sure that the start and end points of the new curve are still at the same level as the base of the support.

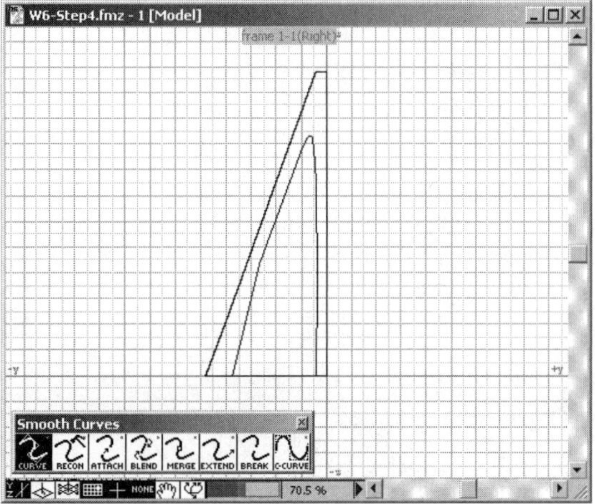

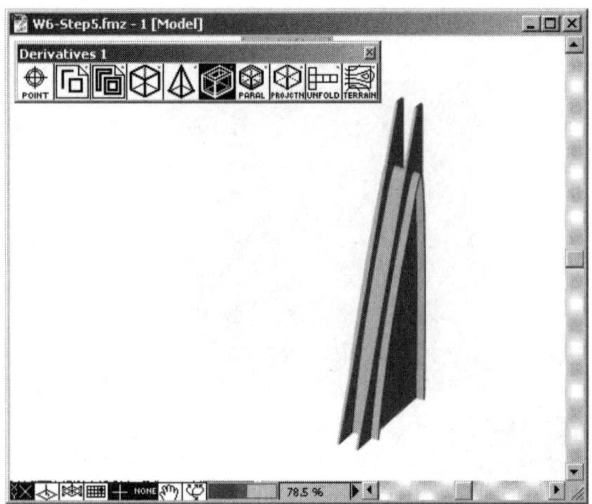

Step 5

Switch back to a non-planar view and apply the 3D Enclosure tool (M-Tool:5a,6) to this curve to extrude it, again in a direction perpendicular to the surface. The enclosure should have the default width of 1'. The extrusion height should be greater than the total width of the twin supports—a value of about 15' should be fine. After the shape has been extruded, position it midway between the supports so that it intersects both of them.

Step 6

Use the Join tool to join the two separate volumes of the twin supports into one object. Then select the B-Split tool and set its Status Of Objects to Keep. Use the default One Way mode to split the joined volume with the curved 3D enclosure you just created.

Delete the original joined support as well as the inside split portions until you're left with just the outer portions. Don't delete the curved 3D enclosure since we still need that.

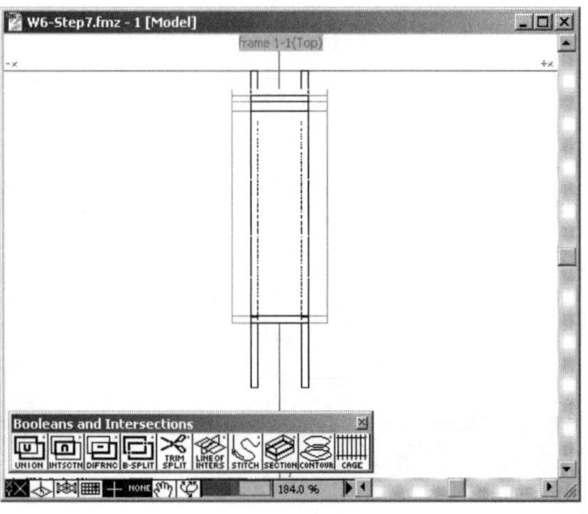

Step 7

Switch to the Top view and zoom in close to the supports. Draw two lines coinciding with the outside ends of the supports; these will be used to trim the parts of the curved enclosure that extend beyond the supports. Use the Trim/ Split tool with the mode set to Trim under With Line and the Stitch option activated for carrying out this task. Remember to set its Status Of Objects back to Ghost.

You should be left with the supports having the hole going through them and the curved extrusion spanning the hole. This configuration will be referred to as the *central support.*

Step 8

Use the Mirror tool in a Copy mode to create a mirror image of the central support, located at a distance of 176' along the Y axis from the original.

We'll now model the *cabled truss* spanning across these two central supports. Switch to the Right view. Use Endpoint snap, with the Project Onto Reference Plane option under Projection Views activated in its dialog, to draw a 2D horizontal line connecting the inner base points of the two supports. Move it vertically by a distance of 80'. Draw another line of length 5' starting from the midpoint of this line, oriented in the Z direction. Finally, draw an arc whose endpoints coincide with the top of the central supports and whose midpoint touches the top of the 5' line. Increase the Display Resolution in its dialog first, so that it looks smooth.

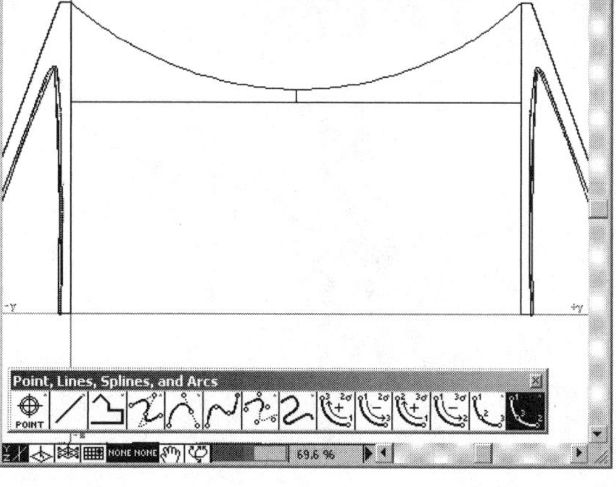

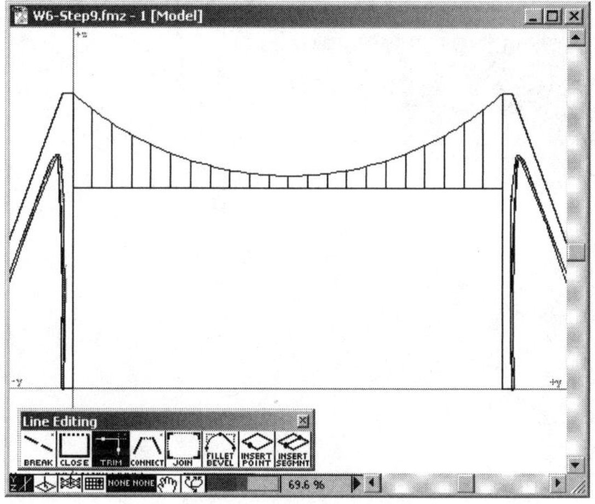

Step 9

Draw a series of vertical lines spaced 8' apart, oriented upwards from the horizontal line. (Draw one and make copies with the Move tool.) Trim this vertical sequence of lines with the arc using the Trim tool with the option set to Trim Segments With Line.

Step 10

Now switch to a non-planar view. All the 2D lines you just created should be in the same vertical plane coincident with the Y axis. Change the active reference plane to YZ. Use the 3D Enclosure tool, with the wall width set to 1'-0", to extrude the horizontal line and the arc by a distance of 1' in the +X direction. Change the wall width to 6", set the Heights menu to a custom value of 6", and extrude all the vertical lines in the same manner.

Switch to the Top view, and use the Align tool (M-Tool:13b,2) to centrally align all these extrusions you just created. Finally, use the Union tool to combine all the individual components of this truss into a single object. Move it to a new layer called central truss.

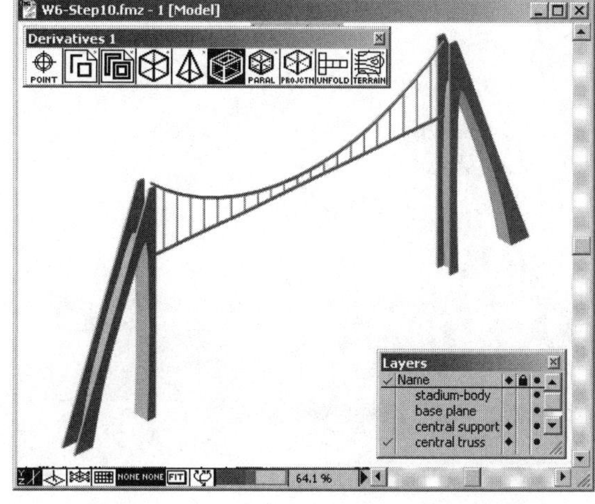

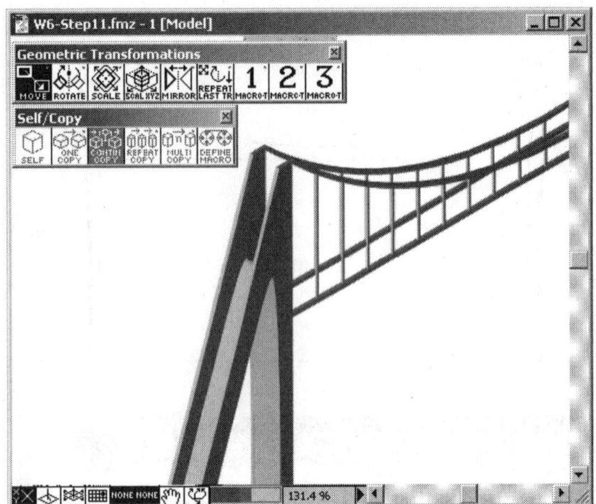

Step 11

Switch to the Right view, and draw a horizontal line connecting the two top ends of the central support. Use this line to trim the top of the arched truss so that its top face is flush with the top face of the central support. You would use the Trim/Split tool with the same settings as in Step 7.

Then switch to the Top view. Use the Move tool in a Copy mode, with Ortho mode and Endpoint snap activated, to make two copies of the truss on either side of the original, touching the two columns of the central support. Delete the original after verifying in a non-planar view that the copies have been correctly positioned.

Step 12

We have to complete the central truss by creating 6" by 6" horizontal bands connecting the two separate trusses at their base. First, create one band in Top view on the XY plane, aligned with one of the vertical bands of the truss, and move it to the required height. Then use the Move tool in Multi Copy mode to create copies of the horizontal band spaced 8' apart, throughout the length of the truss. The objective is to have the horizontal band spacing of the truss match its vertical band spacing.

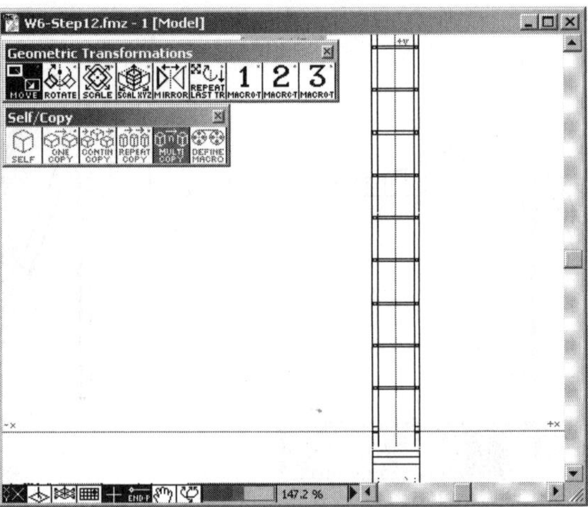

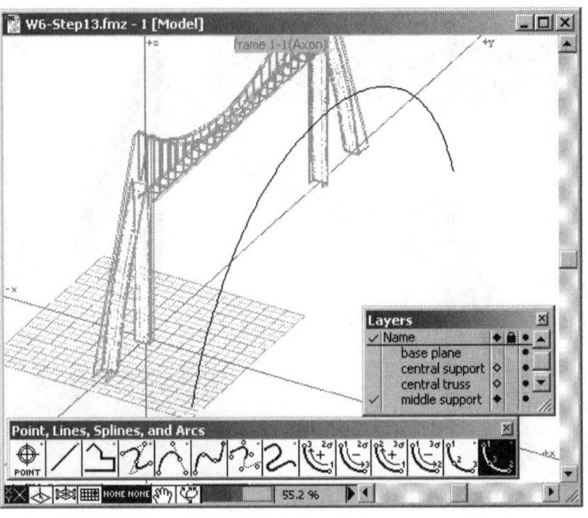

Step 13

We'll now proceed to model the *middle support* located midway between the central support and the end support. Activate a new layer called middle support and switch to the Right view. Ghost the central support and central truss layers. Use the last Arc tool on Row 3 in 2D Surface mode to draw an arc whose endpoints coincide with the outer ends of the base of the central supports and whose midpoint lies 100' above the base plane in the +Z direction.

Switch to a non-planar view. The arc will be coincident with the Y axis because the object snapping option was set to Project Onto Reference Plane. Move it by a distance of 55' in the +X direction.

Step 14

Make a copy of the arc at a distance of 20' in the +X direction.

Select the 3D Enclosure tool and set the Wall Width in its dialog to 1'-6". Switch to the YZ reference plane and extrude the first arc by a distance of 40' in the +X direction.

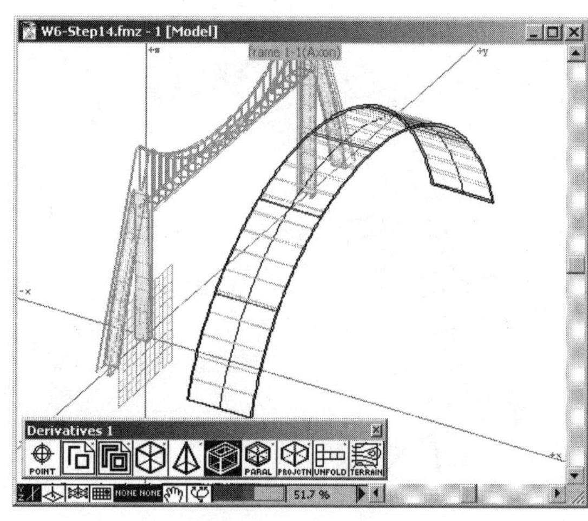

Step 15

Make the central support and central truss layers completely invisible, and switch to the Top view. Draw a line parallel to the Y axis, located 16' inside from the left end of the arched enclosure. Use the midpoint of this line as a reference to draw a 2D arc spanning the endpoints of the extruded arc.

Set the reference plane to XY and the Heights menu to Graphic/Keyed. In the dialog of the 3D Enclosure tool, choose the Left justification option, and specify the Wall Width as 1'. Apply it to the 2D arc you just created, extruding it to a height greater than the extruded arc.

Step 16

Use the Intersection tool to derive the 1' thick intersected volume of these two extruded arched volumes.

Move the straight line you created for drawing the arc in the last step by a distance of 4' in the +X direction. In the dialog of the Mirror tool, set the option to About A Segment and check the Relative To Reference Plane box. Use the Mirror tool in a Copy mode to make a mirror image of the intersected volume about the central straight line.

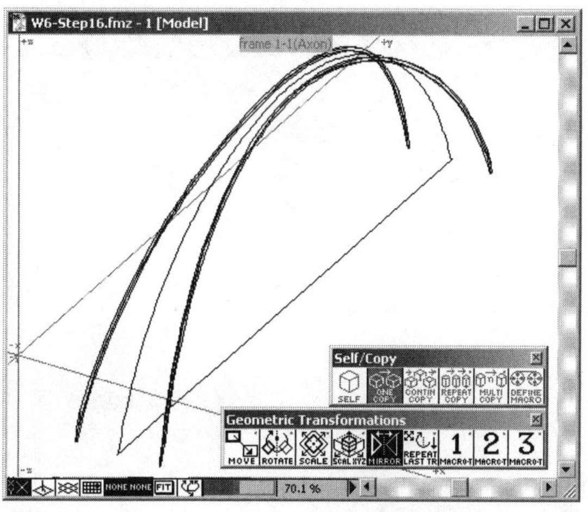

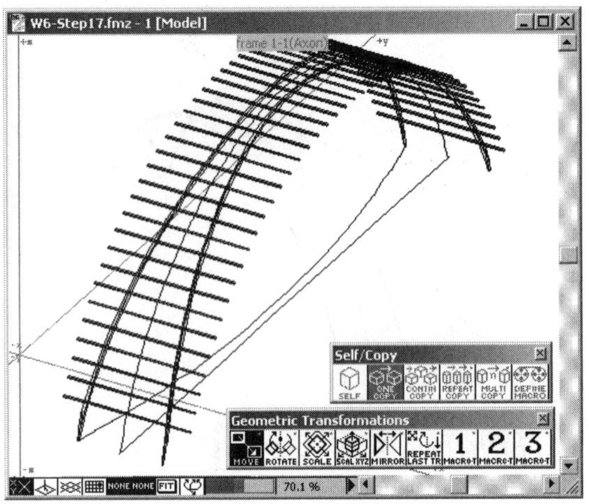

Step 17

Turn on the display of ghosted objects. Use the Unghost tool to unghost the 2D arc on the XY plane you had created in Step 15. Then go back and hide the display of ghosted objects. Create a strut of dimensions 60' by 1' by 6" on the XY plane and move it so that it sits on top of the highest point of the 2D arc that runs between the two arched slices. Use the Move tool in a Copy mode to make copies of it along one side of the arc, at regular intervals. Then mirror them to the other side. Ideally, the Rotate tool should be used in Multi Copy mode for precise spacing, but this requires locating the center of the arc to specify as the center of rotation; instead, we're using the Move tool for a quick approximation.

Step 18

Select all the struts and apply the Join tool to them. Make a mirror copy of the 2D arc on the XY plane (which you retrieved using the Unghost tool in the last step) about the straight line that's still there.

In the dialog of the Trim/Split tool, go to the Status Of Objects tab and choose the Single Object option under New Object Status. The main options should still be set to With Line and Stitch, as in Step 11. Use this tool to trim the ends of the joined struts, first with one of the 2D arcs on the XY plane and then the other. Make sure the reference plane is set to XY if you're in a non-planar view, so that the trimming action happens in the Z direction. Then delete the 2D arc running through the center of the support and the straight line on the XY plane.

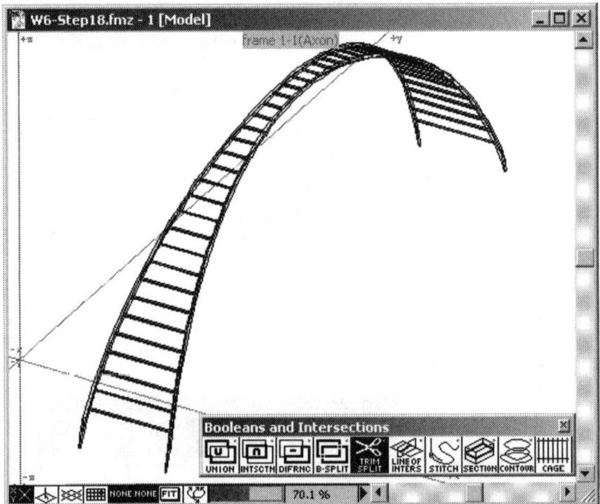

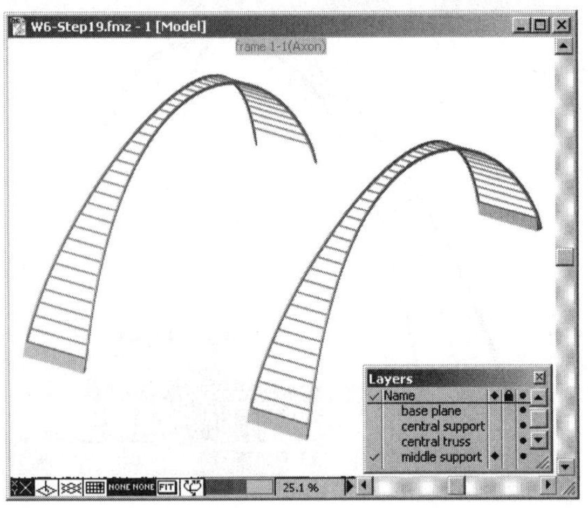

Step 19

All the middle support now needs is a triangular buttress at each end. Create a block of dimensions 40' by 4'-6" and a height of 8' at one end of the support. Use the Extend tool (M-Tool:13b,3) to trim its sides against those of the support and incline its outer side as shown.

Create a mirror copy of the buttress for the other end. Then use the Join tool to combine the buttresses, arched supports, and struts into one object. Create a copy of it at a distance of 150' in the –X direction to position it on the other side of the central support.

Step 20

It's time to move on to the end support, which is relatively simpler than the other supports. Activate a new layer, end support, and turn off the visibility of all the other layers. Use the Vector Line tool in 2D Surface mode to create a closed 2D shape with the following coordinates:

Pt #1: [182,0,0] absolute
Pt #2: [-25,0,0] relative
Pt #3: [0,0,63] relative
Pt #4: [5,0,0] relative
Pt #5: [c] for close

After drawing the shape, switch to the ZX plane and extrude it in the –Y direction by a distance of 3'. Make a mirror copy of this extrusion in the +Y direction, leaving a gap of 176' between the two extrusions.

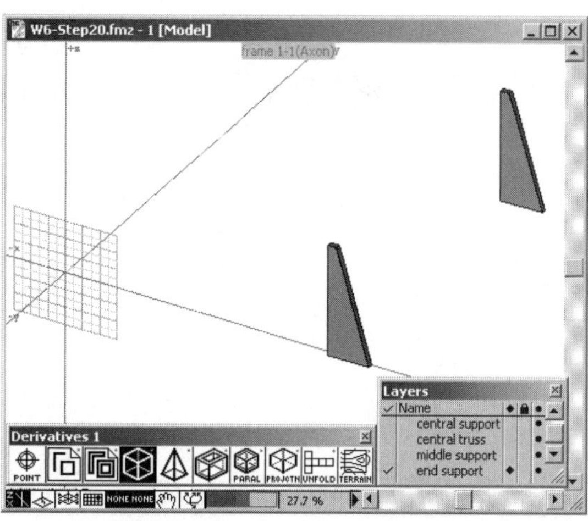

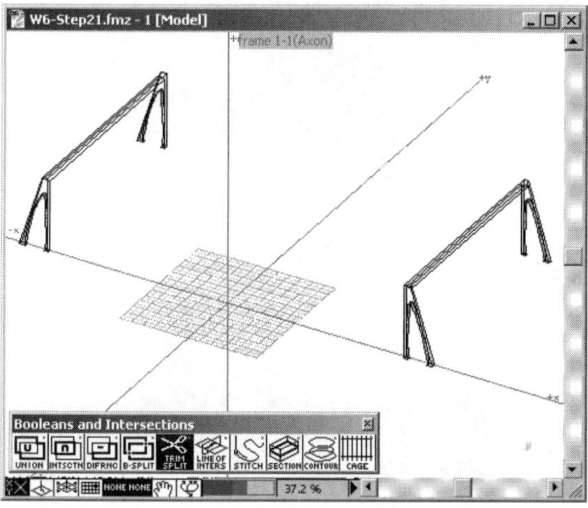

Step 21

Create a block of 5' width and 3' depth running between the two supports. Unite all three entities into one object.

Switch to the Front view, and create a 2D curve cutting through the triangular body of the support. Then apply the Trim/Split tool in the With Line mode to carve this area out of the support.

Finally, make a mirror copy of the support in the –X direction, at the same distance from the Y axis as the original. There should be a gap of 314' between the two supports. With this step, the two end supports are also complete.

Step 22

All that remains is to model the meshed roof covering, spanning across all the supports. This is actually divided into four parts: an identical pair spanning the end and middle supports, and a similar pair spanning the middle and central supports. As usual, we'll model the spans on one side of the central support and copy them to the other side.

Let's start with the roof covering spanning the end and middle support. Activate a new layer, roof1. Ghost the end support and middle support layers and turn off all the others. Switch to the Right view and draw three control lines as shown. They will be used to generate a c-mesh, so make sure their directions are in sync.

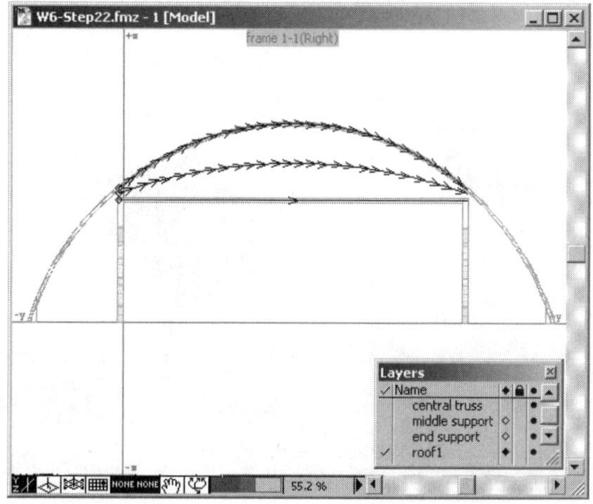

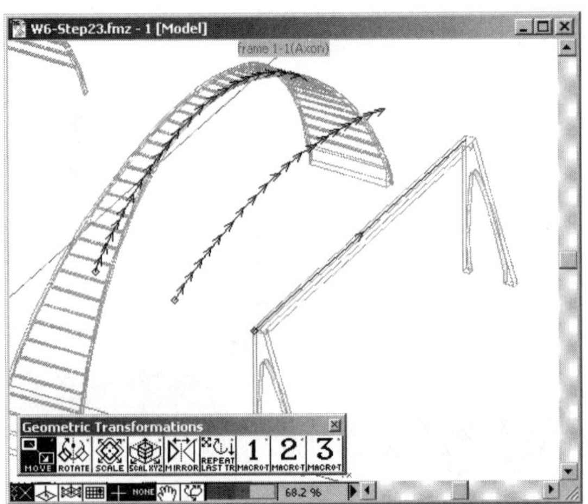

Step 23

Switch to a non-planar view, turn on the Ortho direction snap, and move the control lines along the X axis as shown. The straight line should coincide with the left side of the end support, the large arc with the right side of the middle support, and the smaller arc should be positioned approximately midway between the first two.

Step 24

Invoke the dialog of the C-Mesh tool and set the mesh length and depth to 20 segments. Prepick the control lines in the right sequence and apply the C-Mesh tool. A meshed surface following the shape and location of the control lines will be created.

We need to give a 2" thickness to the meshed surface, for which we'll use the Parallel tool (M-Tool:5a,7). However, to specify such a small value, the Numeric Accuracy in the Working Units dialog has to be reduced. Set this value to 1". Then invoke the dialog of the Parallel tool, set the option to Double Parallel with the Center option, and change all the offset values to 1". Apply this tool to the meshed surface and it will acquire a thickness of 2".

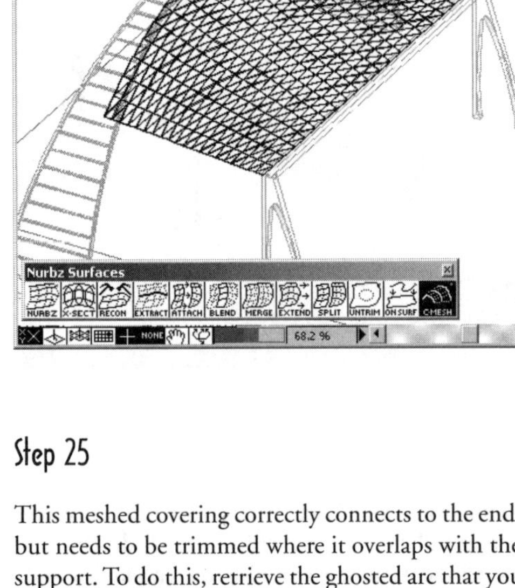

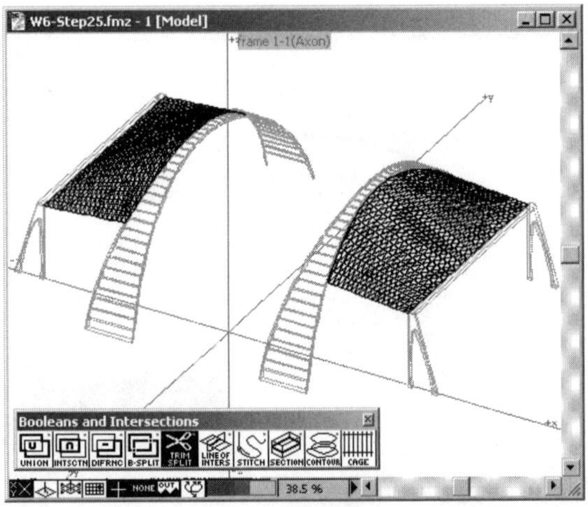

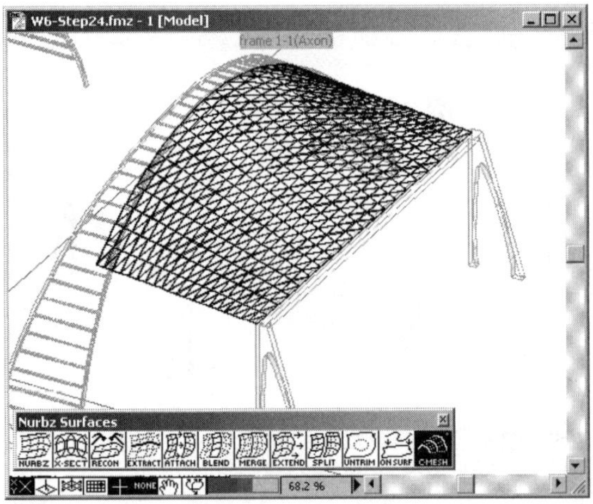

Step 25

This meshed covering correctly connects to the end support but needs to be trimmed where it overlaps with the middle support. To do this, retrieve the ghosted arc that you used in Step 18 for trimming the struts of the middle support on the right side, using the Unghost tool. Then move the arc by 1' in the +X direction so that it's aligned with the outer side of the middle support. Trim the meshed object with the arc using the Trim/Split tool. Check to see that it's correctly trimmed against the middle support.

Make a mirror copy of this meshed covering for the other pair of middle and end supports.

Step 26

Let's move on to the second roof covering spanning the middle and central supports. Activate a new roof2 layer, ghost the middle support and central support layers, and turn off all the other layers. As you did for roof1 in Step 22, create three control lines in the Right view as shown. These lines must start and end at the same Y coordinate values as the control lines you created for roof1.

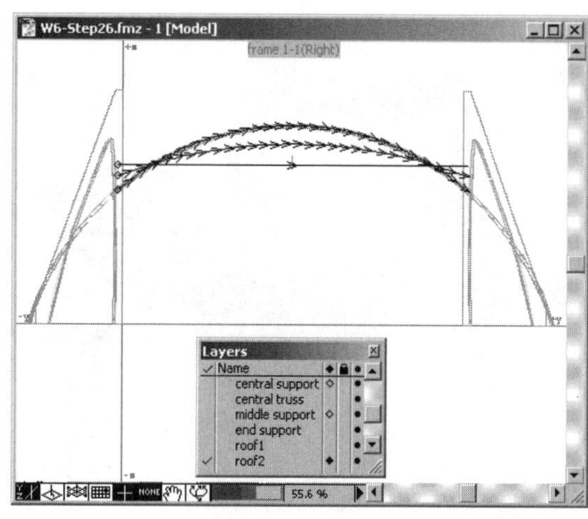

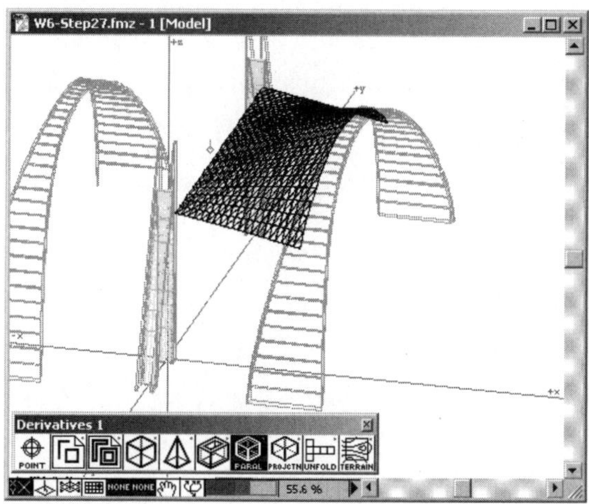

Step 27

Position the control lines appropriately and generate the mesh using the same parameters you used for roof1. As in Step 24, use the Parallel tool to give a 2" thickness to the meshed surface after you've created it.

Step 28

This meshed roof needs to be trimmed against the middle support, just like the earlier roof. As you did in Step 24, retrieve the ghosted arc that was used for trimming the struts of the middle support on the left side, and move it by 1' in the –X direction. Use it to trim the meshed roof so that it properly connects to the middle support.

Then make a mirror copy of it for the other side of the central support, as before.

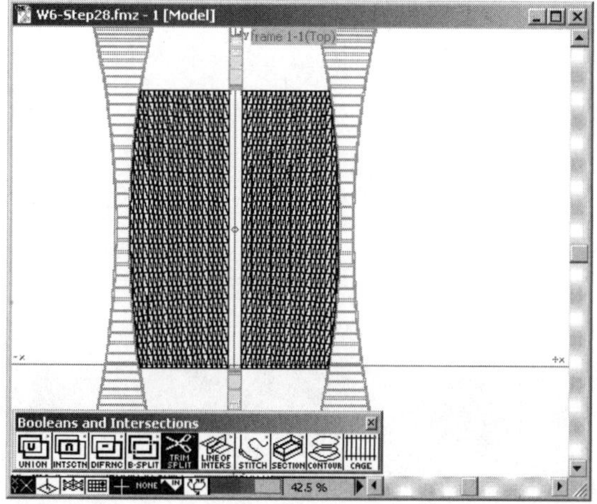

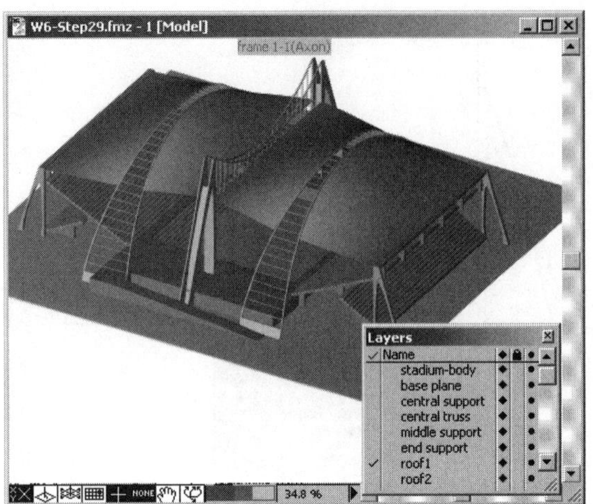

Step 29

With that, your model is complete. Turn all the layers on and color the objects appropriately. Your stadium now has a structurally stable and exciting roof over its head!

Ending with More

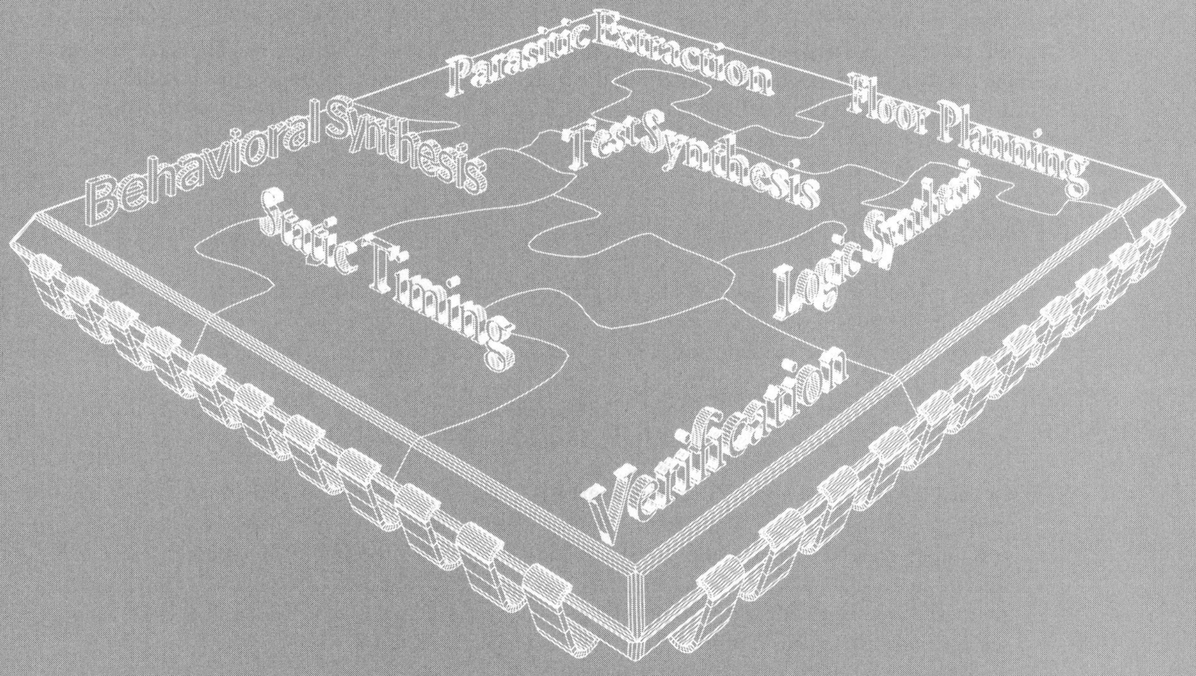

This workshop marks the last step of our long and exciting foray into the 3D world of form•Z. Most of the difficult tools and operations have already been covered, so you can look forward to a relatively easy time as you make your way through this workshop.

You will first be introduced to the amazing realm of 3D text, with which you can populate your models. Then, you'll learn to create and use symbols, or object libraries as they're more commonly referred to. You'll see how the Panoramic view type can be used to generate QuickTime VR movies, and how to generate and play animation sequences of your modeling world. Finally, you'll study some of the common options associated with importing and exporting files of different formats, and how to customize your use of form•Z with plugins and scripts.

EXERCISE 1

Writing in 3D

Very often, you might need to label or annotate different parts of your model. The most obvious solution to this problem, one that you may already have implemented, is to save a rendering of the model as an image file and then take it to any other drawing, painting, or image-editing program to add the text.

There is, however, another option. You can create this text as a 3D object within the modeling environment of form•Z itself, where it will be treated just like any other object and can be moved, scaled, copied, rendered, and so on. At times, you could use such 3D text to enhance the overall visual quality and graphic design content of the image. At other times, such text objects could become the focal points of your model, for instance, in the design of logos, banners, book covers, and so on. In this exercise, you'll see how to create and manipulate various kinds of text objects.

1.1 Placing Text

- Open a new form•Z project. We'll start putting text in it right away. Select the **Text Place** tool (**M-Tool:10a,1**) and watch the instructions in the **Prompts** palette. You'll be asked to specify the *text origin*, or where the text should be placed. Select or key in [0,0,0]—selecting the origin will give you a good reference point for the text placement. After this, the program takes a few seconds to load various kinds of fonts. (This will be done only once during a form•Z session.) You're then presented with the **3D Text Editor** dialog shown in Figure 7.1-a. TEXT PLACE

- In this dialog, you can write over the <Text> in the text box with the actual text you want. For multiple lines of text, use the **return** (Mac) or **Enter** (PC) keys. Go easy, however, on too much text, since these objects do take up space and slow down processing. There are a lot of other options in the dialog that determine the size and placement of the text object, and we'll be studying them in due course. For now, simply change the text and click **OK** to exit the dialog. You should see your text object laid out on the current reference plane, as shown in Figure 7.1-b.

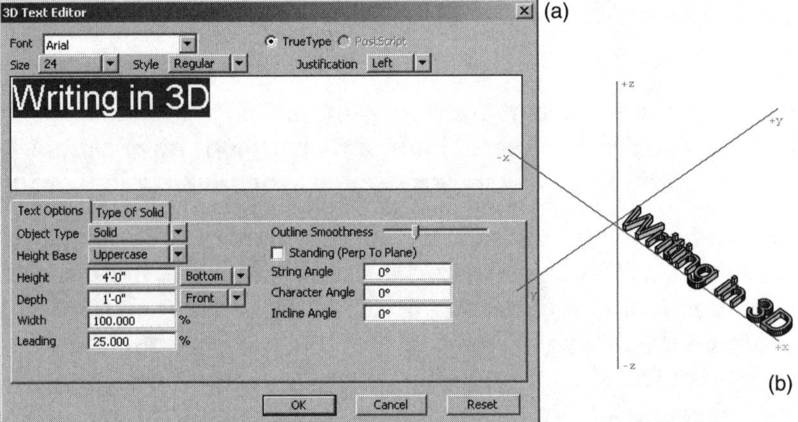

Figure 7.1

Using the Text Place tool. (a) The 3D Text Editor dialog. (b) Text placement using the default options in the dialog.

- Before moving on to see how to edit this text object, invoke the Plot/Print Setup dialog from the File menu. This has an option, Print Text As Paths, which is related to how a text object—such as the one you just created—is printed. This option is off by default, which makes the printer use its own native graphics while printing text, so it usually gives better results. But it might not exactly match what you see on the screen. If that's crucial, you should activate the Print Text As Paths option in the Plot/Print Setup dialog. Then the outline of each character of the text object is sent to the printer or plotter, eliminating any discrepancy between what you see on the screen and the printed output.

1.2 Editing Text

To change the settings for a text object you've already created, you need to use the Text Edit tool, located immediately after the Text Place tool.

- Select the Text Edit tool (M-Tool:10a,2) and apply it to the text object. The same 3D Text Editor dialog you saw earlier will open up, showing the settings for that object.

- Look at these settings more closely now. In the top right corner of the dialog, you can choose between TrueType and PostScript fonts. If no postscript fonts are found, that option will be deactivated. Depending upon the choice you make, the fonts available on your computer for that category will show up in the Font popup list. (Just as with any other application program, take care to ensure that the same fonts are available on other machines when you move your work between computers.) Highlight the text and choose a different font for it from the list. You also have the usual Size, Style, and Justification options for formatting the text. Make the appropriate choices, depending upon how you want your text object to look.
- Move on to the Object Type popup menu in the Text Options tab. This gives you three choices for the kind of object the text should be. The default is Solid, which is why the text object you created had a thickness. If you don't need your text to have this "depth" effect, you can go in for the Surface or Surface Solid options.
- The height of the text object is determined by the Height and Height Base specifications rather than by the font size specified. Keep this in mind, as it's often a source of confusion. The value specified in the Height field determines the actual size of the text object. You can also choose between three justification options—Top, Center, and Bottom—which respectively determine if the object is placed below, at the center, or above the reference line passing through the text origin you selected. The Height Base option determines which part of the text object the Height specifications are applied to. You can choose between an uppercase character (the default), a lowercase character, the actual font height, any character that you specify, or the maximum height of that entire string of text.
- Move on to the next three options. If you've specified your text object type as Solid, you can specify a numeric value for the Depth or thickness of your object. It's accompanied by three additional justification options—Front, Middle, and Back—which are analogous to those you saw for the Height. The Width and Leading percentage values respectively control the width of a character and the space between multiple lines, if any.
- Move on to look at the remaining options on the right side of the Text Options tab. The Outline Smoothness slider bar lets you increase the curvature resolution of your text object. Experiment with both the minimum and maximum values for this and follow the usual policy of settling for the lowest you can get away with, in order to reduce the complexity of the object.

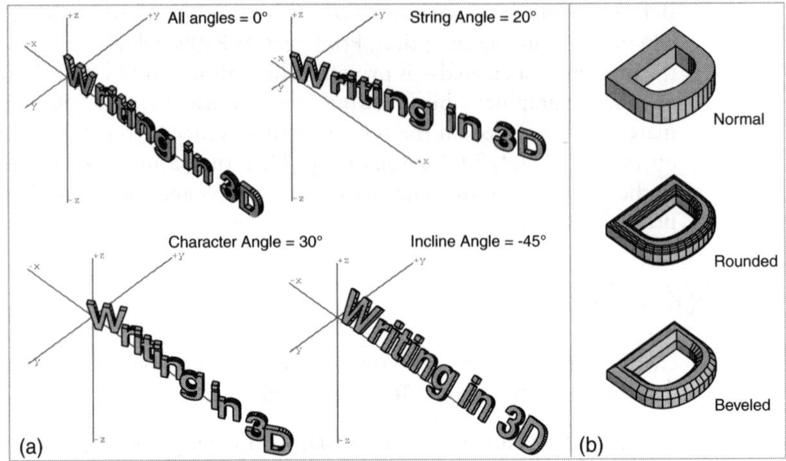

Figure 7.2

Exploring 3D Text editing options. (a) Different Angle options applied to a Standing text object. (b) The three different Type Of Solid options applied to a single character.

- Check the next option, Standing (Perp To Plane), and you'll find that your text object is now positioned standing up rather than lying flat on the reference plane. Experiment also with the following three angle options. With String Angle, you can specify at what angle the text object should be placed about the Z axis at the placement point. The default is 0°, which is the +X direction. The angle is, as usual, measured anticlockwise, unless otherwise specified in your Angle Options dialog. Character Angle will rotate each character about the specified angle rather than the entire text object. And finally, Incline Angle lets you rotate the text object about the line of placement itself. Figure 7.2-a shows examples of all three angle options, applied to a "standing up" text object.

- Let's now look at the options in the Type of Solid tab. These are active only when the Object Type is set to Solid. Ensure that this is the case, and you'll see that you can choose to round or bevel the edges of your text. You have a choice of applying this effect on one or both sides of the text object. Experiment with different values for both rounding and beveling. Keep in mind that the extent to which these operations can be applied is proportionate to the height and depth of the text, and you'll be warned if the specified values are not within the range of what's feasible. If it consistently refuses to work, try using a different font—that usually does the trick. Figure 7.2-b shows both the beveling and rounding effects at close range by zooming in on a single character of the text object. Its font and size were also changed from those shown in Figure 7.1.

We've finished looking at all the options in the 3D Text Editor dialog, and you might think that this is the end of the story as far as 3D text is concerned. Not so! In fact, we still have to look at the most interesting aspect of 3D text—how to twist and mold and curve it in 3D space. You might want, for instance, your text objects to meander gently along a path, or maybe fly out of a box! Let's see how to go about achieving such effects.

1.3 Other Options for Text Placement

- Go back to the Text Place tool and open its dialog (Figure 7.3). You'll see that it contains many options for text placement, of which you've been working with the At Point option under the Text As Object section. Let's see how the other options differ from this default.

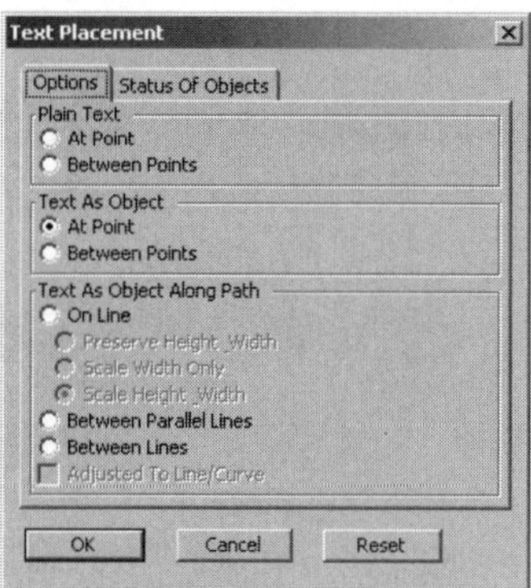

Figure 7.3

The dialog of the Text Place tool.

- Change the text placement option to Between Points under the same Text As Object section. When you now use the Text Place tool, you'll find that the program expects you to input two points rather than just one. The first point selected determines, as before, the starting point for the text. The second point determines the direction of the text. After you finish specifying both points, the 3D Text Editor dialog will open up in the usual manner. The only difference is that the String Angle option is grayed out, since this angle has already been determined by the two points. Verify this by entering some text and observing its location in the window when you exit the 3D Text Editor dialog.

- Get back to the Text Placement dialog and choose the At Point option, but this time under the Plain Text section. Apply the Text Place tool with this setting. Now, you'll find quite a few options grayed out in the 3D Text Editor dialog—Object Type, Depth, and so on. Enter some text and exit the dialog. You'll find that your text appears as a surface object without any thickness. Plain text is useful for labeling or annotating parts of your model, since it's the least complex type of text. Note that you can still edit this text with the Text Edit tool, so it's not a plain object in that sense.

- The Plain Text section also has the same Between Points option you saw earlier for the Text As Object section. It works in the same way. Try it out. Also explore the settings in the Interactive tab of the Wire Frame Options dialog that determine how plain text objects are displayed.

- Get back to the default At Point option under the Text As Object section in the Text Placement dialog and apply the tool. You'll find that there is a Plain Object option in the 3D Text Editor dialog, which wasn't there when the Text Edit tool was used. If you check this option, the object created with the Text Place tool will be a real plain object in the sense that it will lose its control parameters and its capability of being edited with the Text Edit tool. If you also check the accompanying Per Character sub-option in the 3D Text Editor dialog, each character of the text will become a separate plain object. Of course, you could always separate the characters later with the Separate tool (M-Tool:9b,2), whether the text was a plain object or not.

1.4 Placing Text Along Paths

- We'll now move on to the most interesting type of text placement in the Text Placement dialog (Figure 7.3), which is Text As Object Along Path. This lets you place text along a path of *any* shape, rather than just along a straight line. There are three options for this type of text placement. Select the first option, On Line. This has additional sub-options, but let the default of Scale Height & Width prevail for now. Exit the Text Placement dialog to get back to the graphics window.

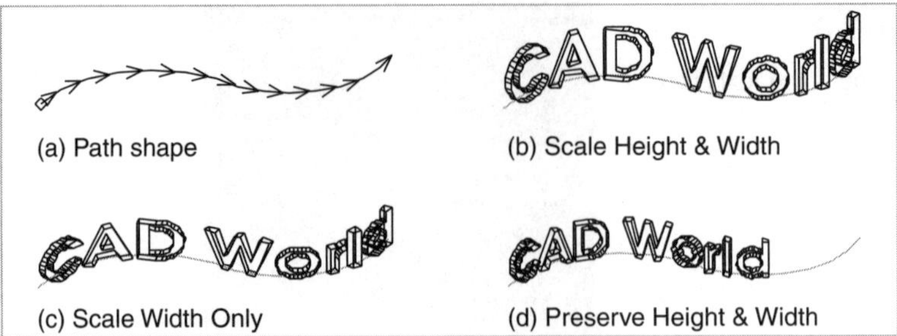

Figure 7.4

Using the On Line sub-options of Text Placement along a path to create a standing up text object. The first point and direction of the path are indicated.

- Create a 2D curved shape as shown in Figure 7.4-a. Then select the Text Place tool and watch the Prompts palette. You'll be asked to select the path along which the text is to be placed. Select the 2D shape you just drew. The 3D Text Editor dialog opens up in the usual manner. Enter some text and change other settings as desired. When you exit the dialog, you'll find that your text is now curved along the path, its direction matching the direction of the path. Moreover, the text has been scaled both in height and width to match the start and end points of the path shape (Figure 7.4-b).

- Undo and place the same text along the same path, but with the On Line option set to Scale Width Only in the Text Placement dialog. You'll find that the text is now scaled to fit the endpoints in width only. The height remains true to what was specified in the 3D Text Editor dialog. This might end up making your text object look somewhat disproportionate (Figure 7.4-c).

- Finally, try the last On Line sub-option, Preserve Height & Width. This preserves all the text size settings and doesn't try to match the endpoints of the path shape (Figure 7.4-d). You'd use this if the size specification was crucial and had to be followed. Make sure that the path is large enough for the text to fit when you work with this option.

- Move on to try the next Text As Object Along Path option, Between Parallel Lines. This is almost similar to the Scale Width Only sub-option for the On Line placement, in the sense that the height remains true to what was specified in the dialog. However, there's a subtle difference in the result, which is illustrated in Figure 7.5. When you select the Between Parallel Lines option, you still select a single control line. But the program automatically generates a line parallel to this at a distance equal to the text height specified and creates a bounding box for each character between the lines. This ensures that individual characters don't touch or overlap even when the path is curved. The Standing (Perp To Plane) option in the 3D Text Editor dialog is deactivated for this type of placement.

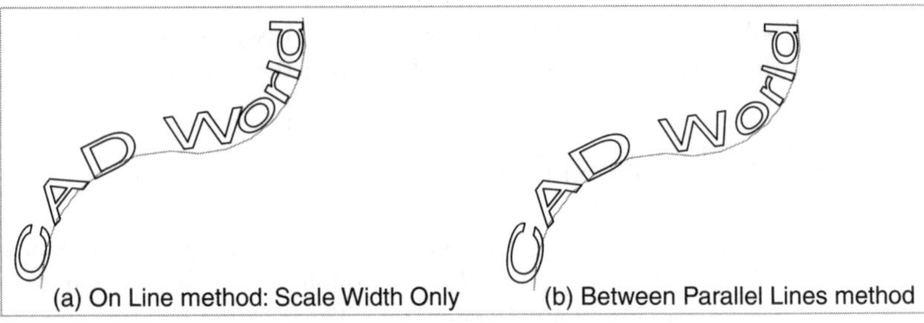

Figure 7.5

Placing the same text on the same control line but using different placement methods.

- Placing text on a line or between parallel lines seems simple enough. But what if you want to place text between paths that are not parallel and want the text to be adjusted appropriately? We'll now work on such a problem. Let's say, for instance, that you'd like to have your text object flying out of a box, getting larger as it emerges. Model the box and then create two 2D shapes that will define the flow of the text, as shown in Figure 7.6. Make sure that the two paths are drawn in the same direction, from the inside to the outside of the box.

- In the Text Placement dialog, select the last Text As Object Along Path option, Between Lines. When you apply the Text Place tool now, you'll be asked to select two paths. Select first the 2D shape that will determine the base of the text. Then select the second shape that will determine the upper boundary of the text. You'll now see your text placed between the two shapes, appropriately sized and curved (Figure 7.6-a).

- The Between Lines method doesn't even require the path shapes to be on the same plane, which gives you a lot of flexibility in placing text creatively. To see how this works, undo the last text placement operation and rotate one of the paths about the vertical axis, so that it's no longer in the same plane as the other path. Then reapply the Text Place tool to see the result (Figure 7.6-b).

- There is an additional option in the Text Placement dialog, Adjusted To Line/Curve, which is relevant to the Between Parallel Lines and Between Lines methods. This option has to do with the shape of the individual text characters. By default, this option isn't checked, so all the characters retain their basic rectangular shapes. Check this option and generate some new text objects using vector lines or curves. You'll find that the shape of the individual characters is now adjusted according to the angles of the line or the curvature of the curve.

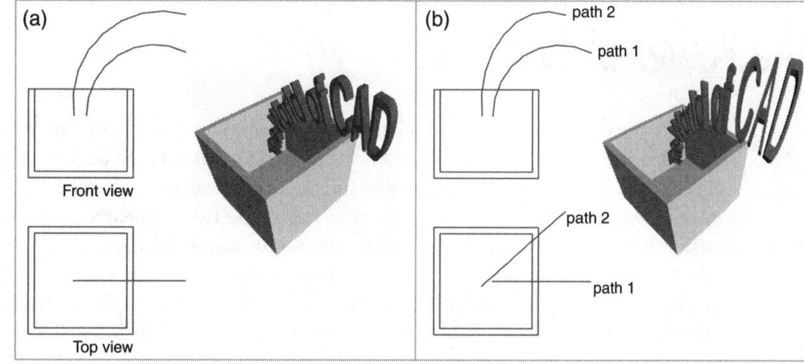

Figure 7.6

Placing text using the Between Lines method. (a) Using two non-parallel paths that lie on the same plane. (b) Using two non-parallel paths that are not on the same plane.

1.5 Editing Text Placement Lines

form•Z not only gives you the ability to place text along paths in many interesting ways, but also lets you edit these paths long after the text has been placed. When you modify a path or paths, the text object is resized and reoriented to match the new configuration.

- Select the Edit Controls tool (M-Tool:4b,2), and apply it to any text object that was placed along a path. You'll now be in the *text line edit mode*, where the original path or paths used for the text placement also become visible (Figure 7.7-a). Click on a path, and its controls become visible. You can move these around to give a new shape to the path; you'll see the text object being rubber-

banded to realign itself with the path as you edit it (Figure 7.7-b). The procedure is similar to how you used the Edit Controls tool to graphically edit the controls of nurbz and patches in Section 5.5 of Workshop 6 (Going Organic). Double-click when you've finished modifying the path to exit the edit mode. This is how you can interactively fine-tune your text object to give it the desired shape.

Figure 7.7

Using the Edit Controls tool to edit the path of a text object and reshape it.

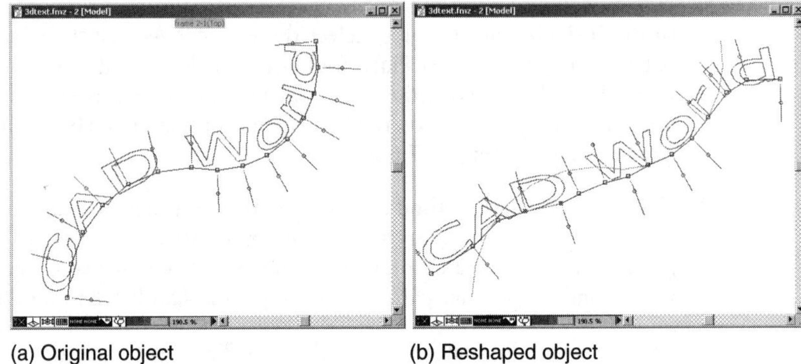

(a) Original object (b) Reshaped object

EXERCISE 2

The Power of Symbols

The concept of an object library must be familiar to you. There are many objects in any design field that are used very frequently across projects. In architecture and interior design, for instance, doors, windows, furniture, fixtures, trees, and so on will almost always be needed. In graphic design, you might create a 3D logo or banner that has to be used repeatedly. There are many such examples in other fields as well. You'd obviously not want to model these objects every time from scratch. You could, of course, model them once and then copy and paste them wherever they're needed. But what if you make a change to the original? You'd like all the copies to automatically update themselves, which would not be possible using the copy-and-paste method.

This is where a "library" of objects comes in useful. All frequently used objects can be created once and then stored in the library. If you need a library object for any project, you simply link to it and place the object in the desired position. One advantage of this already mentioned is the automatic updating ability. The other important advantage is that it reduces the file size of the project, since the object description sits only once in the library and doesn't have to be repeated each time it's used.

In form•Z, an object stored in such a library is referred to as a *symbol*, and the library, consequently, is called a *symbol library*. You can create many symbol libraries containing different categories of objects. All that you need to do to use a particular library for a form•Z project is to load it. Then you can reference any symbol from that library and place it as an *instance* into your project. We'll be looking at all these operations in the course of this exercise. Apart from creating your own symbols and storing them in your own libraries, keep in mind that you can also use predefined form•Z libraries, available on the installation disk or on the form•Z website.

2.1 Creating Symbols from Objects

- Find a suitable object in any of your earlier projects that you need to use frequently in other projects, e.g., a chair, window, 3D logo, and so on. The object itself can be made up of several component objects, i.e., you're not restricted to a single form•Z object. If you don't have such an object, create a configuration of objects in a new file and use that instead.

- Use the Pick tool to select all the individual components of the object that has to be stored as a symbol. Then activate the Symbol Create tool (M-Tool:10b,1). You'll be prompted to click to create a symbol definition from the picked object. Do so but don't just click anywhere in the window, since the selected point will function as the point of placement for the symbol when you recall it in other projects. Instead, click by snapping to an appropriate reference point, for instance, an endpoint, the center of a face, the center of the base of the object, and so on.

- You'll now be greeted with a message telling you that a symbol definition cannot be created since no symbol library has been loaded. You're given two options for dealing with the situation, apart from canceling the operation. Since you haven't yet created any library, Load Existing Library isn't an option you want to use now. (Remember, however, that you could use it in future sessions when you want to create a new symbol in an existing library.) Therefore, click on the Create New Library button. The familiar file save dialog will open up, allowing you to create a new file with an extension of ".zlb," indicating that it's a form•Z library file. Give the file an appropriate name and change the default location if necessary.

- Once you've completed the process of creating a new library file, you'll be prompted to enter a *definition name* for the symbol. Since a library can contain many symbols, it's important for each one to have its own identifying name. Type in a suitable name, and click OK. You've now completed the process of creating a symbol from the selected object.

- How do we know that it worked? There's no visible change in the graphics window. However, go to Options > Symbol Libraries and a dialog will open up, showing you the new library you just created as the active library, along with the object you just created as a symbol in this library (Figure 7.8).

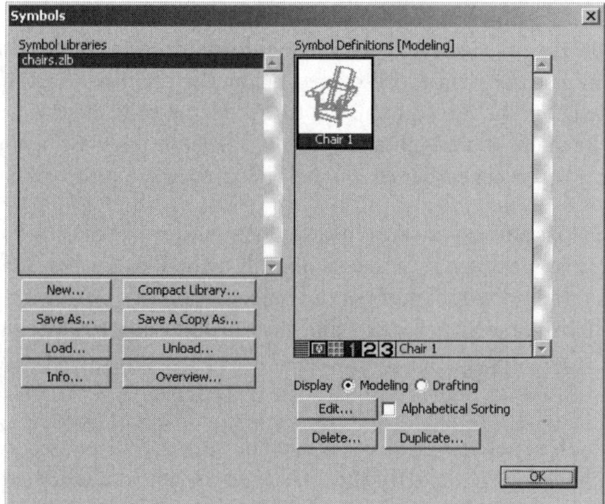

Figure 7.8

The Symbol Libraries dialog, showing the new library with the symbol that was created in it.

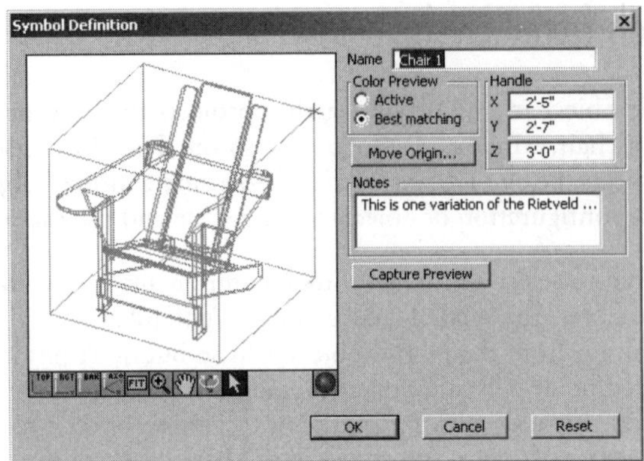

Figure 7.9

The Symbol Definition dialog for the created symbol.

- Spend some time at this stage going through the various buttons and options in the Symbol Libraries dialog. You can create a new library (New), make copies of libraries (Save As) as well as symbols (Duplicate), Load and Unload libraries from the project, get a brief Info as well as a detailed Overview of a particular library, Edit and Delete symbols, and perform an Alphabetical Sorting. Compact Library gives you a couple of options for the memory management of libraries; stick with the defaults for now.

You can load multiple libraries into a project using the Load button.

- Turn to the actual object symbol displayed in the preview window of the dialog. It's highlighted, indicating that it's the active symbol. Double-click on it or hit the Edit button and a second dialog will open up, showing more information about that symbol (Figure 7.9).

- Explore the various options available in the Symbol Definition dialog. You can change the origin—the placement point indicated by the intersection of the three red-colored segments denoting the axes—by moving it graphically with the Pointer tool in the preview area, or numerically through the Move Origin option. You can do the same to what is called the Handle, indicated by the intersection of the three teal-colored segments. How the handle gets created and what it's used for, we shall look at very soon. Any reference information for the symbol can be entered in the Notes area. You can use the icon tools located below the preview window to get a different view of the symbol; then, by clicking on the Capture Preview button, the new view can be registered for display in the main Symbol Libraries dialog. The Color Preview options are relevant when a symbol is placed into a project rather than when it's created, so pass these for now.

- Exit both dialogs and get back to the graphics window. Let's see what has happened to the original object that was transformed into a symbol. Use the Pick tool on it and you'll find that you can no longer select the individual parts of the object—you can only select it as a single entity. Apply the Query tool to this object, and you'll find that its Object Type is listed as Symbol. What has happened is that the original object has been transformed into an instance of the symbol that was created from it.

- Let's now look at what options the Symbol Create tool comes with. Double-click to open its dialog. You have four choices for Origin/Handle Definition, which are self-explanatory. The default of Pick Origin is the most commonly used one. However, if the handle position is important (and we shall soon see when that might happen), you should opt for Pick Origin And Handle. In addition to the placement point, this will ask you to select an additional point for the handle while creating a symbol.

- The Status Of Picked Objects in the Symbol Create Options dialog is set to Replace With Instance by default, which explains why your object was transformed to an instance when a symbol was created from it. You can choose the Status Of Objects option instead and set the Status to Keep. The object will now be retained in its original state after a symbol is generated from it.

2.2 Creating Multiple Definitions of a Symbol

- You'll now create one more symbol in the same library. Find or create a suitable object and apply the Symbol Create tool to it. (Remember to prepick its individual parts first.) If this object is in a different project file, you'll have to take the additional step of loading the library into that project. Give the new symbol an appropriate name. Then open the Symbol Libraries dialog from the Options menu to verify that the library now has two symbols stored in it. Check out also the Symbol Definition for the new symbol to see how the origin and handle have been positioned.

- Back in the Symbol Libraries dialog, look more closely at the iconic tools at the base of the preview window. The first three of these are for different ways of displaying the symbols in the preview window. Try them out. Then turn to the icons marked 1, 2, and 3. These stand for different levels of a symbol. Each symbol can have up to three definitions associated with it. This is useful for storing symbols at different levels of detail. For instance, a window can be stored at one level with its frame, glass and mullions, and on another level as just a flat vertical slab. The level you use will depend upon how closely that object is to be seen in a particular view.

- Notice that level 1 is highlighted, indicating that it's the active level in which symbols will be created and from which they will be placed. Select 2, and you'll find that while there are still two placeholders for the two symbols you've created so far, they're grayed out, indicating that no definitions for these two symbols have been created at level 2.

- Let's create these definitions right away. Ensure that level 2 is still active and get back to the graphics window. Create two simple objects of approximately the shape and size of your two symbols, and apply the Create Symbol tool to each of them in turn. Give them the same names as your first two symbols. If you now look in the Symbol Libraries dialog, you'll have definitions for the two symbols at both levels, 1 and 2.

2.3 Placing Symbol Instances into Projects

- We'll now see how the stored symbols can be placed in a different project. Open a new form•Z project file, or continue with the one you used for Exercise 1. To be able to place a symbol from your saved library in this project, remember that you need to load that library file first. You know that you can do this through the Symbol Libraries dialog, which can be accessed by going to Options > Symbol Libraries. Let's, however, use an alternate and more convenient method. Go to the Palettes menu and open the Symbols palette. It's currently blank since no library is loaded (Figure 7.10-a). Click inside the palette in the top row where the word Library appears. This will invoke the same Symbol Libraries dialog you saw earlier.

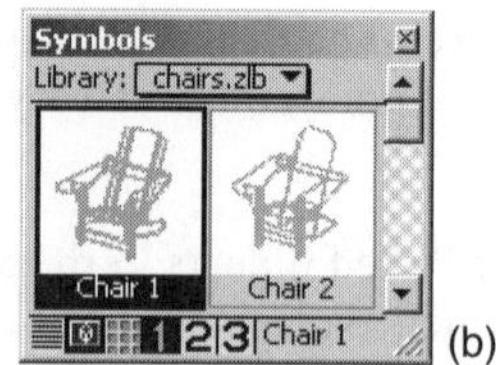

Figure 7.10

The Symbols palette, before and after loading the symbol library created earlier.

- No library has been loaded, so the symbols preview area in the dialog is blank. Click on the Load button and select the library you had saved. It gets loaded into the project and the two symbols it contains appear in the preview area. The first symbol is highlighted by default, indicating that it's the active symbol. Click OK to exit the Symbol Libraries dialog. In the Symbols palette, you'll now see the same symbols preview that you saw in the dialog (Figure 7.10-b). Double-clicking on a symbol in the palette invokes the same Symbol Definition dialog for the symbol you saw in Figure 7.9. The Symbols palette is thus a very convenient interface to the symbol libraries.

- Let's now get down to the business of placing an instance of the active symbol into the project. Select the Symbol Place tool (M-Tool:10b,2). You'll be asked to pick the *instance origin*, or, in other words, the placement point for the symbol. Select a point in the window and watch your first symbol appear there. Keep clicking at different points and see how easily and quickly you can populate your model with instances of the symbol. Switch to the other symbol in the Symbols palette and place instances of that as well into your project. You should have something similar to what is shown in Figure 7.11.

Figure 7.11

Placing instances of the symbols shown in Figure 7.10-b in a project.

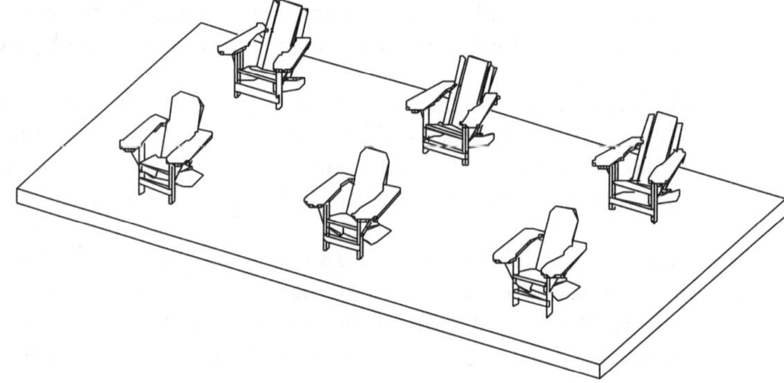

- Notice that the orientation and size of all the instances of a symbol are exactly the same as they were when you created the symbol. What if you wanted some instances to be oriented and sized differently? For this, access the dialog of the Symbol Place tool (Figure 7.12-a), and change the scaling factors and rotation values for symbol placement. Deselect the Scale Lock box if you want to specify different scaling factors for the 3 directions. Reapply the Symbol Place tool and you'll see that the symbol instances now placed follow your specifications rather than the original values.

- The default placement option, as you can see in the Symbol Placement Options dialog, is Pick Origin. There are two other options—Pick Origin And Uniform Scale and Pick Origin And X, Y, and Z Scale—which let you dynamically rotate and scale a symbol instance while placing it. Activate each of them in turn. When you now use the Symbol Place tool, the first point you select is the placement point as usual. But you also go on to select additional points that will determine the orientation and size of the instance, which is rubber-banded as you move the mouse. For both these options, the location of the *handle* in the symbol definition affects this dynamic positioning of the instance. Test this by executing the Symbol Place operation for different handle locations of the symbol.

- By default, the Color Display of a symbol instance is set to its Definition Colors in the Symbol Placement Options dialog, which are the colors in which it was created. This option will import the colors if they don't exist in the project. You could opt for Best Matching Colors, which will instead find the closest match to the colors from those existing in the Surface Styles palette. The third option, Active Color, colors the symbol instance in the active color of the project and also lets you change its color freely later, which the other two options don't.

- Similarly, you can also change the layer settings of the symbol instance in the Layer Display popup menu, but it's a good idea to stick with the default of Active Layer. The other option, Definition Layers, will import all the layers that were used to define the symbol in its project file into the current project, increasing your layer list unnecessarily.

The colors and layers used by a symbol in a project get locked and cannot be modified. Such colors and layers will appear in a read-only mode in their respective palettes, as shown in Figure 7.12-b.

There is one more option at the base of the Symbol Placement Options dialog, Use Lights If Present. This is related to creating symbol lights, which we'll look at in detail in Section 2.6, so skip it for now.

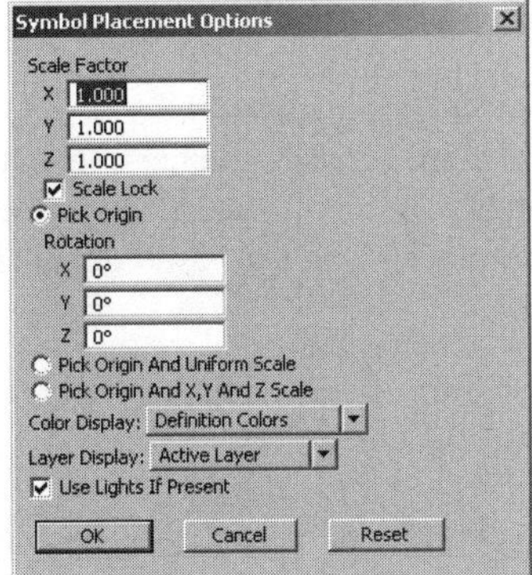

Figure 7.12

(a) The dialog of the Symbol Place tool, showing the default placement values. (b) The Surface Styles and Layers palettes, showing the locked colors and layers.

2.4 Editing and Exploding Symbol Instances

- What if you want to change the scale, position, or orientation of a symbol instance *after* you've already placed it? Try applying the Move, Rotate, or Mirror tools to any of the instances you created and you'll find that you can move, rotate, and mirror them just like any regular object. However, you'll find that both the Scale tools on Row 13 do not work on symbol instances.

- For scaling, you'll have to resort to the special tool reserved for editing symbol instances, Symbol Edit (M-Tool:10b,3). Select this tool and apply it to one of your symbol instances. A dialog will be invoked showing the various parameters for that instance (Figure 7.13).

Figure 7.13

Applying the Symbol Edit tool to a symbol brings up the Symbol Instance Edit dialog.

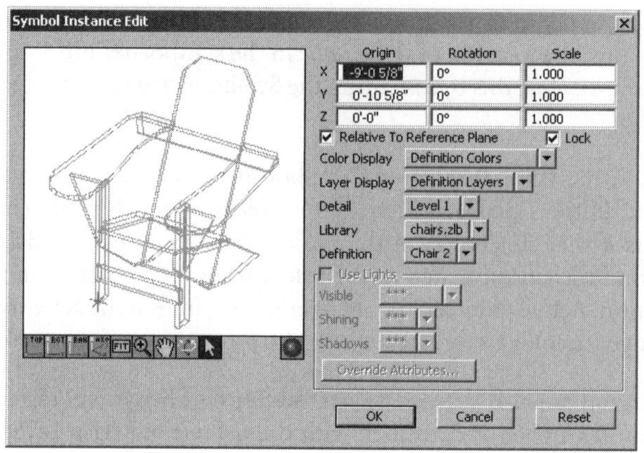

- Edit some of your symbol instances in different ways, as shown in Figure 7.14-a, using the options in this dialog. You can change the origin or placement point of an instance, rotate it, or scale it. To rotate or scale along all three axes independently, deselect the Lock icon. You can change the Color Display and Layer Display settings, which are similar to what you saw earlier in the Symbol Placement Options dialog. You can switch to a different level definition of the same symbol by selecting it from the Detail menu. You can also go to the extent of placing another symbol at the same placement point by choosing it from the Definition menu. If necessary, you can choose a symbol from another library—if it has been loaded into that project—from the Library menu. The set of options related to lights is currently deactivated; we'll be looking at these options soon.

- It's also possible to edit multiple symbol instances at the same time. This is useful when you need to apply the same transformation to many symbol instances. Invoke the dialog of the Symbol Edit tool and select the Edit Simultaneously option. You can now preselect with the Pick tool all the symbol instances you want to modify, then apply the Symbol Edit tool to them.

- If you want to modify only one of the individual parts that make up a symbol instance, you cannot do it using Symbol Edit, since this tool treats the symbol instance as one composite entity. In such a situation, apply the Symbol Explode tool (M-Tool:10b,4) to the instance. This will break the instance down into each one of its constituent parts, and they can now be treated as regular objects—moved, rotated, scaled, colored, and so on, independently of the other parts of the symbol instance.

- When you apply the Symbol Explode tool to a symbol instance to break it down into its constituent parts, it no longer remains a symbol. Test this by trying to apply the Symbol Edit tool to an exploded symbol instance—you'll find that you cannot. You've thus lost the advantage of using a symbol for that particular object, including the automatic updating facility. Therefore use the Symbol Explode tool judiciously, only when you really need to.

2.5 Updating Symbols Dynamically

Suppose that you need to modify an original symbol you had created, and would like the change to be automatically updated in all the instances of that symbol. Let's see how to do this.

- Use File > Open to open the library file which contains the symbol you want to modify. (Remember that a library file can be identified by the ".zlb" extension.) Open the Symbols palette if it's closed, and select the symbol that's to be modified. It will appear in the graphics window, where you can now use the regular modeling tools of form•Z to transform it as desired. You can add more parts to it or modify or delete existing parts. To save the changes to the symbol, click on another symbol in the palette. If the symbol you're modifying needs to have another symbol from the palette placed *within* it, switch the Mode at the top of the Symbols palette temporarily to Place Instance instead of Edit Definition in order to do this. To save the changes to the library file as a whole, you must select Save from the File menu before you close the file.

- Now switch back to the project in which you placed instances of the symbol you just edited. You'll immediately be informed that the library has been modified and will be reloaded. And voila!—your project will be automatically updated, with the changes that you made to the symbol showing up in each one of the instances, even in their edited versions (Figure 7.14-b). Only the exploded symbol instances will remain unaffected.

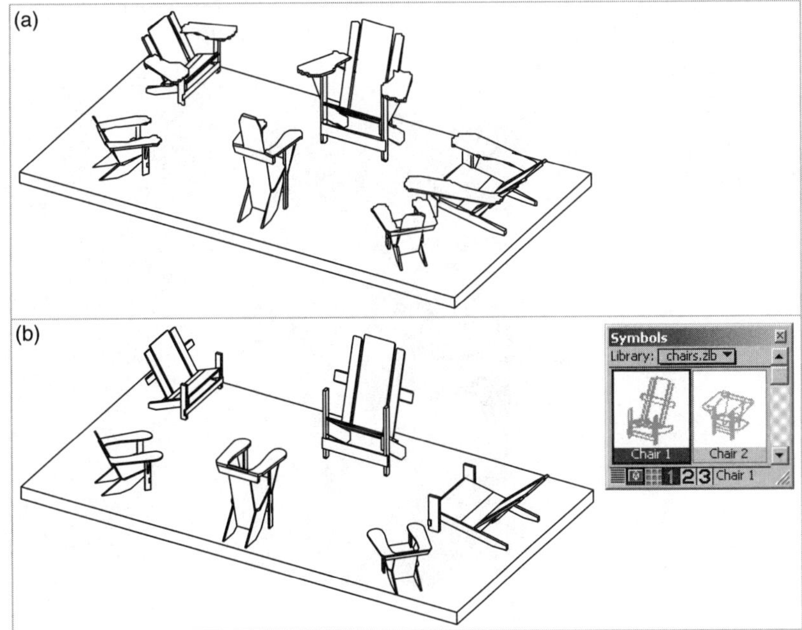

Figure 7.14

(a) Editing the symbol instances shown in Figure 7.11 in various ways using the Symbol Edit tool. (b) Modifying the original symbol automatically updates the symbol instances. The new Symbols palette is also shown.

2.6 Including Lights in Symbols

A lighting fixture is a commonly required symbol in architecture and interior design projects. This is why form•Z allows you to include lights in symbol definitions. Let's see how this works, using the table lamp we created in the Assignment for Workshop 5 (Illuminating, Texturing, and Rendering Your World). Refer to Exercise 2 of that workshop if you need to go over operations such as creating a light and working with the Lights palette.

- Open the form•Z file with the table lamp model and save a copy of it using File > Save As. This is to ensure that the original copy remains intact. Make sure the model includes a light source; if it doesn't, create a point light positioned inside the light bulb. Go to Options > Symbol Libraries, and load the library you had created earlier into this project.

- Select all the individual objects that make up the lamp. Make sure the light source is selected as well. Use the Symbol Create tool to create a new symbol definition from the selected objects in the current library. Give it a suitable name, say Lamp.
- Switch back to the test project in which you were placing instances of the symbols you had defined. Since the library has been modified, it will be automatically reloaded and the Symbols palette will show the new Lamp symbol (see Figure 7.15), alongside the other two symbols you had created before in that library.
- Use the Symbol Place tool to place an instance of the Lamp symbol in the project. Then switch to the RenderZone display mode, and you'll find the light in this symbol instance contributing to the illumination of the scene, as shown in Figure 7.15. Notice also that the Lights palette has an entry for each symbol instance containing a light. Such entries are named with an S followed by the name of the instance in square brackets. The instance name comes from its default object name in the Objects palette, where you can modify it if required.

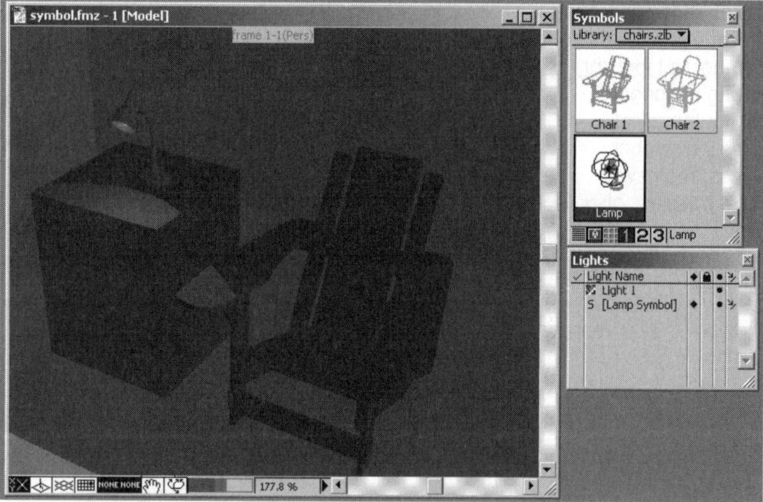

Figure 7.15

Creating a symbol with a light, and placing an instance of it in the project. The Symbols and Lights palettes are also shown.

- Double-click on one of these light symbol entries in the Lights palette. This will invoke the same Symbol Instance Edit dialog (shown earlier in Figure 7.13) that is invoked by selecting a symbol instance with the Symbol Edit tool. We looked at this dialog in detail earlier in Section 2.4. Let's look at the Use Lights section that is now activated, since this symbol includes a light. Here, you can change the visibility, shining, and shadows attributes of the light—the same attributes you can directly manipulate in the Lights palette. You can also choose to override the color, intensity, and other attributes of the light as defined in the symbol, with new settings in a dialog invoked by clicking on the Override Attributes button. If necessary, you can turn off the light in that symbol instance altogether by deselecting the Use Lights option.
- After exploring the Symbol Instance Edit dialog for an instance of the Lamp symbol, turn your attention to the dialog of the Symbol Place tool, shown earlier in Figure 7.12. Notice the Use

Lights If Present option that we had skipped earlier. By default, this option is active, so lights are included with symbol instances when they're placed. If you need to place an instance of a symbol without including its lights, simply deselect this option prior to using the tool.

As you can see, the ability to include lights in symbols is very convenient, and combined with the ability to define custom lights, it can be used to create several libraries of real world lighting fixtures, which you can then use across multiple design projects.

EXERCISE 3

Panoramic Views and QuickTime VR

You were briefly introduced to the Panoramic view type in Workshop 3 (Personalizing Your Environment), when you worked with all the different options under the Views menu. You saw that this isn't an interactive view in which you can carry out modeling operations, which is why all the tools are grayed out when you're in this mode. Panoramic views, however, can be saved as image files and can make for very interesting presentations of design concepts. You can go further and use them for generating QuickTime VR (QTVR) movies, which can then be played by Apple's MoviePlayer or any application that supports QTVR. If you don't have QuickTime installed on your computer—you'll need version 2.0 or later on the Mac and version 3.0 or later on the PC to generate a QTVR movie—you'll find the Installers on your form•Z CD. To play back a spherical panoramic movie—one of the three available movie types you can generate—you would need version 5.0 of QuickTime.

Movies are useful as stand-alone presentations. They can also be embedded in Web pages and then be viewed by anyone with an Internet connection, a Web browser, and the QuickTime VR plug-in. In a world that's increasingly going online, this might conceivably become the dominant mode of presentation of design concepts very soon.

In this exercise, we'll look at how QuickTime VR works. But first, let's explore the Panoramic view options in some more detail.

3.1 Panoramic Views

- Open one of your completed form•Z projects and switch to the Panoramic view under the Views menu. You should see a 360° view of your model, centered by default in a position where you can see most of the model. The view point can be changed, if required, either numerically through the View Parameters dialog, or graphically using Edit Cone Of Vision.

- Let's explore the graphical option first. Go to Edit Cone Of Vision under the Views menu, and you should see something similar to what is shown in Figure 7.16. The grid and axes display was turned off by going to Window > Window Setup, and all the lights in the project were also made invisible. Notice that the Top view (upper left modification window) shows the area of vision as a circle, while the Front and Right views (lower windows) show it as a rectangle. The actual volume of vision is therefore a *cylinder* rather than a cone, as you've encountered for the other view types. At the center of the cylinder is the eye point, and it's connected to the center of interest located at the circumference of the cylinder by a heavy line, which represents the line of sight. This line also indicates the center of the view.

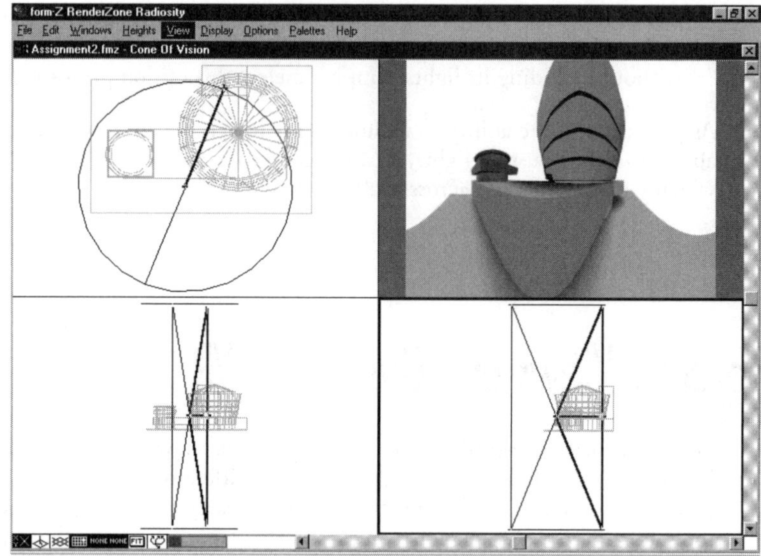

Figure 7.16

Modifying the panoramic cylinder graphically in the Edit Cone Of Vision environment for a Panoramic view.

- Try and modify the panoramic cylinder in the modification windows in various ways, and see the result of the changes in the preview area. The process is similar to the manner in which the cone of vision is modified for other views. Figure 7.16 shows some modifications made to the default panoramic cylinder and the resultant view.

- Some of the modifications can also be fine-tuned numerically. Go to View > View Parameters. You've already explored this dialog in Section 5.6 of Workshop 3 and are familiar with the Eye Point and Center Of Interest options. There are three additional parameters here for the Panoramic view type: Spin, Angle, and Smoothness. The Spin value indicates the tilt of the panoramic cylinder, while the Angle value defines the extent of the panoramic view. The default value of 360° for Angle shows a full panorama, but you can reduce this value depending upon what you'd like to see in your view.

- The third parameter, Smoothness, determines the *resolution* of the view. Unlike the other views, a panoramic view is composed of a sequence of vertical bands, whose width is set by the Smoothness value. Increase this value from the default of 5 pixels to, say, 50 pixels, and you'll see that all the curved lines appear more segmented (Figure 7.17). For final renderings, you can set a very small Smoothness value to get extremely smooth curves. Naturally, the smaller the value, the greater the rendering time.

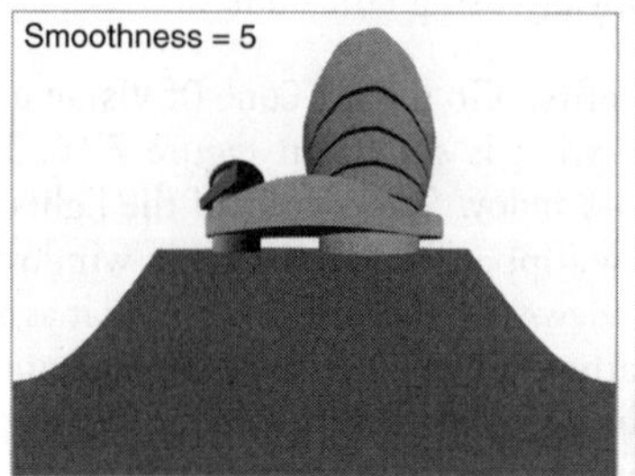

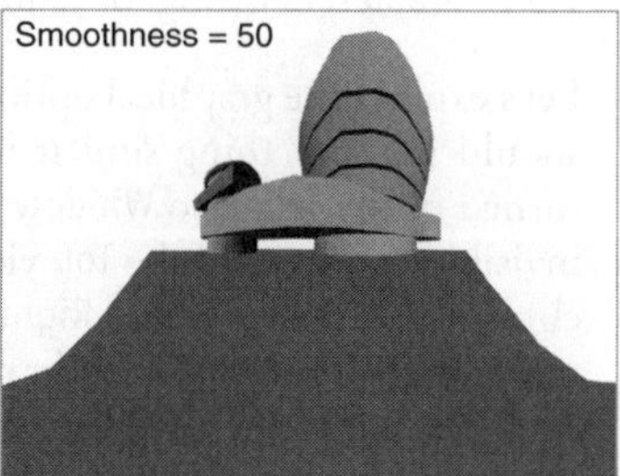

Figure 7.17

The same panoramic view, but with different Smoothness values.

- Modify the parameters of your panoramic view until you're satisfied with the result; then exit the Cone Of Vision environment. Change the display to RenderZone to generate a rendered version of your panoramic view. You can save this as an image file for a presentation, as you learned to do in Section 1.4 of Workshop 5 (Illuminating, Texturing, and Rendering Your World). You can also go on to generate a QuickTime VR movie from this view, which is what we'll look at next.

3.2 Generating Cylindrical Panoramic Movies

- To save your rendered panoramic view as a QuickTime VR movie, go to Display > Generate QuickTime VR. (If QuickTime is not installed on your computer, the command will be grayed out.) This brings up the QuickTime VR Movie Options dialog shown in Figure 7.18-a. You can see that there are three main options, of which Generate Cylindrical Panoramic Movie is selected by default. Let's look at this first. It has two sub-options, letting you create a movie of the current panoramic view, if there is one, or of a new view that it will first create. Since you have a panoramic view currently in the window, stick with the first sub-option, Use Current Panoramic View.

- The two Movie Size values at the base of the dialog will determine the dimensions of the movie window. You can settle for the default size of 300 by 300 pixels for now, so that the generation process doesn't take too long. However, for final presentation movies, you can specify window sizes as large as the size of your monitor, if necessary. The View Movie When Complete option, checked by default, plays the movie as soon as it's generated; you can leave it on. The Compression Options button leads you to a standard operating system dialog, in which you can choose a compression method and the associated color depth and picture quality for the movie. Stick with the default settings for now. Later, you can refer to your operating system manual for more information on the various compression techniques to determine which one is best suited to your needs.

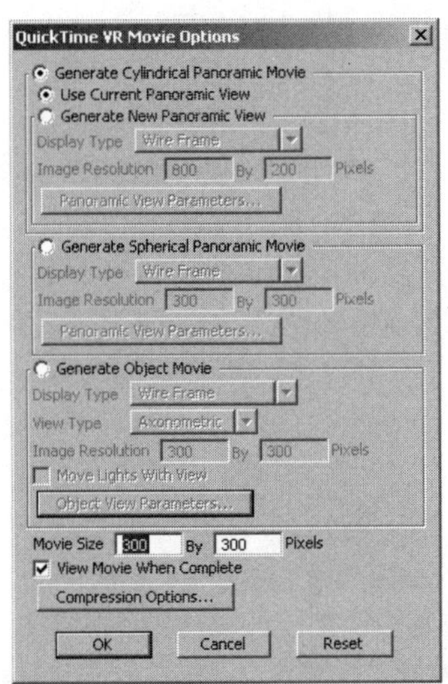

(a)

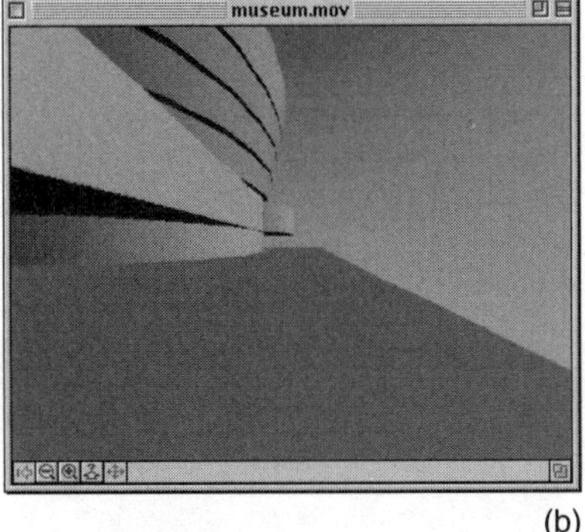

(b)

Figure 7.18

Generating a QuickTime VR movie from the panoramic view shown in Figure 7.17. (a) The QuickTime VR Movie Options dialog. (b) One frame of the movie, seen in the MoviePlayer application window.

- Finally, click OK to begin the generation process. You'll be prompted for a file name for the movie. Specify a suitable name and location. The movie generation process will now be set in motion. It might take quite a bit of time, depending upon the movie size specified and the complexity of the project. When the process is complete, the movie player application on your system will automatically be invoked, showing one frame of the newly created movie (Figure 7.18-b). To navigate through the movie, use the controls of the application. For MoviePlayer, these are located at the base of the window. Refer to your movie application's Help facility for detailed instructions on how to use the navigation options.

- The newly created file is automatically given a ".mov" extension. You can play it outside form•Z by double-clicking on it, or opening it in your movie player program. Within form•Z, you can also play the same file at any time by using the File > View File command.

- Get back to the QuickTime VR Movie Options dialog, and note the second option in the Generate Cylindrical Panoramic Movie section, called Generate New Panoramic View. This lets you generate a new panoramic view for the movie, whose settings you can numerically specify by clicking on the Panoramic View Parameters button. Additionally, you can specify the type of display and the resolution of the image. Needless to say, this option isn't that useful since it would always be preferable to generate a view first, and then decide if you'd like to make a movie out of it.

3.3 Generating Object Movies

Another type of QuickTime VR movie that you can generate is an *object* movie. This kind of movie comprises views of the modeling world from all sides. You can think of it as a large sphere surrounding the objects, with you standing *outside* the sphere and being able to view the objects through any facet of the sphere. In contrast, in a cylindrical panoramic view, you stand *inside* a cylinder and can only see the objects as they're mapped to the vertical sides of the cylinder; you cannot see what is above and below the cylinder.

Since a cylindrical panoramic view consists of a continuous sequence of vertical strips, it can be "unfolded" in a single piece; this is why you can generate a panoramic view without necessarily making a movie out of it. However, the individual facets of the spherical object view cannot be unfolded in one piece; thus, you don't have the option of generating an object view independent of QuickTime VR. Also, the object movie deals with more information than a cylindrical panoramic movie, therefore it takes much more time to generate.

- Select Generate QuickTime VR once again from the Display menu. This time, select the third main option in its dialog, Generate Object Movie. (The second movie type falls somewhere in between the first and third types, so we'll look at it later.) Since this kind of movie is independent of the current display and image settings on your screen, it has several options to specify these settings, as you can see in the QuickTime VR Movie Options dialog in Figure 7.18-a. Let's go through them in brief.

- The first three options are very simple. For the Display Type, you can choose between the eight display types in form•Z. For the View Type, you can choose between Axonometric and Perspective. The two Image Resolution values will determine the width and height of the object movie. Go ahead and make the desired selections for these options.

- Move Lights With View is an interesting option. When it's selected, lights are moved as the view changes, which means that the lighting on the objects keeps changing, depending upon where they're viewed from. It gives the illusion of the lights being fixed while the objects themselves are moving. When this option is deselected, lights remain in a fixed position like the objects, therefore the lighting on the objects also remains constant. You should generate two identical object movies, one with this option turned on and the other with it turned off, and compare the results.

- Next, click on the Object View Parameters button. This brings up a dialog in which you can make more detailed specifications about the object movie (Figure 7.19-a). The first two options, # Of Pan Steps and # Of Tilt Steps, determine the number of facets of the viewing sphere in the horizontal and vertical directions respectively. The names come from *panning* (which refers to the horizontal rotation of the view about the vertical axis) and *tilting* (which refers to the vertical rotation of the view about the horizontal axis). Higher values will lead to more views in the movie, making the navigation through it less jerky. Naturally, the generation time for the movie will also take longer.
- The Center Of Interest option has the usual meaning, and it can be set to desired coordinate values. You can also choose to automatically place it at the center of the scene by clicking on that button. Alternately, you can hit the Current button, which will position it at the point that's the center of interest in the currently active view.
- The field of view settings are used to determine the extent of the view. The default is the whole sphere (Use Complete Field Of View), but you can opt for Custom Field of View and specify the starting and ending angles along both the horizontal and vertical directions.
- The horizontal and vertical axes for panning and tilting are always defined with respect to a reference plane, for which there are four choices grouped under Rotate Relative To. The default is XY Plane, which makes horizontal movement take place on the XY plane and vertical movement along the Z axis. You can opt for the other two predefined planes or settle for the currently active plane, which could also be an arbitrary plane.
- Finally, you can choose between two zoom options. Zoom To Fit Scene will adjust the zoom level to include all visible objects in the views, while Use Current Zoom will use the current zoom setting of the active window.
- After making any desired modifications to these parameters, exit the Object Movie View Parameters dialog by clicking OK. Back in the QuickTime VR Movie Options dialog, make sure that the View Movie When Complete option is selected. Then click OK, and the generation of the object movie will begin. It might take a long time, depending upon the complexity of the model, the type of rendering, and the number of pan and tilt steps specified. When it's complete, the movie will open up in a movie player application window as before (Figure 7.19-b).

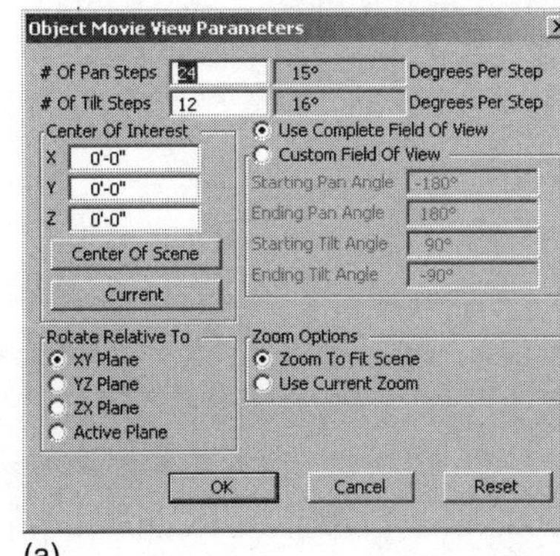

(a)

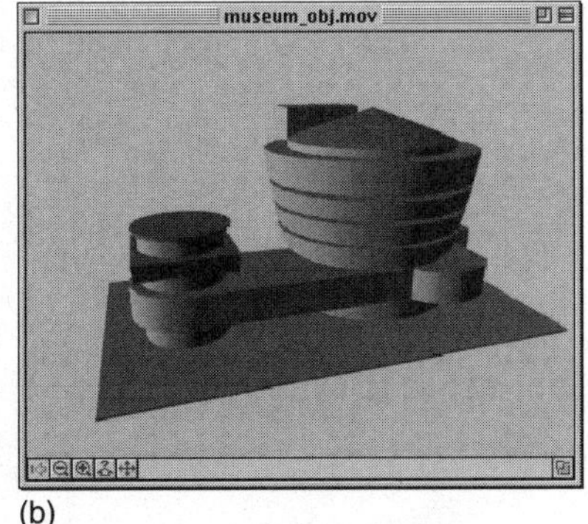

(b)

Figure 7.19

Generating a QuickTime VR object movie. (a) The dialog for specifying the detailed parameters of the movie. (b) One frame of the movie, seen in the MoviePlayer application window.

- Navigate through this movie and see how it's different from the cylindrical panoramic movie you created earlier. In this movie, you can move anywhere and see the scene from all sides, whereas in the panoramic movie, your position is fixed and you can only turn around and see what is immediately visible before you. Of course, you can also zoom in and out in a panoramic view, which gives you the illusion that you're moving, but the viewpoint is actually fixed at the position you saw in the Edit Cone Of Vision environment in Figure 7.16.

3.4 Generating Spherical Panoramic Movies

It's time to look at the second movie type, spherical panoramic movies, which we skipped earlier. As mentioned before, this type of movie falls somewhere in between the cylindrical panoramic and object movie types. Like the object movie, a spherical panoramic movie comprises views of the modeling world from all sides; the difference is that you are now standing *inside* the sphere looking out, rather than standing outside and looking in. In that respect, a spherical panoramic movie is like a cylindrical panoramic movie, except that the volume of vision is a sphere rather than a cylinder. A spherical panoramic view cannot be unfolded in one piece and therefore cannot be generated independently of QuickTime VR—just like an object movie—and it takes longer to generate than a cylindrical panoramic movie. Let's see how it works.

- Get back to the QuickTime VR Movie Options dialog, and select the Generate Spherical Panoramic Movie option. It has the usual Display Type and Image Resolution settings seen for the other movie types. Set these as required.

- Click on the Panoramic View Parameters button. You'll find, not surprisingly, that the options here are almost identical to those in the Object Movie View Parameters dialog you saw in Figure 7.19-a, although they're not as extensive. The only difference is that for a spherical panoramic view, you'll be specifying the Eye Point rather than the Center Of Interest you specified for the object movie. The field of view options for determining the extent of the view are identical to those discussed in the last section for object movies. Make any desired modifications to these parameters; then exit the Spherical Panoramic Movie View Parameters dialog by clicking OK.

- Back in the QuickTime VR Movie Options dialog, click OK to generate the spherical panoramic movie. When it's complete, navigate through the movie and see how it's different from both the cylindrical panoramic and object movies you created earlier. (As mentioned earlier, to play back this type of movie, you'll need version 5.0 of QuickTime; otherwise, you'll see it as a cylindrical panoramic movie.) You'll find that in this movie, your position is fixed, as in the cylindrical panoramic movie, but with a significant difference—you can turn not only sideways, but in any other direction as well, and see what is around you on all sides, including up and down.

Animating Your World

EXERCISE 4

In this exercise, we'll go through the process of generating and viewing animations from a 3D modeling project, which involves a number of steps. Let's use a completed project to experiment with, for instance, the stadium roof structure we modeled as the Assignment for the last workshop. We'll start by looking at the Cage tool, which isn't strictly a part of the animation process, but can be useful in temporarily substituting low resolution objects for high resolution objects to speed up the animation. Once the animation setup is complete, you can go back and substitute the original objects.

4.1 Using the Cage Tool

- Make a copy of the modeling project containing the Assignment for Workshop 6 (Going Organic), and open it. Turn off all layers except the one that has the meshed roof covering. Of the four separate pieces comprising the covering, move one to a separate layer and turn off the original layer. We'll focus on this single meshed object (see Figure 7.20-a), and use it to study the resolution-reducing capability of the Cage tool.

- Select the Cage tool (M-Tool:9a,10) and apply it to the meshed object. You'll find that it gets replaced by an object of lower resolution that approximates the shape of the original along two of the three orthogonal world axes: XY and ZX. Switch to all three planar views to verify this (see Figure 7.20-b). Look at the new object carefully, and you'll find that it has been derived by a threefold process: first, the perimeter of the original object is projected on the XY and ZX planes; then, each of the two projections is extruded in the perpendicular direction, i.e., along the Z and Y axes respectively, starting from and ending at heights corresponding to the other projection; finally, the boolean intersection of the two extrusions is obtained, yielding the final "cage." The last step explains why the Cage tool is grouped along with the other boolean tools.

The original object gets ghosted by default. Unghost it and move it to a separate layer, so that you can use it to replace the low resolution cage once the animation setup is complete.

- Invoke the dialog of the Cage tool to look at its options (Figure 7.21-a). You'll find that the default selection for Extrusion Directions is Y,Z, which is why the low resolution object you just derived is created by the intersection of the projected extrusions along the Y and Z axes. Change the selection to X,Y, and undo and reapply the Cage operation (see Figure 7.21-b). The result is now much more in sync with the original object. Thus, your choice of Extrusions Directions from among the three options available will depend upon the form and orientation of the original object, and usually the reference plane with respect to which it was created. Our meshed roof covering was created with respect to the XY plane, so the X,Y option works best. This isn't, however, a hard and fast rule, and you might have to explore all three options before you get it right.

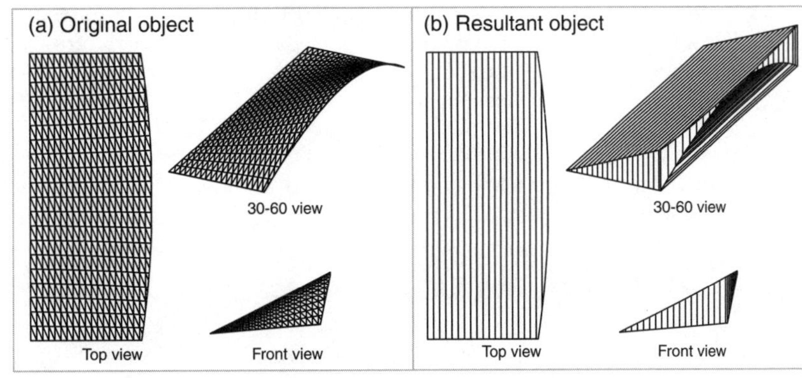

Figure 7.20

Deriving a low resolution object from a high resolution object using the Cage tool.

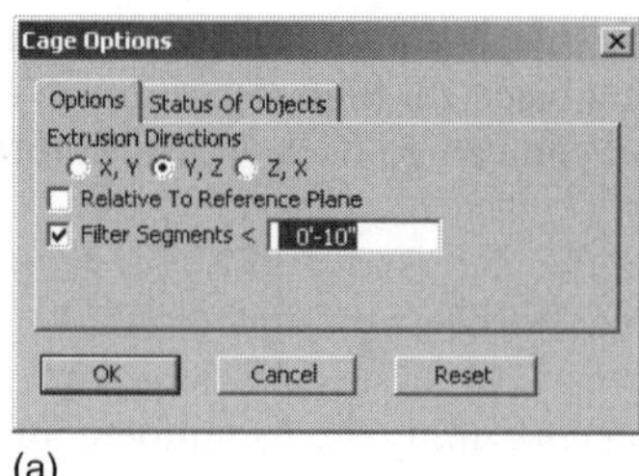

(a)

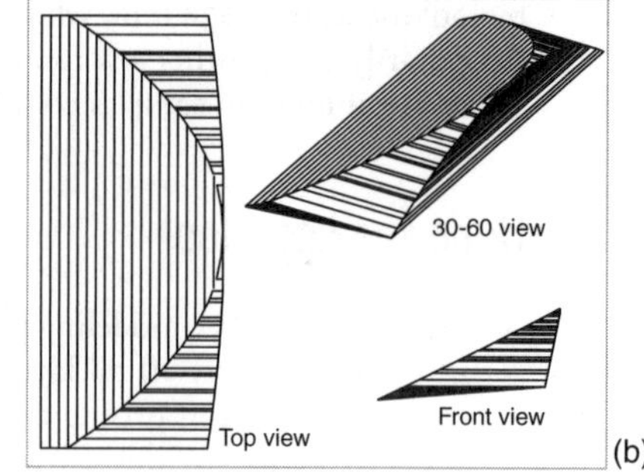

(b)

Figure 7.21

The dialog of the Cage tool, and using the X,Y option for Extrusion Directions on the same object shown in Figure 7.20-a.

- If the original, high resolution object was created with respect to an arbitrary plane, you can check the Relative To Reference Plane option. This will create the low resolution cage by projecting and extruding with respect to the axes of that arbitrary plane rather than the world axes. Just make sure that the right reference plane is activated before applying the Cage tool.

- The last option in the dialog of the Cage tool is used to determine the resolution of the resultant object. When activated, the initial projections are generated such that they don't contain segments larger than the specified value. Thus, the larger the Filter Segments < value, the lower the resolution of the derived cage. Test it out.

The Cage tool can only produce objects with a single volume. So if the original object has holes, they won't be included in the resultant cage.

4.2 Creating an Animation from Keyframes

An animation sequence, as you know, is essentially made up of a large number of separate images, each one of which is slightly different from the previous image in the sequence. The animation is played by changing the image sequence rapidly, conveying the impression of movement due to the *persistence of vision* facility that the human eye is endowed with. Each one of these separate images of the animation sequence is referred to as a *frame*.

Before the age of computers, animators had no choice but to manually create each and every one of the frames required for an animation. With the help of computers, however, the animation process has been accelerated and made a lot less tedious. Now, only the critical or *key* frames of the animation are actually created; the remaining *intermediate* frames, capturing the movement from one keyframe to the next, are generated automatically by the computer using interpolation.

The same procedure is followed in form•Z as well. Once your 3D model is ready for animation, the first step that you need to undertake is to set up the keyframes. These are basically views of the modeling world that are created and saved in the Views palette. form•Z then generates all the intermediate frames by interpolation to create the desired animation sequence. Let's see how it works for the sample project we've chosen.

- Set the view type in the Views menu to Perspective. Then select Edit Cone Of Vision from the same menu. In this environment, create a sequence of different views that will define the path of your animation. Each subsequent view should differ from the previous view in the sequence in the location of its eye point, or its center of interest, or both. Save each view in the Views palette as you create it. While you can define as many views as you want, at least two are needed for generating the animation sequence. Exit the Cone Of Vision mode when you've completed this task to get back to the regular modeling environment.

- The next step is to identify all these views you just saved as the keyframes of your animation. In order to do this, first make each one of these views visible by activating the corresponding visibility icons in the Views palette. Then select these views in the sequence in which the animation has to be generated, either graphically by using the Pick tool, or by clicking in the first column of the Views palette.
- Once the keyframes are selected in the right sequence, the animation can be generated. To do this, go to Views > Animation From Keyframes. This will invoke the familiar View Parameters dialog where you can modify the default parameters of the animation (see Figure 7.22). If necessary, change the View Name, which here stands for the name of the animation sequence. All the other options on the left side of the dialog apply to the individual keyframes rather than to the entire animation. These are already familiar to you from Section 5.6 of Workshop 3 (Personalizing Your Environment), so we needn't go over them again.
- Turn your attention to the options on the right side of the View Parameters dialog. Notice that both the Camera View and Animated Camera options are selected by default for the animation. Be careful not to deactivate them, otherwise the animation will no longer be recognized as an animation. You've already studied the Standard and Custom options under Camera View, when applicable to a regular view, in Workshop 3. They work in the same fashion for defining the camera settings of an animation.
- All the options under the Animated Camera section are really what we need to focus on for defining our animation, so let's go over them one by one. We'll start with three interrelated parameters: Duration, Frames, and Frames Per Second. The Duration is the total time period required for playing the animation, specified in the format, *hours* : *minutes* : *seconds* : *frames (within last second)*. The last number must obviously be less than the value specified for Frames Per Second. The value of Frames represents the total number of frames in the animation, and has to be equal to the Frames Per Second value multiplied by the Duration in seconds. Thus, changing the Frames Per Second or Duration value automatically changes the number of Frames, while changing the Frames value automatically adjusts the Duration value.

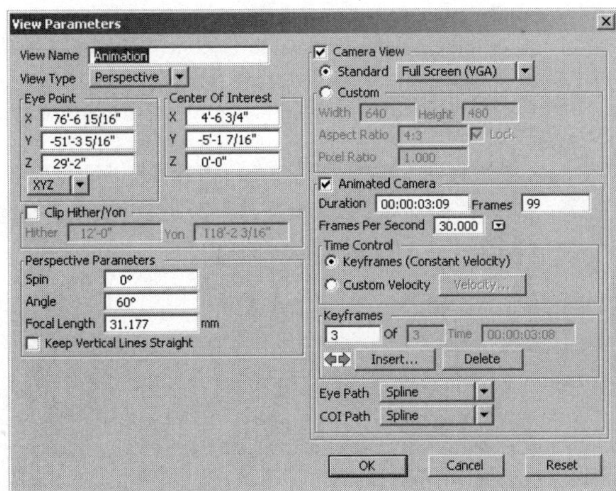

Figure 7.22

The View Parameters dialog, showing the default parameters for generating an animation from the selected keyframes.

The higher the Frames Per Second value, the smoother the animation. However, more frames will be required for the specified duration, so more time will be required to generate the animation. A Frames Per Second value of 30 is sufficient for the human eye to experience a non-jerky, flicker-free animation.

- The next parameter, Time Control, determines the rate of change or *velocity* of the animation—how the camera moves from the first to the last keyframe in the specified duration. This velocity can be specified in two ways, the first of which, Keyframes (Constant Velocity), is active by default. Using this method, the time at which the camera arrives at each keyframe is specified under the Keyframes subsection (which we'll soon study). The camera then moves at a constant velocity between one keyframe to the next. In contrast, the second option, Custom Velocity, is far more sophisticated, letting you specify the velocity by means of a time-distance curve. To see and manipulate this curve, activate the Custom Velocity option and click on the accompanying Velocity button. This will bring up the Velocity Control dialog shown in Figure 7.23-a.

- The velocity curve in the Velocity Control dialog is in the form of a graph with the number of frames and the time represented along the horizontal axis, and the distance along the vertical axis. The default curve, as you can see in Figure 7.23-a, is almost linear, representing a constant velocity. It can be reshaped by manipulating the accompanying *controls*—indicated by the unshaded circles—to apply different velocities to different portions of the curve. This is illustrated in Figure 7.23-b. A gentler slope (more horizontal) represents a slower speed, while a steeper slope (more vertical) represents a faster speed. At any time, you can click on the Constant button at the base of the dialog to revert back to a linear curve representing a constant velocity.

- Notice that the curve initially has two *points* indicated by shaded circles, one at each end, to which the controls you just manipulated are attached. A new point can be inserted on the curve, if further adjustments are desired, by clicking on the Insert button next to the Constant button. Try it. If a point is no longer needed, you can get rid of it by selecting it and clicking on the Delete button.

- Notice that intermediate points inserted on the curve are accompanied by their own controls. While moving a control reshapes the curve without changing the position of the point it belongs to, a point itself can also be selected and moved. The two endpoints can be moved along the vertical axis only, while the intermediate points can be moved in any direction. How exactly the selected point gets edited depends upon which Curve Type is selected from the popup menu above the graph. Additionally, the editing can be done in five different ways, depending upon which icon is selected in the upper left corner of the Velocity Control dialog. These icons get activated only when a point on the curve is selected, and are dimmed out when a control is being manipulated. Experiment with each one of these five icons and see how it affects the movement of the selected point.

Figure 7.23

The Velocity Control dialog invoked by activating the Custom Velocity option. (a) The default velocity curve. (b) The modified curve.

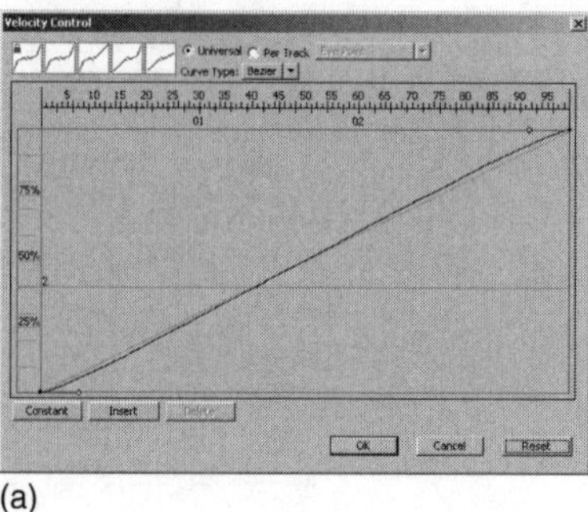

(a)

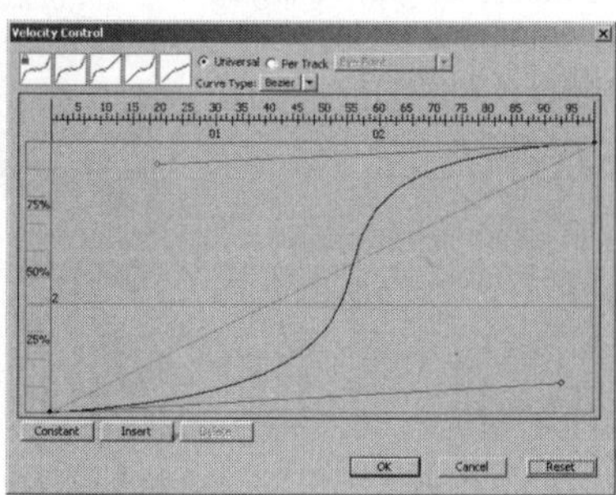

(b)

- The only options remaining in the Velocity Control dialog for us to explore are Universal, and its alternate, Per Track, located at the top of the dialog. The default selection is Universal, which means that a single velocity curve exists which controls *all* aspects of the animation. The curves shown in Figure 7.23 are universal curves. In contrast, when you select the Per Track option, you'll see a number of curves displayed in the graph, one controlling each *separate* aspect of the animation such as the eye point, center of interest, view angle, and so on. All these aspects are listed in the popup menu accompanying the Per Track option. Selecting an aspect activates the respective curve, which can then be edited in the same fashion as the universal curve we saw. Essentially, selecting the Per Track option as opposed to the Universal option is useful when you want to incorporate complex effects in your animation, such as moving the eye point very slowly but the center of interest very rapidly, and other interesting variations.
- Now that we've finished exploring all the options in the Velocity Control dialog, exit it to get back to the View Parameters dialog, where we need to explore the remaining parameters of the animation.
- Turn your attention to the Keyframes subsection. Here, you can navigate through each keyframe of the animation by using the left and right arrow keys, and edit its parameters listed on the left side of the dialog if necessary. (Remember that a keyframe is essentially just a view.) Additionally, you can specify the time at which the camera should arrive at the current keyframe, if the Time Control in the previous subsection has been set to Keyframes (Custom Velocity). Needless to say, the time for the first and the last keyframe cannot be changed, as the animation must finish within the specified Duration. For an intermediate keyframe, you also cannot go beyond the time of its previous or next keyframe.
- It's possible to insert a new keyframe into the animation sequence, before or after the current keyframe, by clicking on the Insert button in the Keyframes subsection. The location and parameters of this new keyframe are interpolated automatically between the two keyframes it's inserted between, but you can edit them as required in the left side of the dialog. New frames cannot be inserted before and after the first and last keyframes respectively. The Insert button is accompanied by a Delete button, which can be used to delete the current keyframe if it's not required.
- The final set of parameters in the View Parameters dialog, Eye Path and COI Path (COI stands for *center of interest*), determine how the frames that are automatically generated between successive pairs of keyframes are actually interpolated, in terms of the paths of the eye point and the center of interest from one keyframe to the next. There are six choices for each path parameter, available in the accompanying popup menu: Point (Fixed) causes the path to remain static rather than change over time; Linear causes the path to be linear from one keyframe to the next; Linear (Closed) is the same as Linear except that the line loops back to the first keyframe after the last; Spline curves the path in the form of a spline between keyframes, leading to a smoother transition, and is the default option; Spline (Closed) loops the curved path back to the first keyframe; and finally, Use Object is similar to Point except that it uses the local origin of an existing object, which is selected from the accompanying dialog, to fix the path.

If you're a design professional whose primary interest lies in the modeling of the design, and animation is just one more presentation medium you use out of many, you should find that the default settings for an animation in the View Parameters dialog work just fine for you. In that case, you don't really need to explore these parameters in great detail to make any modifications. But if you're a professional animator, you'll almost always need to modify the basic settings to achieve the creative and special effects you're aiming for. If so, you should spend a lot of time experimenting with all the animation parameters and see how they affect the final output.

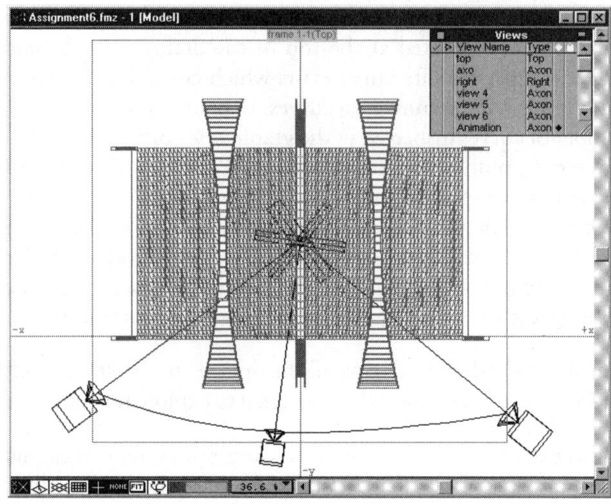

Figure 7.24

Making the animation visible in the graphics window by turning on its visibility icon in the Views palette.

- After making any desired modifications, exit the View Parameters dialog to return to the modeling environment. You'll find the animation you just created listed as a view in the Views palette. Turn on its visibility icon and switch to a view, preferably a planar one, in which you can clearly see all the individual views or keyframes of the animation. You'll find the path of the animation also illustrated if you've used the default of Spline for the Path parameters (see Figure 7.24). Just like any other entry in the Views palette, the View Parameters dialog for the animation can be invoked by double-clicking on its name in the palette. You can create as many animations as you want in the same project file; just give them different names and they will all be accessible from the Views palette.

4.3 Previewing Animations Using the Animation Palette

In the last section, you accomplished the task of setting up keyframes and generating an animation sequence from them. You still have to render the animation frame by frame, and finally, play it in order to view it. We'll look at both these tasks in the next section. In this section, we'll explore the Animation palette and see how it can be useful in previewing an animation to verify that it's satisfactory. This is an extremely important step and should be undertaken so that the time-consuming task of rendering the animation is executed only when you're reasonably sure that it will turn out the way you want.

- Open the Animation palette, if it's closed, using the Palettes menu. Notice that the palette is blank when a regular view is activated in the Views palette. Go ahead and activate the animation you saved in the last section by clicking in the first column before its name in the Views palette. The Animation palette will now be activated and will display the animation controls of the selected animation. The function of each of these controls is illustrated in Figure 7.25.

- The Animation palette essentially displays the *time line* of the animation and the corresponding frames in the form of a ruler. The red marker on this ruler stands for the current time. Initially, it's positioned at the beginning, i.e., at the first keyframe, but you can move it to any frame of the animation by clicking on its position along the time line. The view in the graphics window gets updated to show the current frame. You can also click and drag the current time marker along the time line, which causes the view to be rapidly updated to show each passing frame, giving you the actual effect of an animation. Thus, you can preview your animation in any manner, forwards or backwards, through a portion of the frames or through the entire time line, by manipulating the current time marker. Just make sure that you're in the Wire Frame display mode, otherwise the view cannot be updated very rapidly and the preview won't be very useful.

Keeping the Shift key pressed while moving the current time marker will delay the redrawing of the view until the key is released. This can be useful when the animation is complex.

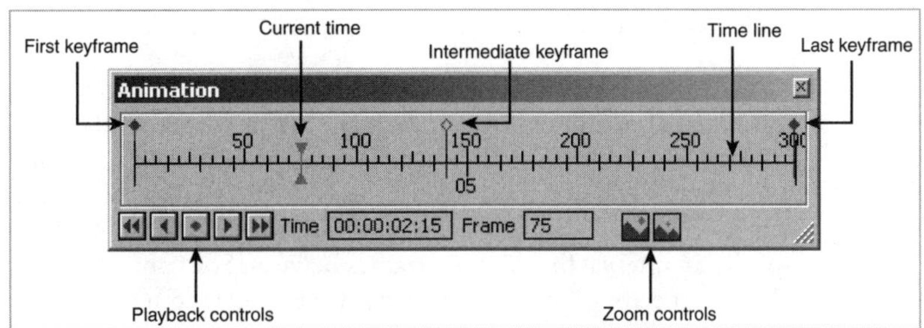

Figure 7.25

The Animation palette, showing the controls of the animation that's activated in the Views palette.

- Instead of dragging the current time marker along the time line yourself, you can also use the VCR-like controls located in the lower left corner of the Animation palette to preview the animation. You can play the animation forwards or backwards, or move through it one frame at a time. Try out all these controls to preview your animation.
- Look closely at the markings along the time line in the palette again. If you had selected the Keyframes (Constant Velocity) option in the View Parameters dialog, you'd find that the start and end keyframes of the animation are represented by solid diamond markers. These are fixed and cannot be moved. However, intermediate keyframes, which are represented by hollow diamond markers, can be moved to a different location along the time line by clicking on and dragging their markers. You can also make a copy of a keyframe at a different location by holding down the option key (Mac) or Ctrl+Shift keys (PC) as you move it. If you had selected the Custom Velocity option, you'd find that all the keyframes are represented by numbers on the time line. Their positions are fixed and cannot be changed.
- You'll have already noticed the two convenient time and frame display boxes located at the base of the Animation palette, which get updated to show the current time and frame of the animation. Next to these are two Zoom buttons that you can use for zooming in and out of the time line, when necessary. Try them out. If you're zoomed in, you'll be able to scroll horizontally through the time line by using the control key (Mac) or Ctrl+Alt keys (PC).

4.4 Generating and Playing Animation Files

After creating an animation sequence from keyframes and previewing it to make sure that it's satisfactory, the next step is to actually render each frame of the animation and store the results in an animation file. The animation can then be viewed by opening and playing that file. Let's see how both these steps are performed.

- In the Views palette, activate the animation sequence you had saved earlier and which you previewed in the last section. Then go to Display > Generate Animation. This brings up the dialog shown in Figure 7.26, containing a number of options for rendering and storing the animation.

- The rendering options in the Animation Generation dialog are fairly straightforward. You can make your choice of the type of rendering for the animation at the top of the dialog, and access its Options dialog using the accompanying Options button. There are some additional rendering options you can choose to apply: Super Sampling will lead to improved antialiasing; Motion Blur reduces flickering and jerkiness by blurring objects that move fast in the animation; and Blur Filter applies an overall blur which reduces flickering caused by areas of high contrast. The Statistics button takes you to a dialog that provides useful information about the resolution and frames—both actual and sampled—in the animation.

- As far as which frames are actually rendered, you have two basic options. If you were generating the final animation, you'd naturally choose to render all the frames. For prefinal previews, you could choose to render only some critical frames of the animation. This can be done in two ways. The Frame Range method lets you specify the starting and ending frames, with the option of setting any one of them to the current frame in the Animation palette. Additionally, you can specify an interval for skipping frames between Start and End. In contrast, the Frame List method lets you specify a variable list of frames that can contain single frames as well as a range—for example, 20, 45–60, 89.

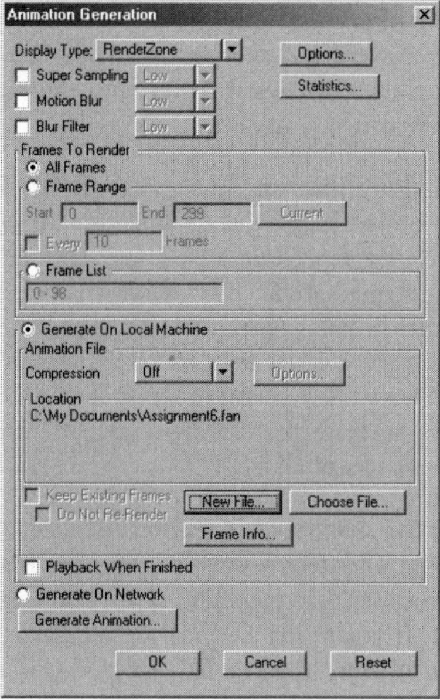

Figure 7.26

The Animation Generation dialog, showing the settings for rendering and saving an animation.

- The Animation File section in the Animation Generation dialog contains the options for saving the file that will be generated if it is to be generated locally. The default file name and location is listed in the box; it can be changed by clicking on the New File button. An extension of ".fan," standing for *form•Z animation*, is automatically appended to the file name. The Choose File button allows you to open an existing form•Z animation for generation. You can choose one of the Compression options if you're short on disk space; this, however, will make the playback slower. The Keep

Existing Frames option can be checked if you'd like to retain frames that were rendered in a previous version of the same animation file, and substitute only certain frames with new ones. This can be useful if only minor adjustments are made to the animation and you don't want to spend time and resources re-rendering all the frames. There's also a Frame Info button, which gives you information on the total number of frames in the file and those still remaining to be rendered. Finally, there's a Playback When Finished option that can be selected to play the animation as soon as it's generated locally. There is, however, a separate command for playing the animation that we shall soon look at, so don't bother with this option for now.

- When you have finished setting up all the animation parameters in the Animation Generation dialog, click on the Generate Animation button at the base of the dialog. As soon as you do this, the rendering of the selected frames begins, with a progress bar showing the status of the rendering. The graphics window gets periodically refreshed to show the current frame; the Animation palette is also updated to show the corresponding time and frame number. All the rendered frames are stored in the specified animation file. If you chose the Generate On Network option in the Animation Generation dialog, you will be presented with an intermediate dialog for specifying the server, network settings, file name and location, and so on, before the animation generation process is set in motion.

- The animation you just saved is in a format native to form•Z, as indicated by the ".fan" extension to the file name. You can export this to a different file format using the Export Animation command under the File menu. The supported file formats fall into two basic categories: QuickTime Movie (Mac and PC) and AVI (PC only) are animation files; the others such as EPS, JPEG, etc., are image files. In the first case, the form•Z animation file is converted to another animation file like itself, while in the second case, it's converted to a set of independent image files, one for each frame of the animation.

- To play the form•Z animation file you just generated, select the Play Animation command, located just below the Generate Animation command under the Display menu. This will invoke the standard File Open dialog from which you can select the .fan file that's to be played. Once you do this, the Animation Playback dialog is invoked, containing a number of playback options (see Figure 7.27).

- There are two options for Playback Method; the one you choose will depend upon the memory that's available to play the animation. If you opt for the Play All Frames method and all the frames of the animation don't fit into the available memory, only the frames that fit will be played; the animation will then pause to load the next set of frames. This can make the playback jerky. The situation can be somewhat improved by selecting the associated Load Frames During Playback sub-option, which loads the frames into memory *while* the animation is playing, slowing it down a little but avoiding the jerkiness at intervals. On the other hand, if you opt for the Play Only Frames That Fit In Memory method, playback is good without being jerky, but the entire animation may not be played.

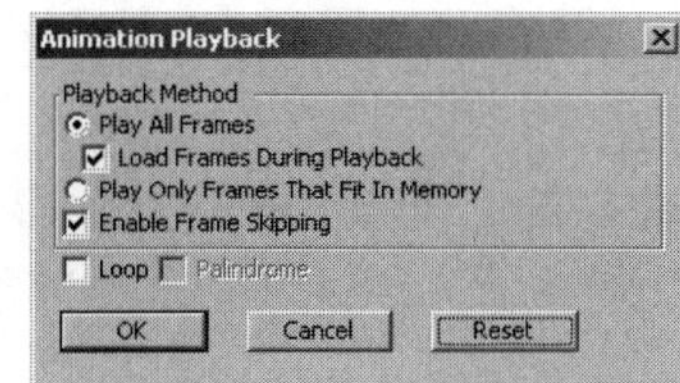

Figure 7.27

The Animation Playback dialog, showing the settings for playing a form•Z animation file.

- The additional option, Enable Frame Skipping, which applies to both playback methods, is used to ensure that the playback remains on schedule, even if it means skipping frames that take too long to load. If this option is turned off and your hardware cannot process the frames at the required rate, every frame will nevertheless be shown, increasing the duration of the animation. For a final animation, you should disable this option at least once in order to see all the frames.
- The final playback option is Loop, which is used to make the animation go back to the beginning when it reaches the end frame, rather than come to a stop. The Palindrome sub-option for Loop makes the animation play back in reverse from the end frame to the start frame when the end is reached, rather than always loop back to the beginning.
- After selecting the required options in the Animation Playback dialog, click OK to exit it. This sets the animation playback in motion, clearing everything else from the screen. How long the animation will play depends upon the playback options you've selected. There are several key combinations you can use to control the playback: the Esc (Mac and PC), command+period (Mac), or Ctrl+period (PC) keys to stop the playback and restore the screen to its previous status; the space bar to pause the playback, and again, to resume the playback; and, the left and right arrow keys to move backwards and forwards by one frame respectively when the playback is paused. Try out all of them while you play your animation.

You can also play form•Z animation files by opening them using the File > View File command.

EXERCISE 5

Internal and External Communication

form•Z allows you to read from and write to a large variety of file formats used by other CAD and graphics programs, referred to as *object* and *image* file formats respectively. In this exercise, we'll look at an overview of these various formats, common import and export options, and the plugins and scripts that extend the functionality of the program. We'll start, however, by looking more closely at the options for working with files in the *native* form•Z formats.

5.1 Working with Native File Formats

- In the course of this and previous workshops, you've already come across a variety of file formats created and used by form•Z itself. A good way to recapitulate these is to go to File > Open, and open up the Files of Type popup menu (see Figure 7.28). Here, you'll see all the native file format types that you can open, including the main form•Z project file (.fmz), form•Z backup file (.fzb), form•Z Imager Set (.fis), form•Z symbol library (.zlb), form•Z suspended rendering (.spd), form•Z Autosave file (.fza), and an additional file type you have encountered so far but will study in the next exercise, form•Z script file (.fsl). This list does not include a form•Z animation file (.fan), which, as you saw in the previous exercise, can be opened by going to Display > Play Animation or File > View File.

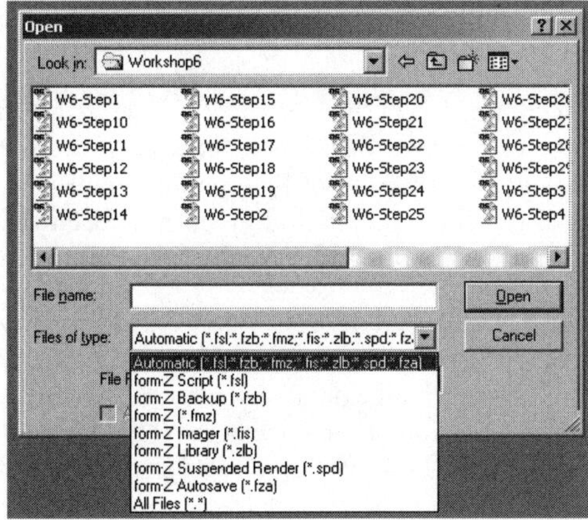

Figure 7.28

The Open dialog, showing the various native form•Z file formats that can be opened.

- Notice the Add To Project option in the Open dialog. This is enabled when a form•Z project file is selected. If you choose it, the selected file's contents will be added to the current project instead of being opened.

- Exit the Open dialog, and open up the File menu to look at all its commands. The first three New commands let you create a new form•Z modeling project, drafting project (which you'll be learning about in the Appendix), and Imager Set respectively. You've already looked at the Open command. The last command in the first group, Open Recent, displays the recently opened native form•Z files, so you can conveniently open them.

- The next set of commands is for closing and saving native form•Z files. Open up any form•Z project file, then select the Save A Copy As command from the File menu. In the dialog that opens up, you can, of course, save a copy of the file in the form•Z format. But there's more to it. Click on the Options button, and you'll find a number of options for saving the file (see Figure 7.29). You can choose to save it for an older version of form•Z; note, however, that this doesn't change the file extension, which remains ".fmz." You can limit the selection of entities that are saved using different options, and also conveniently include the symbol libraries, image files, and fonts used in the project.

Let's move on to look at the options for working with non-native file formats.

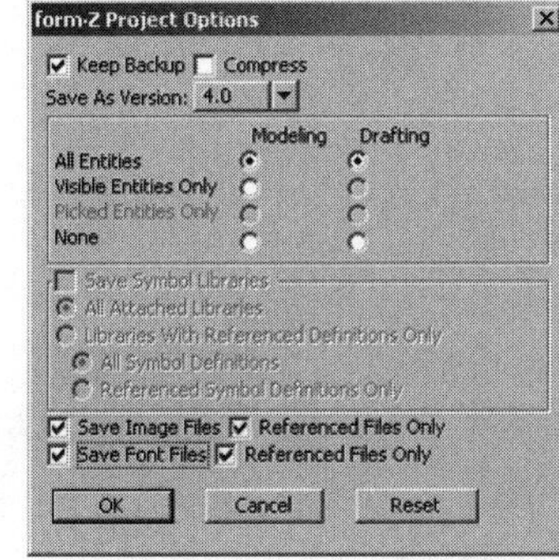

Figure 7.29

The different options available for saving a copy of a form•Z project file.

5.2 Importing and Exporting Object File Formats

▣ Look at the third set of commands in the File menu. These are for importing and exporting all the files that are not native to form•Z, but which form•Z can read from and write to. Select the Import command, and open up the Files of Type popup menu as you did for the Open command. You'll see an extensive list of file types, including both object and image formats. We'll focus on the object file formats in this section, and leave the image file formats for the next.

Object file formats include DXF, DWG, 3DS, OBJ, SAT, 3DGF, 3DMF, DEM, IGES, VRML, and others. Just like the native FMZ format, these contain vector-based information about geometric entities, and can thus be used to exchange data between form•Z and other applications that support these file formats. A detailed discussion of each one of these file formats and its import/export options is beyond the scope of this book. However, let's look at the import and export options that are common to all formats.

▣ In the Import dialog, select a common object file format from the Files of Type popup menu, say DXF, of which you have a sample file on your computer or on your network. Browse to the folder where this is located, and select it (see Figure 7.30). Before we look at its import options, notice the other options listed at the base of the dialog. The Add To Project option works the same way as described in the last section, adding the contents of the imported file to the current project instead of opening the file as a new form•Z project. You can also choose between the Import Model and Import Draft options to import the file as 3D modeling data or 2D drafting data in form•Z's modeling and drafting components respectively. Note that all file formats may not have both modeling and drafting data, in which case the non-supported option will be dimmed.

▣ After setting up these options, click on the Open button in the Import dialog. This will invoke the Modeling Import Options dialog for the selected file format, which in our case is DXF. As you can see in Figure 7.31, the upper section of this dialog contains an extensive set of import options that are common to all object file formats, while the lower section contains options specific to the selected format. The first two unit options determine whether the incoming information will be interpreted as English or Metric units and how it will be formatted. The next section contains modeling options or drafting options, depending upon whether the Import Model or Import Draft option was active in the Import dialog. We selected the former, which lets us explore the various modeling import options common to all object file formats.

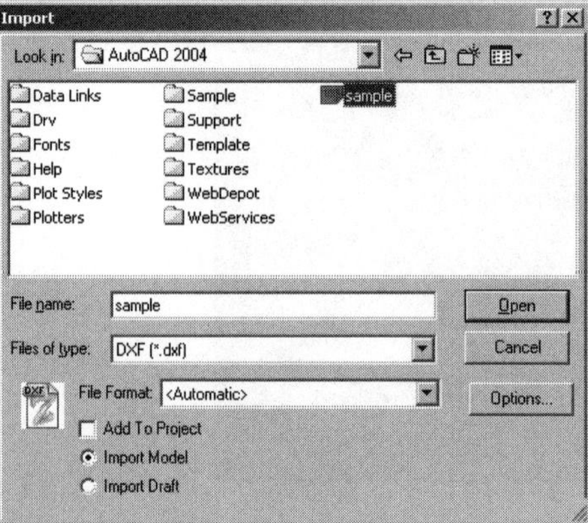

Figure 7.30

The Import dialog with the Files of Type set to DXF.

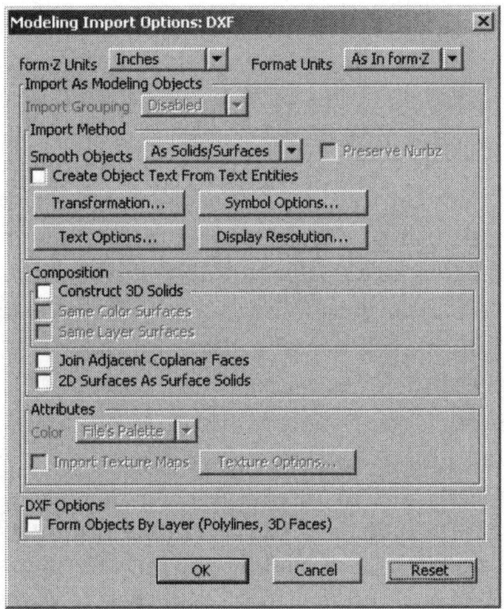

Figure 7.31

The Modeling Import Options dialog for the DXF file format.

- The Import Grouping option is active only for the FACT and VRML file formats, and allows grouping information to be constructed as groups or as layers in form•Z. The Import Method section contains various options that determine how smooth objects, text objects, and symbols are imported and displayed. Browse through all of them. If the imported data is not oriented correctly with respect to the form•Z coordinate axes, you can use the Transformation option to flip axes or swap planes, or even to scale, rotate, or move the imported entities by specific values. The Composition section contains options determining whether 3D solids should be constructed from 3D surface data, whether 2D surfaces should be imported as surface solids, and so on. The final section, Attributes, contains options relating to the color and texture maps of the imported entities. Not all of these options will be applicable to all the object file formats; those not relevant to the selected format will be deactivated.

- You can see that the only import option for DXF, listed at the base of the dialog, is related to whether objects should be formed by polylines and 3D faces created on the same layer. Whether this option should be checked or not will depend upon how the geometric entities have been created in the original application.

- Once you've specified the import parameters, exit both the dialogs by clicking on their OK buttons. The file you selected will open up as a new form•Z project, or get added to the current project, depending upon the Add To Project setting in the Import dialog. If the results are not satisfactory, repeat the import process with different settings. You might have to make a few trial runs with different import parameters, until you can pinpoint the exact combination that serves your purpose. Needless to say, you must also have a good understanding of the application that created the original file to specify the import parameters accurately. As usual, you can rely on the default settings in most instances.

- Let's look at the other import/export commands in the File menu. The Import Recent command displays the recently opened imported files, so you can conveniently open them again. The next command, Export, is used to export form•Z data in an object file format. You can open up the accompanying sub-menu to see the entire list. Select a specific file format, say 3Dstudio, and specify a name and location. Hit the Save button, and you'll be presented with the Modeling

Export Options dialog for the selected file format, as shown in Figure 7.32, where you can modify the default export parameters, if required.

- The Modeling Export Options is similar to the Modeling Import Options dialog in that it has the options common to all object file formats in the upper section, and any options specific to the selected format in the lower section. For the 3Dstudio format, as you can see, there are only the common options. These are similar to the import options, and determine various aspects such as how objects are grouped in the exported file, and how all the different object and model types—plain and parametric, facetted and smooth—are exported. There is the same Transformation option you found in the import dialog, and a Decomposition option that is the reverse of the Composition option for importing. If the file includes symbols, the Symbol Options button is active and gives you some options for exporting them. You can activate different Attributes settings, and decide whether to export Textures as wrapped, rendered, or turned off altogether.

Just as for the import options, you might need to run some iterations using different export settings until you figure out the exact combination that works. Also, keep in mind that it is difficult to achieve perfect interoperability between applications developed by different vendors, so some amount of tweaking might be needed to get results that you can work with, both in form•Z for imported data, and in the application you are exporting form•Z data to.

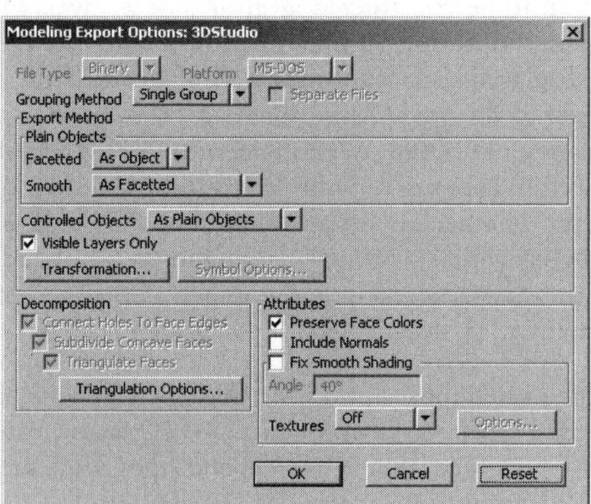

Figure 7.32

The Modeling Export Options dialog for the 3DStudio file format.

5.3 Importing and Exporting Image File Formats

- Select the Import command again, and this time, choose an image file in a format such as BMP, EPS, TIFF, Illustrator, JPEG, and so on. You'll find that the raster image formats such as BMP, TIFF, JPEG, etc., only allow the data to be imported as drafting elements, so the Import Model option will be deactivated. For vector image formats such as Illustrator, Windows Metafile, etc., the data can be imported as modeling elements or drafting elements, just like object file formats.

- Once you select an image file to import, the Import Options dialog is invoked, allowing you to change the default import parameters. This dialog follows the same convention of listing the common image import options at the top and the ones specific to the selected format below. As you can see in the Import Options dialog for the Illustrator file format in Figure 7.33, the common options are limited to specifying the scale and color settings of the imported elements. Other options are related to how text and paths from Illustrator will be imported, along with grouping and positioning options. In the case of vector file formats such as Illustrator, you could use the imported 2D elements as the base objects from which to generate 3D objects.

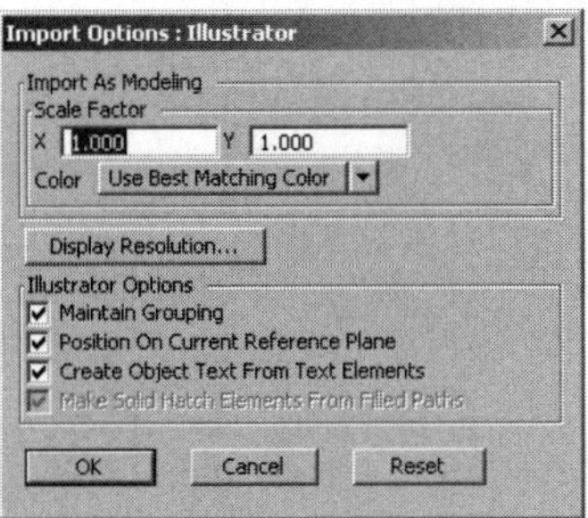

Figure 7.33

The Import Options dialog for the Illustrator file format.

- Next, turn to the Export Image command in the File menu, which is used to export form•Z data in various image file formats. Recall from Section 1.4 of Workshop 5 (Illuminating, Texturing, and Rendering Your World) that while all kinds of images can be saved to raster file formats such as JPEG, TIFF, Targa, etc., line-based displays such as Wire Frame, Hidden Line, and Surface Render can also be saved as vector-based images in file formats such as Illustrator. The export options are relatively straightforward for most of the image formats. Thus, for a hidden line drawing being exported to Illustrator, you can specify settings such as the line weight and whether the background should be included or not.

- Notice that the Export Image command has some formats in its sub-menu, such as Piranesi and HPGL, which were not available as formats for importing image data. A brief explanation of these formats is in order. Piranesi is a specialized application for architectural sketch rendering, that uses the EPX (Extended Pixel) file format, in which each pixel stores depth and material information in addition to color. This means that the individual 2D planes making up a 3D scene exist and can be separately selected and applied a color or texture; the program automatically adjusts the size of a texture and the shade of a color along the plane according to its depth. You can directly export a form•Z file in the EPX format to Piranesi for applying artistic rendering effects.

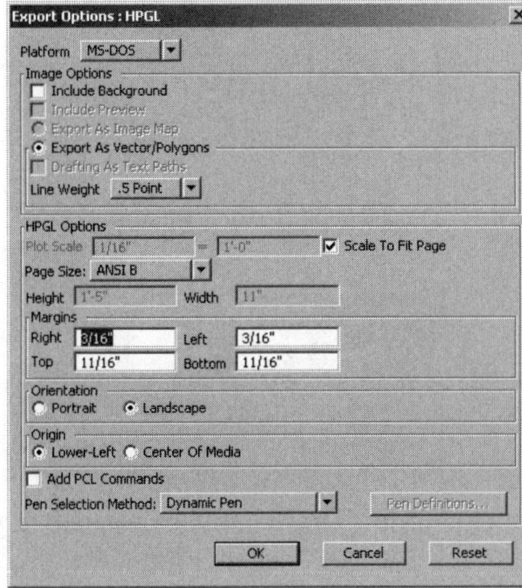

Figure 7.34

The Export Options dialog for the HPGL file format.

- In contrast, an HPGL (Hewlett-Packard Graphics Language) file contains pen plotting commands, to be used by HP plotters and other plotters supporting the same language. Exporting a form•Z file in the HPGL format involves a fairly extensive set of options, as shown in Figure 7.34. There are the standard Image Options settings applicable to all image formats. The HPGL Options include settings such as the plot scale, paper size, margins, paper orientation and origins, addition of PCL commands which can then be sent to an HP laser printer, and finally, different ways of selecting the physical pens needed for carrying out the plotting.

5.4 Plugins and Scripts

Many of the external file formats you saw in the Import and Export menus use file translator *plugins* to communicate with form•Z. There are different kinds of plugins extending the functionality of the program: file translators, as you have seen, that import and export data to different object and image formats; RenderZone shaders, that define shaders for the different attributes of a surface style; new tools and commands, such as the Sketch Render display mode and the Re-engineer tool; drivers for interfacing with hardware digitizers; and so on. Some plugins are automatically installed with the program. Others, such as Sketch Render and Re-engineer, have to be installed separately.

Figure 7.35

Generating a nurbz surface from a set of point cloud data with the Re-engineer tool.

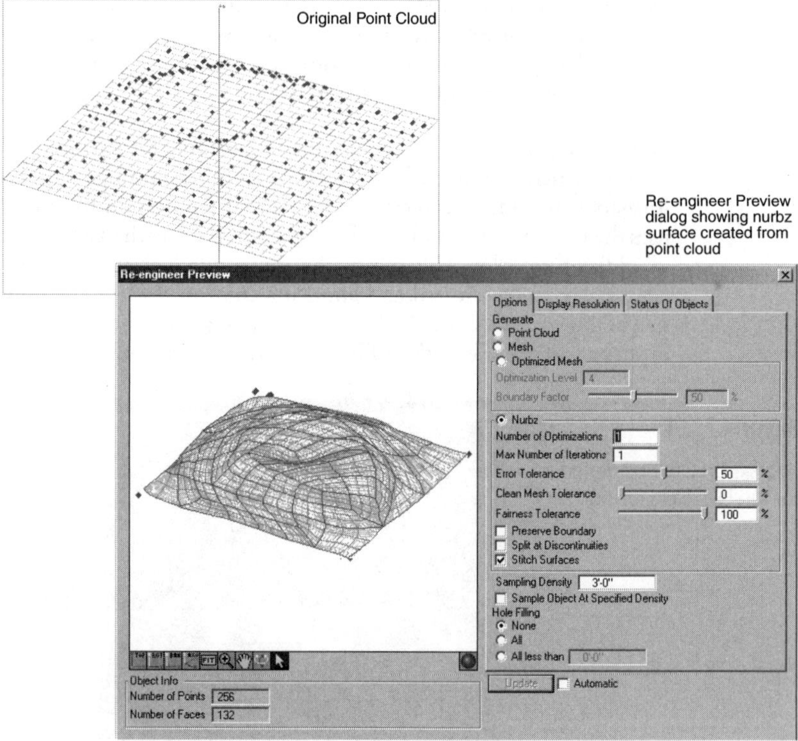

You have already worked with the Sketch Render plugin in Section 1.3 of Workshop 5 (Illuminating, Texturing, and Rendering Your World). The Re-engineer plugin, when installed, appears as the last tool in the left toolset of Row 6 of the modeling tool palette. It is most useful for converting a set of

point cloud data, such as that generated by 3D scanning devices, into modeling surfaces from which that objects may be re-engineered and eventually manufactured. An example of a nurbz surface created from a set of points with the Re-engineer tool is shown in Figure 7.35. As you can see from the preview dialog, the tool can also be used as a reduction tool to simplify form•Z objects or to convert meshed objects to nurbz objects.

In addition to plugins, form•Z also allows extensions to its functionality in the form of *scripts*; these are instructions in a specific language stored in a text file (.fsl) or a binary file (.fsb). Unlike plugins, scripts are interpreted rather than compiled, so they're slower in execution; also, they are platform independent, unlike plugins, which cannot be moved between operating systems. Scripts can be used, just like plugins, to define different types of RenderZone shaders, and to perform other tasks. Eventually, the ability to create user-defined custom scripts will also be provided.

- To view and manage plugins and scripts, select the last command from the Edit menu, Plugins And Scripts. This invokes the dialog shown in Figure 7.36, where all the plugins and scripts known to the application are listed. Along with the name of the plugin or script, you can also see additional information such as its type, version, and vendor. The column on the left allows you to enable or disable a particular plugin or script. Any changes that you make will take effect only after form•Z has been restarted.

Figure 7.36

The Plugins and Scripts dialog.

- Browse through the list to see the different types of plugins and scripts. To find out more about any item in the list, double-click on it. This will invoke a dialog showing more detailed information about the plugin or script, including its ID number, file name, path, and so on.

- The group of options under Selected Sets in the lower part of the Plugins And Scripts dialog allows you to define a new set of plugins and scripts, select a previously defined set, and delete the current set if it isn't the default set. The New Plugins and New Scripts options let you specify whether plugins and scripts new to form•Z should be automatically loaded, not loaded, or loaded after issuing a prompt. And finally, the Search Paths option lets you add and remove folders where form•Z should look for plugins and scripts to load.

Plugins and scripts were introduced only in version 4.0 of form•Z, which is why the list you see in Figure 7.36 is quite limited. Subsequent versions should have many more plugins and scripts that extend the functionality of the program in various ways and allow you to customize it as required.

With that, we come to the end of the exercises for this last workshop. Let's proceed to see what is in store for us in the Assignment for this workshop.

ASSIGNMENT 7

3D Graphic for Book Cover Design

Design a 3D graphic that can be used as the cover image for a book. It should, of course, reflect the theme of the book.

The actual exercise of modeling the 3D graphic shown here will now be demonstrated step by step. It is the cover image for a book on computer chip design, and is comprised of 3D text placed on a computer chip that has been divided like a jigsaw puzzle. After a sequence of progressively tougher modeling assignments, this is a relatively simple modeling assignment.

You can refer to the form•Z files for each step of this assignment in the accompanying CD-ROM, under the folder Assignments > Workshop 7. A color rendered image of the 3D graphic is in the Assignment7.tif file in the same location.

Setup

Open a new form•Z project. The exact size of the objects in this kind of project does not matter, as long as they're in proportion to each other. So we'll use dimensions that are convenient rather than those that accurately represent the size of a computer chip.

Go to Options > Working Units. Make sure the Data Scale is set to Medium (Building). Set the units to Feet under the English measurement system, Numeric Accuracy to 1", and Angle Accuracy to 1°. Ensure that the Window Setup under the Window menu is set to a grid module of 8'-0" with four subdivisions, and set the Display Scale to 1/16" = 1'-0".

Step 1

The first step is to model the base block of the computer chip, which is profiled on all sides. We can easily use the Sweep tool to model it. Switch to the Top view. Draw a 2D square of size 48', which will serve as the path shape. For the source, use the Vector Line tool to draw a two-segment profile shape as shown. The length of the upper segment is 2'-2", the length of the lower segment is 2'-4", and the angle between them is 120º.

Change the name of the layer on which these shapes are created to chip-body.

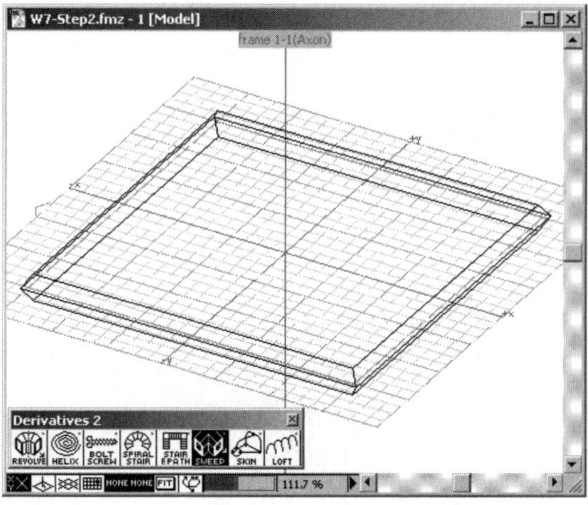

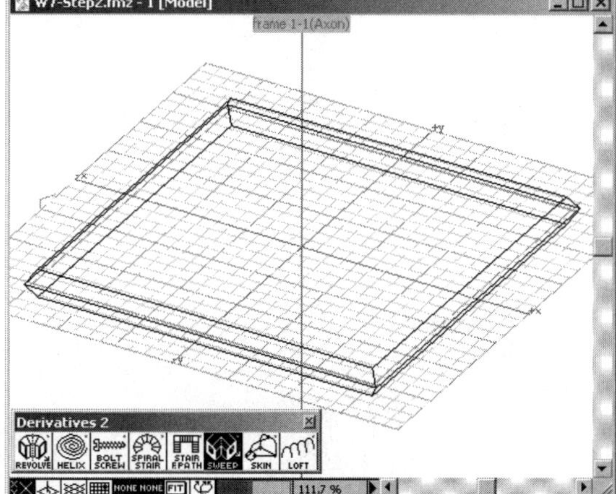

Step 2

Access the dialog of the Sweep tool, and set the Type to Boundary Sweep. Apply it to the configuration of source and path you have created, accepting the default options in the Sweep Options dialog, including the Facetted model type.

Step 3

Apply the Plain Rounding tool, with a radius of 3", to round off all the faces and segments of the base block of the chip.

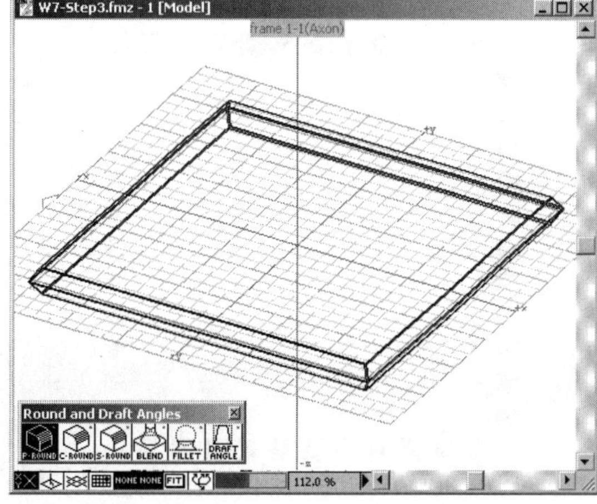

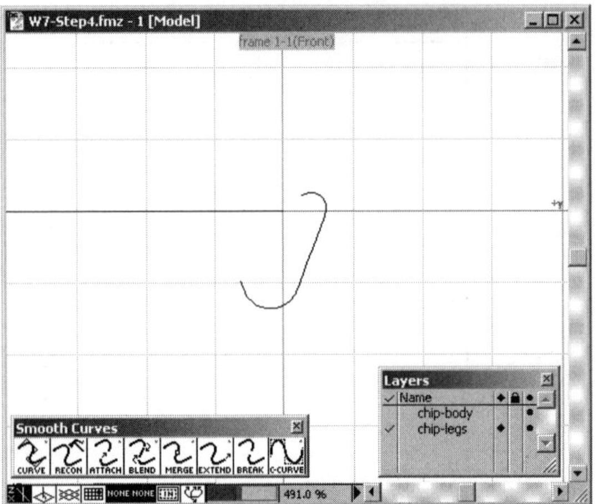

Step 4

Next, we'll model the "legs" that are attached to the base block on all sides. Activate a new layer, chip-legs. Unghost the original 2D square of size 48' used in the Sweep operation, and copy it to the chip-legs layer. Then turn off the chip-body layer.

Switch to the Front view, and draw a 2D profile, positioned close to one end of the square and oriented as shown. You can use any drawing tools you prefer. We'll call this shape the *chip profile*.

Step 5

Switch to a non-planar view and draw a 2D rectangle on the XY plane of size 3" along the X axis and 2' along the Y axis. Set the mode of the Front view back to Axial Sweep, and sweep the rectangle along the chip profile shape. This will give you one of the chip legs.

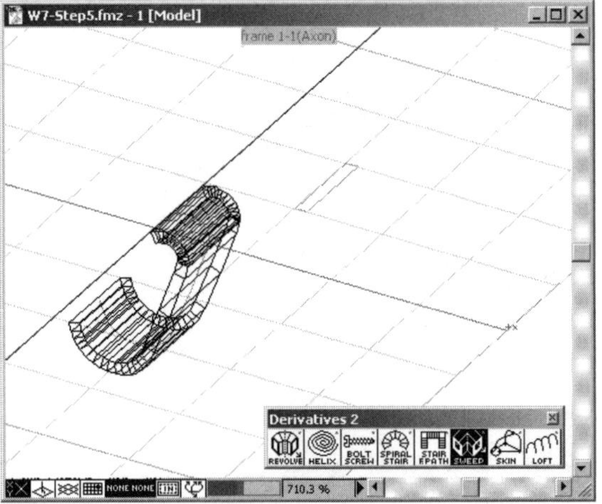

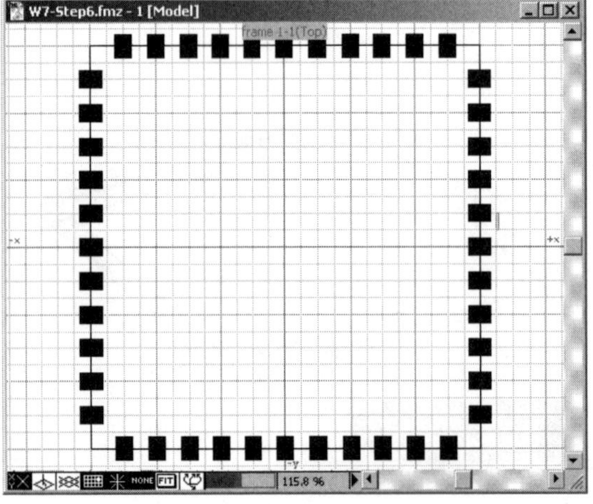

Step 6

Switch to the Top view. Use the Move and Mirror tools in Copy tools to make copies of the chip leg all around the 2D rectangle. There should be 11 legs on each side, equally spaced about the middle leg, which is positioned at the middle of each side of the rectangle.

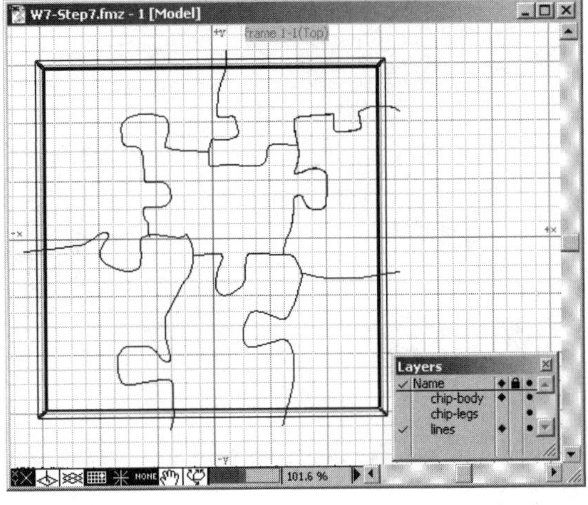

Step 7

Ghost the 2D rectangle, since we don't need it any more.

Activate a new layer, lines. Turn off the chip-legs layer, but turn the visibility of the chip-body layer back on. Still in the Top view, use the base block as a guide for drawing 2D lines simulating a jigsaw puzzle as shown. These lines will be used to cut the base block into multiple pieces, so make sure the lines extend beyond the boundary of the block. Again, use your preferred drawing tool for creating the lines.

Step 8

Select the Trim/Split tool, and set its mode to Split under With Line and check the Stitch option. Under Status Of Objects, ensure that the Object Per Volume option is selected for New Object Status.

Use the Trim/Split tool to progressively cut the base block with each line, until the base block is completely divided into separate pieces following the line markings. Color the pieces with different colors so that the distinction between them is clear in a rendered display.

Step 9

The next step is the model the 3D text objects standing up on top of the individual jigsaw pieces. Activate a new layer, text. Create lines for text placement at the appropriate position and height relative to the pieces. Using the Text Place tool with the option set to the On Line option under Text As Object Along Path, place the required text on each line. The height of the text should be specified as 2'-6", and make sure you check the Standing (Perp To Plane) option.

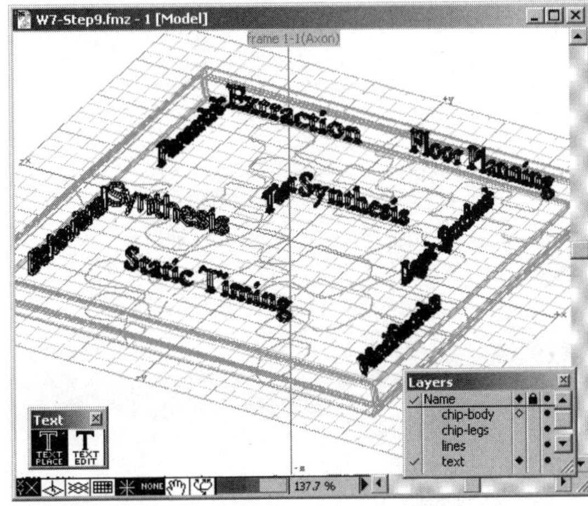

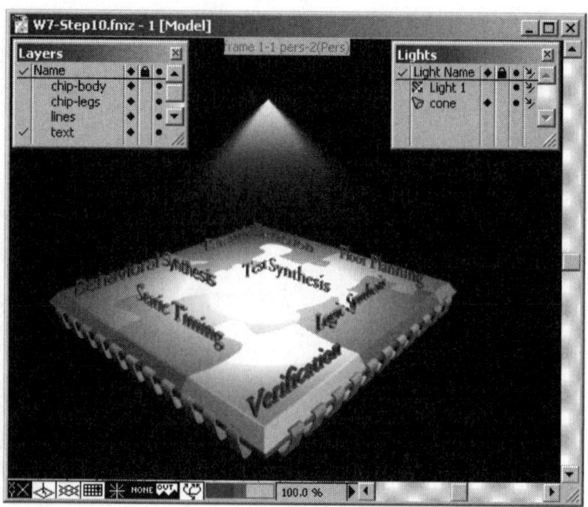

Step 10

As the final step, place a point light source in the scene shining on top of the chip configuration. Turn on all the layers. Color all the objects appropriately, and set the background color to black. Create an appropriate perspective view. A simple RenderZone display will now create the 3D graphic that is needed.

Brief Overview of the Drafting Module

The drafting module of form•Z is provided mainly in support of its modeling environment. After 3D models have been created, they may need to be communicated to others for presentation or construction. For this, you might need to add text and dimensions to the images derived from 3D models, use a variety of line types and line thicknesses, apply hatch patterns, and so on. All of these tasks can be done in the drafting environment of form•Z, which basically emulates a traditional 2D CAD program like AutoCAD.

You can also draw directly in the drafting module. These drawings can serve as the base objects for the generation of 3D solids when you transport them to the modeling environment. This is useful on those occasions when the base 2D object is quite complex and you'd like to create it accurately before proceeding to 3D modeling. The modeling environment, of course, does provide you with all the tools for creating 2D shapes, but you'll find that the drafting module has a few extra tools which just might make the task a little simpler.

This appendix will give you a brief overview of the drafting module of form•Z. Since it has lots of similarities with the modeling environment, mastering the drafting module should not be a difficult task, and you should be able to go beyond the information provided here quite comfortably.

1. From Modeling to Drafting

Let's start by going through the process of how objects—or their 2D plans, sections, and elevations—can be transported from the modeling to the drafting environment.

Opening a Drafting Window

For every project in form•Z, just as you can open up one or more associated modeling windows using `Window > New Model Window`, you can open up one or more associated drafting windows using `Window > New Draft Window`. Such draft windows can be used to contain all the drafting work related to that modeling project and will automatically be saved when the project is saved. Don't expect, however, these associated drafting windows to automatically display 2D views of the objects that exist in the 3D modeling component of the project; there's no such correspondence between the two.

You can also simply open up a new drafting project using `File > New[Draft]` for creating the work related to one or more modeling projects. This will now be an independent project that has to be saved separately, just like any other modeling project that you've worked with so far.

The advantage of using an associated drafting window is that all the relevant settings such as working units, window setup, colors, and so on, that you specified for the modeling project will be automatically applied to the associated drafting windows. If you use a new drafting project, on the other hand, you'll have to specify the settings again if they're different from the defaults.

Whatever method you choose, a drafting window will switch you to the drafting environment when it's activated. This environment looks similar to the modeling environment, except that some of the tools and palettes are different. A drafting window will also have the label [Draft] or [Draft Layout] appearing in the window title bar next to the project name, so there should be no confusion about which environment—drafting or modeling—you're currently in.

Copying Modeling Objects into the Drafting Module

Transferring objects between the modeling and drafting modules is a simple process. Simply select all that you want to transfer, go to Edit > Copy, open up a drafting window by either one of the two methods described in the last section, and select Edit > Paste From Modeling. The selected objects will now be pasted into the draft window, in the same position with respect to the origin as in the original model. (For copying objects from drafting to modeling, the corresponding paste option is Edit > Paste From Drafting.)

Notice from the asterisk (*) sign that the Paste From Modeling item under the Edit menu has a dialog associated with it. This can be opened in the usual manner—select this item while holding down the option key (Mac) or Ctrl+Shift keys (PC). You can see from Figure A.1 that the default option is Each 3D Segment As A Single Line. This will lose the connectivity information between the individual segments of a 3D object, which means that a rectangle will be imported as four separate segments rather than as a rectangle. Thus, you cannot apply a hatch operation to this set of segments in the draft module until you reconnect them with the Join tool into a closed rectangle. If you check the associated sub-option, Remove Duplicate And Overlapping Lines, the many coincident segments that can exist in a planar view of a 3D object are automatically removed. To retain segment connectivity information, you should select the alternate Each Face/Outline As A Polyline option. But keep in mind that there's no option to delete duplicates automatically with this method, so you'll have to remove them yourself step-by-step.

3D objects can be transferred from the modeling to the drafting environment either in planar or in non-planar views. The first is essential if you want to dimension your objects correctly, such as for plans, sections, etc. Of the non-planar views, recall that only in an Isometric or Oblique view do objects retain their actual dimensions, and there, too, only along the direction of the axes. In an Axonometric or Perspective non-planar view, none of the object dimensions will be correct. Since the 3D model is being projected onto a flat 2D surface, the dimensions of the original and the projection will match only for planar views such as Top, Front, etc. Thus, non-planar views are generally used for annotating rather than dimensioning when copied across to the drafting module.

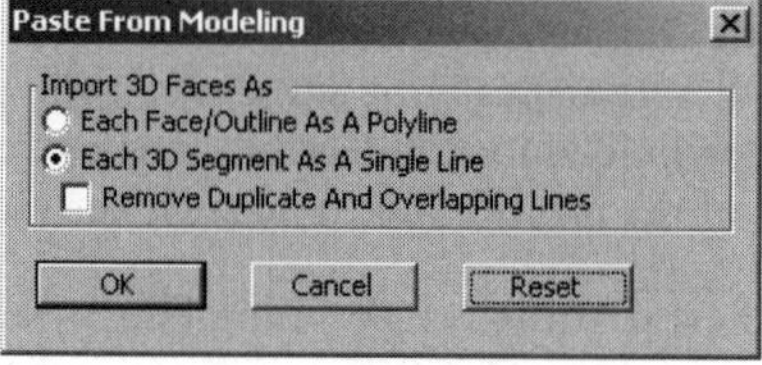

Figure A.1

The Paste From Modeling options dialog.

Generating Sections of Modeling Objects for Drafting

You've already seen how you can use the Section tool (M-Tool:9a,8) in the modeling environment, in either the 2D mode or the 3D mode, to generate sections of objects along a cutting plane. Once the Section operation is complete, those parts of the objects that should not appear in the desired planar view can be temporarily deleted. You can then switch to the view, and copy and paste the objects in a draft window. These *plans* and *sections* can now be annotated, dimensioned, and so on.

If some of the objects in your modeling project have non-planar faces, the Section tool won't be able to operate on them. In this case, you can make use of the Edit Cone Of Vision option to generate the desired sections by following the procedure described below. In fact, you might even find this method more convenient than using the Section tool.

Depending upon the plan or section you're trying to generate, switch to the appropriate planar view in your modeling project. Then go to Views > Edit Cone Of Vision. Here, adjust both the front and back clipping planes so that you see only the required portion of the model for the given plan or section. To turn the clipping action on, activate the Clip Hither/Yon option in the Views menu. You should now see only the clipped portion of your model in the preview window, as shown in Figure A.2. Save this view, and generate more sections, if necessary, following the same sequence of steps. Exit the Cone Of Vision environment when you're done.

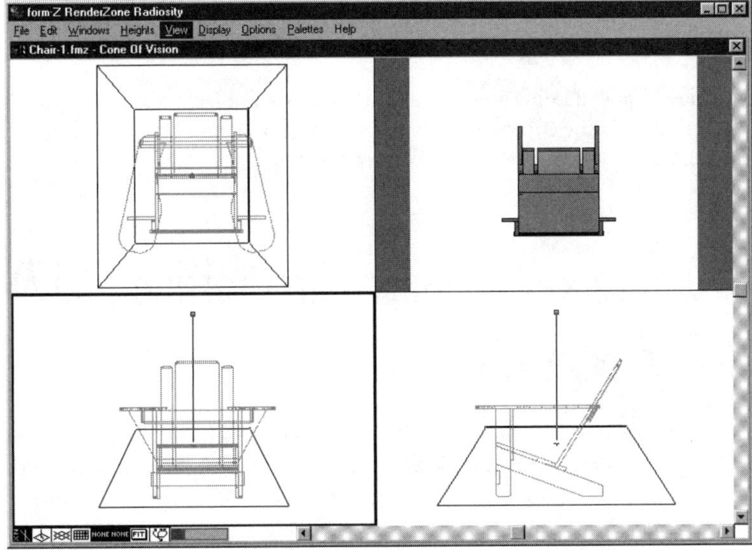

Figure A.2

Adjusting the clipping planes in the Cone Of Vision environment to see only the desired section of a model.

Back in the graphics window, you'll find that in Wire Frame you see the complete object rather than the clipped portion. Change to Quick Paint but it is still the same. Only when you switch to Hidden Line, Surface Render, and the higher rendering modes, is the view restricted to the clipped portion. Settle for the Hidden Line or Surface Render modes of display.

Now that you have obtained a result similar to what you'd have if you had used the Section tool, you might think of simply copying and pasting the clipped modeling objects into the draft module. This, however, won't work, since the clipping is just a visual effect rather than an actual cut. Thus, you'll be copying and pasting the complete objects and not just the cut portions. Try it. Obviously, we need to do something else in order to transfer these clipped images to the drafting environment.

The solution is simple—you can save what you have into a 2D vector-based file format and then *import* that into a drafting window. Before saving it, go to Window > Window Setup and turn off the displays of all the axes and grids. This will leave only the modeling objects in the window, without all the background objects. Now go to File > Export Image and save what you have in a vector-based file format such as Illustrator, PICT (Mac only) or Metafile (PC only). Bitmapped file formats won't be useful since you want to transport the objects in a form that you can also dimension, which you can't do for a bitmapped image. Stick with the default options for the file format when you save the file.

After saving the file, open a new draft window and use File > Import to choose the file you just saved, with the Import Draft option. Your objects will be transported, clipped just the way they were in the modeling view that you had saved. The only catch is that the dimensions of what you now have in the draft window will no longer match the actual dimensions of the objects in the original model.

Getting around this problem is relatively simple. Find out the dimension of a particular segment using the Query tool in both the draft and model windows, divide the modeling dimension by the drafting dimension to get a scaling factor, and use the Uniform Scale tool in the draft window to scale all the objects by this factor. You'll now have an accurate sectioned drawing of your model in a draft window. This additional step of scaling is, of course, not needed when the Copy command is used to transfer objects from modeling to drafting.

Now that you know how to transfer sections of objects from the modeling to the drafting environment, let's look at the components of this environment and how they differ from the modeling environment that we know so well from all the workshops.

2. Differences Between the Drafting and Modeling Environments

The drafting environment of form•Z has an interface similar to the modeling environment. It's comprised of the main pulldown menu, the drafting tool palette on the left, the window tool palette at the bottom, a number of floating palettes, and of course, the graphics window. Most of the commands and tools are identical to what you've already seen for the modeling environment. However, there are some differences. Let's see what they are.

Main Menu and Graphics Window

In the main pulldown menu, you'll notice that there's no Heights menu. Since the drafting module contains only 2D objects, the concept of *heights* does not exist. The Views menu, likewise, has very few commands. There's no concept of seeing the objects from different angles—you can see 2D objects only head-on. Thus the graphics window always looks the same. You can choose to rotate it using the different rotation angles in the Views menu, or zoom and scroll through it using the various window tools, but you'll always be looking at it in exactly the same *view*.

Also notice that under the Display menu, there are no display modes, except for a Replot command. Since there are no 3D objects, there's nothing to render. All that you might want to do is refresh the screen occasionally, which is what the Replot command does.

Tool Palettes

The drafting tool palette located on the left of the graphics window is revised to meet the requirements for drafting, and we'll briefly go through each row of tools of the drafting palette in Section 4.

The window tool palette is essentially the same as in the modeling environment, except that the tools not applicable to drafting—Reference Planes, Perpendicular Lock, and so on—are grayed out. The Grid Snap and Direction Snap, as well as the Zoom & Pan tools, remain the same. The Object Snap options are almost the same, except that the Face snap is deactivated.

Floating Palettes

The drafting module has fewer floating palettes as compared to the modeling environment. Of these, four are unique to the drafting module (see Figure A.3). These are Colors, Hatch Patterns, Line Weights, and Line Styles. The others are identical to the corresponding palettes in the modeling environment. Notice that there's also a Views palette, although you cannot really have different views, as such, of 2D objects. But you can zoom the graphics window in and out, rotate it, and scroll through it—each of these can be saved as a separate view in the Views palette.

The Colors palette for drafting corresponds to the Surface Styles palette for modeling. Since there's no concept of rendering in 2D, there can obviously be no concept of textures and texture mapping. But you can apply different colors to 2D objects by highlighting different colors in the Colors palette. You can create new colors or delete existing ones in the same manner as you did for surface styles.

The other three palettes are self-explanatory. Hatch Patterns contains various kinds of patterns that you can apply to the interior of an object using the Hatch tool. Line Weights and Line Styles allow you to choose between various line thicknesses and styles an object can be drawn in. Appropriate tools for modifying all these attributes of an object exist in the drafting tool palette, which we'll soon look at.

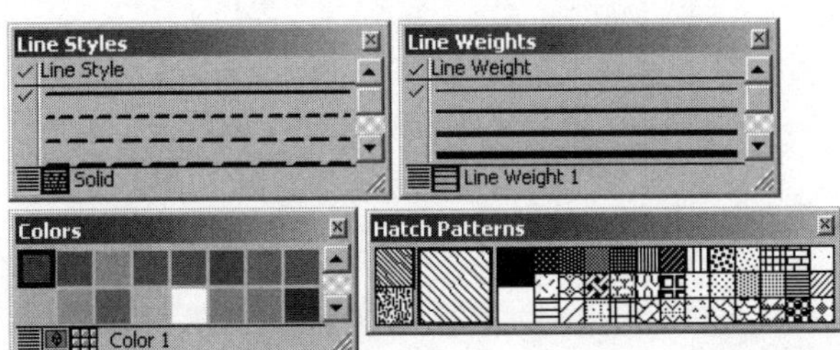

Figure A.3

The four palettes unique to the drafting environment of form•Z.

3. Draft Space Versus Layout Space

In its drafting module, form•Z gives you the option of working in two different modes. The one you see as soon as you open a new draft window is the *draft space* mode. This is the regular working mode, in which you have a graphics window where you create various entities, just as in the modeling environment. Any change made to the view, layer settings, and so on affects the entire window.

The alternate mode, *layout space*, is useful for composing a set of drawings for printing. One *pane* can be created for each drawing. A number of such panes can be composed, in combination with text and other graphic elements, as shown in Figure A.4. A pane is essentially a *window* into the draft space. You can create your separate drawings in different parts of the draft space, or on different layers. Then, in the layout space, each pane can be set to "see" a different part of the draft space or a different layer, so as to have different drawings visible in different panes. Keep in mind that a *drawing* does not have to be something necessarily created within the drafting environment; it can also be a set of modeling objects or even a rendered image imported into the drafting environment. Examples of panes containing different kinds of drawings are shown in Figure A.4.

By default, you're in the draft space mode, as you can see. To enter into the layout space mode, go to Display > Draft Layout Mode. The only visible change is that all your drafting elements will disappear, presenting you with a blank window. Look carefully and you'll notice that the word Draft has been replaced by the words Draft Layout in the title bar of the window.

The next step is to add panes in the window for the number of drawings you want to compose. This is done by setting the object generation mode in the drafting tool palette to Pane—the second tool in the right column of the first row—and using the regular drawing tools. Panes can be of any shape and size. As soon as a pane is drawn, the elements in the draft space will be visible through it.

To manipulate what you see through this pane, activate it by selecting it with the Pick Pane tool—the second tool in the right column of the fourth row. It gets highlighted in gray. You can now change its zoom, layer, and display settings to compose your drawing properly within it. You can even create or modify entities in the draft space *through* this pane, although it's better to be in the draft space mode to do this.

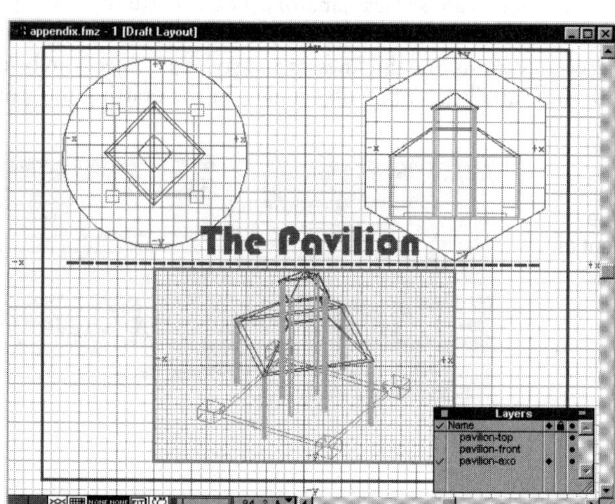

Figure A.4

Panes in the layout space of the drafting environment, showing various aspects of the project composed for printing.

When no pane is activated, changes in the zoom and display settings are applied to the entire layout space window. Any entities that you draw or text that you place are created in the layout space and will not be visible in the draft space. Thus you can format the layout window for printing in any manner, maintaining a clear separation between the entities in the project and the elements added only for printing.

Once created, panes can be moved, resized, deleted, and so on like regular drafting elements by selecting them with the Pick tool (*not* the Pick Pane tool) and applying the desired operation.

To exit the layout space mode, select the same command, Draft Layout Mode, from the Display menu.

4. The Drafting Tool Palette

The layout of the drafting tool palette is similar to that of the modeling tool palette. The different rows of tools are shown in Figure A.5. This section will provide you with a brief overview of these tools. Many of these are identical to the modeling tools covered in the main workshops. So we'll concentrate only on where and how the drafting palette differs from the modeling palette. Note that a similar notation will be used to refer to the tools. Thus, D-Tool:1a,1 refers to the first tool in the left column of the first row of the drafting tool palette.

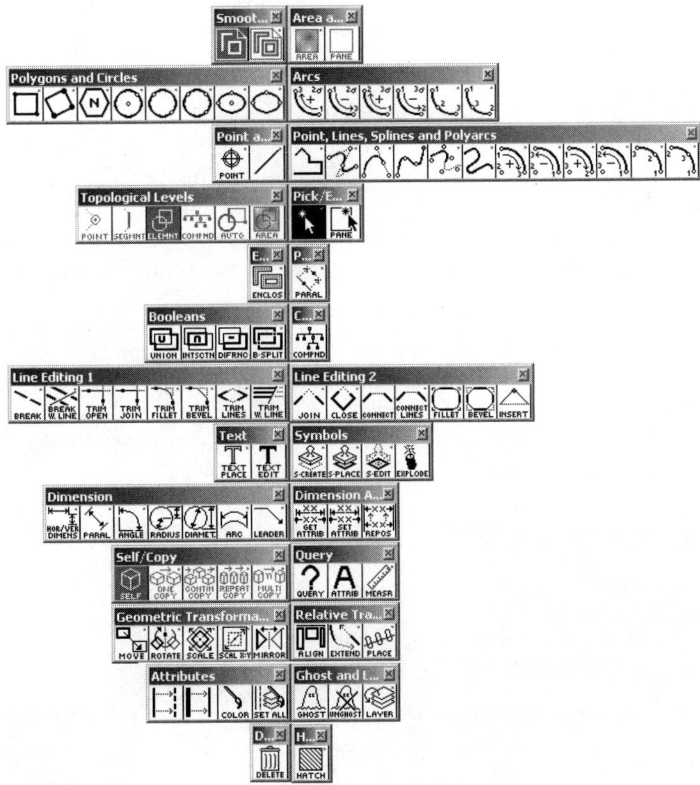

Figure A.5

The 13 rows of tools, arranged in two columns, of the drafting tool palette.

Row 1: Element Generation Modes

These tools determine the type of element that will be generated by the drawing operators located in the next two rows. (Note that the term *element* in the drafting environment corresponds to *object* in the modeling environment.) The tools in the left column are the familiar single-line and double-line modes. Of the two tools in the right column, we've already looked at Pane in Section 3. The remaining tool is the Area Generation mode, which will be discussed now. It's used for creating a special element unique to the drafting environment known as an *area*. This is a temporary element, used not for creating entities, but for the identification of other drafting elements to which some operation can subsequently be applied.

An area element is generated through the same set of drawing operators on Rows 2 and 3 as the other element types. It can be of any shape, but is required to always be *closed*. Thus, polylines are automatically closed in the area mode, while open arcs are not acceptable at all. The area is displayed on the screen with a gray fill, which clearly distinguishes it from other drafting elements (see Figure A.7-a). It plays an auxiliary role only and doesn't appear in the final drawing. Also, there can only be a *single* area element in a project at any given time. Generating a new area element replaces the previous one, if any.

Once created, an area element can be moved or modified just like any other shape. The boundary of the area splits the drawing into two portions: the *inside* and the *outside*, forming two separate groups. The area's main function is to *pick* other drafting elements in this manner, identifying them for a particular operation such as move, rotate, copy, etc. This operation can be applied to either the inside or the outside group, the choice of which is made in the dialog of the Area tool, under the Area Type section (Figure A.6).

There's an additional section in this dialog called Boundary Type, which has three options. The first, In/Out Only, will select only those elements that lie completely inside or completely outside the boundary of the area (for Area Type settings of Inside and Outside respectively). The second, On/Crossing, will also select elements that touch or cross the boundary of the area. The third option, Clip To Area, enables the area to be used as a clipping tool. With this option, elements that cross the boundaries of the area are broken at their points of intersection when an area is picked.

To actually select the elements thus designated or clipped by an area, the topological level on Row 4 needs to be set to Area (D-Tool:4a,6). Any transformation such as Move will now be applied to the elements selected by the area. This is illustrated in Figure A.7-b, where the Clip To Area and Inside options were selected in the Area dialog, and the Move tool was applied with the topological level set to Area. (Note that if the topological level is set to Element, the area *itself* will be moved, rather than the elements it selects.)

Figure A.6

The dialog of the Area element generation tool.

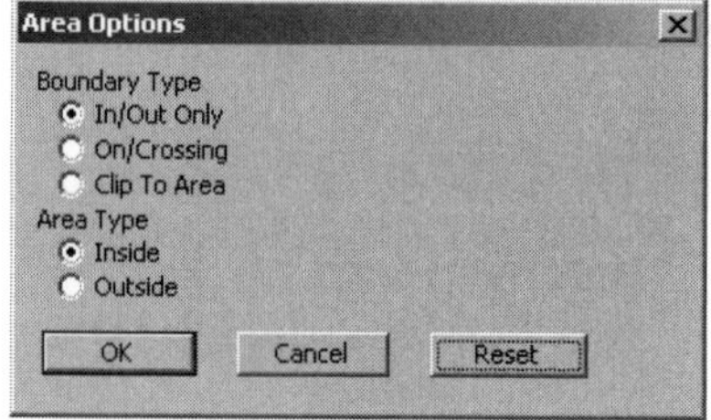

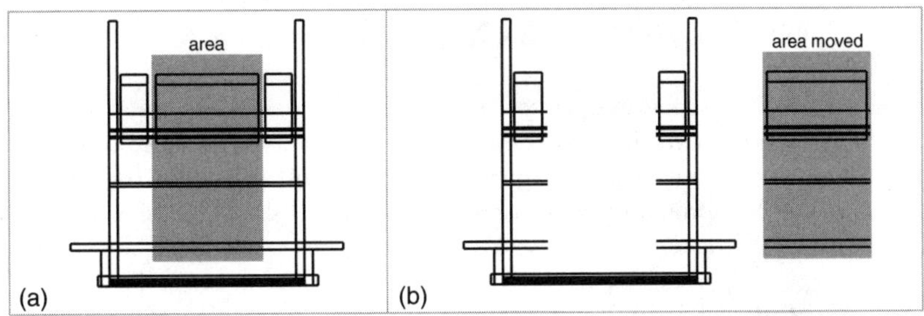

Figure A.7

Working with an area element. (a) A rectangular area created in a drawing. (b) Moving the area along with its enclosing elements.

Rows 2 and 3: Drafting Operators

These tools can be used to draw polygons of any type, circles, ellipses, polylines, curves, points, and arcs. They are identical to those found in the modeling environment and work in the same fashion.

Notice that there are two seemingly identical sets of Arc tools, located on Row 2 as well as Row 3. The difference between the two sets is that the ones on Row 2 are *elemental arcs*, i.e., they're not comprised of a series of segments that can be selected by setting the topological level to Segment. (However, these arcs still appear to be segmented, based on the resolution specified in their Options dialog.) On the other hand, the Arc tools on Row 3 create *polyarcs*, i.e., arcs comprised of a sequence of segments that can be individually selected and manipulated.

Row 4: Topological Levels and Picking

The tools in the left column establish the topological level at which the subsequently executed operators will be applied, just as in the modeling environment. You're already familiar with Point, Segment, and Auto. Element corresponds to Object of the modeling environment. Compound is similar to Group of the modeling environment—it acts on elements that have been linked into a compound element using the Compound tool on Row 6. And finally, Area, as we've seen, refers to the area element that can be drawn using D-Tool:1b,1.

The tools in the right column are Pick, which is identical to its counterpart in modeling, and Pick Pane, which was discussed earlier in Section 3.

Row 5: Deriving Enclosures and Parallel Offsets

The Enclosure tool in the left column generates a double-line element out of a single-line element. The thickness of the double line is specified in its dialog.

The Parallel tool on the right creates a new element that is parallel to the selected element. The offset—the distance of the new element from the original—can be graphically specified by a mouse click. Alternately, a specific offset distance can be set in the tool dialog.

Row 6: Booleans and Compounding

The four boolean operators in the left column—Union, Intersection, Difference, and B-Split—work identically to their modeling counterparts. In the right column, there's the Compound tool, which works on the same principle as the Group tool of the modeling environment. Compounded elements can be restored to their original "ungrouped" status by using the Explode tool on Row 8.

Row 7: Line Editing

Both the left and right columns contain a number of tools for the manipulation and editing of lines in various ways. They're practically identical to the line editing tools in the modeling environment that you worked with in Section 5.3 of Workshop 2 (Bringing a Sense of Scale). The only difference is that the various options in the dialogs of those tools appear as separate tools in the drafting environment. So, for instance, the options and sub-options of the Trim tool (M-Tool:11a,3) in the modeling tool palette appear as six separate tools—Trim Open, Trim Join, Trim Fillet, Trim Bevel, Trim Lines, and Trim With Lines—in the drafting tool palette.

Row 8: Placing Text and Symbols

Here are the operators for placing and editing text and creating and placing symbols. They work identically to the text and symbol tools in the modeling environment. The text, of course, won't be 3D text but regular 2D text, which you can place at a point or between two points. The choice is made in the dialog of the Text Place tool. There are a number of options related to text display in the Text tab of the Drafting Display Options dialog, invoked from the Display menu. Be sure to check them out. One useful option is to use a *stick font* for the text, which helps to speed up screen regeneration while working in the drafting module.

The symbols that you place using the Symbol Place tool have to be drafting symbols, i.e., they must be created in the drafting module and then transformed to symbols using the Symbol Create tool. Both drafting and modeling symbols, however, can be placed in the same library. Only the drafting symbols will show up in the Symbols palette when such a library is loaded in the drafting module. If a library contains only modeling objects, it won't be useful when you're working in the drafting environment.

The Explode tool accompanying the other symbol tools in the right column doesn't work just on symbols in the drafting environment, as in the modeling environment. It also operates on other drafting elements, reducing their structure by one level. Thus polylines, polycurves, and polyarcs get broken down into their constituent segments; rectangles and arcs into polylines; dimensions into their constituent lines and text; and leader lines into their constituent segments. (Dimensions and leader lines will be covered next.) The most elementary entities are single segments and text, which cannot be exploded further.

Row 9: Dimensions

This row contains all the tools needed for placing and editing dimensions and leader lines. It's unique to the drafting module, since there's no concept of dimensioning in 3D modeling. The first six tools in the left column allow you to apply different kinds of dimensioning on elements: horizontal and vertical, parallel, angular, radial, diametric, and circular. An example of each one of these is shown in Figure A.8.

To create a dimension using the first two tools, you can select any number of points and double-click after you have finished making the selection. A dimension line will be rubber-banded. Click to position it where you want it to be. The distances between all the selected points will appear as dimensions. The Parallel dimension tool creates dimensions parallel to the segments between the selected points, in contrast to the Horizontal/Vertical tool, which marks horizontal and vertical dimensions only.

The Angle dimension tool is used by selecting any three points. This will dimension the angle subtended by the first and third points at the second point. The Radius, Diameter, and Arc dimension tools work on circles and arcs only, giving you their radius, diameter, and length respectively. Keep in mind that these three tools won't work on the polyarcs created using the drawing tools on Row 3, only on the arcs created with the tools on Row 2.

Once a dimension is created, it gets attached to the element it's dimensioning. Thus, it moves when the element is moved, gets deleted when the element is deleted, is updated automatically when the element is resized, and so on. This makes dimensions very simple and convenient to use.

Dimensions can also be placed that do not reference any particular element. These are referred to as *non-attached* or *non-associative dimensions*. To place such dimensions, simply select the required points in the graphics window. Such points are known as *non-associative points*, and are displayed by default. They can be selected for repositioning by setting the topological level to Point—the dimension will be automatically updated. The display of such points can be turned off in the Dimension Display section under the Elements tab of the Display Options dialog.

Very often, you'll find that the overall appearance of a dimension may not be quite what you had in mind. There are many components to a dimension, which are illustrated in Figure A.9-a. Each one of these components has its own options, listed under separate tabs in the dialogs of the dimension tools (Figure A.9-b). You can explore each one of these component attributes and see how it affects the appearance of the dimension. For instance, you can choose whether the dimension text should show unit indicators or not, use dots or slashes instead of arrows as the dimension terminators, and so on. In addition to exploring the component attributes, also explore the main options under the Options tab for each dimension tool dialog, as shown in Figure A.9-b, before doing any serious work with dimensions.

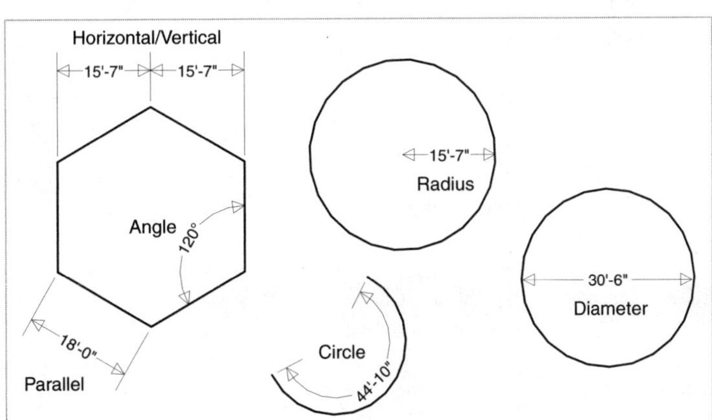

Figure A.8

The six kinds of dimensions that have dedicated dimension tools in form•Z.

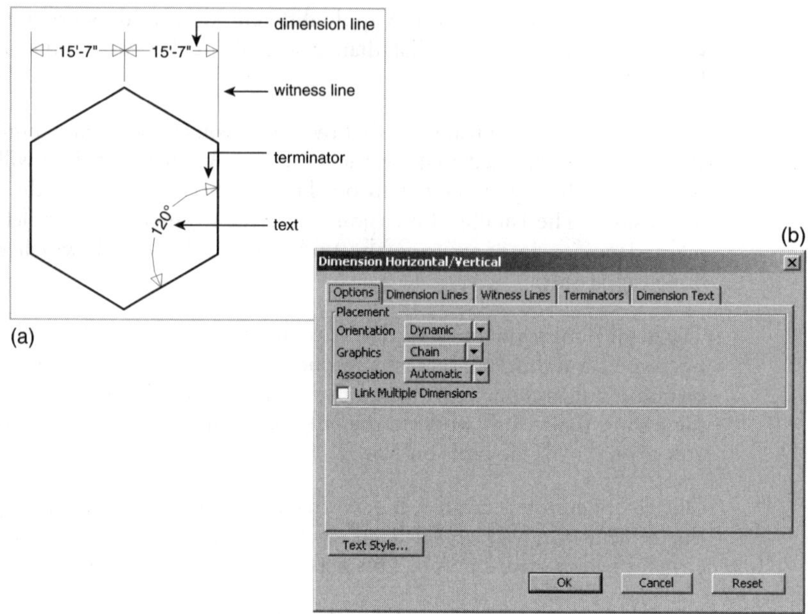

Figure A.9

The various components of a dimension element, and one of the dimension tool dialogs through which they can be modified.

Note that you can't change the attributes of dimensions that have already been created by modifying them through the tool dialogs. You have to take the additional step of applying the Set Dimension Attributes tool (D-Tool:9b,2) to these dimensions. As you would expect, the attribute settings in the dialog shown in Figure A.9-b are also provided in the dialog of the Set Dimension Attributes tool.

You can also conveniently copy the attributes of one dimension element to another dimension element. First, select the dimension whose attributes are to be copied with the Get Dimension Attributes tool (D-Tool:9b,1). What this effectively does is change all the dimension attribute settings based on the attributes of the selected dimension. This combination of attributes can now be applied to any other dimension element by selecting it with the Set Dimension Attributes tool.

There are two remaining tools on Row 9, one in the left column and one in the right. The Leader tool, located in the left column, is simply used to draw lines that have an arrow or some other kind of terminator at one or both ends. Such lines are often used for annotating various parts of a drawing. The choice of terminator, as well as the end on which the terminator should appear, is made in the dialog of the Leader tool. The Reposition Dimension tool in the right column is used to reposition the dimension line of a dimension element. This is contrast to the Move tool, which when applied to a dimension element, moves the whole element.

Finally, keep in mind that dimensions and leader lines are elements just like any other drawing element, and can be deleted, colored, etc. in the usual fashion.

Row 10: Self-Copy Modifiers and Query

These sets of tools are exactly identical to those found in the modeling environment. There's no Define Macro tool, however, since macro transformations are not provided in the drafting environment.

Row 11: Geometric Transformations

The tools in the left column execute translations, rotations, scalings, and reflections, operating directly on the original element or in creating one or more copies of it, depending upon the setting of the self-copy modifier. These tools are already familiar to you from the modeling environment.

In the right column are the Align, Extend, and Place tools, with similar abilities and functions as their counterparts in modeling. Note that the Extend tool works with polylines and arcs only. It extends or shrinks them, retaining the original orientation of the polyline or the radius of the arc.

Row 12: Attribute Assignment

These tools are used to modify various element attributes such as line weight, line type, color, layer, and ghosting. All of these operators can be applied at the Element level only.

The desired line type and line weight have to be set in their respective palettes. They can then be applied to any element using the first two tools on Row 12: Line Type and Line Weight. You are already familiar with the Color tool. The fourth tool in the left column, Set All, simultaneously changes the line type, line weight, color, and layer of the selected element to the current settings of these attributes.

Ghost, Unghost, and Set Layer in the right column work in an identical fashion as in the modeling environment.

Row 13: Delete and Hatch

The Delete tool in the left column of this last row deletes entities, prepicked or postpicked, just as in the modeling environment.

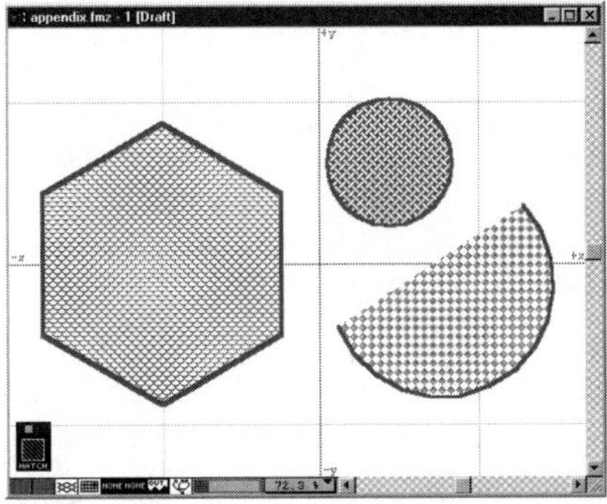

Figure A.10

Different kinds of hatch patterns applied to various elements. The line weight of the elements has also been increased.

The Hatch tool in the right column, however, is unique to the drafting module. This lets you apply a selected pattern from the Hatch Patterns palette to an element. The element can also be an open shape, as shown in Figure A.10, as long as it encloses some amount of area. Obviously, you won't be able to apply a hatch pattern to a straight line. Once a hatch is created, it can be selected with the Pick tool independently of the element to which it has been applied. This makes it possible to select it and delete it if required, which is useful because there is no "unhatch" command. You should take care to delete old hatch patterns before applying new ones to an element, since the Hatch tool doesn't do this automatically. If you're not able to select the hatch (which can sometimes happen for open shapes) but want to delete it, apply the white hatch pattern to the element as a short-term solution.

This concludes our brief overview of the drafting module of form•Z.

Index

D

E

F

G

H

I

J

K

L

M

N

Q

R

S

X

Y

Z

About the Author

Lachmi Khemlani, Ph.D., is the author of the earlier *Into 3D with form•Z*, also published by McGraw-Hill. She has taught form•Z workshops and other CAD courses for a number of years at the University of California, Berkeley, where she earned her doctorate in architecture, specializing in computer applications. She works as an independent consultant and writes extensively on CAD and modeling solutions, including articles, product reviews, tutorials, and a biweekly newsletter. Her credentials include a professional B.Arch. (Honors) degree from the Indian Institute of Technology, Kharagpur, India, and an M.Phil. in Architecture from the University of Cambridge, England. She has also worked on numerous design projects as a practicing architect.

CD-ROM WARRANTY

This software is protected by both United States copyright law and international copyright treaty provision. You must treat this software just like a book. By saying "just like a book," McGraw-Hill means, for example, that this software may be used by any number of people and may be freely moved from one computer location to another, so long as there is no possibility of its being used at one location or on one computer while it also is being used at another. Just as a book cannot be read by two different people in two different places at the same time, neither can the software be used by two different people in two different places at the same time (unless, of course, McGraw-Hill's copyright is being violated).

LIMITED WARRANTY

Customers who have problems installing or running a McGraw-Hill CD should consult our online technical support site at http://books.mcgraw-hill.com/techsupport. McGraw-Hill takes great care to provide you with top-quality software, thoroughly checked to prevent virus infections. McGraw-Hill warrants the physical CD-ROM contained herein to be free of defects in materials and workmanship for a period of sixty days from the purchase date. If McGraw-Hill receives written notification within the warranty period of defects in materials or workmanship, and such notification is determined by McGraw-Hill to be correct, McGraw-Hill will replace the defective CD-ROM. Send requests to:

McGraw-Hill
Customer Services
P.O. Box 545
Blacklick, OH 43004-0545

The entire and exclusive liability and remedy for breach of this Limited Warranty shall be limited to replacement of a defective CD-ROM and shall not include or extend to any claim for or right to cover any other damages, including, but not limited to, loss of profit, data, or use of the software, or special, incidental, or consequential damages or other similar claims, even if McGraw-Hill has been specifically advised of the possibility of such damages. In no event will McGraw-Hill's liability for any damages to you or any other person ever exceed the lower of suggested list price or actual price paid for the license to use the software, regardless of any form of the claim.

McGRAW-HILL SPECIFICALLY DISCLAIMS ALL OTHER WARRANTIES, EXPRESS OR IMPLIED, INCLUDING, BUT NOT LIMITED TO, ANY IMPLIED WARRANTY OF MERCHANTABILITY OR FITNESS FOR A PARTICULAR PURPOSE.

Specifically, McGraw-Hill makes no representation or warranty that the software is fit for any particular purpose and any implied warranty of merchantability is limited to the sixty-day duration of the Limited Warranty covering the physical CD-ROM only (and not the software) and is otherwise expressly and specifically disclaimed.

This limited warranty gives you specific legal rights; you may have others which may vary from state to state. Some states do not allow the exclusion of incidental or consequential damages, or the limitation on how long an implied warranty lasts, so some of the above may not apply to you.